ART IN FOCUS

Second Edition

Honoré Daumier. *Advice to a Young Artist.* **Probably after 1860. Oil on canvas, 0.41 x 0.33 m [16⅛ x 12⅞"]. The National Gallery of Art, Washington, D.C. Gift of Duncan Phillips, 1941**

ART IN FOCUS

Second Edition

Gene A. Mittler

Professor of Art
Texas Tech University

GLENCOE PUBLISHING COMPANY

BENNETT & McKNIGHT DIVISION

To Maria Luisa, Carmen, Teresa, and Pilar

Copyright © 1989 by Dr. Gene Mittler

Published by Glencoe Publishing Company, a division of Macmillan, Inc.

Send all inquiries to:
Glencoe Publishing Company
15319 Chatsworth Street
P.O. Box 9509
Mission Hills, California 91345-9509

Printed in the United States of America

ISBN 0-02-662271-8 (Student Text)

3 4 5 6 7   93 92 91 90 89

If acknowledgments to any museum or gallery have inadvertently been overlooked, the author extends his most sincere apologies. Proper acknowledgment will be made in future editions of this text.

Drawings by Vernon Dargel

Cover designed by Benoit Design

Cover illustration: Claude Monet, HAYSTACK AT SUNSET NEAR GIVERNEY, 1891. Oil on canvas, approx. 74.9 × 94 cm (29½ × 37″). Courtesy of the Museum of Fine Arts, Boston. The Juliana Cheny Edwards Collection, 25.112. Bequest of Robert J. Edwards in memory of his mother.

Preface

This book is designed primarily for use by students in art history, art criticism, art appreciation, humanities, or a course including studio art, although it could serve as a resource book in several other kinds of classes as well. It is hoped that it will, in some small way, aid teacher efforts to expand content in art to include opportunities for students to engage in criticism and history operations. If this occurs, the art class may be more appealing to students who are not typically attracted to it because of a real or imagined lack of artistic ability. A class which incorporates criticism and history experiences along with studio may cause these students to question their preconceptions of the art class. As a result, they may no longer regard it as a place reserved for the talented few who exhibit an aptitude for making art.

Enticing as many students as possible to the art experience is a goal of every art teacher, and this art teacher is no exception. All students can profit from such an experience, provided that it includes ample opportunity for them to respond to as well as create art. Art classes which promote learning in studio, criticism, and history are more likely to succeed in expanding student knowledge, understanding, and sensitivity in and about art. The products of such classes are students who can draw upon that knowledge, understanding, and sensitivity to enrich the quality of their lives.

The book is divided into two parts, with the first part containing introductory material to be used throughout the rest of the text. The art-criticism and art-history operations introduced in Part I will be applied in study of the artworks in Part II. In Part II, the focus is on art criticism and art history, from cave paintings to art of the present day. Two chapters on art of non-Western cultures are also included.

At the start of each chapter, the student will find a pronunciation guide to artists' names and a few significant facts about the artists whom the reader will meet in that chapter. Important and/or unusual words have been defined and included in the Glossary. Enrichment footnotes which expand on items mentioned in the text will help increase student understanding and awareness. A Time Line will aid students in reviewing important artists and works with reference to their historical

context. Criticism and history experiences, which the student will find at the end of the book, are geared to each chapter and will help students to review concepts.

An important section at the end of each chapter will outline several studio experiences for students. Complete, detailed lesson plans for these studio segments will be found in the Teacher's Guide. Thus, the text will meet the needs of teachers who wish to include studio work in their courses. Each studio segment is based upon what students have learned during their reading. *The studio content is directly related to learning in aesthetics, art criticism, and art history.* The result is a comprehensive program that focuses on both the response and production goals of visual arts education. With this program, students first complete their reading of each chapter in the text and examine the works discussed from critical and historical points of view. They are then better prepared to identify the ideas and feelings they would like to express in visual form. Next, they engage in studio experiences that are designed to (1) help them clarify and refine those ideas and feelings, (2) expand their understanding of the elements and principles of design, and (3) develop their skills with a variety of art media and techniques.

The text also provides a listing of books recommended for further reading as well as a brief discussion of possible careers in art and art-related fields. The careers section has been included as an aid to students contemplating further study and eventual careers in art.

Given the limited parameters of time and space, it is impossible to list here all those people who assisted in the preparation of this book. However, let me hasten to add that I have no difficulty whatsoever identifying for special consideration the one person whose work over the years has had a decided impact upon my own approach to the study and teaching of art—Edmund B. Feldman of the University of Georgia. I recall an evening many years ago in the home of Manuel Barkan where I first heard Dr. Feldman discussing informally his views on art criticism and art history. While the memory of that evening has no doubt long since faded from his mind, I have cherished it over the years. I suspect that the idea of writing this book was born that evening, although it has certainly been nourished by continued exposure to Dr. Feldman's many articles and his monumental *Varieties of Visual Experience*.

I would also like to express my gratitude to Arthur Efland, The Ohio State University; David Templeton, Western Washington State University; Evan Kern, Kutztown State College; and the late Manuel Barkan, all former teachers at The Ohio State University, and to Willard Wankelman and Otto Ocvirk who served in the same capacity at Bowling Green State University along with Hugh Broadly, Arizona State University. Few students could claim the same good fortune in having teachers equal to these.

Help and encouragement were also provided by Earl Floyd and Guy Hubbard, Indiana University; Jessie Lovano-Kerr, Florida State University; and Marvin Moon, Texas Tech University. And I would be remiss if I did not mention Phil Demott, an art teacher in Martinsville, Indiana, who, until now, may never have realized how much I appreciated his willingness to question, to challenge, and to reserve judgment.

This book could not have been written without the assistance of a great many people in museums, art galleries, and agencies who helped provide the many photographs required. In this category too are Nancy Reed, Terry Zeller, and Susan Talbot, Texas Tech University; Michael Gilliatt, Virginia State University; Pauline Ahmad, Ball State University; and Denis Pett, Indiana University, all of whom supplied photographs for this book.

Certainly the members of the editorial and production staff of the Bennett & McKnight Publishing Company deserve recognition here. Special thanks are reserved for Michael Kenny for his confidence and friendship and Ramona Gibbs for her great patience and attention to detail. Whatever clarity is to be found in this book is due largely to her untiring efforts.

Finally, I want to acknowledge the contributions of my wife and daughters. Without their constant encouragement, this project would never have progressed beyond the level of wishful thinking.

Gene A. Mittler

Contents

Preface 5

Part I: Learning to See 9
    Chapter 1: An Overview 10
        The Purpose of This Book, 11; Gaining Information from Works of Art: Art
        Criticism, 11; Gaining Information about Works of Art: Art History, 12; How
        to Use This Book, 13

    Chapter 2: Learning a Visual Vocabulary 14
        Understanding Art, 14; The Elements of Art, 16; The Principles of Art, 30;
        Discovering Design Relationships in Art, 37

    Chapter 3: Seeing, Knowing, Understanding, and Judging 39
        Learning about Works of Art, 39; The Art-History Approach, 41; The
        Art-Criticism Approach, 48; When to Use Art History and Art Criticism, 60;
        Studio Experiences, 62

Part II: Seeing to Learn 63
    Chapter 4: The Magic Picture: Prehistoric Art in Western Europe 64
        Life in Prehistoric Times, 64; Cave Painting: The Bison from Altamira, 64;
        History of the Cave Paintings: Lascaux and Altamira, 66; Studio Experiences,
        71

    Chapter 5: Art for Eternity: The Art of Ancient Egypt 72
        The Growth of Egyptian Civilization, 72; Architecture, 75; Sculpture, 78;
        Relief Sculpture and Painting, 82; Studio Experiences, 86

    Chapter 6: The Age of Beauty: Greek Art 87
        The Birthplace of Western Civilization, 87; The Greek Contribution to
        Architecture, 89; Sculpture in the Archaic Period, 94; Sculpture in the
        Classical Period, 96; Sculpture in the Hellenistic Period, 101; Stylistic Changes
        in Sculpture, 104; Painting and the Greek Love for Color, 104; The Demand
        Elsewhere for Greek Artists, 106; Studio Experiences, 107

    Chapter 7: Age of the Conquerors: Roman Art 108
        The Rising Power of Rome, 108; Roman Architecture, 108; Roman Sculpture
        and Painting, 120; The Declining Power of Rome, 123; Studio Experiences,
        124

    Chapter 8: In Quest of Salvation: Early Christian and Byzantine Art 125
        Early Christian Art, 125; Basilicas, 127; Decline of the Classical World, 130;
        Growth of the Byzantine Culture, 131; Studio Experiences, 136

    Chapter 9: The Age of Faith: Early Medieval and Romanesque Art 137
        Centuries of Change, 137; The Early Medieval Period, 138; The Romanesque
        Period, 146; Studio Experiences, 159

    Chapter 10: The Age of Faith Continued: Gothic Art 160
        End of the Feudal System, 160; Emergence of the Gothic Style, 160;
        Innovations in Cathedral Architecture, 161; Gothic Church Construction,
        166; Sculptural Decorations, 167;. Illustrated Books, 171; The Spread of
        Gothic Architecture, 174; Italian Church Painting, 174; Studio Experiences,
        179

    Chapter 11: A Time of Titans: Renaissance Art in Italy 181
        The Emergence of a New Age, 181; Blending of Early Renaissance and
        Gothic Ideas, 185; A New Style Emerges, 188; New Levels of Excellence,
        195; Women and Art, 206; Studio Experiences, 208

    Chapter 12: With Sight and Feeling: Fifteenth-Century Art in the North 209
        Continuation of the Gothic and the International Style, 209; The Flemish
        Influence, 210; The Combining of Emotionalism and Realism, 213; Studio
        Experiences, 219

Chapter 13: Crisis and Transition: Art of the Sixteenth Century 220

The Art of Venice, 221; Mannerism, 225; Northern Art: A Conflict of Styles, 233; Studio Experiences, 242

Chapter 14: A World of Light and Shadow: Baroque Art 243

The Role of Art in the Counter-Reformation, 244; New Style Reflected in Church Architecture, 244; Emphasis on Mood and Drama in Sculpture, 246; Emphasis on Motion Changes Painting, 248; Dutch Art Takes a New Direction, 254; Religious Subjects Continue in Spanish Art, 261; Church Division Has Lasting Effect on Art, 266; Studio Experiences, 267

Chapter 15: In Search of Pleasure: Rococo Art 268

Courtly Beginnings, 268; New Directions in French Painting, 269; The Movement in England, 274; Spanish Rococo Art: Francisco Goya, 278; Breaking the Bounds of Tradition, 280; Studio Experiences, 281

Chapter 16: Era of Change: New Styles in Nineteenth-Century Art 282

Looking to the Past, 283; Neoclassicism, 283; Romanticism, 288; English Landscape Painting, 291; Realism, 294; Impressionism, 298; Studio Experiences, 312

Chapter 17: A Time for Rebels: Art of the Later Nineteenth Century 313

Europe in the Late Nineteenth Century, 313; America in the Late Nineteenth Century, 323; Studio Experiences, 358

Chapter 18: A New Vision: Art of the Early Twentieth Century 332

European Art, 333; Mexican Art, 346; American Art, 348; European and American Architecture, 352; Studio Experiences, 331

Chapter 19: New Directions: Art to the Present 359

Art in the Past Few Decades, 360; Painting in Europe: Dada, Surrealism, and Fantasy, 360; Painting in America: A Mixture of Styles, 364; Sculpture in Europe and America, 379; Architecture in Europe and America, 386; Art Today—A Never-ending Quest for New Visual Experiences, 391; Painting in Canada: A Passion for Nature, 398; Studio Experiences, 398

Chapter 20: Centuries of Tradition in the East: The Art of China and Japan 400

The Beginnings of Chinese Civilization, 400; The Arrival of Buddhism during the Han Dynasty, 401; The Powerful T'ang Dynasty, 403; A Period of Stability and Great Art, 405; The Art of the Ming Dynasty, 408; The Early Development of Japanese Art, 409; Temple Construction, 410; A Japanese Painting Style, 413; The Kamakura Period, 413; The Fall of the Kamakura Rulers, 414; A Rich Era of Art, 416; Studio Experiences, 421

Chapter 21: Out of the Shadows: The Art of Other Non-Western Cultures 422

The Art of Tribal Africa, 422; The Art of Islamic Spain, 427; Pre-Columbian Art, 435; Studio Experiences, 439

Criticism and History Experiences 440

Appendix: Art Related Careers 449

Glossary 454

Books for Further Reading 465

Chronology of Selected Periods, Styles, and Artists 469

Index 472

List of Studio Experiences Included in the Text 479

Picture Credits 480

PART I

LEARNING TO SEE

TO LOOK IS ONE THING,
TO SEE WHAT YOU LOOK AT IS ANOTHER,
TO UNDERSTAND WHAT YOU SEE IS A THIRD,
TO LEARN FROM WHAT YOU UNDERSTAND IS STILL
SOMETHING ELSE:
TO ACT ON WHAT YOU LEARN IS ALL THAT
MATTERS.

Taoist saying

Chapter 1

An Overview

"I like paintings of things that I can recognize. Why, the apples in that painting we saw a moment ago looked so real I felt as if I could reach out and touch them."

"I don't see what this painting is supposed to mean."

"Artists today don't seem to take the time to paint like the artists of the past."

"I may not know anything about art, but I certainly know what I like."

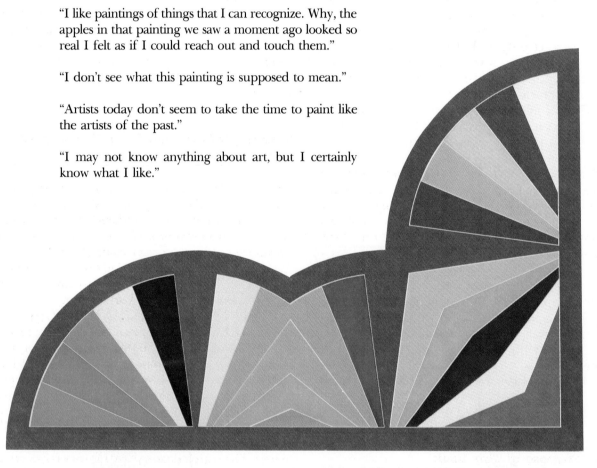

Figure 1.1 Frank Stella. *Agbatana III.* **1968. Fluorescent acrylic on canvas, 3.05 x 4.57 m [10 x 15′]. Allen Memorial Art Museum, Oberlin College, Oberlin, Ohio. Ruth C. Roush Fund for Contemporary Art and National Foundation for the Arts and Humanities Grant, 68.37**

(This painting is discussed on page 395.)

Sound familiar? Most people at one time or another have made or overheard statements like these about art. Sometimes they are heard over the hum of a projector in a darkened classroom as students view slides of artworks. Such statements are rather common in galleries and museums where they are whispered as if for the very first time. Often, such statements are met with smiles and outright laughter, or with furrowed brows and heads nodding in agreement.

The comments people make about art usually reflect the past experiences they have had with art. These experiences influence what they see in a work of art and how they will react to it. Like everyone else, you have inherited some parts of your cultural heritage. But your unique experience with that cultural heritage means that you will be prepared to see and react differently from others to the same work of art. Thus, a work you feel is outstanding may cause others to shake their heads disapprovingly. But, by openly discussing your point of view with others, you might see some things you missed before, or learn to interpret works from a completely different angle. When this happens, everyone benefits.

Fortunately, people always seem ready and willing to express their opinions about art. This is true whether they have a broad background in art, or know nothing at all about it. Point to a work of art in a museum and make a statement about it to friends and they will quickly respond with statements of their own. This is a good sign. After all, it shows that they are interested enough to make a statement or offer an opinion. However, merely stating an unsupported opinion about a work of art is not enough if that work is going to have more than passing interest. If a work of art is to be appreciated, opinions about it should be based upon knowledge and understanding.

The Purpose of This Book

The purpose of this book is to help you acquire the knowledge and understanding you will need to make and support your own personal decisions about works of art. In order to do this, you must first learn the vocabulary of art and how to use it. Artists use many different colors, values, lines, textures, shapes, forms, and space relationships to create their works. These are called the "elements of art," and they are used by artists in countless combinations. If you are to fully understand a painting, a sculpture, or a building, you will need to recognize the elements within each and find out for yourself how they are being used. In Chapter 2 you will learn how to do this. It will not only add to your understanding of how others create, but will also help you to express yourself through art. A visual vocabulary is essential when you are trying to do the following:

• Gain insights into the artworks produced by others.

• Create your own artworks with different media and techniques.

Once you have mastered a vocabulary of art, you will be ready to learn how art criticism and art history can be used to gather information from and about works of art. The following paragraphs will introduce you to these two different kinds of information-gathering operations.

Gaining Information from Works of Art: Art Criticism

Many people seem to think that art criticism is very complicated and difficult. This is simply not true. In fact, it can be quite uncomplicated, is easily learned, and will add a great deal of interest and excitement to your encounters with all kinds of art. You could say that art criticism is an orderly way of looking at and talking about art. It helps to direct you to information found within works of art.

To gain information from a work of art, you must know two things: what to look for and how to look for it. This will be covered in Chapter 3. You will be shown the aesthetic qualities that you should look for when examining a work. Those qualities represent the "criteria," or standards for judgment, you will need when making and supporting decisions about art. A search strategy, or way of looking, will make the task of looking for those qualities much easier. The search strategy will consist of four steps:

• **Description:** Through which you try to find out what is in the work.

• **Analysis:** Through which you discover how the work is organized or put together.

• **Interpretation:** Through which you try to determine the feelings, moods, or ideas communicated by the work.

• **Judgment:** Through which you make your own decisions about the artistic merit of the work.

Gaining Information about Works of Art: Art History

Artworks are not created in a vacuum. Your understanding of them cannot be complete until you determine who made them as well as when, where, how, and why they were made. You can add greatly to your knowledge and understanding of a work by learning something about the artist and what caused that artist to select and paint certain subjects in certain ways. Every great work of art reveals something seen, plus something seen into it. Claude Monet portrayed haystacks as no one before him had portrayed them, as you will see in Figure 16.14, page 300. Paul Cézanne painted a rather ordinary mountain in southern France over and over again (Figure 1.2 and Figure 17.4, page 317). No one saw and painted the suffering of a repressed people as Francisco Goya did. An example of this can be found in Figure 15.11, page 279. To understand and appreciate such works, you must know something about the environment that influenced the sight and the insight of the artists who created them.

Art history can add to the knowledge you have gained from artworks during criticism. It also enables you to check some of the decisions you made during art criticism. For example, during art criticism you will make some preliminary decisions about the meaning and merits of a certain work of art. After this you will be ready, perhaps even eager, to find out what meaning and merits others have found in the same work. Facts about the artist, the period, the country, the artistic style, and the subject matter will help you to check your decisions. How historians value a work could have an impact upon your final judgment. Thus, by referring to art history, you can confirm, change, or reject all or some of the decisions you made during art criticism.

A search strategy can be just as useful to you in art history as it is in art criticism. Furthermore, it can consist of the same four steps used in an art-criticism search strategy. However, you must remember that when it is applied to art history this search strategy operates from a different point of view. It is used to gain information about a work of art rather than gain information from the work. As used in art history, the search strategy would look like this:

- **Description:** Through which you try to find out when, where, and by whom the work was done.
- **Analysis:** Through which you discover the unique features of a work of art.
- **Interpretation:** Through which you try to determine how the artist was influenced by the world in which he or she lived and worked.
- **Judgment:** Through which you make a decision about the work's importance in the history of art.

Figure 1.2   Paul Cézanne. *Mont Sainte-Victoire.* 1885-87. Oil on canvas, 65.5 x 81.7 cm [25¾ x 32⅛"]. The Metropolitan Museum of Art, New York. The H. O. Havemeyer Collection. Bequest of Mrs. H. O. Havemeyer, 1929

How to Use This Book

In this book, art criticism and art history are used in a sequence beginning with art criticism. Part I is an introduction to the methods you will be using to sharpen your skills as art critic and historian. In Part II you will be able to put these skills to work. Before reading each chapter in Part II, you will first need to examine all the illustrations in the chapter carefully. Then read the captions labeled "criticism." You will find questions included in these captions which you should try to answer. They are there to help you sharpen your art-criticism skills as you gain information from works of art. These questions will also encourage you to make some personal decisions about each work. Of course, not every question dealing with criticism will be included in these captions. Others will no doubt occur to you as you examine each work. In fact, as you gain experience, you will find yourself asking more and more questions on your own. This will be a sign that you are trying to see and think as an art critic.

The second thing to do before beginning your reading is to select a work of art from the chapter. The work of art you select is to be studied carefully in depth. This means that you will describe, analyze, interpret, and judge the work in a deliberate, thorough way. Doing this will enable you to establish a personal relationship with the work of art. It will give you an opportunity to determine in your own mind what you think about the work and why you think about it in that way.

When the two art-criticism activities have been completed, you will be ready to read the text of the chapter. There you will learn about the artworks illustrated as well as the artists who created them.

When you have completed your reading, you will have an opportunity to play the role of an art historian. First, reexamine all the illustrations and read the captions labeled "history." These captions will include questions dealing with facts and information about the works of art and the artists discussed in the chapter. Answering these questions will help you review the material covered in your reading.

Next, return to the artwork you selected earlier to study in depth. Your study of this artwork will continue as your try to find out as much as you can about it and the artist who created it. To do this, you

will have to consult as many sources as possible. Some of these will be books and magazines found in your school or community libraries. A nearby museum may be another source of information.

As you become absorbed in these criticism and history activities, you will find that you will want to share what you have learned with others. It is the same thing that happens after you have seen an especially good movie or play. You can hardly wait to pass on to others the same excitement you experienced. Sharing your perceptions, insights, and judgments enables you to learn from each other.

When describing and discussing with others the various aspects of a work, you will need to use words that are precise and accurate. If you do not, you run the risk of being misunderstood. Further, a refined art vocabulary will prepare you to see even more in the next work of art you examine. In other words, an expanded vocabulary helps you to see. And the more you see, the more you will need to expand your vocabulary.

At the end of each chapter are several studio experiences. You will discover that these studio segments are based upon material covered in the chapters. They are provided so that you can create your own art forms while learning from and about the art forms created by others. Each of these studio experiences will help you in several ways. They will aid you in finding and refining your ideas for art. They will help you learn how to use the visual vocabulary to express those ideas in visual form. And, finally, they will enable you to polish your skills with a variety of art media and techniques.

At the end of the book, you will find a number of criticism and history experiences for each chapter. These will help you review concepts and become more knowledgeable and skillful in art criticism and art history.

One of the most difficult things about writing a book like this is deciding which artists and which artworks to include. Of course, it is impossible to include every artist and every masterpiece. Many are certain to be excluded. Thus, this book's success will be measured by the number of its readers who continue, after they have finished this book, to read about and study art. If you are one of these, you have a great deal to look forward to—a lifetime acquaintance with some of the most fascinating and unique individuals in history, united by their determination and their ability to create art.

Chapter 2

Learning a Visual Vocabulary

The young girl strolling through the museum paused before a large fifteenth-century jewelry chest. Its highly lacquered surface and the miniature paintings which decorated each of the many drawer fronts had caught her eye. Fascinated, she bent down to examine the chest more closely. She was so absorbed in her examination that she failed to notice the guide come up beside her.

"It is a beautiful chest isn't it?"

The girl looked up and nodded. "I was just thinking that at one time it must have held a great many valuable things. But it seems odd that not all the drawers can be locked with a key."

"Don't jump to conclusions," said the guide. "Here, this drawer has no lock, but try to open it."

The girl took hold of the drawer handle and pulled, but it would not give. She pulled harder, but even though the drawer felt loose, it would not come out. "I don't understand," she said finally. "Why won't it open?"

"Because," the guide answered, "it wasn't made to pull open. Watch."

Ignoring the drawer the girl had been trying to pull open, the guide removed the entire drawer next to it. This allowed him to slide the first drawer front easily to one side, exposing the interior.

"You see," he said, "you just have to know what to look for."

Understanding Art

Art objects are unique arrangements of the obvious and the not so obvious. In order to understand any art object, you must be willing to go beyond the obvious and examine the not so obvious as well. To do this, you must, like the guide in the story, know what to look for (Figure 2.1).

One of the most important things to look for in works of art is the way those works have been designed or put together. To do this means you must know what the

Figure 2.1 This girl is examining the painting before her very carefully. Because she knows what to look for, she will learn much about the work.

elements and principles of art are and how they are used to create art objects.

The elements of art are the building blocks of art. They are what artists use to express their ideas. We are not referring to the media the artist uses here, media such as paint or clay or stone, but to the *visual vocabulary* used by the artist. This visual vocabulary is used in much the same way that writers make use of a verbal vocabulary. However, writers use an extensive verbal vocabulary composed of thousands of words. Artists, on the other hand, must depend on a limited vocabulary composed of seven elements: *color, value, line, texture, shape, form,* and *space.*

If the elements of art are what artists use to express their ideas, what are the principles of art? The principles are the different ways artists can use the elements to create unified works of art. Again, we can make a comparison with writers who must do more than just select words if they are to communicate their ideas to others. They must also organize those words to form phrases, sentences, and paragraphs. Then they must carefully arrange these into meaningful sequences. After all, a book composed of words haphazardly placed on each page would be of little value to anyone. The words must be organized so that the reader will be able to understand the writer's ideas. Like books, works of art are also organized so that artists' ideas and feelings can be understood by viewers. When organizing their artworks, artists make use of such principles as *balance, emphasis, harmony, variety, gradation, movement, rhythm,* and *proportion.*

Artists carefully select and use the art principles to arrange the elements. In this way, they are able to achieve *unity* in their works. Unity refers to the look and feel of wholeness or oneness in a work of art. In works where unity is evident, the elements and principles work together to show harmony and completeness. Where unity is lacking, the works may look disorganized, incomplete, or confusing.

You may find it useful to think of unity in terms of a basketball team. When there is team unity, each player works toward a common goal. That goal is to score as many points as possible while preventing the opposing team from scoring. This goal may not be realized if the players act more like individuals than a team. If they are more concerned with their own performances than with the team's performance, their game will suffer. Try to picture such a team playing in your school gym. The players would be running wildly up and down the floor, calling for the ball, shooting at every opportunity, and ignoring their defensive responsibilities. Their confused play would make it easy for a well-organized team to beat them.

Of course, artists have goals too. They want their works to look complete and whole. If a color, a shape, or some other element does not contribute to unity, they will eliminate it or change it in some way. Disorganized basketball teams often find themselves playing before a great many empty seats. And few people are willing to view and respond favorably to disorganized works of art.

Artworks owe much of their uniqueness to the ways artists have used the elements and principles. No doubt you have heard people talk about an artist's "style." More often than not, they are referring to the special way an artist used the elements and principles to organize a work.

Many artists place great importance on the use of the elements and principles to achieve unity in their art products. They deliberately try out different principles, or ways to use each element. These artists are not satisfied until a certain way looks right to them. Other artists choose to use the elements of art in a more spontaneous or intuitive manner. They do not make deliberate decisions regarding the principles of art. Rather, these artists instinctively select and organize the art elements in their works. They are satisfied with the unity of the work if it feels right to them. Just as there are different styles in writing, there are different styles in painting, sculpture, and architecture.

Some authors write books that can be read with ease, even by younger readers. However, other authors produce books that are more demanding to read. They are more difficult because the ideas expressed are more complicated. In addition, the words and sentence structures may be more sophisticated. Years of education and a good dictionary are often needed for the reader to fully understand such books. In much the same manner, some artists try to express their ideas in simple, easy-to-understand artworks. At the same time, others choose to present their ideas in a more complicated form. Often, the degree of complexity in an artwork depends upon the number and type of principles used to organize the elements. You could say then that there is a difference in the level of difficulty involved in "reading" paintings. This is similar to what you may have found in reading books. Some paintings and some books are easy to read and understand. Others, however, require a great deal of preparation and careful reading and rereading in order to understand them completely.

The Elements of Art

Often, people looking at works of art stop looking once they have examined the subject matter, or "content." They recognize the people, objects, and events shown but pay little attention to the elements of art used in the works. They overlook the fact that a painting is made up of colors, values, lines, textures, shapes,[1] and spaces. In a landscape painting, for example, these art elements are combined to look like trees and hills and fields and sky. While you may admire the way the artist painted such a realistic scene, you should not limit your attention to the subject matter alone. If you do, you might miss seeing other important and interesting things in the work. For instance, you might miss the way the artist used the elements of art to create that realistic scene (Figure 2.2). Furthermore, in paintings where subject matter is *not* shown, you should be prepared to examine what *is* shown. In those cases, the elements of art are especially important.

Actually, you are already familiar with the elements of art even if you have never taken an art course or read a book about art. Pick up any object and study it for a minute or two. Now, imagine yourself trying to describe the object to a friend over the telephone without naming it. What things would you include in your description? No doubt you would find yourself talking about the object in terms of color, value, line, texture, shape, form, and space. If your comments about these art elements are clear and detailed, your friend would have a good chance of identifying the object.

Suppose for a moment that you are listening to a description of an object over the telephone. Could you guess what that object is after hearing a description that includes the following list of art elements?

• It has height, width, and depth and occupies actual *space.*

• Abrupt changes in light and dark *values* indicate that it is made up of flat planes at right angles to each other.

• It is a flat, three-dimensional *form* with six sides.

• It is rectangular in *shape* when viewed directly from any side or from the top or bottom.

• Three sides are a rich, leather-brown *color;* the remaining three sides are white.

• Three sides are hard and smooth in *texture;* this contrasts with the fine ridged texture of the remaining three sides.

Figure 2.2   Lee Ables. *View of Puente la Reina, Spain.* 1978. Watercolor. Private Collection

• The three sides with the ridged texture are made up of a series of thin, parallel *lines.*

Did you correctly identify the object as a book? It is unlikely that you guessed that it was an umbrella, or a shoe, or a tennis racquet even though those items also contain the art elements of color, value, line, texture, shape, form, and space. However, those items are distinguished by having *different* colors, values, lines, textures, shapes, forms, and spaces. To test your understanding of the art elements, select a common object. Then, describe it to a friend in terms of its art elements. Now have your friend do the same for you.

There is always a problem of interpretation with any language, and this seems to be especially true with regard to a visual language. When you use the term "line," for example, you will want to be sure that the person to whom you are talking has the same understanding of the term as you do. If this bond of understanding is missing, confusion will occur. In order to avoid this, each of the elements of art will be examined and defined in some detail.

Color

Color is an element which is made up of three distinct qualities: hue, intensity, and value. When talking about a color or the differences between two or more colors, you can refer to any one or all of these qualities.

---

[1] Form is another art element, but it is more often referred to during discussions of three-dimensional works such as sculpture and architecture.

Hue

Hue refers to the name of a color. The term is used to point out the difference between a blue and a green, or a red and a yellow. Imagine that you have gone into a department store and have asked to see a selection of blue sweaters. You would not expect the salesperson to return with several *yellow* sweaters. The name "blue" should be enough of a color description for the salesperson to know what color you have in mind. Examples of twelve different hues are shown in the color diagram on page 18 (Figure 2.3).

Intensity

Now assume for a moment that while checking the store's stock of sweaters, the salesperson discovers that there is a variety of blue sweaters in your size. Some seem to be brighter, purer blues than others. These could be described as the "bluest blues." It is this quality of brightness and purity that is called a color's *intensity*. When a hue is strong and bright, it is said to be high in intensity. When that same color is faint and dull, it is said to be low in intensity. Perhaps the salesperson brings a selection of blue sweaters out for you to see. Unsure which you like best, you arrange them on the counter in a row, from those that are the most intense to those that are the least intense. Your arrangement would reveal the differences in color intensity. All the sweaters on the counter would be blue, but some would appear to be *more* blue, or higher in intensity. Others would be *less* vivid. In fact, it might even be difficult to call them blue because they would be nearly neutral. These would be referred to as being low in intensity. The differences in color intensity of these sweaters might resemble the range of intensities shown in the chart below.

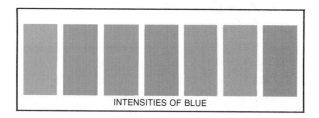

INTENSITIES OF BLUE

Value

The salesperson now brings out more blue sweaters. Some of these sweaters are darker and some are lighter than those you have just seen. You arrange this second group of sweaters in a row from darkest to lightest. Your awareness of the lightness and darkness of the blues would mean that you have recognized the differences in their *values*. Whenever the term *value* is used to describe a hue, it refers to that hue's lightness or darkness. Value changes are often obtained by adding black or white to a particular hue. The chart below, for example, shows the range of dark and light values created when various amounts of black and white were added to blue. The differences in color value that you found in the sweaters might resemble the range of color values shown in this chart.

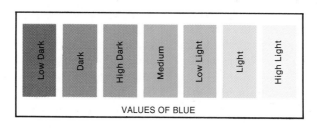

VALUES OF BLUE

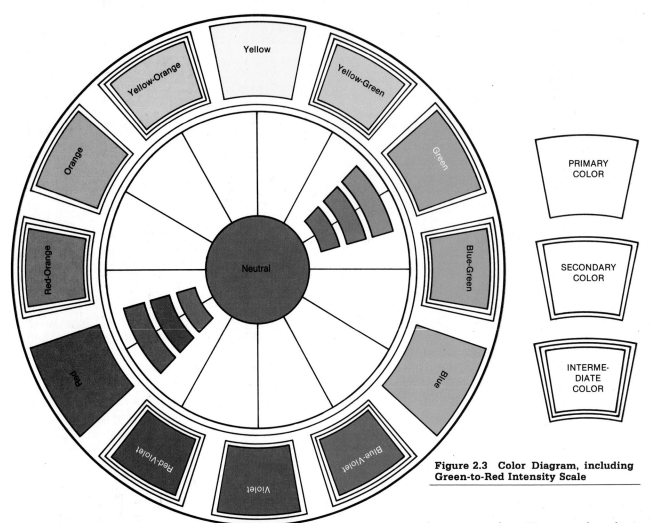

Figure 2.3 Color Diagram, including Green-to-Red Intensity Scale

The Color Diagram

COLOR DIAGRAM

Often an understanding of color is aided by the use of a color diagram (Figure 2.3). Notice, first of all, the three *primary colors:* red, yellow, and blue. These are called primary colors because they can be mixed to make all the other colors, but they cannot be made by mixing other colors.

The *secondary colors* are orange, green, and violet and are located midway between the primary colors on the diagram. Each of the secondary colors is made by mixing two primary colors. Orange is made by mixing red and yellow; green, by mixing blue and yellow; and violet, by mixing blue and red. Adding more red to the combination of red and yellow will produce a red-orange. Adding more yellow will produce a yellow-orange. Red-orange and yellow-orange are examples of *intermediate colors.* By varying the amounts of the two primary colors used, it is possible to create a number of these intermediate hues. (In some books you may find that the intermediate colors are referred to as "tertiary colors." Both terms, *intermediate* and *tertiary,* refer to the colors found between the primary and secondary colors on the color diagram.)

Colors that are opposite each other on the color diagram are called *complementary colors.* Thus, red and green are complementary colors. However, these hues are opposites in a more fundamental way: there is no green hue at all in red and no red in green. You can say then that no other color in the diagram is as different from green as red.

When two complements are mixed in equal portions, they will cancel each other out to form a neutral gray tone. But, the addition of only a small amount of a hue's complement will lower its intensity. In other words, a green can be made to look less green—and move by degrees closer and closer to a neutral tone—by the addition of its complement, red (see the scale above).

Colors that are next to each other on the color wheel and are closely related are called *analogous* colors. Examples of analogous colors are blue, blue-green, and green.

The terms *warm* and *cool* are applied to certain colors on the color wheel. Cool colors are those often associated with water, sky, and foliage and suggest coolness. These are the colors which contain blue and green and appear on one side of the color wheel opposite the warm colors. Warm colors are often associated with fire and sun and suggest warmth. These are colors which contain red and yellow and appear on one side of the color wheel opposite the cool colors. Cool colors appear to recede in space, while warm colors seem to advance.

18

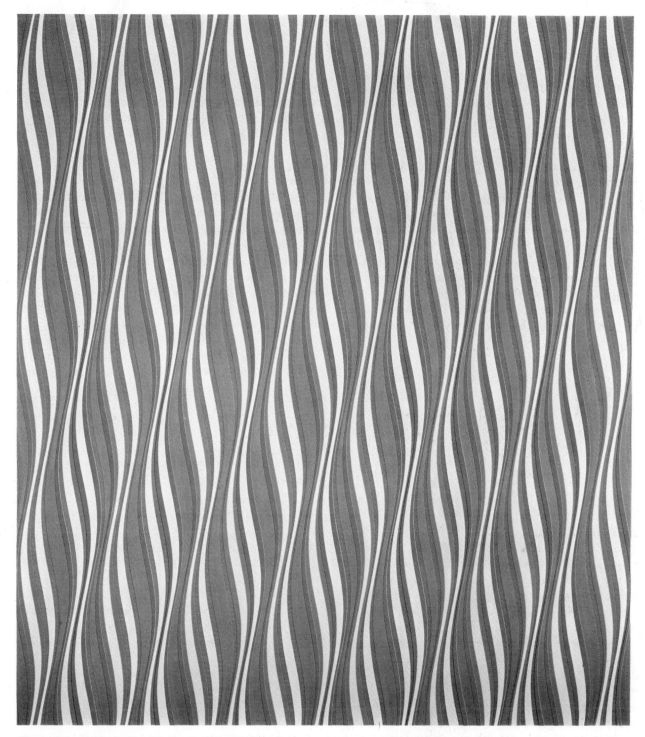

Figure 2.4   Bridget Riley. *Entice 2.* **1974. Acrylic on canvas, 1.5 x 1.8 m [60¾ x 54⅛″]. Courtesy of the Sidney Janis Gallery, New York**

Over the centuries, artists have used color in many different ways. Some have tried to reproduce exactly the colors of the objects they have painted. Others have freely changed colors in order to emphasize a certain feeling or mood. Bridget Riley, a contemporary British artist, creates works that are composed of completely unexpected changes in color (Figure 2.4). Sometimes these color changes are sudden, sometimes gradual, but they are found everywhere in her paintings. If you look into one of her pictures long enough, you will find that your eye begins to wander over waving lines of color, seeking a place to pause and rest. But there is no resting place. Eventually the surface seems to rise and fall, and you find it difficult to think of the painting as flat and still. The surface seems to have a life of its own as it reaches out to stimulate and perhaps even disturb you.

Value Apart from Color

There are times when *value* is found to be an important element in works of art even though color is absent. This is certainly the case with drawings, woodcuts, lithographs, and photographs. It is just as true with most sculpture and architecture. Abrupt or gradual changes in value can add greatly to the visual effect of these art forms. Abrupt value changes can suggest planes at various angles to each other. Gradual value changes can indicate concave or convex surfaces. However, they can do more than this. Changes in value can also be used to help the artist express an idea. For example, Nathaniel Kaz uses sudden changes of value to illustrate the complex nature of one of his subjects (Figure 2.5). *Cyrano* is a portrait of a sensitive poet destined to live his life in a ridiculous, awkward body. The contrast be-

tween Cyrano's personality and his appearance is reflected in a sculpture that emphasizes dramatic contrasts of light and dark values.

Line

Line is an element that is difficult to describe. However, most people know what it is and can easily think of several ways to make it. Perhaps the simplest way to describe line is to say that it is a continuous mark made on some surface by a moving point. The marks made by a ball-point pen moving across a sheet of paper are lines. So are the marks made on canvas by a moving paintbrush, or the marks made by the sculptor's finger moving across a clay surface.

Artists use several different types of line in their works to identify and describe objects and their movements and directions. Different effects are created through use of these different types of line.

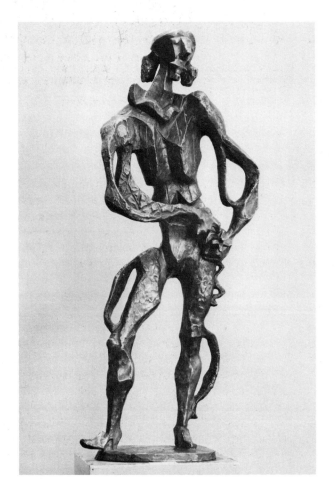

Point to abrupt changes of value in this sculpture. Would your impressions of this work change if the value changes were smooth and gradual? How would they change?

Figure 2.5 Nathaniel Kaz. *Cyrano.* **1950. Bronze, 86.9 x 35.6 x 25.4 cm [34¼ x 14 x 10″]. Collection of the Whitney Museum of American Art, New York. Wildenstein Benefit Purchase Fund**

Point to the different kinds of lines found in this painting—straight and curved, heavy and thin, dark and light. Can you find any other painting in this chapter which also makes use of line as an important element?

Figure 2.6   Drawing by a Six-Year-Old Child

Figure 2.7   Henri de Toulouse-Lautrec. *A Corner of the Moulin de la Galette.* 1892. Approx. 1 x 0.89 m [39½ x 35⅛"]. The National Gallery of Art, Washington, D.C. Chester Dale Collection, 1962

Emphasizing Line

One type of line shows the edges or contours of an object. This is called a *contour line*. Such a line is familiar to anyone who has tried to draw. It is, in fact, one of the most common forms of line used by children. When children pick up pencils or crayons and make their first, uncertain marks on paper, they are using line. This is the beginning of a long association with line as a way of reproducing on a flat surface the things they see around them. As children grow older, they use a combination of lines—straight and curved, thick and thin, long and short—to show figures, houses, trees, and flowers. Usually, children draw these objects in outline form. That is to say, they draw the edges of the objects. They draw this way because their finished pictures seem to match the way the real objects look to them (Figure 2.6).

Artists often use contour lines in much the same way to identify and describe different objects in their drawings and paintings. They do this even though they know that these outlines are not actually a part of the real object. However, the contour line helps to identify the object in a work. The contour line separates the object from the background and from other objects in the same work.

You will find that some artists place great importance on contours or outlines. They use them as a way of adding interest or unity to their paintings. The works created by such artists are frequently called *linear*.

Notice, for example, how the French artist Henri de Toulouse-Lautrec used black outlines to add clarity and interest to his painting of people in a Paris music hall (Figure 2.7). Because of these outlines, every figure is clearly defined and stands out on its own. But more importantly, the black outlines add a decorative accent that increases the picture's appeal.

De-emphasizing Line

Of course, not all artists emphasize line in their work. Some even try to eliminate or hide the outline of objects in their pictures. The term *painterly* is used when describing works by these artists. Claude Monet was such an artist, and you can see why when you look at his painting of haystacks (Figure 16.14, page 300). Monet was interested in recording the fleeting effect of light playing on the various surfaces of objects. In order to do this, he used short brushstrokes to create a shimmering effect in which the contour lines seem to disappear.

Lines Used in Sculpture

Linear and *painterly* are not terms reserved only for discussions about paintings. They are also applied to sculptures. Henry Moore was interested in using a continuous flowing contour line in his sculpture of a reclining figure (Figure 2.8). But Nathaniel Kaz was less interested in contour when he created his sculpture of *Cyrano* (Figure 2.5). He concentrated instead on the light and dark contrasts within the form. These contrasts accent the various parts of the work and their relationships to one another.

It is usually inappropriate to attach labels to artists and their works. However, terms like *linear* and *painterly* can help you see more clearly a quality found in works of art. Thus, when told that a painting or sculpture is linear, you know immediately that the element of line has been stressed. The term *linear* produces a mental image that is quite different from the image that comes to mind when a work is described as painterly.

Lines Suggesting Movement

In addition to defining and describing objects in works of art, line can also serve to suggest movement in some direction. This movement could be horizontal, vertical, diagonal, or curved. Certain feelings or sensations are associated with each of these movements. *Vertical* suggests strength and stability. *Horizontal* suggests calmness. *Diagonal* suggests tension. *Curved* suggests flowing movement. Sometimes the feelings suggested by the lines in a picture can influence your reactions to it. The lines in one picture may help you feel calm and relaxed (Figure 16.8, page 293), while the lines in another may create a tense and uneasy feeling (Figure 14.8, page 251).

Describe the movement of your finger if you could trace it around this sculpture—would it jump about and change direction suddenly, or travel in a smooth, flowing manner?

Figure 2.8   Henry Moore. *Reclining Figure. (Hand).* **1979. Bronze, 2.2 m [7′ 4″] long. Wichita State University, Endowment Association Art Collection, Edwin A. Ulrich Museum of Art, Wichita, Kansas**

An *axis* line can be helpful when you are trying to determine movement and the direction of movement in a work of art. This is an *imaginary* line that is traced through an object or several objects in a picture. It can show you if the object or objects have been organized in a particular direction. For example, examine the painting by Jacob Lawrence in Figure 2.9. Use your finger to trace the movement and direction of the three sailors trudging up the gangplank of their ship. Notice how your finger moves upward in a diagonal direction from the lower left-hand corner to the upper right-hand corner of this painting. The axis line is the line that would have been made if your finger had left a mark on the picture as it moved along this strong diagonal. You should remember that the axis line is not a real line that can actually be seen in a work of art. Rather, it is an imaginary line that you invent and use to trace the direction of movement in a work.

How do the contour lines help to emphasize the strong diagonal movement of these figures?

Figure 2.9   Jacob Lawrence. *War Series: Another Patrol.* 1946. Egg tempera on composition board, 40.6 x 50.8 cm [16 x 20″]. Collection of the Whitney Museum of American Art, New York. Gift of Mr. and Mrs. Roy R. Neuberger

Figure 2.10   Sandro Botticelli. *The Adoration of the Magi.* **c. 1481-82. Approx. 0.7 x 1 m [27⅝ x 41″]. The National Gallery of Art, Washington, D.C. Andrew W. Mellon Collection, 1937**

Some artworks make use of a single axis line. However, others make use of several. When more than one is found, you should determine how these relate to one another. For example, in Sandro Botticelli's painting of *The Adoration of the Magi* (Figure 2.10), four axis lines are combined to form a large "W." Can you find it? Why do you suppose the artist arranged his composition in this manner? The answer becomes obvious when you find that the most important figures in this painting are placed at the point in the center of this "W." It is at that point that the Madonna and Christ Child are located. Even though they are not the largest figures in the picture, they are the most important. Botticelli has skillfully arranged his lines to guide your eye to them.

Axis lines can be just as important in sculpture and architecture as they are in painting. They can help you recognize the rigid, vertical pose of one sculpture (Figure 6.10, page 96), or the active, twisting pose of another (Figure 6.11, page 97). Axis lines can also help

you define the principal vertical emphasis of one building (Figure 2.11), or the horizontal emphasis of another (Figure 2.12).

Texture

Whenever you talk about the surface quality or "feel" of an object, you are referring to its *texture*. In painting, some works have an overall smooth surface in which even the marks of the paintbrush have been carefully concealed by the artist. There are no textural "barriers" or "distractions" to get in the way as your eyes sweep over the smooth, glossy surface. Other paintings have a more uneven surface. This occurs where a heavy application of paint has been used to produce a rough texture that you sense with your eyes and can feel with your fingers. Both types of painting are examples of actual texture because you can actually feel the smooth surface of one and the rough surface of the other.

Figure 2.11   Cathedral of Toledo, Spain. Begun 1227

Sometimes artists glue materials such as paper, cloth, or other real objects to the surfaces of their works to create another kind of actual texture. This technique is known as collage and was introduced around 1911 by a group of French artists known as Cubists (see Chapter 18, page 342). It is a technique that has been widely used ever since. One artist who made use of textures in this way was the American painter Lee Krasner. Some of her paintings (Figure 2.13) include pieces of works that she did many years earlier.

Figure 2.13   Lee Krasner. *Between Two Appearances*. 1981. Oil on canvas with paper collage, 119.4 x 145.4 cm [45 x 57¼"]. The Robert Miller Gallery, New York

Figure 2.12   Frank   Lloyd   Wright. Robie House, Chicago. 1909

Figure 2.14   Gerard Ter Borch. Detail of *The Suitor's Visit*. c. 1658. Oil on canvas, 80 x 75 cm [31½ x 29⅝"]. The National Gallery of Art, Washington, D.C. Andrew W. Mellon Collection, 1937

However, there are many paintings where the surface is smooth to the touch but the sensation of different textures is *suggested* by the way the artist painted some areas. In a picture entitled *The Suitor's Visit* (Figure 2.14), the artist, Gerard Ter Borch, obviously delighted in painting as accurately as possible a range of different textures. There is a distinctive "feel" to the smooth silk of the women's dresses. Another texture is suggested in the suitor's crisp linen collar and cuffs. Still other textures are shown in the soft velvet of the chair and the rough nap of the Turkish carpet on the table. Yet if you were to pass your fingers lightly over this painting, you would find that it is smooth all over. The carpet actually feels as smooth as the white silk dress. When artists try to make different objects in their pictures appear rough or smooth, they are using *simulated texture*. (Of course, you

would never actually do the experiment described in this paragraph, since even the lightest touch could damage the aged and delicate surface of a valuable painting. Usually, you can observe differences in the textures of a painting by examining it closely with your eyes.)

Because three-dimensional forms seem to invite touch, texture is especially important to sculptors. They recognize the urge to touch a sculptured surface and often encourage this by providing rich textural effects. José de Creeft creates obvious contrasts in rough and smooth textures in his sculpture of *The Cloud* (see Figure 2.16, page 28). These different textures are emphasized by the effect of light playing across the surface of the work. In this way, de Creeft has added variety as well as increased textural interest in his sculpture.

Sculptors must not overlook the natural textural qualities of the materials they choose to work with. They know that wood, marble, and bronze all have unique textural qualities of their own. It is necessary to keep this textural quality in mind when they choose the material for a particular work.

Once a sculptor selects the material, it is necessary to decide upon the technique to be used. The technique should make the best use of the textural potential of the material. If a hard, slick, and highly polished surface is desired, the sculptor would probably reject clay or wood as the medium. Instead, a fine marble might be used since this could be filed, sanded smooth, and then polished to a high luster.

Shape and Form

The term *shape* refers to an area of a real or imaginary object which is defined and determined by other elements such as value, line, color, texture, and space. In painting, shapes may take on the appearance of solid three-dimensional objects although they are in fact limited to two dimensions, length and width. This two-dimensional character of shape distinguishes it from "form," which has a depth as well as length and width. Thus, a form is an actual three-dimensional object.

Shapes can be created deliberately in drawing and painting by joining a single continuous line or several lines to enclose an area. For example, when two parallel horizontal lines are joined to two parallel vertical lines, a square or rectangular shape is made.

Usually, when trying to visualize a shape, the first thing that comes to mind is an area surrounded by lines. Yet line is not always needed to create shapes. Many shapes are formed in a more indirect manner without the aid of lines. When an artist paints an area of a picture with a particular color, a shape is created. When an area is isolated by making it texturally different from its surroundings, a shape is created. In both instances, shapes are made without the use of contour lines. However, an imaginary outline might be added later by the viewer to help distinguish those shapes.

Many painters have tried to create the illusion of solid, three-dimensional objects in their works. Frequently, the look of solidity and depth is achieved by painting shapes with light and dark values. For example, a circular shape could be made to look three dimensional by gradually changing its value from light to dark. This technique is effective in reproducing the effect of light on the surface of a round object. When this is combined with a dark shadow cast by that round object, the desired three-dimensional effect is realized (Figure 2.15).

A *form* can be thought of as a shape in three dimensions since it possesses the added dimension of depth. You cannot actually feel around a shape in a painting, but you are able to do so with the forms found in sculpture and architecture.

Two important features of form are *mass* and *volume*. Mass refers to the outside size and bulk of a form, while volume refers to the space within a form.

When discussing the *mass* of a sculpture or a building, the vocabulary of solid geometry is used. This allows you to describe more clearly a three-dimensional work as resembling a cube, a sphere, a pyramid, a cylinder, or a cone. However, this does not mean that a sculpture or a building must be solid. You can use these terms when talking about a simple, block-like stone sculpture or a pyramid, both of which are solid. And you can use them when describing a contemporary sculpture made of transparent plastic and wire or a cathedral. Both of these enclose space, but the sculpture in this instance does not have solid, opaque surfaces or walls, while the cathedral does.

How are the flat shapes in this painting made to look like round, three-dimensional forms?

Figure 2.15   Leon Kroll. *Still Life with Lemon Tree.* 1918. Oil on canvas, 58.4 x 49.5 cm [23 x 19½"]. Allen Memorial Art Museum, Oberlin College, Oberlin, Ohio. Gift of Mrs. Malcolm L. McBride, 42.25

The term *volume* is used during discussions of interior space. In architecture, volume refers to the space within a building. This inside space is determined by the exterior mass of the building. Sometimes volume can be small and confining as in a tiny chapel. At other times it can be huge and expansive as in an enormous cathedral. But you should not limit your concern for volume to buildings alone. You can also refer to the volumes that are created between and within sculptural masses. For example, you might comment on volume when speaking of the areas enclosed by the body, arms, and legs of a reclining abstract figure created by Henry Moore (Figure 19.18, page 380).★

Occasionally it is convenient to describe a sculpture or a building in terms of its shape as well as its form. This is done when you are concerned with the two-dimensional outline or silhouette of a sculpture or building seen from a fixed position. In this way, a sculpture may be found to offer several interesting shapes as you walk around it and view it from different angles. And a building that looks small and square when viewed directly from the front might prove to be very large and rectangular when viewed from one side.

Space

Space can be thought of as the distance or area between, around, above, below, or within things. In art, space is an element that can be described as being either three-dimensional or two-dimensional.

Space that is three-dimensional is recognized as having height, width, *and* depth. Three-dimensional space is known as *actual* space. It is the type of space found in art forms that are themselves three-dimensional. This would include, for instance, sculpture, ceramics, and architecture. For example, when studying José de Creeft's sculpture of *The Cloud* (Figure 2.16) in its museum setting, the viewer can move about freely in the space that surrounds the sculpture. Only then can the viewer see the way this work changes when viewed from different positions. Not only does it offer different shapes, but different images and meanings as well. From one angle the sculpture resembles a cloud. From another, it changes to look like a woman. And from another, it appears to be a mother and child. The work does more than just occupy space. Like a real cloud, it

seems to be moving through space, constantly forming new shapes and suggesting different images as it is blown by the wind. Certainly an understanding of this sculpture would be incomplete if a viewer insisted on examining it from a single point of view rather than walking completely around it.

As noted earlier during the discussion on volume, architecture too is concerned with three-dimensional space. In fact, architecture is an art form devoted to the enclosure of space. To truly appreciate this art form, you must carefully consider the way in which space is treated in different structures.

Unlike three-dimensional artworks, the space in flat, two-dimensional works is limited to height and width. There is no actual depth or distance in such works. However, artists have devised several techniques to create the *illusion* of depth or distance on flat or nearly flat surfaces. These include the following:

• Overlapping the shapes in a work.
• Making distant shapes smaller and closer shapes larger.
• Placing distant shapes higher and closer shapes lower in the picture.

Figure 2.16   José de Creeft. *The Cloud*. 1939. Greenstone, 34.3 x 31.8 x 21.6 cm [13½ x 12½ x 8½"]. Collection of the Whitney Museum of American Art, New York

★ **Enrichment** Abstract art refers to artworks which stress the importance of the elements and principles of design rather than subject matter. Abstract artists select and then exaggerate or simplify the forms suggested by the world around them.

Of course, this painting is flat, but does it *look* flat? How is the illusion of space created? What has the artist used to carry your eye back to the distant hills? How are the hills made to look as if they are far off in the distance?

Figure 2.17   Giorgione. *The Adoration of the Shepherds.* c. 1505-1510. Approx. 0.9 x 1.1 m [35¾ x 43½"]. The National Gallery of Art, Washington, D.C. Samuel H. Kress Collection, 1939

• Using less detail on distant shapes and greater detail on closer shapes.

• Using duller, less intense hues for shapes in the distance.

• Coloring distant shapes with hues that appear more blue to suggest the layers of atmosphere between the viewer and those shapes.

• Slanting the lines of shapes (buildings and other objects) inward to make them appear to extend back into space.

Many of these techniques were used by Giorgione when he painted his *Adoration of the Shepherds* (Figure 2.17). With these techniques, the flatness of the picture plane seems to be destroyed. The viewer is transported into what appears to be a world of actual space, atmosphere, and three-dimensional forms. Giorgione's picture may be an illusion, but it is a very convincing illusion.

Working with the Elements

Typically, artists are faced with the challenge of considering several elements with each step taken in creating a work of art. They cannot, for example, work effectively with color without considering other elements. They must realize that the selection and application of one hue in one part of a painting will have an impact upon the hues, shapes, lines, and textures used in other parts of the work. Some artists respond to this challenge in a deliberate, thoughtful manner, while others are more spontaneous and intuitive. It will be important for you to understand and appreciate the different ways in which different artists respond to this challenge. To do this, you will need to be familiar with the elements of art.

The Principles of Art

Artists "design" their works by controlling and ordering in some way the elements of art. When trying to combine these different elements into an organized whole, they use the principles of art. These principles are balance, emphasis, harmony, variety, gradation, movement, rhythm, and proportion. A skillful blend of elements and principles results in a unified design, a design in which all the parts hold together to produce the best possible effect. Without this overall principle of unity, the work would "fall apart," or appear less successful to the viewer.

The principles of art then describe the different ways artists can use each element. When artists add the element of shape to their paintings, for example, they deliberately or instinctively decide how this element will be used. The placement of certain shapes in the right places might help *balance* the picture. Or a combination of large and small, light and dark shapes could be used to add *variety* to a composition. Some shapes might also be repeated in a way that suggests *movement* or *rhythm* in the picture. A decision might be made to include a series of shapes that change gradually, or in a *gradation,* from round to angular. Or an angular shape might be placed in the midst of many round shapes, a contrast which would create *emphasis.* The difference in *proportion* between a large, important shape and smaller, less important shapes helps to highlight that importance. When working with shape, or any other element, artists seek variety without chaos, *harmony* without monotony. The elements must fit together and work together to make a complete and *unified* whole.

If you were to draw a line down the center of this picture and compare the two halves, what would you find? Can you find any other pictures in this chapter that use this same kind of symmetrical balance?

Figure 2.18   Josef Albers. *Homage to the Square: "Ascending."* 1953. Oil on composition board, 1.1 x 1.1 m [43½ x 43½"]. Collection of the Whitney Museum of American Art, New York

If you were to ask several artists to write down the principles of art, you would probably find that their lists would differ. Some lists would be quite long, while others might contain only a few principles. Perhaps, as in the case of highly intuitive and spontaneous artists, no principles at all would be listed. If questioned, these artists might say that they organize the elements of art by instinct. They are saying, in other words, that they use color, value, line, texture, shape, form, and space in certain ways because the composition "feels right" that way.

In order to understand works of art, you will need to know how the principles of art are used. You will use this knowledge whether you are examining works created by artists who deliberately use a variety of art principles, or by artists who create by instinct. Failure to do this may keep you from recognizing and enjoying one of the most fascinating things about works of art: how they are put together.

The following principles should help you determine how the elements of art can be used to produce art. Remember, each of these principles describes a unique way of combining or joining elements to achieve different effects.

Balance

Balance refers to a way of combining elements to add a feeling of equilibrium or stability to a work of art. Balance can be of two kinds: symmetrical or asymmetrical.

Symmetrical balance means a formal balance in which two halves of a work are identical; one half mirrors exactly the other half (Figure 2.18). This is the simplest kind of balance and is usually found to produce the least interesting composition.

Asymmetrical balance is more informal and takes into account such qualities as hue, intensity, and value in addition to size and shape. All these qualities have an effect on the apparent "weight" of objects in a work of art. It is possible to balance a large white shape at one side of a picture with a similar large white shape at the other side. However, a smaller black shape may accomplish the same result. The result is a "felt balance." The dark value of the smaller shape makes it appear heavier and equal to the task of balancing the larger white shape (Figure 2.19).

What is used to balance the weight of the woman at the far left of this picture? Do you think the "felt balance" found here is more, or less, interesting than the formal balance noted in *Homage to the Square: "Ascending"* by Josef Albers? Can you find any other pictures in this chapter that use asymmetrical balance?

Figure 2.19   Richard Diebenkorn. *Woman by a Large Window.* 1957. Oil on canvas, approx. 1.8 x 1.6 m [70⅞ x 65″]. Allen Memorial Art Museum, Oberlin College, Oberlin, Ohio. R. T. Miller, Jr. Fund, 58.118

In what ways do the shapes contrast in this painting? Can you find contrasts of hue and line as well?

Figure 2.20   Marsden Hartley. *Painting Number 5.* **1914-15. Oil on canvas, 1 x 0.8 m [39½ x 31¾″]. Collection of the Whitney Museum of American Art, New York. Anonymous gift**

Emphasis

Emphasis or contrast is a way of combining elements to stress the differences between those elements. Often, contrasting elements are used to direct and focus the viewer's attention on the most important parts of a design. Artists try to avoid making works of art in which the same colors, values, lines, shapes, forms, textures, and space relationships are used over and over again. They know that such works may be monotonous and uninteresting. To avoid this, they introduce obvious contrasts which establish centers of interest in their works. In *Painting Number 5* (Figure 2.20), Marsden Hartley creates these centers of interest with bold colors and circular shapes. These centers of interest stand out because their colors and shapes contrast with the colors and shapes found in the rest of the painting. Try to imagine how this picture would look without these centers of interest. If they were missing, the picture would lack a great deal of visual interest and it is unlikely that it would hold your attention very long.

Harmony

Harmony refers to a way of combining similar elements in an artwork to accent their similarities. It is accomplished through the use of repetitions and subtle, gradual changes. Complex, intricate relationships are avoided in favor of a more uncomplicated, uniform appearance. Often, a limited number of like elements is used in a effort to tie the picture parts together into a harmonious whole. This is certainly evident in Fritz Glarner's work entitled *Relational Painting* (Figure 2.21). Notice how similar colors, shapes, and values are repeated throughout the painting in an effort to emphasize the overall unity of the picture surface.

Can you find any shapes in this work that are *not* rectangular? How many hues are there? Name them. What are these hues called?

Figure 2.21   Fritz Glarner. *Relational Painting.* 1949-51. Oil on canvas, 1.6 x 1.3 m [65 x 52″]. Collection of the Whitney Museum of American Art, New York

Describe the shapes in this work—are they rounded, angular, or a combination of both? How many hues can you
count? Do these hues differ in value and intensity? Point to
areas with different textures.

Figure 2.22   Max Weber. *Chinese Restaurant.* **1915. Oil on canvas, approx. 1 x 1.2 m [40 x 48″]. Collection of the Whitney
Museum of American Art, New York**

Variety

Variety is a way of combining elements in involved ways
to create intricate and complicated relationships. It is
achieved through diversity and change. Artists turn to
this principle when they want to increase the visual
interest of their works. A picture made up of many
different hues, values, lines, textures, and shapes would
be described as complex (Figure 2.22).

A carefully determined blend of harmony and variety
is essential to the success of almost any work of art.
Artists who concentrate on harmony but ignore variety
may find it easier to achieve balance, but do so at the
expense of interest. Their finished works may look static
and lifeless. On the other hand, artists who overlook
harmony in their quest for variety may find that their
works are too complex and confusing to viewers.

Both harmony and variety must be taken into account during the creative process. Harmony aids efforts to blend the picture parts together to form a unified whole. And variety enables the artist to add visual interest to this unified whole. It is this visual interest which attracts and holds the attention of viewers.

Gradation

Gradation refers to a way of combining elements by using a series of gradual changes in those elements. For example, a gradual change from small shapes to large shapes, or from a dark hue to a light hue, would be gradation. Unlike emphasis, which often stresses sudden and abrupt changes in elements, gradation refers to an ordered, step-by-step change (Figure 2.23).

Movement and Rhythm

Movement is a way of combining elements to produce the look of action or to cause the viewer's eye to sweep over the work in a certain manner. Of course, in a two-dimensional artwork, any look or sensation of action or motion is only an illusion: a horse pictured at full gallop gives only the impression of motion. However, some three-dimensional artworks actually do move. They allow the viewer to study the constantly changing relationships of colors, shapes, forms, lines, and textures found in the artworks. Movement is also used to direct the viewer's attention to a center of interest (emphasis), or to make certain that the main parts of the work are noted. This movement is achieved through placement of elements so that the eye follows a certain path, as the curve of a line, the contours of a shape, or the repetition

Point to the step-by-step change from large to smaller shapes. Can you find any other examples of gradation in this painting?

Figure 2.23   Joseph M. W. Turner. *Mortlake Terrace.* c. 1826. Oil on canvas, 0.92 x 1.22 m [36¼ x 48⅛″]. The National Gallery of Art, Washington, D.C. Andrew W. Mellon Collection, 1937

of certain colors, textures, or shapes (Figure 2.24). Closely related to movement is the principle of *rhythm*. Rhythm is often realized through the careful placement of repeated elements in a work of art to create a visual tempo or beat. These repeated elements invite the viewer's eye to jump rapidly or glide smoothly from one to the next. For example, the same shape may be repeated several times and arranged across the picture to create the sensation of movement in a certain direction. As the viewer's eye sweeps from one shape to the next, this sensation is heightened, as seen in Figure 2.24. Sometimes visual contrasts set up a rhythm when repeating elements are combined with contrasting colors, values, shapes, lines, or textures. For instance, a certain color may rush forward, then backward, or light values may clash with darker values, all the while moving the viewer's eye through the work, as in Figure 2.24.

Proportion

Proportion refers to the relationship of certain elements to the whole and to each other. Often proportion is closely allied to emphasis. If there are more intense hues than dull hues, or more rough textures than smooth, emphasis is suggested. In a similar manner, the large size of one shape compared to the smaller sizes of other shapes would create a visual emphasis. The viewer's eye would automatically be attracted to the larger, dominant shape.

In the past, artists often relied on the principle of proportion to point out the most important figures or objects in their works. The more important figures were made to look larger than the other, less important figures. This was the case in the thirteenth century when a sculptor carved the scene that took place in Christ's tomb following the Resurrection (Figure 2.25). The artist made the sleeping guards at the bottom of the composition much smaller than the other figures. This was done to show that they are not the major perform-

---

Describe the shapes used here. Do these shapes appear to be moving? If so, do they look as if they are moving slowly or rapidly? Can you find another painting in this chapter where repeated shapes have been used to create the illusion of movement?

Figure 2.24   Gabor Peterdi. *Tidal.* **1955. Oil on canvas, approx. 1.3 x 2 m [50 x 80″]. Collection of the Whitney Museum of American Art, New York. Gift of Walter Bareiss**

Figure 2.25 *The Three Marys at the Tomb.* Relief carving from the main portal, Church of the Holy Sepulchre, Estella, Spain. Thirteenth to fourteenth centuries

ers in this drama. They are only supporting actors. The main characters are above, acting out the familiar Easter story. The size of these main characters is as effective as a spotlight in emphasizing their importance.

Unity of the Work

Although *unity* was discussed earlier, its importance demands additional comment here. Unity may be thought of as an overall concept—or principle. It describes the total effect of a work of art. All artists draw from the same reservoir of elements and principles, but few are able to take those elements and principles and fashion works of art that are unique, exciting, and complete. Those who do, achieve what is referred to as unity. Any of the works illustrated in this chapter can be studied in relation to this overall principle.

Discovering Design Relationships in Art

A Design Chart (Figure 2.26) can help you identify the many possible relationships between elements and prin-

Figure 2.26
DESIGN CHART

ELEMENTS OF ART		PRINCIPLES OF ART						
		Balance	Emphasis	Harmony	Variety	Gradation	Movement/Rhythm	Proportion
	Color: Hue							
	Intensity							
	Value							
	Value (Non-Color)							
	Line							
	Texture							
	Shape/Form							
	Space							

UNITY

Note: Do not write on this chart.

ciples in works of art. The first step in determining how a work is put together is to ask the right questions about it. The Design Chart helps identify these questions. For example, begin with any element and then, referring to the chart, ask yourself how this element is used in a work. The questions you come up with will link the element with each principle. You might begin an examination of a painting with the color quality of hue. Then, referring to each principle in order, you would ask and then answer such questions as these:

• Are the hues in the picture *balanced* formally or informally?

• Are contrasting hues used to direct the eye to areas of *emphasis*?

• Is *harmony* achieved through the use of similar hues which are repeated throughout the picture?

• Are different hues employed to add *variety* to the composition?

• Do any of the hues change gradually, or in a *gradation,* from one to another?

• Are the hues arranged to create a feeling of *movement* or *rhythm*?

• Is the presence of any one hue out of *proportion* to the other hues used in the picture?

Once you have completed an examination of hue, you would turn to the next quality of color, which is intensity, and repeat the procedure with all the principles. An analysis carried on in this manner would help you gain the knowledge and understanding needed to determine how the parts of a picture have been put together to achieve *unity.* In the next chapter, you will find that a Design Chart can be a very helpful aid when you are trying to learn as much as you can from a work of art.

A work of art is made up of many different colors, values, lines, textures, shapes, forms, and space relationships. The artist who creates it must combine these elements into an organized whole, and this takes a great deal of knowledge and skill. When viewing a work of art, you must determine how the artist has done this, and that too takes a great deal of knowledge and skill. Without this knowledge and skill, you merely *look* at art, you do not *see* it. And you may never learn to fully appreciate it.

Chapter 3

Seeing, Knowing, Understanding, and Judging

Learning about Works of Art

People have always shown a great deal of interest in art, although in recent years this interest has increased dramatically. Signs of this increased interest are everywhere. Bookstores display attractive new books on art and artists. Motion picture studios produce major films on such artists as Michelangelo, Vincent van Gogh, and Paul Gauguin. Television networks present prime-time specials on art. The discovery of a lost masterpiece is a front-page item in newspapers across the country. Meanwhile, museum officials report that attendance continues to rise every year. Special exhibitions bring out thousands of people willing to wait in long lines to gaze at masterpieces by Rembrandt, Rubens, and Picasso.

Discussions about art are no longer confined to whispered comments in quiet museum corridors, or lively exchanges of opinion at noisy gallery openings. People talk about art every day in homes, schools, and shopping malls—wherever pictures are hung to be seen. For example, a group of students strolling through a shopping mall notice a large art print in the window of a bookstore. They stop to look at it and for a few moments are engaged in a lively discussion about the print. A passerby might hear such statements as these: "Now that's something I wouldn't mind hanging in my room." "Not me; I think it's a mess!" "Well, I think there are some good things to say about it." "There are? Name one!" "I don't care what you say, I like it." "That's fine—you can have it."

You may have noticed that all these statements have something in common. Look again and you will see that they all deal with likes and dislikes. This is a common feature of many conversations about art. As long as the discussion centers on what people like or dislike, everyone participates. However, the talk trails off quickly after everyone has had a chance to voice an opinion.

What is your first impression of this painting? Why do you think you respond to it in that way? Do you think you could learn enough about this work during a brief examination, or would you like to study it more carefully?

Figure 3.1   Meindert Hobbema. *A Pond in the Forest.* **1668. Oil on panel (oak), 60 x 84.5 cm [23⅝ x 33¼"]. Allen Memorial Art Museum, Oberlin College, Oberlin, Ohio. Bequest of Mrs. F. F. Prentiss, 44.52**

People with little experience in art usually have no special way of looking at paintings or sculptures. Often they do not know what to look for in a work of art. They may glance at the work and decide at once if they like it or not. If they do, they may take time to look at it more closely. On the other hand, if their first impression is not favorable, they probably will not take time to examine the work of art further. A realistic landscape by Meindert Hobbema (Figure 3.1) might cause a group of museum visitors to stop and express their admiration with such a statement as "You feel as though you are really there in the picture." On the other hand, a quick glance and a whispered "What's that supposed to be?" may be enough as they hurry past an abstract work by Stuart Davis (Figure 3.2).

Unfortunately, people who do this miss out on a great deal. For one thing, they fail to experience the joy of discovering how these two artists responded to different situations in different ways. Hobbema succeeded in giving us a glimpse of a Dutch landscape just as it must have looked over three hundred years ago. Davis, however, did not try to make his painting look real. Instead, he combined flat, geometric shapes and bright colors in a composition that suggests the sights, sounds, and chaos of a twentieth-century American city. His work is certainly different from Hobbema's. But this does not mean that Davis' work is less successful and cannot be appreciated. Both works can be appreciated, but for *different reasons.*

Many people seem willing to point to artworks that they think are good or successful. However, they often have trouble when it comes to offering good reasons for their decisions. Some might say that a work of art is good if it looks real; others, because it was painted by a famous artist. But these reasons are not convincing. After all, not all successful artworks are realistic, nor were they always done by well-known artists.

In order to make and support intelligent judgments about a work of art, you must first learn as much about the artwork as you can. Learning leads to understanding. Only when you understand a work of art is it possible to make a decision about it and to defend that decision with good reasons. But how do you learn about the work of art? Where do you turn to find information about it?

Two ways of looking and learning in art are art history and art criticism. You can use an art-history approach when you want to learn *about* a work of art. An art-criticism approach will help when you want to learn *from* a work of art. When both of these approaches are used, they can help you understand and appreciate many different kinds of art. But before you can do this, you should become familiar with the differences between these two ways of looking and learning in art. For this purpose, you will be introduced to two imaginary characters. One is an art historian named Helen, and the other, an art critic named Robert.

The Art-History Approach

As an art historian, Helen is mainly interested in identifying and learning about works of art. She tries to place them within a framework of time and place. When studying a work of art, she tries to find out such things as these:

- When was it done?
- Where was it done?
- What style of art does it represent?
- What artists or works of art influenced the artist?
- What impact did the artist or the work have upon artists and works that followed?

To learn all these things, Helen realizes that it is helpful to have a plan of action. Helen's plan makes use of four steps, or operations, which she calls *Description, Analysis, Interpretation,* and *Judgment.*
In Helen's plan,

- Description means discovering when, where, and by whom the work was done.
- Analysis means discovering the unique features of a work of art.

Can you identify any subject matter in this picture? Does it annoy you that most of the objects illustrated here do not look lifelike? Can you point out and name any of the elements of art used in this work? Do you suppose that the selection and arrangement of these elements was more important to the artist than trying to paint a realistic picture of a city?

Figure 3.2 Stuart Davis. *Owh! in San Paõ.* **1951. Oil on canvas, 1.3 x 1.06 m [52¼ x 41¾"]. Collection of the Whitney Museum of American Art, New York**

Figure 3.3 Pierre Auguste Renoir. *A Girl with a Watering Can.* 1876. Oil on canvas, 1 x 0.7 m [39½ x 28¾"]. The National Gallery of Art, Washington, D.C. Chester Dale Collection, 1962

• Interpretation means discovering how artists are influenced by the world around them.

• And Judgment means making a decision about a work's importance in the history of art.

Because Helen will apply these steps from the art historian's point of view (discovering facts *about* a work of art), she will call them *art-history operations.* Later, you will see that these steps, applied in a different way, can also be used for art criticism (or learning facts *from* a work of art).

Observe how an art historian works as you follow Helen's use of these four operations. She is examining a painting of a young girl with a watering can (Figure 3.3).

Description: Discovering When, Where, and by Whom the Work Was Done

During this first operation, Helen tries to find out who painted the work as well as learn when and where it was done. In this instance, her knowledge of art history enables her to immediately identify the artist. Helen does not even have to refer to the signature in the lower right-hand corner of the picture to know that it was painted by the well-known French artist Pierre Auguste Renoir. A date next to the signature reveals that the painting was done in 1876. Since Renoir was born in 1841, Helen realizes that this picture was painted when the artist was thirty-five years old.

At other times Helen might not recognize the artist so easily. Then she would carefully examine the work to see if the artist had signed it. Usually a signature would be found, although it might be the name of an artist

Rouault's unique style involved the use of a heavy, dark outline enclosing brightly colored shapes. As a result, his pictures look like stained-glass windows.

Figure 3.4   Georges Rouault. *Three Clowns.* c. 1933. Oil on cardboard, 36.2 x 23.2 cm [14¼ x 9⅛"]. Allen Memorial Art Museum, Oberlin College, Oberlin, Ohio. Gift of Mr. and Mrs. Joseph Bissett, 56.22

unknown to Helen. This would require her to do research on the artist. She would examine books, magazine articles, newspaper clippings, and letters to learn as much as possible about the artist. In most cases, the needed information is found in readily available sources. However, sometimes a great deal of additional time and effort must be put into research before all the important facts are uncovered.

There are times, of course, when no signature is found on a work of art. Even after a long investigation, it might be impossible to say for certain who created the artwork. Then Helen would make a well-informed guess. She would base her guess upon the information gathered during her investigation. You may have noticed on your trips to museums that some identification labels state that the works are "attributed to" or are "from the school of" this or that artist. These are instances where historians have not yet been able to identify the artist with certainty.

Analysis: Discovering the Unique Features of a Work of Art

Great artists have special ways of seeing and, with their art, they develop their own ways of showing us what they see. Historians call this the artist's individual style. For Georges Rouault (Figure 3.4), this individual style consisted of using a bold, dark outline around brightly colored shapes. Paintings by this artist look like stained-glass windows. In this case, the artist's painting style is as personal and unique as a signature (see also Figure 18.3, page 336).

Following many years of study, historians are able to recognize the main features of an artist's style. They also learn that this style often develops gradually as the artist's special way of seeing matures and as his or her painting skills are perfected. A historian who has studied the development of an artist's style can usually tell if a painting was done early or late in the career of that artist.

During Analysis, the historian tries to learn about the style of an artwork by examining its features. When Helen examines the painting of the girl with a watering can, she sees certain features which she has learned to associate with Renoir's individual style. For example, she notes that strong, pure colors are used in the painting. Also, the edges and details seem to be blurred. Only the child's face is painted in sharp detail. Everything else seems fuzzy as if slightly out of focus. Helen knows that this was the artist's way of showing what the eye sees at first glance. The viewer's eye is attracted to the girl's face, and so this is painted with the most detail. With its rosy cheeks and blue eyes, the face is the center of attention. In contrast, the rest of the picture gives only a general impression. The child's body and the flowers in the garden seem to blur together in the bright sunlight. Renoir's picture shows what you might expect to see if you glanced up a garden path and suddenly spied a girl standing alone in the dazzling afternoon sun.

During Analysis, Helen also tries to group Renoir's painting with other pictures having the same features but painted by other artists. She knows that many works of art have a "family resemblance" which allows historians to group them in the same category. Such works are said to have a group style.

A group style is evident to Helen as she continues to study the painting by Renoir. She observes that the picture is made of bright-colored paint applied in small dabs and dashes. She also notes that some colors are carefully placed next to their complementary colors. This technique makes the bright colors seem even brighter. For example, the red flowers at the top of the picture and the girl's hair ribbon seem more brilliant because they are surrounded by green, the complementary color to red.

Helen knows Renoir's reason for using dabs of paint and carefully selecting and placing the hues in his picture. He was trying to show the flickering effect of sunlight on the child, the grass, and the flowers. She is convinced that light is an important part of this picture, perhaps even the most important part. This decision enables her to group the painting with other works in which the effect of light on subject matter is a major feature. Paintings of this kind were first done in the nineteenth century by a group of French artists. Helen and other art historians now refer to the group style developed by those artists as *Impressionism*. One of the most famous artists in this group was Pierre Auguste Renoir.

Interpretation: Discovering How Artists Are Influenced by the World around Them

When interpreting a work of art, historians consider the influence of time and place upon the artist. They know that pictures of the same subjects painted at the same time but in different countries often reflect different traditions and values. As a result, these pictures may look quite different. A picture of the Madonna and Christ Child painted in Italy during the fifteenth century (Figure 3.5) may be quite different from a picture of the same subject painted in Germany at about the same time (Figure 3.6). Moreover, historians know that pictures of the Madonna and Child painted in the same country but at different times may also have little in common. Works of art are created in real-world settings which have a strong influence on artists. The setting contributes to the ideas formed by artists and the

Observe how these figures are modeled in light and dark values so they appear solid, round, and lifelike. Except for the halos, they look and act like real people. The mother lightly holds her child with one hand. The thumb and forefinger of this hand are slightly curved to lend support to the child's head should it suddenly fall forward. Meanwhile, the child seems a bit restless. Perhaps he is tired of sitting still for so long. He has raised one leg and now grips one of his mother's fingers with his left hand. What could be more natural?

Figure 3.5 Fra Filippo Lippi. *Madonna and Child.* **1440-45. Approx. 80 x 51 cm [31⅜ x 20⅛"]. The National Gallery of Art, Washington, D.C. Samuel H. Kress Collection, 1939**

techniques they choose to interpret those ideas. It even influences the tools and materials artists use to put their ideas into visual form.

In an effort to discover how time and place influenced Renoir, Helen turns to sources of several types. She uses history books, biographies, magazine articles, and published interviews with the artist or people who knew him. From these sources, she learns that when he was thirteen Renoir was already earning a living by working in a porcelain factory painting scenes on china. He used the money earned in this way to pay for his studies at a famous art school in Paris. It was there that he met two other young artists, Claude Monet and Alfred Sisley, and the three became friends. Monet and Sisley convinced Renoir that he should leave his studio and paint outdoors in natural sunlight. Soon Renoir was painting alongside his friends trying, as they were, to capture in his pictures the fleeting, shimmering effects of sunlight on subject matter. In 1874, these three painters were among a group of artists who held a famous exhibition of their work. But the critics scorned and laughed at their paintings. It was these critics who first called the artists *Impressionists* because their works showed a general impression of subject matter. The name was meant to belittle them, although time has changed that. Today, paintings by the Impressionists are among the most admired in the history of art.

The Impressionists were influenced by many things in their world. These influences included new scientific theories about light, the relationship of colors, and the way people see. The recently discovered camera also had an impact on them. They began to paint what seemed to be unstudied, candid views that looked like snapshots. Many of their pictures look as if the artist had come upon an interesting scene and was able to sketch it in a few minutes.

No subject was too small or unimportant for the Impressionists. They left their dark studios and ventured out into the sunlight to record all aspects of life around them. They painted simple scenes of common people going about their daily routines. Of little interest to them were the rousing battle scenes, famous national heroes, and solemn religious events favored by more traditional artists. Some of the Impressionists even found beauty in railway stations and the factory smoke that filled the sky over a nation that was becoming more

Do these look like real people in a real-world setting? Of course not. The figures may be detailed and very charming, but you certainly would not say that they are lifelike. A gold background closes off the space behind so that any similarity to a real-world setting is denied. These figures are placed in an imaginary, heavenly setting.

Figure 3.6   Stephen Lochner. *The Virgin of the Rose-Bower*. c. 1430-35. Approx. 50 x 40.6 cm [20 x 16″]. Wallraf-Richartz-Museum, Cologne

and more industrialized. Renoir, however, preferred to paint the world at its happiest and most beautiful. He refused to include ugliness or evil or sickness in his pictures. It is not surprising then that he decided to paint a simple but happy scene of a little girl holding some flowers and a watering can.

Judgment: Making a Decision about a Work's Importance in the History of Art

Helen's examination of Renoir's painting concludes with her decision about its historical importance. She realizes that some paintings are more important than others because they pioneered many of the new ideas or techniques that inspired artists who followed. She also knows that some works are valued because they are excellent examples of a great artist's fully developed individual style.

The date of Renoir's painting, 1876, tells Helen that it was done when the artist was most interested in the goals of Impressionism. She remembers that Renoir later moved away from Impressionism and painted pictures with more solid forms and clear outlines. But this painting has all the features of the mature Impressionistic style. Perhaps the most important of these features is the use of many colors applied in dabs and dashes to show the effect of sunlight flooding a casual, everyday scene. For this reason, Helen decides that the painting is an excellent example of Renoir's fully developed Impressionistic style. She places great historical importance on it.

As you can see, it is possible to learn a great deal about a work of art if you use the four art-history operations. During each of these operations, you can gather facts and information about the work and the artist who created it. Facts and information of this kind can be called *external*, or "outside," *cues*. ("Cue" is another word for "key" or "clue.") Figure 3.7 shows the external cues you should look for in each of the art-history operations.

At this point you may be wondering why historians devote so much effort to the study of artworks. Perhaps Helen is on the staff of a museum where Renoir's picture is on display. Her research may be the first step leading to a publication on Renoir which museum officials want to have ready for a major exhibition of his work. Or the results of her study might be presented in the form of gallery notes which are made available to museum visitors. These notes are found in many museums. They can be very enlightening to people who know little about Renoir, his style of painting, or his historical importance.

Of course, Helen may not work in a museum at all. She might be a professor of art history at a college or university. Her study of Renoir's painting may have been done as part of her preparation for a lecture on Impressionism. Or perhaps she is planning to write an article on the artist for an art-history journal. In the article, she would share with other scholars what she has learned.

There are many reasons why historians do what they do. They also do it in many different settings. But the important thing to remember is that their knowledge and skill will be a help to you in your appreciation of art. They provide the facts and information about art that contribute so much to others' understanding and enjoyment of it.

Looking Further: Arshile Gorky

Perhaps you are still not quite certain that facts and information about an artist or a work of art can have an effect upon your reaction to that work. If so, examine the painting by Arshile Gorky showing a boy standing beside a seated woman (Figure 3.8). How do you react to this painting? If you were to see it in a museum, would you stop to look at it closely or quickly move on to something more interesting? What relationship do these

Figure 3.7
CHART OF ART-HISTORY OPERATIONS

| External Cues | Art-History Operations | | | |
	Description	Analysis	Interpretation	Judgment
	When, *where*, and by *whom* the work was done.	Unique features of the work of art, compared to features found in other works, to determine its *artistic style*.	How artists are influenced by the world around them, especially by *time* and *place*.	Facts relevant to making a *decision* about the work's importance in the history of art.

Figure 3.8   Arshile Gorky. *The Artist and His Mother.* **1926-29. Oil on canvas, 1.52 x 1.27 m [60 x 50″]. Collection of the Whitney Museum of American Art, New York. Gift of Julien Levy for Maro and Natasha Gorky in memory of their father**

two figures have with one another? How do you think *they* feel and how do *you* feel after looking at them? A brief look into the life of the artist and the circumstances leading up to his painting this picture might well change some of your answers to questions of this kind.

Gorky was born in the mountain forests of Turkish Armenia in 1904. When he was four years old, his father emigrated to the United States to avoid service in the Turkish army. He left Gorky and his sisters in the care of their young mother. Four years later, Gorky and his mother posed for a photograph that was sent to his father in Providence, Rhode Island. Not long after that, in 1915, a bloody conflict between Turks and Armenians living within Turkish borders caused Gorky and his mother to flee Turkey. They marched 240 km [150 miles] to reach safety in what is now Soviet Armenia. That difficult trek and the hardships they endured in Russia were too much for Gorky's mother to bear. In 1919, just four years after their arrival in Russia, she

died of starvation in her son's arms. She was only thirty-nine years old.

Not long after his mother's death, Gorky managed to emigrate to the United States. There, using the photograph taken years before as his inspiration, he painted a haunting double portrait of himself and his mother.

Look at Gorky's painting again. Has your reaction to it changed because of what you have learned about it? Do you think you might still casually pass it by if you came across it on a museum visit? Or would you now stop and look deeply into those haunting eyes to share some of the sorrow the artist must have felt as he painted it?

Of course, this does not mean that every work of art will have a story behind it that will affect your reactions to the work. However, if you fail to look for such a story, you may be missing important information. In your quest for knowledge and understanding, this may not be a risk you wish to take.

The Art-Criticism Approach

Critics, like historians, have their own way of studying works of art. It enables them to find and respond to as much in the artwork as possible. Often, they use the same four operations used by historians: Description, Analysis, Interpretation, and Judgment. However, critics work from a different point of view. They use these operations to gain information *from the work* rather than from books, articles, letters, and other external sources. Art history focuses attention on external cues, or cues found outside the work of art. Art criticism, on the other hand, directs a person's attention to *internal cues,* that is, cues discovered *inside* the work. When examining a painting, critics try to answer such questions as these:

- What is shown in the work?
- How is it organized?
- What does it mean?
- How good is it?

Exploring internal cues as opposed to external cues is the major difference between these two ways of studying works of art. However, there is an added dimension to

Figure 3.9   Rembrandt van Rijn. *The Mill.* **c. 1650. Oil on canvas, approx. 0.88 x 1.06 m [34½ x 41½″]. The National Gallery of Art, Washington, D.C. Widener Collection, 1942**

the art critic's search. The cues which the critic is looking for are more commonly referred to as "aesthetic qualities." During the steps of Description, Analysis, and Interpretation, the critic searches especially for three main types of internal cues, or aesthetic qualities:

- Literal.
- Visual.
- Expressive.

Some of the cues found during Description are *literal qualities* and some, *visual qualities*. Those found during Analysis are *visual qualities*. Those found during Interpretation are *expressive qualities*. Going through these steps before coming to a final judgment can be very helpful. It enables the critic to identify and respond to as many aesthetic qualities as possible in the work.

In order for you to fully understand different works of art, you will need to look at them carefully. This will help you recognize and understand the qualities that make them unique. Once you have identified those qualities in a work, you will be on your way to understanding it. And when you understand the work of art, the chances are that you will begin to enjoy and appreciate it.

To understand more clearly how the critical and historical approaches differ, follow along as the art critic named Robert examines a painting. The work in question is a landscape featuring a windmill silhouetted against a golden sky (Figure 3.9). You will be studying the way Robert uses the operations of Description, Analysis, Interpretation, and Judgment to examine this painting. In this way you will learn *how to look at works of art*. And by studying the three types of aesthetic qualities Robert searches for in the painting, you will learn *what to look for in works of art*.

Description: Discovering What Is in the Work

The first thing that Robert does is to make a complete list of all the things he sees in the painting. In other words, he takes inventory of the *literal qualities* in the work. He makes sure to include everything on his list no matter how small and unimportant it might seem. In this way, he notices the solitary dark windmill and the way it stands out against the sky. Houses and stone barns surround the mill, which is perched on a curved rampart overlooking a quiet river. A glowing sunset is reflected in the still water of the river below.

Looking closer, Robert begins to identify details in the picture. Almost lost in the deepening shadows of dusk are the dim figures of a woman and a child at the lower left. They have crossed a small bridge and walk slowly in the direction of two figures at the river's edge. One of these figures is a man who leans lazily against a small hill. The other figure seems to be a woman who may be washing clothes carried to the river in the basket resting on the ground behind her. A boat glides silently into the picture at the far right. Its sail is furled and a man tends the oars. In the lower half of the picture, shadows creep over the scene. Overhead, the approaching night moves forward to extinguish the golden glow of the setting sun.

Satisfied that he has found all the important details in the picture, Robert turns his attention to listing the *elements of art* used. These, along with the principles of art, constitute the artwork's visual qualities. (The principles of art will be explored in the section on Analysis.) As he studies the painting, he makes note of the different hues, values, shapes, textures, and space relationships in it. He is surprised to find that there are few hues in the work. In fact, the picture has just three main hues—brown, yellow, and blue. There are, however, different values of these hues. They are dark in some places and light in others. Robert also notices that the large brown shapes in the lower half of the picture have strong outlines which help to separate them from the sky behind. The glow in that sky is a deep glow created with a heavy application of paint. This also adds to the painting's rich textural surface.

Robert has now completed his description of the painting. Having found all the important details in the picture, Robert feels confident that his study of its literal qualities is complete. He has also identified the art elements found in the work. Robert is now ready to move on to Analysis, which may be the most difficult of the art-criticism operations.

Figure 3.10
DESIGN CHART

PRINCIPLES OF ART — UNITY

ELEMENTS OF ART	Balance	Emphasis	Harmony	Variety	Gradation	Movement/Rhythm	Proportion
Color: Hue			X (#1)		X (#2)		
Intensity							
Value			X (#4)		X (#3)		
Value (Non-Color)							
Line							
Texture				X (#5)			
Shape/Form		X (#6)	X (#7)				
Space						X (#8)	

Note: Do not write in this book.

Analysis: Discovering How the Work Is Organized or Put Together

During Analysis, Robert tries to learn how the elements of art found in the picture are organized. To do this, he concentrates on the *principles of art*. When he has determined how well the elements have been organized, Robert will have an understanding of the painting's *visual qualities.*

Robert decides to complete a *Design Chart* which will help him analyze this picture. (This same Design Chart was discussed in Chapter 2. There it was pointed out that such a chart can help you discover how a work of art is organized or put together.) This chart will act as a checksheet. Robert can use it to identify the relationships between elements and principles found in the work. If you were to look over Robert's shoulder, you might see him working on a Design Chart like the one in Figure 3.10.

Robert's Design Chart records the most important relationships between elements and principles observed in the picture. Notice, for example, that the first mark (#1) is placed at the intersection of hue and harmony. This reflects his decision that an uncomplicated, uniform appearance is due mainly to the fact that the yellow and brown hues in particular are distributed throughout the entire composition. Gradation in both hue (#2) and value (#3) is noted in the sky where pale yellow and pale blue towards the center change gradually to dark brown at the left and top.

Robert's chart also indicates that the dark values in the sky are repeated in the lower half of the work, adding harmony to the painting (#4). Texture is accounted for by a mark under variety (#5). Variety in texture has been achieved by a difference in the way the sky and the shadow area have been painted. The sky reveals a thick application of paint, while the shadow area is more thinly painted. This change in texture helps to increase the visual and tactile interest of the work.

The dark shape of the solitary windmill is clearly the center of interest in this painting. This is achieved by the dramatic contrast between the windmill and the lighter value of the sky behind. For this reason, Robert placed a mark at the intersection of shape and emphasis (#6). He also decided that shape and harmony are related (#7). The principal shapes in the work are unified by their similarity in value.

Observing that overlapping shapes were used to lure the viewer's eye deeper and deeper into the work, Robert placed a final mark at the intersection of space and movement (#8). As he did so, he saw that this illusion of space is accented by the differences in values noted earlier (#3). The darker parts of the sky appear to be much closer, while the lighter parts seem to extend far back into the picture.

Of course, Robert could have gone on to identify additional design relationships in the picture had he chosen to do so. Many other, more subtle relationships could have been uncovered with further analysis. And, having done this many times before, Robert had developed fully his skills at analysis. (Although he remembers how difficult it had seemed when he was learning how to analyze works of art.) However, on this occasion, he is satisfied with his identification of the most important and obvious design relationships. Now, having done this, he is ready to move on to an interpretation of the work.

Interpretation: Discovering the Meaning, Mood, or Idea in the Work

Robert is eager to interpret the picture because he knows that this is the most exciting and the most personal of the art-criticism operations. Here he takes everything he learned about the work during Description and Analysis and tries to determine what it all means. His concern then centers on identifying the *expressive qualities* in the picture. However, Robert realizes that a work of art is often very complicated. It can be interpreted in different ways by different people. For this reason he does not believe that his interpretation will be the only one possible. He knows that his interpretation will be a personal one, based upon information he has gathered from the picture.

For a time, Robert viewed the painting as a possible symbol or idea. Perhaps, he thought, the windmill, steadfastly silhouetted against the sky, was meant to represent and honor the patriotism of a brave people or nation. But the longer he viewed the picture, the more Robert began to feel that it spoke more eloquently of peacefulness and stillness. It is evening and the day's work is done. The only sounds are the occasional creaking of the old mill, the gentle splash of boat oars, the muffled voice of a mother talking to her child. Darkness has started to settle over a drowsy world. In the shadows, half-hidden figures can be seen moving slowly as though weary after a long day's activity. But, in addition to peacefulness, there is a feeling of solitude and loneliness in the picture. This feeling can be traced to the single idle windmill outlined dramatically against the fading sunset. The great sweep of the sky seems to overwhelm the windmill and adds to its isolation. Robert finally decides that the picture presents a mood of peaceful silence. This mood, he feels, is tempered by a strain of loneliness and melancholy. It is a mood that he finds both comforting and restful. His examination of the painting's qualities is complete.

Imitationalism requires that a work of art look real or lifelike in order to be considered successful. Do you think that this painting would be appreciated by someone using that theory of art?

Figure 3.11 Marie Louise Elisabeth Vigée-Lebrun. *The Marquise de Peze and the Marquise de Rouget with Her Two Children.* 1787. Oil on canvas, 1.23 x 1.56 m [48⅝ x 61⅜"]. The National Gallery of Art, Washington, D.C. Gift of the Bay Foundation in memory of Josephine Bay Paul and Ambassador Charles Ulrick Bay, 1965

Judgment: Making a Decision about the Work's Success or Lack of Success

Judgment is the final art-criticism operation. It is the step in which all the information gathered earlier can be put to use. Of prime importance in these earlier operations have been three types of aesthetic qualities: the literal, the visual, and the expressive. They will also play important roles in the final art-criticism operation.

Reasons for Studying These Aesthetic Qualities

You may wonder why the literal, visual, and expressive qualities have been singled out for discussion here. It is because these three seem to be the aesthetic qualities often referred to by critics during discussions about art. Some critics feel that the literal qualities of a painting make it successful. They feel that the most important thing about a work of art is the realistic presentation of subject matter. It is their feeling that a work is successful if it looks like and reminds the viewer of what he or she sees in the real world. People with this view feel an artwork should *imitate* life, that it should look lifelike before it can be considered good (Figure 3.11). Their theory is called *imitationalism*. On the other hand, some feel that the visual qualities must be dominant for a painting to be successful. They contend that the most important aspect of a work of art is the effective arrangement of the art elements according to the principles of art. Their theory is known as *formalism*. It holds that an effective organization depends upon how well the artist has arranged the colors, values, lines, textures, shapes, forms, and space relationships used in the work (Figure 3.12). Works of art that use these elements successfully are said to have unity. Still others deny both imitationalism and formalism. They claim that no object can be considered art if it fails to

Do you think that this is a lifelike painting? Of course not. But while an imitationalist might ignore or reject it for this reason, a formalist might call it highly successful. Why? Because it demonstrates an effective use of the elements and principles of art to create a flat, decorative, unified design.

Figure 3.12 Henri Matisse. *Young Girl Seated.* 1936. Oil on canvas, approx. 62 x 51 cm [24¼ x 20"]. Allen Memorial Art Museum, Oberlin College, Oberlin, Ohio. Gift of Mr. and Mrs. Joseph Bissett, 59.120

Some viewers may feel that the elements and principles do not contribute to a unified design in this work. The colors, shapes, and lines exaggerate the depth of the picture, and this interferes with the picture's overall balance. The work seems to ignore the literal and visual qualities in an attempt to communicate a powerful message. Concentrating on the expressive qualities enables viewers to identify that message. When doing so they might ask such questions as the following: Why is the foreground mirrored in the background? Does this scene resemble the Brooklyn identified in the title? Is that resemblance important? Who are the women in the capsule, and why are they weeping? Why does the lamppost look like a dagger? Answers to these questions might help the viewer discover an emotional message in the work. This could lead to a positive judgment of the work by someone using the emotionalist theory.

Figure 3.13 Louis Guglielmi. *Terror in Brooklyn.* 1941. Oil on canvas, 86.4 x 76.2 cm [34 x 30"]. Collection of the Whitney Museum of American Art, New York

communicate with the viewer. The expressive quality is most important to them. Their theory, called *emotionalism*, places greatest importance on the feelings, moods, and emotions communicated, or expressed, to the viewer by the work of art (Figure 3.13).

These three theories of art, summarized in Figure 3.14, can be very useful when you look for different aesthetic qualities in works of art. Keep in mind, though, that each of these theories stresses some aesthetic qualities and rejects others. (Of course, there are other theories of art in addition to imitationalism, formalism, and emotionalism. But these three seem to account for the aesthetic qualities often referred to in art discussions.)

Figure 3.14

CHART OF ART THEORIES AND AESTHETIC QUALITIES

Aesthetic Qualities	Theories of Art		
	IMITATIONALISM	FORMALISM	EMOTIONALISM
	Literal Qualities:	Visual Qualities:	Expressive Qualities:
	The most important thing about a work of art is the realistic presentation of subject matter. A work is successful if it looks like and reminds us of what we see in the real world.	The most important thing about a work of art is the effective organization of the elements of art through the use of the principles.	The most important thing about a work of art is the vivid communication of moods, feelings, and ideas to the viewer.

Formalism, which stresses the importance
of the elements and principles of art,
would be very helpful when you are trying
to gain an understanding of a painting
like this.

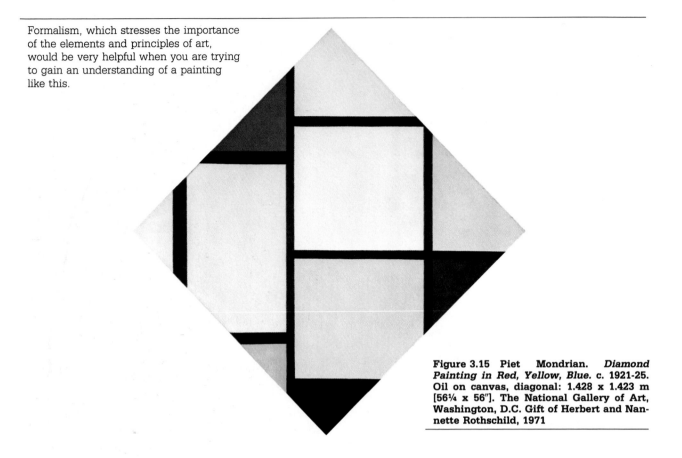

Figure 3.15 Piet Mondrian. *Diamond Painting in Red, Yellow, Blue.* c. 1921-25. Oil on canvas, diagonal: 1.428 x 1.423 m [56¼ x 56″]. The National Gallery of Art, Washington, D.C. Gift of Herbert and Nannette Rothschild, 1971

Importance of Trying More than One Theory

It is during Judgment, the last art-criticism operation, that Robert must make a decision about the merits of the painting entitled *The Mill*. He knows that some art critics would call a painting successful only because of its outstanding literal qualities. Others would do so because of the painting's superb visual qualities. Still others would do so because of its fine expressive qualities. Robert knows, however, that if he always uses the same theory with its emphasis only on certain qualities, he may be doing the artwork an injustice. He will be in danger of overlooking other important qualities stressed by the other theories.

This will also be true of you if you rely on a single art theory. It will cause you to limit your search for information to just those qualities favored by the theory you are using. This will place you at a disadvantage, especially when you examine different works of art. Imitationalism, for example, may be very helpful when examining works that are realistically painted. However, it would be useless when examining paintings where there is no realistic subject matter. In such cases, it would be wise to turn to one or both of the remaining theories.

To illustrate this last point, examine the painting by the Dutch artist Piet Mondrian (Figure 3.15). There is no recognizable subject matter in this painting. It is a work in which colors, lines, and shapes have been used to create simple vertical and horizontal units. These units have been arranged in a precise and formal order. Since there is no subject matter, imitationalism, which emphasizes literal qualities, would not be useful here. Insisting on using this theory would result in rejecting Mondrian's painting as a successful work of art. In order to avoid this and gain an understanding of this painting, you would have to turn to another theory for help. Of the two remaining theories discussed, formalism and emotionalism, which do you think would be the most useful in helping you to understand this painting? Formalism, with its emphasis on the elements and principles of art, would be the most helpful here. Why? Because the painting ignores both realistic subject matter and the expression of a mood or feeling. Instead, it favors a balanced arrangement of carefully selected colors, shapes, and lines.

However, consider the painting by Matthias Grüne-wald in Figure 3.16. It seems to ignore the rules of good design stressed by formalism. Yet, it would still be regarded as an outstanding work of art if another theory were used. This painting succeeds in communicating a powerful message to the viewer. By using emotionalism as a guide, the viewer is able to "read" this message of violence and suffering.

Always remember that a single theory of art can point out some qualities in some works of art, but it will fail to point out all the qualities in all works of art. For this reason you should develop the habit of trying out *all three theories* of art each time you examine a painting. When you do this, you will be more likely to discover more aesthetic qualities in the work. And a knowledge of these qualities is essential if you are to understand and appreciate the work of art.

An Art Critic's Decision

For his part, Robert decides that *The Mill* is a good work of art. He feels he can defend that decision by referring to everything he learned about it during the earlier criticism operations.

During the descriptive operation, he was impressed by the literal qualities of the work. These were the qualities emphasized by imitationalism. Robert was impressed with the authentic look of the ancient windmill, the surrounding houses and barns, the small figures, and the golden sunset. He also liked the way light and shadow were used to lure his eye deeper and deeper into the work. When he analyzed it, Robert saw how well the painting was organized. Using the formalistic theory, he focused on the principles of art. Among the things he observed during Analysis was the way hues, values, and shapes were used to add harmony to the picture. This harmony was balanced with variety in the form of different rough- and smooth-textured surfaces which added visual and tactile interest to the work. And, Robert was especially impressed with the way the windmill stood out boldly against the glowing sky. Clearly, the windmill was meant to be the center of interest in this painting. The result was a painting that to Robert seemed simple, monumental, and majestic. At the same time, he felt it was a composition in which all the elements contributed to an overall sense of wholeness and unity. But Robert was most pleased by the expressive qualities stressed by emotionalism. These were the aesthetic qualities that became apparent as he interpreted the work. He was struck by a feeling of calmness he found in the picture, a calmness which seemed to creep silently across a weary world. It seemed to emerge in the same quiet way that the lengthening shadows of night advanced softly to wrap all things in darkness. To

Using emotionalism as a guide helps you focus attention on the powerful feelings and emotions contained in this painting.

Figure 3.16   Matthias Grünewald. *The Small Crucifixion.* **c. 1510. Approx. 61.6 x 46 cm [24¼ x 18⅛"]. The National Gallery of Art, Washington, D.C. Samuel H. Kress Collection, 1961**

Robert, the work clearly showed that moods and feelings can be communicated by a painting in which human subjects play a minor role.

Clearly, Robert made certain that he considered all three theories of art as he progressed through the criticism operations. By doing so, he felt confident that he had attended to a range of different aesthetic qualities found in the painting.

His examination of the painting finished, Robert might now wish to look at what others have had to say about it. No doubt he would want to know what historians like Helen had written about the work. It is at this point that Robert concerns himself with certain external cues. These would include the name of the artist, when and where the picture was painted, and the artistic style it represents. Of course, as an experienced critic with a broad education in art, Robert knew many of these things before he began his study of the work. He had realized at once that the painting was done by Rembrandt, one of the most famous of all painters. However, he made a conscious effort to disregard these cues during his examination. He knew that if he took these external cues into consideration too soon they might influence his study of the internal cues and color his judgment.

Keep in mind that the critic's main objective is to gain an understanding of the work of art. In order to do this, a systematic approach to art criticism is used. The outline in Figure 3.17 summarizes the four operations involved in such a systematic approach.

Why Critics Study Art

Earlier in this chapter, some of the reasons why historians study art were briefly discussed. Having observed a critic examine a painting, you might be curious about the purpose of such efforts. Robert, for example, might be on the staff of a newspaper or magazine where he writes a column about art. Perhaps he was assigned to write an article on *The Mill* because it was included in a major exhibition of Rembrandt's work held at the local art museum. His published critique of the painting would make use of clear and precise language. This would allow him to share with his readers what he saw and experienced in the work.

Or perhaps Robert is an art consultant rather than a newspaper critic. As such he would be called upon to offer advice to clients who want to buy or sell works of art. His list of clients would include individuals who are interested in collecting. It could also include small businesses and large corporations which maintain their own collections. By doing this, businesses and corporations not only encourage the arts, but also provide a more attractive setting for their employees. Then again, Robert might work side by side with art historians in a museum. There the things he learned from the painting of *The Mill* could be combined with information about the artist gathered by historians. It is possible that their joint effort might lead to the production of an art film or television program. In whatever situation he finds himself, Robert, like all critics, realizes that his primary goal is to aid others in their search for meaning and pleasure in art.

Combining a Way of Looking with a Knowledge of What to Look For

The art critic, then, combines a way of looking with a knowledge of what to look for. The critic uses the four art-criticism operations as an aid in looking for cues to the work's aesthetic qualities. These, in turn, are keys to judging the work's success. Now consider using this process to your own advantage in judging a work of art.

Figure 3.17
CHART OF ART-CRITICISM OPERATIONS

| | | Art-Criticism Operations | | | |
		Description	Analysis	Interpretation	Judgment
Internal Cues		What is in the work, discovered through an inventory of the *subject matter* and/or *elements of art* found in the work.	How the work of art is *organized* or put together; concern centers on how the principles of art have been used to arrange the elements of art.	Possible *feelings, moods,* and *ideas* communicated by the work of art.	Facts relevant to making a *decision* about the degree of artistic merit in the work of art.

Figure 3.18

USING ART-CRITICISM OPERATIONS TO DISCOVER DIFFERENT AESTHETIC QUALITIES IN WORKS OF ART

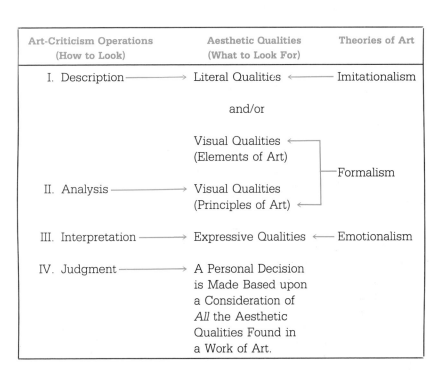

Art-Criticism Operations (How to Look)	Aesthetic Qualities (What to Look For)	Theories of Art
I. Description ⟶	Literal Qualities ⟵	Imitationalism
	and/or	
	Visual Qualities (Elements of Art) ⟵	
		Formalism
II. Analysis ⟶	Visual Qualities (Principles of Art) ⟵	
III. Interpretation ⟶	Expressive Qualities ⟵	Emotionalism
IV. Judgment ⟶	A Personal Decision is Made Based upon a Consideration of *All* the Aesthetic Qualities Found in a Work of Art.	

How the Process Can Work for You

Imagine yourself standing before a painting. You know that you should try to find as many aesthetic qualities in that painting as you can. Because you are now familiar with literal, visual, and expressive qualities, you are interested in seeing if these qualities are in the work. But what is the best way of finding them? Then you remember the four art-criticism operations: Description, Analysis, Interpretation, and Judgment. These steps form a search strategy which will help you find those aesthetic qualities. The first three operations are used to find the different aesthetic qualities stressed by imitationalism, formalism, and emotionalism. The approach, outlined in Figure 3.18, will help you in your search. It makes sure that you will take into account the aesthetic qualities favored by each of these theories when you examine the painting before you. Using this method will help you to make and support wise judgments about it.

During Description, you should list the literal qualities stressed by imitationalism. You should also list the elements of art favored by formalism. If the painting does not have recognizable subject matter (as in Mondrian's painting, Figure 3.15, page 54), then you would list only the elements of art used. Later, during Analysis, your attention would shift to the principles of art also stressed by formalism. When interpreting the work, concern would center on the expressive qualities emphasized by emotionalism. Judgment, the fourth and final criticism operation, would require a personal decision on your part. You would have to decide if the various aesthetic qualities in the work are used effectively.

In this way, you might decide that the painting is successful because of the skillful handling of realistic subject matter (literal qualities). Or you might decide the painting is a success because it provides an effective and pleasing arrangement of art elements (visual qualities). Or perhaps you feel it is successful because it offers a clear and powerful idea in visual form (expressive qualities). The painting might be considered successful for any *one or more* of these reasons.

Examine this painting carefully and then make a judgment about it. To which aesthetic qualities—literal, visual, or expressive—did you refer when making your decision? Did you turn to more than one of these qualities?

Figure 3.19 John Constable. *A View of Salisbury Cathedral*. c. 1825. Oil on canvas, 73 x 91 cm [28¾ x 36"]. The National Gallery of Art, Washington, D.C. Andrew W. Mellon Collection, 1937

Using the Process on Specific Artworks

For example, assume that the painting you have been studying is *A View of Salisbury Cathedral* by John Constable (Figure 3.19). You might decide that this painting is successful because it offers a well-done, realistic treatment of the subject matter. After all, the picture captures the fleeting effects of sky, light, and atmosphere. It makes you feel almost as if you are actually there looking at the real thing. However, you might also praise the picture because of the way the artist has arranged the elements of art to produce a unified design. Constable's combination of light and dark values could be a major reason why you thought this work was successful. Also, you may have noticed that he did not paint his trees and meadows in one uniform green. Instead, he used a rich pattern of light- and dark-green values that helps bind the picture parts together into a unified composition. The light area of the sky and cathedral is joined visually with the light-green areas of the foreground. But the combination of light and dark values contributes even more than this to the picture's effectiveness. The dark-green values, which contrast with the lighter area of the sky and cathedral, also serve to frame the center of interest. Thus, the viewer's attention is drawn to the distant spire of a great cathedral. Finally, you might feel this painting is successful because it communicates a feeling of peacefulness or calmness. You can almost feel the pleasant warmth of the summer sun, the inviting coolness of the shaded areas beneath the trees, the gentle breeze which stirs the leaves and grass. It is a casual, no-rush world that Constable paints. His picture allows you to experience that world and feel relaxed and refreshed as a result of that experience.

Following Description and Analysis, try to interpret the feeling or mood you receive from this building. Is it serious and forbidding? Gay and inviting? Dark and mysterious? What kind of people would live in such a house? What does this building tell you about the kind of lives they might lead?

As you can see, a work such as Constable's *View of Salisbury Cathedral* can be judged in terms of its literal qualities, its visual qualities, or its expressive qualities. Moreover, it can be judged with *all* these aesthetic qualities in mind. You might decide that it is successful (or unsuccessful) because of the way it deals with one, two, or all three of these qualities.

The same procedure would be followed when you critically examine an example of architecture. During Description, you should concentrate on identifying the principal features of a building—doors, windows, towers, and building materials. You could then list the elements of art used. When analyzing a building, you would note how the principles of art have been used to organize the elements. The meaning or purpose of the building would be probed during Interpretation. At this point, you would discover that some buildings, like paintings and sculptures, can communicate unmistakable moods and feelings (Figure 3.20). As in judging other forms of visual art, judgments about architecture should be based upon how well the various aesthetic qualities have been used.

Figure 3.20   John Nash. The Royal Pavilion. Brighton, England. c. 1816-22

When to Use Art History and Art Criticism

Earlier it was stated that when you use both art history and art criticism, you are more likely to learn as much as possible about and from a work of art. But when you are standing before a painting or looking at a reproduction of one in a book, where do you start? Do you first use art history or art criticism? Should you begin by determining who painted it, where and when it was painted, and what style it represents? Or should you first identify the aesthetic qualities used and then decide for yourself if these qualities have been used to create a successful work of art?

If a work of art is going to mean anything special to you, then you must become personally involved with it. You should avoid depending entirely upon others to tell you whether it is good or bad. Rather, you should be prepared to make your own decisions about it. Only after you have made these personal decisions will you want to turn to what others have said about the work. You may recall that Robert did not consider what others had to say about the painting of *The Mill* until after he had finished his own examination of it.

It is suggested then that when you study a work of art, you should begin with the art-criticism operations. Concentrate on finding the internal cues which will enable you to learn as much as you can from the work. When this has been done, you will be ready for the art-history operations. They will help you to find the external cues about the work and the artist who created it. During the art-history process, you will have a chance to make additional decisions about the work. This time, those decisions will relate to its historical importance. After you have done this, you can compare your decisions to those expressed by others. Remember, however, that the final decision is *yours* to make and defend. If you forget this, it is doubtful that your experience with the work of art will be personally rewarding.

In your reading about art and during visits to museums, you will encounter many works that you will want to examine closely. These examinations will be more valuable to you if you follow the sequence of art-criticism and art-history operations outlined in Figure 3.21.

Figure 3.21

A SEQUENCE OF ART-HISTORY AND ART-CRITICISM OPERATIONS

		Description	Analysis	Interpretation	Judgment
I.	Art Criticism	Make an inventory of the subject matter and/or the elements of art.	Determine how the work of art is organized or put together; concern centers on the principles of art.	Identify the feelings, moods, and ideas communicated by the work of art.	Make a personal decision about the degree of artistic merit of the work of art.
II.	Art History	Determine when, where, and by whom the work of art was completed.	Identify the features in the work and compare these to features found in other works to determine its artistic style.	Investigate the influence of time and place upon the artist who created the work of art.	Make a decision about the work's importance in the historical development of art.

Review

The sequence of steps you will be using in your study can be summarized briefly as follows. Describing the work from the art critic's point of view, you will discover what is in the work of art. You will look for the literal qualities (stressed by imitationalism) and the elements of art (stressed by formalism). As you analyze the work, you will discover how it is organized. You will look for the principles of art, which, along with the art elements, constitute the visual qualities (stressed by formalism). The Design Chart shown in Figures 2.26 and 3.10 can be of help to you during Analysis. Using it as described on pages 38 and 51 will aid you in checking the relationships between elements and principles in a work of art. As you interpret the work, you will discover its meaning, mood, and underlying idea. You will look for the expressive qualities (stressed by emotionalism). As you judge the work, you will make a decision about the work's success or lack of success.

Describing the work from the art historian's point of view, you will discover when, where, and by whom the work was done. As you analyze the work, you will discover its unique features. As you interpret the work, you will learn how the artist was influenced by the world around him or her. As you judge the work, you will make a decision about its importance in the history of art.

The first time you attempt this process it may seem difficult and time consuming. However, each time after that will be easier and faster. You may be surprised to discover how much you can learn from and about a work of art by doing this. And you may be pleased to find how much meaning, pleasure, and excitement you can receive from that work once you understand it.

Studio Experiences

Lesson One: A Still Life with an Emphasis on Literal Qualities

Examine Vigée-Lebrun's *The Marquise de Peze and the Marquise de Rouget with Her Two Children* (Figure 3.11) and Chardin's *Still Life with Rib of Beef* (Figure 15.4, page 272). Acting as a critic using imitationalism as your guide, discuss the literal qualities in these paintings. Notice how both artists went to great lengths to present a faithful duplication of their chosen subject matter. Next, use tempera paint to produce a still life which includes no less than three familiar objects. These objects should first be drawn and then painted as accurately as possible. Like Vigée-Lebrun and Chardin, your attention should focus upon completing a painting in which the literal qualities are stressed.

Safety Note

When using tempera paint or other art materials, make certain that the container or package bears one of the following safety labels: AP (Approved Product); CP (Certified Product); or CL (Certified Label). The AP and CP labels certify that the product contains no material in sufficient amounts to be toxic or dangerous to the user. The CP label also indicates that the product meets specific quality standards. A CL seal is used to certify art products which are appropriate for older students (over twelve years of age) and adults. If you find a CL on a product label, read the rest of that label carefully. It will contain cautionary statements required by law, and these should be understood and adhered to when using the product.

Lesson Two: A Still Life with an Emphasis on Visual Qualities

Identify and discuss the visual qualities noted in Matisse's *Young Girl Seated* (Figure 3.12) and Braque's *Blue Guitar* (Figure 18.13, page 345). Refer to the Design Chart on page 37, which identifies different ways of combining the elements and principles to create a work of art. Identify at least five of these relationships on which to concentrate while completing a second still-life painting. Use the same objects employed in the first painting. However, do not concern yourself with painting those objects to look real. Instead, abide by the five decisions you made on the Design Chart as you plan and complete your painting. In this way your work will stress the visual qualities.

Lesson Three: A Nonobjective Composition with an Emphasis on Expressive Qualities

Study Guglielmi's *Terror in Brooklyn* (Figure 3.13) and Kandinsky's *Improvisation 28* (Figure 18.8, page 340). What expressive qualities (ideas, moods, or feelings) can you identify in these paintings? Using watercolors, torn magazine illustrations, and glue, create your own expressive composition. This composition should attempt to communicate a one-word idea such as lonely, happy, terrified, or sad. To do this, arrange on a section of 31 x 46-cm [12 x 18-inch] poster board a variety of shapes torn from newspapers and magazines. The illustrations and words on these torn shapes should reflect your one-word idea, *but in subtle terms.* Arrange your shapes to create a center of interest and glue them in place. Then use opaque and transparent watercolors to tone down distracting or unimportant areas and emphasize important areas. Several layers of paper and watercolor may be needed before you are satisfied with your composition.

PART II
SEEING TO LEARN

"A country could be perfectly governed, immensely powerful and without poverty; yet if it produced nothing of its own in architecture, sculpture, music, painting, or in books, it would some day pass into the twilight of history, leaving only the traces of a creditable political record."

Booth Tarkington

Before proceeding with Part II, review Chapter 1, page 13, "How to Use This Book."

Chapter 4

The Magic Picture: Prehistoric Art in Western Europe

You are inside the cave of Altamira in northern Spain walking down a wide passageway carved by an ancient underground river. You have been in the cave only a few minutes when you come upon a large, low chamber on your left. Your guide signals you to stop and quietly whispers that you are about to enter what one French scholar called the Sistine Chapel* of prehistoric art. You hesitate a moment. Having seen pictures of prehistoric cave paintings, you think you are prepared for what you are about to experience. But a few seconds later, gazing upward, you realize that no picture could have prepared you for what you see. You are struck by the visual impact of huge, powerful animals parading silently across the rough ceiling of the cavern . . .

Life in Prehistoric Times

One of humanity's earliest achievements was art. Long before they could write or fashion utensils and weapons from metal, early humans were painting and scratching pictures of animals on the uneven walls of their caves and rock shelters. This was a remarkable achievement when you consider what it must have been like to live in a world where each person fought a daily battle for survival. The lives of prehistoric people were filled with danger, hunger, ignorance, and fear. Winter found them searching for shelter from the cold and snow, and in the summer they suffered from the heat and sudden rains that flooded their cave dwellings. Those who were

fortunate enough to survive were old in their early forties, and few lived beyond their fiftieth year. It is difficult then to understand why these people took time to produce art. Certainly it would be reasonable to expect that the artworks they did create would be primitive and crude. But are they? This is a question you should answer for yourself. However, before you do this, it is necessary to examine thoroughly an example of prehistoric art. Such an example is a painting of a bison from the ceiling in Altamira (Figure 4.1).

Cave Painting: The Bison from Altamira

To help you in your examination of this painting it is suggested that you use the art-criticism operations to describe, analyze, interpret, and judge it. You will recall that these operations were discussed in Chapter 3. In that chapter it was suggested that you gather as much information as possible from a work by looking for the answers to certain questions about it ("the Art-Criticism Approach," pages 48-59). Finding the answers to these questions will add to your understanding and enjoyment of the work of art.

Describing the Work

As you examine the bison from Altamira, try to describe the animal to yourself. You can do this by asking and answering questions about the various features of the animal. For example, where is the head and what position is it in? Are the legs clearly defined? Are the legs extended or are they pulled upward? Does the animal seem to be motionless, or is movement suggested? As you scan the picture further, you might notice that just a few details were used to highlight the most important features of the bison.

★ **Enrichment** This is the famous chapel in the Vatican, the headquarters of the Pope in Rome, where paintings by Michelangelo decorate the entire ceiling and one wall.

Did you notice that the animal is not placed in a setting? Indeed, there is no hint of the ground beneath its hooves, nor are there signs of trees or hills or sky behind the bison. What effect does this have upon the animal's apparent size and its position in space?

Before moving on to Analysis, you should ask yourself about the elements of art found in this painting. What hues are noted? What kinds of values and lines are employed? How would you describe the shapes that are used—are they rounded, angular, or both? Do you think that the rough texture of the stone surface on which it was painted adds to the overall effect of the animal? Does it look flat or does it seem to extend out from the ceiling into space?

After you have asked and answered Description questions, you might be inclined to say that this painting of a bison is surprisingly lifelike. But how was this lifelike quality achieved? To find the answer, you'll need to consider how the principles of art are used in arranging the art elements to achieve a realistic appearance.

Analyzing the Work

Using a copy of the Design Chart illustrated in Chapters 2 and 3, pages 37 and 50, will help you determine how the art elements were used to create this painting of a bison. Refer to the painting as you consider each relationship of element and principle indicated on the Design Chart. For example, notice how the rich reddish hue is applied in such a way that the three-dimensional mass or volume of the animal is suggested. Gradual value changes in the body of the bison add to the illusion of a fully rounded form projecting outward in space. On the Design Chart, this discovery is indicated with a checkmark at the intersection of "color: value" and "gradation." Did you also observe how a dark outline, which varies from thick in some places to thin in others, defines the simple, compact shape of the animal? If you did, you would place a checkmark for "line" under "variety" and another for "shape" under "harmony." But your analysis is not yet complete. Do you see how smaller shapes of contrasting values are used to call

Criticism

Does this painting look lifelike? What kind of animal is it? Can you identify its main features? What do you think it is doing—standing still, lying down, or running? What makes you think so? Does this animal seem meek or fierce, slow or swift, helpless or powerful?

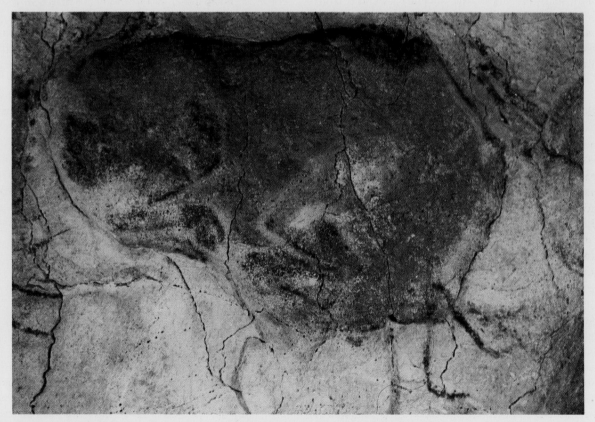

Figure 4.1   Bison (cave painting), Altamira. c. 15,000-10,000 B.C. Near Santillana, Spain

attention to such vital details as the head, legs, and hump? How would this be indicated on the Design Chart? Since this discovery points out how value and shape have been used to emphasize the most important parts of the animal, the answer is obvious.

Of course, not *all* the relationships of elements and principles found in this bison have been discussed. Only the more obvious relationships have been touched upon. You can, and should, go on to determine other, more subtle, relationships for yourself to complete your understanding of this painting. But, you should be warned. This kind of "detective work" can be habit-forming. Each new discovery will add to your eagerness to learn even more about the work of art.

Interpreting the Work

You are now ready to interpret this painting. You will recall that this means discovering the meaning, mood, or idea of the work. Even though this work was made in prehistoric times, it will still be possible to interpret it.

At first glance you might have thought it would be difficult to guess the size and character of this animal. After all, the bison is isolated and not placed in a scene with other animals or objects with which to compare it. But by the time you have reached this point in your study, you should have little difficulty choosing from such interpretation statements as "large and powerful," "small and helpless," or "slender and frail."

Having observed that the head of the bison is lowered and the legs pulled upward, your curiosity might be aroused. What is the animal doing? Obviously it is not standing, and so you might be tempted to say that the animal is lying down. Another possibility is that it is in motion, perhaps charging at full speed toward some unseen enemy. Or, it may be galloping away from some unknown danger. The wide-open eyes and lowered head seem to support the idea that the bison is alert and in motion rather than weary and inactive. Nevertheless, after examining all the evidence, you alone must decide which interpretation seems best.

Judging the Work

You should now be prepared to make an intelligent judgment about this painting. Would you say that it is crude and primitive? Or do you think it was painted by a skilled artist who succeeded in producing a lifelike image of a bison? Does the painting call to mind the bison's untamed nature and its unique attributes? Has a thorough examination of it uncovered signs of the animal's fierceness, gentleness, strength, and speed? Remember, this painting can only become personally meaningful to you if you supply answers to questions of this kind.

You have now provided answers to some questions by critically examining this painting of a bison, but you have not covered all the important questions concerning this work. You have yet to consider questions *about* the work, questions such as "Who painted this picture?" "How and when was it done?" "Was it painted to serve some special purpose and, if so, what was that purpose?" For answers to questions of this kind, it is necessary for you to turn to art history.

History of the Cave Paintings: Lascaux and Altamira

As you know, the art-history operations can be used to describe, analyze, interpret, and judge a work of art. Some of these operations will be more helpful in discovering facts about the cave paintings than others. However, you should try out all the operations to see which ones are most helpful and to be sure your study of the cave paintings is complete. The art-history operations were discussed in Chapter 3, pages 41-47, "The Art-History Approach."

Origins of the Paintings

There is much uncertainty among historians and archaeologists about the early dates of human development. However, some experts believe that it was during an age which began some thirty thousand years ago that the earliest known works of human achievement were made. This book relies on the early dates determined by these experts because they are the best dates available. ★

★ **Enrichment** The age of cave paintings and artifacts produced thousands of years ago can be determined by several means. One way is to date the artifact according to the age of the surrounding earth layer. Another way is radiocarbon dating of once-living objects found near the artifact. In general, all living organisms maintain a known amount of radioactive carbon-14. After the organism's death, the carbon-14 loses its radioactivity at a known rate. By measuring how much radioactivity is left in charcoal or carbonized bones, for instance, it is possible to discover their age. And when these objects are found in caves where prehistoric paintings are located, scholars are able to arrive at the approximate date the paintings were produced. However, dating methods are constantly being improved, and this may mean that scholars will eventually have to revise some of their estimates.

Since a study of the history of art must start somewhere, this book will go back in time to the age just described, called the Old Stone Age or the Paleolithic period. This age is believed to have lasted from 30,000 B.C. until about 10,000 B.C. There you will find these earliest works—the vivid, lifelike pictures of animals painted on the rough ceilings and walls of caves.

In caves found in southern France and northern Spain are numerous paintings, so well preserved and skillfully done that they caused great controversy among scholars when they were discovered. The reason for this controversy becomes clear if you look closely at one of the animal paintings found at the cave of Lascaux in the Dordogne region of southern France (Figure 4.2). Is it possible that cave people working with the most primitive instruments could have produced such splendid works of art? Or are these the work of skilled artists from a more recent time? Perhaps, as some have suggested, they are the work of tramps or shepherds who took shelter in the caves. On the other hand, if they are truly the creations of prehistoric artists, why were they done and how did they survive?

Today scholars agree that the paintings discovered at Lascaux and at Altamira are the work of prehistoric artists. However, it is unlikely that they are the first works of art ever created. They are too sophisticated for that. No doubt they were preceded by hundreds,

perhaps thousands, of years of slow development about which nothing is known still. Of course, this does not keep people from speculating about how art may have started . . .

Deep inside the cave, the man sat down for a moment to rest. After several minutes, he raised his torch high above his head to examine his surroundings. Curiosity had driven him to explore deeper into the cave than he had ever ventured before, even though he and his family had lived at the mouth of the cave for many weeks. The light of his torch cast long shadows on the rough stone walls of the cave, and the man noticed that some of the shadows looked like the animals he hunted daily in the fields. Idly, he bent down and picked up a piece of soft stone and walked to a place on the wall where the surface seemed to swell outward like the round body of an animal. With a few awkward strokes of stone, he added crude legs and then a head to the body. Finished, he stepped back to admire his work. It was crude, but it did look something like a bison. And the man, standing alone in the dark, silent cave, suddenly became frightened by the strange image he had created on the wall. He turned and made his way back to the mouth of the cave. It would be many days before he gathered enough courage to return to the mysterious drawing on the wall . . . and he would take others with him to see it. They would all agree that what he had done on the wall of the cave was magic . . .

While this story is imaginary, it is quite possible that prehistoric cave painting started this way. And, because these paintings of animals were done deep inside caves, far from the living quarters near the entrance, scholars now feel that they must have had something to do with magic rituals.

Use of the Paintings in Hunting Rituals

During prehistoric times, art was almost entirely limited to the drawing of animals. This was probably due to the prehistoric people's dependence on animals for food. The painting of animals almost certainly played a part in some kind of magic ritual which would help them in the hunt.

Of course, hunting in prehistoric times was quite different from what it is today. Primitive spears and clubs were the only weapons known, and these had to be used at close range. This made the hunting of large game very dangerous. Often hunters were seriously injured or killed. When this happened, the rest of the family was in danger of starving.

Before taking up their clubs and spears, prehistoric hunters may have turned to magic to place a spell over their quarry. This was intended to weaken it and make it easier to hunt. The magic may have involved a ceremony in which an image of the animal was painted

History

Were paintings like this done by prehistoric artists to decorate the walls of their cave dwellings? Why would it be accurate to refer to pictures like these as a kind of trap or snare? Why did prehistoric artists insist on painting pictures of animals?

Figure 4.2 Cave paintings, Lascaux. c. 15,000-10,000 B.C. Dordogne, France

Most of the cave sites used by prehistoric families were situated on a rise because if offered a view of the surrounding hills and valleys. These sites may have been selected because they enabled them to follow the movement of game below.

Figure 4.3   View of the Spanish countryside around the Altamira Cave in northern Spain

on the wall or ceiling of the cave. Prehistoric people must have had difficulty distinguishing the difference between painted animals and the real thing. They probably believed that by drawing a lifelike picture of an animal they were capturing some of that animal's strength and spirit. This would make it easier for them to find and overcome the real animal in the fields.

These prehistoric people may have thought that the animal could be weakened even more if, during the magic ceremony, they frightened it or struck the painted image with their spears and clubs. The presence of spears painted into some of the animals suggests that efforts were made to weaken the animals before the hunt took place.

These prehistoric hunting rituals may sound unusual and even amusing to you at first, but they were probably very effective. No doubt they bolstered the confidence and the courage of the hunters who were convinced that their quarry would be weaker and easier to kill. And, in some ways, these prehistoric rituals were not unlike some of the rituals we practice today. A school pep rally with its rousing cheers and inspiring music serves the same purpose. It builds confidence and courage in football players just as the hunting ritual did for prehistoric hunters.

Why the Paintings Survived

Utensils, bones, and charcoal from numerous campfires found at the mouths of caves suggests that the Stone-Age occupants lived there to take advantage of the daylight and ventilation. A special place further back in the cave was set aside for their magic rituals, and this was where the paintings were done. There they were protected from the wind and rain, and for this reason many paintings have survived to the present day. Unfortunately, many others were washed away by underground rivers. Only a few stone tools and utensils have been found, and scholars now look sadly at the barren walls and try to imagine what wonders might have once been painted there.

How the Paintings at Lascaux and Altamira Were Discovered

The discoveries of prehistoric paintings at both the caves of Lascaux in 1941 and Altamira in 1879 were quite accidental. The Lascaux caves were found by two boys playing in a field with their dog. A ball was thrown to the dog, and, in his eagerness to retrieve it, the dog failed to notice a small hole in the ground. The boys were startled to see the dog disappear and rushed to investigate. They quickly found the hole and saw that the dog was trapped within a cave. Frantically the boys searched for a way to reach the dog and finally discovered another, larger hole nearby. Cautiously they crawled down into it. Imagine how their hands must have trembled as they lit matches and illuminated the magnificent paintings of animals on the cavern surfaces.

It is a curious fact that another dog played a similar key role in the finding of the caves of Altamira some seventy years before the discovery at Lascaux. One morning in 1869 a man living in northern Spain took his gun, called for his dog, and set out to hunt in the green, open countryside near the quaint village of Santillana in the northern province of Santander (Figure 4.3). There was little about the day to stir much

interest, although the hunter later reported that his dog had fallen into a hole. The hole proved to be the blocked entrance to an unknown cave. Fortunately, he had been able to find the dog and pull him free. The incident was soon almost completely forgotten.

Several years later, an amateur archaeologist named Marcelino de Sautuola heard the hunter's story and decided to explore the cave. For four years he excavated inside the cavern, uncovering a number of flint and stone tools which he realized were made in prehistoric times. These discoveries kept drawing him back to the cave where he hoped to make a more important find.

One day de Sautuola's five-year-old daughter went along with him to the cave. They entered and made their way to a low-roofed chamber which the archaeologist had examined many times before. The father had to bend over as he went into the chamber, but the little girl was able to walk upright. The light from the candle in her father's hand made strange shadows on the walls of the cave and these amused the child. Then she glanced up at the ceiling and screamed for joy as she saw something more than shadows. Her father turned and saw her looking upward and, with some difficulty, raised his own gaze to the ceiling just a few centimeters [several inches] above his head. There he saw for the first time the painted images of bison, boar, wild horses, and deer. He held his candle closer, and the light revealed the sleeping, galloping, crouching animals which had been hidden for centuries in the dark chamber (Figure 4.4). De Sautuola knew at once that this was the great discovery he had been hoping for.

History

In what part of the cave were pictures like this done? How have they survived up to the present day? Why was it so difficult for scholars to accept paintings like these as the work of prehistoric artists?

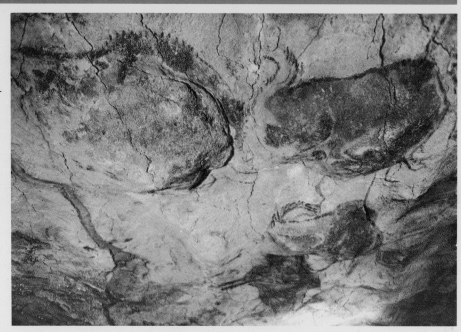

Figure 4.4 Cave paintings, Altamira. c. 15,000-10,000 B.C. Near Santillana, Spain

De Sautuola knew that the cave had only been visited by a few hunters since its discovery. He was convinced from the outset that the paintings dated from the Stone Age. He believed they were the work of the same prehistoric people who had made the tools found earlier in the cave. However, when he reported his discovery, it was greeted with widespread disbelief. Most people felt that the paintings were too sophisticated to be the work of Stone-Age artists. Only after similar paintings were uncovered in southern France in 1896 was de Sautuola's amazing discovery recognized as authentic.

Skills of the Prehistoric Artists

If you could visit Altamira today, you would see a low ceiling covered with animals painted in shades of red, brown, and black. Looking carefully, you would be able to count at least sixteen bison grouped in the center of the ceiling. Surrounding them are two boars and a deer. A smaller deer painted over a horse is located nearby. It was not uncommon for Stone-Age artists to paint on top of earlier paintings when space ran out.

The way in which many of the animals have been painted on the uneven rock surfaces seems to accent the swelling muscles and hollows of their bodies. But perhaps the most surprising thing about the paintings is their size. A deer at the far end of the chamber is almost 2 m (meters) [6.5 feet] long (Figure 4.5), while most of the other animals average around 1.5 m [5 feet].

Should you look closely at any animal on this ceiling, you would be impressed by its fresh, vivid color. This makes it seem as if the animal had just been painted. The pigments, or coloring mixture, were made from lumps of clay and soft stone which were ground into fine powder. They were then mixed with animal fat, blood, or some other medium. In some caves this pigment was applied to the smoothest walls with the fingers, although at Altamira the technique was more advanced. There the artist first scratched in the outline of the animal on the stone and then filled in the lines with black or dark brown pigment to give it a strong edge. The animal was then filled in with different shades of reddish-brown hue. This shading technique added to the impression of a three-dimensional form projecting outward from the ceiling. Finally, realistic details were added. These details suggest that the artist made a careful study of the animals before painting them. Such a study would explain why they seem so lifelike.

The painting technique may have made use of some kind of reed or bristle brush. Perhaps the animal was colored in by wiping the paint on with a piece of fur or a moss pad. Even with these crude instruments, prehistoric artists were able to demonstrate a knowledge and an affection for the animals they hunted. What they knew and felt was combined with a sensitive artistic instinct. This enabled them to capture in paint the power of a bison, the fleetness of a horse, the gentleness of a deer. Such is the impression that lingers long after you have left the darkness of the prehistoric Altamira cave and returned to the bright sunshine of the Spanish countryside.

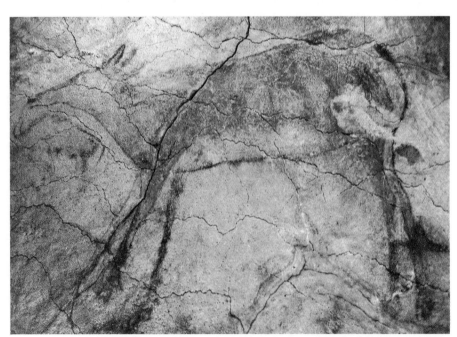

Figure 4.5   Deer (cave painting), Altamira.   c.   15,000-10,000   B.C. Near Santillana, Spain

Studio Experiences

Lesson One: Creating the Appearance of Three Dimensions

In your reading you learned that prehistoric artists painted animals to make them look as lifelike as possible. This lifelike quality was observed in paintings of a bison (Figure 4.1) and a deer (Figure 4.5) found at Altamira, Spain. In both works, gradual changes of value were used to make the animals look three-dimensional. Complete a large, simple contour drawing of an animal of your own choosing on a sheet of 31 x 46-cm [12 x 18-inch] white drawing paper. Mix a single tempera color and paint your animal using gradations of value to make it appear three-dimensional. Gradations of value are obtained by adding white or black tempera to the single color you decided to use.

Lesson Two: Modeling a Three-Dimensional Animal in Clay

In their paintings, prehistoric artists tried to capture the traits or characteristics of animals. Can you identify the traits associated with the bison (Figure 4.1) and the deer (Figure 4.5) from Altamira? Model a compact animal form in clay which exhibits the traits typically associated with that animal. The animal should be shown in a reclining or sitting position. Begin this sculpture by forming one of the basic geometric forms to represent the body of the animal (sphere, cone, cylinder). Add other smaller forms to represent the head, legs, and tail. Now use even smaller forms to suggest other features of the animal. After the major features have been joined to the basic geometric form, details can be added and refinements made. When attending to these details and refinements, make certain that your animal exhibits the traits for which it is known (power, grace, gentleness). Realism and tactile interest can be heightened by applying an actual texture to the soft surface of the clay piece. Finished works should be hollowed out, allowed to dry thoroughly, and fired.

Safety Note

If you are asthmatic, the dust that results from clay work may cause additional breathing difficulties. You should consult your physician to determine whether or not to engage in an art experience that will expose you to clay dust.

Chapter 5

Art for Eternity: The Art of Ancient Egypt

The Growth of Egyptian Civilization

Like most people, you probably know something about the pyramids. If nothing else, their appearance is certainly familiar to most. In fact, it may be so familiar that you no longer take the time to look at the pyramids closely. When you see them in books and films (Figure 5.1), your eyes may scan the pyramids just long enough for you to recognize them before moving on to examine more novel objects in the picture. "Oh yes," you think to yourself, "a pyramid. But what is that strange-looking thing in front of it?"

It would be a different story if you could see an actual pyramid rather than just a picture of one. If you were standing before the pyramids, the chances are that your eyes would not stray from them quickly. Their tremendous size and bulk would command your complete attention.

Unfortunately, you may never have the opportunity to see the pyramids firsthand. This means that your knowledge of them may have to come largely from books and pictures. This does not mean, however, that because you may never actually see the pyramids you cannot understand and appreciate them. This book gives you the chance to engage in a careful investigation which will enable you to do just that. But, to carry on this investigation, you must be prepared to look closely at pictures of pyramids and ask yourself questions about

History

Many people are so accustomed to seeing pictures of the pyramids that they are no longer impressed by them. But try to picture this pyramid as it once was: covered with a smooth layer of polished white limestone, it was a massive, pure-white monument standing solidly before a backdrop of constantly shifting brown sand and blue sky.

Figure 5.1 Sphinx and Pyramid of Khafre, Giza. c. 2600 B.C.

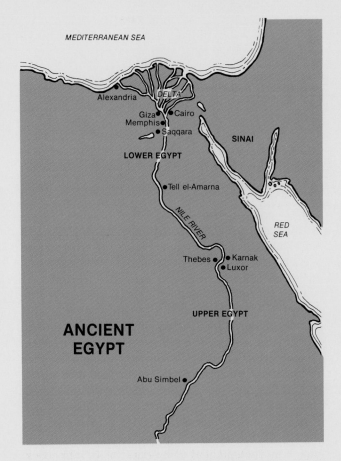

MEDITERRANEAN SEA

Alexandria

DELTA

Giza • Cairo
Memphis •
• Saqqara

SINAI

LOWER EGYPT

• Tell el-Amarna

NILE RIVER

RED SEA

Thebes • • Karnak
• Luxor

UPPER EGYPT

**ANCIENT
EGYPT**

Abu Simbel •

them. Your experience with art-criticism questions in the chapter on prehistoric art should help you here.

Traveling up the Nile River in Egypt today you would be amazed by the mighty monuments seen at almost every bend in this great river. Most of these huge stone monuments are tombs and temples, reminders of a once-powerful ancient Egyptian civilization.

Who were these Egyptians who were able to build such impressive monuments? Where did they come from? What were they like? Your search for answers to these questions will lead you back in time to prehistoric periods when people first came to inhabit the lands bordering the Nile.

Early Inhabitants along the Nile

Sometime around 5000 B.C., perhaps seeking the animals they depended upon for food, prehistoric hunters and their families came upon and settled in the fertile valley of the Nile River (see map of Ancient Egypt, this page). As far as experts can tell, these people came from western Asia. Since there is no evidence that they moved on or were somehow destroyed, they are regarded as the direct ancestors of most European peoples. The Nile River valley in which they settled was about 1207 km [750 miles] long, but measured no more than about 50 km [31 miles] at its widest point. In some places, it was not much more than 16 km [10 miles] wide. It was lined on both sides by cliffs ranging in height from

around one hundred to three hundred meters [a few hundred to a thousand feet]. Beyond these cliffs was nothing but desert.

Each summer the Nile River would flood its banks and deposit layers of fertile soil. This soil had been carried for thousands of kilometers [miles] from the African interior.* In some places, these rich soil deposits reached a depth of more than 9 m [30 feet]. In this fertile environment, people gradually changed from food gatherers to food producers. Discovering that the wild vegetables and grains they gathered grew from seeds, they began to gather these seeds and planted them in the fertile soil of the valley. This soil was so productive that as many as three crops could be raised in a single year on the same land.

The people continued to hunt animals for food, but came to rely more and more on the animals they raised themselves. This gave them a decided advantage over their ancestors. They were no longer entirely dependent upon the game they hunted for survival. Because they no longer had to move from one location to another in search of game, they could give up the practice of living temporarily in caves. Instead, they began to build more permanent houses of mud, wood, and reeds.

This settled existence brought about an increase in population and led to the growth of villages and towns. Some towns grew so strong that they took control of neighboring villages and, in this way, formed kingdoms. As the prehistoric period came to a close, there were only two large kingdoms in Egypt.** One of these was Lower Egypt, which included the fan-shaped delta region at the mouth of the Nile. The other was Upper Egypt, which was the valley carved in the desert by the river (see map of Ancient Egypt).

Thus, an Egyptian civilization grew up along the banks of the Nile over three thousand years before the birth of Christ. It continued in existence for nearly three thousand years. During that period, Egypt became a

---

★ Enrichment The river overflowed its banks for at least three months. During that time, the area between the river and the cliffs on both sides became a lake.

★ Enrichment The prehistoric period ended and history ★ began with the development of writing some five thousand years ago. It should be noted, however, that all dates in Egyptian history before 200 B.C. are approximate. This is why the dates found in many books vary so much. It is quite possible that the dates given are actually in error by as much as several centuries.

thriving nation in which Pharaohs, or kings, ruled with complete authority. Agriculture and trade grew; art flourished; and majestic monuments and temples were constructed.

The Three Major Periods of Egyptian History

It is customary to divide the long history of Egypt into three periods: the Old Kingdom, the Middle Kingdom, and the New Kingdom, or Empire. These kingdoms are further divided into dynasties. Dynasties were periods during which a single family provided a succession of rulers.

One reign ended and another began with the death of a Pharaoh and the crowning of a successor from the same royal family. For this reason, every precaution was taken to keep the blood of the royal family pure. One of these precautions was to forbid the Pharaoh to marry outside of the immediate family.

The Old Kingdom

The earliest dynastic period began around 3100 B.C. when Upper and Lower Egypt were united by a powerful Pharaoh named Menes. Menes established his capital at Memphis and founded the first of the thirty-one Egyptian dynasties. The Old Kingdom dates from the start of the third of these dynasties, in about 2686 B.C. It ended about five hundred years later. The end came when the strong centralized government established by the Pharaohs was weakened by the rise of a group of independent nobles. These nobles split the country into small states. Soon civil war and disorder broke out between these states, and the authority of the reigning Pharaoh collapsed.

After a long period of turmoil, the nobles in Thebes, a city on the upper Nile, were able to gain control of the country. They managed to unify Egypt once again into a single state, and order was restored to their troubled land. The success of these nobles marked the beginning of the Middle Kingdom, an approximately 250-year period from around 2050 to 1800 B.C.

The Middle Kingdom

The Middle Kingdom was a time of law and order and prosperity in Egypt. This was true even though the Pharaoh, while still the supreme head, was not as powerful as Pharaohs had been during the Old Kingdom. Then, around 1800 B.C., Egypt was overrun for the first time by foreign invaders. The Hyksos from western Asia, using horses and chariots, swept across the country. They easily defeated the Egyptians fighting on foot. The Hyksos inhabited Lower Egypt and for two hundred years forced the Egyptian people to pay them tribute. Finally, the Egyptians, having learned how to use horses and chariots from the Hyksos, drove the invaders from their country and restored independence.

The New Kingdom

The third and most brilliant period of Egyptian history is known as the New Kingdom, or Empire, and began in 1570 B.C. Warrior Pharaohs used their knowledge of horses and chariots to extend Egypt's rule over neighboring nations. The greatest of these warrior Pharaohs was Thutmose III. He reigned for fifty-four years and was such a great military leader that he is often referred to as the Napoleon of Egypt.

Under a later Pharaoh, Amenhotep III, the New Kingdom reached the peak of its power and influence. Thebes, the royal capital, became the most magnificent city in the world. But Amenhotep's son and heir, Amenhotep IV, broke suddenly with tradition. He tried to bring about changes in Egyptian religion which for centuries had recognized many different gods. Amenhotep IV moved the capital from Thebes to Tell el-Amarna where he established Aton, symbolized by the sun disk, as the one supreme god. In honor of his god, Amenhotep changed his name to Ikhnaton (also spelled Akhenaton), which meant "It is well with Aton." Unfortunately, while Ikhnaton was absorbed in his new religion, Egypt's enemies began to whittle away pieces of the once-mighty nation.

Ikhnaton's new religion did not survive after his death. Tell el-Amarna was destroyed, the capital was returned to Thebes, and the old religion was restored. Other Pharaohs after Ikhnaton tried to recapture the glories of the past. However, Egypt's long chapter in history was coming to an end. In 332 B.C. Egypt was conquered by Alexander the Great of Macedonia, bringing the New Kingdom to a close. There followed several centuries of Hellenistic rule.★ Finally, in 30 B.C., Egypt was made a province of Rome.

But the greatness of ancient Egypt has not been forgotten over the centuries. Works of art of all kinds remain. They range from huge pyramids and tombs to skillfully formed stone statues, carved and painted reliefs, and wall paintings.★★ These and other treasures remain as fascinating reminders of the magnificent civilization that flourished on the banks of the Nile some four thousand years ago.

★ **Enrichment** *Hellenistic* means "relating to Greek culture after Alexander the Great."

★ **Enrichment** A *relief* is a type of sculpture in which
★ forms project from a background.

Criticism

Does this structure seem taller than it is wide, or wider than it is tall? Which two words best describe the contour lines: curved, rigid, vertical, straight? Does this structure appear to be fragile and small, huge but flimsy, or large and strong? Why are there no doors or windows? What purpose do you think it served? Do you feel it served this purpose well? Why or why not?

Figure 5.2 Pyramid of Khufu, Giza. c. 2650 B.C.

Architecture

The structures which the ancient Egyptians built remain as testimonies to the genius and skill of those ancient architects. It is clear to anyone visiting the great pyramids at Giza or the Temple of Amon-Re at Karnak that these ancient people were master planners and builders with great resources at their command.

The Pyramids

It would be impossible to discuss the glories of ancient Egypt without talking about the pyramids. One's most vivid image of Egyptian life usually includes those familiar stone monuments located at Giza, which were largely built during the period of the Old Kingdom. Photographs fail to capture the full impact of the three pyramids. They can only hint at the tremendous effort that must have gone into the Pyramids' construction. Still, when examining a photograph closely, certain questions about these mysterious structures almost always come to mind: What purpose did they serve? How were they built? How long did it take to build them? What is inside?

Before considering these questions, however, an effort should be made to bring your mental picture of these pyramids into sharper focus. When viewing the Pyramid of Khufu (often called "Cheops," its Greek name) (Figure 5.2), you may be attracted first by its great size. Rigid, straight contour lines clearly define and accent the simple triangular shape of this monumental structure. To begin to appreciate its massive size, consider the fact that the Pyramid of Khufu covers an area of 5.3 ha (hectares) [13 acres]. This may not seem very impressive at first. However, it means that the five largest cathedrals in the world could be placed within its base with room to spare. It was made by piling 2.3 million blocks of stone, each averaging 2.3 t (metric tons) [2.5 tons], to a height of 146.3 m [480 feet]. This makes the pyramid about as high as the Washington Monument.

The pyramid was built on an almost perfectly square ground plan. The base, which measures more than 228.6 m [750 feet] on each side, is much greater than the height. Because the pyramid is wider than it is tall, it lacks an upward movement. Rather than a vertical, soaring quality, the shape and proportions of the pyramid suggest solidity and permanence.

Looking at it from the outside, you might expect the inside of the pyramid to be spacious. This is not the case. Except for passageways and a few small rooms called *galleries*, the pyramid is made of solid limestone. Perhaps your curiosity is aroused. Why build such a massive building and then provide such little space inside for rooms? To answer this question you must first learn something about the religious beliefs of the ancient Egyptians. As you will see, religion influenced every phase of Egyptian life.

The Influence of Religion

Egyptian religion placed great importance on the resurrection of the soul and eternal life in a spirit world after death. The Egyptians believed that the soul, or *ka*, as it was called, came into being with the body and remained in the body until death. At death, the ka would leave the body for a time. However, eventually it would return and unite with the body again for the journey to the next world and immortality. If the body were lost or destroyed, the ka would be forced to spend eternity in aimless wandering. For this reason, the Egyptians went to great lengths to preserve and protect the body after death. Following a complicated embalming process, the body was wrapped in strips of cloth and placed in a fortress-like tomb where it would be safe until the ka's return. Thus, a strong tomb was a kind of insurance against final death.

The most impressive tomb was built for the most important person in Egyptian society, the Pharaoh. The Pharaoh was not only a king, but, in the eyes of the people, he was also a god. When he died, the Pharaoh was expected to join other gods, including Re, the sun god; Osiris, the god of the Nile and ruler of the underworld; and Isis, the great mother god. The pyramid was built to house and protect the body of the Pharaoh and the treasures he would take with him from this world to the next.* His body was sealed in a stone coffin called a *sarcophagus*. It was then placed in a burial chamber located in the very center of the pyramid. Dead-end passages and false burial chambers were added to the building. These were meant to confuse tomb robbers and enemies who might try to destroy the Pharaoh's body. For an Egyptian, the destruction of the body was the most horrible form of vengeance.

Evolution of the Pyramid Shape

Probably the now-familiar pyramid shape developed gradually over a long period of time. Originally, the Egyptians buried their dead in hidden pits and piled sand and stone over the top. Later this practice changed, and they began to use sun-dried bricks to build low, flat tombs called *mastabas*. These rectangular tombs had sloping sides and contained a chapel and a false burial chamber in addition to the true one hidden deep inside. In time, several mastabas of diminishing size were stacked on top of each other to form a step

pyramid (Figure 5.3). Finally, they were built without steps, and a point was added to the top. With this, the true pyramid form was completed.

Thousands and thousands of paid workers and slaves toiled for decades to build a single pyramid. Stone was quarried and dragged to the construction site and then carefully fitted into place.* How the Egyptians managed to lift and fit these huge blocks of stone into place remains unclear. Some scholars believe that the stones may have been dragged up ramps of earth and sand that were raised with each level of the structure. They believe that when finished, the pyramid was almost completely covered with sand. The final task, then, was to remove this sand, exposing the finished structure for the first time.

By the time of the Middle Kingdom, the weakened position of the Pharaohs and the threat of invasion made large-scale structures such as the pyramid impractical. Many small pyramids and mastabas may have been built during this period. However, these were probably made of mud bricks which soon crumbled and disappeared. More permanent tombs prepared for the Pharaoh were cut into the rock cliffs of a valley across the Nile from the capital city of Thebes.

The Temples

If the pyramids are evidence of the skill of Old Kingdom builders, then the architects of the New Kingdom could point to the great temples they constructed as proof of their own genius. The practice of burying Pharaohs and nobles in tombs hidden in the cliffs west of the Nile continued throughout the New Kingdom. Meanwhile, architects took on more important tasks. Temples were erected along the eastern banks of the river near Thebes, and these became more and more elaborate. Each of these temples was built by command of a Pharaoh and was dedicated to the Pharaoh's favorite god or gods. When the Pharaoh died, the temple became a funeral chapel where people could bring offerings for the Pharaoh's ka. Often, a temple built to honor a particular god was enlarged by several Pharaohs until it reached tremendous proportions. The ruins of the Temple of Amon-Re at Karnak (Figure 5.4), dedicated to the all-powerful chief god of Thebes, will give you an idea of what these gigantic structures must have looked like.

★ **Enrichment** It is possible that the Pyramids served another purpose as well—as monuments dedicated to the sun god, Re. As the tallest structures in Egypt, they received the first rays of the sun each morning. This was a daily reminder to the people that Re was constantly watching over them.

★ **Enrichment** Many of these stones were so perfectly fitted that you would find it impossible to slip the blade of a knife into the joint.

Structures of this kind were one step in a long tradition of Egyptian tomb building. Can you recall the kinds of tombs that were built before and after this type was constructed?

Why were tombs such an important concern for the Egyptians?

Figure 5.3   Step Pyramid of King Zoser, Saqqara. c. 2750 B.C.

Can you determine how this huge temple was constructed? Posts and crossbeams called *lintels* were used to support the heavy stone slabs of the ceiling. Posts and lintels were also used to form the openings for windows and doors. This method of construction originated in prehistoric times when trees and bundles of lotus or papyrus stalks were used as post and lintels.

Figure 5.4   Hypostyle Hall, Temple of Amon-Re, Karnak. c. 1280 B.C.

The approach to the Temple of Amon-Re was a wide avenue which led directly up to the massive sloping front of the structure. A great doorway flanked by obelisks (tall, four-sided, pointed stone shafts), statues of the Pharaoh, and huge banners opened onto an uncovered courtyard. Directly across from this courtyard was the entry to the great hall, perhaps the largest ever built.★ This hall was filled with massive stone columns, the tallest reaching a height of nearly 21 m [70 feet]. Beyond this hall was the sanctuary, the small, dark, and mysterious chamber where only the Pharaoh and certain priests were allowed to enter.

A walk from the courtyard to the sanctuary at Karnak must have been a moving experience. You would move gradually by stages from spacious, bright, warm areas to areas which were smaller, darker, and cooler. No doubt this created the impression that you were leaving the real world behind and, with each step, were moving nearer and nearer to another, spiritual world beyond.

Sculpture

Despite every precaution, the fortress-like pyramids and tombs of the Pharaohs were soon broken into and robbed of their treasures. Frequently the mummified bodies of the Pharaohs were mutilated or destroyed in the process. To make certain that the ka would have a body to live in even if this happened, sculptors were commanded to carve the king's portrait out of hard stone. These sculptures were then placed in the tomb near the Pharaoh's sarcophagus where they acted as substitutes for the body inside. The Egyptians believed that even if the real body were destroyed, the ka would still have the stone substitute to enter for the journey to the next world. In fact, one of the Egyptian words for sculptor translates to read, "He who keeps alive."

Portrait of Khafre

The strength and dignity that were a trademark of the pyramids also characterized the sculptures produced during the Old Kingdom. In the seated portrait of the Fourth Dynasty Pharaoh Khafre (the Greek "Chephren") (Figure 5.5), the figure keeps the solid, block-like form of the hard diorite stone from which it was carved.★ The Pharaoh is shown sitting erect and attentive on a throne inscribed with symbols proclaiming him the king of Upper and Lower Egypt. He wears a simple, pleated garment which fastens at the waist. A cloth headdress covers his forehead and falls over his wide shoulders. His left hand rests on his knee, while the right hand forms a fist which must have once gripped some symbol of his high office.

But Khafre is more than just a powerful king. He is also a god, the descendent of Re, the sun god. To show the Pharaoh's divinity, the sculptor has added a falcon representing Horus, god of the sky. Can you find it? It is placed at the back of the Pharaoh's head where its wings partly encircle and protect his head.

The head of Khafre is not as stiff or rigid as the body. Even though it is simplified, the head has a more lifelike appearance. Khafre looks straight ahead and seems to be completely motionless, although the eyes seem alive to events taking place around him. And could that be the beginning of a smile at the corners of the firmly set mouth? Perhaps, but there is also an aloofness about him that makes such a question difficult to answer. In studying Khafre's portrait, you have the feeling that the Pharaoh is aware of, but above, the concerns of ordinary mortals. It is this quiet aloofness that makes this portrait a symbol of eternal strength and power —befitting a king and a god.

★ **Enrichment** Egyptian temples were known for their immense proportions. The temple at Karnak was about 396 m [1,300 feet] long and covered the largest area of any religious structure ever built. The great hall could accommodate almost any of the great cathedrals of Europe.

★ **Enrichment** This sculpture was one of several carved for Khafre's temple located near his pyramid and the Sphinx at Giza.

Criticism

Describe this figure's pose and expression. Does he seem relaxed and natural? Why or why not? Is the overall form more like a block or a cylinder? Viewed from the front, is this figure balanced formally or informally? Does this figure look angry, excited, bored, or dignified? Do you think this is a portrait of an important person? If so, what makes you think so?

Figure 5.5   Khafre. c. 2600 B.C. Egyptian Museum, Cairo

Figure 5.6   Great Sphinx, Giza. c. 2600 B.C.

Perhaps the most familiar and impressive example of Old-Kingdom sculpture is the Great Sphinx (Figure 5.6). Carved from rock at the site, the Sphinx presents the head of the Pharoah, probably Khafre, placed on the body of a reclining lion. It towers to a height of almost 20 m [65 feet]. Its massive size was no doubt intended to demonstrate the power of the Pharaoh. But why was the Pharaoh's head placed on the body of a lion? Perhaps it was done to show that the Pharaoh possessed the courage and strength of a lion.

Portrait of a Middle-Kingdom Ruler

You may recall that the Middle Kingdom was a time of law and order that followed a long period of internal strife and civil war. It lasted only about 250 years, from around 2050 to 1800 B.C. when Egypt was invaded by the Hyksos.

Much of the sculpture produced during the Middle Kingdom was destroyed by the invading Hyksos as well as the New Kingdom rulers who followed. The works that have survived range in quality from those that are quite crude to others which were skillfully done. A small fragment of a portrait of a Middle-Kingdom ruler is an example of the skill and sensitivity demonstrated by the best of these Middle-Kingdom carvers (Figure 5.7).

Figure 5.7   *Fragment of a Head of King Sesostris III.* 1887-49 B.C. Quartzite, 16.5 cm [6½″] high. The Metropolitan Museum of Art, New York. Carnarvon Collection, Gift of Edward S. Harkness, 1926, 26.7.1394

The expression on this surprisingly realistic face suggests none of the confidence and aloofness noted in the portrait of Khafre. In this work, the firmly set mouth shows determination and strength. However, the eyes indicate that this ruler is also troubled and weary. The great Pharaoh Khafre would never wear such an expression in public. But Khafre ruled during the Old Kingdom, a time when no one dared question the Pharaoh's divine power or authority. Conditions had changed by the Middle Kingdom when this Pharaoh's portrait was carved. Much of his power had been taken away from him, and his authority depended largely upon his personality, strength, and cunning. His expression tells you that he is keenly aware of this.

Portraits of Ikhnaton

By about 1570 B.C., all of the conquering Hyksos who had not been destroyed or enslaved had been driven out of the country. Egypt then entered into a period of expansion and prosperity known as the New Kingdom. Apparently the Egyptians' military success against the Hyksos resulted in a desire for more victories. The powerful army created to defeat the invaders was already in place, and it must have seemed appropriate for the Egyptians to make use of it. A series of successful raids into Palestine and Syria followed. Eventually all opposition in Syria was eliminated. Egypt then found itself in control of a vast territory extending from the upper Nile to the Euphrates River.

The expansion of the Empire brought new wealth to the country, and this encouraged artistic activity. During the New Kingdom, sculptors were commissioned to complete a variety of works. These ranged from huge tomb sculptures carved in the native rock to smaller pieces used to decorate temples. Statues of Pharaohs were often gigantic, reaching heights of 27.4 m [90 feet]. Sometimes these were painted and the eyes made with rock crystal to add to their realistic appearance.

It was during the New Kingdom that an unusual man appeared and briefly challenged the centuries-old traditions of Egyptian life. This was the Pharaoh Amenhotep IV, or Ikhnaton, mentioned earlier. You will remember that he was the rebel who refused to follow the religious customs of his ancestors. Many of Ikhaton's portraits show him as a homely man with a strange, elongated head, pointed chin, heavy lips, and a long, slender neck (Figure 5.8). Of course, as Pharaoh he could have demanded that his artists portray him in a more flattering manner. But perhaps he did not object to these portraits because they showed him as he really

Criticism

Provide an adjective that best describes the following features of this man's portrait: head, chin, lips, nose, neck. Does he seem solemn and stiff, or natural and lifelike? Why does the eye seem to be inaccurate? In your opinion, what is most successful about this work? What is least successful?

Figure 5.8   *Ikhnaton (Amenhotep IV).* c. 1360 B.C. State Museum, Berlin

History

This portrait of Ikhnaton's queen is made of painted limestone. Do you think it looks lifelike? Did this more realistic approach to art continue after Ikhnaton's death?

Figure 5.9   *Queen Nefertiti.* c. 1360 B.C. State Museum, Berlin

looked. Indeed, much of the art that was done during Ikhnaton's reign took on a more realistic look. Instead of the solemn, stiff likenesses favored by earlier Pharaohs, Ikhnaton's portraits are more natural and lifelike. They often show him in common, everyday scenes in which he is playing with his daughters or strolling with his wife, Nefertiti (Figure 5.9).★

Ikhnaton's revolutionary religious ideas died with him. However, much of the art produced after Ikhnaton continued to exhibit the realistic, relaxed poses favored during the reign of this unusual king.

Relief Sculpture and Painting

Just as much can be learned about the ancient Egyptians from their free-standing sculpture, so a great deal can also be learned from their relief sculpture and painting.

Relief Sculpture: Portrait of Hesire

About forty-seven hundred years ago, an official to the Pharaoh Zoser died. Following traditional burial rites, his mummified body was carried to a mastaba and sealed in a small chamber hidden below ground level. Several relief panels from wooden doors in this tomb have survived, and they tell a great deal about this proud official whose name was Hesire. But more importantly, these panels tell about an artistic style that was practiced without change throughout the long history of Egyptian art.

One of these wooden panels shows Hesire standing erect with a baton in his right hand, which indicates his high office (Figure 5.10). His left hand holds a staff and writing materials. This suggests that Hesire must have been a secretary to the Pharaoh. But have you noticed that something seems "wrong" with the way this figure is shown? Perhaps you have observed that the head, arms, legs, and feet are in profile, but the shoulders and eye are shown as if seen from the front. It even appears as though Hesire has two left feet since a big toe is on the outside of each foot. Furthermore, the figure looks as if it has been twisted in some way, making it look flat —notice how all parts of the body seem to be at the same distance from your eye.

★**Enrichment** The famous portrait of Queen Nefertiti was found among the debris of a sculptor's studio. Work on it had ceased after the death of her husband, the Pharaoh.

Do you think the artist who carved this panel simply lacked the skill needed to make his portrait more lifelike? This argument is not very convincing after examining the figure more closely. The head, for instance, is skillfully modeled and looks realistic. Also, the body is correctly proportioned and details at the neck, shoulders, and knees show that the sculptor could

Criticism

Describe this figure, paying particular attention to any unusual features it might have. Do you think these unusual features were due to the artist's lack of skill, or were they intentional? Point to contrasts of texture found in this work. Can you find any horizontal lines which help balance the strong verticals of the figure and staff?

Figure 5.10 *Portrait of Hesire.* c. 2700 B.C. Egyptian Museum, Cairo

carve realistically when he chose to. He was also aware of how to achieve effective design relationships. The deeply etched texture of the hair offers a pleasing contrast to the smooth surface of the face. Harmony is noted in the way the rich texture of the garment around Hesire's waist repeats the texture of his hair. This texture contrasts with and helps to emphasize the smoothness of the body. Notice also how the strong verticals of the figure and staff are balanced by the horizontals of the baton, waistband, shoulders, and hair.

Rules of Egyptian Art

The skill of the artist in handling realistic detail and design relationships makes one thing clear: the carving's unusual features are not due to a lack of ability. Instead, they are the result of a strict set of rules followed by all Egyptian artists. These rules required that every part of the body must be shown from the most familiar point of view. For this reason, the head, arms, legs, and feet were always shown in profile, while the eyes and shoulders were presented as if seen from the front. Following these rules meant that paintings and relief sculptures of the body looked distorted and unnatural. However, it is a credit to the skill of Egyptian artists that this distortion was kept to a minimum and did not take away from the appealing appearance of their works.

You may be wondering why these unusual rules were established. It is necessary to refer again to the Egyptian concern for life after death for an answer. Like sculptures, paintings and relief sculptures of the dead were meant to act as substitutes for the body. When artists created images of the Pharaoh, they wanted to make sure that all parts of the body were clearly shown. This was more important to them than making the image beautiful or accurate. A complete image was vital. After all, if an arm were hidden behind the body in a relief sculpture or painting, it would mean that the ka would enter a body without an arm. He would then be forced to spend eternity in a deformed body. Thus, over the years a strict set of rules were formed to make sure that all parts of the body were shown correctly in sculptured and painted images. As you can see, the artist who carved Hesire's portrait followed those rules carefully.

At one time, it was customary for the Pharaoh to have his wife, servants, and slaves sealed in the tomb with him when he died. Then, when he arrived in the next world, he would have his loved ones and servants with him for eternity. They would make sure that his new life would be just as pleasant as the old one. In time, this practice of burying others with the Pharaoh was discontinued. Instead, painted relief sculptures or sculptures in the round were substituted for real people and placed in the tomb with the dead king.

The ka was expected to pass through the door painted on the wall of this tomb. What was the ka, and why would it enter here? What are the figures on either side of the door doing? What would happen to the ka if it could not find its body or a substitute for the body? Why were paintings and relief sculptures of family members and servants placed in the tomb?

Figure 5.11   Wall painting from the Tomb of Nakht: *Ceremonial Door.* **Thebes. c. 1450 B.C. [The Metropolitan Museum of Art, Photography by Egyptian Expedition]**

Why are some figures larger than others? Do all the figures look stiff and solemn? Point out those that do not. What are these figures doing?

Figure 5.12   Wall painting from the Tomb of Nakht: *Nakht and His Wife.* **Thebes. c. 1450 B.C. [The Metropolitan Museum of Art, Photography by Egyptian Expedition]**

Painting: Portraits of Nakht and His Wife

Eventually the tomb of every important or wealthy person was enriched with painted relief sculptures. But when it became difficult and costly to carve reliefs on the rough, hard walls of cliff tombs during the Middle Kingdom, painting came into its own as a separate art form. The rough walls of the cliff tombs were first carved and scraped until they were flat. Then they were smoothed over with a coating of plaster. When this was done, the artist went to work by drawing a series of horizontal straight lines on the plastered wall. Figures and animals were carefully arranged along these lines to tell a story, usually an event from the life of the deceased. The pictures were then colored in with rich red and yellow hues, with black and blue-green added for contrast. Typically, little shading was used, and so the figures tend to look flat, as if they had been cut from paper and pasted to the wall. This method of arranging pictures in horizontal bands and using bright colors with little shading resulted in a style that looks very much like contemporary comic strips.

A look inside a New-Kingdom tomb prepared for a priest named Nakht will add to your understanding of Egyptian painting (Figure 5.11). Painted on a wall of the small chapel within this tomb is a false door. The priest's ka was expected to pass through this door in search of offerings. Arranged in bands on either side of the door are painted substitutes for servants bearing offerings of food and drink for the ka. An assortment of offerings is painted in the strip directly below the door where the ka would be sure to find them when he entered.

The way in which the figures have been painted should look familiar to you. The style used to paint them is much like the style used in the relief portrait of Hesire. The artists who did both these works were bound by the same set of rules. These rules even told artists how they were to paint the skin colors of men and women. Women were painted with a lighter skin color than men.

Standing portraits of Nakht and his wife are found on one wall of this chapel (Figure 5.12). They are surrounded by busy servants engaged in different farming chores on the priest's land. The figures of the priest and his wife are much larger than the other figures to show that Nakht and his wife are more important. They are also stiff and solemn because the Egyptians believed that such a pose was fitting for people of high rank. In contrast, the smaller servants are shown in more natural positions as they labor in the fields and care for the animals.

Egyptian artists were content to echo the art of the past until influenced by new ideas from outside sources such as Greece and Rome. As the impact of these new ideas grew, Egyptian art lost much of its unique character—and the art of the Pharaohs perished.

Studio Experiences

Lesson One: Painting with Flat Shapes and Monochromatic Color

The Egyptian painting style is easily recognized because, among other things, it denies space and emphasizes the two-dimensional arrangement of flat shapes. You observed these stylistic features in the wall paintings found in the Tomb of Nakht (Figures 5.11 and 5.12). What would happen if you were to adopt those same features when completing a painting of your own? To find out, complete a line drawing of houses and other buildings making sure not to include any illusions of depth. Do not draw any forms in three dimensions, overlap forms, or show size differences related to distance. Houses and other objects (trees, telephone poles, sidewalks, signs) should be shown as though they are all on the same plane. These should be arranged to fill an entire sheet of 23 x 30-cm [9 x 12-inch] white drawing paper. Paint your picture using a monochromatic color scheme. That is, use only a single color throughout. Value changes can be obtained by adding white or black tempera to this one color.

Lesson Two: Designing a Sarcophagus Cover in the Egyptian Style

You have learned that Egyptian artists adhered to a rigid set of rules when carving and painting portraits. The artist who carved the Portrait of Hesire (Figure 5.10) was bound to follow those rules. Assume that you are a painter living in Egypt at the same time as that artist (about 2700 B.C.) You have been hired to design a sarcophagus cover for a deceased Pharaoh. This cover is to show the entire figure of the Pharaoh and tell something about him. He may have been a tyrant, a scholar, or a great spiritual leader. Assuming that he was one of these, how might he look? What kind of personality would you associate with him? What might some of his accomplishments be? On a sheet of 23 x 30-cm [9 x 12-inch] white drawing paper, complete two drawings in pencil which reflect your answers to questions like these. On each drawing make certain that every part of the body is shown from its most familiar point of view (head, arms, legs, and feet in profile; eye and shoulder from the front).

Lesson Three: Painting a Sarcophagus Cover in the Egyptian Style

Examine the sarcophagus cover designs completed in the previous lesson and select the one that most appeals to you. On a sheet of 23 x 61-cm [9 x 24-inch] poster board, outline the shape of a sarcophagus cover that has the following dimensions:

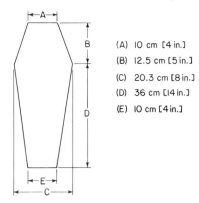

(A)   10 cm [4 in.]
(B)   12.5 cm [5 in.]
(C)   20.3 cm [8 in.]
(D)   36 cm [14 in.]
(E)   10 cm [4 in.]

Fit your design into this shape by drawing lightly with pencil. Use tempera to paint your design, making certain to select intense colors for the figure and contrasting dull colors for the background. This will enable you to emphasize the figure. Avoid gradations in hue, intensity, and value in order to capture the flat quality noted in Egyptian painting.

Chapter 6

The Age of Beauty: Greek Art

Artists you will meet in this chapter

(Correct pronunciation of the artists' names is given in parentheses, with accented syllables indicated by italics. This practice has been followed throughout the book where appropriate.)

Myron (*my*-run), fifth century B.C. His sculpture of the *Discobolus* suggests that he must have spent long periods of time studying athletes in action.

Phidias (*fid*-ee-us), fifth century B.C. One of the greatest Greek sculptors, he created a colossal statue of a goddess using more than .9 t [1 ton] of gold.

Polyclitus (pol-ee-*kly*-tus), fifth century B.C. His sculptures of athletes suggest strength and agility even though action is kept to a minimum.

Exekias (ex-*ee*-kee-us), sixth century B.C. Ancient Greek paintings have been lost, but some idea of what they may have looked like is provided by the vase paintings done by Exekias and others.

The Birthplace of Western Civilization

Why do historians place so much importance on events that happened over thirty centuries ago in a country not much larger than the state of Arizona? And why are the names of such artists as Myron, Phidias, and Polyclitus still held in esteem even though none of their works are known to exist today? The answer is simply that the country—Greece—was the birthplace of Western civilization. Furthermore, its contributions to art have had a profound effect upon artists up to the present day.

The long story of ancient Greece begins around 2000 B.C. At that time it is believed the earliest Greek tribes entered the land. The descendants of these primitive peoples remained there, and in about five hundred years a strong culture known as the Mycenaean had formed. However, the power of the Mycenaeans eventually gave way to that of a stronger people. After a series of invasions, the warlike Dorians took over the land, in about 1100 B.C. This meant in many areas a changed way of life as the conquerors mingled with the native populations. Towns eventually grew into small

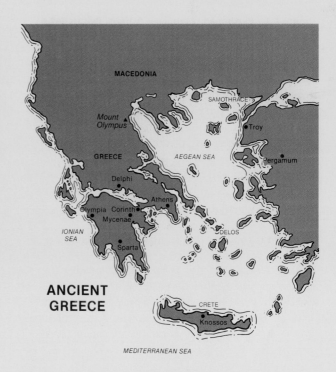

ANCIENT GREECE

Criticism

What kind of roof was used here—flat, round, gabled, or domed? Greek architects favored the post-and-lintel method of construction; can you find the posts and lintels in this building? Is this structure an example of formal (symmetrical) or informal (asymmetrical) balance? What is the overall effect of this building—distorted and awkward, or balanced and graceful?

Figure 6.1   Parthenon, Acropolis. Athens. Begun 447 B.C.

independent city-states. Many other civilizations began as a collection of city-states which then joined together to form kingdoms and empires. But this did not happen in Greece. Instead, the city-states remained fiercely independent. One reason for this may have had to do with geography. Greece is a country cut into pieces by mountains, valleys, and the sea, and this made communication difficult. In addition to these natural barriers were the social barriers of local pride and jealousy. These factors combined to keep the Greek city-states from uniting to form a nation.

Although there was a great rivalry between the city-states, not one of them was able to grow strong enough to conquer the others. Their rivalry was so intense that they could never agree about anything or work toward a common goal. It was even difficult for them to join together for mutual defense. Fear alone finally united them long enough to fight off invaders from Persia during the fifth century B.C. Then, suspecting still further invasions by the Persians, several city-states joined together to form a defensive alliance. This alliance came to be known as the Delian League. It was so called because its treasury was kept on the island of Delos. The larger cities contributed ships and men to this alliance, while the smaller cities gave money.

Because it was the most powerful member of the Delian League, Athens was made its permanent head. Athens was put in charge of the fleet and was authorized to collect money for the treasury. But, when the threat of invasion lessened, Pericles, the Athenian leader, moved the treasury from Delos to Athens. No doubt this angered the other city-states, but Pericles insisted that the treasury would be safer in Athens. However, he used the money to rebuild and beautify Athens, which had been badly ruined by the Persian invaders.

Athenian greatness was not destined to last long. The actions of Pericles were bitterly resented by the other members of the Delian League, especially Sparta and

Corinth. Finally, in 431 B.C., this resentment led to the Peloponnesian War. At first, Pericles successfully withstood the challenge of Sparta and the other city-states. But in 430 a terrible plague struck which killed a third of the Athenian population. A year later, Pericles himself was a victim of this great plague. With the death of its leader, Athens was doomed.

Unfortunately, the Greeks never learned the lesson of unity which enabled them to defeat the Persians. After Athens was defeated, a century of bickering and conflict followed. First one, then another city-state gained the upper hand. This conflict so weakened the country that it was helpless before foreign invaders. Finally, in 338 B.C., Greece was conquered by Macedonia.

Despite a history of rivalry, wars, and invasions, the Greek people managed to make many important contributions to art. Their accomplishments in architecture, particularly temple architecture, were among their most enduring legacies to Western civilization.

The Greek Contribution to Architecture

The Greeks thought of their temples as dwelling places for gods. They believed that these gods looked and often acted like humans. The gods controlled the universe and the destiny of every person on earth. For the Greeks, a perfect life was the highest goal, and a perfect life meant doing what the gods wanted them to do. As a result, fortune tellers and omens were very important in the Greek religion because they helped people discover the will of the gods.

The earliest Greek temples were made of wood or brick, and these have disappeared. As the economy prospered with the growth of trade, stone was used. Limestone and finally marble became the favorite building materials. But even though changes were made in building materials, the basic design of Greek temples did not change over the centuries. Unlike the Egyptian pyramid which evolved from mastaba to step pyramid to true pyramid, the design of the Greek temple remained the same. Greek builders chose not to alter a design that served their needs and was also pleasing to the eye. Instead, they made small improvements upon the basic design in order to achieve perfection. Proof that they realized this perfection is found in temples such as the Parthenon (Figure 6.1). It was built as a house for Athena, the goddess of wisdom and guardian of the city named in her honor.

The Parthenon

In 447 B.C., using funds from the treasury of the Delian League, Pericles ordered work to begin on the Parthe-

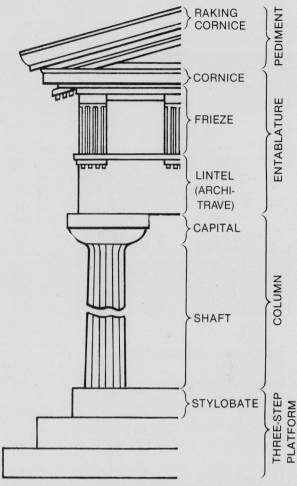

Figure 6.2   Features of temple construction

non. Ten years later the building was basically finished, although work on outside carvings continued until 432 B.C. The construction of such a building in just a decade is itself a wonder. Still, it was finished none too soon. The last stone was hardly in place before the Peloponnesian War started.

Like most Greek temples, the Parthenon is a simple rectangular building placed on a three-step platform (Figure 6.2). The top step of this platform is called the *stylobate*. From the stylobate rose columns, or posts, the tops of which were called *capitals*. The columns supported crossbeams, or *lintels*, and these held up a series of members which culminated in a sloping roof. The lintel, also referred to as the *architrave*, was part of the upper portion of the building called the *entablature*. Another component of the entablature was the *frieze*, a series of decorations forming an ornamental band around the building. Also included in the entablature was a horizontal member called a *cornice*, which was positioned across the top of the frieze. The cornice, along with a sloping member called a *raking cornice*, framed a triangular section called the *pediment*. A covered colonnade surrounded the entire porch. Thus the Parthenon

Criticism

How many rooms are in this building? What must you do to enter one room from the other? Does this seem convenient? Does this plan suggest that these two rooms served two different purposes?

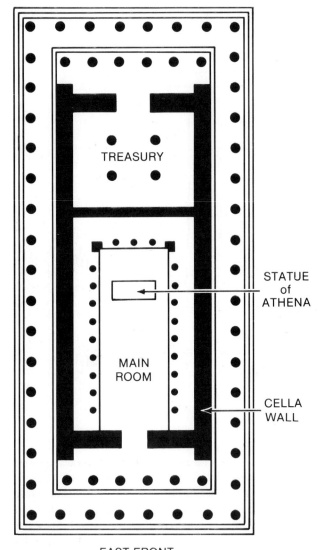

EAST FRONT

Figure 6.3   Plan of the Parthenon

made use of the most familiar features of Greek architecture: post-and-lintel construction; a sloping, or gabled, roof; and a colonnade. And, like all Greek buildings, the parts of the Parthenon were carefully planned to be balanced, harmonious, and beautiful.

The Parthenon had just two rooms (Figure 6.3). The smallest held the treasury of the Delian League, while the other housed a colossal gold and ivory statue of Athena. However, few citizens ever saw this splendid statue. Only priests and a few attendants were allowed inside the sacred temple. Religious ceremonies attended by the citizens of Athens were held outdoors in front of the building.

Of course, the details of these religious ceremonies are not known. Perhaps the people gathered before the temple to sing hymns of praise or hymns which asked for help from the goddess. At some point in the ceremony, a procession may have formed to carry offerings up to an altar. Food, pottery, and other gifts would be placed before the altar, and, on special occasions, animals may have been brought forward to be sacrificed.

Since few people were allowed inside the temple, there was no need for windows or interior decorations. Instead, attention centered on making the outside of the building as attractive as possible. It is hard to see with the naked eye, but there are few, if any, perfectly straight lines on the entire structure. The three-step platform and the entablature around the building *look* straight but actually bend upward in a gradual arc, so that the center is slightly higher than the ends. This means that the entire floor and ceiling is a low dome a few centimeters [several inches] higher in the middle than at the edges. The columns also curve outward slightly near their centers. Like muscles, they bulge a bit as they hold up the great weight of the roof. In addition, each column slants inward toward the center of the building. The columns were slanted in this way to prevent a feeling of top-heaviness and to add a sense of stability to the building. The slant is so slight that if the lines of the columns were extended they would meet about 4 km (kilometers) [2.5 miles] above the center of the Parthenon.

What was the "Acropolis" and where was it located? What was built there? Were the buildings here erected during the Archaic period or the Classical period?

Figure 6.4   View of the Acropolis today

The Greeks did not like the cold whiteness of their marble buildings. For this reason, they painted large areas with bright colors. Blue, red, green, and yellow were used most often, although some details were coated with a thin layer of gold. Today little of this color remains since the painted surfaces were exposed to the weather and have been worn away. But if you look closely at the more protected places of these ancient buildings, you might still find a few faint traces of blue paint.

The Parthenon has been put to a variety of uses over its long history. It was a Christian church in the fifth century and a mosque in the fifteenth century. Its present ruined state is due to an explosion which took place in the seventeenth century. The structure was being used as an ammunition storehouse by the Turks when an artillery shell fired by a Venetian ship landed in the center of it. The building has now been restored as far as possible with the original remains.

The Parthenon was only one of the several buildings erected on the sacred hill, or *Acropolis*, of Athens (Figure 6.4). The Acropolis is a mass of rock that rises abruptly 150 m [500 feet] above the city. Like a huge pedestal, it was crowned with a group of magnificent buildings that symbolized the glory of Athens. Covering less than 3.2 ha [8 acres], it was filled with temples, statues, and great flights of steps. On the western edge was a huge statue of Athena that was so tall that the tip of her gleaming spear served as a beacon to ships at sea. The statue was created by the legendary sculptor Phidias, and it was said to have been made from the bronze shields of the defeated Persians. Today, the crumbling but still impressive ruins of the Acropolis are a reminder of a great civilization and the achievements of the original and inspired artists it produced.

Which was the earliest of these orders? Which was the most elaborate? Which order was used on the Parthenon (Figure 6.1)?

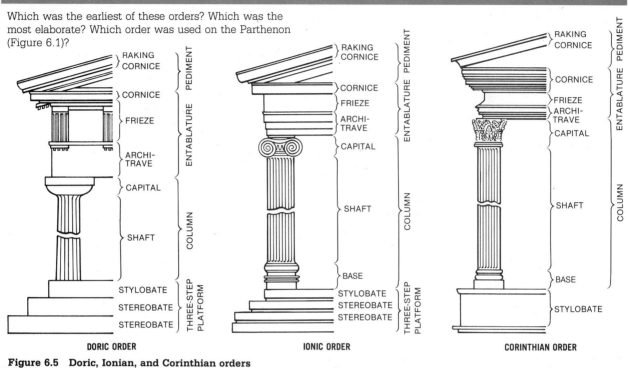

Figure 6.5   Doric, Ionian, and Corinthian orders

The Three Orders of Decorative Style

The Parthenon was built according to a particular order, or decorative style, known as the *Doric order*. This was the earliest of three orders developed by the Greeks (Figure 6.5). Its principal feature is a simple, heavy column without a base, topped by a broad, plain capital.

Later, the Greeks began making use of another order called the *Ionic*. This order employed columns which were more slender and higher than the Doric. The Ionic column had an elaborate base and a capital carved into double scrolls that looked like the horns of a ram. This was a more elegant order than the Doric, and for a time architects felt that it was only suitable for small temples. Such a temple was the little shrine to Athena Nike built on the Acropolis between 427 and 424 B.C. (Figure 6.6). But the more they looked at the new Ionic order, the more the Greeks began to appreciate it. Soon they began making use of it on larger structures such as the Erechtheum, a temple located directly opposite the Parthenon. This building was named after Erechtheus, a legendary king of Athens who was said to have been a foster son of Athena.

An unusual feature of the Erechtheum is the smallest of two porches added to its sides. Called the "Porch of the Maidens," the roof of this porch is supported by six columns carved to look like female figures (Figure 6.7).

Compare this temple with the Parthenon (Figure 6.1). How do these two temples differ from one another?

Figure 6.6   Temple of Athena Nike, Acropolis. Athens. 427-424 B.C.

History

What order of columns is found here? What unusual feature do you see on this building?

Figure 6.7   Erechtheum, with detail of the Porch of the Maidens, Acropolis, Athens: 421-405 B.C.

The most elaborate order was the *Corinthian*, developed late in the fifth century B.C. It was believed that this order was suggested by a wicker basket overgrown with large leaves found on the grave of a young Greek maiden. At first, Corinthian columns were used only on the inside of buildings. Later, they replaced Ionic columns on the outside. A monument to Lysicrates (Figure 6.8) built in Athens about three hundred years before the birth of Christ is the first known use of this order on the outside of a building. The Corinthian columns surround a hollow cylinder which once supported a trophy won by Lysicrates in a choral contest.

History

Can you identify the order of columns used on this monument? Describe the form of this structure. How does it differ from the form used for the Temple of Athena Nike (Figure 6.6)?

Figure 6.8 *Monument to Lysicrates*. Athens. c. 334 B.C.

The buildings on the Acropolis were constructed during the fifth and fourth centuries B.C. This was a time in Greek history known as the Classical period. Like architecture, Greek sculpture also reached its peak during this Classical period. But to understand and appreciate Greek accomplishments in sculpture it is necessary to turn the pages of history back to an earlier time known as the Archaic period.

Sculpture in the Archaic Period

From around 600-480 B.C., Greek sculptors were busy carving large, freestanding figures known as *Kouroi* and *Korai*. *Kouroi* is the plural form of *Kouros*, meaning "youth," and *Korai* is the plural of *Kore*, or "maiden."

The Kouros

A Kouros was a male youth who may have been a god or an athlete (Figure 6.9). In some ways, the stiffness and frontal pose of this figure brings to mind Egyptian statues. The only suggestion of movement is noted in the left foot which is placed slightly in front of the other.

You may have noticed that even though the figure is stepping forward both feet are flat on the ground. Of course, this is impossible unless the left leg is longer than the right one. This problem could have been corrected if the right leg had been bent slightly, but it is perfectly straight. Later, Greek artists learned how to bend and twist their figures to make them appear more relaxed and natural.

Except for the advancing left foot, the *Kouros* is symmetrically balanced. Details of hair, eyes, mouth, and chest are exactly alike on both sides of the figure just as they are on Egyptian statues. But, unlike Egyptian figures, the arms of the Kouros are separated slightly from the body and there is an open space between the legs. These openings help to break up the solid block of the stone from which it was carved.

No one knows for certain what the *Kouros* was meant to be. Some say he represents the sun god Apollo, while others insist that he is an athlete. If he is an athlete, he may be stepping forward to receive an award for a victorious performance in the games that were such an important part of Greek life. The wide shoulders, long legs, flat stomach, and narrow hips support the claim that he is an athlete. But the dreamy facial expression with its curious smile seems to suggest that he knows something that we ordinary mortals could never hope to know. In that case, he may indeed have been a god.

The face of the *Kouros* is interesting for another reason: it has a number of unusual features which were

Criticism

How is movement suggested here? Do you notice anything unusual about the position of the feet? Does this figure seem natural and graceful? Why or why not? Do you think this is a portrait of a particular person? Was this sculpture designed to be viewed from all sides or from the front only? Does it make effective use of three-dimensional space?

Figure 6.9   *Kouros*. c. 600 B.C. The Metropolitan Museum of Art, New York. Fletcher Fund, 1932, 32.11.1

used over and over again on early Greek sculptures. Among these are the bulging eyes, square chin, and a mouth with slightly upturned corners. This same mouth with its curious smile can be found on scores of early Greek sculptures. You may find it strange and even amusing, but this smile may have been a first step in the direction of greater realism. Greek sculptors wanted their figures to look more natural, and what could be more natural than a warm, welcoming smile? However, it took them a while to learn how to make that smile look more natural. But this is not too surprising—if you look at the work of beginning sculptors today, you will surely see that same strange smile on the faces of some of their figures.

The Hera of Samos

Korai were clothed women, often goddesses, which were also carved during the Archaic period. One of these goddesses, the *Hera of Samos* (Figure 6.10), looks a great deal like a stone cylinder. It has the same frontal pose as the *Kouros*, but its arms are held lightly against the body and the feet are placed tightly together. The left arm is bent and may have once held a small animal received as an offering. There is no deep carving here and no open spaces. Perhaps the artist was afraid to cut too deeply into the stone for fear of breaking it. Instead, a surface pattern of lines is used to suggest the garments and add textural interest to the simple form. Straight vertical lines are repeated to suggest a light lower garment. These contrast with the more widely spaced and deeper lines of a heavier garment draped over her shoulders. The folds of the garments gently follow the subtle curves of the figure. There is little to suggest action or movement; the figure stands perfectly upright and still. Over 1.8 m [6 feet] tall, it must have been an impressive symbol of authority and dignity to all who saw it.

Criticism

Can you find any deep carving or open spaces on this sculpture? Is movement suggested in any way? Which art element seems most important here? Point out the different ways line has been used. What is the purpose of the lines?

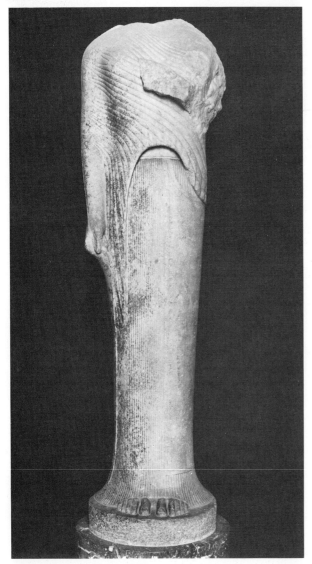

Figure 6.10 *Hera of Samos.* c. 570-560 B.C. Over 1.8 m [6'] tall. The Louvre, Paris. [Cliché des Musées Nationaux, Paris]

Sculpture in the Classical Period

With each new generation, Greek artists became bolder and more skillful. During the Classical period, they abandoned the stiff frontal pose and made their figures appear to move in space.

Myron's Discus Thrower

You can see how successful they were by examining a life-size statue of a discus thrower, or *Discobolus*, by a sculptor named Myron (Figure 6.11). Gone is the blocky, rigid pose of the earlier Kouroi and Korai. Myron has skillfully captured one of the rapidly changing positions required of an athlete throwing a discus. The athlete's weight is placed on his right leg, and the other is posed and ready to swing forward. He is frozen for a split second at the furthest point of the backswing.

But have you noticed something unusual about the face of Myron's figure? You would think that at this instant, just before vigorously hurtling the discus, the athlete's face would be tense and strained. He is about to put all his strength into a mighty throw, and yet his face is completely calm and relaxed. In this respect, the figure is more idealistic than real.

Few facts about Myron the man are known, but his work says a great deal about Myron the artist. It reveals that he had a thorough understanding of anatomy (how the body is structured) and that he delighted in the expression of motion. Myron's work also reveals that he must have spent many hours studying athletes in action and that he had complete confidence in his skills as an artist. Today he is generally regarded as one of the most important of the ancient Greek sculptors.

Myron's chief material was bronze, although it was said that he also created huge figures of gold and ivory.

What is this figure doing? Does he seem to be in action *at this exact moment*? Trace the axis line that begins at the tip of the right hand—where does it take you? In what way does the face fail to reflect the tenseness and strain of the body? Do you think this makes the figure seem real, or idealistic?

Figure 6.11 Myron. *Discobolus (Discus Thrower).* **Roman copy of a bronze original of c. 450 B.C. Life-size. Museo Nazionale Romano, Rome**

As far as is known, he did not work in marble. However, knowledge of his sculptures comes from marble copies produced in Roman times. A dependence on Roman copies for information about Greek sculptures is not unusual. Today there no longer exists a single certified original work by the great sculptors of Greece. Bronze works which once numbered in the thousands were melted down for different reasons long ago. Even marble sculptures were mutilated, lost, or ruined by neglect. What is known of those ancient works comes from copies made later by Romans who used them to decorate their public buildings, villas, and gardens.

Figure 6.12 Interior of Parthenon with the sculpture of Athena by Phidias. Restored model. The Metropolitan Museum of Art, New York

Phidias' Sculptures for the Parthenon

It is through Roman copies and descriptions by ancient writers that the works of Phidias are known. He was one of the greatest of all Greek sculptors and the creator of the gigantic statue of Athena in the Parthenon. Photographs of Roman copies of Athena are not very impressive, however (Figure 6.12). You will have to use your imagination to appreciate the full impact of this work. Walking into the darkened room of the Parthenon, you would face this colossal goddess, towering over you to a height of over 10 m [35 feet]. Her skin was of the whitest ivory, and over 0.9 t [1 ton] of gold was used to fashion her armor and garments. Precious stones were used for the eyes and as decorations for her helmet. A slight smile softened a face that looked as if it could turn cruel and angry at any moment. You might fear her or admire her, but it is unlikely that you would ever forget this powerful vision of Athena fashioned by Phidias.

In addition to creating the statue of Athena, Phidias also supervised the decorations on the outside of the Parthenon. One of these decorations was a large relief sculpture made up of 350 people and 125 horses taking part in a religious parade.

Criticism

Find two diagonal axis lines in this relief sculpture. Does the use of these repeated diagonals suggest a movement or rhythm? If so, what is the direction of this movement? How have these figures been made to look more round and solid? Describe the expression and gesture of the first horseman. What do you think he is saying to the rider behind? What is the second rider doing? What aesthetic qualities would you use when making and supporting a judgment about this carving?

Figure 6.13   *Horsemen,* **from the west frieze of the Parthenon. c. 440 B.C. Marble, approx. 109 cm [43″] high. British Museum, London**

A parade today is an exciting and colorful event whether you are participating in it or watching as it passes by. It must have been just as exciting and colorful in ancient Athens. On a 141 m [525 foot] band, or frieze, running around inner walls of the Parthenon, Greek sculptors directed by Phidias show you how a parade looked to them over twenty-four hundred years ago.★

Every four years, the citizens of Athens held a great celebration in honor of Athena. As part of this celebration, a procession was held. The people in this procession carried new garments and other offerings to Athena in the Parthenon. These were the city's gifts thanking the goddess for her divine protection. The procession was formed in the city below the Acropolis and moved slowly up a winding road through a huge gateway, the entrance to the sacred hill. Then it wound between temples dedicated to various gods and goddesses and past the huge bronze statue of Athena. The procession finally stopped at the entrance to the Parthenon where, during a solemn ceremony, the presentations were made.

The processional frieze is no longer on the Parthenon. In fact, it is not even in one piece. Badly damaged parts of it are housed in museums in London, Paris, and Athens. This is unfortunate since they were intended to go together to form a single work of art. Since you cannot see it in one piece, try to picture it as it must have looked when it was completed centuries ago.

To see the frieze you would have had to climb the three steps and pass through the row of outside col-

---

★ **Enrichment** With the other carvings on the outside of the Parthenon, this frieze makes up the largest surviving group of Classical sculpture.

umns surrounding the Parthenon. Inside are the walls of the temple. The frieze, which was over 1 m [3 feet] high, ran around the top of these walls like a giant stone cartoon strip. It must have been difficult to see because it was so high and, placed just below the ceiling, poorly lit.

The scene begins on the western side of the Parthenon. There the procession is seen taking shape in the city. A feeling of anticipation is in the air as riders prepare to mount their prancing horses. Others, preparing to march on foot, are seen standing about impatiently, lacing their sandals or adjusting their garments. Further on, mounted and unmounted youths, charioteers, city officials, and sacred animals are moving forward—the parade is underway. As they move, the figures bunch up in some places and spread out in others as paraders often do. At one point, an irritated horseman turns and raises his hand in warning to the horseman behind him, who has come up too quickly and jostles his mount. The rider behind responds to the warning by reining in his rearing horse (Figure 6.13). All along the parade, there is a strong sense of movement. It is evident in the spirited prancing of the horses and the lighthearted pace of the figures on foot. This pace seems to quicken as the procession draws nearer to

its destination. But perhaps movement is best suggested by the pattern of light and shadow in the carved drapery. This pattern of alternating light and dark value contrasts creates a flickering quality which becomes even more obvious when contrasted with the empty spaces between the figures.

Finally, the procession slows down and becomes more serious as it approaches a group of seated gods and goddesses watching the scene. They may be guests enjoying the parade at the invitation of Athena. Nearby, a number of standing figures stop the parade at a point just over the main door of the temple (Figure 6.14). You will recall that, in reality, it was here at the main entrance to the Parthenon that the gifts and offerings were made to Athena.

There are many legends about Phidias, but few reliable facts about his life. One story says that he was accused of stealing gold that was to be used for the statue of Athena. This charge apparently was not proved, but it was followed by another—that he had included his portrait and that of Pericles in the design on Athena's shield. For this act of blasphemy, he was thrown into prison where he died of disease or, as some said, of poison.

Criticism

Is harmony an important principle here? How is it achieved? Is the rhythm or movement noted here swift or slow? How has the movement from right to left been slowed down? How has value been used to create greater interest in the drapery? Would you say these figures are excited, or solemn?

Figure 6.14 *Head of the Procession,* **from the east frieze of the Parthenon. c. 440 B.C. Marble, approx. 109 cm [43″] high. The Louvre, Paris. [Cliché des Musées Nationaux, Paris]**

Sculpture from the Temple of Athena Nike

Another relief sculpture, this one from the Temple of Athena Nike, may remind you of Myron's discus thrower since it also shows a figure frozen in action (Figure 6.15). The unknown sculptor has carved the goddess of victory bending over to fasten her sandal. A graceful movement is suggested by the thin drapery which clings to and defines the body of the goddess. As you analyze this work, you will see how the flowing folds of the drapery and the line of the shoulder and arms create a series of oval lines that unifies the work. And if you compare the handling of the drapery here with that of the *Hera of Samos*, you can appreciate more fully the great strides made by Greek sculptors over a 150-year period.

Polyclitus' Spear Bearer

The second most famous Classical Greek sculptor after Phidias was Polyclitus. His specialty was creating statues of youthful athletes such as his *Doryphorus* (or *Spear Bearer*) (Figure 6.16). Often his figures are shown in a pose that has come to be known as "contrapposto." In such a pose, the weight of the body is balanced on one leg, while the other is free and relaxed. In the *Doryphorus*, the left leg is bent and the toes lightly touch the ground. The body turns slightly in a momentary movement that gives the figure a freer, more lifelike look. The right hip and left shoulder are raised; the head tips forward and turns to the right. The result is a spiral axis line, or line of movement, that begins at the toes of the left foot and curves gently upward through the body to the head. Action is kept to a minimum, but there is an unmistakable feeling of athletic strength and prowess here. The figure seems to be doing little more than just standing around at the moment. Perhaps he is waiting his turn to test his skill in the spear-throwing competition. If so, he certainly does not look nervous or tense. On the contrary, he looks completely relaxed and confident. There is no doubt in his mind—or the viewer's—that he will be victorious.

History

In what way is this carving similar to the *Discobolus* (Figure 6.11)? What *shape* is created by the axis lines found in this sculpture? Do you have the impression that a real body exists beneath the drapery?

Figure 6.15 *Nike Fastening Her Sandal,* from the Temple of Athena Nike, Acropolis. Athens. c. 410 B.C. Marble, approx. 107 cm [42″] high. Acropolis Museum, Athens

Criticism

What makes this figure seem so lifelike? Is the figure's weight carried on both legs? Draw an imaginary axis line down the center of this figure. Is this axis line straight, or does it form a spiral? Would you say that the mood of this figure is tense and anxious, or relaxed and confident? Is this a successful work of art? Why or why not?

Figure 6.16   Polyclitus. *Doryphoros (Spear Bearer).* Roman copy of an original of c. 450-440 B.C. Life-size. Museo Nazionale, Naples. [Photo Alinari]

Sculpture in the Hellenistic Period

The Peloponnesian War left the Greek city-states weakened by conflict. To the North lay Macedonia ruled by Philip II, a military genius who had received a Greek education. Having united his own country, Philip turned his attention to the disunited and bickering Greek city-states. Their disunity was too great a temptation to resist, and in 338 B.C. Philip defeated them to realize his dream of controlling the Greek world. Before Philip could extend his empire further, he was assassinated while attending the wedding of his daughter. His successor was his twenty-one-year-old son, Alexander the Great, who soon launched his amazing career of conquest.

Alexander, whose teacher had been the famous Greek philosopher Aristotle, inherited his father's admiration for Greek culture. Alexander's admiration was so great that he was determined to spread this culture throughout the world. As he marched through one country after another, the Greek culture that he brought with him blended with other, non-Greek, cultures. The period in which this occurred is known as the Hellenistic age. It lasted about two centuries, ending in 146 B.C. when Greece was again conquered, this time by Roman legions.

Sculptors working during the Hellenistic period were extremely skillful and confident. They showed off their skills by creating dramatic and often violent images in bronze and marble. The face was especially interesting to them because they felt that the face was a mirror of inner emotions. Beauty was less important to them than the expression of these inner emotions. Their works left little to the imagination, and often lacked the precise balance and the harmony of Classical sculptures.

What do you think has happened to this figure? What features make it look so real? How does this sculpture make you feel? What theory or theories of art seem especially appropriate here?

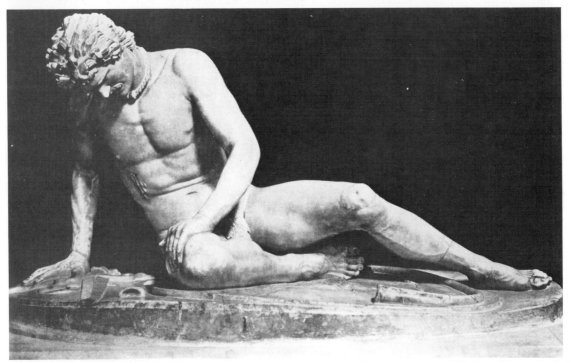

Figure 6.17 *Dying Gaul.* Roman copy of a bronze original of c. 240 B.C. from Pergamum. Life-size. Museo Capitolino, Rome

The Dying Gaul

Many of the features of the Hellenistic style can be observed in a life-size sculpture known as the *Dying Gaul*[1] (Figure 6.17). A Roman copy shows a figure that was once part of a large monument erected in the ancient Greek city of Pergamon. The monument was built to celebrate a victory over the Gauls, fierce warriors from the North. In this sculpture, you witness the final moments of a Gaul who was fatally wounded in battle. The fighting has swept by and in the stillness that follows, a once-feared warrior gallantly fights one final battle, one he cannot win. Blood flows freely from the wound in his side. Life seems to have already left the legs crumbled beneath him, and he uses what little strength he has remaining to support himself with his right arm. He has difficulty supporting the weight of his head and it tilts downward. Pain and the certain knowledge that he is dying distort the features of his face. In a few moments, no longer able to hold himself up, he will sink slowly to the ground.

Works like the *Dying Gaul* were intended to touch the emotions of the viewer. You are meant to become involved in this drama of a dying warrior, to share and feel his pain and loneliness and marvel at his quiet dignity at the moment of death.

The Nike of Samothrace

About twenty-one hundred years ago, an unknown sculptor completed a larger-than-life marble sculpture to celebrate a naval victory (Figure 6.18). The finished sculpture of a winged Nike (goddess of victory) stood on a pedestal made to look like the prow of a war ship. She may have held a trumpet to her lips with her right hand while waving a banner with her left. Loudly trumpeting victory, her wings outstretched, she lands lightly on the ship. Clearly the vessel is underway, speeding to meet and defeat some enemy. A brisk ocean breeze whips Nike's garments into ripples and folds adding to a feeling of forward movement. Her weight is supported

[1] Unfortunately, the name of the sculptor who created this dramatic work is unknown.

by both legs, but the body twists in space creating an overall sense of movement.

It is not known for certain what great victory this sculpture was meant to celebrate. Likewise uncertain is its original location. It was found in 1875, on a lonely hillside of Samothrace, headless, without arms, and in 118 pieces. Pieced together, it is now known as the *Nike (or Victory) of Samothrace.* It stands proudly once more, welcoming visitors to the Louvre, the great art museum in Paris.

The Seated Boxer

Ten years after the *Nike of Samothrace* was found, a bronze sculpture of a seated boxer (Figure 6.19) was unearthed in Rome. It is not as dramatic as the *Dying Gaul* nor as spirited as the "Winged Victory," but it has an impact on the emotions of anyone pausing to look at it carefully. The unknown artist does not present you

with a victorious young athlete, but a mature, professional boxer seen resting after what must have been a brutal match. Few details are spared in telling you about the boxer's violent occupation. The swollen ears (a boxer's trademark), scratches, and perspiration are signs of the punishment he has received. He turns his head to one side as he prepares to remove the leather boxing glove from his left hand. The near-profile view of his face reveals his broken nose and battered cheeks. What is he looking at? Of course, it is impossible to know for certain, but there is no mistaking the joyless expression on his face. Perhaps he is listening to the decision of the judges. They may be telling him what he already knows: an old boxer, well past his prime, he has just suffered another bitter defeat.

Criticism

What is this person's occupation? What clues helped you identify his occupation? What is he doing at this moment? What are your feelings about him? Is emotionalism an appropriate theory to use here? If you use that theory, how would you judge this work?

History

What has the artist done to create a feeling of forward movement here? Does this work suggest excitement and action, or calmness and dignity? What do you think this figure represents?

Figure 6.18 *Nike of Samothrace.* c. 190 B.C. Marble, approx. 2.4 m [8'] high. The Louvre, Paris. [Cliché des Musées Nationaux, Paris]

Figure 6.19 *Seated Boxer.* c. 50 B.C. Bronze. Museo Nazionale Romano, Rome

Stylistic Changes in Sculpture

The development of Greek sculpture can be traced through an examination of the cavalcade of gods, goddesses, and athletes created from the Archaic period to the Hellenistic period. Sculptured figures produced during the Archaic period were solid and stiff, but by the Classical period they had achieved near perfection in balance, proportion, and sense of movement. During Hellenistic times, sculptures emphasized even greater movement in space and added an emotional appeal intended to actively involve the viewer.

Perhaps this development can be illustrated best by looking again at several sculptures which made use of the same subject matter. The *Kouros*, the *Discus Thrower*, the *Spear Bearer*, and the *Seated Boxer* are all sculptures of male athletes,[2] but each reflects different objectives stressed at different periods in Greek art history. The *Kouros* was created at a time when artists were seeking greater control of their materials in order to make their statues look more real. The *Discus Thrower* shows that they eventually gained the knowledge and skill needed to do this. From there, they went on to improve upon their works, striving for the balance, harmony, and beauty noted in works such as the *Spear Bearer*. And finally, their interest shifted to more dramatic and emotional subjects, such as the *Seated Boxer*.

Painting and the Greek Love for Color

Painting was just as valued as sculpture in Greece. This is not unexpected since it is known that the Greeks had a great affection for color. In fact, they liked color so much that they painted their statues as well as their buildings. Some sculptures have been found with their colors still preserved. Unfortunately, none of the great paintings have survived. They are known only through descriptions passed on by ancient writers.

Concern for Realism

It is likely that Greek painters had the same concern for realism as did sculptors. The Roman historian Pliny the Elder supports this notion.★ He tells of a great competi-

How does this early Greek vase differ from vases that were done later?

Figure 6.20 *Geometric Jug,* **from the Greek Islands. Seventh century** B.C. **Clay, 41 cm [16¼"] high. Courtesy of the Indiana University Art Museum, Bloomington, Indiana**

★ Enrichment In his thirty-seven books on natural history, Pliny compiled an encyclopedia of the arts, crafts, zoology, and botany. He claimed to have drawn twenty thousand topics from more than two thousand books by 473 authors. However, despite the wealth of material in it, the work is of limited value because Pliny seemed unable or unwilling to distinguish between fact and fable. Pliny died in A.D. 79 while trying to observe closely an eruption of the famous volcano Vesuvius.

---

[2] It should be mentioned again that the identity of the *Kouros* is uncertain. While it may be an athlete, there is equal justification in claiming that it represents a god instead.

tion which took place in the fifth century B.C. The purpose of this competition was to determine which of two famous painters was more skilled in producing lifelike paintings. The painters, Zeuxis and Parrhasius, faced each other with their works covered by curtains. Zeuxis confidently removed his curtain to reveal a painting of grapes that was so natural that birds were tricked into pecking at it. Certain that no one could outdo this feat, he asked Parrhasius to reveal his work. Parrhasius answered by inviting Zeuxis to remove the curtain from his painting. But when Zeuxis tried, he found he could not—the curtain was the painting.

Vase Decoration

Of course, Pliny's story is probably more fiction than fact. A more accurate idea of what Greek painting was like may be provided by the pictures found on ancient Greek vases. The earliest Greek vases were decorated with bands of simple geometric patterns covering most of the vessel. (The label *Geometric Period* refers to the period in which geometric decorations were used.) Eventually the entire vase was decorated in this way (Figure 6.20). Early in the eighth century B.C., artists began to add figures to the geometric designs on their vases (Figure 6.21). Some of the best of these figures were painted on large funeral vases. These vases were used in much the same way as tombstones are used today, as grave markers. It was customary to pour oil into them as offerings for the dead. Holes in the bottom allowed the offerings to sink into the earth. The figures on these vases are made of triangles and lines, and look like simple stick figures. Often they are placed on either side of a figure representing the deceased as though they were paying their last respects. Their hands are raised upward pulling on their hair in a gesture of grief and despair.

Criticism

How are the patterns and figures organized on this vase? What kind of event is taking place—a battle, a wedding, or a funeral? How do you know?

Figure 6.21 *Vase* (with detail), from the Dipylon cemetery, Athens. Eighth century B.C. 72.3 cm [40½"] high. The Metropolitan Museum of Art, Rogers Fund, 1914

In time, vase figures became more lifelike and were placed in story-telling scenes. An excellent example of this kind of painting is provided by a vase showing two figures engrossed in a game (Figure 6.22). It was created by an artist named Exekias.

Criticism

What are the two figures painted on this vase doing? Can you determine their occupation and their importance from the clues provided? How has the artist arranged this scene to complement the shape of the vase on which it is painted? What makes this an effective design?

Figure 6.22   Exekias. *Vase with Ajax and Achilles Playing Draughts.* c. 540 B.C. **Vatican Museums, Rome**

Have you ever become so caught up in a game that you failed to hear someone calling you? It happens to everyone, no matter how important the person being called or how urgent the summons. Exekias painted such an event on a vase over twenty-five hundred years ago. Two Greek generals are seen playing a board game, probably one in which a roll of the dice determines the number of moves around the board. The names of the generals are written on the vase. They are two great heroes from Greek literature, Ajax and Achilles. The words being spoken by these warriors are shown coming from their mouths just as they appear in modern cartoon strips. Ajax has just said "tria," or "three," and Achilles is responding by saying "tessera," or "four." Legend says that these two great heroes were so involved in this game that their enemy was able to mount a surprise attack.

Exekias has tried to show the informality of this simple scene. Shields have been set aside, and Achilles, at the left, has casually pushed his war helmet to the back of his head. Ajax, forgetting for a moment that they are at war, has removed his helmet and placed it out of the way on top of his shield. For a few moments, the Greek heroes are just two ordinary people lost in friendly competition.

Exekias also made an effort to add details to his scene to make it seem as realistic as possible. An intricate design decorates the garments of the two generals. Also, the facial features, hands, and feet are carefully drawn, although the eyes are shown from the front as they were in Egyptian art. However, Exekias was not so concerned with realism that he ignored good design. The scene is carefully arranged to complement the vase on which it was painted. The figures lean forward, and the curve of their backs repeats the curve of the vase. Also, notice how the lines of the spears continue the lines of the two handles and lead your eye to the game which is the center of interest in the composition.

The Demand Elsewhere for Greek Artists

In 197 B.C., the Romans defeated Macedonia and gave the Greek city-states their freedom as allies. But the troublesome Greeks caused Rome so much difficulty that their freedom was taken away and Corinth burned. Athens alone continued to be held in respect and was allowed a certain amount of freedom. But even though the great creative age had passed its peak, Greek artists were sought in other lands where they spread the genius of their masters.

Studio Experiences

Lesson One: Drawings of Buildings with Greek Features

Your reading pointed out many of the features of Greek architecture, including posts and lintels, gabled roofs, colonnades, capitals, and stylobates. (You may wish to review these and other features by reexamining Figures 6.2, 6.5, 6.6, 6.7, and 6.8.) Armed with this information, look for buildings in your community which exhibit some of these same features. Complete a detailed drawing of all or part of such a building. Use value gradation and emphasis to add to the three-dimensional quality of your drawing. Dots, lines, diagonal shading, cross-hatching, or individualized linear patterns can also be used to create a variety of values and simulated textures in your drawing.

Lesson Two: Functional Coil Vases

The Greeks developed a variety of vase, or vessel, forms designed to serve specific purposes (Figures 6.20, 6.21, and 6.22). Some were intended as drinking vessels, others as mixing bowls, and still others as storage containers for oil, honey, and grain. On sketch paper complete several designs for a vase intended to serve a particular purpose. Make certain to identify this purpose *before* beginning work on these designs. Select your best sketch and make a cardboard template, or pattern, of it. When cut out, this template should measure no less than 25.4 cm [10 inches] in height. Starting with a clay disk 1.27 cm [½ inch] thick, add clay coils one on top of the other to form your vase. Coils should measure about 1 cm [⅜ inch] in thickness and are joined together with coats of slip between them. (Slip is a mixture of clay and water used in the making of pottery to cement together parts that have been formed separately.) After each coil is in place, position your template along the clay wall to make certain the vase is progressing according to plan and is symmetrically balanced. Various clay tools can be used to create a rich, overall texture on the soft surface. When the vase is completely dry, it can be fired, and later, if you wish to do so, it may be glazed.

Lesson Three: Clay Slab Pitcher with Sgraffito Design

"Sgraffito" comes from an Italian word meaning "to scratch." During this lesson you will scratch a design onto a clay slab pitcher of your own making. The vase by Exekias in Figure 6.22 showed a scene of two ancient heroes playing a game. When you studied this work, you noticed that this scene complemented the shape of the vessel. Bear this in mind as you sketch several ideas for a pitcher which will have on it a decorative line design. Also, make certain that your sketches show pitchers with spouts and handles. With a rolling pin, flatten out a slab of clay to a uniform thickness of 1.3 cm [½ inch]. From this, cut out a rectangle measuring no less than 35.6 x 15.2 cm [14 x 6 inches]. When it has stiffened slightly, place this rectangle into an upright position and fold it into an oval shape. The two ends of the slab are firmly pinched together to close the form and provide the material needed for the handle. Seal the inside seam with your fingers. Measure, cut, and add a 1.3-cm [½-inch] slab of clay to the bottom of your pitcher. Then shape the form for the handle and cut out the opening. Next, form a simple spout with your fingers. When it is as hard as leather, the surface should be coated with a layer of slip, or *engobe,* of a different color than the clay used to make the pitcher. When this coating is firm but still soft, scratch or cut your design into it, revealing the contrasting clay body beneath. Make certain that this "sgraffito" design takes into account and complements the form of the pitcher. When dry, the vase can be fired.

Safety Note

Always use non-lead glazes on your ceramic pieces, especially if they are intended to hold food or drink. *Avoid* lead glazes. Certain liquids, such as coffee, can pull the lead out of such a glaze and affect the health of the person using the vessel.

Chapter 7

Age of the Conquerors: Roman Art

The Rising Power of Rome

Long before the Roman Empire rose to greatness, Italy was the home of a mysterious ancient people called the Etruscans. No one is sure where these dark, sturdy people came from. Some claim they were a seafaring people from Asia Minor, while others believe that Italy was their native land. But one thing is certain, of all the peoples in Italy they were the most civilized and the most powerful. In time, they conquered much of Italy north of the Tiber River. Among their conquests was the hill town of Rome.

Under the rule of Etruscan kings, Rome grew in size and importance. By the end of the sixth century B.C., it had become the largest and richest city in Italy. However, the Romans were never happy under Etruscan rule, and in 509 B.C. they drove the Etruscans from the city and established a republic.

Ridding themselves of the Etruscans did not end Rome's problem. Finding itself surrounded by enemies, it was forced to fight for survival. As nearby enemies were defeated, more distant foes tried to conquer the young republic. But Rome managed to defend itself against these threats and extended its power until all of Italy was under its control.

An early victory over Carthage, its chief rival, won Rome its first overseas province—Sicily.★ But that was just the beginning. Before it was finished, Rome ruled over every civilized land in Europe and Africa. Eventually, it controlled territory from Britain in the west to Mesopotamia in the east. So extensive was its rule that Romans proudly referred to the Mediterranean as *"mare nostrum—our sea."*

Roman Architecture

It is difficult to talk about "Roman Art" because so much of it was copied from the Greeks. From the very first,

---

★ Enrichment Carthage was an ancient city and state in northern Africa founded by the Phoenicians in about 800 B.C. near the present site of Tunis. After a period of a hundred years, Rome defeated Carthage in the Punic Wars.

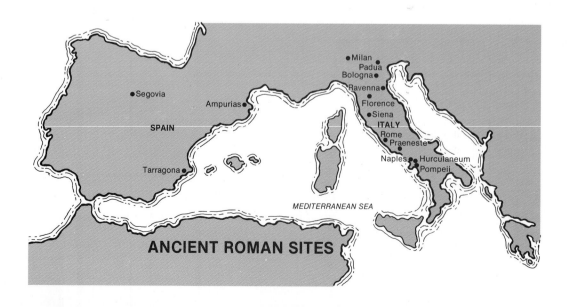

ANCIENT ROMAN SITES

Do all the columns here act as structural supports? If not, what purpose do they serve? Can you find another structure in this chapter that uses engaged columns in this same way? What elements of art can you identify? Do you think these elements are used effectively? Have you seen buildings before that looked something like this? Where?

Here Roman builders constructed staircases leading to a series of seven terraces built into a hillside. How did this differ from the way Greek builders used a hill site for the Acropolis?

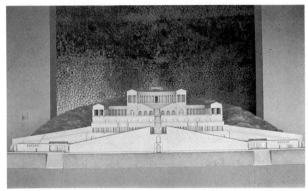

Figure 7.2 Reconstructed model of the Sanctuary of Fortuna Primigenia at Praeneste (Palestrina). Original, c. 80 B.C.

Figure 7.1 Temple of Fortuna Virilis, Rome. Late second century B.C. [Photo Alinari]

well-born and cultured Romans exhibited a great admiration for Greek art forms of every period and style. They imported Greek works by the shipload and even brought Greek artists to Rome to work for them. Generally, the Romans were content with being heirs of Greek art. Except for architecture, they made few original contributions of their own in art. Because they were excellent planners and engineers, the Romans were destined to make their mark as the first great builders of the world.

The Temples

Many early Roman temples made use of features developed earlier by others, especially the Greeks. But these features were used by Romans to satisfy their own needs and tastes. For example, while the Greeks used columns as structural supports, the Romans added them to their buildings as decoration without structural purpose.

The Greek influence can be seen in a temple built in Rome during the last years of the second century B.C. (Figure 7.1). At first, the rectangular shape and Ionic columns make this building look like a Greek temple. But when you look closer, you will see that free-standing columns do not surround the entire building as they do Greek temples such as the Parthenon. Instead, they are used only for the porch at the front. Along the sides and

back of the building, half-columns are attached to the solid walls to create a decorative pattern.

The Romans did not limit themselves to borrowing solely from the Greeks. The Roman temple is placed on a podium or platform which raises it above eye level. This was a feature the Romans borrowed from the Etruscans who built their temples in this way.

Another early Roman temple which made use of Greek features is found in the foothills of the Apennines, a short distance from Rome. The route to this temple is along an ancient Roman road called the Appian Way. This road was once lined with the grand villas and tombs of wealthy Roman citizens. Many chose to be buried here since a law prohibited burials within the city. A two-hour trip over this historic road will take you to the site of the ancient town of Praeneste (now the modern city of Palestrina). This town was said to have originated when a peasant found a mysterious tablet in the woods nearby.★ It was reported that on this tablet was recorded the history of the town, even though it had not yet been built. The people were so impressed that they erected a temple (Figure 7.2) to hold a statue of Fortuna, the goddess of good fortune, and the mysterious tablet was placed within this statue. Eventually the temple became the home of a famous oracle who attracted people from great distances who came to have their futures revealed to them.★★

★ Enrichment A tablet is a flat piece of stone with an inscription on it.

★ Enrichment An oracle was a medium or priest be-
★ lieved to be in communication with the gods.

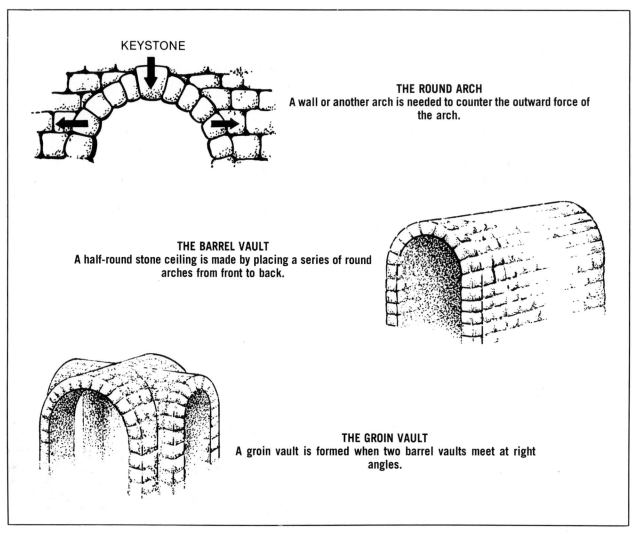

KEYSTONE

THE ROUND ARCH
A wall or another arch is needed to counter the outward force of the arch.

THE BARREL VAULT
A half-round stone ceiling is made by placing a series of round arches from front to back.

THE GROIN VAULT
A groin vault is formed when two barrel vaults meet at right angles.

Figure 7.3 Features of Roman architecture

People wishing to consult with the oracle at the Temple of Fortuna Primigenia had to climb a series of ramps and terraces until they reached a great courtyard. From there, a flight of stairs led to the semicircular colonnade of the main temple. The entire complex was made up of many circular and semicircular temples, terraces, colonnades, arches, and staircases. To span openings, the builders made use of the arch. To roof large areas, they placed a series of arches from front to back to form a barrel, or tunnel, vault (Figure 7.3). This made it possible for them to cover huge rooms and halls with half-round stone ceilings. Because these ceilings were so heavy, thick windowless walls were needed to support them.

Innovations in Structure and Material

If you look closely at a Roman arch (Figure 7.3), you will see how it improved upon the post-and-lintel system favored by the Greeks. The post and lintel limited builders in terms of the space it could bridge. A stone lintel could not be used to span a wide space because it would break. Under pressure, stone does not bend; it snaps. Unlike a lintel, an arch is made of a number of bricks or cut stones. These are held in place by a wooden form until the top stone, called a *keystone,* is fit into place. The space that can be spanned in this manner is much greater than the space bridged by a lintel. However, an arch needs the support of another arch or a wall. If this support is not provided, the outward force of the arch will cause it to collapse. For this reason, the Romans created a series of smaller arches to replace the single large arch (Figure 7.4).

Concrete, one of the most versatile of building materials, was used in the Temple of Fortuna Primigenia. Although it had been used in the Near East for some time, the Romans were the first to make extensive use of this material. Coupled with their knowledge of the arch, concrete enabled the Romans to construct buildings on a large scale.

After Rome became Christianized, the oracle at Praeneste was banished and the temple destroyed. Eventually it was forgotten and, after the fall of Rome, a town was built on the site. It was not until a bombing raid in World War II destroyed most of the houses that the ruins of the huge temple were discovered.

History

How was the arch used here an improvement on the post-and-lintel system used by the Greeks? Can you point to the keystone in one of these arches? What was done here to prevent the arches from collapsing?

Figure 7.4   Roman aqueduct. Segovia, Spain. c. First century A.D.

This amphiteater was built alongside the sea, using the natural slope of the hillside for the tiers. Can you think of any present-day building that resembles this ancient structure?

Figure 7.5 Ruins of a Roman amphitheater. Tarragona, Spain. c. First century B.C.

Wherever the Roman legions went, they introduced the arch and the use of concrete in architecture. With these they constructed great domes and vaults over their buildings and covered these with marble slabs or ornamental bricks. Even today, the remains of baths, amphitheaters (Figure 7.5), temples, triumphal arches, and aqueducts (Figure 7.6) are found throughout countries once part of the Roman Empire.

Figure 7.6 Roman aqueduct. Tarragona, Spain. c. First century B.C.

One of the challenges facing the Romans was to provide an adequate water supply for the cities of the empire. Channels with a continuous, gradual decline were constructed to bring water from mountain streams to the cities. Arches were built to carry these channels over valleys and gorges. At Segovia, 118 arches were constructed, reaching a height of 28 m [92'].

Figure 7.7 Roman aqueduct (two views). Segovia, Spain. c. First century, A.D.

The Aqueducts

Their aqueducts demonstrate how the Romans were able to combine their engineering skills with a knowledge of architectural form. The aqueducts were constructed by placing a series of arches next to each other so they would support each other and carry the weight to the ground. While attractive, these aqueducts were designed for efficiency rather than beauty. They carried water from mountain streams into cities by using gravitational flow. Eleven were built in and around Rome alone. These ranged from 16 km [10 miles] to 96.6 km [60 miles] in length and carried about 1 billion liters [270 million gallons] of water into the city every day.

One of the best-known aqueducts is found in Segovia, Spain (Figure 7.7). It brought water to the city from a stream 16 km [10 miles] away. Constructed of granite blocks laid without mortar or cement, the aqueduct made use of many angles to break the force of the rushing water. Many regard this as the most important Roman construction in Spain.

Today only the walls of this huge complex remain. At one time these walls supported vaults forming an enclosure that could accommodate fifteen hundred bathers. Landscaped gardens surrounded the main buildings, and these were lined by shops, restaurants, gymnasiums, and libraries. Here, for a small fee, Romans could while away an entire day bathing, gossiping, studying, shopping, and relaxing.

Figure 7.8 Aerial view, Baths of Caracalla. Rome. c. A.D. 215

Public Buildings

Roman emperors were constantly building and rebuilding the cities of their empire.★ As long as there was money to do so, baths, circuses, forums, and amphitheaters were constructed for the enjoyment of the people. Of course, there was a reason for such generosity. By providing beautiful monuments and places for public recreation, the emperors hoped to maintain their popularity with the people. As a result, Roman monuments and public buildings were numerous and impressive. An ancient guidebook to Rome, published in the middle of the fourth century A.D., claims that there were 424 temples, 304 shrines, 80 statues of gods made from precious metals, 64 of ivory, and over 3,700 bronze statues scattered throughout the city.

The Baths

Among the most popular of the Roman public buildings were the baths. These were much more than just municipal swimming pools. They were vast enclosed structures that contained libraries, lecture rooms, gymnasiums, shops, restaurants, and pleasant walkways. These made the baths a social and cultural center as well as a place for hygiene. In many ways, they were like the shopping malls of today.

Every large Roman city had its baths. Although they differed in ground plan and details, these baths had certain features in common. They all contained a series

★ **Enrichment** The Emperor Augustus boasted that he found Rome a city of brick and stone and left it a city of marble. His boast was justified. He not only rebuilt the forum, or public square, but restored eighty-two temples as well.

You can see here how a long barrel vault was intersected by three shorter barrel vaults to make groin vaults. What advantges did this offer over the use of a single long barrel vault? Can you think of anything today that reminds you of this structure?

Figure 7.9 Central hall of the Baths of Caracalla (restoration drawing)

of rooms that were progressively cooler. The "calidarium" with its hot water pool was entered first. From there one walked to the "tepidarium" where a warm bath awaited. The last room was called the "frigidarium," and there a cool bath was provided. The different water and room temperatures were made possible by furnaces placed in rooms beneath the building. These were tended by scores of workers and slaves.

One of the most famous baths was built by the Emperor Caracalla in the early part of the third century A.D. (Figure 7.8). It sprawled out over 12.1 ha [30 acres] and had a bathhouse which measured 228.6 m [750 feet] by 115.8 m [380 feet]. A huge central hall over 54.9 m [180 feet] long and 23.5 m [77 feet] wide was spanned with concrete groin vaults (Figure 7.9). A groin vault is formed when two barrel vaults meet at right angles (Figure 7.3, page 110). In this structure, a barrel vault that ran the length of the hall was intersected at right angles by three shorter barrel vaults producing the groin vaults. The use of these groin vaults allowed the builders to cover a very large area. It also permitted the use of windows, which was not possible with barrel vaults requiring thick, solid walls.

Buildings for Sports

Although the Romans enjoyed many different athletic events, the chariot races were easily their favorite spectator sport. As many as one hundred fifty thousand cheering spectators would gather at the Circus Maximus to cheer on their favorite teams. These races became so popular that eventually they were scheduled sixty-four days a year.

Almost as popular as the chariot races were the armed contests. These were held in large arenas or amphitheaters such as the Colosseum (Figure 7.10). The Colosseum was built in the second half of the first century A.D. It owes its name to a colossal statue of the Roman emperor Nero which once stood nearby. The huge structure covers 2.4 ha [6 acres]. It forms a complete oval measuring 187.4 m [615 feet] by 155.4 m [510 feet]. The structure is so large that during the Middle Ages people moved within its protective walls and erected a small city.★

★ **Enrichment** The period from about 500 to 1500 is called the Middle Ages or the Medieval period.

Criticism

How many stories do you see on this structure? Repetition is an important aid to harmony here—what elements are repeated on the outside of this building? What do you think was the purpose of this building? With that purpose in mind, do you think the structure was successful? What do you consider the best features of this structure?

Figure 7.10   Colosseum. Rome. A.D. **72-80**

History

What was used to support the tiers of seats inside the Colosseum—posts and lintels, barrel vaults, or groin vaults? The best seats were in the first tier; who do you think sat in those seats? In this arena, Romans were treated to lavish spectacles. At one time the arena was filled with water, and a naval battle involving more than three hundred participants was held.

Figure 7.11   Colosseum, interior

Over the centuries, rulers, popes, and nobility carried off large masses of stone from the Colosseum to construct new buildings. Only after many of the stones had been removed did Pope Benedict XIV put a stop to this destruction. But it was too late. Today the great amphitheater is little more than a broken shell.

The outside of the Colosseum consists of four stories constructed of stone, brick, and concrete. Each story makes use of a different column type borrowed from the Greeks. The lower level uses the Doric, which is the heaviest and sturdiest of the columns. The Ionic is used on the second story and the Corinthian on the third. At the fourth level, Corinthian columns flat on one side are attached to the wall between a row of small holes. Poles were placed in these holes to support a canvas awning which was used to protect the spectators from the sun and rain.

At the ground level, eighty arched openings enabled spectators to enter and leave the Colosseum so efficiently that it could be emptied in minutes. Seventy-six of these openings were used by the general public. One was reserved for the emperor, and another was used by priestesses. Another door, named the "Door of Life," was reserved for victorious gladiators. The bodies of the slain gladiators were carried through the final door which was called the "Door of Death."

From inside the Colosseum, you can see clearly how it was built (Figure 7.11). The arches are the openings of barrel vaults that ring the amphitheater at each level. These vaults supported the sloped tiers of seats. These seats are gone now, but once there were enough to accommodate fifty thousand people.

Securing a seat for a particular event at the Colosseum must have been much like buying tickets for a football game today. The more you were willing to pay, the better your seat. The best seats were in the first tier and were reserved for the emperor and state officials. The upper classes sat in the second tier, while the general public crowded into the upper tiers. A high stone wall separated the spectators from the gladiators and the wild animals fighting in the arena. As a further protection, archers, nets, and a second wall made sure that no energetic animal would leap up among the onlookers.

The floor is gone now, but you can still see the walls of passageways and rooms. For what were these rooms used?

Figure 7.12   Colosseum, interior

Beneath the floor of the Colosseum (Figure 7.12) were compartments and passages serving a number of purposes. There were places to hold caged animals, barracks for gladiators, and rooms to hold the machinery needed to raise and lower stage sets and performers.

In the third century B.C., the Romans revived an Etruscan spectacle in which slaves were pitted against each other in battles to the death. In 264 B.C., the first contest between armed gladiators was held in the forum.★ The purpose was to celebrate the funeral of an important nobleman. It was a modest contest between three pairs of battlers. However, it was so popular that soon contests between hundreds of gladiators were being staged in the Colosseum before thousands of spectators.

Not all Romans approved of these brutal contests. But they were so popular with the masses that most objectors were afraid to express their feelings. For instance, when Cicero, the famous orator and statesman, had to attend, he took his secretary and notebooks with him and refused to watch. He was an exception, however. The amphitheater was always filled to capacity for events in which as many as five thousand pairs of gladiators fought to the death and eleven thousand animals were killed in a single day.

★ Enrichment The forum was the public square or marketplace of the city. It was the central gathering place for the people, a place to raise and discuss topics of public interest and carry on trade. It contained state buildings, monuments, temples and open courtyards. In the cities of Medieval Europe, the use of a forum was continued as a square, usually placed in the heart of the city.

The Pantheon: A Marvel of Design

One of the marvels of Roman architecture is the Pantheon (Figure 7.13). Designed as a temple dedicated to all the Roman gods, it was later converted into a Christian church. This explains why it is in such excellent condition today.

From the outside, the Pantheon looks like a low, gently curving dome resting on a cylinder. However, from street level the building can no longer be viewed as it was intended. The level of the surrounding streets is much higher now, and the steps that once led up to the entry porch are gone. The building loses much of its original impact today because you are forced to look straight at it rather than lifting your eyes up to it.

It may not be as impressive as it once was from the outside. However, the interior of the Pantheon is certain to have an impact on you. Passing through the entrance hall, you step suddenly into the great domed space of the interior (Figure 7.14). Raising your eyes upward, you discover that the dome that looked so shallow from the outside is actually a true hemisphere. Made of brick and concrete, this huge dome soars to a height of 43.9 m [144 feet]. This is exactly the same measurement as the diameter.

The inside of the Pantheon is divided into three zones. The lower zone has seven *niches,* or recesses, in the wall. These may have contained statues or altars dedicated to the Roman gods of the heavens: Sol (sun), Luna (moon), and gods of the five known planets.

Above this, another zone contains the twelve signs of the zodiac. Finally, rising above all, is the magnificent dome representing the heavens. The surface of the dome is covered with *coffers,* or indented panels. These are more than just a decorative touch. They also lessen the weight of the dome.

You may be surprised to find that the interior of the Pantheon is well illuminated, although there are no windows. Walls up to 6.1 m [20 feet] thick were needed to support the dome, and windows would have weakened these walls. In addition to the door, the only source of light is a round opening at the top of the dome. Although it may look small from floor level, this opening is almost 9.1 m [30 feet] across. It fills the interior with a bright, clear light and enables you to see a section of sky at the top of a dome. But what happens when it rains? Surely rain water would come through the openings. It does, of course, but the Romans anticipated this problem. They built the floor so that it was raised slightly in the center, causing the water to drain off quickly to the sides.

The Basilicas

The Romans also constructed spacious rectangular buildings called *basilicas.* Designed as public meeting halls, these were often a part of the forum, or public square. Basilicas are important because they combined in one structure many of the architectural advances

Which of the following descriptions fits this building:
It is a high rectangle with a round roof.
It is a low cube with a shallow dome.
It is a cylinder with a low dome.
Would you refer to this building as heavy and sturdy, or light and graceful? For what do you think this building was used?

Figure 7.13   Pantheon.   Rome.   A.D. 118-25

made by the Romans. But they are important for another reason. Later they were to serve as models for generations of Christian church builders.

The basilica was a functional building made to hold large numbers of people. On the inside, slender columns divided the space into a long, wide center aisle called a *nave* and two or more narrower side aisles (Figure 7.15). The roof over the center aisle was usually higher than the roofs over the side aisles. This allowed the builders to install windows to let sunlight in. The Roman basilica had a side entrance and one or more *apses*, or semicircular areas, at the end of the nave.

Wooden roofs were used for most basilicas. The roof over the center aisle was peaked, while those over the side aisles sloped gently downward. An exception was the Basilica of Constantine (Figure 7.16), where stone was used to construct barrel and groin vaults. These replaced the wooden crossbeams and peaked timber roofs used in other basilicas.

History

What are the advantages of such a plan? Can you think of any buildings today that make use of such a plan?

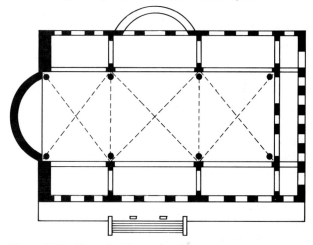

Figure 7.15   Plan of a Roman basilica

Criticism

What surprises did you find on the inside of this building? How does light enter? Why do you suppose there are no windows along the sides? The walls look very thick—why was it necessary to build them that way? What do you think is the most impressive thing about this interior?

Figure 7.14   *Interior of the Pantheon*, a painting by Giovanni Paolo Panini. c. 1740. Oil on canvas, 1.28 x 0.99 m [50½ x 39″]. The National Gallery of Art, Washington, D.C. Samuel H. Kress Collection, 1939

History

What type of vaults were used here? What was the advantage of using stone rather than timber for these vaults?

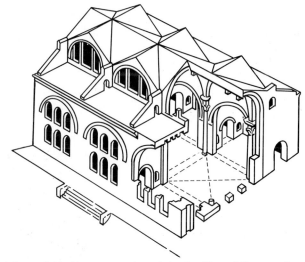

Figure 7.16   Reconstruction of the Basilica of Constantine. Rome. c. A.D. 310-20

The Triumphal Arches

The Romans loved celebrations and often marked their successful military campaigns by building triumphal arches. After a great victory, the general and his troops would pass through a heavily decorated arch to the cheers of thousands. These arches often consisted of a large central opening and two smaller openings on each side. The general and his officers rode chariots and horses through the central opening, while unmounted troops marched through the smaller ones. It was not unusual for the troops to carry posters showing the major events of the campaign.

The Arch of Constantine (Figure 7.17) was the largest and most elaborate of these triumphal arches. It was decorated for the most part with sculptures and reliefs taken from earlier monuments dedicated to other emperors. Of course, this meant that the sculptures showing the emperor had to be changed to look more like Constantine.

The Romans built triumphal arches throughout their empire. The Arch of Bara in Spain (Figure 7.18) differed from most because it was not meant to glorify a military campaign. It was built with funds left in the will of a Roman general and advisor to the Emperor Trajan, and its purpose is not known. It has only one large passageway and does not make use of sculptured reliefs. The decoration is limited to two grooved *pilasters* on either side of the passageway.* The Arch of Bara owes its beauty to its simplicity, the excellence of its workmanship, and its fine proportions.

Roman Sculpture and Painting

In sculpture and painting, the Romans preferred realism. This is especially true in the case of sculptured portraits. A desire for lifelike portraits can be traced back to the earliest periods of Rome's history. At that time, wax masks of deceased family members were made to be carried in funeral processions. These masks were then displayed in small shrines in the home. But masks made of wax were not permanent, and a more durable material was sought. Stone and marble were found to be perfect. Soon artists who could carve portraits from these materials were in great demand.

★ **Enrichment** Pilasters are flat, decorative columns attached to a wall.

Criticism

Would you refer to the design here as simple and harmonious, or complex and varied? What elements of art were used to create this effect? What was the function of this structure—was it a dwelling, a temple, or a monument of some kind? Why were columns used here—for support or decoration?

Figure 7.17   Arch of Constantine. Rome. A.D. 312-15

Portrait Sculpture

Many of the sculptors who worked in Rome came from Greece. These artists worked in the Greek tradition, but adapted that tradition to meet Roman demands. The Greeks preferred idealistic portraits. However, the Romans wanted theirs to look real. Perhaps this was because Greek portraits were almost always designed for public monuments, while Roman portraits were meant to serve private needs. Romans wanted their sculptures to look and remind them of specific people. This explains why most of their portraits seem so natural and lifelike. They felt that the character of a person could best be shown by facial features and expressions. Therefore, they often commissioned portrait heads rather than sculptures of the entire figure. The Greeks, on the other hand, rarely made sculptures of parts of the body. For them, a sculpture of a head or bust (head and shoulders) was not complete.

History

In what ways does this arch differ from the Arch of Constantine? Columns were used on the Arch of Constantine —what was used here instead? Why were they used?

Figure 7.18 Arch of Bara. Tarragona, Spain. Second century A.D.

Criticism

Would you say that this portrait was lifelike or idealized? Point out the things about it that will support your decision. Does the man seem happy, angry, sad, or bored? Do you think that this is a successful portrait? Why?

Figure 7.19 *Portrait of a Roman*. Late first century B.C. **Terracotta, 35.6 cm [14″] high. Courtesy of the Museum of Fine Arts, Boston. Purchased by contribution, 01.8008**

A Roman portrait sculpture (Figure 7.19) gives the feeling that you are looking at a real person. The figure may even look familiar. He may remind you of someone you met somewhere, although it is difficult to remember exactly where or when. He could be a high-school football coach, a teacher, or a fast-food restaurant manager. Like all Roman portrait sculptures, it is an exact duplicate of a real person with all the wrinkles and imperfections intact and an expression suggesting a definite personality.

121

Figure 7.20   Mosaic floor from a Roman villa. Ampurias, Spain. c. First century B.C.

Mural Painting

Wealthy Roman families lived in luxurious homes with courts, gardens with elaborate fountains, rooms furnished with marble walls and mosaics on the floors (Figure 7.20), and numerous works of art. They did not like to hang paintings on the walls of their homes. Perhaps they felt that this ruined the interior decorations. Instead, they used entire walls and parts of walls for large murals. The artists who painted these murals tried to reproduce as accurately as possible the world around them. They painted landscapes and pictures of buildings that suggested a world beyond the walls of the room. Often these scenes create the impression that you are gazing out a window overlooking a city (Figure 7.21). Oftentimes, as in the example shown here, the artist painted window frames and columns to make the artificial window look more realistic.

Of course, not all Roman paintings were noteworthy. This is evident in many paintings found in houses in Pompeii and neighboring cities which were covered by ashes when the volcano Vesuvius erupted in A.D. 79.

History

What happens when you try to place yourself in this scene? It turns out to be an impossible maze. There is no logic to the placement, size, and relationship of the buildings. The artist did not know how to show space and depth in a realistic manner.

Figure 7.21   Architectural view, wall painting from the cubiculum of a villa at Boscoreale, near Pompeii. First century B.C. **The Metropolitan Museum of Art, New York. Rogers Fund, 1903, 03.14.13**

When the well-preserved ruins of these cities were discovered and excavations began, it was found that almost every house had paintings on its walls. Many are quite ordinary and were done by painters of limited ability. But a surprising number of fine works were also found. Among these is a painting of a maiden pausing in mid-stride to pluck a flower to add to her bouquet (Figure 7.22). A breeze stirs her garments as she turns her head and daintily removes a blossom from the tip of a tall bush. Charming and beautiful, this work hints at the level of skill and sensitivity that must have been reached by many Roman painters. Unfortunately, the paintings they produced no longer exist for viewers to admire.

Criticism

What is this woman doing? Does the figure seem to be standing still, or moving? How do you know? What gives this figure such a graceful, dainty look? How does this picture make you feel—sad, happy, angry, or serious?

Figure 7.22 *Maiden Gathering Flowers.* **Wall painting from Stabiae, a Roman resort on the Bay of Naples. First century** A.D. **[Photo Alinari]**

The Declining Power of Rome

It is difficult to pinpoint exactly what brought about the decline of the great Roman Empire. No doubt, an important factor was the transfer of the capital of the Roman Empire from Rome in the West to the site of the ancient Greek city of Byzantium in the Eastern provinces. In A.D. 330 the Emperor Constantine I dedicated his new capital, which was renamed "Constantinople," in the Eastern Roman Empire. This move marked the beginning of the long history of what would eventually be known as the Byzantine Empire. But from that time on, the Western section of the Roman Empire was marked by weakness and decline. Eventually, invaders from the North came down to overrun the once-powerful Western Empire. In 410, Alaric, king of the Visigoths, took Rome, and after that followed wave after wave of barbarian invasions. By the last of the fifth century A.D., the Roman Empire in the West had come to an end, and the barbarian kingdoms of the Middle Ages took its place.

Studio Experiences

Lesson One: Drawing Exterior Views of Buildings—As They Are

Briefly review the architectural features introduced in this chapter, features such as columns, arches, keystones, barrel vaults, groin vaults, and domes. As part of this review examine again the temples, baths, amphitheaters, and arches built by ancient Roman architects (Figures 7.1, 7.2, 7.4, 7.9, 7.10, 7.13, and 7.17). Conduct a study of the buildings in your community and determine which among them are in need of improvement. Complete three pencil drawings showing different exterior views of one of these buildings. Make certain that your drawings are as accurate and detailed as you can make them. Prepare a written report in which you describe the building and point out its shortcomings. Also indicate what you feel would have to be done to improve the appearance of the building.

Lesson Two: Drawing Exterior Views of Buildings—As They Could Be

Refer to the written report you completed as part of the previous lesson. Redraw the building discussed in this report as it might look if all your suggestions for improvement were acted upon. Use gradation and contrasts of value to enhance the three-dimensional appearance of this pencil drawing. Finally, design and assemble a display consisting of your "before and after" drawings and your written report.

Chapter 8

In Quest of Salvation: Early Christian and Byzantine Art

Early Christian Art

The Christian religion was not legal for many years. This meant much hardship and persecution for its followers. Finally, in A.D. 313, it was made legal by the Roman Emperor Constantine with the Edict of Milan. However, pictures with Christian meanings were being painted long before that time. Many of those early paintings were made on the stone walls of narrow underground passageways. These passageways were called *catacombs*.★ When persecuted by Roman emperors, the Christians dug these catacombs beneath the city as places to hold religious services and bury their dead (Figure 8.1).★ In time, the catacombs grew into a vast maze of tunnels. These tunnels were lighted and ventilated by skillfully constructed air shafts.

★ Enrichment The catacombs beneath Rome were discovered by accident in 1578.

★ Enrichment The Christians were persecuted more for political and social reasons than for religious motives. They were considered disloyal and even dangerous because they seemed more interested in a life after death than a life in the present. Also, they refused to take the customary oaths in court or to take part in civic religious ceremonies. Other factors were their idea of meekness and their criticism of the excesses of the rich. In addition, their practice of holding what many thought were secret meetings made the Romans suspect them as enemies of established law and order.

History

What were the catacombs? Who built them and what purpose did they serve? Why was it necessary to build them in the first place? Do you have any idea why the recesses were carved in the walls?

Figure 8.1 Catacomb of Saint Domitilla. Rome. Founded at the end of the first century A.D.

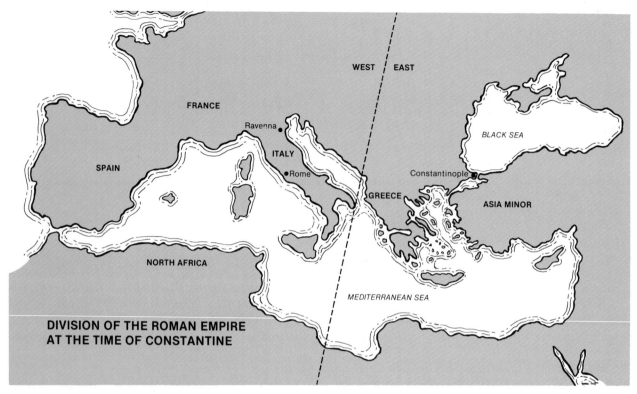

DIVISION OF THE ROMAN EMPIRE
AT THE TIME OF CONSTANTINE

Note: Names of countries are present-day.

Over 1,650 years ago, an unknown Christian artist completed a painting on the rough ceiling of a gallery in one of those catacombs. The painter was not greatly skilled and worked with the crudest of instruments. The flickering light of a flame torch and a constant fear of being found by Roman authorities no doubt made the task more difficult. The finished painting (Figure 8.2) can tell you a great deal about the Early Christians' outlook on life and offers insights into the characteristics and purpose of their art.

Early Christians viewed life in a way that was quite different from views held by believers in the Roman religion. The Christians believed Christ to be the Savior of all people and hoped to join Him in heaven after death as a reward for following His teachings. They had little interest in gaining fame and fortune in the world. Instead, they sought an eternal reward in the form of a life after death. For this reason, Early Christian paintings of people showed little interest in the beauty, grace, and strength of the human body, which were so important to Greek and Roman artists. Christian art was intended to illustrate the power and glory of Christ. It was also meant to tell, as clearly as possible, the story of His life on earth. Christ's life story was very important because it was the model for people to follow as the surest way to attain salvation.

The Early Christians' view of life on earth as a preparation for the hereafter is reflected in the artworks they produced. These works may have *looked* Roman, but the beliefs and ideas they passed on to other Christians were not Roman beliefs and ideas—they were Christian. For example, a picture or sculpture of a shepherd was a popular subject for both Roman and Christian artists. But when a Christian artist painted a shepherd, it was as a symbol for Christ as the Good Shepherd.

Christian artists used symbols as a kind of code.★ Familiar figures or signs were used to represent something else. Catacomb paintings are filled with images of animals, birds, and plants, which are also found in Roman art. But when Romans looked at one of these, perhaps a painting of a goldfinch, they saw only the goldfinch. Christians looking at the same painting saw a great deal more. They remembered that the goldfinch was fond of eating thistles and thorns, and plants of that

★ Enrichment Symbols are still widely in use today. For example, the dove or olive branch stands for peace; the lion, for courage; a heart, for love; four-leaf clover or horse shoe, for good luck; and a skull and crossbones, for danger.

kind reminded them of Christ's crown of thorns. Thus, the goldfinch was a symbol of Christ's passion and death. Over time, birds, animals, and plants came to symbolize different Christian ideas. The peacock became the symbol for immortality because it was believed that the flesh of that bird never decayed. A dog was used as a symbol of faithfulness because of its watchfulness and loyalty. And ivy, because it is always green, was associated with eternal life.

The artist who painted on that rough catacomb wall borrowed heavily from art forms seen all over Rome. But these forms were given new Christian meanings. A great circle was painted to represent heaven. Within this circle is a cross, the most important symbol of the Christian religion. The shepherd in the center circle represents Christ. The sheep around Him symbolize His faithful followers. Christians knew that Christ, as the Good Shepherd, was willing to lay down His life for them, His flock. The lamb on Christ's shoulders symbolizes those people who need additional help on the difficult road to salvation.

The arms of the cross end in half-circles in which the Old Testament story of Jonah and the whale is told. This was another favorite subject in Early Christian art because, like the Good Shepherd, it illustrated God's power to protect the faithful from danger. Beginning at the left, Jonah is seen being thrown from his ship to be swallowed by the whale. On the right, he is being released by the whale at God's command. In the final scene at the bottom, he is shown recalling his adventures and thanking God for His mercy.

Between these scenes are standing figures with their hands raised in prayer. They represent all the members of the Church pleading for God's assistance and mercy in their own struggles for salvation.

You probably noticed that this picture contains only enough detail for you to understand the story. The figures are sketchy and there is little to suggest depth or the world in which the figures lived. The artist was clearly not interested in painting a realistic picture. Instead, interest was centered on illustrating the Christian story so that the faithful could read it easily and meditate upon its meaning.

Basilicas

Not long after this painting was completed, things began to improve for the new Christian religion. Christianity had spread rapidly across the entire Roman Empire, and the Emperor Constantine had granted Christians the freedom to practice their faith openly. This meant that they had to decide upon the kind of building to use as a church. In this matter, the Christians again borrowed from the Romans. Christian builders selected as their model the basilica. This was the long, spacious building that the Romans had used for their public meeting halls. It was a practical choice since such a building could accommodate the large numbers of people crowding into it to worship.

Criticism

Describe the figure in the center. What is this figure doing? Describe the other figures, beginning at the left and moving clockwise. Do these figures look lifelike? Why or why not? Identify the different shapes found in this work. How are these shapes tied together? Is harmony an important principle here? If so, point to places where it has been used. Who do you think the figure in the center represents? What could the sheep represent? Can you identify the Old Testament story told in the half-circles? Do you think this painting was meant only to decorate a ceiling, or did it have some other purpose?

Figure 8.2 Painted ceiling from the Catacomb of Saints Pietro and Marcellino. Rome. Fourth century A.D.

Retreats from the World

Early Christian church builders made no attempt to imitate the grandeur of Roman temples. Christian churches were intended as retreats from the real world where worshipers could go to take part in a deeply spiritual event. The outside of these churches was quite plain (Figure 8.3), especially when compared to Classical temples.★ The addition of a bell tower, or *campanile*, later did little to change the outer simplicity of these early churches.

Sundays and holy days the people gathered for services in the church. No doubt they looked forward to leaving their humble dwellings for what must have seemed like a brief visit to heaven itself. In contrast to the plain exterior, the inside of the church was designed for dramatic effect (Figure 8.4). As in the Roman basilica, rows of columns divided the huge space into a main corridor, or nave, and narrower aisles on either

★ **Enrichment** *Classical* here means "relating to the ancient Greek and Roman world."

side. And also, as with the earlier model, windows were inserted in the space between the wooden roofs over the side aisles and the higher roof over the nave. However, unlike the Roman basilica, the main entrance was at one end of the nave, and at the other was a single apse. The light from the windows streamed into the nave and illuminated the avenue leading from the main entrance to the apse, where the main altar was placed. At this altar the priest solemnly celebrated the Mass, while the faithful silently followed each movement with their eyes.

"Houses of Mystery"

Occasionally, when eyes did stray from the altar, they rose to view walls richly decorated with *mosaics* (Figure 8.5). These were decorations made with small pieces of glass and stone set in cement. This ancient medium had been very popular in Rome. There it had been used to decorate the floors of Roman villas rather than walls. Christian artists saw the potential of the medium and placed mosaics on walls where the light from windows and candles caused them to flicker and glow mysteriously. This may be one of the reasons why Early Christian churches came to be known as "Houses of Mystery."

Most of the Early Christian churches are gone now, victims of a variety of man-made and natural misfortunes over the centuries. But from the few that have survived, it is clear that they served as the basic model for church architecture in western Europe for centuries.

History

How does this church of the Early-Christian type compare with the temples erected earlier by Greek and Roman builders? Point to the campanile. What was its purpose? Did it help to make the exterior of this church more ornate?

Figure 8.3 Sant' Apollinare in Classe. Ravenna. A.D. 533-49

How does the decoration inside this church differ from the decoration found on the outside? Why was so much effort made to create such an impressive interior? What is used to divide the space in this building? Point out the nave and the apse. Where is the altar placed? Do you think the design of this church was suited to its purpose? Why or why not?

Figure 8.4 Sant' Apollinare in Classe, interior, looking toward the apse

What was used to decorate the walls of this apse? Where have you seen this same technique used before? Why do you think it was so effective here on the walls of the church? Can you identify any of the symbols used here?

Figure 8.5 Apse decorations from Sant' Apollinare in Classe. c. A.D. 549

How does this church differ from the hall-like basilica plan used in the Western Empire? Of which Roman building are you reminded when looking at this structure?

Figure 8.6   Hagia Sophia. Constantinople. A.D. **532-37**

Decline of the Classical World

After the dedication of Constantinople in A.D. 330, with some exceptions during the fourth century, the Roman Empire functioned as two separate sections, East and West (see map, page 126). There was an emperor in each section, although the emperor in the East was much more powerful.

In the West, the emperors gradually lost their influence and prestige. At the same time, the Church, governed by the popes, grew in power. Eventually, the Church replaced the emperor in the West as the central authority. This did not happen in the East, where the emperors were recognized as heads of both the Church and the State.

In theory, the Roman Empire was still united. However, as time passed, the two sections drifted further and further apart, separated by differences in language, politics, and religion. The western half finally fell to barbarian invaders from the North during the fifth century A.D. During the long struggle with these northern invaders, cities in the West were abandoned by frightened inhabitants who sought refuge in the countryside. The population of Rome dwindled from 1.5 million to about three hundred thousand. Magnificent temples, palaces, and amphitheaters were torn down and the stone used to erect fortifications to keep out the invaders. But it was useless. Once-proud cities were overrun and their art treasures destroyed or carried off.

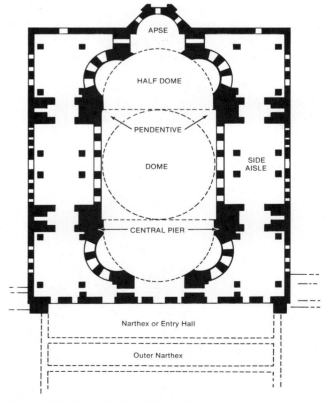

Figure 8.7   Ground plan of Hagia Sophia

Growth of the Byzantine Culture

The Classical world came to an end with the fall of the Western Roman Empire in the fifth century. However, the eastern half of the empire, now called the Byzantine Empire, continued to thrive for another thousand years. The city of Constantinople soon surpassed Rome in both size and wealth. It became the largest city in the Medieval world and was a great cultural center with grand public buildings and fabulous art treasures.

Constantinople

Constantinople became the cauldron in which Roman, Greek, and Oriental influences were blended to produce a rich and brilliant art. Above all, this art glorified the Christian religion and served the needs of the Church. It set the standard for artistic excellence in western Europe until the twelfth century.

Byzantine Architecture: Hagia Sophia

The best examples of the Byzantine style were great churches like the domed Hagia Sophia (Figure 8.6). Western architects favored the hall-like basilica plan for their churches, but those in the East preferred a central plan (Figure 8.7).* Hagia Sophia, built in the sixth century A.D. by the Emperor Justinian, was the greatest of these centrally-planned churches. It replaced another church which had been ruined during political rioting some years before. Rebuilding it gave Justinian a chance to outdo Constantine. The latter had arranged for the original building.

Strangely, Justinian did not turn to architects. He chose instead two Greek math experts to design Hagia Sophia. The finished church beautifully blends the engineering skills of the Romans with a Greek sensitivity for carefully balanced proportions. Its most impressive feature is the huge dome. Almost 30.5 m [100 feet] across, it is 9.4 m [31 feet] higher than the one used for the Pantheon. It differs from the Pantheon dome in other ways as well. The dome over the Pantheon is placed on a massive concrete drum made with thick, concrete walls. But Hagia Sophia's dome rests on four huge piers which support arches made of cut stone (Figure 8.8). By using this method of construction, the builders were free to erect thinner walls and add more windows to light the interior of the church. This method also creates the appearance of lighter weight. The great dome seems to soar over a row of windows placed around its base. As you look up at it, it is easy to understand how an astonished observer once said that it seemed as if the dome hung from heaven itself on a golden chain.

★ **Enrichment** In a hall-like basilica church, the axis runs horizontally through the center of the building from the front entrance directly to the altar. In a central plan, the axis is vertical from the center of the floor area up to the dome. The logical place for the altar in such a church was in the center of the building beneath the dome. However, this presented problems. The clergy felt it was contrary to tradition to have the congregation placed behind the altar. Thus, in many churches with a central plan, the altar was placed off center against an apse.

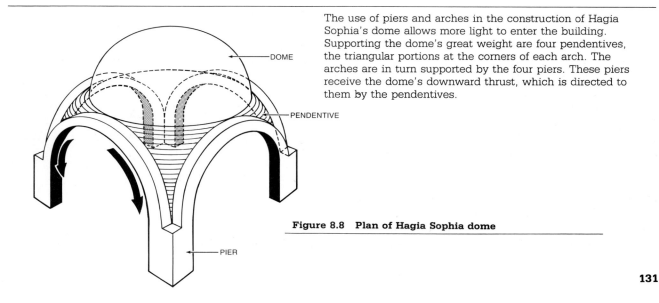

The use of piers and arches in the construction of Hagia Sophia's dome allows more light to enter the building. Supporting the dome's great weight are four pendentives, the triangular portions at the corners of each arch. The arches are in turn supported by the four piers. These piers receive the dome's downward thrust, which is directed to them by the pendentives.

Figure 8.8   Plan of Hagia Sophia dome

Criticism

Describe in detail the interior of this building. What do you think are its most impressive features? What principles of art help in unifying this interior? Does this building seem barren and cold, or heavy and forbidding, or dark and plain, or rich and dazzling? Do you think it was intended to remind people of their life on this earth, or suggest the world awaiting them in the life after death?

Figure 8.9   Interior of Hagia Sophia

The Mosaics of Hagia Sophia

Inside, Hagia Sophia's dim lighting and richly shimmering surfaces combine to produce a dream-like setting (Figure 8.9). Walls of stone and marble brought from Egypt and Italy are decorated with gold, silver, ivory, and gems. Worshippers are treated to a dazzling display of red and green marble piers, polished marble slabs, brilliant murals, and gleaming mosaics. Light filters into the church through rows of windows placed at several levels. Light from these windows illuminates the different colors of stone and marble, creating a spectacular effect.

Churches as huge as Hagia Sophia required special decorations on the inside. They had to be brightly colored and large enough to be seen from great distances. Mosaics were found to be the best way of meeting these needs. These brightly colored mosaics became a trademark of Byzantine churches. They were created to tell in glowing colors the familiar stories from the Old and New Testaments. Often these stories made use of symbols which were readily understood by the faithful. In Hagia Sophia, for example, a mosaic shows the Virgin and Christ Child between two figures (Figure 8.10). The figure on the left is the Emperor Justinian carrying a small church, while the figure on the right is the Emperor Constantine bearing a small city. The meaning of the mosaic is clear. The emperors are proclaiming the loyalty and dedication of Church and State to the Virgin and Child.

Criticism

Two men on either side of the mother and child appear to be bearing gifts. Do these men look important? How can you tell? Identify the gifts that they are carrying. What do you think these gifts represent? These and other mosaics in this church are large and brilliantly colored—why were they made that way?

Figure 8.10   *The Virgin and Child with the Emperors Justinian and Constantine.* Mosaics from Hagia Sophia. Probably A.D. 986-994

Criticism

Does this appear to be a basilica-type building? Would you say that there is a variety of shapes used here? Point to contrasts of curved and straight lines, flat and curved forms. Do these add to the visual interest of this building? Having examined it from the outside, are you curious about how this building looks on the inside?

Figure 8.11   San Vitale. Ravenna. A.D. 526-47

Ravenna

The Byzantine style was not limited to just the eastern half of the empire. Contacts between East and West were not wholly broken off when Constantine moved his capital to Constantinople. They were maintained until the middle of the fourth century A.D. Also, trade between Constantinople, Venice, and other Italian towns lasted through the Middle Ages. But nowhere in Italy is the Byzantine style more obvious than in the city of Ravenna.

Ravenna had become the capital of the Western Roman Empire early in the fifth century A.D. The Roman Emperor had moved to Ravenna because it was isolated and seemed to be a safe refuge from barbarian invaders. He was mistaken. Ravenna was captured in A.D. 476. With this, the last emperor of the West was forced to surrender his authority to the barbarian conquerors. Later, in A.D. 540, Justinian, the Eastern emperor, recaptured the city. It remained under Byzantine control for the next two centuries.

The Mosaics of San Vitale

Justinian had long dreamed of equaling the achievements of early Roman emperors. He saw his chance with the capture of Ravenna. He was determined to erect a great church in the city, a church that would rival anything his predecessors had built. When it was finished, the church was named San Vitale (Figure 8.11). It became the most famous church of that time.

How many figures are there here? Who are these people? Do they look lifelike? Why or why not? Identify the most important figure in this group. Why do you think that this is the most important figure? What makes these figures seem to float? They seem to be engaged in some kind of ceremony—would you say that this is a civic, social, or religious ceremony? What clues did you use to make your decision?

Figure 8.12 *Justinian and Attendants.* Mosaics from San Vitale. c. A.D. 547

Inside San Vitale, artisans created two mosaics on opposite sides of the apse. One of these shows the Emperor Justinian with the archbishop, deacons, soldiers, and attendants (Figure 8.12). You should have no difficulty finding the emperor. His elegant attire, crown, and halo clearly set him apart from the others. The figures are tall and slender and have small feet and oval faces. They turn to face you and stare boldly through huge, dark eyes. Perhaps you find it odd that all the figures seem to float before a gold background. The gold color was used to add a supernatural glow to the scene. The gold makes it seem heavenly rather than worldly. A feeling of weightlessness is heightened by the lack of shadows and the position of the feet which hang downward. Some of the figures are even stepping on the toes of their companions. But, since they are floating, there is no sign of pain or annoyance by any of the injured parties. The bodies of the most important people overlap those of the lesser ones. However, the archbishop beside Justinian places his leg in front of the emperor's cloak. Perhaps this was meant to show that in spiritual matters the archbishop was the leader of all the people, including the emperor.

On the opposite wall facing the emperor and his party is his wife, the Empress Theodora, and her attendants (Figure 8.13). Like Justinian, she is dressed in magnificent robes and wears the imperial crown. Observing her, you would never guess that this grand and powerful woman was the daughter of a bear-keeper and was once a popular actress. Writers of her day agreed that she was charming, intelligent, and beautiful. However, on the wall of San Vitale, Theodora is shown as the equal of any saint in heaven. The great halo around her head is similar to her husband's. It is a symbol of their virtue and innocence and tells you that they are marked for future sainthood.

Would you describe these figures as flat and stiff, or graceful and natural? Find the main figure in this group. List the reasons why you believe it is the main figure. What does their clothing tell you about these people? What do you think is more important in this work—its literal qualities or its expressive qualities?

Figure 8.13 *Theodora and Attendants.* Mosaics from San Vitale. c. A.D. 547

The emperor and empress are part of a solemn religious procession leading to the altar. They bear items used in the celebration of the Mass. Justinian carries a flat, gold plate called a *paten,* which was used to hold the Communion bread. Theodora holds a chalice containing the Sacramental wine. For almost fifteen centuries, their quiet, never-ending march to the altar has stirred religious feelings in countless worshipers visiting San Vitale. Few could resist being impressed by the sight of these great and powerful rulers humbly serving their God.

You would probably not describe the figures on the walls of San Vitale and other Byzantine churches as realistic or natural. They are flat and stiff and more abstract and formal than Early Christian art. The figures give little suggestion of three-dimensional forms moving about in real space. Certainly they lack the beauty, grace, and lifelike qualities you observed in Greek and Roman figures. But these qualities were not sought by Byzantine artists. Their pictures were intended to be religious lessons presented as simply and clearly as possible. Thus, the lesson presented on the walls of San Vitale could be easily learned by anyone looking at the mosaics. Important to this lesson were the people shown in the mosaic. There was a reason for showing emperors and empresses and leaders of the church and military. Likewise, there was a reason for including important court dignitaries. It was necessary to show that people of their position were paying homage to God in order to gain salvation. And if they had to do so, then ordinary people could do no less.

The quest for eternal salvation touched every Christian. No matter how mighty or humble, all were influenced. To see how much importance was attached to this quest, look into the life of Justinian. He was a brilliant and ambitious emperor. His worldly accomplishments were many and his power, great. However, as his life drew to a close, he turned away from worldly luxury and power. He spent his last days in a monastery praying and meditating.

Studio Experiences

Lesson One: Making Ceramic Tesserae

In this chapter you learned that brilliantly colored mosaics were used to decorate the interiors of many Byzantine churches (Figures 8.5, 8.10, 8.12, and 8.13). These mosaics were made with small pieces of glazed clay known as *tesserae*. And, as you will discover in this studio experience, tesserae can still be used to create exciting works of art. But before you can make something from them, you must make the tesserae. To do this, first complete several 30.5 x 30.5-cm [12 x 12-inch] pencil sketches showing different designs for a mosaic wall plaque. On the best of these designs apply a color scheme consisting of at least five hues. Crayons or colored pencils may be used for this purpose. Then divide the design into small sections with a ruler to determine the number of tesserae that will be needed for your plaque. These sections should measure about 1.3 x 1.3 cm [½ x ½ inch]. Clay slabs, *one for each color,* are then prepared. These thin (about 0.6 cm [¼ inch]) slabs are liberally coated with glaze and, when firm, are cut into sections with a fettling knife. (A fettling knife is a special knife for working with clay.) Allow the tesserae to dry slowly (to prevent warping) and fire.

Lesson Two: Using Ceramic Tesserae to Make Mosaic Wall Plaques

Transfer the mosaic plaque design completed in the previous lesson to a waterproofed 30.5 x 30.5-cm [12 x 12-inch] panel. The panel can be cut from 1.5-cm [⅝-inch] marine plywood or 1.3-cm [½-inch] tempered hardboard. Household cement is used to attach the tesserae to this panel. If you have a circular design, it is advisable to begin at the center. Make certain that the tesserae do not touch because they may buckle as the cement dries. When all the tesserae are in place, grout is applied. (Grout is a mortar used for filling cracks and crevices.) The tesserae are moistened with water, and the grout, mixed to a creamy paste, is rubbed into the grooves between them. After the grout sets a few minutes, the excess can be sponged off. Keep the mosaics under wet cloths for three days to prevent cracking and powdering.

Safety Note

The dust resulting from mixing grout may be harmful to some students with breathing difficulties. For safety's sake, the instructor should mix the grout into paste form in an area away from the class. Skin contact with grout should also be avoided since it may cause irritation or, in some instances, burns and rash.

Chapter 9

The Age of Faith: Early Medieval and Romanesque Art

Centuries of Change

For some time, foreign aggression and internal conflicts had marked the lands to the west. For this reason, Justinian and other Byzantine emperors gave up their dream of reconquering those lands. In time, most of the territory in Italy that had been recaptured had to be given up. However, the Byzantine Empire managed to survive for about one thousand years, while the Western Roman Empire rapidly crumbled. During this period, the court of Constantinople with its power, wealth, and learning had no equal in the West. Meanwhile, western Europe struggled through a period of change. It began with the fall of Rome and ended with the beginning of modern culture in the fifteenth century. This period from about 500 to 1500 is known as the Middle Ages or the Medieval period.

At one time the Middle Ages were known as the "Dark Ages," a label suggesting that they represented so many blank pages in the history of Western civilization. However, a closer look has helped to fill in those pages with an impressive list of accomplishments. During this period, many of the important features of our modern world were born: parliamentary government and common law evolved; universities were started; present-day languages were born; and national states began to take shape. In art, the period was anything but dark. It was the most splendid of all periods for bookmaking. In addition, it was a time of a great architectural revival that led to the construction of magnificent structures known as Gothic cathedrals. The "Dark Ages" also saw sculpture grow in importance until it joined with architecture as an equal partner. And these same times witnessed the painting genius of an artist named Giotto whom you will meet in Chapter 10.

Perhaps a more accurate label for this period would be the "Age of Faith." The hearts and minds of our Medieval ancestors were fixed on one all-important goal—the preparation for eternal life after death. And, aiding them in the quest for that goal was the Church.

The Church was the only stable institution remaining in western Europe after the collapse of the Roman Empire. Its power and influence had an impact on the lives of kings and peasants alike. Political boundaries simply did not exist where the Church was concerned. Virtually everyone was born into the faith and was expected to place loyalty to the Church above everything else. This loyalty was freely given because the priceless gift of salvation was promised in return.

Because of its length, it is helpful to divide the Middle Ages into three overlapping periods. The first is the Early Medieval, which dates from about the last quarter of the fifth century to the middle of the eleventh. The second is the Romanesque, which, in most areas, took place during the eleventh and twelfth centuries. The third period is the Gothic, which overlapped the Romanesque and continued in some areas into the sixteenth century. The remainder of this chapter will deal with the Early Medieval and Romanesque periods. Chapter 10 will focus attention on the Gothic period.

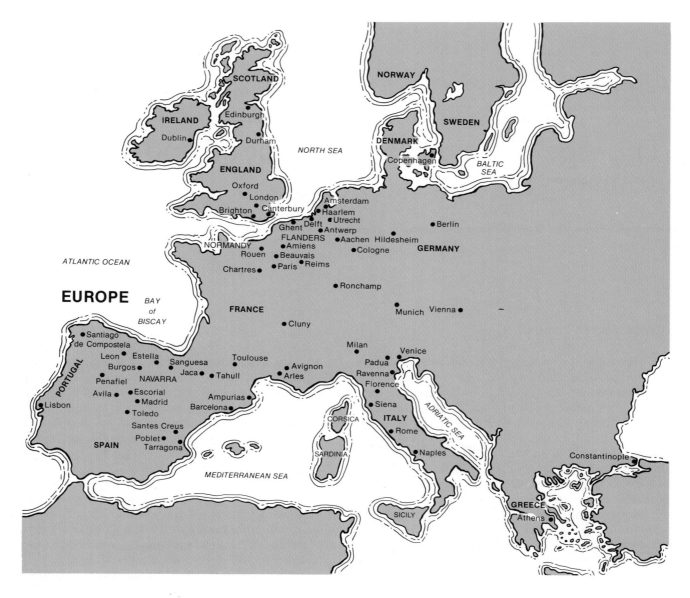

The Early Medieval Period

The fall of Rome is considered the start of the Early Medieval period. This was a time of great uncertainty because the strong central government which had assured law and order to all Roman subjects was gone. The period was marked by conflicts, open warfare, and mass migrations of foreigners into and across lands formerly controlled by the Romans. Under these trying conditions, the Carolingian Dynasty was founded.★ Although it survived less than 150 years, this dynasty managed to bring about the revival of a strong, efficient government. Furthermore, it stimulated a renewed interest in learning and the arts.

★ Enrichment As noted in the earlier discussion of Egyptian art, a *dynasty* is a period marked by the succession of strong rulers, usually members of the same family.

The Role of Charlemagne

One man was largely responsible for the many accomplishments of the Carolingian Dynasty. His name was Charles the Great, better known as Charlemagne. Already King of the Franks, Charlemagne was crowned emperor by the Pope on Christmas Day in the year 800.★ Thus he became the first of the Holy Roman Emperors, although he chose not to use the title.

It seemed that Charlemagne was destined to restore the political unity that had existed during the time of the Roman emperors. His domain grew until it included all of the western part of the old Roman Empire except Britain, Spain, southern Italy, and Africa. Furthermore, his subjects enjoyed an efficient government and a remarkable level of law and order.

★ Enrichment The Franks were a mixture of different German tribes whose empire eventually included much of what is now France, Germany, and Italy.

Beyond creating a great empire, Charlemagne did everything he could to encourage learning and the arts. He ordered every monastery and abbey to establish a school where students could learn arithmetic, grammar, and the psalms. But his most important achievement may have been the preservation of ancient manuscripts. He invited scholars from England and Ireland to his court to rewrite old texts and prepare new ones.★ It is to Charlemagne's credit that many of the ancient documents we have today were copies made by scholars working under his command.

★ **Enrichment** This activity also resulted in a revised form of handwriting in Europe. It is from this new form that our alphabet is derived.

History

The capital of Charlemagne's empire was Aix-la-Chapelle. It was here that he built his palace and tried to recapture the glories of which of the following: ancient Egypt, Greece, or Rome?

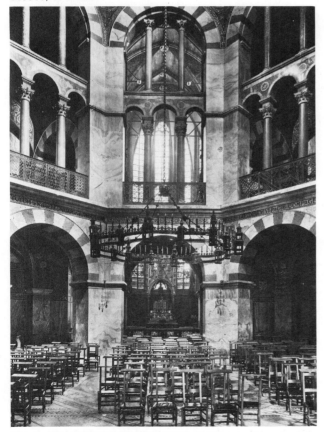

Figure 9.1 Palace Chapel of Charlemagne, interior. Aachen, Germany. 792-805

The center and capital of Charlemagne's empire was Aix-la-Chapelle, now the German town of Aachen. Here he set up his court and tried to restore the splendors of ancient Rome. Statues were brought from Italy, baths were constructed, and a chapel was built that closely resembled the famous Roman church at Ravenna (Figure 9.1).

Unfortunately, Charlemagne's empire and the strong central government which the empire enjoyed ended shortly after his death in 814. By the close of the ninth century, civilization in western Europe was in a shambles once again. Weak central government and the need for protection led to the formation of a governmental system known as *feudalism.*

The Rise of Feudalism

Feudalism was a system in which weak noblemen gave up their lands and much of their freedom to more powerful lords in return for protection. The lord allowed the former owner to remain on the land as his administrator. The administrator was the servant, or vassal, to the lord and pledged total loyalty to him.

Most of the people, however, were poor peasants, or *serfs,* who did not have land to give in return for protection. These people worked the land and went along with it when it was handed over from one nobleman to another. Serfs lived in small villages and toiled in the open fields nearby. In payment for protection, they were required to turn over a share of their annual harvest to the lord or his vassal. The peasants were allowed to keep only enough food to feed themselves and their families.

For the serf, life consisted of hard work, heavy taxes, the simplest living conditions, and little variety of food. The serf's routine was determined by the seasons. Everyone in the village went through the same yearly routine of planting, tending, and harvesting crops. A system in which they shared fields and pastures forced them to do the same things at the same time.

Church Building

Like their Early Christian ancestors, Medieval church builders used Roman models. The Roman civic basilica continued to be the most popular type of structure for religious services. You may recall that the basilica featured a rectangular plan which was divided on the inside to form a nave, or central aisle, and two or more side aisles. Light from windows in the walls of the nave above the side aisles lit the interior of the building.★ As in the Early Christian church, at one end of the nave was the main entrance, and at the opposite end was a semicircular area known as the *apse*. An alter was placed in the apse in plain view of the people who assembled in the nave.

During Charlemagne's time, a few changes were made in the basic basilica plan. Some churches were built with another aisle added which cut directly across the nave and the side aisles. Called a *transept*, this aisle was placed between the apse and the nave and extended beyond the side aisles. Seen from above, the addition of this aisle gave the church the shape of a cross. Thus the transept not only increased the space inside the building —it also added to its symbolic appearance. Occasionally, towers were also added to the outside of the churches. These towers were to influence church construction in western Europe for centuries (Figure 9.2).

Unfortunately, most of the churches erected during the Early Medieval period were made of timber. Accidental fires and warfare during the ninth and tenth centuries destroyed most of these. Today, only a few heavily restored buildings remain.

The Spread of Monasticism and Religious Art

Throughout the long Medieval period, there were people who labored in the service of learning and art. Charlemagne was the most famous of these, but there were others whose names have not come down to us. Many were monks, devoted religious men who lived under a strict set of rules in remote communities called *monasteries*.

Monasticism refers to a way of life in which individuals gathered together to spend their days in prayer and self-denial. It had its roots in the Near East as early as the third and fourth centuries A.D. At that time, some people began to feel that the Church had become too worldly. As a result, they sought lives of quiet contemplation and prayer in the wilderness or desert. Eventually, in Egypt groups of men with the same

★ **Enrichment** The portion of the walls of the nave which were located above the side aisles and through which light entered was called the *clerestory*.

Often, the church was the only stone building in a town, and the church tower could be seen from a great distance. Of what other type of Medieval building does this church remind you? In what ways were they similar?

Figure 9.2 Village church. Ujue, Spain. Eleventh century.

spiritual goals banded together. They formed religious communities far removed from the rest of society. Each monk was provided with little more than an isolated, barren cell or cave where he spent his time in prayer and sacrifice. Occasionally there were gatherings of the community, but these were called for purposes of group worship, manual labor, and scriptural readings.

Monasticism spread to western Europe by way of Italy. It was a familiar institution by the end of the fourth century. In 526, St. Benedict drew up a set of rules that outlined the basic organization for most western European monasteries. St. Benedict's rules required many sacrifices and hardships, but many chose to live by them. After all, such sacrifices made it possible

Judging from its outside appearance, do you think the inside of this monastery was very comfortable? What kind of sites were preferred for monasteries? Was the life of a monk an easy one? Why did men choose to become monks? What contributions did monasticism make to Medieval society?

Figure 9.3   Monastery of San Juan de la Peña. Near Jaca, Spain. c. 922

to live a life that would be rewarded for eternity in heaven. Thinking this, many men turned their backs on society to become monks.

According to St. Benedict's rules, any man wishing to become a monk had to take the vows of poverty, chastity, and obedience. Every part of his daily routine was regulated. Each day included six to seven hours of labor. The monk was also required to take part in eight daily religious services which began at dawn and ended at dusk. Talking was always kept to a minimum, but at certain times of the day it was forbidden entirely. Everyone in the monastery ate, went to bed, and rose at the same time. It was a simple life, but a useful one as well. Monasteries offered peace of mind for each monk, but the monks also made valuable contributions to the world. From them have come advances in agriculture, animal husbandry, learning, and art.

Because they wanted to remove themselves from the temptations of the world, monks built their monasteries in remote places. Often they were carved out of deep forests or were perched on the rocky slopes of mountains. Surrounded by steep stone walls, they were self-sufficient communities. The ideal site for a monastery was one that was isolated and near the sea or a river. Since meat was forbidden on Fridays and many fast days, fish was the customary fare.★ If the monastery was inland, the fish in a nearby river could be caught for this purpose.

The Monastery of San Juan de la Peña

Most of the earliest Medieval monasteries have long since crumbled away. But in northern Spain, deep in the forests covering the foothills of the Pyrenees Mountains, you can still visit the ruins of one of these ancient monasteries. Even today it is isolated and difficult to find, but the search is well worth the effort. Positioned dramatically within a huge cave at the end of a narrow gorge, it still manages to stand proudly after nearly nine hundred years—the Monastery of San Juan de la Peña (Figure 9.3).

★ **Enrichment** Fast days were special days set aside for sacrifice and self-denial. On these days people were to avoid all food or certain foods such as meat.

141

Centuries of neglect have allowed the once-fertile fields and lush pastures of San Juan de la Peña to return to the wild. Here and there among the weeds, a few stones piled one on top of another are the only remnants of walls erected by industrious monks. Silent now, the monastery was once filled with the solemn chants of monks at prayer. But the monastery is not entirely silent. It still whispers to the sensitive ear stories of a glorious past.

Like many ancient structures, the history of San Juan de la Peña is shrouded in legend. One story has it that its origins can be traced back to the day a young nobleman went hunting in the forest above the cave . . .

Spying a deer, he fired an arrow and saw it strike home. The wounded animal crashed through the heavy underbrush with the young hunter not far behind. Reaching the crest of the cliff above the cave, the crazed deer failed to stop and

plunged over. The hunter coming up swiftly saw the danger, but it was too late. Poised at the crest of the cliff, about to fall over, he cried out to St. John the Baptist for help. Of course, this would be a strange legend indeed if the young hunter's plea had gone unanswered. But it was not, and he was miraculously pulled to safety.

Later, having regained his composure, the hunter made his way to the base of the cliff in search of the deer. There he discovered the cave and inside, the remains of a hermit. Writing on the wall of the cave indicated that the hermit had been devoted to St. John the Baptist. Returning home, the young nobleman told his story to his brother. Both were so moved by the experience that they gave all their possessions to the poor and returned to the cave to spend the rest of their lives in prayer. They were soon joined by others, and the first stones of the monastery were put into place.

History

What was the name for the covered walkway surrounding a pleasant garden within the monastery? What was it used for?

Figure 9.4   Monastery of San Juan de la Peña

There are other legends associated with San Juan de la Peña and they are all interesting, but none are more interesting than the building itself. From the outside, the thick stone walls and small windows give it the look of a fortress. Inside it is dark and damp. Walking through it you soon find that the windows are too small and too few for light or ventilation. It is difficult to make out details in the dim light as you pass from dining hall to kitchen to dormitory to church. Dark smoke stains on the walls tell you that torches were once used to light the interior. The rooms are empty; no furniture remains, of course, but there was little to begin with. You remember that the monks took a vow of poverty, but standing in the barren gloomy interior of San Juan de la Peña you can appreciate the full meaning of that vow.

You make your way to a flight of stairs which leads to an upper story. There an arched doorway beckons. Stepping through it, you find yourself in the sunlight once more, standing in an open court with the massive, projecting wall of the cliff overhead. This open court was the *cloister.* It is as quiet and peaceful now as it was centuries ago when the monks, weary from their work in the fields, would come here to pray.

Much emphasis was placed on private prayer and contemplation in the monastery. Typically, this was done in the cloister, where the monks spent several hours each day. The cloister was a covered walkway around an open court or garden (Figure 9.4). Generally, it was attached to one side of the church linking it to the other important buildings of the monastery. Here, in all kinds of weather, the monks came to pray, meditate, and read from books they received from an adjoining "library."

No doubt you would be surprised by the appearance of a Medieval library. Frequently it was little more than an alcove located off the cloister. The number of books on its shelves was modest, perhaps only twenty or so. At the beginning of Lent, each monk received a book from this library, and he was required to read the volume thoroughly.★ As you might guess, these books were always religious writings. No time limit was set to complete the reading, although the monks were expected to return their books no later than the first Monday of the next Lent. Any monk who had not finished his book during that period was required to make a public confession of his failure.

★ Enrichment Lent is an annual season of fasting and penitence beginning on Ash Wednesday and lasting until Easter Sunday.

Why are illuminated manuscripts so important to us today? How were they produced? Who produced them? Do you think this was an enjoyable task?

Figure 9.5 *St. John,* from the *Franco-Saxon Gospels.* c. 850. The Pierpont Morgan Library, New York

Manuscript Illumination

Perhaps no other art form captures the spirit of the Early Medieval period better than the *illuminated manuscript* (Figure 9.5). Until the development of the printing press in the fifteenth century, all books had to be copied by hand. Usually this was done by monks working in the *scriptoria,* or writing studios, of monasteries. These monks were often men of great skill who took pride in their beautifully designed letters. Often they decorated manuscript pages with delicate miniature paintings done in silver, gold, and rich colors. For nearly one thousand years, these *illuminations* were the most important paintings produced in western Europe. It is surprising then that today many people pass them by in museums with little more than a fleeting glance. Perhaps, too, they fail to realize that these manuscripts contain the precious ideas of the past. They contain ideas preserved for later ages by dedicated men who were so humble that they rarely identified themselves.

What is this figure doing? Can you identify the object in his left hand? Describe his facial features. Point to the different lines found in this work. What effect is created by the use of these lines? Does this person look calm and collected, or active and excited? Do you think he regards his task as an important one? How can you tell? Is he receiving any help? What seems to be more important here, the literal qualities or the expressive qualities?

Figure 9.6   *St. Matthew*, from the *Gospel Book of Archbishop Ebbo of Reims.* c. 830. Approx. 25.4 x 20.3 cm [10 x 8″]. Bibliothèque Municipale, Epernay, France

Sheltered from the rest of the world by mountains and forests, writing painstakingly in Latin, Medieval monks were skilled in the use of words. They sought to pass on the ideas of Classical writers and church fathers. Often they phrased these ideas in beautiful and complex ways. The inspiration and skill that they gave to their work was no less than that offered by the painter, the sculptor, or the architect.

After examining one of these manuscripts, you might conclude that writing it was no simple task. A statement written by a monk named Florencio in 945 should confirm that decision: "He who knows not how to write thinks that writing is no labor, but be certain, and I assure you that it is true, it is a painful task. It extinguishes the light from the eyes, it bends the back, it crushes the viscera and the ribs, it brings pain to the kidneys and weariness to the whole body. Therefore, o reader, turn ye the leaves with care, keep your fingers from the text, for as a hail storm devastates the fields, so

does the careless reader destroy the script and the book. Know ye how sweet to the sailor is arrival at port? Even so for the copyist is tracing the last line."[1]

Throughout the Medieval period, it was customary to illustrate manuscripts of the Gospels with small paintings of the four Evangelists. A symbol was usually used to help the reader identify each of these Gospel writers. Matthew was symbolized by an angel; Mark, by a lion; Luke, by a bull; and John, by an eagle. A painting of Matthew (Figure 9.6) from a ninth-century Gospel book created in Reims, France, shows the Evangelist hard at work on his vision of the life of Christ. The Evangelist is seated before a small writing table. His left hand holds

[1] Clara Louisa Penny, "Manuscripts and Books," in *The Hispanic Society of America Handbook of Museum and Library Collections,* ed. Elizabeth du Gue Trapier (New York: Hispanic Society of America, 1938), pp. 353-407.

an ink container shaped like a horn, while a quill pen is clutched in the right. However, it is clear that the artist who painted this picture was interested in presenting more than a realistic portrait of Matthew. This is not a picture of a scholar calmly recording his thoughts and ideas. It is a painting of an inspired man frantically writing down the words of God. The entire scene is filled with a dramatic vitality that sets everything in motion. The drapery swirls around the figure, while sketchy lines behind seem to push upward. Motion and not form is the main ingredient here. You are invited to share Matthew's excitement as he works furiously at the moment of inspiration to record the sacred message. But he is only human. He fears that the words will be forgotten before he can write them down. His wide-open eyes, furrowed brow, and rumpled hair are clues to his intense concentration. A huge, clumsy hand guides the pen rapidly across the pages of his book. He struggles to keep up as an angel, Matthew's symbol, reads from a scroll on which is written the sacred text. It is Matthew's responsibility to pass these words on to the world. His expression and actions show that he is painfully aware of this responsibility.

The Church was the center for art and learning as well as religion during the Medieval period. It favored art which could teach and inspire the people in their faith. This was especially important at a time when most people could not read.★ The written portions of manuscripts were meant for the few people who could read, while the illustrations were intended for those who could not. The messages contained in the illustrations had to be simple and familiar so everyone could understand them. For this reason, the pictures often told the same Scripture stories that the people heard every Sunday in church sermons.

Other Religious Art

These Scripture stories were not just told on the pages of manuscripts. Early in the eleventh century, a bishop in the German town of Hildesheim ordered a pair of great bronze doors for his cathedral named in honor of St. Michael. A scene from one of those doors illustrates a well-known story from the Bible: Adam and Eve Reproached by the Lord after the Fall (Figure 9.7). The simplicity and directness noted in manuscript illustrations is also evident here. The Lord points an accusing finger at Adam, who cringes in shame and passes the blame on to Eve. However, Eve is not about to take responsibility for disobeying God. Instead, she quickly points to the serpent at her feet as the real villain.

The efforts of Medieval artists may seem crude and even amusing to you today. However, you should not make the mistake of judging them solely in terms of their literal qualities. Rather, they should be judged for their expressive qualities—for the feelings and ideas that they tried to pass on to the people who veiwed them.

★ **Enrichment** During this period, reading and writing were a convenience but not a necessity. Most peasants did without these skills for centuries.

Criticism

Do these look like real people? Why or why not? Describe their actions and expressions. Why are they pointing at each other? Is there any suggestion of depth or space in this work? Since it is neither realistic nor beautiful, must this work be considered unsuccessful? Can you think of a reason why it could be called a successful work of art? What is your reason?

Figure 9.7 *Adam and Eve Reproached by the Lord after the Fall.* **From the bronze doors of Bishop Bernward for Saint Michael's Cathedral, Hildesheim, Germany. c. 1015. Approx. 58.4 x 109.2 cm [23 x 43″]**

The Romanesque Period

The art of the Early Medieval period began to take on new features and abandon others until a new artistic style known as Romanesque emerged.★ This new style was especially apparent in architecture. Churches began to dot the countryside in greater numbers, and most of these had many features in common. Of course, it is impossible to say when the Early Medieval style left off and the new style began, but by the eleventh century the Romanesque appears to have been accepted throughout most of western Europe. It continued to thrive until the middle of the twelfth century when another style, Gothic, appeared on the scene.

The Effects of Feudalism

The feudal system which had originated in the ninth century reached its peak during the Romanesque period. It contributed to the constant disputes and open conflict that continued to mar the Medieval period. Under this system, land was the only source of wealth and power, but the supply was limited. A nobleman hoping to add to his estate might do so by marriage, but this was not always possible. If he was already married or there was no suitable bride, he often turned to a second course of action—war. Nobles, lords, and kings were constantly fighting each other in order to protect or add to the land under their control.

Life in the Castles

With warfare unchecked, nobles found it wise to further fortify their dwellings. Towers of stone were built by the late eleventh century, and by the twelfth century the now-familiar stone castle had evolved (Figure 9.8). With its tower, walls, moat, and drawbridge, the castle became the symbol of authority during the Romanesque period.

Although the life of the nobles centered around the castle, it could hardly have been a comfortable place. Its main purpose was defense, and this eliminated the possibility of windows. The thick outer walls were pierced only by narrow slots through which archers could fire upon attackers. Stairs were steep and passage-ways dark and narrow, making movement difficult. The drafty rooms were usually sparsely furnished and lacked decoration. Occasionally tapestries were hung, which helped relieve the monotony of the gray stone walls.★ However, these were intended to keep the dampness out rather than add a decorative touch to the gloomy interior. In cold weather, the only warmth came from fireplaces, the largest of which was in the great hall where the family gathered and meals were served.

★ Enrichment The tapestries were intricate pictures made of tightly woven colored fabric illustrating scenes from the Bible or popular legends. Weavers, both men and women, often spent years completing a large tapestry for a church or palace.

History

Why did nobles find it necessary to fortify their dwellings? Do you think the people inside this fortress were well protected? Point to the features that made this castle so secure. Why did the builders choose not to add more windows for light and ventilation?

Figure 9.8   Castle at Peñafiel, Spain. c. Fourteenth century

★ Enrichment The name "Romanesque" comes from the word "Roman." This style was thought to have come from regions where Roman culture had previously existed. However, this was not accurate since a different style, the Byzantine, developed in the Eastern Roman Empire, while the Romanesque style reached areas never touched by Roman culture.

Eventually, castles became obsolete and were abandoned. What happened to cause this? Where did the people who once lived in or around these castles go when the castles were abandoned?

Figure 9.9   Castle ruins. Near León, Spain. Thirteenth century

In addition to the great hall, there were a kitchen, storage rooms, and bedrooms. Again, there was little furniture beyond a large canopied bed. Heavy curtains hung from the canopy to keep out drafts at night after the fire died out. Often the bedroom was home for any number of hounds, birds, and even farm animals. It was not uncommon for noblemen to keep their favorite horse in the bedroom. More often than not, the task of feeding it fell to their wives. As you might expect, not all wives took kindly to this assignment. It was said that one became so angry that she fed her husband's horse nothing but bran so that it would tire quickly in battle and her husband would be wounded or killed.

The Growth of Cities

Castles remained important as long as the feudal system flourished. But the growth of trade and industry in the thirteenth century brought about an economy based on money rather than land. Cities sprang up, and castles became more and more obsolete. Mighty stone walls which had withstood seige and assault against the castles fell victim to time and neglect (Figure 9.9).

Why was it necessary to build walls like these around Medieval towns? These walls also created some problems for town dwellers; what were these problems?

Figure 9.10   City walls. Avila, Spain. c. Eleventh century

Town Walls

The still-unsettled times made it necessary to erect barricades around the towns. Wooden walls were used at first, but these were replaced during the twelfth and thirteenth centuries by more sturdy stone barricades. An early example of such a stone wall still surrounds the historic city of Avila in Spain (Figure 9.10). Often referred to as one of the most ambitious military constructions of the Middle Ages, it measures more than 2.4 km [1.5 miles] and contains eighty-eight towers and nine gates.

Overcrowding

Town walls may have succeeded in keeping out plunderers, but they created problems as well. As more people moved into a town, space ran out and overcrowding resulted. To solve this problem, buildings were built higher, sometimes reaching heights of seven stories or more. The amount of space inside was increased by building each story so that it projected out more and more over the street. As a result, it was not unusual for people on the top floor of one building to carry on a conversation easily with those living at the same level in the building across the street.

Of course, this method of construction made the narrow streets below very dark. However, that was hardly the most serious problem. People developed the annoying habit of throwing their refuse out the windows onto the street below. Pedestrians had to keep a sharp eye turned upward to avoid being showered by someone's trash. In a noble gesture to protect their ladies' clothing, gentlemen formed the habit of walking on the outside. Their ladies' clothing was in danger not only from the refuse raining down from overhead, but from the water splashed by passing carriages. The custom of walking on the outside was continued in western European countries over the centuries and was even carried to America. In many places, it is practiced to the present day.

Increased Church Building

Every town had one thing in common—in its center stood the church (Figure 9.11). During the Romanesque period, the Church increased its influence on the daily lives of the people. It offered comfort in this life and, more importantly, it provided the means to salvation in the next. It is not surprising then that the entire community joined in when the need for a new church rose. The richly decorated stone churches of the eleventh and twelfth centuries are a testimony to the power of the Church, the faith of the people, and the skill of the builders.★

Pilgrimage Churches

The Church at this time placed great importance on piety and encouraged people to take part in journeys to holy places. These journeys, called *pilgrimages,* were a visible sign of religious devotion. People would band together and travel under often hazardous conditions to pay homage to saints and relics in far-off churches. They believed that by praying before the sacred remains of a saint, a plentiful harvest could be assured, diseases could be cured, and personal problems solved. But the greatest reward for these journeys was the promise of eternal salvation.

★ **Enrichment** Romanesque church builders were often master masons who performed as both architects and bricklayers—and were more highly respected and better paid than sculptors or painters.

History

Why was the Church such an important institution in Medieval society? In what ways did the Church help art?

Figure 9.11 Church of Santa Maria. Sangüesa, Spain. Twelfth to thirteenth centuries

History

Who were the pilgrims who made the dangerous journey to visit this famous cathedral in northwest Spain? What brought them here? What did they hope to receive in return for making this journey? Why was it necessary to build churches this large?

Figure 9.12 Cathedral of Santiago de Compostela, Spain. Eleventh to thirteenth centuries

The Holy Land and Rome were the destinations for many of the early pilgrimages. However, the long journey to the Holy Land was very dangerous and was undertaken at great risk. A pilgrimage to the shrine of St. James at the Cathedral of Santiago de Compostela (Figure 9.12) in northwest Spain became an acceptable substitute. Soon churches and shelters were being built along this pilgrimage route in southern France and northern Spain. Builders continued to use the Roman basilica plan, but the churches were made larger to hold the great number of pilgrims that visited them.

Chapels projecting out from churches were a familiar fea-ture of Romanesque architecture. Why was it necessary to build these tiny chapels? These chapels were built inside the church along what two areas?

Figure 9.13   Church of San Sernin, radiating chapels. Tou-louse, France. c. 1080-1120

Enlargement of the Romanesque Church

In order to increase the size of a Romanesque church, the nave and transept were extended and two more aisles were added, one on each side. Often, an aisle curving around behind the main altar was added as well. This aisle, called an *ambulatory,* made it easier for religious processions and groups of pilgrims to move about inside the building.

Large numbers of priests also took part in pilgrimag-es, and they were required to say Mass every day. This meant that more altars had to be provided in the churches along the pilgrimage routes. These altars were placed in small curved chapels built along the transept and the ambulatory. The chapels, projecting out from the building, became a familiar part of a Romanesque church (Figure 9.13).

One of the biggest problems faced by Romanesque builders was how to construct stone roofs over their huge churches. They solved the problem by again turning to methods developed by the Romans. The Romans had been able to roof large areas by creating a series of arches to make a barrel vault. Romanesque builders used this same technique. However, it meant that they had to build thick, solid walls and huge pillars to support the outward and downward pressure of the heavy stones above. The weight of the roof made it dangerous to place windows in the walls because this would weaken them. But even though great care was taken, Romanesque builders were not always successful. In 1255, part of the roof of Cluny Abbey in France suddenly collapsed because the walls were not strong enough to support it.

List some of the main features of this building. In what ways is this church like a castle? Do you think the inside is light and graceful, ornate and gay, or dark and massive? On what do you base your decision?

Figure 9.14   Two views of San Sernin

How were stone ceilings like this built? Who originally developed this method of construction: the Egyptians, the Greeks, or the Romans? What was the main reason for building ceilings of stone rather than wood?

Figure 9.15   San Sernin, interior, looking toward the apse

Using this plan, point out the following features of a Romanesque church: nave, side aisles, transept, apse, ambulatory, and radiating chapels.

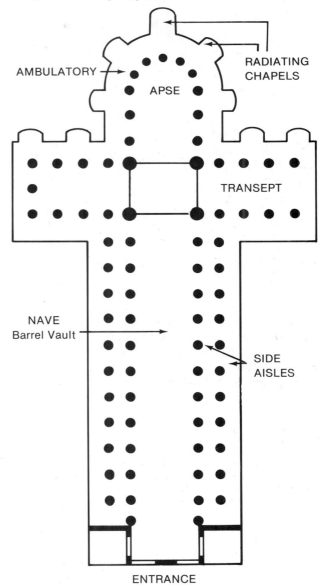

Figure 9.16   Plan of a Romanesque church

The Church of San Sernin in Toulouse

It was in France that the Romanesque style reached its peak in architecture. Perhaps no structure better illustrates this style than the Church of San Sernin in Toulouse (Figure 9.14).

Surveying this church from the outside, you would probably be impressed by its large size and solid appearance. A huge octagonal tower rises from the center of one end of the structure. With its small windows and lack of ornamentation, this tower gives the building a fortress-like appearance. It is no wonder that churches like this came to be known as "Fortresses of God."

Inside, the church is spacious, but dark and gloomy. A few steps lead down into the wide nave; on either side are two side aisles. A series of massive, closely spaced piers line the nave and separate it from the aisles on either side. These form a majestic arcade of arches leading from the main entrance to the altar at the far end of the church (Figure 9.15). Above, barely visible in the dim light, is the rounded ceiling of the barrel vault.

There are no surprises inside such a church. The nave, side aisles, transept, apse, and ambulatory are quickly identified. After a short stroll through it, you could easily sketch a plan of the building. Such a sketch would reveal that the church is laid out in the form of a huge cross (Figure 9.16).

The half-round panel above the doorway of a church was an ideal place for relief carvings. What is this panel called? What was the purpose of these carvings? Why were carvings like this designed with a large figure in the center and smaller ones on either side? Is this an example of formal or informal balance?

Figure 9.17   West portal, Leyre Monastery. Province of Navarra, Spain. Twelfth century

Many feel that the overall impression of San Sernin is one of quiet strength and dignity. Indeed, there is little about it to suggest lightness and grace. Nor could you describe it as fancy or ornate. It is as simple and direct as a military command. With its massive walls, small windows, and durable tower, it has the look and feel of a stone castle.

What goings-on would you have witnessed if you had walked inside this Romanesque church on a typical Sunday morning over eight hundred years ago? No doubt you would be surprised at some of the things you would see . . .

As you enter the cool, dim interior of the church, you are struck by the contrast with the warm, bright sunlight outside. In those first few moments while your sight adjusts to the darkness, your other senses are sharper. The first thing you become conscious of is the noise. Your ears are flooded with all kinds of sounds, such as rustling, humming, and clattering. Next you are struck by the strong scent of incense and candle wax. Finally, aided mainly by the small, high windows and rows of flickering candles, your eyes begin to take in the activities around you. People are seated in small groups loudly exchanging bits of gossip gathered during the week. A knight struts by, stopping only long enough to threaten the snarling hounds at his heel. Beggars wend their way slowly through the congregation with outstretched hands to receive offerings. In return, they promise to say prayers for any ailment, problem, or desire. Merchants earnestly discuss the past week's business and argue over prospects for the next. Yet, in spite of the apparent disrespect, you observe that everyone's gaze constantly returns to the apse at the far end of the nave. There, before a richly decorated altar where the greatest number of candles glow, a priest solemnly celebrates the Mass. . . .

The Revival of Sculpture

The revival of the sculptor's craft was one of the important achievements of the Romanesque period. Many of the churches along the pilgrimage routes used relief sculptures as another way to teach the faith to people who were largely illiterate. Like manuscript illustrations, these stone carvings reminded people of the familiar stories from Scripture.

Two architectural features were found to be ideal places for relief carvings: the *tympanum* (plural: *tympana*) over the doorway of the church and the capitals of columns inside.

Criticism

Find the most important figure; observe what he is doing with his right hand. How do the figures on his right differ from those on his left? What do you think all this means? The four small figures in the center seem to be blowing trumpets—what event are they announcing? At the far right is a figure with a scale; what is he doing? Did you find this work easy or difficult to interpret?

Figure 9.18   Tympanum, Church of Santa Maria. Sangüesa, Spain. Twelfth to thirteenth centuries

Tympanum Reliefs

The tympanum on the outside of the church was the half-round panel that filled the space between the lintel and the arch over the doorway (Figure 9.17). This was an area to which people naturally lifted their eyes as they entered the building. It was a perfect location for relief sculpture, and artists were quick to take advantage of it. The shape of the tympanum seemed to demand a large figure in the center, which became the focus of attention. Smaller figures were placed on either side of this central figure. It was soon found that a subject such as the Last Judgment was especially well-suited for this arrangement.

On the tympanum of the pilgrimage church of Santa Maria in Sangüesa, Spain (Figure 9.18), God the Father is placed in the center. He is surrounded by angels trumpeting the news that the final judgment has arrived. The row of figures below includes Mary holding the Christ Child, with the twelve apostles at either side. God is shown welcoming the chosen at His right. But, with a down-pointing left arm (not visible in the illustration), He condemns sinners. In a far corner, St. Michael is seen weighing souls to determine who is worthy to enter heaven. The drama of this event is suggested by the upright stance of the saved and the contortions of the condemned. Notice how the sinners are either falling or are being pulled backward to their doom.

Efforts were made to fit as many stories as possible into the space available on the front of Romanesque churches. This was certainly the case at Santa Maria in Sangüesa (Figure 9.19). There you will even find one of the few carvings of the hanged Judas Iscariot, as shown in the detail of Figure 9.19. Judas is the figure to the far right in the bottom row of figures, which flank the door on either side.

Most of the church carvings at this time showed scenes from the lives of Christ, Mary his mother, or the saints. A relief found on the façade of San Miguel in Estella, Spain, for example, presents an account of the events that took place immediately following Christ's Resurrection (Figure 9.20). Although the celebration at Easter of Christ's rising from the dead was the most important event in the Christian religion, the Resurrection itself was rarely shown in works of art before the thirteenth century. Instead, it was symbolized by showing the three Marys before an empty tomb.

In the San Miguel relief, the story is clear and easy to "read." The three holy women approach the tomb bearing boxes of ointments with which to annoint the body of Christ. This was in keeping with the custom at that time. An angel greets them, raising his hand in a typical Medieval gesture to show that he is speaking. He tells the women that Christ is no longer there, but has risen. The first woman seems to be speaking to the angel, while the other two talk with one another. A second angel is seated on the edge of the sarcophagus. The second angel raises the cover and points to the empty shroud confirming the first angel's announcement that Christ has risen. Two sleeping guards are placed in the foreground directly in front of the sarcophagus. You might think it odd that these two figures are so small. However, since they do not have major roles to play in the drama, it was not necessary to make them as large as the principal figures.

History

Why were Romanesque church facades like this known as "Bibles in Stone"?

Figure 9.19 Santa Maria

Criticism

Do these look like solid, round figures in a realistic setting? What makes them look so flat? Which element of art is used to create the decorative details? Can you identify the figures and the event? What is the angel at the left pointing to? Why are the figures below the angels so small?

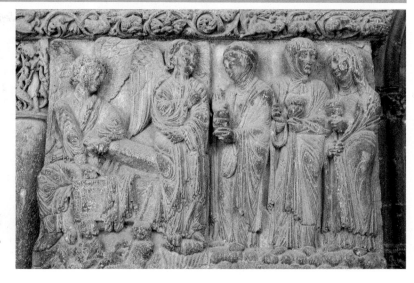

Figure 9.20 *The Three Marys at the Tomb.* Relief carving from the north portal, San Miguel. Estella, Spain. Twelfth century

The carving here is clear and direct. Nothing is hidden from view or left to the imagination. However, there is little to suggest that these are solid figures in a realistic setting. Instead, a flat decorative effect is noted. The flatness is due to the fact that the figures project only slightly from the wall, a carving technique referred to as "low relief," or "bas-relief."* This flatness is in harmony with the flat walls of the church on which the relief is placed. Line is used to form the decorative details. The flowing, curving lines representing the folds of the garments create an overall pattern that holds the work together. Line then contributes both decoration and unity to the work. The effect is pleasing to the eye, but, more importantly, it does not interfere with an immediate understanding of the story. Lord and serf alike could gaze upon this relief and visualize at once the miraculous event that was the first Easter.

There is one feature of Romanesque carvings that might seem strange and out of place to you. But it occurs often enough that once people are aware of it they begin to look for this feature, and they are rarely disappointed. There lurking among carvings of the

Holy Family, church fathers, apostles, and saints are fantastic creatures, half man and half animal (Figure 9.21). They may be evil spirits or devils. Perhaps the artists who created them were trying to tell us that these spirits lie in wait everywhere hoping to snare the unwary. Or these grotesque combinations of animal and human forms may be a sign that artists were beginning to use their imaginations once more.

History

Romanesque sculptors often included fantastic creatures among their carvings. What reasons could they have had for creating these unusual creatures?

Figure 9.21   Relief carving from the cloister, Santes Creus Monastery. Near Tarragona, Spain. Twelfth century

★ **Enrichment** When carved forms stand out from the background, the carving technique is called "high relief."

Criticism

Identify the animals found in this relief carving. There are two scenes to the story being told here. Reading from left to right, what is happening in each scene? What message or meaning do you receive from this story?

Figure 9.22 Capital carving from the cloister of the Cathedral at Tarragona, Spain. Twelfth to thirteenth centuries

Capital Decoration

Inside churches and in cloisters, the capitals of columns were another excellent place for carvings. Here, where the weight of the ceiling was met by the upward thrust of columns, the roving eyes of the faithful came to rest. Many Medieval sculptors served their apprenticeships by carving these capitals with biblical scenes, human figures, birds, and animals. Once they had developed their skills, they moved on to carving larger scenes.

Romanesque capitals are often a curious mixture of skilled craftwork and quaint storytelling. For example, in a capital relief carving in the cloister of the cathedral at Tarragona, Spain (Figure 9.22), rats are seen carrying a "dead" cat to its grave. But the wily cat is only pretending to be dead as it is carried on the litter. In the next panel, it is shown jumping from the litter to claim its careless victims. There are several explanations for this carving. Some claim it is a rare example of Medieval humor. Others say it was inspired by an old Spanish proverb which says, "The mouse is wise, but the cat is wiser." Then again it may be a reference to the Resurrection itself indicating that Christ's return from the dead will result in the destruction of His enemies. Of course, you may have your own interpretation for this scene. If so, you would join a legion of viewers who have tried for centuries to unravel the meaning behind this curious carving.

On a single capital in Pamplona, Spain, the artist presents a series of scenes in carved relief which deal with the Passion and death of Christ (Figure 9.23). The work is carefully designed to lead the viewer's eye around the capital from one scene to the next. The stories are clearly told, but not at the expense of unity.

The relief is "low"—nothing projects beyond the contour of the capital. Its compactness adds to a monumental quality. This quality combined with a vivid narrative are trademarks of Romanesque sculpture.

Miniature Painting in Religious Manuscripts

Miniature painting in religious manuscripts continued to be an important activity throughout the Romanesque period. The flattened look seen in figures carved in stone is even more obvious in these paintings. There are no shadows and no suggestion of depth. Certainly Romanesque painters possessed the skill to reproduce more accurately what they saw, but they chose not to do so. Shadows and depth were simply not necessary. Painters were concerned mainly with the presentation of easy-to-understand religious symbols and not with the imitation of reality. This flattened quality is evident in an illumination from a gospel produced around the middle of the twelfth century in Swabia, a small territory in southwest Germany (Figure 9.24). Here an angel appears before a woman who raises her hands in surprise. Above the woman's head, a dove descends from a cloud.

The faithful had no difficulty recognizing this scene as the Annunciation. The angel, with his hand raised to show that he is speaking, has just announced to Mary that she is to be the mother of the Savior. The dove over Mary's head is a symbol for the Holy Spirit. The easy-to-read message, flat, colorful shapes, and a bold use of line are common features in this and all other Romanesque paintings.

Criticism

Can you identify the events from the life of Christ that are taking place here? How has the artist used pointed fingers to lead your eye from one scene to the next? Do you think this work is noteworthy because of its fine, precise carv-ing, or because it presents a familiar story in a clear, easily understood way? Is this an effective design for a capital? Why or why not?

Figure 9.23 Capital carving, with detail, from the cloister of the Cathedral at Pamplona, Spain. Twelfth to thirteenth centuries

Criticism

List the literal qualities found here. How is this work similar to the carved reliefs you have been examining? Which art element is especially important here? Which of the two figures seems to be speaking? What makes you think so? Point to the clues that tell you that this is a religious painting.

Figure 9.24 *Annunciation.* Illustration from a Swabian Gospel Manuscript. c. 1150. Landes-Bibliothek, Stuttgart, Germany

Make a list of the colors found in this painting. Describe the lines used; are they straight, curved, heavy, thin, dark, or light? How would you feel if you saw this huge figure peering down at you in a darkened church? Do you think this is a successful work? Would you support your decision by referring to the literal qualities, visual qualities, or expressive qualities found here?

Figure 9.25 *Christ in Majesty.* **Wall painting from San Clemente. Tahull, Spain. Twelfth century**

Church Wall Painting

Large paintings decorating the inside walls of churches were also done during this period. Often artists were required to fit their paintings into a specific area. At San Clemente in Tahull, Spain, the painter took a familiar Byzantine theme and tailored it to fit within the apse of the church. (Figure 9.25). Christ as Ruler of the Universe is seated on an arch with His feet resting on a semicircular shape. His right hand is raised in blessing, while His left holds an open book proclaiming His title as Supreme Ruler. He is surrounded by the four Evangelists. Below are several apostles and Mary holding the Holy Grail, the cup used by Christ at the Last Supper. The background is decorated with broad bands of color, a common feature of Medieval wall paintings. A bold use of line, brilliant colors, and a sensitive feeling for pattern are reminders of the manuscript illuminations produced during the same time. It is likely that many works like this one were painted by artists who also decorated the pages of Medieval manuscripts.

Studio Experiences

Lesson One: Crayon Etching in the Style of Romanesque Manuscript Illustrations

Take a moment to reexamine two of the manuscript illustrations discussed in this chapter (Figures 9.6 and 9.24). Observe in particular the variety of lines found in the *St. Matthew* and the flat shapes of the figures in the *Annunciation*. With this in mind, complete a crayon etching which will employ a variety of thick and thin lines and intensely colored, flat shapes. The subject for this crayon etching will be two people engaged in a spirited conversation: one is speaking while the other is listening intently. Draw your version of this conversation in pencil on 23 x 30.5-cm [9 x 12-inch] white paper. Then go over the major pencil lines using a fine brush and India ink. Vary the pressure on the brush to produce a variety of thick and thin lines. Use a thick application of crayon to color your entire composition. The colors used should be light and intense. A coating of India ink should then be brushed over the entire crayon drawing and allowed to dry. Now use a sharp instrument to scratch out an intricate design on the inked surface. This will expose the contrasting lines and brightly colored, flat shapes of the crayon drawing beneath.

Lesson Two: Woodblock Prints of Fantastic Creatures

Romanesque artists often included fantastic creatures in their carvings and manuscript illustrations. You saw examples of these in the carvings at Santes Creus Monastery (Figure 9.21) and the cloister of the Cathedral at Tarragona (Figure 9.22). Give full reign to your imagination by sketching a fantastic creature of your own. This sketch can then be transferred to a wood block with pencil and carbon paper. Study your design carefully and identify the positive and negative shapes. Then cut away the negative shapes, leaving the positive shapes intact. When you have finished carving the wood block, squeeze a small amount of water-soluble printer's ink onto a smooth, nonporous surface and pass a brayer through it several times. Then roll the brayer over the carved wood block until it is completely and evenly covered with ink. Now place the inked block face down on a sheet of white paper and press firmly by hand, producing a print. On the print the shapes that have been cut away (negative) will not print, while those that have been left intact (positive) will.

Safety Note

When carving your wood block, make certain that the hand holding the block is always kept away from the path of the carving tool. Also, make all cuts in the direction of the wood grain. Cuts across the grain can bind the carving tool and may splinter the wood.

Chapter 10

The Age of Faith Continued: Gothic Art

Artists you will meet in this chapter

Duccio (*doo*-chee-yo), c. 1255-c. 1318. People were so impressed with his huge painting for the altar of the Cathedral of Siena that they carried it in triumph through the city streets to the cathedral.

Giotto (*jot*-toe), c. 1266-1337. Not only did his paintings of people look lifelike, but their gestures and expressions suggested real emotions.

End of the Feudal System

A revival of cities during the late stages of the Romanesque period gradually changed the character and tempo of life in western Europe. These new cities drew large numbers of serfs away from their rural villages with the promise of a better life. They made it possible for a former serf to realize a more comfortable existence as an artisan or merchant. By the beginning of the thirteenth century, thriving cities could be found in northern Italy, southern France, and Flanders.* Some of these surpassed cities of the old Roman Empire in size and wealth. By 1200, the Flemish towns of Bruges, Ghent, and Lille boasted populations numbering in the thousands.** And, by the late thirteenth century, the population in Florence, Italy, had reached forty-five thousand. These, and other cities, were the center of most of the intellectual and artistic progress during the late Medieval period.

★ **Enrichment** Flanders is a region in western Belgium, northern France, and a southwestern portion of the Netherlands. In the thirteenth century, it covered an area in the southwest portion of the Low Countries, which are now called the Netherlands, Belgium, and Luxembourg.

★ **Enrichment** People who lived in Flanders were re-
★ ferred to as "Flemish."

It is difficult to say if cities contributed to the revival of trade or trade brought about the rebirth of cities. It is certain though that the growth of trade kept pace with the growth of cities throughout the thirteenth and fourteenth centuries. Trade routes were established between existing cities, and new cities sprang up along these routes. Trade, the growth of cities, and the increasing power of kings combined to bring to an end the feudal system where serfs were bound to the land which they tilled for the nobility.

Emergence of the Gothic Style

The name "Gothic" is used to identify a period which began around the middle of the twelfth century and lasted to the end of the fifteenth century and, in some places, into the sixteenth. It was a name coined by later critics who scorned the art of the period because it did not hold to the standards of ancient Greek and Roman art. Since the Goths and other barbarian tribes had brought about the fall of Rome, the term *Gothic* was given to buildings which replaced Classical forms. The name then is misleading. The buildings constructed during this time were not actually built by the Goths at all.

Like many cathedrals in western Europe, this one began as a Romanesque church. Gothic innovations were added as it was being built. The center section is Gothic, while the sections on either side are Romanesque. Even though work continued for nearly two centuries, this cathedral was never finished.

Figure 10.1 Cathedral of Tarragona, Spain. Begun in the twelfth century

Why do you think the Gothic cathedral is called Medieval architecture's greatest triumph? How does its appearance differ from Romanesque churches? In what other ways did the Gothic cathedral differ from Romanesque churches? What words would you use to describe this exterior—low or soaring, light or heavy, fortress-like or graceful? In what ways was the construction of a cathedral a community effort?

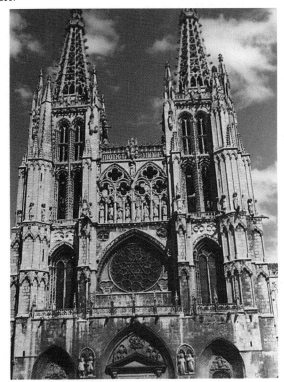

Figure 10.2 Cathedral of Burgos, Spain. Begun in the thirteenth century

It would be a mistake to think that the Romanesque style died as the Gothic was born. Romanesque prepared the way for the Gothic and, in most areas, merged with it as smoothly as dawn dissolves into a new day. In fact, many buildings that were begun as Romanesque were completed as Gothic (Figure 10.1). The lessons learned in producing Romanesque churches were put to good use during the Gothic era. This experience enabled builders to erect the most complex and ambitious art form ever created. If the greatest of the Medieval arts was architecture, then the Gothic cathedral was Medieval architecture's greatest triumph (Figure 10.2).

Innovations in Cathedral Architecture

Gradually, Gothic architecture moved away from Romanesque heaviness and solidity toward lightness, grace, and even frailty. Romanesque builders never learned how to build churches with walls which could contain many windows and still be strong enough to support a heavy stone roof. As a result, their churches were low, thick-walled, and dimly lit. This was changed in France during the thirteenth century by the introduction of the pointed arch and the flying buttress. These innovations enabled builders to erect the slender, soaring Gothic cathedral.

Were slender interior columns like these enough to support the stone roof of a cathedral? If not, what else was used?

Figure 10.3   Burgos Cathedral. Interior, showing one of the supporting columns, or piers

Pointed Arches and Flying Buttresses

Gothic builders discovered that they could reduce the sidewise pressure, or thrust, of a stone roof by replacing the round arch with a pointed one. Because the curve of a pointed arch is more vertical, the thrust is directed downward. This downward thrust is then transferred to slender supporting columns, or piers, within the building (Figure 10.3). Additional support is provided by braces, or *buttresses,* outside the building. Because they often had to reach over the side aisles of the church, these braces came to be known as "flying buttresses" (Figure 10.4). The use of pointed arches, piers, and flying buttresses created a thrust, counter-thrust system that supported the ceiling. This system eliminated the need for solid walls. As a result, the space between the supporting piers could be filled in with stained-glass windows.

A support that reaches out to absorb the outward thrust of the heavy roof of a Gothic cathedral is called which of the following: tympanum, pointed arch, lintel, or flying buttress?

Figure 10.4   Burgos Cathedral

To more clearly visualize this Gothic support system, picture in your mind a giant bird cage. The wires across the top of this cage represent the arches which support the roof. These arches become piers when they turn downward to form the sides of the cage. The spaces between these piers are places where stained glass could be used. The only things missing in the bird-cage illustration are the buttresses on the outside which act as a counter-thrust to the outward push of the arches.

Stained-Glass Windows

The walls of glass which builders were now free to use between the piers let light flow into the cathedrals. But it would be a mistake to think that these windows did nothing more than let light in. They were an ideal way of impressing and instructing the faithful. The light streaming through them made these windows richer and brighter than the dull surface of a wall painting. With their stories from the lives of Christ, the Virgin, and saints, they bring to mind the beautifully colored illuminations found in Medieval manuscripts. In cathedrals such as those at Chartres and Reims in France and León in Spain, huge areas were devoted to stained glass. At the cathedral in León, for example, 1124 m² (square meters) [12,917 square feet] of glass were used (Figure 10.5).

What innovations enabled Gothic builders to use so much stained glass in their cathedrals? Were these windows only decorative, or did they have other purposes as well? If the latter, what were these purposes? What effect do you think was created inside the cathedral when light filtered through these stained-glass windows?

Figure 10.5   Cathedral of León, Spain. Thirteenth to fourteenth centuries. Interior, showing walls of stained glass

Here pieces of colored glass were cut to shape, details
were painted on, and the pieces were fired to fuse the
painting with the glass. The pieces were held together
with lead strips and reinforced with iron bars. In this
section from a large window, Mary Magdalene is shown
carrying a container of oil that she would use to anoint the
feet of Christ. Why didn't Romanesque builders use as
much stained glass in their churches as Gothic builders
did?

**Figure 10.6   Mary Magdalene, detail from a stained glass
window in the Cathedral of León, Spain. Thirteenth to
fourteenth centuries**

**Figure 10.7   Cathedral of Chartres, France. Begun 1194.
Exterior and interior with detail of stained glass**

Do you think you could see everything in this cathedral from a fixed position, or would you have to move from one position to another? How is this interior similar to that of a Romanesque church? How is it different? Which element of art dominates here? Does this interior seem appropriate for a church? Why or why not?

Figure 10.8   Cathedral of Reims, France. Begun c. 1225. Exterior and interior views

The making of stained glass was one of the greatest of Medieval art forms. Medieval stained glass was of such high quality that it has not been matched since. For color, artisans added minerals to the glass while it was still in a molten state. In this way, the glass was stained rather than painted and was very bright. Small pieces of this stained glass were then joined together with lead strips and reinforced with iron bars. Often, the lead strips and iron bars were made a part of the design (Figure 10.6).

The Gothic Interior

Gothic interiors required no more decoration than the vertical lines of the architecture, the richly colored stained glass, and the colorful flow of light. Romanesque churches had to be lighted from within by candles and lamps. Gothic interiors, on the other hand, were bathed in tinted sunlight passing through walls of stained glass. Thus, the flickering candlelight of Romanesque churches gave way to a rainbow of color in Gothic cathedrals.

A Gothic cathedral such as the Cathedral of Chartres (Figure 10.7) or the Cathedral of Reims (Figure 10.8) is just as impressive on the inside as it is on the outside. It is so huge that it forces the viewer to become physically involved in looking. It cannot be examined from one spot because no single point offers a view of the entire structure. Instead, the viewer must move from one position to another to gain a picture of the whole. Walking through such a cathedral, you would soon find that your eye is constantly moving in all directions. A beautifully carved relief sculpture captures your attention for a moment, but then an immense expanse of stained glass draws your eyes upward. Tilting your head back as far as it will go, you see an arched stone ceiling that seems to float lightly overhead.

165

While these Gothic interiors are always striking, they are even more so at sunset. At that time of day, when the rays of the sun strike low and filter through the many colors of the window, the effect is breathtaking. As the sun settles lower and lower, the light on the columns and walls rises slowly. It seems to penetrate even the darkness of the furthest reaches of the lofty nave. Then, suddenly, the sun dips below the horizon. At this moment, the church is filled with a deep purple twilight that accents a strange silence. Not surprisingly, it was once said that the mysterious light in Gothic cathedrals would lead the souls of the faithful to the light of God.

Gothic Church Construction

Romanesque churches were usually built in rural settings. However, Gothic cathedrals were products of the new and prosperous cities. They were meant to serve as churches for bishops, and their construction included all in the community. Not only were they an expression of religious devotion, but they were products of civic pride as well. Rival bishops and cities vied for the right to claim that their cathedral was the biggest, the tallest, or the most beautiful. After the citizens of Paris built the nave of Notre Dame Cathedral 35 m [115 feet] high,

builders of the Amiens Cathedral raised their roof to almost 45 m [147 feet]. Builders of the cathedral at Beauvais, not to be outdone, raised theirs to almost 48 m [157 feet], the tallest of them all. But there was a limit. Twelve years after the last stone was laid in place, the roof at Beauvais collapsed.

Criticism

Do these figures seem lifelike, or are their proportions elongated and stretched out of shape? Describe the position of the feet—does this create the impression that these figures are standing firmly on the ground, or rising upward? With your finger, trace along the repeated lines of these sculptures. In what direction do the lines lead you? Would you say these figures are heavy and clumsy, or light and graceful?

Figure 10.10   Statues from the west portals, Chartres Cathedral. Early thirteenth century

History

Priests, peasants, and nobility alike raised their eyes with pride and praise to these towers soaring high above the rooftops and ordered their day by the regular tolling of the cathedral's great bells.

Figure 10.9   Burgos Cathedral

The money to finance these huge structures came from a variety of sources. Countless fund-raising activities were planned and individual contributions sought. One person might pay for a pillar; another, for a door. A wealthy family might contribute the money needed to roof a side aisle. It also became fashionable to leave one's earthly possessions to the construction fund. Everything, no matter how humble, was gladly accepted. Thus, it was reported that one gentleman willed his razor and several cushions, while another left a selection of choice arrows. People who had nothing to give donated their time and effort. Artists and craftspersons offered their knowledge and skills. And the clergy promised to reward everyone who helped by praying for them.★

Sculptural Decorations

Seen from the narrow streets of Medieval cities, the spires of Gothic cathedrals stretched upward to heaven (Figure 10.9). This upward tendency is noted everywhere. The pillars, pointed arches, and windows are unified in the upward surge. A statue of normal size and proportions attached to such a structure would have detracted from this soaring quality. To avoid this, sculptures were *elongated,* or stretched out (Figure 10.10). The long folds on their sculptured garments emphasized the vertical movement of these figures. Not even the feet were permitted to rest flat on the ground. Often, the figures stand on globes with their toes pointing downward to create the impression that they are rising upward.

★ **Enrichment** Piety was not the only reason behind the contributions made to church construction. Occasionally, personal pride entered into the transaction. One wealthy Italian offered to provide the Church of San Croce with a new façade but then withdrew the offer when he was told that he could not put his coat of arms on it.

Criticism

Would you describe these figures as excited and active, or calm and dignified? Do they seem flat and attached to the building? What is there about them that gives these figures the appearance of being real? Can you identify the figure which is second from the left?

Figure 10.11   Statues from the west portals, Tarragona Cathedral. Thirteenth century

Romanesque carvers made their figures appear to be firmly attached to the wall. Gothic sculptors, by contrast, made theirs project outward into space. Further, each figure was clearly identified in some way and easily recognized by anyone familiar with the Bible. Thus, a figure holding keys was immediately identified as St. Peter, since he was entrusted with the keys of the heavenly kingdom. Another bearing stone tablets was recognized as Moses: engraved on the tablets were the Ten Commandments given to him by God on Mount Sinai (Figure 10.11).

Criticism

Point to the most important figure. How do you know that this is the most important figure? Does he seem to be angry and menacing, or calm and gentle? How many seated figures can you count along the bottom of this tympanum? Does this number provide a clue to their identity?

Can you identify the figures (accompanied by their symbols) surrounding the central figure? What are these figures doing? Why were they designed to bend over their desks like this? Is this an example of formal (symmetrical) or informal (asymmetrical) design?

Figure 10.12   Sarmental portal, Burgos Cathedral. Thirteenth century

The Growing Concern for Reality

But Gothic sculptors wanted to do more than present sacred symbols of biblical figures. Increasingly, they tried to make these figures look like real people. The figures appear to move and look about, and the drapery looks as though it is covering a real three-dimensional body.

Although it still recalls the spirit of the Romanesque, the south door of the Burgos Cathedral reveals this growing concern for reality (Figure 10.12). In the tympanum are the twelve apostles and above them a calm and serene Christ in Majesty. Christ is not shown as a menacing judge of doomsday, but a majestic, thoughtful, and approachable man. He is surrounded by the four Evangelists who are bowed over their writing desks, allowing them to fit into the triangular shape of the tympanum. Their symbols take up the rest of the available space.

Like Romanesque tympana, the one at Burgos makes use of a formal balance. But as the Gothic style developed further, an informal, more natural balance was sought. This informality is observed in a fourteenth-century tympanum in the cathedral cloister in Pamplona, Spain (Figure 10.13). Here fifteen figures surround a bed on which rests the lifeless body of the Virgin. Again, the figures are carefully designed to fit within the tympanum. Christ is the largest figure and, if you look closely, you will see that He holds a small version of Mary. This is her soul which He is preparing to carry to heaven. Small angels hover overhead holding garments with which to clothe Mary in glory. A sign of the growing concern for human emotions is noted in the sorrowful expressions on the faces of the mourners around the deathbed. These are more than mere symbols for religious figures. They are real people expressing a genuine grief at the loss of a loved one.

History

In what ways does this tympanum differ from that of the Sarmental Portal at Burgos (Figure 10.12)? Find the most important figure in this group. What is that figure holding in his hands? What do you think this represents? Describe the behavior of the other figures.

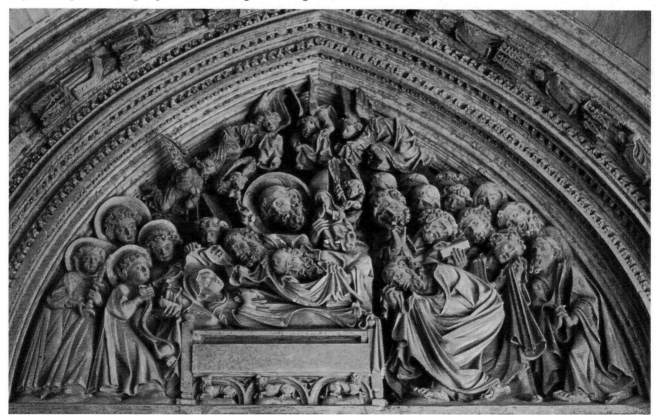

Figure 10.13 *Death of the Virgin.* **Cloister, Cathedral of Pamplona, Spain. Fourteenth century**

History

What was so special about this sculpture to make it so famous? How is this pose similar to that of such Greek sculptures as the *Spear Bearer* by Polyclitus? Describe the expression on the Virgin's face. Does this expression make her seem warm and friendly, or cool and stern?

Figure 10.14 *Golden Virgin*, **from the south portal of the Cathedral of Amiens, France. c. 1250-70**

Veneration for the Virgin Mary

Veneration for the Virgin grew steadily during the Gothic period. This was especially true in France, where great cathedrals were erected in her honor in Paris, Chartres, Rouen, and other cities. God the Father was usually thought of and pictured as a stern judge. God the Son seemed far removed from the day-to-day routine of this world. And God the Holy Spirit was scarcely understood at all. But Mary, who had experienced the happiness and sorrows of any mother, could be counted on to help anyone in need.

History

What is the name for this type of Medieval sculpture? On what part of a building, specifically, are sculptures like this to be found? What purpose do they serve? What do they represent?

Figure 10.15   Gothic gargoyle, Cathedral of León, Spain. Thirteenth to fourteenth centuries

On the south portal of Amiens Cathedral is an almost freestanding sculpture of Mary holding the Christ Child (Figure 10.14). Originally covered in gold, it came to be known as the Golden Virgin. People weary from long hours of work or facing problems of various sorts found comfort in her warm, welcoming smile. The figure is both elegant and noble. Its gentle human features and friendly expression made it one of the most famous sculptures in Europe.

There is one other sculptural feature of Gothic cathedrals that has not been mentioned yet, although it is a feature you would certainly notice and be curious about. This unusual feature is the *gargoyles* (Figure 10.15), the grotesque flying monsters that project out from the upper portions of the huge churches. They look as if they are about to unfold their wings and fly off to some far-off land of mystery. Made of carved stone or cast metal, these gargoyles are rain spouts intended to carry rainwater from the roofs of the churches. Why were they made to look like frightening monsters? Perhaps because someone—someone with a very fertile imagination—thought it would be a good idea to make rainspouts look more interesting. And so they were made to look like evil spirits fleeing for their lives from the sacred building.

Illustrated Books

The new style in architecture which substituted stained glass for solid walls eliminated the need for wall paintings in churches throughout most of western Europe. With no walls to decorate, artists had to find other ways to use their talents. Some turned to designing stained-glass windows, while others preferred to create graceful and colorful illuminations for manuscripts.

A demand for illustrated books containing psalms, Gospels, and other parts of the liturgy grew steadily during the thirteenth and fourteenth centuries. These books were called "psalters" and were the prized possessions of the wealthy. Artists used tiny, pointed brushes and bright colors to illuminate these psalters with scenes from the life of Christ.

The Influence of Stained-Glass Art

During the thirteenth and fourteenth centuries, manuscript illumination showed the influence of stained-glass art.★ Often these illustrations were placed within a painted architectural framework which resembled the frames used for stained-glass windows. In addition, the elegant figures found in these manuscript illuminations were drawn with firm, dark outlines, suggestive of the lead strips used to join sections of stained glass. With these features, plus rich, glowing colors, the illuminations closely resembled the stained-glass windows set into Gothic cathedral walls.

The influence of stained glass can be seen in a series of illuminations found in a fourteenth-century English book of prayers known as *Queen Mary's Psalter*.★★ An illumination from this book (Figure 10.16) shows a very small Christ Child teaching in the temple. Seated on a high stool between two arches, He is conversing with Church scholars who surround Him. It is clear by their expressions and gestures that the scholars are astonished by the wisdom of the child's words. At the left, Christ's parents have just entered the scene. They too exhibit amazement at the child's words and actions. They draw back slightly and whisper excitedly to each other. Perhaps they are unsure about what to do next.

★ Enrichment It is quite possible that, in some cases, stained-glass windows and illustrated manuscripts were produced by the same artists.

★ Enrichment *Queen Mary's Psalter* was so named be-
★ cause it was presented to Mary Tudor, wife of Louis XII of France, in 1553. However, it was made in the first half of the fourteenth century for some other member of nobility.

Should they interrupt and take their child home, or allow Him to continue with His teaching?

While the illustration from *Queen Mary's Psalter* is simple and easy to read, its style is certainly not very realistic. The gold background and absence of shading on the figures denies the existence of space and makes everything seem flat. The faces of the scholars are all alike, and the Christ Child hardly looks like the twelve-year-old described in the well-known Bible story.

Criticism

What is there about this picture that makes it seem so unrealistic? Why does it seem so flat? How is the small child emphasized in this design? Do you see anything unusual about the men's faces? Describe the actions of these men. Why do you suppose they are acting like this? Describe the actions of the child. What does he appear to be doing?

Figure 10.16 *Christ Child in the Temple,* **from** *Queen Mary's Psalter.* **Fourteenth century. The British Library, London**

Criticism

Does this work contain a great many details? Is it a religious picture? What time of year is it? Are these people peasants, members of the clergy, merchants, or nobility? How did you make your decisions? Do you see anything strange in the way the woman in green is sitting on her horse? What is the mood of the people in this picture? Why do you think they feel this way? Why are the men at the left blowing their trumpets? If you had to limit your comments about this work to a single word, what would that word be: realistic, graceful, or solemn?

Figure 10.17   The Limbourg Brothers. *May,* **a page from a book of hours painted for the Duke of Berry** *(Les Très Riches Heures du Duc de Berry).* **1413-16. Musée Condé, Chantilly, France**

The International Style

In the years that followed, painters began to exhibit a greater concern for realistic detail in their works. But even more important than this was a desire to make their painted figures more graceful and colorful. They took delight in painting elegant and beautiful subjects with the same care and precision as that of a skilled goldsmith. So successful were they that their pictures glowed on the pages of manuscripts like rare and delicate jewels. This elegant art style appealed to the tastes of the wealthy throughout western Europe, and the demand for manuscripts illustrated in this manner grew. Because of its widespread popularity, this style of painting came to be known as the International Style.

Among the greatest of the artists working in the International Style were the Limbourg brothers. These three brothers from Flanders had settled in France where their patron was the Duke of Berry, the brother of the French king. Early in the fifteenth century, the brothers produced a luxurious book of prayers, or "book of hours," for the duke. Included in this book were a series of elaborate pictures illustrating the cycle of life through scenes from each of the twelve months. In an illustration for *May* (Figure 10.17), lords and ladies are shown enjoying a carefree ride in the brilliant, warm sunshine. The cold, gray winter months, which meant confinement within castle walls, have finally come to an end. The lords and ladies have donned gay attire and crowned themselves with leaves and flowers to welcome spring. Trumpeters announce the new season's arrival; lively horses prance about excitedly; and the people exchange warm and friendly words.

The precision found in paintings of this kind is fascinating. The artists must have relished the chance to demonstrate in paint their powers of observation. Beautiful women and handsome men dressed in elaborate costumes and wearing fine jewelry are perched atop steeds decked out in the finest bridles and saddles. Behind them the trees of a forest are painted with such exactness that each branch and many of the leaves stand out clearly. The same concern for minute detail is observed in the ornate castle beyond. To paint such detail, the Limbourg brothers must have held a magnifying glass in one hand and a very fine brush in the other.

You may have noticed that the desire for rich detail and gracefulness is stressed at the expense of realism here. The finely dressed ladies sit regally on their horses, unmindful of the fact that their positions are not very secure. They look as if they could slide off their mounts at any moment. But this matters little. Of greater importance is that they look graceful, sophisticated, and beautiful. At the same time, however, they look posed. Much of the movement suggested in the work is a result of the flowing lines of the drapery rather than any action on the part of the figures themselves.

What Gothic features can be seen in the cloister of this monastery? Earlier you learned that cloisters like this served a valuable purpose. What was that purpose?

Figure 10.18   Monastery of Poblet, Spain. Thirteenth century

The Spread of Gothic Architecture

Like the International Style in painting, the Gothic style of architecture spread from France, the land of its birth, to other western European countries. In each country, it was altered to meet different needs and tastes. The church continued to be the most characteristic large structure of the period. However, Gothic architectural features were not limited to cathedrals. These features were also incorporated into the construction of monasteries (Figure 10.18), town halls, and other secular buildings.

Italian Church Painting

Italy was one country that refused to be impressed by the new Gothic style in architecture. The extensive use of windows did not appeal to Italian builders, who continued to construct churches in a modified Romanesque style during the Gothic period. Perhaps the warmer climate of their country caused them to prefer the darker, cooler interiors of the Romanesque building. Instead of stained-glass windows, they continued to commission artists to decorate the large wall spaces in their churches with murals.

Duccio

In addition, paintings on wooden panels were also used to decorate the interiors of Italian churches. One of the most famous of these panel paintings was created by an artist named Duccio di Buoninsegna for the altar at the Cathedral of Siena. It was known as the *Maestà* (or "majesty") *Altarpiece* and was actually a combination of several panel paintings.⋆ The Virgin in Majesty was the subject of the main panel. This painting was done on a large central panel almost 3.4 m [11 feet] high and

---

⋆ **Enrichment** An altarpiece was a painting placed behind and above an altar. Often it was made up of several panels which were joined together and could be opened and closed.

List the things in this painting that look realistic. List the things that do not look realistic. Which list is longer? Point to the figure that looks calm and peaceful. Which figure looks surprised? How would you describe the third figure? Is there any clue to suggest that these figures are communicating with each other? What is it?

Figure 10.19   Duccio. *The Calling of the Apostles Peter and Andrew*, detail of the *Maestà Altarpiece*. Between 1308 and 1311. Panel, 43.5 x 46 cm [17 ⅛ x 18 ⅛"]. The National Gallery of Art, Washington, D.C. Samuel H. Kress Collection, 1939

showed the Madonna enthroned as the Queen of Heaven. Below and above this panel and on the back were a series of smaller panels on which Duccio painted scenes from the lives of the Virgin and Christ. When the *Maestà* was completed and the people saw it, they were so impressed that they carried it in triumph through the streets of Siena to the cathedral. It remained there until the eighteenth century when it was dismantled. Two of the panels are now in the National Gallery of Art in Washington, D.C.

One of the *Maestà* panels in the National Gallery shows Christ calling to Peter and Andrew, inviting them to join Him as His apostles (Figure 10.19). The extensive use of gold in the background of this picture calls to mind the rich mosaics of Byzantine art. The intense colors, two-dimensional figures and shallow space are futher reminders of the Byzantine style. A Byzantine influence is not surprising since Italy had been a part of the Byzantine world for a long time. Byzantine art was both familiar and popular in Italy.

You may recall that the Byzantine style stressed the spiritual and ignored references to the real world. Byzantine artists stripped reality to its essentials and avoided suggestions of depth and volume in their works. The mosaics which these artists created in their churches were not intended to be realistic or decorative. Instead, they were to aid the people in understanding their faith. These mosaics were noteworthy for the depth and intensity of the religious feelings they expressed.

Unfortunately, this art style proved to be very conservative. Byzantine artists did not attempt to improve upon the efforts of earlier artists. Indeed, they felt obliged to paint religious figures in the same way as their ancestors did. By doing this, they thought they were continuing a tradition which began at the time of Christ, when artists painted the actual portraits of the Savior, saints, and martyrs. It is not surprising then that by Duccio's time the Byzantine style had become little more than a formula. It had become a method artists used to record the appearance, but not the vitality, of the earlier works. The depth and intensity of those earlier works had been replaced by a monotonous sameness. Yet, because the tradition had been popular for so long, it took time for artists like Duccio to break away from the once-dynamic art style.

Duccio's painting avoids the typical Byzantine stiffness and introduces a more realistic, relaxed look. The three figures seem solid, and the details in their faces and gestures give them a natural appearance. It is unlikely that Duccio followed a formula when painting these figures. Instead, they suggest that he studied real men before he attempted to paint them. Christ reaches out with one hand to the two men in the boat, while Peter, surprised, returns His gaze. The gestures are natural and not forced. The serene expression on Christ's face is contrasted by the startled look of Peter and the hesitancy of Andrew. The two fishermen, dumbfounded by Christ's sudden summons, are pictured at the moment of decision. Should they ignore the stranger calling to them from the shore and pull in their net filled with fish? Or should they leave everything to follow this man speaking gently to them about being fishers of men?

Giotto

While Duccio struggled to free himself from Byzantine conservatism, another artist was covering the walls of a small chapel in Padua with murals that were destined to change the future course of Italian painting. The subjects for those paintings were not unusual. They were the familiar stories from the lives of Christ and the Virgin. But they were illustrated with realistic-looking people who moved about in what seemed to be real space. The man who painted those murals was a poet, sculptor, architect, and painter by the name of Giotto di Bondone.

A popular legend tells us that Giotto was a poor shepherd who learned to draw on flat stones in the fields. One day the famous artist Cimabue came across Giotto at work on one of his drawings. He was so amazed at the boy's skill that he took him into his studio as his pupil.

As Giotto's fame grew, stories about his great talent captured the imagination of his contemporaries. It was said that when he was still studying with Cimabue he painted a fly on the nose of one of the master's figures. The fly was so realistic that when Cimabue returned to work on the picture he tried several times to brush it off before discovering that it was a painting by his mischievous student.

The Fresco Technique

Most of Giotto's paintings were murals painted on the inside walls of churches in a *fresco* technique. In order to make a fresco, he first made a charcoal drawing on the wall. Then, taking as much of the drawing as he could finish in a single day, Giotto spread a thin coat of wet plaster over the dry wall and then retraced the charcoal lines which he could barely see underneath. Paint, mixed with water and white of eggs, was applied directly to this fresh plaster.★ The paint and wet plaster mixed together to form a permanent surface. Sometimes artists painted over this surface after it had dried, but this repainting usually flaked off in time. If a mistake was made, the whole surface had to be cleaned off and the section done again.

This fresco technique did not allow Giotto time to include many details in his pictures. The paintings had to be completed quickly while the plaster was still wet. This meant that only the most essential details could be included. As a result, Giotto's fresco paintings were usually simple, but very powerful.

★ **Enrichment** The Italian word for fresh is "fresco." Since fresh plaster is used in this painting technique, fresco seemed to be an appropriate name for it.

Criticism

Are there a great many details in this painting? Which art elements have been used to make the figures look more round and solid? In what ways is this picture like a stage play? Point to the two main characters. Identify at least three ways in which your eye is directed to these characters. Describe the different emotional reactions of the other figures. What is the purpose of the dead tree? Do you think that this is a successful work of art? What aesthetic qualities would you use to defend your judgment?

Figure 10.20   Giotto. *Lamentation.* Fresco. c. 1305. Arena Chapel, Padua, Italy. [Photo Alinari]

Concern for Realism

One of Giotto's frescoes in Padua testifies to his monumental talent. It is entitled *Lamentation* and shows a group of mourners around the body of Christ following the Crucifixion (Figure 10.20). The figures are modeled in light and dark so that they look as solid and round as sculptures. There is a feeling that real bodies exist beneath those robes. The picture is made to look more real by the addition of a natural background of blue sky, rocky ledge, and dead tree. Gone is the flat, gold background that was a standard feature of earlier works. The purely spiritual does not interest Giotto. He vigorously pursues a more realistic course.

Expression of Emotions

Giotto's concern for realism led him to study human emotions, and he tried to show those emotions in his paintings. In the *Lamentation,* anguish, despair, and resignation are noted in the expressions and gestures of the figures surrounding Christ. In the foreground, framed by the two massive seated figures, you can see the dead Christ in the arms of a grieving woman. She is undoubtedly Christ's mother, Mary. To the left are several other mourners. The two women at the front of this group are especially noteworthy. One throws her hands upward and her lips part as if to release a cry of sorrow, while the other clasps her hands in anguish and suffers in silence. To the right, the bent-over figure of a young man dominates. He throws his hands back dramatically in a violent gesture of horror and disbelief. His actions seem even more dramatic when compared with the two men at the far right who endure their sorrow without an outward trace of emotion.

Dramatic Effect

Giotto arranged his scene carefully with an eye for dramatic effect, much like a director placing the actors in a play. Even though the fresco technique did not permit him to use many details, it is unlikely that he would have done so anyway. No, Giotto would still have used only a few details or "props" to enhance his story. In the *Lamentation,* he offers a solitary rock ledge rather than a mountain range; he presents a single tree instead of a forest. Neither of these objects is decorative; they are there for a purpose. They direct your attention to the players acting out the great tragedy of Christ's death on a narrow stage. The ledge guides your eye to the most important part of the picture—the faces of Christ and His mother. The tree visually balances the figure of Christ in the opposite corner and also serves as a symbol for His eventual Resurrection. It appears to be dead, but, like Christ, it will rise up in the spring. And in the background is the sky, as flat and solid as a wall. It forces you to focus your attention on the scene in front of it. From a position between the two seated figures, you can see for yourself the weeping mother, the dead son. You do not "read" this story as you would a Romanesque carved relief. Instead, you *experience* it as a silent, helpless, totally involved witness.

The Spreading of Giotto's Fame

Giotto's fame eventually spread to Rome where the Pope was preparing to decorate St. Peter's Basilica with paintings. His curiosity aroused, the Pope sent a messenger to Florence to gather more information about the artist. It was reported that the messenger found Giotto at work in his studio and told him of the Pope's plans for St. Peter's. When the messenger asked Giotto for a sample of his work to take back to the Pope, the artist took a pencil and, with a quick turn of his hand, produced a perfect circle on a scrap of paper. He handed this to the startled messenger, who thought Giotto was joking. "Is this what you want me to take to the Pope?" he asked. Giotto nodded, saying, "It is enough and more than enough." Reluctantly, the messenger took the drawing of the circle to the Pope and presented it to him along with a description of how it was made. The Pope looked at the circle and immediately summoned the artist. When Giotto arrived in Rome, he was received with great honor, having demonstrated with a twist of his wrist that he was one of the outstanding artists of his time.

Giotto was admired by intellectuals and adored by the common people. No doubt his ready wit contributed to his great popularity. Once the King of Naples said to him: "Giotto, if I were you on such a hot day, I would leave my painting for a while." Giotto immediately replied: "So would I, if I were you."

Giotto died in 1337. Later, one of the most powerful men in Italy, Lorenzo de Medici, had a stone statue erected in Giotto's honor in a church in Florence. The final lines of the Latin inscription are a fitting epitaph to this great artist: "I am Giotto, that is all. The name alone is a triumphal poem."

Today, Giotto's works may seem quaint and even awkward to you. But you should remember that artists ever since Giotto have continued to build upon the ideas and techniques that he originated. He painted realistic figures, actions, and emotions studied directly from life and not copied from traditional models as before. This was a revolutionary break with Byzantine art. Giotto identified new goals in art, goals that were to guide artists for generations. It is a further testimony to his greatness that not until Masaccio one hundred years later was there an artist who could match Giotto's power and skill.

Studio Experiences

Lesson One: String Print of a Gothic Cathedral

Take time to reexamine some of the Gothic cathedrals discussed in this chapter, especially the Cathedral of Burgos (Figures 10.2 and 10.4), the Cathedral of Chartres (Figure 10.7), and the Cathedral of Reims (Figure 10.8). Can you identify the major features of those buildings? On sketch paper, complete several line drawings of an imaginary Gothic cathedral. Make certain that each drawing exhibits the following features:

- A central portal and two side portals.
- One or more tympana.
- A large, elaborate rose window.
- No less than eight other windows with pointed arches.
- At least two tall, richly decorated pointed towers or spires.

Reproduce your best line drawing on a piece of corrugated cardboard measuring about 30.5 x 46 cm [12 x 18 inches]. Cut and glue lengths of heavy string or cord over all the lines in your drawing. As you do this, make sure that you capture the strong vertical emphasis of the lines in your cathedral. Using a brayer, apply a water-soluble printing ink to your composition. When the string or cord is thoroughly covered with ink, place a sheet of white or contrasting colored construction paper over your composition and rub it firmly with your fingers or a spoon to produce a print. Try several prints. With this technique, later prints will usually be more successful than the first.

Lesson Two: Drawing Personal Tympana

Compare the carved Gothic tympana of the Cathedral of Burgos (Figure 10.12) and the Cathedral of Pamplona (Figure 10.13) with the Romanesque tympana of Leyre Monastery (Figure 9.17, page 152) and Santa Maria in Sangüesa (Figure 9.18, page 153). In what ways do the Gothic tympana differ from those done during the Romanesque period? Complete several sketches which show you involved in different school activities—at a dance, participating in or viewing a sports event, studying in the library. Other figures and objects should be included in your sketches, but be sure that you are the center of interest. Set your sketches aside long enough to cut a half-round or triangular shape from a large sheet of newsprint. This shape should measure about 30 cm [12 inches] in length and 20 cm [8 inches] in height. Redesign the best of your sketches to fit within this shape. As you do so, determine whether your "tympanum" composition is to be balanced symmetrically (as Romanesque and early Gothic sculptors balanced theirs) or asymmetrically (as later Gothic sculptors balanced theirs). Complete your pencil drawings using a heavy uniform line.

Additional Suggestion: If you wish to do a *finished* tympanum drawing, use a better quality of paper and concentrate on the following art principles while drawing:

- *Balance* (symmetrical or asymmetrical).
- *Emphasis,* to direct attention to the center of interest in your composition—*you.*
- *Variety* in the way you use such elements as line, shape, and value to add visual interest to your drawing.
- *Gradation* in values to suggest three-dimensional forms.
- Contrasts in *proportion* to emphasize the center of interest.

Lesson Three: Carving Personal Tympanum Reliefs in Clay

With a rolling pin, flatten a slab of clay between two wood strips measuring 2.54 cm [1 inch] in thickness. This method will provide you with a slab of uniform thickness. Place the tympanum drawing completed in the previous lesson on this slab and trace over the lines with a sharp pencil. In this way your design will be transferred to the soft clay surface. Use modeling tools (tools for working with clay) to "carve" your picture out of the clay. Follow the lines of your design and remove, or "subtract," clay where necessary to create forms in three dimensions. You will not be adding clay onto the surface of your design, only subtracting it. This "subtractive" technique will enable you to complete a panel in high relief. When you are finished carving and refining your tympanum and before the clay hardens, add a textured surface to heighten the tactile appeal of your work. Include no less than six contrasting textures to add variety to the clay surface. When your relief is finished, it should be fired.

Additional Suggestion: If you wish to add a bronze-like finish after firing, mix black powdered tempera paint with a paste wax and rub this over the relief with a cloth. A second mixture of green or blue-green powdered tempera and paste wax should then be applied lightly over the blackened surface so that raised portions of the carving are highlighted. Finally, polish the relief lightly with a clean, soft cloth.

Safety Note

When using powdered tempera paint, make certain to keep the dust to a minimum. It may affect others who might be sensitive to dust in the air.

Chapter 11

A Time of Titans: Renaissance Art in Italy

Artists you will meet in this chapter

Masaccio (ma-*saht*-chee-oh), 1401 to c. 1428. His painting of the Holy Trinity was so lifelike that when people saw it for the first time they became frightened and ran from the church.

Fra Angelico (frah ann-*jay*-lee-coe), c. 1387-1455. A monk and a painter, it was said that he never started a painting without a prayer.

Lorenzo Ghiberti (loh-*ren*-zo gee-*bair*-tee), c. 1378-1455. His bronze doors for the Baptistry of the Cathedral of Florence were so beautiful that Michelangelo called them the Gates of Paradise.

Filippo Brunelleschi (fee-*leep*-poh brew-nell-*less*-key), 1377-1446. He abandoned sculpture for architecture and designed the famous dome for the Cathedral of Florence.

Paolo Uccello (*pah*-oh-lo oo-*chell*-loh), c. 1397-1475. His pictures reveal an obsession with perspective and foreshortening.

Piero della Francesca (pee-*air*-oh *dell*-ah fran-*chess*-kah), c. 1416-92. He reproduced in paint the effects of sunlight on figures and landscapes.

Donatello (doh-nah-*tell*-oh), 1386-1466. His sculptures were so lifelike that it was reported that he commanded them to speak!

Sandro Botticelli (*sand*-roe bought-tee-*chel*-lee), c. 1444-1510. He used line to organize his highly decorative designs.

Leonardo da Vinci (lay-oh-*nar*-doe da *vinn*-chee), 1452-1519. What did he mean when he said that people of genius sometimes produced the most when they seemed not to be working at all?

Michelangelo Buonarroti (my-kel-*an*-jay-loe bwon-nar-*roe*-tee), 1475-1564. His talents were so great that people said that he must be a descendant of some super race.

Raphael Sanzio (*rah*-fa-yell *sahn*-zee-oh), 1483-1520. At the peak of his glory and productivity, this young genius died at the age of thirty-seven.

Sofonisba Anguissola (so-foe-*niss*-bah ahn-gue-*iss*-sole-ah), c. 1532-1625. An early art historian claimed that her portraits were so lifelike that they lacked only speech.

The Emergence of a New Age

During the Middle Ages, people in western Europe thought of themselves as being helpless and unimportant. The Church was the center of their existence, guiding them over the rough road of life to salvation. But by the beginning of the fifteenth century, people were beginning to rediscover the world around them and realize that they were an important part of that world. It was as if blinders were slowly removed from their eyes allowing them to see, little by little, the wonders before them. The idea that life in this world was little more than a preparation for heaven slowly gave way to an interest in the world of here and now. This change of view and the period in which it took place is referred to as the Renaissance.

The fifteenth century was a time of great growth and discovery. Commerce spread, wealth increased, knowledge multiplied, and the arts flourished. In Italy, a number of cities grew to become important trading and industrial centers. Among these was Florence, which rose to become the capital of the cloth trade and boasted of having the richest banking house in Europe.

During this period, scholars and artists began to show an interest in the art and literature of ancient Greece and Rome. Artists greatly admired the lifelike appearance of Classical works and longed to capture the same quality in their own works. They turned to a study of nature and the surviving Classical sculptures in an effort to make their artworks look more realistic.

In the middle of the fifteenth century, a German printer named Gutenberg perfected the printing press, an invention which ranks as one of the most important

Criticism

Which *words* best describe these figures—flat? round? dainty? solid? lifelike? Why are the two kneeling figures made to look larger then the others? This painting was done on a flat wall, and yet it seems as if you are looking into another room—how has line been used to create this illusion of depth?

Figure 11.1   Masaccio. *The Holy Trinity.* **Fresco. c. 1428. Santa Maria Novella, Florence**

contributions of the Renaissance. Before long, thousands of presses were in operation in Germany, France, England, and Italy. A flood of books poured from these presses. This made available to great numbers of readers the works of ancient Greek and Roman writers, religious books, and volumes of poetry and prose. While the clergy and nobility bought their share of these books, the biggest market was the growing middle class in the cities. Wealthy from trade, finance, and industry, the middle class was eager to improve its lot. Education was seen as the surest way to do this.

Masaccio

In Florence, the wealthy and better-educated citizens grew in number and began to show a lively interest in the arts. Beginning in the fourteenth century and continuing through the fifteenth century, they made their city the artistic capital of Italy. It was in Florence that an absentminded, carefree, and clumsy young painter known as Masaccio brought about a revolution in art equal to that of Giotto.

Masaccio is regarded as the first important artist of the Italian Renaissance, although he certainly did not look the part. Completely devoted to his art, he paid little attention to his appearance or to the events going on around him. It was said that he was so carefree that he never bothered to collect the money others owed him unless he was in great need. People laughingly called him "Masaccio," or "Clumsy Thomas," instead of his real name, Tommaso, but he was unruffled. No matter what they called him, no one denied his genius with a brush, and that was all that mattered to him. He took the innovations of Giotto and developed them further to produce a style that became the trademark of the Italian Renaissance. It was a style that owed a great deal to the fresco painting technique that continued to be popular throughout Italy.

You will recall that the Gothic architectural style, which was flourishing in other countries, never was widely popular in Italy. The walls of glass common to this style did not appeal to the Italians. They liked instead the solid walls and cool, dark interiors of the Romanesque style. The walls of their churches were covered with bright mosaics and large frescoes. At this time, northern artists were making intricate stained-glass windows and small manuscript illustrations. Italian artists, on the other hand, were doing huge wall paintings on the insides of their churches.

The Holy Trinity

Masaccio worked in fresco when he created one of his greatest works in the Florentine Church of Santa Maria Novella. The painting was *The Holy Trinity* (Figure 11.1),

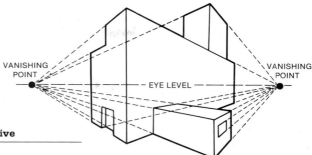

VANISHING POINT   EYE LEVEL   VANISHING POINT

Figure 11.2   An example of linear perspective

and Masaccio was just twenty-one years old when he painted it. Like Giotto before him, he ignored unnecessary detail and focused his attention on mass and depth. He wanted his figures to look solid and real, so he modeled them in light and shadow. To show that some of these figures were at different distances from the viewer, he overlapped them. To increase the lifelike appearance of his painting even more, Masaccio created the illusion of a small chapel. In it he placed the Holy Trinity, St. John, and the Virgin Mary. On either side of this chapel, he added two figures, members of the wealthy family that had commissioned him to paint the fresco. These two figures are life-size. However, the figures inside the painted chapel are smaller to show that they are further back in space.

Shortly before Massacio painted *The Holy Trinity*, an architect and friend named Filippo Brunelleschi made a discovery known as *linear perspective*. This was a geometric system that showed artists how to create the illusion of depth on a flat surface. Using this system, an artist is able to paint figures and objects so that they seem to move deeper *into* a work rather than across it. Slanting the lines of buildings and other objects in the picture inward makes them appear to extend back into space (Figure 11.2). If these lines are lengthened, they will eventually meet at a point along an imaginary horizontal line representing the eye level. The point at which these lines meet is called a *vanishing point*.★

Masaccio made brilliant use of Brunelleschi's discovery when he painted *The Holy Trinity*. He placed all his figures several feet above the floor of the church and slanted the lines of the ceiling and capitals of the columns downward and inward so they would meet at a vanishing point below the foot of the cross.★ As a result, you are made to believe that you are looking into a real chapel with real people in it, when actually the entire scene is painted on a flat wall.

If you find Masaccio's painting lifelike, imagine how it must have appeared to the people of his time. Never having seen realism of this kind in art before, they were stunned by the work. It was even reported that some fled from the church in fright. They thought they had gazed upon the real thing.

★ **Enrichment** Some scholars speculate that Brunelleschi used a mirror to discover and perfect his method of linear perspective. A mirror reveals features of perspective which are not observed by the naked eye, features such as the horizontal lines of a building which appear in the mirror to come together in the distance. Indeed, with a mirror the three-dimensional relationships are automatically represented on a two-dimensional surface just as they are in a drawing using linear perspective.

★ **Enrichment** Below Masaccio's fresco is the tomb of the two donors seen in the painting. The Italian inscription on this tomb gave the faithful something to think about. It read, "What you are, I once was; what I am, you will be."

Criticism

How has light been used to make these figures seem round and solid? Point to the perspective lines that lead your eye *into* this painting. How have hue, value, and intensity been used to heighten the illusion of deep space? In what ways is this picture like a play?

Figure 11.3   Masaccio. *The Tribute Money*. Fresco. c. 1427. Brancacci Chapel, Santa Maria del Carmine, Florence. [Photo Alinari]

The Tribute Money

Not too long after finishing *The Holy Trinity,* Masaccio began working on a number of large frescoes in another Florentine church. *The Tribute Money* (Figure 11.3) is one of these frescoes. In it he grouped three scenes to tell a story from the life of St. Peter. In the center, Christ tells St. Peter that he will find a coin in the mouth of a fish with which to pay a tax collector. The tax collector is shown at Christ's left with his back to you. At the left side of the picture, you see St. Peter again, kneeling to remove the coin from the mouth of the fish. Finally, at the right, St. Peter firmly places the coin in the tax collector's hand.

As in his earlier painting of *The Holy Trinity,* Masaccio wanted to create a picture that would look true to life. Depth is suggested by overlapping the figures of the apostles gathered around Christ. With linear perspective, he slanted the lines of the building to lead the viewer's eye deep into the picture. He also made distant objects look bluer, lighter, and duller, heightening the illusion of deep space. This method of using hue, value, and intensity to show distance in a painting is known as *aerial* or *atmospheric perspective.*★ In *The Holy Trinity,* aerial perspective was not needed because the illusion of space was limited to a chapel interior. But, in *The Tribute Money,* an outdoor setting offered Masaccio the opportunity of using aerial perspective to create the impression of endless space.

★ **Enrichment** Think of yourself on a flat desert looking off toward some mountains in the distance. The atmosphere between you and the mountains would make their color seem bluer, lighter, and duller. The mountains would also seem more blurred and less distinct than objects that are closer to you. When artists try to capture this same effect in their paintings, they are said to be using aerial or atmospheric perspective.

You probably noticed in *The Tribute Money* that Masaccio again modeled his figures so that they seem to be as solid as statues. To achieve this effect, he used a strong light which strikes and lights up some parts of his figures while leaving other parts in deep shadow. Then he placed these figures before a faint background. This not only makes them seem even more solid, but much closer to you as well. Added to this is the fact that the figures are quite large in relation to the rest of the picture and are shown standing at the front of the scene rather than farther away. Because these figures are so large and so near, you can see clearly what Masaccio was trying to do. He was concerned with showing how the body is put together and how it moves. But he does not stop here in his quest for reality. Notice the natural and lifelike gestures and poses of the apostles around Christ. Now look at the face of St. Peter at the left. In his effort to bend over and take the money from the fish's mouth, his face has turned red. And finally, at the right, observe how St. Peter hands over the coin with a firm gesture while the tax collector receives it with a satisfied expression on his face. The actions, gestures, and expressions here are what you might expect from real people.

His Early Death

There is no way of knowing what further advances Masaccio might have made to art had he lived a long life. Unfortunately this young genius, who thought of little beyond his painting, died at the age of twenty-seven. His death was so sudden and shocking that rumors circulated that he had been poisoned, perhaps by another, lesser artist jealous of Masaccio's great talent.

Blending of Early Renaissance and Gothic Ideas

Not all Italian artists accepted the innovations made by Masaccio. Many chose to use some of his ideas and ignore others. Italian art at this time was a blend of the progressive ideas of the Early Renaissance and the conservative ideas of the Gothic period. Two artists who worked in this way were the painter Fra (or "brother") Angelico and the sculptor Lorenzo Ghiberti.

Fra Angelico

Fra Angelico was described by people who knew him as an excellent painter and a monk of the highest character. A simple, holy man, he never started a painting without first saying a prayer and never painted a crucifixion without crying. He also made it a practice not to retouch or try to improve a painting once it was finished. He felt that to do so would be tampering with the will of God.

A few years after Masaccio's death, Fra Angelico painted a picture in which the Angel Gabriel announces to Mary that she is to be the mother of the Savior (Figure 11.4). This painting shows that he was familiar with Masaccio's ideas and did not hesitate using some of them in his own work. Fra Angelico's earlier paintings had been done in the Gothic style and were filled with figures and bright colors. But in this painting there is a simplicity that calls to mind the works by Masaccio. Rather than filling his picture with figures and a colorful background, Fra Angelico uses just two figures, placing them in a modest, yet realistic, architectural setting.

History

Are these figures as lifelike as the figures painted by Masaccio (Figure 11.3)? Does this artist show the same concern for deep space as Masaccio does? What seems to be the most important concern here—realistic subject matter, or a clear, easily understood story?

Figure 11.4   Fra Angelico. *The Annunciation.* Fresco. c. 1440-45. San Marco, Florence. [Photo Alinari]

While he makes some use of perspective, it is clear that Fra Angelico was not greatly interested in creating an illusion of deep space in his picture. The figures of Mary and the angel do not overlap as do the figures in Masaccio's paintings. Instead, they are separated and placed within a limited area marked off by arches. A full arch in the background surrounds Mary's head like a second halo. A half-arch above Gabriel's head serves the same purpose. Fra Angelico chose not to use Masaccio's modeling techniques to make his figures look round and solid. There is little to suggest that real people exist beneath the garments he paints.

There are no surprises or sudden movements depicted in Fra Angelico's paintings. The gestures and facial expressions are easy to read. Like Gothic artists before him, Fra Angelico painted the religious story so that it could be understood by those who saw it. This religious story was more important to Fra Angelico than making his picture seem true to life.

And how did the people of his time react to Fra Angelico's paintings? Giorgio Vasari, a sixteenth-century biographer, claimed that Fra Angelico's paintings of the Madonna were so devout, charming, and well made that they were like the products of heaven and not man.★

Figure 11.5   Lorenzo Ghiberti. *The Sacrifice of Isaac.* 1401-02. Gilt bronze, 53.3 x 43.2 cm [21 x 17″]. Museo Nazionale, Florence

Lorenzo Ghiberti
Like Fra Angelico, Lorenzo Ghiberti combined elements of the new Renaissance style with the earlier Gothic style. A sculptor, Ghiberti is best known for the works he made for the Baptistry of the Florence Cathedral.

The Baptistry Doors Competition
In 1401, the city council of Florence decided to sponsor a contest. The purpose was to find an artist to decorate the north doors of the Baptistry of the cathedral. This Baptistry, built in the twelfth century and dedicated to St. John the Baptist, was one of the most important buildings in the city. It was here that every child was baptized and officially brought into the Church. In 1330, an artist named Andrea Pisano had been selected to decorate the south doors of the Baptistry with scenes from the life of St. John the Baptist. Pisano had done so by creating a series of bronze reliefs in the Gothic style of that period. Now the city decided to decorate the north doors as well and offered a challenge to the leading artists of the day. Sculptors were asked to design a sample relief panel in bronze. The subject for the relief was the Sacrifice of Isaac. This subject was chosen because it seemed like a good test for an artist. It was a religious scene of great dramatic interest, and it would have to include several figures in motion. Entries were turned in by hopeful artists and were carefully examined.★ Finally Ghiberti was declared the winner. He spent the next twenty-one years of his life completing the twenty-eight panels used on the doors. His reliefs are a great feat of artistic skill. This is especially evident when one considers that he was just past twenty years of age when he began.

★ **Enrichment** Giorgio Vasari was the first modern art historian. In 1550 he wrote a series of biographies of the Italian artists of the previous three hundred years. Today it is one of the most important, though often debated, sources for information about Renaissance art.

★ **Enrichment** Only two of these bronze competition panels have survived—those produced by Ghiberti and Brunelleschi.

When you compare Ghiberti's winning relief panel with one produced by his chief rival in the competition, Filippo Brunelleschi,[1] some interesting similarities and differences are noted. Ghiberti's panel (Figure 11.5) and Brunelleschi's panel (Figure 11.6) both are marked by the Gothic influence. However, Ghiberti's shows that he was aware of the new trends in art.

A requirement of the competition was that all the panels had to employ the same Gothic frame used by Pisano on the south doors of the Baptistry. At first glance, this frame makes the panels created by Brunelleschi and Ghiberti both look like little pictures from a Medieval manuscript. But a close inspection reveals that only one panel retains the Gothic style throughout.

[1] This is the Brunelleschi who is credited with discovering linear perspective.

Brunelleschi formed each of his figures separately without concerning himself too much with how these figures related to each other. His panel also shows a Gothic flatness, which you can see in the way the figures have been arranged *across* the front plane. In fact, Brunelleschi's panel can be divided horizontally into three layers which are placed one on top of the other. Ghiberti, on the other hand, tried to pull the different parts of his work together to form a more unified whole. The figures and objects in his work overlap each other in a more natural way. Moreover, his figures turn and move freely across and *into* the work. They seem to be communicating with each other by glances or gestures. There is indeed movement in Ghiberti's panel. However, much of this movement is suggested by the flow of the draperies rather than by the figures themselves. By this you can see that Ghiberti did not choose to abandon completely the flowing lines and graceful gestures that were the trademarks of earlier Gothic figures.

History

Compare this relief panel with the one created by Ghiberti (Figure 11.5) and decide which panel

• has figures that turn and move across and *into* the work.

• seems to be a collection of separate figures that do not relate well with each other.

• is arranged in a flat pattern *across* the panel.

• can be divided horizontally into three layers placed one on top of the other.

• has figures and objects which overlap each other in a natural way.

Figure 11.6 Filippo Brunelleschi. ***The Sacrifice of Isaac.*** **1401-02. Gilt bronze, 53.3 x 43.2 cm [21 x 17″]. Museo Nazionale, Florence**

Why was there no competition for these second doors to the Baptistry? Which famous artist referred to these doors as "The Gates of Paradise?"

Figure 11.7   Lorenzo Ghiberti. East doors of the Baptistry of Florence Cathedral. 1425-52. Gilt bronze, approx. 43.2 cm [17″] high. [Photo Alinari]

"The Gates of Paradise"

Ghiberti drew more heavily upon new Renaissance ideas later in his career when he worked on a second set of doors for the Baptistry. Everyone had been so pleased with his first doors that there was no competition for this second set. These doors showed scenes from the Old Testament. For them, Ghiberti abandoned the Gothic frame used in earlier panels and made his reliefs rectangular. He also introduced a greater feeling of space by using linear perspective. This made the buildings and other objects appear to extend back into the work. Finally, he modeled his figures so that they stand out from the surface of the panel and seem almost fully rounded (Figure 11.7). The effect was so impressive that when Michelangelo gazed upon these doors he said they were worthy of being used as the gates to heaven. There seems to have been no argument then, nor is there now—Ghiberti's doors are still referred to as "The Gates of Paradise."

A New Style Emerges

While Fra Angelico and Ghiberti were finding it difficult to break completely with the old Gothic style, other artists were eagerly accepting Renaissance ideas. However, some of these artists were unable to grasp the full meaning of the bold new style. Instead, they concentrated on certain innovations and ignored the rest.

Criticism

Why does this picture fail to look realistic? Is there a great deal of movement and action here, or do the figures seem stiff and frozen? Find places where contour and axis lines have been used to lead your eye into the work.

Figure 11.8   Paolo Uccello. *The Battle of San Romano.* c. 1455. Tempera on wood panel, approx. 1.8 x 3.2 m [6′ x 10′5″]. Reproduced by courtesy of the Trustees of the National Gallery, London

Paolo Uccello

Paolo Uccello was one of these. He became so enthusiastic about perspective that he devoted all his time and energy to it. It excited him so much that he would work far into the night arranging the perspective lines in his paintings. When his wife begged him to go to sleep, he would only reply, "Oh what a delightful thing is this perspective!"[2]

Uccello's concern for perspective is evident when you analyze his painting of *The Battle of San Romano* (Figure 11.8). Bodies and broken spears are placed in such a way that they lead your eye into the picture. Horses and men are posed at daring angles as Uccello uses every chance to show space and distance. And yet, even with all its depth, you would never say that this work looks realistic. It is more like a group of puppets arranged in a mock battle scene. By concentrating on perspective, Uccello failed to include movement and zest in his painting. The world that he painted is not a real world at all, but a strange, fairy-tale world.

[2] As quoted in Giorgio Vasari, *Lives of the Artists,* abr. & ed. with Commentary by Betty Burroughs (New York: Simon & Schuster, 1946), p. 56.

Piero della Francesca

Fra Angelico and Ghiberti could not turn their backs entirely on the Gothic style. Uccello's interest in the Renaissance style was solely in perspective. It was up to a fourth artist, Piero della Francesca, to break with tradition and fully embrace the new style. By doing so, he carried on the ideas that started with Giotto and were continued by Masaccio.

The *Baptism of Christ* (Figure 11.9) shows how Piero painted figures that have the same three-dimensional aspect found in figures painted by Giotto and Masaccio. Christ is a solid form placed in the center of the picture. The hand of St. John the Baptist and a dove representing the Holy Spirit are placed directly over His head. The figures show little movement or expression. They are serious, calm, and still. The tree and the figures in the foreground provide a strong vertical emphasis. The effect of this vertical emphasis is softened by the artist's use of contrasting horizontals and curves. The horizontals are found in the clouds and the dove. The curves are seen in the branches, stream, and horizon line.

Criticism

What has been done to make these figures look solid and three-dimensional? How is the main figure emphasized and made to look more important than the others? Two gently curving arches frame the face of the main figure—can you find them? What words best describe the mood of this picture: excited or peaceful? serious or lighthearted? loud or quiet?

Figure 11.9   Piero della Francesca. *Baptism of Christ.* **c. 1445. Reproduced by courtesy of the Trustees of the National Gallery, London**

Why did the sculptor stretch the upper part of the body here? What happens when you look up at this sculpture from below? Which artists contributed to Donatello's interest in perspective?

In what ways is this figure similar to Classical Greek sculptures? Was this similarity accidental, or did this artist study the works of ancient sculptors? Describe the expression on the young knight's face. Would you say he is frightened, angry, determined, or confused?

Figure 11.10 Donatello. *St. Mark.* 1411-13. Marble, approx. 2.4 m [7′ 9″] high. Or San Michele, Florence. [Photo Alinari]

Figure 11.11 Donatello. *St. George.* 1415-17. Marble, approx. 2.1 m [6′ 10″] high. Museo Nazionale, Florence

Did you observe how Piero used two gently curving arches to frame and draw your attention to Christ's face? One of these arches curves over Christ's head. It is formed by a tree branch and the hand and arm of John the Baptist. A second arch, representing the horizon line, dips down below Christ's head.

Piero is well known for the way he used light and color in his paintings. His use of light and color gave solidity to his figures and added a new realism to the space around them. He captured the look of fresh, clear morning air which brightens the wide landscape and flows around the people in his pictures. Piero went further than any artist of his time by studying and reproducing in paint the effects of sunlight on his landscape and figures.

Donatello

One of the assistants who worked for Ghiberti on the first set of doors for the Baptistry of Florence was to go on to become the greatest sculptor of the Early Renais-

sance. A good friend of Brunelleschi, he also shared Masaccio's interest in realistic appearances and perspective. His name was Donatello.

You might think it strange to talk about perspective in sculpture, but Donatello used it when carving figures that were to be placed in churches above eye level. In such figures, he made the upper part of the bodies longer so that when viewed from below they would seem more naturalistic (Figure 11.10). This kept his sculptures from looking short and awkward.

Donatello's sculptures became famous for their vitality and lifelike qualities. Even he was delighted by their realism. Vasari tells of one incident in which Donatello, while working on one of his sculptures, commanded it again and again to speak to him. You can see this remarkable realism for yourself in Donatello's sculpture of *St. George* (Figure 11.11). The young knight seems to lean forward in anticipation as he stares intently ahead.

The plan for constructing the dome of this cathedral was based on building techniques developed by which of the following: (a) Egyptian architects, (b) Greek architects, (c) Roman architects, or (d) Gothic architects? Brunelleschi was also credited for making an important discovery—what was it?

Figure 11.12 Filippo Brunelleschi. Dome of Florence Cathedral. 1420-36

Perhaps he is watching the advance of an enemy and is preparing for his first move. He certainly looks ready to leap forward at any moment to do battle.

In many ways, the sculpture of St. George is similar to Classical Greek sculptures. Its slightly twisting, contrapposto pose may remind you of the *Spear Bearer* by Polyclitus (Figure 6.16, page 101). Even though Donatello's figure is clothed, there is no mistaking the presence of a human body beneath the garments. With works like this, Donatello reveals that he admired, studied, and mastered the techniques of the great Greek and Roman sculptors.

Donatello lived a long, productive life and created works of art in several Italian cities. Everywhere he went, people were so amazed by his talent that they did everything possible to persuade him to stay. Finally, back in his native Florence and eighty years old, it was obvious to all that the famous sculptor was nearing death. Some of his relatives visited him and told him it was his duty to leave them a small estate that he owned. Donatello's reply to them tells a great deal about the character of this famous artist. He listened patiently to his relatives. Then he told them he was going to leave the property to the peasant who had cared for it faithfully over the years. After all, he explained, the relatives had done nothing to the property but desire it. For this they were not entitled to it.

Filippo Brunelleschi

You may be wondering what became of Filippo Brunelleschi. He was, you will recall, the artist credited with discovering linear perspective. You may also recall that he was Ghiberti's major rival for the right to design the doors for the Baptistry in Florence. When he lost the contest to Ghiberti, Brunelleschi was very disappointed. In fact, it caused him to abandon sculpture for a career in architecture. He could not accept the idea that

Ghiberti was a more gifted artist than he was. Once, when asked to name the best thing Ghiberti ever did, he answered by saying, "Selling his farm."[3] He was referring to a worthless piece of property for which Ghiberti had paid too much. Ghiberti finally sold it in disgust when it failed to produce anything.

But sixteen years later, the two rivals faced each other again in another competition. This time they were asked to submit their designs for a huge dome for the Cathedral of Florence. Work on the Cathedral had been underway for generations. Everything had been completed except a dome which would span the huge opening above the altar. But no one was able to design a dome to cover such a large opening. Many claimed that it could not be done. Brunelleschi was one of those who claimed that it could. He submitted a plan based on Gothic building techniques and was awarded the opportunity to try.★

Brunelleschi's plan called for the use of Gothic ribs which met at the top of the dome and were joined by horizontal sections around the outside of the dome at its base. The surface between the ribs was then filled in with bricks. The eight major ribs can be seen on the outside of the dome, five of which can be plainly seen in Figure 11.12. For extra height, the entire dome was placed on a drum. Circular windows in this drum allowed light to flow into the building.

[3] As quoted in Giorgio Vasari, *Lives of the Artists*, abr. & ed. with Commentary by Betty Burroughs (New York: Simon & Schuster, 1946), p. 84.

★ **Enrichment** There are several stories associated with Ghiberti's work on this dome. One version has it that Brunelleschi and Ghiberti were asked to work together on the project. However, Ghiberti soon tired of it and withdrew, leaving the task entirely to Brunelleschi.

It took sixteen years to build the dome, but when it was finished Brunelleschi's reputation as an architect and engineer was made. The towering dome dominated Florence and soon became a symbol of the city's power and strength. It was so spectacular that later, when designing the great dome for St. Peter's in Rome, Michelangelo borrowed ideas from it.

Before he began work on the dome, Brunelleschi agreed to design a chapel for the Pazzi family. They were one of the wealthiest and most powerful families in Florence. In this chapel, he rejected the Gothic style. Instead, he chose a new architectural style based upon his studies of ancient Roman buildings. Inside the Pazzi Chapel (Figure 11.13), you will not see soaring pointed arches or a long, high nave leading to an altar. The vertical movement was not stressed. Rather, Brunelleschi wanted to achieve a balance between vertical and horizontal movements. He preferred a gently rounded curve rather than a tall, pointed arch. Dark moldings, pilasters, and columns were used to divide and organize the flat, white wall surfaces. The overall effect is not dramatic or mysterious as in a Gothic cathedral, but simple, calm, and dignified. Its beauty is due to the carefully balanced relationship of all its parts.

History

How does this church interior differ from interiors built in the Gothic style? What has been used here in place of tall, pointed arches? How are the white wall surfaces divided and organized? Would you describe this interior as dramatic and mysterious, or quiet and dignified?

Figure 11.13   Filippo Brunelleschi. Exterior and interior views of the Pazzi Chapel. Begun c. 1440. Santa Croce, Florence. [Photos Alinari]

Criticism

Which of the art elements is stressed here? How would you describe the contour lines—crisp and sharp, or soft and vague? What has been done to guide you into the picture to the main figures? What shape is formed when you draw a line around these main figures—a square, a rectangle, or a triangle? Who do you think these people are and what are they doing?

Figure 11.14   Sandro Botticelli. *The Adoration of the Magi.* c. 1481. Approx. 0.7 x 1 m [27⅝ x 41″]. The National Gallery of Art, Washington, D.C. Andrew W. Mellon Collection, 1937

Sandro Botticelli

Unfortunately, Brunelleschi never saw the completed Pazzi Chapel. He died in 1446, and the chapel was finished much later in the 1460s. His life overlapped by just two years that of a remarkable painter by the name of Sandro Botticelli. Botticelli was born in 1444 and died quietly in Florence some sixty-six years later. Not many took note of his passing, and his name was even misspelled in the official register. Forgotten for centuries, this artist's paintings are now ranked among the most admired of the Renaissance period.

When he was a boy, Botticelli angered his father by ignoring his schoolwork. Art seemed to be the only thing that interested the boy, and so his father finally placed him, as an apprentice, in the studio of a goldsmith. Later, Botticelli studied in the workshop of a well-known painter. Then, like so many painters, sculptors, and architects of that time, he worked for the powerful Medici family of bankers and wool merchants. Apparently the Medici family thought of him as a decorator, for they had him paint a number of ornamental pictures for bed fronts and chests. Work of this kind had an effect on the development of his unique, decorative style of painting.

When you describe and analyze a painting by Botticelli, you find yourself drawn into a unique world of flowing lines and graceful forms. In his *Adoration of the Magi* (Figure 11.14), an aisle bordered by kneeling figures leads you to the Holy Family. They are surrounded by the Magi and their attendants all dressed in garments worn during Botticelli's time.★ The Magi are presenting their gifts to the Christ Child seated on Mary's lap. The figures are drawn with crisp, sharp contour lines, and their garments have folds that twist and turn in a lively decorative pattern. Clearly Botticelli was less interested in the literal qualities than in the visual qualities that enabled him to create a decorative design. For example, you may find that the figure of Mary seems stretched out of shape, but this was a feature of Botticelli's graceful style. He thought that by elongating the form and tilting the head he would make Mary look more elegant.

★ **Enrichment** These figures are probably portraits of real people. It was common for people having a religious painting done to ask the artist to paint them into it as devout worshipers. In that way, they could show proof of their piety. Then, even when they were engaged in misconduct, their painted images would still be seen praying humbly before the Holy Family.

Botticelli relied on the element of line to organize and add interest to his painting. Notice what happens when you draw a line around the principal figures. It forms a large triangle with the Madonna and Child at the apex, or top. When you include the Magi's attendants who fan outward on both sides, a large "W" is formed. Above, the diagonal lines of the ruined Classical building guide your eye to the central figures. Thus, Botticelli tied all the parts of his picture together into a unified whole and directed your attention to the most important parts.

But why did Botticelli choose to place the Madonna and Child in the ruined remains of a Classical building? Of course, there is no way of knowing for certain, although he may have wanted to tell us that Christianity was born among the crumbling ruins of paganism.

Before leaving Botticelli's painting, one last question seems to beg for an answer. Where is the famous star that guided the Magi on their long journey? The star itself is not included in the painting, but the artist provides a clue indicating that it is present somewhere overhead. Did you notice this clue? You would be correct if you pointed to the young man at the far right. He looks upward in awe as though struck by the brilliance of the star hovering over the scene.

New Levels of Excellence

One of the most remarkable things about the Renaissance was its great wealth of artistic talent. During this period lived the artistic giants Leonardo, Michelangelo, and Raphael. Each of them alone would have set any period apart as something special, but all three lived in Italy during the Renaissance. Like all artists before them, these great masters dreamed of achieving new levels of excellence. Unlike most other artists, they each succeeded in their own way.

Leonardo da Vinci

Even when he was a child, people saw that Leonardo da Vinci was blessed with remarkable powers. He had gracious manners, a fine sense of humor, and great physical strength. Leonardo also had a curiosity that drove him to explore everything. As he grew older, he studied architecture, mathematics, sculpture, painting, anatomy, poetry, literature, music, geology, botony, and hydraulics. It is estimated that he completed 120 notebooks. These notebooks were filled with drawings surrounded by explanations (Figure 11.15). They reveal a driven man moving abruptly from one area of study to another. The subjects range from anatomy to storm clouds to rock formations to military fortifications. He dissected cadavers at a time when the practice was outlawed and subject to severe punishment. This enabled Leonardo to learn how arms and legs bend and how muscles shift as the body moves. But he was especially interested in the head, particularly how the eye sees and how the mind reasons. He searched for that part of the brain where the senses meet, believing that this was where the soul would be found.

History

Leonardo's sketchbooks reveal his remarkable curiosity. Can you name some of the subjects that interested him? Were all of his experiments successful? Name one that was not.

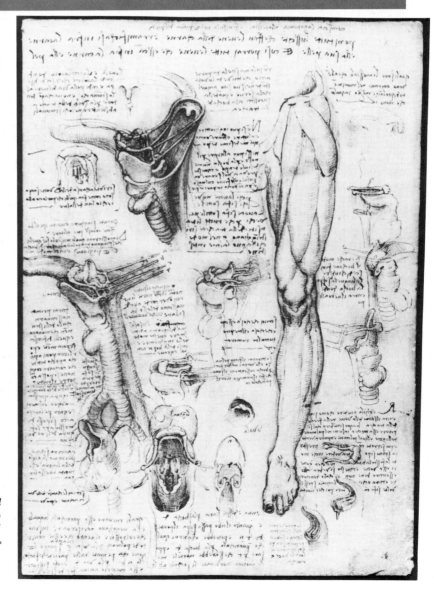

Figure 11.15 Leonardo da Vinci. *Anatomical Studies.* **(Date unknown.) The Royal Library, Windsor Castle. Reproduced by Gracious Permission of Her Majesty Queen Elizabeth II**

Criticism

Describe the setting, the figures, and the event portrayed in this painting. Are all the figures at this table arranged in small groups? Which one is isolated and alone? Are all the figures gesturing and talking? Which one is not? With your finger, trace along the straight lines of the walls and ceiling—where do they lead you? Can you find a curved line among the lines of the architecture (see enlargement below)? Why is this line important? Did you notice anything unusual about the way the figures are seated at the table? Why do you think they are painted this way?

Figure 11.16 Leonardo da Vinci. *The Last Supper*, with detail. Fresco. c. 1495-98. Santa Maria delle Grazie, Milan. [Photo Alinari]

The Last Supper

Leonardo's artworks are limited in number. He left many projects unfinished because the results did not please him or because he was eager to move on to some new task. But, in addition to this, he was always experimenting, and many of these experiments ended in failure. Perhaps his greatest "failure" is his version of *The Last Supper* (Figure 11.16). This was a magnificent painting that began to flake off the wall shortly after he applied his final brushstroke.

The Last Supper had been painted many times before, and so Leonardo probably welcomed the challenge of creating his own version. He had an entire wall to work on. It was a wall in a dining hall used by monks in the Monastery of Santa Maria delle Grazie in Milan. Using linear perspective, Leonardo designed his scene so that it would look like a continuation of the dining hall. Christ is the center of the composition. All the lines of the architecture lead to Him silhouetted in the window.

He has just announced that one of the apostles would betray Him, and this news has unleashed a flurry of activity around the table. Only Christ remains calm and silent, and this effectively separates Him from the others. At His right are John, Judas, and Peter. John, Christ's favorite, looks as if he is about to faint. Peter bends forward in shock, unable to believe what he has just heard. Judas leans on the table and stares at Christ, his expression a mixture of anger and defiance.★ The other apostles, stunned, shrink back and express their denials and questions in different ways.

As you examine Leonardo's painting, you may be struck by an unusual feature. All the apostles are crowded together on the far side of the table. Certainly they could not have been comfortable that way, and yet none has moved to the near side where there is ample room. Leonardo chose not to spread his figures out because that would have reduced the impact of the scene. Instead, he jammed them together to accent the action and the drama.

Leonardo broke with tradition by including Judas with the other apostles. Earlier works usually showed him standing or sitting at one end of the table, apart from the others. But instead Leonardo placed him among the apostles but made him easy to identify with a dark profile, suggestive of guilt. This was to show that Judas was separated from the other apostles in a spiritual way rather than in a physical way.

Vasari says that the prior of the monastery became impatient with Leonardo while he was painting *The Last Supper*.★ He thought the artist was taking much too long to finish the painting. He became especially upset when he noticed that Leonardo spent long periods of time staring at the picture rather than working on it. Angry, the prior went to the Duke of Milan to complain. Leonardo was then summoned to appear before the Duke. After hearing the complaints made against him, Leonardo said that men of genius sometimes produce the most when they do not seem to be working at all. The Duke found no reason to argue with that. Therefore, Leonardo continued by saying that two heads in the composition were providing him with some difficulty—Christ's and Judas's. He would search for a model for Judas, he said, but was not hopeful that he could ever find anyone so wicked and depraved as the man who betrayed Christ. But, he hastened to add, he could always paint in the head of the troublesome prior!

It is fortunate indeed that Leonardo's painting of *The Last Supper* still exists. It has suffered a great deal of abuse and neglect in the centuries since it was completed. After Leonardo's death, other artists tried to repair it but used the wrong colors. Years passed and the painting grew more and more faint. At one point, a monk in the monastery ordered a door placed in the wall. The mark from that door can still be seen at the bottom of the picture. Later, Napoleon's army swept into Italy, and the dining hall was turned into a temporary barracks. The bored soldiers amused themselves by throwing their boots at the figure of Judas. Then, during World War II, the monastery was bombed, and the dining hall suffered a direct hit. Only one wall, protected by sandbags and a steel frame, was left standing—the one with Leonardo's masterpiece. Still safe, but badly scarred, the painting was covered by a canvas. But moisture gathered under the canvas, and when it was removed the entire wall was found to be covered with a white fungus. After the war, it took two years of work to save the painting. Work on this great painting continues to the present day.

★ Enrichment Did you notice the overturned saltcellar in front of Judas? At this time in history, the spilling of salt was considered to be unlucky. It was a sign of certain tragedy to come. After spilling it, the spiller had to throw a small amount over the left shoulder to avoid misfortune. Why the left shoulder? Because the left side was thought to be sinister—it was thought to be the place where evil spirits gathered.

★ Enrichment A prior was the second in command of a monastery, next in line to the abbot.

One of Leonardo's paintings is famous for its haunting smile—what is the name of that painting? What is the most interesting feature on *this* face? Can you find anything unusual about this feature? How would you describe the mood of this woman?

Figure 11.17 Leonardo da Vinci. *Ginevra de' Benci.* c. 1474. Oil on wood, approx. 38.8 x 36.7 cm [15¼ x 14½"]. The National Gallery of Art, Washington, D.C. Ailsa Mellon Bruce Fund

Portrait of Ginevra de' Benci

The only painting by Leonardo in the United States may be a portrait of Ginevra de' Benci, the daughter of a rich Florentine banker (Figure 11.17). In his famous picture entitled the *Mona Lisa,* Leonardo created a mysterious, haunting smile. However, in this portrait of Ginevra de' Benci the eyes command attention. At first they seem to focus on you, but in the next instant they appear to stare at something behind you. Suddenly you are aware that there are no eyelashes. And why did Leonardo paint a heavy shadow under the upper eyelids? He may have done this to draw your gaze to the pupils, which have been painted with layer upon layer of transparent paint until they appear to glow. It is not known why he placed so much importance on the eyes in this picture. However, it may have had something to do with his curiosity about the mind and how it worked. Leonardo may have come to regard the eyes as windows to that mind.

An "Unfinished" Masterpiece

Leonardo was a genius who showed great skill in everything he tried. This was his blessing and his curse, for he jumped suddenly from one undertaking to the next. His curiosity and constant experimenting often kept him from remaining with a project until it was completed. A perfectionist, he was never entirely satisfied with his efforts. When he died, he still had in his possession the *Mona Lisa* portrait. He had been working on it for sixteen years and yet claimed that it was still unfinished. That painting, which he regarded as unfinished, is now one of the most famous works of art ever created.

Criticism

Why is the woman so much larger than the other figure? Does she seem to be struggling under the weight of her burden? The face of the woman seems to be expressionless—so how does she express her sorrow? To which aesthetic qualities would you refer when judging this work? Do you think it is a successful sculpture?

Figure 11.18   Michelangelo. *Pietà*. c. 1500. Marble. St. Peter's, Rome

Michelangelo

Ranked alongside Leonardo as one of the greatest artists of the Renaissance was Michelangelo Buonarroti. Like Leonardo, Michelangelo was gifted in many fields, including sculpture, painting, and poetry.

Pietà

A measure of his early genius is provided by his *Pietà* (Figure 11.18), carved when he was still in his early twenties.★ In this over-life-size work, the Virgin is presented as a beautiful young woman seated at the foot of the Cross. She holds in her lap the lifeless form of the crucified Christ. Gently, she supports her son with her right arm. With her left, she expresses her deep sorrow

---

★ **Enrichment**   "Pietà" is a name given to a picture or sculpture of the Virgin Mary mourning over the dead body of Christ.

with a simple gesture. The Virgin's face is expressionless. It is a beautiful face, but small when compared to her huge body. In fact, you may have noticed that Mary's body is much larger than that of Christ. Why would Michelangelo make the woman so much larger than the man? Probably because a huge and powerful Mary was necessary to support with ease the heavy body of her son. Michelangelo wanted you to focus your attention on the religious meaning of the figures and the event, not on Mary's struggle to support the weight of Christ's body.

Soon after the *Pietà* was placed in St. Peter's Basilica in Rome, Michelangelo overheard some visitors discussing it. He became dismayed when it became clear that they did not know who had created it. Later, he returned with his carving tools, and, on the band across Mary's chest, he carved "Michelangelo Buonarroti of Florence made this." As word of his talent spread, it became obvious to all that only Michelangelo could have carved such a masterpiece.

What makes this work seem more like a carving than a painting? Which property of color—hue or value—is stressed here? How would you describe the actions and gestures of these figures?

Figure 11.19 Michelangelo. Ceiling of the Sistine Chapel, with detail of *The Creation of Adam*. Fresco. 1508-12. The Vatican, Rome

The Ceiling of the Sistine Chapel

Everything that Michelangelo set out to do was on a grand scale. For this reason, many projects were never completed. Asked by Pope Julius II to design a tomb for him, Michelangelo created a design calling for forty figures. However, only a statue of Moses and some figures of slaves were ever finished. While Michelangelo was still preparing for this project, the Pope changed his mind and decided not to spend any more money for it. Instead, he assigned the artist the task of painting the immense ceiling of the Sistine Chapel in the Vatican (Figure 11.19). This chapel was about 12 m [40 feet] wide and about 40 m [133 feet] long and had a rounded ceiling. It looked impossible to paint, and Michelangelo protested. It was not just the difficulty of the task. No doubt his pride was hurt as well. Ceiling paintings were considered less important than wall paintings, but the walls of the Sistine Chapel had already been painted by Botticelli and other well-known artists.★ Furthermore, what could he paint on such an immense ceiling so high above the heads of viewers? And finally, Michelangelo was angry because he thought of himself as a sculptor and not a painter. But all his protests were in vain. In the end, the proud, defiant artist gave in to the stubborn Pope.

★ **Enrichment** The Sistine Chapel had been built in 1480, and the famous frescoes on its walls had been painted from 1481 to 1483 by Botticelli, Signorelli, and Perugino.

Before he could begin work on the ceiling, Michelangelo had to build a high scaffold stretching the length of the chapel. Then, refusing the aid of assistants, he bent over backwards and lay on his back to paint on the wet plaster applied to the ceiling. He divided the ceiling into nine main sections and in these painted the story of humanity from the Creation to the Flood.

Looking up at this huge painting you can see that Michelangelo the Sculptor left his mark for all to see. It looks more like a carving than a painting. There is little color, and the figures are highly modeled in light and shade to look three-dimensional. They are shown in violent action, twisting and turning until they seem about to break out of their niches and leap down from their frames.

For over four years, Michelangelo toiled on the huge painting over 20 m [68 feet] above the floor of the chapel.★ Food was sent up to him, and he only climbed down from the scaffold to sleep. He became so involved with this task that he did not take off his clothes or boots for weeks at a time. When he finally removed his boots, the dead, outermost skin of his feet peeled off with them. But perhaps his greatest difficulty was being forced to see and work while bending backward in a cramped position. He grew so accustomed to this that when he received a letter he had to hold it overhead and bend over backward to read it. He claimed that after working on the Sistine Ceiling he was never able to walk in an upright position again. When he was finished, he had painted 145 pictures with over three hundred figures, many of which were 3 m [10 feet] high. Only a man of superhuman strength and determination—only a Michelangelo—could have produced such a work.★★

Moses

As soon as the Sistine Ceiling was finished, Michelangelo returned to work on the Pope's tomb. Attacking the stone blocks with mallet and chisel, he said that he was "freeing" the figures trapped inside. In about two years, he carved the life-size figures of two slaves and a seated *Moses* (Figure 11.20).

Michelangelo's *Moses* shows the prophet as a wise leader, but capable of great fury. Indeed, here Moses seems to be about to rise up in anger. His head turns as if something has caught his attention. Perhaps, as many have suggested, he sees his people worshiping a false god and is about to unleash his wrath upon them. It is a powerful and commanding portrait, so striking that once you see it, it is difficult to picture Moses looking any other way.

Michelangelo's Energy and Spirit

Popes and princes admired Michelangelo, and everyone stood in awe before his works. His talents were so great that people said that he could not be human, that he must be a descendant from some super race of beings. But he had some very human characteristics as well. He had strong views about art, and this caused him to disagree with other artists, including Leonardo. A violent temper made it difficult for him to work with assistants. And a suspicious nature caused him to suspect everyone of cheating him. He placed his art above everything else. Only death, at age eighty-nine, could silence the energy, the spirit of the man regarded by many as the greatest artist in a time of great artists.

★ **Enrichment** There were many complications and delays. The Pope was often busy with other matters and unavailable to approve of Michelangelo's progress so that he could continue. The Vatican clergy complained about the noise and dust. Mold appeared on some of the finished work, making it necessary for the artist to repaint the affected areas. At one point, the stubborn Michelangelo refused to continue working until he received an overdue payment from the Pope.

★ **Enrichment** Twenty-two years after painting the ceil-
★ ing of the Sistine Chapel, Michelangelo returned to paint a scene on the altar wall. It was to be his famous version of *The Last Judgment*. In it he showed people of all kinds huddled together in groups pleading for mercy moments before they are to be judged by a wrathful Christ.

Criticism

Is this seated figure relaxed and peaceful? If not, how would you describe him? What do you feel is the most impressive feature of this sculpture? Why do you find that feature so impressive?

Figure 11.20   Michelangelo. *Moses.* c. 1513-15. Marble, 2.3 m [7′ 8 ½″] high. San Pietro in Vincoli, Rome

Raphael

Michelangelo was a lonely, tragic figure, but the opposite was true of Raphael Sanzio. Raphael was successful, wealthy, and admired throughout his brief but brilliant career. Born in a small town in central Italy, he probably had his first art lesson from his father, who was a painter at the court of the Duke of Urbino. While still a child, he was apprenticed to an artist named Perugino. This man taught him to use soft colors, simple circular forms, and gentle landscapes in his paintings.

Having learned all he could from Perugino, the young, ambitious Raphael traveled to Florence to study the works of the leading artists of the day. He was an excellent student and learned a great deal by studying the works of others, especially Leonardo and Michelangelo. From Leonardo he learned how to use shading to create the illusion of three-dimensional form. From Michelangelo he learned how to add vitality and energy to his figures. As an inventor and original thinker, Raphael could not equal either of those masters. But by skillfully blending the ideas of those artists in his own works, he arrived at a style that made him the most typical artist of the Renaissance.

Criticism

How many figures are in this picture? Describe the background. How have these figures been made to look lifelike? What clues can you find which reveal that this is a religious picture? What three hues are used? What do we call these hues—primary colors, secondary colors, or complementary colors? How are hue, value, and intensity used to create the look of deep space? Describe the expression on the woman's face—is it happy or sad? Why do you think she feels this way? Who do you think these people are? In your opinion, is this a good work of art? Why or why not?

Figure 11.21   Raphael. *The Alba Madonna.* c. 1510. Diameter, 94.5 cm [37¼"]. The National Gallery of Art, Washington, D.C. Andrew W. Mellon Collection, 1937

The Alba Madonna

In 1508, when Raphael was twenty-five years old, Pope Julius summoned the artist to Rome to paint frescoes for the papal palace in the Vatican. It was while he was working on these frescoes that Raphael probably painted the well-known *Alba Madonna* (Figure 11.21). This is an excellent example of the kind of pictures that were painted in Italy at the peak of the Renaissance. For this reason, it is well worth discussing at some length.

The painting shows three figures, a woman and two children, placed in the foreground with a peaceful and calm landscape stretching back into the distance. You will find no other figures in the painting. In fact, the only other signs of people are the steep-roofed farm houses in the distance. The figures seem round, solid, and lifelike, a result of Raphael's subtle shading technique. The unclothed child in the center turns in the woman's lap and reaches out for a cross held by the second child, dressed in animal skins. The woman is seated on the ground leaning against the trunk of a tree. In her left hand she holds a book, which she must have been reading. A finger holds her place in the book as she glances away. The facial expressions are serious as all eyes focus on the cross. There is no sign of joy or happiness on these faces. Instead, the figures seem to be lost in their own private thoughts.

There is a balanced use of hue in the painting. Raphael has used the three primary colors—red, yellow, and blue—which represent a balance of the color spectrum. Blue dominates: it is used throughout the work and, in the background, adds to the illusion of deep space. This illusion is heightened further by the use of duller hues in the background.

A gradual change from light to dark values adds a feeling of roundness and mass to the shapes. The shapes that make up the three figures combine to form a single large *trapezoid* which is placed slightly off center in the circular composition.★ You can identify this trapezoid by drawing an imaginary line around the contour of the three figures (Figure 11.22). The repeated horizontal lines in the background help to balance and hold this large trapezoid in place.

The halos and cross immediately suggest a religious theme. The woman and unclothed child are identified as the Madonna and the Christ Child. The second child is probably St. John the Baptist. The camel's-hair garment that he wears fits the description of the garment he wore later while preaching in the desert. St. John holds a small cross, the symbol of salvation made possible by Christ's death. The Christ Child takes the cross and appears to be turning and moving on His mother's lap. He twists around in a way that suggests that He wants St. John, representing all people, to follow Him.

At first you may think that this painting is little more than a gentle picture of Christ, His mother, and St. John the Baptist enjoying a pleasant outing in the sunshine. But there is an undercurrent of tension in the work that becomes obvious the more you study it. This tension is best noted in the faces. Everything else is calm and peaceful, but the faces fail to show signs of happiness or contentment. A sadness veils Mary's face as she lifts her eyes from her book. Perhaps something she has read causes her to turn her attention to the cross in her child's hand. All three figures stare intently at this cross, and their thoughts drift to the future. Do they recognize the meaning of the cross, or are they only concerned with the unexpected uneasiness it stirs up within them?

Once you have described, analyzed, and interpreted Raphael's painting, you may find that your own judgment echoes that of Vasari who wrote the following: "Other masters painted pictures, but Raphael paints life itself."

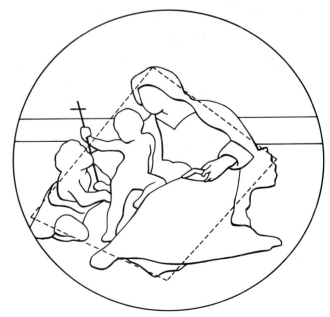

Figure 11.22   Diagram of *The Alba Madonna* by Raphael

★ **Enrichment** A trapezoid is a shape with four sides, two of which are parallel.

"He Who Is Here Is Raphael"

In the spring of 1520, Raphael fell ill with a violent fever. Friends told him that it was nothing serious, but Raphael knew he was dying and calmly went about putting his affairs in order. He died on his thirty-seventh birthday and was buried with full honors in the Pantheon in Rome. His epitaph, in Latin, says simply, "He who is here is Raphael." No other words were necessary; the name alone was enough to testify to his greatness.

Women and Art

You may have noticed that in the coverage of art periods up to this point there has been no mention of women artists. The reason for this is that few works by women artists completed before the Renaissance have come to light. Furthermore, it was not until the Renaissance had passed its peak that women artists were able to make names for themselves as serious artists. And even in that enlightened period, it was not easy for women to succeed as artists because of the obstacles that had to be overcome.

During the Medieval period, women were expected to tend to duties within the household. Their first responsibilities were those of wife and mother. If that failed to occupy all their time, they were required to join their husbands in the backbreaking chores awaiting in the fields. There seemed to be no reason for women to seek an education or learn a trade because there were few opportunities for them to work outside the home. They were, in general, excluded from the arts because, as women, most of them were prevented from gaining the knowledge and skills needed to become artists. Their involvement in art was limited, for the most part, to making embroideries and tapestries and occasionally producing illustrated manuscripts.

During the Renaissance, artists came into their own as valued and respected members of society. However, the new importance attached to artists made it even more difficult for women to pursue a career in art. Artists at that time were required to spend longer periods in apprenticeship. During this time, they studied mathematics, the laws of perspective, and anatomy. Serious artists were also expected to journey to major art centers. There they could study the works of famous living artists as well as the art of the past. This kind of education was out of the question for most women in the fifteenth and sixteenth centuries. Only a handful were talented and determined enough to overcome all these barriers and succeed as serious artists. One of these was Sofonisba Anguissola.

What sets this artist apart from those you have learned about up to this point? This artist's international reputation was based upon an ability to paint which of the following: still lifes, landscapes, portraits, religious subjects?

Figure 11.23   Sofonisba Anguissola. *Double Portrait of a Boy and a Girl of the Attavanti Family.* **(Date unknown.) Oil on panel; diameter, 40 cm [15¾"]. Allen Memorial Art Museum, Oberlin College, Oberlin, Ohio. Gift of the Kress Study Collection, 61.84**

Sofonisba Anguissola

Anguissola was the first Italian woman to gain a worldwide reputation as an artist. She was the oldest in the family of six daughters and one son born to a nobleman in Cremona about twelve years after Raphael's death. At that time, art was flourishing in Cremona. Sofonisba's father was no doubt pleased to find that all his children showed an interest in art or music. He encouraged them all, especially his oldest daughter. Sofonisba was allowed to study with local artists where her skills were quickly recognized. Her proud father even wrote to the great Michelangelo about her. The response was words of encouragement and a drawing which Sofonisba could study and copy as part of her training.

Many of Sofonisba's early works were portraits of herself and members of her family. However, she is known to have done a few religious paintings as well. Her father was always eager to spread the word about his talented daughter. He sent several of her self-portraits to various courts, including that of Pope Julius III. Publicity of this kind contributed to her growing reputation. In 1559, while she was still in her twenties, Sofonisba accepted an invitation from the King of Spain, Philip II. He asked her to join his court in Madrid as a lady-in-waiting. For ten years, she painted portraits of the royal family. After this time, she met and married a nobleman from Sicily and returned to Italy with him. She took with her a fine assortment of gifts presented to her by the appreciative Spanish king.

Many of Sofonisba's portraits deserve to be included among the best produced during the late Renaissance. The reason will be clear when you examine her portrait of the son and daughter of a wealthy Florentine family (Figure 11.23). You can then appreciate Vasari's claim that her pictures were "so lifelike that they lacked only speech." Speech is hardly necessary in this straightforward painting of a boy gazing up thoughtfully from an open book he has been reading. As he does so, his sister places her arm around him. The artist seems to be telling us that the boy not only knows how to read, but is intelligent enough, even at this young age, to think seriously about what he has read. His sister's gesture and expression are signs of her affection and her pride.

Studio Experiences

Lesson One: Painting a Landscape with Gradations of Value to Emphasize Space

In this chapter you learned that many Italian Renaissance artists sought to create the illusion of space in their paintings. The measure of their success was noted in such works as Masaccio's *The Tribute Money* (Figure 11.3), Botticelli's *The Adoration of the Magi* (Figure 11.14), and Raphael's *The Alba Madonna* (Figure 11.21). Compile a list of objects that might be included in a landscape painting which will emphasize the element of space. Your list should be lengthy and could include such items as houses, trees, hills, fields, sky, and clouds. Select at least eight objects from this list and arrange these as *overlapping but two-dimensional* shapes on a 23 x 30.5-cm [9 x 12-inch] sheet of white paper. Paint this composition with a range of light and dark values obtained by mixing white and black tempera paint. Begin by applying the darkest value to the nearest object in your composition. Paint the remaining objects progressively lighter in value. The lightest value should be reserved for the shape located furthest back in the composition.

Lesson Two: Painting a Landscape with Gradations of Intensity to Emphasize Space

Follow the same procedure as in the previous lesson, but paint your landscape with a range of color intensities obtained by mixing two complementary colors. The highest intensity should be used to paint the nearest object. The remaining objects should be painted with progressively duller intensities. The object located furthest back in the composition should be painted with a neutral obtained by mixing equal amounts of the two complementary colors.

Chapter 12

With Sight and Feeling: Fifteenth-Century Art in the North

Jan van Eyck (*yahn* van *ike*), c. 1385-1441. Every object in his pictures, no matter how small or unimportant, was painted with utmost precision and care.

Rogier van der Weyden (roh-*jair* van der *vy*-den), 1399-1464. He wanted to show people expressing their feelings and emotions.

Hugo van der Goes (*hoo*-go van der *goose*), c. 1440-82. The figures in his most ambitious work defy the rules of logic. Was he mad, or did he have a reason for painting them this way?

Continuation of the Gothic and the International Style

The fifteenth century saw commerce and industry thrive in the North just as in Italy. This contributed to the growth of cities and a vigorous middle class. The people of this new middle class did not exhibit the same interest in the spiritual life as had their Medieval ancestors. Their thoughts were fixed on the here and now rather than on an enternal life after death. They placed their faith in a future on earth and preferred to enjoy the pleasures and material possessions of this world instead of preparing for spiritual rewards in the next.

Throughout the century, most artists in northern Europe remained true to the traditions of the Late Medieval period. This was especially true in architecture. The construction of churches and government buildings in the Gothic style lasted on into the next century. However, the progress of painting in the North during this time was more complicated.

The change from a Medieval art style to a more modern art style began later and progressed more slowly in northern Europe than it did in Italy. Northern painters showed little interest in the Classical art of ancient Greece and Rome. While Italian artists were busy studying ancient art, northern artists carried on and developed further the International Style. For this reason, their paintings continued to show a great concern for accurate and precise details. Artists spent countless hours painting a delicate design on a garment, the leaves on a tree, or the wrinkles on a face. At the same time, symbolism, which was so important in Gothic art, grew even more important. Many of the details placed in a picture had special meanings. For example, a single burning candle meant the presence of God; a dog was a symbol of loyalty; and fruit signified the innocence of humanity before the Fall in the Garden of Eden.

Development of the Oil-Painting Technique

Up to this time, European artists were accustomed to using a paint made of dry pigments, or colors, which were mixed with a binding material. Typically, this binding material was egg yolk, although gum and casein were also used. Known as *tempera,* this paint was applied to a surface, often a wooden panel, which had been prepared with a smooth coating of gesso. Gesso was a mixture of glue and a white pigment such as plaster, chalk, or white clay. This painting method produced a hard, brilliant surface, which was used for many Medieval altarpieces.

In the fifteenth and sixteenth centuries, the northern artist's concern for precision and detail was aided by the development in Flanders of a new oil-painting technique. Oil paints consisted of a mixture of dry pigments with oils and sometimes varnish. With such a mixture, artists could produce either a transparent, smooth glaze, or a thick, richly textured surface.

The change from tempera paint to oil was not a sudden one. At first, oil paints were used as transparent glazes placed over tempera underpaintings. The solid forms of figures and objects were modeled with light and dark values of tempera. Then oil glazes were applied over them, adding a transparent, glossy, and permanent surface. Later, artists abandoned the use of an underpainting and applied the oil paint directly to the canvas, often building up a thick, textured surface in the process.

One of the more important advantages of the oil-painting technique was that it slowed down the drying time. This gave artists the chance to work more leisurely. With the new technique, there was no need to hurry as the Italian artists had while working in fresco. Thus, artists had time to include more details in their pictures. Also, the layers of transparent glazes added a new brilliance to the colors so that finished paintings looked as if they were lit from within. The artist usually given credit for developing this new painting technique was the Flemish master, Jan van Eyck.

The Flemish Influence

The art of Jan van Eyck and his successors made Flanders the art center of northern Europe. Throughout the fifteenth century, the art produced by Flemish artists was a great influence on other artists in Europe, from Germany to Spain. But nowhere did it reach the lofty heights achieved by van Eyck and two other Flemish artists, Rogier van der Weyden and Hugo van der Goes.

Jan van Eyck

Jan van Eyck was mostly a product of the late Middle Ages, although he went beyond the older traditions of the International Style to introduce a new painting tradition. Like other northern artists, he did not turn his back on the International Style as did many Italian artists at this time. Instead, he used it as a starting point. As a result, his break with the past was not as sudden as that of Italian artists such as Masaccio.

Giovanni Arnolfini and His Bride

One of van Eyck's best-known works is a painting of two people standing side by side in a neat, comfortably furnished room (Figure 12.1). The room is modest in size and illuminated by a subdued light entering through an open window at the left. But who are these people and what are they doing? The man is Giovanni Arnolfini and the woman at his side is his bride. You are witnessing in this extraordinary painting their marriage ceremony.

Giovanni Arnolfini was a rich Italian merchant who lived in Flanders. Since he was from the city of Lucca, it is probable that he became wealthy by selling the beautiful silk brocade for which that town was famous. But, like many other Italians in Flanders, he no doubt sold other luxury goods as well and may have worked as a banker. When Giovanni Arnolfini decided to marry Jeanne de Chenay in 1434, he looked for the best artist available to paint a picture of their wedding. He found that artist in Jan van Eyck, who made him, his bride, and their wedding immortal.

The wedding couple solemnly faces the witnesses to the ceremony. Giovanni raises his right hand as if he is saying an oath, while his bride places her right hand in his left. Her frail body seems lost in the full, green, fur-lined dress. Her curving posture may look odd, but at that time it was considered quite fashionable to stand that way. Both figures look real, but frozen in their poses. The face of the bride is white and smooth as a china doll's. However, Giovanni's is much more natural. Given the opportunity to examine the actual painting, you would see the stubble on his chin.*

★ Enrichment Many of the details in van Eyck's painting are so small that they are not visible in reproductions. They require a close examination even when looking at the original.

How would you describe this room to a friend? Are these people well-to-do or poor? From their expressions, do they appear amused, bored, angry, or solemn? What are they doing? In what ways is this picture lifelike? Symbolism is an important feature of this painting; can you find any examples of symbolism?

Figure 12.1 Jan van Eyck. *Giovanni Arnolfini and His Bride.* 1434. Panel, 83.8 x 57.2 cm [33 x 22.5″]. Reproduced by courtesy of the Trustees of the National Gallery, London

Van Eyck's picture is rich in detail; every part of it is painted with a precision rarely equaled in art. Did you notice the mirror on the far wall of the room? In this mirror are shown the reflection of the room, the backs of Giovanni and his bride, and two other people standing in the doorway. These two people face the bride and groom and are probably the witnesses to the exchange of vows. Above the mirror is a Latin inscription that reads, "Jan van Eyck was here." Could van Eyck be one of those witnesses seen in the mirror? What do you think?

Numerous symbols can be found in van Eyck's painting. The couple have removed their shoes as a sign that they are standing on holy ground. It is holy because of the blessed event taking place there. The burning candle in the chandelier tells you that God is present at this solemn ceremony, while the little dog represents the loyalty which the husband and wife pledge to each other. Innocence is suggested by the fruit on the table and window sill.

Criticism

Are there many details in this work? Has it been organized to direct your attention to a particular spot? What do you find at this spot? How has hue been used to create the illusion of deep space? When judging this work, did you refer more to its literal qualities or its expressive qualities?

Figure 12.2   Jan van Eyck. *Adoration of the Lamb* (with detail), central panel from the *Ghent Altarpiece.* 1432. St. Bavo, Ghent, Belgium

Detail of 12.2, Copyright A.C.L. Brussels

Adoration of the Lamb

Van Eyck's painting of the *Adoration of the Lamb* (Figure 12.2) is the central lower panel of a large (4.4 × 3.4 m [14.5 × 11 feet]) altarpiece containing twelve panels.★ It shows angels, saints, and earthly worshipers coming from all directions through a green valley toward a sacrificial altar. A lamb, one of the symbols of Christ, stands on this altar. Blood from the lamb flows into a

★ Enrichment Known as the Ghent Altarpiece, this work by van Eyck was involved in one of the most famous art thefts of the twentieth century. Two panels from this altarpiece were stolen from the Church of Saint Bavo in Ghent in 1934. Eventually the thief returned one of the panels along with a note demanding a huge ransom for the second panel. However, he was apprehended and confessed to the crime. Unfortunately, he died of a heart attack before he could reveal the location of the missing panel. The whereabouts of this panel remains a mystery to this day.

chalice. In the foreground is a fountain from which flows the pure water of eternal life. Most likely this painting was inspired by a passage from the Bible which refers to Christ as the Paschal, or sacrificial, Lamb. The picture tells you that eternal salvation is possible for all because of Christ's willingness to sacrifice His life on the Cross. His death made possible the water of eternal salvation received by the faithful at baptism

The scene is carefully organized so that the lamb is the obvious center of interest. The placement of the angels kneeling at the altar and the prophets and other worshipers around the fountain serves to lead your eye to this center of interest. Other groups of saints and worshipers move toward it from each of the four corners of the painting.

Like Masaccio, van Eyck controls the flow of light and uses atmospheric perspective to create the illusion of deep space in his work. However, unlike that in Masaccio's work, the light in van Eyck's painting is crystal clear. It allows you to see perfectly the color, texture, and shape of every object. Van Eyck was less interested in telling the viewer how he felt about things. Instead, he took pride in demonstrating his ability to see and pass on to others the wonders he discovered in the world around him.

The details in van Eyck's picture are painted with extraordinary care. The soft texture of hair, the glitter and luster of precious jewels, and the richness of brocade are all painted with the same concern for precision. Every object, no matter how small or insignificant, is given equal importance. This attention to detail enabled van Eyck to create a special kind of realism—a realism in which the color, shape, and texture of every object were painted only after long study.

Even with all the advantages of modern science, it is still not known how van Eyck was able to achieve many of his effects. Somehow, by combining a study of nature with a sensitive use of light and color, he was able to produce paintings which others admired but could not duplicate. No painter has ever been able to match van Eyck's marvelous precision and glowing color.

Comparison with Masaccio

Earlier you studied Masaccio's painting of *The Tribute Money* (Figure 11.3, page 184). It was painted at about the same time as van Eyck's *Adoration of the Lamb*. When you compare these two works, you should be able to see some important differences. These differences show how Flemish paintings of the early fifteenth century differed from Italian paintings of the same time. Look again at the paintings by these two artists. Then decide which of the statements in Figure 12.3 apply to van Eyck and which to Masaccio.

The Combining of Emotionalism and Realism

Gradually, northern fifteenth-century art developed into a style that combined the realism of Jan van Eyck with the emotionalism and attention to design found in works done during the late Gothic period. This style is best seen in the works of Rogier van der Weyden.

Rogier van der Weyden

Jan van Eyck had been concerned with painting every detail with careful precision. Rogier van der Weyden continued in this tradition, but also added some new ideas of his own.

Figure 12.3

COMPARISON OF VAN EYCK AND MASACCIO

1. This artist painted his scenes in broad, simple shapes.

2. This artist used the International Style as a starting point, and his work still shows a strong resemblance to that earlier style.

3. This artist's concern for detail was made possible by the development of the oil-painting technique.

4. This artist's figures look like three-dimensional sculptures.

5. This artist's colors seem to glow as if illuminated from within.

6. This artist's work is based on a fresco tradition.

7. This artist's work shows that he had great patience when observing and copying nature.

8. This artist's works are reminders of the paintings done by Giotto a century before.

9. This artist used linear perspective to help create the illusion of deep space in his paintings.

10. This artist's works are noted for their bold outlines and for shapes that are modeled in light and dark.

Criticism

How many figures are in this picture? Even with all these figures, does it seem too crowded? How are the figures made to look lifelike? Are the faces the same, or are they different? Do the facial expressions and gestures differ, or are they all alike? Can you find any repeated, curved axis lines? Why are these lines important to this composition? How does the background force you to keep looking at the figures?

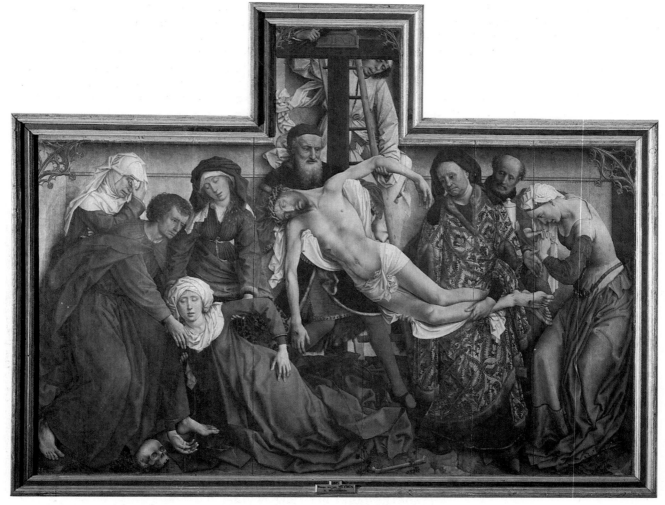

Figure 12.4 Rogier van der Weyden. *Descent from the Cross.* c. 1435. Panel, approx. 2.2 x 2.6 m [7′ 2⅝″ x 8′ 7⅛″]. The Prado, Madrid.

Descent from the Cross

In Rogier's painting of the *Descent from the Cross* (Figure 12.4), you will see more emotion and a greater concern for organization than you will find in van Eyck's pictures. In this instance, organization is achieved through use of repeating curved axis lines. Observe how the two figures at each side of the picture bend inward and direct your attention to Christ and His mother. In the center of the picture, Christ's lifeless body forms an "S" curve, which is repeated in the curve of His fainting mother. Unlike van Eyck, Rogier made no attempt to create a deep space. Space is restricted as if to compress the action across the surface of the painting. Rogier managed to group ten figures in this shallow space without making them seem crowded. By placing these figures on a narrow stage and eliminating a landscape behind, he forces you to focus your attention on the drama of Christ's removal from the Cross. The figures and the action are brought very close to you, forcing you to take in every detail. This enables you to see that the faces clearly differ from one another just as the faces of real people do. Every hair, every variation of skin color and texture, and every fold of drapery is painted in with care.

But Rogier does not stop there. Just as much attention is given to the emotions exhibited by the different facial expressions and gestures. No two people react in the same way. In fact, the entire work is a carefully designed and forceful grouping of these different emotional reactions to Christ's death. Yet, one of the most touching features is also one of the easiest to miss. The space between the two hands—Christ's right and Mary's left—suggests the void between the living and the dead. It may seem like a minor point, but once you notice those hands, so close and yet so far apart, you are not likely to forget them or their meaning.

Portrait of a Lady

Rogier van der Weyden was a very popular artist, and many people wanted their portraits painted by him. One of those people was a young woman, unknown to us today, whose portrait (Figure 12.5) Rogier painted some twenty years after the *Descent from the Cross*. The woman's face, framed by a white, starched headdress, stands out boldly against a dark background. Light flows evenly over it, revealing a pleasant, but not beautiful, woman. The headdress is thin and transparent, allowing you to see the line of her shoulder and the back of a chair or sofa at the left. Her other shoulder is also seen through the headdress at the right.

Criticism

This picture contains sharp and subtle contour lines—can you find examples of each? What has been done to make this face stand out? What does this picture tell you about this woman's personality? Do you think she was wealthy or poor? What makes you think so? What, in your opinion, is the most impressive thing about this portrait?

Figure 12.5   Rogier van der Weyden. *Portrait of a Lady*. c. 1455. Approx. 37 x 27 cm [14½ x 10¾″]. The National Gallery of Art, Washington, D.C. Andrew W. Mellon Collection, 1937

You might not think so at first, but this is a remarkable portrait. Look at it closely. Now, what does this painting tell you about the *personality* of the woman? Do you think she was loud, outgoing, perhaps even rude? Or was she quiet, shy, and devout? Does she appear to be bold and active, or frail and reserved? Rogier provided you with clues to answer questions like these. The lowered eyes, tightly locked fingers, and frail build all suggest a quiet dignity. The young woman is lost in thought, her clasped hands seemingly resting on the frame. She must have been wealthy but does not flaunt her good fortune. A gold belt buckle and rings are the only signs of luxury. Even though it is not known who the woman was, Rogier has left us with a vivid impression of the kind of person she must have been.

Rogier's Influence

Rogier van der Weyden performed a valuable service by preserving the Gothic concerns for good design and vivid emotion. Those concerns could have been lost in the rush to use van Eyck's new oil-painting technique to produce highly detailed pictures. But Rogier's paintings set an example for other artists. When he died in 1464 after being the most famous painter in Flanders for thirty years, his influence was second to none outside Italy.

Hugo van der Goes

One of the artists who continued in the direction taken by Rogier was Hugo van der Goes. Hugo combined the emotionalism of Rogier with the realistic detail of Jan

---

History

How is this work similar to works created by Jan van Eyck and Rogier van der Weyden? How does it differ? What are the major differences between this painting and one completed by Sandro Botticelli in Italy at about the same time? What has the artist done to make you feel as though you are a witness to this event? Point to things in the picture that make it seem as if you are seeing it as a dream or a vision. Identify some symbols in this work and explain their meaning.

Figure 12.6   Hugo van der Goes. *The Adoration of the Shepherds,* central panel of the *Portinari Altarpiece.* c. 1476. Approx. 2.5 x 3 m [8′ 3″ x 10′]. Galleria degli Uffizi, Florence [Photo Alinari]

van Eyck. In addition, he made his own unique contribution: he was not afraid to alter or distort nature if it would add to the emotional impact of his picture.

Hugo van der Goes rose to fame as an artist in Bruges, one of the wealthiest cities in Flanders. At the peak of his popularity and while he was still a young man, he entered a monastery near Brussels where he remained the rest of his life. However, he did not retire to a strict life of prayer and meditation when he entered the monastery. Apparently, he was regarded as something of a celebrity and enjoyed special favors. He continued to work as a painter and enjoyed a great many luxuries. But he suffered from fits of depression and thought that he was destined to everlasting punishment in the next world because of his sinful ways. Hugo van der Goes, the unhappy genius, died in 1482, seven years after entering the monastery.

The Portinari Altarpiece

Hugo's most ambitious work was an altarpiece completed in 1476 for the Italian representative of the Medici bank in Bruges. This huge work is known as the "Portinari Altarpiece" after the name of this banker. It is especially important because it was sent to Florence soon after it was completed. There it was a great influence on late-fifteenth-century Italian artists who were deeply impressed by Hugo's ability to portray human character and feeling.

Unlike van Eyck, Hugo decided not to organize the space in his picture so that it would look real. Instead, he took liberties with space to increase the emotional appeal of his picture. In the central panel of his altarpiece showing *The Adoration of the Shepherds* (Figure 12.6), he tipped the floor of the stable upward. This not only gives you a better view but makes you feel as though you are an on-the-spot witness to the event. But a clear view of Hugo's version of the Nativity leads to some strange discoveries. Where is the joy and gladness usually associated with the birth of Christ? Joseph and Mary both seem strangely withdrawn, even sad. Odd behavior for such a joyous event. Could it be that they are thinking ahead to the suffering in store for their son? Of course, you cannot know for sure what Joseph and Mary are thinking, but one thing is certain: Hugo's picture succeeds in arousing your curiosity. He makes it difficult for you not to think ahead in time to the tragic events awaiting the Christ Child.

More strange discoveries await you in Hugo's painting. For example, did you notice the unusual differences in the sizes of the figures? The angels closest to you, for example, should be much larger than the figures further back in space. Instead they look much smaller. Also, the three shepherds at the right are about the

same size as Mary even though they are further away. It is unlikely that these differences in size are due to this artist's lack of skill. There must be some other explanation. Could Hugo have been trying to paint this scene as if he were seeing it in a dream or a vision? This is a possibility, since the figures in a dream would not have to follow the rules of logic. Large and small figures could be placed next to each other or could even float about in space.

One of the most fascinating things about Hugo's painting is his portrayal of the three shepherds. (Figure 12.7). More than anything else, their behavior and expressions set this painting apart from countless other Nativity scenes produced since the Early Christian period. It was Hugo's painting of these shepherds that later caused so much excitement among the Italian artists who saw this picture. They had never seen figures painted like this before. Hugo's shepherds are not saints, or angels, or elegant noblemen. They are ragged, coarse peasants from the lowest level of society. They represent the great masses of common people in the world who are as interested in salvation as anyone else.

History

Why do you think the artist's treatment of these three shepherds caused much excitement among the Italian artists who saw this painting? Describe the appearance, expressions, and actions of these figures. How do they set this work apart from earlier pictures of the same event?

Figure 12.7   Hugo van der Goes. *The Adoration of the Shepherds,* detail

What event is shown in this Medieval relief carving? Can you identify the animals in the relief? What is each animal doing? How do their actions reflect the different ways people reacted to this important religious event?

Figure 12.8   Nativity, relief carving, the Village Church, Ujue, Spain. Eleventh century

Their crudeness, curiosity, and blind faith contrasts with the quiet dignity and grace of the adoring angels. One of the kneeling shepherds clasps his hands reverently, while another spreads his in wonder. Meanwhile, the standing shepherd presses forward to peer over their heads, his mouth open in amazement. In different ways, each of these shepherds shows his surprise at finding himself witnessing a grand and glorious event. But it is an event they cannot fully understand. With these poor, rough shepherds, Hugo presents a new kind of piety. It is a piety expressed by the ordinary uneducated people of the world, a piety based on blind faith rather than on knowledge and understanding.

In the manner of Jan van Eyck, the Portinari Altarpiece is enriched by the addition of symbols. A sheaf of wheat in the foreground symbolizes the bread of the Eucharist. The bouquets of iris and columbine are traditional symbols for the sorrows of Mary. And the shoe at the left? You will recall the same symbol in van Eyck's *Giovanni Arnolfini and His Bride*. It is a reminder of God's words to Moses from a burning bush on Mount Sinai: ". . . put off your shoes from your feet, for the place on which you are standing is holy ground."

The donkey and the ox standing behind the manger also had a symbolic meaning in this painting. In Medieval times these two animals were often used to illustrate the different ways in which people reacted to Christ. The donkey symbolized those who failed to recognize Christ as the Savior, while the ox represented those who did. In earlier works, the unconcerned donkey was sometimes shown eating or, at other times, even tugging on the swaddling clothes of the Christ Child. It was either too ignorant or too stupid to understand the meaning of Christ's birth. In contrast, the enlightened ox was frequently shown kneeling in adoration before the Child. In this painting, the donkey is idly eating the straw in the manger, while the ox is solemnly surveying the miracle of Christ's birth.

The End of a Period
The art of Hugo van der Goes marks the end of a period. The innovations of Jan van Eyck and Rogier van der Weyden began to lose ground by the end of the fifteenth century. They were replaced by new ideas spreading northward from Renaissance Italy.

ANSWERS TO STATEMENTS ON PAGE 213:

1. Masaccio	6. Masaccio
2. van Eyck	7. van Eyck
3. van Eyck	8. Masaccio
4. Masaccio	9. Masaccio
5. van Eyck	10. Masaccio

Studio Experiences

Lesson One: Expanding Detail Drawing

Northern Renaissance artists showed a concern for details and precision in their paintings. This concern is evident in the works of Jan van Eyck (Figures 12.1 and 12.2) and Rogier van der Weyden (Figures 12.4 and 12.5). Select an interesting and intricate object as the subject for a detailed and precise pencil drawing. Such items as an old laced boot, a kerosene lantern, or a complex machine part will do very well. Beginning at or near the center of a sheet of 23 x 30.5-cm [9 x 12-inch] white paper, draw a part of your object as accurately as possible. Continue to add details as you expand your drawing until it reaches all four edges of the paper. Use varied and complex lines and shapes to show the intricate nature of your subject matter. You may also wish to use contrasts and gradations of value for added realism.

Lesson Two: Designing a Visual Symbol

Jan van Eyck, Hugo van der Goes, and other northern Renaissance artists often included symbols in their religious paintings. Symbols are still used today, but for different reasons. Contemporary companies often use symbols to establish their corporate image. Assume that you have been commissioned to design a symbol for an important organization such as The Society to Save America's Trees or The Agency to Eliminate Unemployment. (Or you may wish to create your own fictitious company.) The symbol is to be unique and easily interpreted by the public. Anyone seeing it must be able to tell immediately what the symbol stands for. Prepare several pencil sketches for this symbol. Select the best of these and continue to refine them until one emerges as the most successful. Complete a final version of this symbol in India ink. Use simplified shapes and bold contrasts of value as a way of drawing attention to your symbol.

Chapter 13

Crisis and Transition: Art of the Sixteenth Century

Artists you will meet in this chapter

Giorgione da Castelfranco (jor-*joh*-nay da cah-stell-*frank*-oh), 1478-1510. He was one of the first European painters to emphasize the importance of the landscape in his pictures.

Titian (*tish*-un), c. 1488-1576. He was nearly as famous during his long lifetime as the great Michelangelo.

Parmigianino (par-mi-jah-*nee*-noh), 1503-40. His famous painting of the Madonna and Child was like a riddle with many different solutions. Which one will you choose?

Tintoretto (tin-toe-*reh*-toe), 1518-94. In his paintings he tried to capture the excitement of an event—and make you a part of it.

El Greco (el *greh*-koh), 1541-1614. He succeeded in making his paintings of saints and martyrs look supernatural.

Matthias Grünewald (mah-*tee*-ahs *green*-eh-valt), c. 1480-1528. He painted powerful visual sermons that will stir your emotions.

Albrecht Dürer (*ahl*-brecht *dur*-er), 1471-1528. His curiosity was as great as Leonardo's. During a journey to satisfy that curiosity, he died.

Hieronymus Bosch (heer-*ahn*-ni-mus *bosh*), c. 1450-1516. His pictures told stories on the subject of good and evil, but they contained traces of humor as well.

Pieter Bruegel (*pee*-ter *bree*-gl), c. 1525-69. One of his paintings stands as a warning to those who blindly follow the lead of others.

Hans Holbein (hans *hole*-bine), 1497-1543. He painted the portraits of three women who married King Henry VIII.

The Art of Venice

Artists in Florence and Rome looked to the Classical monuments of Greece and Rome, which they still saw around them, for much of their inspiration. Venetian artists, lacking these monuments close by, turned to other sources of inspiration. One of the most important of these sources was their beautiful and unique island city.

Venice could be described then, as now, as a city of constantly changing lights and reflections. On clear days, brilliant sunlight poured down on colorful buildings which were mirrored in the rippling waters of its famous canals.* These reflections softened contours, lessened the contrast between lights and darks, and broke up shapes into patches of shimmering color. But on overcast days, colors and shapes were dimmer and seemed to melt in a silvery mist. Artists had only to look around them as they made their way down the streets and canals of Venice to discover new ways of making their painted forms glow with color.

Centuries of close contact with the East had also left their mark upon the appearance of Venice. The dazzling mosaics that decorated Venetian churches; the different-colored buildings; and the Venetians' pervading love of color, light, and texture can be traced to the Byzantine art style of the East. The Byzantine influence on Venetian art was far different from that of Classical Greece and Rome on the Renaissance cities of Florence and Rome. Unlike their Classical counterparts, Byzantine artists were not mainly interested in portraying a world of solid bodies and objects existing in space. Instead, they sought to present a world of carefully designed surfaces and brilliant colors. Byzantine art did not try to mirror the present world. It wanted to offer a glimpse of the next.

Venetian artists skillfully adapted the Byzantine use of color, light, and texture to their own painting. But at the same time, they were not blind to the new Renaissance concern for reality that characterized the art of Florence and Rome. This concern for reality, originating in Florence, had spread throughout Italy. It eventually reached Venice near the close of the fifteenth century. When it did, it touched off a revolution in painting. Venetian artists successfully combined the best of the Byzantine with the best of the Renaissance. This produced the greatest school of color and pure painting that Europe has seen.

Giorgione

One of the first great Venetian masters was Giorgione da Castelfranco, who died of the plague while he was still in his early thirties. Unfortunately, very little is known about him. Art experts can point to no more than a handful of pictures that were definitely painted by him. These reveal that he was among the first artists in Europe to place importance on the landscape. Before, artists had used the landscape to fill in the spaces around their figures. Giorgione used it to create a mood or feeling in his paintings.

Giorgione also used oil paint to add a new richness to his colors.* This medium was more suited to the Venetian taste than the cold, pale frescoes of Florence and Rome. For one thing, it was more vivid and allowed the artist to create delicate changes in hue, intensity, and value. Further, the artist could linger over his painting to produce a glowing effect with colors that stayed wet and workable for days. Giorgione, inspired by his radiant Venetian surroundings, eagerly used this new medium to make his pictures glow. He avoided hard edges and lines and bathed his subjects in a soft, golden light.

★ **Enrichment** Cut in two by the twisting Grand Canal, the island city of Venice is crisscrossed by some 170 smaller canals.

★ **Enrichment** A painter from Sicily named Antonello da Messina is said to have brought the Flemish secret of oil painting to Italy. However, this story, recounted by Vasari, is questioned today by scholars cross-checking dates and events.

Criticism

How many people are in this painting? What is each one doing? How are the two seated men dressed? What does their clothing tell you about them? Are the hues intense or dull? Are the contour lines sharp or blurred? How is color used to draw your attention to the center of the composition? Point to places where value gradation is found. What mood or feeling does this picture communicate to you?

Figure 13.1   Giorgione (sometimes attributed to Titian). *The Concert.* c. 1508. Oil on canvas, approx. 1 x 1.4 m [43 x 54″]. The Louvre, Paris. [Cliché des Musées Nationaux, Paris]

The Concert

One of Giorgione's most beautiful and haunting paintings is *The Concert* (Figure 13.1).★ No matter how long you study it, you will still find it difficult to determine exactly what is going on in this picture. This adds to its charm and mystery and keeps luring you back for another look, another guess about its meaning. And as you search for a meaning, you will find yourself falling under the spell of the work's mood, or feeling. It is this

★ Enrichment This painting has had several other names including *Pastoral Symphony, Fountain of Love,* and *Country Feast.* Some scholars today even believe that it was the work of two artists, Giorgione and Titian, who may even have worked on the painting at the same time. Others feel it may even have been painted by Titian working alone.

mood, rather than the uncertain meaning, that you will remember most about this work. It is a calm, gentle mood, although there is a touch of sadness here as well . . .

On a peaceful summer day, two weary travelers meet and pass some time together in the lengthening shadows alongside the road. They may be strangers coming from different backgrounds and going in different directions. One is dressed simply and is barefoot. He listens intently as the second, dressed in rich garments, plays a lute. As for the two women, they are a mystery. Perhaps they are not flesh and blood at all, but exist only in the minds of the two young men. Their imaginary images may have been suggested by the tune being strummed gently on the lute. Perhaps in a few moments the song will end, and they will vanish. Then the two men will rise, bid each other a reluctant good-bye and go their separate ways. It will signal the end of a rare, enchanted moment that can never be repeated.

Giorgione's scene appears to glow in the warm rays of a setting sun. The edges of his figures are blurred as though a light mist is settling around them. This mist surrounds and blends together the green and blue shadows and softens the red accents of a cloak and a hat. It also dulls the other colors found further back in space. Giorgione's treatment of the landscape and his use of color enabled him to create a picture that is as haunting as the strains of an unforgettable melody. It may be just such a melody that the young traveler plays on his lute.

Titian

Giorgione's approach to painting was carried on after his untimely death by another Venetian artist, Titian.★ Titian's career reportedly started when, as a child, he painted a Madonna on the wall of his father's house with the juice of flowers or fruit. Unlike Giorgione,

---

★ **Enrichment** Titian is the anglicized version of this artist's real name, which was Tiziano Vecelli. He was said to have been named for a saint who, as a bishop, had served in a chapel that later belonged to the Vecelli family. Because of this, Tiziano was a rather common name in the Vecelli family.

Titian lived a long life. He was almost one hundred years old when he died, not of old age as you might expect, but of the plague. A nobleman's artist, Titian's patrons included Lucrezia Borgia, the Duchess of Farrara; Pope Paul III; and the Emperor Charles V, who made Titian a knight and a count. According to Vasari, there was hardly a noble of high rank, scarcely a prince or lady of great name, whose portrait was not painted by Titian.

The Entombment

From Giorgione, Titian learned how to use landscape to set a mood. He also learned to use oil paints to make works that were rich in color and texture. However, while Giorgione's figures always seem to be inactive —sleeping, dreaming, or waiting—Titian's are wide awake, alert, and active. Observe how the figures in his painting of *The Entombment* (Figure 13.2) are more powerfully built and more expressive than those of Giorgione. When Titian combined Giorgione's lighting and color with these sturdy figures, he created a highly emotional scene. The mourners carrying the crucified Christ to His tomb turn their eyes to Him and lean forward under the weight of the lifeless body. This helps to direct your gaze to Christ between them. The rapidly fading light of day bathes the scene in a mellow glow. It heralds the approach of night and accents the despair of the figures in this tragic scene.

History

In what ways are Titian's paintings similar to those of Giorgione? How are they different? Why is Titian often referred to as a nobleman's artist? Although he painted religious subjects like this, Titian is best known for another kind of painting. What is it? Why do you think Titian is regarded as one of the greatest painters in history? Do you agree with that assessment? Why or why not?

Figure 13.2 Titian. *The Entombment.* **c. 1525. The Louvre, Paris. [Cliché des Musées Nationaux, Paris]**

Where does the curving row of buttons lead your eye? Would you describe this man as gentle and content, or powerful and stern? On what do you base your opinion? Is this a successful work of art? Why or why not?

Figure 13.3   Titian. *Doge Andrea Gritti.* **c. 1540. Oil on canvas, approx. 1.3 x 1 m [52½ x 40⅝"]. The National Gallery of Art, Washington, D.C. Samuel H. Kress Collection, 1961**

Curiously, Titian placed the head and face of Christ in deep shadow. Why do you suppose he would do this with the most important person in the painting? Before trying to answer this question, you might ask yourself if you have seen this done before. Look again at Giorgione's painting of *The Concert* and you will find that the faces of the two young travelers also are placed in shadow. Both artists used this technique to arouse your curiosity and get you involved with their paintings. They challenge you to use your imagination to complete the most important part of their pictures—the faces of the main characters.

Doge Andrea Gritti

Titian's greatest fame was as a painter of portraits. One of his most forceful was of Andrea Gritti, the doge, or ruler, of Venice (Figure 13.3). Gritti ruled during troubled times when Venice was involved in a series of wars and conflicts. During this period, Venetian sea power was the only barrier between threatening Muhammaden invaders and Christian Europe. In spite of his advanced age (he was over eighty years old when Titian painted him), Gritti took an active role in the fighting. It was this fierce determination and power that Titian captured in his portrait. The doge is shown as if he is about to burst from the frame. A curving row of buttons curls up the robe leading to the stern, defiant face. Titian leaves no doubt that this was a fierce, iron-willed leader. But if the face somehow fails to communicate that impression to you, look at the powerful right hand. It was modeled after the hand on Michelangelo's heroic statue of *Moses* (Figure 11.20, page 203). Titian knew of this hand even though he did not visit Rome until about five years after completing his picture of the doge. A cast had been made of it and brought to Venice by a sculptor named Jacopo Sansovino. Titian realized that such a hand could communicate as well as any facial expression. For this reason, he enlarged it and showed it clutching the heavy robe. It is neither delicate nor relaxed, but as strong and tense as the man.

Titian's Enduring Fame

All the important people of his day were eager to have their portraits painted by Titian. As a result, he lived like a prince, traveling far and wide to complete his commissions, accompanied by numerous servants, admirers, and students. It was said that after Titian had finished his third portrait of Charles V, the Emperor exclaimed, "This is the third time I have triumphed over death!" Titian's many great paintings assured his own victory over death. In his lifetime he became nearly as famous as the legendary Michelangelo, and his fame has not lessened over the centuries. In the nineteenth century, the great French painter Delacroix said of him, "If one were to live for 120 years, one would prefer Titian to everything." His talents are no less admired today. Artists, historians, and critics without exception list Titian among the greatest painters of all time.

Mannerism

Artists like Giorgione and Titian made Venice a great art center that rivaled and then surpassed Florence and Rome. In Rome, art suffered a decline. Its artists struggled to find new avenues of expression in the vacuum left by the passing of Leonardo, Michelangelo, and Raphael. The period in which this struggle took place is referred to as the Mannerist period.

Today, *Mannerism* is thought of as a deliberate revolt by artists against the goals of the Renaissance. But why would Mannerist artists turn against the art of the Renaissance? To answer this question you must compare the Italy in which the Renaissance masters lived with the Italy in which Mannerist artists lived.

When Raphael painted the *Alba Madonna* around 1510, Italy was at peace and the Church continued to be the unchallenged seat of authority. Most people were still absorbed in seeking eternal salvation and were certain that the Church would help them toward this goal. It was a period of confidence and hope, and this was reflected in the artworks that were created. Artists like Raphael produced works that were carefully thought out, balanced, and soothing. But then a series of events took place that shook the confidence and replaced the hope with uncertainty. Within the space of a few decades, the religious unity of Western Christendom was shattered. Having endured almost without challenge for centuries, it was destroyed in 1517 by Martin Luther and the Protestant Reformation. This movement, along with the French invasion of Italy in 1524 and the sack of Rome in 1527, brought about an era of tension and disorder. It was in this setting that Mannerist art was born and matured.

Mannerism was an effort by artists to show through their art what was going on in their minds during this period of crisis. An art of balance and harmony could hardly be used to express the instability and tension around them. Thus, where the art of the Renaissance tried to achieve balance, Mannerism preferred imbalance. The calm order found in works like the *Alba Madonna* was replaced by a restlessness. Mannerism was a nervous art, created in and mirroring a world filled with confusion. Its artists painted the human figure in strange new ways, twisting it into impossible poses and stretching it to unreal proportions. Gone was the three-dimensional fullness sought by Masaccio, Michelangelo, and other Renaissance artists. Mannerist artists preferred figures that were slender, elegant, and graceful. Gradually, these figures began to look less natural and more supernatural.

Parmigianino

This new style is evident in the work of Francesco Mazzola, called Il Parmigianino, who was among the first generation of Mannerists in Rome. Born in Parma, Parmigianino went to Rome four years after Raphael's death. There he found artists working in a number of different styles. His own very personal art style developed as he took and combined features found in the work of other artists.

Criticism

Look closely at the woman and child. What unusual features can you find in this woman? How would you describe the child and his position on the woman's lap? How many other figures are in the picture? What are they doing? Do you find anything surprising about these figures? If so, what? Is this an indoor or an outdoor scene? How can you tell? Do you think all the unusual things in this work were done intentionally, or is this simply a poor painting? Defend your answer. How does this picture make you feel—calm and relaxed, or confused and tense?

Figure 13.4 Parmigianino. *The Madonna with the Long Neck.* c. 1535. Oil on panel, approx. 2.2 x 1.3 m [85 x 52"]. Galleria degli Uffizi, Florence. [Photo Alinari]

The Madonna with the Long Neck

After the sack of Rome in 1527, Parmigianino fled to Bologna, but after several years returned to his native Parma. It was there that he painted his best-known work, *The Madonna with the Long Neck* (Figure 13.4). You will not get too far into a description of this painting before a number of disturbing questions arise. For one thing, is this an interior or an exterior setting? It is difficult to say for certain because the drapery at the left and the columns at the right suggest a background that is both interior and exterior. And what purpose do the columns serve? It seems as if some confused builder went to a great deal of trouble to construct this row of tall, slender columns and then forgot why and abandoned the whole project. Now look at the unusual figures of the Madonna and Christ Child. The Madonna is seen from a low vantage point and seems to be sitting, although no throne or chair is indicated. She is enormous and towers over the other figures in the picture even though she is seated and they are standing. If this were not enough, she also has a small head, long neck, wide hips and long legs that taper down to small, delicate feet. It looks as if she is about to stand, and this places the child on her lap in real danger. Notice how the baby already seems to be slipping from the mother's lap. Curiously, the mother shows no concern. Her eyes remain half-closed and she continues to look content and quite pleased with herself.

It is unlikely that you would describe the Christ Child as robust and full of life. Actually, the Child looks lifeless; His flesh is pale and rubbery, and His proportions are unnatural. The Madonna's left hand conceals the Child's neck, and this, coupled with the position of the head, makes it look as if the head is not attached to the body. Crowding in tightly at the left side of the picture are a number of figures who have come to admire and worship the Christ Child. However, they pay little attention to Him at all. Instead, they look about in all directions—one even stares out of the picture directly at you.

Before leaving this crowded group of figures, look at the leg in the left corner. To whom does this leg belong? You might be inclined to say that it belongs to the figure with the unusual urn who looks up toward the Madonna. But, if this is his leg, he is indeed unfortunate because he would have almost no waist at all and his leg would be attached to his body at a most unusual place.

The foreground space occupied by the Madonna and other figures is crowded; everyone seems jammed together here. But when your gaze moves to the right side of the picture, you plunge into a deep background where you encounter the strange row of columns and the small figure of a man reading from a scroll. The size of this man indicates that he is far back in space, but there is no way of determining the distance between him and the foreground figures. Who is this man and what is he doing? Perhaps he is a prophet reading from ancient documents which prophesied the birth of Christ. It is impossible to be certain since the artist gives no clues to his identity. Nor do you know to whom he is directing his reading—the frame of the painting cuts his audience off from view.

The questions do not stop after you have described and analyzed Parmigianino's painting. They continue as you move on into interpretation. Is it just an accident that the Christ Child looks lifeless, or that His arms are outstretched in the same position He would take later on the Cross? Could the mother be a symbol of the Church? After all, it was common to refer to the Church as the spiritual mother to all. But why does she seem so unconcerned even though her child seems to be slipping from her grasp? And then, why are all those people crowding in at the left—at first you might think that they are only interested in catching a glimpse of the Child, but only one is looking at Him. The painting dares you to make sense out of all this. What is Parmigianino trying to say? Could he be criticizing the Church and the people for their growing worldliness? Was he trying to say that they were becoming so concerned with their own well-being that they had forgotten the sacrifices made for them by Christ? Of course, you can never know for certain what Parmigianino meant by this picture. Only one thing is clear: he has left you with the pieces of an unforgettable puzzle. You can put these pieces together to arrive at many different solutions, but you will never know if any one of them is right. Parmigianino's painting raises a great many questions and offers very few answers. No doubt, that is exactly what it was intended to do.

In many ways, Parmigianino's life was as unusual as his painting. According to Vasari, toward the end of his short life (he died when he was thirty-seven years old), Parmigianino changed. He let his hair and beard grow, turned his back on the world, and became an almost savage wild man.

Tintoretto

Mannerism established itself later in Venice than in other parts of Italy. The best-known Venetian artist to work in this style was Tintoretto. He was able to combine the goals of Mannerism with a Venetian love of color.

Tintoretto's real name was Jacopo Robusti, but since he was the son of a dyer he became known as "Tintoretto," the Italian word for "Little Dyer." He was born, lived, and worked all his life in Venice. He taught himself to paint by copying sculptures and the works of other artists. Eventually he developed a style that featured quick, short brushstrokes and a dramatic use of light.

Presentation of the Virgin

When you look at Tintoretto's painting of the *Presentation of the Virgin* (Figure 13.5), you will see some of the qualities that make it a Mannerist work. Among these are the elongated figures with their dramatic gestures, the odd perspective, and the strange, uneven light that touches some parts of the picture and leaves other parts in deep shadow. Almost everyone in the picture is watching the young Mary as she climbs solemnly up the stairs to the temple. The woman in the foreground points to the small figure of Mary silhouetted against a blue sky. This woman's gesture is important because without it you might not notice Mary at all. Mary may be the most important person in the picture, but Tintoretto made her look small and unimportant. He may have done this because he wanted you to become actively involved in finding her.

Tintoretto is interested in doing more than merely describing another event in the life of the Virgin. He tries to capture the excitement of the event and make you a part of it. He wants you to feel as though you are actually there, to put yourself on the stairs to the temple. Imagine how it would be . . .

Like the men resting in the shade to your left, you stop what you are doing and look upward. A young girl has neared the top of the stairs and is being greeted by the high priest. Who is she? What is so special about her? The little girl in front of you may be asking the same questions of her mother. You cannot hear the mother's reply but notice that she urges her daughter forward and points upward. Suddenly an old man at your left breaks from the shadows to call others to witness the event. Truly something important is going on here. Only a woman seated at your right seems unmoved and uninterested, but her lack of concern only underlines the excitement exhibited by everyone else around you. It is impossible for you not to become excited as well, and you begin to climb rapidly up the steps. If there is something special about that girl at the top of the stairs, you are determined to learn what it is.

Criticism

Can you find the main character in this picture? What clues did you use to find this character? Is this a symmetrically balanced composition? How would you interpret the gesture of the woman at the bottom center—casual, excited, or tragic? How do her actions differ from those of the seated woman at the right?

Figure 13.5   Tintoretto. *Presentation of the Virgin.* **c. 1550. Church of Santa Maria dell' Orto, Venice. [Photo Alinari]**

Huge and simple, you would have to walk about 16 km [10 miles] to visit every room in this palace built for King Philip II of Spain. What part did this king and this palace play in luring El Greco to Spain?

Figure 13.6   The Escorial, east façade. Near Madrid. 1563-84

El Greco

Highly emotional religious pictures by Mannerists like Tintoretto were welcomed by the Church during this troubled period. The Church was placing a renewed emphasis on the spiritual in order to counter the Reformation.

Art could aid this effort by working on the emotions of the people, reminding them that heaven awaited those who followed the Church's teachings. Nowhere was this more evident than in Spain. It is there that you will find the last and most remarkable of the Mannerist artists, El Greco.

El Greco's story ends in Spain, but it begins in Crete, the Greek island where he was born and christened Domenico Theotocopoulos.★ Around the middle of the sixteenth century, he left Crete to continue his art studies in Venice. There he came under the influence of Titian and Tintoretto. From Titian the young artist learned how to use contrasts of light and dark to heighten the drama in his works. Tintoretto taught him to add an active movement to his compositions. El Greco's curious elongated treatment of the human figure may also have been inspired by Tintoretto.★

After spending some ten years in Venice, El Greco moved to Rome where he became familiar with the work of Michelangelo. However, the work of that great genius failed to overwhelm El Greco. He claimed that if Michelangelo's *Last Judgment* were to vanish from the Sistine Chapel he could do it over again just as well. According to El Greco, Michelangelo was a good man, but he did not know how to paint. No doubt, statements like these did not make El Greco a popular figure in Roman art circles where Michelangelo's talents were legendary. In any event, he left Italy for Spain in 1577, probably hoping to find work at the court of Philip II. At that time, the Spanish king was looking for artists to decorate the Escorial, his huge new palace outside Madrid (Figure 13.6).

★ **Enrichment** After he left Crete, people found this name too difficult to pronounce, so they simply called him "El Greco"—"the Greek."

★ **Enrichment** El Greco's unusual treatment of the human figure was not caused by defective vision as was once claimed—in fact, at one time special spectacles were made to be worn to correct the distortion caused by his "flawed vision." To prove to yourself that El Greco had no such vision problem, look at any horizontal line or shape in one of his paintings. You will find that he did not stretch these lines or shapes vertically. However, he did deliberately elongate his figures to give them a supernatural grace. He wanted his saints and martyrs to look supernatural and not natural.

Which two Italian artists influenced El Greco? What was his opinion of Michelangelo's paintings? What does this tell you about his self-confidence as an artist? Why did Philip II reject this painting by El Greco? How is this painting regarded today?

Figure 13.7 El Greco. *The Martyrdom of St. Maurice and the Theban Legion.* 1580. The Escorial, near Madrid

The Martyrdom of St. Maurice and the Theban Legion

Unfortunately, El Greco's dream of working for Philip did not last long. In 1580 he was commissioned to paint two pictures for the king. One of these, *The Martyrdom of St. Maurice and the Theban Legion* (Figure 13.7), so displeased the king that he refused to have it hung in the Escorial. El Greco never again received a royal commission. And what of his painting of St. Maurice? Today it is regarded as one of his greatest works.

In order to understand this painting, you should know something about Maurice, his soldiers, and their fate. Maurice and the troops in his legion were Christian and loyal subjects of the pagan Roman emperor. A serious problem arose when the emperor ordered everyone in the army to worship the Roman gods or face execution. Maurice and his soldiers could not do this and remain Christian, but they did not want to be disloyal to the emperor. Their solution to the problem was to accept death.

El Greco's picture blends the three parts of this story into a single scene. In the foreground, Maurice is seen explaining the situation to his officers. Further back, he and one of his officers are shown watching their men being beheaded. They calmly offer their encouragement knowing that shortly they will face the same end. At the top of the picture, the heavens open up and a group of angels prepare to greet the heroes with the laurels of martyrdom.

At first, Philip seemed to like El Greco's picture and ignored complaints that the artist was spending too much money on materials for it. But later he came to dislike it and finally judged it a failure. It was hidden away as a disgrace until found by another great Spanish artist, Velázquez, who finally had it hung in the Escorial.

Describe the dress, actions, and expressions of the figures in the bottom half of this picture. What event is taking place? What is used to divide the picture in half? How does the top half differ from the bottom half? What is the winged angel in the center carrying? Where is he carrying it? With your finger, trace along the axis and contour lines that lead your eye to the top of the painting. What important figure is found there? What aesthetic qualities did you use when making a judgment about this work?

Figure 13.8   El Greco. *The Burial of Count Orgaz.* 1586. Oil on canvas, 4.88 x 3.66 m [16 x 12′]. Santo Tomé, Toledo, Spain

The Burial of Count Orgaz

Disappointed after his experience with Philip, El Greco went to Toledo where he spent the rest of his life. He was well on the way to becoming a successful and popular artist when the Church of St. Tomé hired him to paint a most unusual picture. El Greco was asked to paint the burial of a man who had died two hundred years before. The huge painting, entitled *The Burial of Count Orgaz* (Figure 13.8), took him two years to paint —and another two years to collect his fee. But El Greco called it his greatest work.

Many people think that El Greco included his own portrait in *The Burial of Count Orgaz.* What would cause them to believe that the face in the center of the painting is the artist's? From your reading, what is known about El Greco's life?

Figure 13.8A   El Greco. Detail of *The Burial of Count Orgaz.* Santo Tomé, Toledo, Spain

Just who was the Count of Orgaz and why would anyone want a picture of his burial? The count had been a deeply religious man who had commanded his subjects to contribute money, cattle, wine, firewood, and chickens to St. Tomé each year. When the count died, so it was said, St. Stephen and St. Augustine came down from heaven and placed the count in his tomb with their own hands. The villagers of Orgaz continued to pay their annual tribute to St. Tomé for generations, but then, feeling that they had done enough, stopped. Officials at St. Tomé protested and a church trial was held. After all the testimony was heard, it was decided that the villagers should continue making their payments. El Greco's painting of the count's funeral was meant to be a reminder of their eternal debt to St. Tomé. In his contract, El Greco was instructed to show witnesses to the miracle, a priest saying Mass, and heaven opened in glory.

You will discover a great deal when you study a complicated painting like this. As a starting point, observe the boy in black at the lower left who seems to be introducing you to the scene. This boy's pointed finger directs your attention to the richly dressed figures of the two saints, a young St. Stephen and a much older St. Augustine. The saints bend over and support the body of the count dressed in armor. His lifeless pose and pale color show that he is dead; the two saints are lowering him into his grave. A monk in a gray habit at the left and a priest reading from an open book at the right frame this tragic scene. Between them, a row of black-robed figures silently witness the event. Their faces, set off by white ruffles at the neck, separate the quiet funeral scene from the swirling action overhead. The gaze of a priest at the right leads your eye to a winged angel who carries something in his hands. Upon closer examination, you will see that he is carrying a small, cloud-like figure—the soul of the dead count. The clouds part, giving the angel a clear path to the figure of Christ seated in judgment at the top of the painting. Saints and angels have gathered before Christ to ask that the count's soul be allowed to join them in heaven.

El Greco has done a masterful job of tying all the parts of this complex picture together. He divides the painting into two parts, heaven and earth, by using a horizontal axis line made up of the heads of the witnesses. Then he unites the two parts with another axis line that begins at the right shoulder of St. Stephen. Tracing this line you will find that it passes down the arm of the saint and through the arched body of the count. It continues to curve upward through the body of St. Augustine to the wing of the angel and on to the soul of the dead count. The contour lines of the clouds at either side of the angel guide your eye even higher to the figure of Christ. Thus, with the aid of axis and contour lines, El Greco takes you on a journey from the bottom of the painting to the top. He also makes sure that along the way you meet the most important figures: the two saints, the dead count, the angel, the count's soul, and Christ.

Details about El Greco's life are sketchy. Some people think that the woman who occasionally appears in his paintings—here shown as the Virgin—may have been his wife. That is uncertain, although it is quite likely that the boy in this picture is his son. On a paper sticking out of the boy's pocket, El Greco has painted his son's birthdate. El Greco may have included his own self-portrait in this picture as well. Many feel that he is the thin man a bit left of the center just above the fingers of an upturned hand. (Figure 13.8A) This man and the boy stand out in this painting because they are the only figures looking out at the viewer.

An interesting story about El Greco makes an appropriate postscript to this brief examination of his famous painting of Count Orgaz's burial. It seems that one beautiful sunny day a friend found El Greco in his house working in a room with the curtains drawn. He chided the artist for being in the dark and invited him for a stroll in the sun. But El Greco refused saying the sunlight would destroy the light shining within him. He need not have worried; his light continues to shine from paintings that startle, mystify, and amaze those who gaze upon them.

The End of a Period

El Greco carried Mannerist ideas as far as they could go. His intense emotionalism and strong sense of movement could not be imitated or developed further.★ Thus, the final chapter in the development of the Mannerist style was written in Spain; in Italy, the new Baroque style was already beginning to appear. However, an examination of that new style must wait. It is time to look north.

Northern Art: A Conflict of Styles

During the fifteenth century, most of the artists north of the Alps remained indifferent to the advances made by the Italian Renaissance. Since the time of Jan van Eyck, they had looked to Flanders and not to Italy for leadership. However, this changed at the start of the next century. Artists began to make independent journeys to Italy and other countries and became aware of what was happening there. Eventually, the lure of Italian art became so strong that a trip to Italy to study the great Renaissance masters was seen as essential for artists in training.

The spread of the Renaissance style across western Europe was further aided by powerful monarchs with a thirst for art. These monarchs were eager to attract well-known artists to their courts to work for them. Some Italian artists were invited to visit other countries. They helped to spread the Italian influence wherever they went. Artists from other countries were also asked to visit Italy. When they left Italy to return home or to go to other lands, these artists carried with them what they had learned of Italian Renaissance ideas. In response to such an invitation, Leonardo da Vinci left Italy and journeyed to France. Albrecht Dürer, the famous German artist, visited Italy. And Hans Holbein, another German artist who visited Italy, also visited and then settled in England.

But not all northern artists were willing to accept the new Italian Renaissance style. Early in the sixteenth century, a conflict of styles developed between those remaining faithful to the Late Gothic and those in favor of adopting Italian Renaissance ideas as quickly as possible.★ This conflict continued until the Renaissance point of view triumphed later in the century.

Matthias Grünewald

By comparing the work of two great northern painters of that time, Matthias Grünewald and Albrecht Dürer, this conflict of styles can be brought more clearly into focus. Both these German artists felt the influence of the Italian Renaissance. They understood the rules of perspective, and could paint figures that looked solid and real. But one continued to show a preference for the dreams and visions favored by Gothic art. He used Renaissance ideas only to make his pictures of these dreams and visions more vivid and powerful. This artist was Matthias Grünewald.

★ **Enrichment** El Greco's art was forgotten for centuries. He was treated as nothing more than an interesting footnote in the history of art. Some writers even went so far as to call him "the painter of the weird." But at the beginning of the twentieth century, El Greco and his works were rediscovered. Historians and critics alike finally realized how important he was. Three centuries before the beginning of modern art, he dared to disregard appearances. At a time when other artists were still concerned with reproducing reality, El Greco had the courage to distort images to express emotions. Like Michelangelo, and the Mannerists who followed El Greco, he argued that intuition—not imitation—was the true purpose of art.

★ **Enrichment** You will recall that a similar conflict of styles took place in fifteenth-century Italy. Some Italian artists quickly accepted the new, progressive ideas of the Renaissance, while others stubbornly held fast to the more conservative ideals of the Gothic style.

What do you find most impressive about this work—its realism or its expression of intense agony and sorrow? How has color been used to heighten the drama here? How would a light blue sky have changed the effect of this picture?

Figure 13.9 Matthias Grünewald. *The Small Crucifixion.* **c. 1510. Approx. 61.6 x 46 cm [24¼ x 18⅛]. The National Gallery of Art, Washington, D.C. Samuel H. Kress Collection, 1961**

The Small Crucifixion

In his small painting of the *Crucifixion* (Figure 13.9), Grünewald used an active imagination to create a powerful version of the familiar Christian subject. His aim was the same as that of generations of earlier Medieval artists, that is, to provide a visual sermon.

How differently a Renaissance artist like Raphael would have painted this same scene. Raphael would have used a balanced composition. His story would have been told with a calm dignity rather than with frenzied action. He would have tried to present the event as a reminder of Christ's sacrifice. But it would have been a gentle reminder, told in a whisper. Grünewald's mes-

sage, however, is neither calm nor gentle. It is a booming sermon forcefully describing Christ's passion and death. It spares none of the brutal details that Italian artists preferred to avoid. The pale yellow of Christ's body is the color of a corpse. The vivid red in the garments is the color of blood. And the cold, black sky behind the figures is a dark curtain against which the tragic scene is played.

Much of the impact of Grünewald's painting comes from the way in which it was painted. Look at the figure of Christ. The ragged edge of His cloth garment repeats and emphasizes the savage marks of the wounds covering His body. Now, focus your attention on the hands.

Notice how the fingers twist and turn in the final agony of death. Like everything else in the work—color, design, brushwork—this contributes to an expression of intense agony and sorrow. The calm balance of the Renaissance has been ignored. Instead you see a forceful representation of the Crucifixion which seeks to seize and hold your emotions.

Albrecht Dürer

Almost every German artist at this time followed the same course as Grünewald. Only Albrecht Dürer turned away from the Gothic style to embrace the Renaissance. Dürer was born in Nuremberg, Germany, in 1471, the second son in a family of eighteen children. Since he was the son of a goldsmith, it was assumed that he would follow in his father's profession. But Dürer showed such skill in drawing that he was apprenticed to a local painter at the age of fifteen. A trip to Italy when he was in his early twenties introduced Dürer to Renais-

sance painting and the Renaissance ideal of the artist as an intellectual. He returned to Nuremberg with a fresh view of the world and the artist's place in it. Dürer made up his mind to make the new Renaissance style his own and set about educating himself in all fields of learning that went with this new approach to art. He studied perspective and the theory of proportions in order to capture the beauty and balance found in Italian painting. Then he applied what he learned to his own art.

Knight, Death, and the Devil

This does not mean though that Dürer did nothing more than imitate the Italian Renaissance style. His studies enabled him to pick out the most interesting and impressive features of that style and combine them with his own ideas. For example, in his engraving entitled *Knight, Death, and the Devil* (Figure 13.10), the horse and rider exhibit the calmness and the solid, round form of Italian painting. But the figures of Death and the Devil

History

Point to features in this work that show that Dürer was influenced by the Italian Renaissance. Can you also identify some features found in northern Gothic paintings? What had the greatest influence on Dürer—the works of Late Gothic artists, or works created by artists of the Italian Renaissance? What trait did Dürer have in common with Leonardo da Vinci? In what ways does this picture reveal some of the conflicts experienced by the artist who created it? Do you feel that this work can be considered important in the historical development of art? Why or why not?

Figure 13.10   Albrecht Dürer [Nurenburg, Germany, 1471-1528]. *Knight, Death, and the Devil.* **1513. Engraving, approx. 24.6 x 19 cm [9½ x 7½″]. Courtesy of the Museum of Fine Arts, Boston. Harvey D. Parker Fund. 68.261**

Point to the only two men in this picture. Do you see any similarities in these two men? Could they be the same man at different times in his life? Who are the other figures? What are they doing? This picture tells a story but does not give it an ending—the man in the bed has to make an important decision. What is the decision he must make? Why must he make this decision quickly? How do you think this story will end? Is this story sad, humorous, or both?

are reminders of the strange creatures found in northern Gothic paintings. The brave Christian soldier is shown riding along the road of faith toward the heavenly Jerusalem seen at the top of the work. The knight's dog, the symbol of loyalty, gallantly follows its master. This is no easy journey—the knight is plagued by a hideous horseman representing Death, who threatens to cut him off before his journey is complete. And behind lurks the Devil, hoping the knight will lose his courage and decide to turn back. But the knight knows full well where he wants to go and what he must do to get there. His journey through life on the road to heaven may be lined with danger, but he rides bravely forward, never turning from the Christian path, no matter how frightening the dangers along the way.

At this time, Dürer found himself in the center of the conflict between Martin Luther and the Roman Church. He accepted Luther's principles and became a strong supporter of the Reformation. He took his place, so he said, alongside those who were looked down upon as heretics. His engraving of the *Knight, Death, and the Devil* may have been his way of showing the tremendous tensions he experienced during that turbulent period of history.

A Curiosity like Leonardo's

Throughout his life, Dürer exhibited a curiosity much like that of Leonardo. This curiosity led him to collect and study all kinds of strange and rare objects. Hearing of a whale stranded on a beach in the northwest part of the Netherlands, he set off to see it for himself. He died on the return journey. As for the whale, Dürer never saw it. It decomposed before he got there.

Hieronymus Bosch

One of the most interesting artists of the late fifteenth and early sixteenth centuries was the Flemish painter Hieronymus Bosch. He picked up and carried on the emotional quality noted in the works of Rogier van der Weyden and Hugo van der Goes. Bosch's paintings, like those of the Italian Mannerists, mirrored the growing fears and tensions of the people during that uneasy period. Many felt that the increasing religious conflicts were a sign that the evil in the world had reached new

Figure 13.11 Hieronymus Bosch. *Death and the Miser.* **c. 1485-90. Oil on oak, approx. 93 x 31 cm [36⅝ x 12⅛"]. The National Gallery of Art, Washington, D.C. Samuel H. Kress Collection**

In what ways is this artist's work like that of Jan van Eyck and other Flemish artists? How does it differ from Italian Renaissance paintings? Does this mean that Bruegel was unaware of the Italian Renaissance style, or did he consciously choose not to paint in the same way as the Italians? What message do you think Bruegel was trying to communicate with this painting? Do you feel he was successful in getting his message across? Is this, in your opinion, a good work of art? Do you think it is an important work of art? Why or why not?

Figure 13.12   Pieter Bruegel. *The Parable of the Blind.* 1568. Tempera on canvas, approx. 0.86 x 1.52 m [34 x 60″]. Museo Nazionale, Naples. [Soprintendenza per i Beni Artistici e Storici di Napoli]

highs. It was only a matter of time, they felt, before an angry God would punish them all.

Bosch's pictures were meant to be viewed in two ways—as stories and as symbolic messages. His stories clearly focused on the subject of good and evil. But his symbolic messages are more difficult to understand because the meanings for many of his symbols have been forgotten over the years. Many of these symbols probably came from magical beliefs, astrology, and the different religious cults that were popular in his day. Even though his paintings are often frightening or difficult to understand, they are not without traces of humor. Bosch often pictured the Devil as a fool or a clown rather than as the sinister Prince of Darkness.

Death and the Miser

Bosch's skills as a storyteller as well as his sense of humor are evident in his painting of *Death and the Miser* (Figure 13.11). He uses the picture to tell you that no matter how evil a man has been during his lifetime, he can still be saved if he asks for forgiveness before dying. An old miser is shown on his sickbed as Death enters the room and prepares to strike. Even at this final moment, the miser is torn between good and evil. An angel points to

a crucifix in the window and urges the miser to place his trust in the Lord. At the same time, a devil tempts him with a bag of money. Who will the miser listen to? It is difficult to say; he seems about to look up at the crucifix, although his hand reaches out for the money at the same time. He cannot make up his mind. At the bottom of the picture is a scene from an earlier period in the miser's life. Here too Bosch shows that the miser cannot make a decision between good and evil. The man fingers a rosary in one hand, but adds to his hoard of money with the other.

Pieter Bruegel

Bosch's unique art style did not pass away with his death in 1516. Forty years later, another Flemish artist turned away from the landscapes he had been painting to create pictures that owe a great deal to Bosch's influence. The artist's name was Pieter Bruegel.

The Parable of the Blind

Bruegel's pictures are often based on the unsettled conditions in the Netherlands during the sixteenth century. But what could he have had in mind when he painted *The Parable of the Blind* (Figure 13.12)? Five blind beggars are seen walking in a line; the sixth—their leader—has stumbled and is falling over the bank of a ditch, and the others are destined to share his misfortune. Like Bosch's work, Bruegel's painting can be seen as a story and as a symbolic message. It illustrates the proverb which reads "And if the blind lead the blind, both shall fall into a ditch." The picture could be interpreted as a warning to those who blindly follow the lead of others. Such people should be prepared to suffer the same fate. Bruegel's beggars follow a road leading to eternal suffering rather than the one leading to salvation. In their blindness they stumble past the distant church cleverly framed by trees and the outstretched staff of one of the beggars. The ditch they are about to tumble into could represent hell. It would represent the only possible end for those who allow themselves to be led down the path of wickedness. Bruegel warns that anyone can be misled; even the blind man wearing a showy cross as proof of his piety is being led astray.

Bruegel demonstrates a keen sense for detail—no less than five different eye diseases were once identified by a French physician after studying the faces in this picture. Also, observe the variety of expressions the figures show. They range from the confusion of the man at the far left to the fear of the figures at the right.

This concern for detail ties Bruegel more firmly to Jan van Eyck and other Flemish painters than to any Italian Renaissance artist. At a time when many Flemish artists were freely adopting the Renaissance style, Bruegel followed his own path. He chose to do this even though he was well aware of the work of Michelangelo and other Renaissance masters. It is known that Bruegel visited Italy and even spent a lengthy period in Rome while Michelangelo was still alive.★ But he did not return to Flanders to paint as an Italian artist might. The Renaissance Italians ignored what they thought to be excessive details. Bruegel, by contrast, emphasized them. The Italians also placed little importance on symbolism. Bruegel, on the other hand, used it in much the same way as the Medieval artist did in illustrating stories from the Bible. His blind men are symbols painted with accurate details to give them a more lifelike appearance.

Hans Holbein

Several years after the death of Grünewald and Dürer, another German artist named Hans Holbein left his native country to settle in England. Carrying a letter of recommendation from the great scholar Erasmus, Holbein hoped to escape from the strife of the Reformation. Known for his lifelike portraits, he became the court painter for King Henry VIII. He was the king's favorite painter and eventually painted portraits of Henry and three of his wives. The king was so impressed by Holbein's talent that he once remarked that he could make seven lords from seven peasants, but he could not make a single Holbein, not even from seven lords.

★ **Enrichment** Michelangelo was a contemporary of Bruegel even though he painted the Sistine Chapel ceiling more than a decade before the Flemish painter was born. Michelangelo died just five years before Bruegel's death in 1569.

History

How did this artist help spread the Renaissance style across western Europe? For what famous king did he work? Does the child in this picture look and act childlike? Why did the artist choose to show him acting more like an adult than a child?

Figure 13.13   Hans Holbein. *Edward VI as a Child.* c. 1538. Oil on wood, approx. 57 x 44 cm [22⅜ x 17⅜"]. The National Gallery of Art, Washington, D.C. Andrew W. Mellon Collection

Edward VI as a Child

As a New Year's gift in 1539, Holbein presented Henry with a portrait of his fourteen-month-old son, Edward (Figure 13.13). The birth of this son had been widely acclaimed in England because it meant that the king finally had a male heir to the throne. It was partly due to Henry's desire for a son to succeed him as king that he had divorced his first wife, Catherine of Aragon. This act had thrown the whole country into confusion. The Pope condemned the action, and Henry broke with the Church, taking his country with him. Unfortunately, Henry did not father a son while married to his second wife either. The future King Edward was born while he was married to his third wife, Jane Seymour.

Holbein painted the young Edward in royal garments and placed a gold rattle in his hand. Even though the face and hands are childlike, Edward hardly looks like a child not yet two years of age. The artist probably wanted to impress Henry by showing the child's royal dignity rather than his infant charms.

The Latin verse below Edward's portrait asks him to follow the path of virtue and to be a good ruler. Unhappily, the young king had little opportunity to do either. He was never strong and died of tuberculosis at the age of sixteen.

Criticism

List the things found in this work that make it seem so lifelike. Point out and describe the different textures found in this painting. Do you think this man is a king, a sea captain, a clergyman, or a merchant? What clues helped you discover his occupation? What is he looking at? Describe the expression on his face. Does he seem posed or natural?

Figure 13.14   Hans Holbein. *George Gisze.* **1532. Oil and tempera on panel, 96.5 x 83.8 cm [38 x 33 inches]. Staatliche Museen Preussischer Kulturbesitz, Gemäldegalerie, Berlin (West)**

George Gisze

Holbein's skills as a portrait artist⋆ are more clearly seen in his painting of *George Gisze* (Figure 13.14). In this work he combines the northern European love for detail with the solid, three-dimensional forms favored by Italian Renaissance artists. Holbein presents a proud young merchant surrounded by the tools of his trade. The business papers, seals, writing materials, and other objects are painted with great precision. The same concern for accuracy is seen in the way the artist has painted the different textures. Everything has its own unique "feel": the hard, cold smoothness of glass, the soft richness of velvet, the coarse roughness of wood.

But the most interesting feature of this work is the pose and expression of the sitter. Holbein has him glancing out of the corner of his eye in your direction. It is as if you have just entered his office—perhaps a bell above the door has signaled your arrival. The young merchant, interrupted at his work, looks up and is about to smile a welcome. The figure is so realistic that you almost expect to hear him say "hello" and invite you to sit down as he will be with you in just a moment. Unfortunately, you cannot wait. You have an important appointment with a number of Baroque artists in the next century.

⋆ **Enrichment** It seems appropriate that this great portrait painter fell victim to the plague and died in London in the fall of 1543 while he was at work on a picture of Henry VIII.

Studio Experiences

Lesson One: Bizarre Creatures from Expanded Paper Shapes

The works of Dürer and Bosch often include unusual creatures that are sometimes frightening (Figure 13.10) and sometimes humorous (Figure 13.11). In this studio assignment you will have a chance to create your own frightening or humorous creature. To do this, follow these steps:

1. Cut out a simple, free-form solid shape from a piece of 15 x 23-cm [6 x 9-inch] white paper, using most of the paper for your shape.

2. Cut this shape into three smaller shapes, each of which has curved contours.

3. Cut each of the three shapes into five smaller shapes. Again, make sure that all contours are curved.

4. Arrange all the shapes on a sheet of 30 x 46-cm [12 x 18-inch] colored construction paper so they again form the large shape you started with.

5. Expand this shape by carefully spreading out the smaller shapes—but make certain that each shape continues to touch at some point the shape or shapes from which it was cut.

6. Glue all the shapes in place.

7. Study your expanded shape from every angle. Does it suggest the beginning of a bizarre creature?

8. When you have discovered the beginning of your creature, develop it further by adding eyes, ears, nose, mouth, teeth, legs, scales, tail, etc. During this last step, give your imagination free reign as you try to illustrate the most unusual creature possible.

Safety Note

Since this studio activity involves gluing, and since rubber cement is often used for this purpose, a word of caution is in order. Rubber cement contains solvents which are potentially harmful. The inhalation of solvent vapors may injure lung tissue or be absorbed into the bloodstream. For this reason, rubber cement is *not* recommended for use in the classroom.

Other adhesives that do not contain solvents are readily available and should be used in place of rubber cement. In the event it is used, every precaution should be taken to do so in a large, well-ventilated room. (Other art materials that contain solvents include aerosol sprays, cleaning solvents, silk-screen inks and their solvents, permanent markers, shellacs, lacquers and their thinners, paint thinner, paint and varnish removers, turpentine, and the wide variety of solvent-based glues and adhesives.)

Lesson Two: Modeling Expressive Figures in Clay

Mannerist painters were interested in communicating ideas, moods, and emotions to viewers. Works by Parmigianino (Figure 13.4), Tintoretto (Figure 13.5), and El Greco (Figures 13.7 and 13.8) did this with exaggeration, distortion, and movement. Can you identify any other paintings illustrated in this chapter that make use of these same techniques? In this studio experience, you will be asked to use these techniques to model an expressive clay figure. To begin, complete several quick sketches of seated or reclining figures which communicate a specific emotion or feeling. Make certain to use exaggeration, distortion, and movement to enhance the emotion or feeling portrayed. Now choose your best sketch and interpret it in clay (approximate size: 25 x 18 cm [10 x 7 inches]). Model the torso of the figure first and then add the head, legs, and arms. Avoid details during the first stages of your modeling. Concentrate instead on general forms, proportions, and gestures. Then progressively smaller details may be added. Finally, create a rich and varied textured surface on your figure by using different marking tools such as combs, toothbrushes, and saw blades. When the figure is thoroughly dry, it can be fired. Finished pieces may be rubbed with linseed oil and waxed. Or, shoe polish may be applied and rubbed to a shine with a soft cloth.

Chapter 14

A World of Light and Shadow: Baroque Art

Artists you will meet in this chapter

Francesco Borromini (fran-*sess*-coe bore-oh-*mee*-nee), 1599-1667. This architect never overlooked any opportunity to create a sense of movement in the buildings he designed.

Fra Andrea Pozzo (ahn-*dray*-ah *pots*-soh), 1642-1709. When looking up at his ceiling painting of *The Entrance of St. Ignatius into Paradise*, it is difficult to determine where the painting and sculptural effects end and reality begins.

Gianlorenzo Bernini (jee-ahn-low-*rents*-oh ber-*nee*-nee), 1598-1680. His sculptures show that he was able to capture in stone the precise moment of highest drama.

Michelangelo da Caravaggio (my-kel-*an*-jay-loe da car-ah-*vah*-jyoh), 1573-1610. He shocked viewers by introducing common, even crude, people into his religious paintings.

Artemisia Gentileschi (ar-tay-*mee*-zee-ah jen-ti-*less*-key), c. 1597-c. 1651. She was the first woman in the history of Western art to have an important effect upon the art of her time.

Peter Paul Rubens (*pee*-ter *pawl roo*-benz), 1577-1640. His paintings make you feel like a participant in the action rather than just an onlooker.

Frans Hals (*frahns hahls*), c. 1580-1666. He demonstrated in his portraits the ability to show a robust laugh, a shy smile, or a sly snicker.

Rembrandt van Rijn (*rem*-brant van *ryne*), 1606-69. This son of a humble miller became one of the best-known artists in history. Few artists have been so successful in arousing the viewer's curiosity.

Jan Steen (*yahn stayn*), 1626-79. A skilled storyteller, he organized his pictures so that no part of his stories would be overlooked.

Jan Vermeer (*yahn* verr-*mair*), 1632-75. Forgotten for almost two hundred years, he is now regarded as one of the greatest painters of all time. This is remarkable since fewer than forty of his pictures are known to exist!

Judith Leyster (jew-*dith lie*-stir), 1609-60. The art world was stunned in 1893 when a picture thought to have been done by a famous artist turned out to be the creation of this gifted, but little-known, woman painter.

Jusepe de Ribera (zhoo-*say*-pay day ree-*bay*-rah), 1591-1652. This Spanish painter spent most of his career in Italy where, because of his stature, he was known as "The Little Spaniard."

Diego Velàzquez (dee-*aye*-goh vay-*lass*-keth), 1599-1660. For over three hundred years, viewers have been trying to decide what is happening in his painting of *The Maids of Honor*. Perhaps you will have some ideas of your own.

Bartolomé Esteban Murillo (bar-toh-loh-*may ess*-tay-bahn mou-*ree*-yoh), 1618-82. A deeply religious man, many of his paintings were done for monasteries and convents. While working in a convent, he fell from a scaffolding and died of his injuries.

Criticism

Which of the following terms would you include in your description of this building: wide or tall, flat or soaring, plain or ornate? Point to a feature on this building that you have not seen before. Do you think the purpose of this feature was decorative or structural?

Figure 14.1 Il Gesù, Rome. c. 1575. [Photo Alinari]

The Role of Art in the Counter-Reformation

Late in the sixteenth century and early in the seventeenth century, a more relaxed and confident attitude replaced the tension and doubts of the Mannerist period. By the start of the seventeenth century, the Catholic Church had gained back much of its power in Italy. It was now answering the challenge of the Protestant Reformation with a reform movement of its own. This movement is known as the Counter-Reformation.

Art played a major role in this Counter-Reformation. It was seen as an important weapon in the struggle to stamp out heresy and lure people back to the Church. For this reason, artists and architects were called to Rome to create works that would restore religious spirit and make the city the most beautiful in the Christian world. Once again, Rome became the center of the art world, just as it had been during the height of the Renaissance a century before.

New Style Reflected in Church Architecture

In architecture, the Counter-Reformation brought about a revival of church building and remodeling. One of these new Roman churches, Il Gesù (Figure 14.1), was among the first to use features which signaled the birth of a new art style. While many of its features are familiar, one certainly is not. The huge, sculptured scrolls at each side are something you have not seen before. They are used here to unite the side sections of the wide façade to the central portion of the building. This sculptural quality on buildings like Il Gesù was an important feature of an architectural style which rose quickly to brilliant heights. The style is called Baroque, and, over the next one hundred years, it spread across a large part of Europe.★

★ **Enrichment** It is not clear where this name originated. Some historians suggest that it comes from the Portuguese word *barroco*, which means "an irregularly-shaped pearl." At first, it was used to label works that were felt to be bizarre or grotesque. This has changed, and now "Baroque" is used when referring to the period from 1600 to about 1700 and the style of art that was practiced during that period.

An excellent example of the mature Baroque style in architecture is a tiny Roman church designed by an emotionally unstable architect named Francesco Borromini who died by suicide in 1667.★ The church that made Borromini famous worldwide was San Carlo alle Quattro Fontane (Figure 14.2). The façade of this church is a continuous flow of concave and convex surfaces. This makes the building seem elastic and pulled out of shape. It also adds a sense of movement to the façade. The push and pull that results creates a startling pattern of light and shadow across the building. The façade is three-dimensional, almost sculptural. The moldings, sculptures, and niches with small framing columns add three-dimensional richness and value contrast. Borromini boldly designed this façade to produce an overall effect of movement, contrast, and variety.

★ **Enrichment** Borromini became ill during the summer of 1667 and, in a fit of delirium, stabbed himself with a sword. He died the next day, but not before repenting his action.

Criticism

You could not call this façade flat or soaring—how would you describe it? In what ways is it like sculpture? This building is said to produce an effect of movement. How is this effect achieved? Do you think this façade is dramatic and exciting, or calm and dignified? Point to things on the building that support your interpretation.

Figure 14.2   Francesco Borromini. San Carlo alle Quattro Fontane. Rome. 1665-76

The artist who painted this ceiling placed a small mark on the floor beneath it. When people stood on this mark and looked up, they had the best view of this amazing painting. It looks as if the roof of the church has been removed, allowing viewers to witness the triumphant entrance of St. Ignatius into heaven. Can you tell where the building ends and the painting begins? What kind of feeling is generated by this work? What makes this a "Baroque" painting?

Figure 14.3   Fra Andrea Pozzo. *The Entrance of St. Ignatius into Paradise.* 1691-94. Sant' Ignazio, Rome. Conway Library, Courtauld Institute of Art, London

Emphasis on Mood and Drama in Sculpture

Throughout the Baroque period, sculptors showed the same interest in movement, contrast, and variety as did architects. They placed great importance on the mood or feeling expressed by their work and tried to capture the moment of highest drama and excitement. Less interest was shown in portraying realistic beauty. Drapery, for example, no longer suggested the body beneath. Instead, it offered artists a chance to show off their skills at complex modeling and reproducing different textures. Deep undercutting was used to create shadows and sharp contrasts of light and dark values. This added to the dramatic impact of the work. Colored marble replaced white marble or somber bronze as the preferred sculptural medium. Frequently, however, several materials were used together in a single work.

Criticism

Which of the following phrases best describes this work: (a) stiff, strong, and dignified, (b) precise balance and harmony, (c) dramatic movement in space, or (d) a flat, decorative effect? Point to as many features in this work as you can to support your choice.

Figure 14.4   Gianlorenzo Bernini. *The Ecstasy of St. Theresa*. 1645-52. Marble, life-size. Cornaro Chapel, Santa Maria della Vittoria, Rome

During this time, sculptures were made which seemed to break out of and flow from their architectural frames. They projected out in different directions. This created an effect that was like that found in murals and ceiling paintings done at the same time (Figure 14.3).★ The results overwhelm and even confuse the viewer. Sometimes the viewer has trouble seeing where the painting or sculpture ends and reality takes over.

★ **Enrichment** Andrea Pozzo, who painted the impressive ceiling fresco shown in Figure 14.3, had been so moved by a sermon that he joined the Jesuit order twenty years before this work was done. His painting of St. Ignatius entering paradise took three years to complete and established him as one of the most important decorative artists of the Baroque period.

Gianlorenzo Bernini

A fine example of this feature of Baroque sculpture is seen in Gianlorenzo Bernini's altar containing the famous *Ecstasy of St. Theresa* (Figure 14.4). This altar shows Bernini's skill in combining sculpture and architecture. It was dedicated to St. Theresa, a sixteenth-century Spanish nun who was one of the great saints of the Counter-Reformation. In one of her books, St. Theresa described a vision in which an angel pierced her heart with a fire-tipped golden arrow symbolizing God's love. This vision served as the inspiration for Bernini's sculpture. The angel and saint are carved in white marble and placed against a background of golden rays radiating from above. This scene is lit from overhead by a concealed yellow glass window that makes the figures seem to float in space within a niche of colored marble. The figures do more than just occupy space, however.

Criticism

What is this figure doing? What clues helped you determine this? How was this work designed to encourage a viewer to move around it rather than view it from one spot? Do you think that this is a successful work? To which aesthetic qualities would you turn when defending your judgment?

Figure 14.5 Gianlorenzo Bernini. *David*. 1623. Marble, life-size. Galleria Borghese, Rome

They appear to move about freely within that space. This new relationship with space sets Baroque sculpture apart from the sculpture of the previous two hundred years.

This new relationship of active figures with space is observed in Bernini's sculpture of *David* (Figure 14.5). If you compare this work with a Renaissance sculpture such as Donatello's *St. George* (Figure 11.11, page 191), you will quickly recognize the Baroque sculptor's love of movement within space. Donatello's St. George remains still and calm as he plans his first move, but Bernini's David has already decided what he must do and is doing it. The theme in Bernini's work is movement. David's body is twisting in space as he prepares to hurl the stone at the mighty giant, Goliath. The coiled stance, flexed muscles, and determined expression are clues to his mood and purpose. But where is David's enemy; where is Goliath? Although he is not shown, his presence is suggested by the action and the concentration of David. It is clear that he is watching his enemy approach and is about to release the shot that must be on target or he is doomed. The space in front of David which would be occupied by Goliath thus becomes an important part of the work. The dramatic action of the figure forces you to use your imagination to place Goliath in that space.

Emphasis on Motion Changes Painting

The forms and figures of Baroque art twist, turn, and spiral in space. As a result, everything seems to be in motion. Architects, sculptors, and painters of this period all used more action in their works than had their predecessors and this increased the excitement of their creations. Furthermore, they used dramatic lighting effects to make vivid contrasts of light and dark. This magnified the action and heightened the excitement.

Michelangelo da Caravaggio

More than any other artist, Michelangelo da Caravaggio gave Baroque art its unique look and feeling. The paintings he produced during a brief and stormy career were an important influence on artists throughout Europe. Rather than drawing his inspiration from the Renaissance artists who preceded him, Caravaggio chose to study and paint the world around him. He made light an important part of his painting, using it to illuminate his figures and expose their imperfections. By showing their flaws, he made his figures seem more real and more human. There is little about his figures to remind you of the supernatural beings found in Mannerist pictures.

The Conversion of St. Paul

Caravaggio's *Conversion of St. Paul* (Figure 14.6) is a fine example of his painting style. Only St. Paul, his horse, and a single attendant are shown. The saint has been thrown from his horse and lies on his back with his arms outstretched. His companion grips the bridle of the uneasy horse and looks on in surprise. The entire scene is pushed forward on the canvas so that you are presented with a close look. There is no detailed landscape in the background to distract your attention from this scene. In fact, you can see nothing but darkness behind the figures. Instead of stretching back into the picture, space seems to project outward from the picture plane to include you as an eyewitness to the event.

At first the religious meaning of this picture may be overlooked. It does look as if the artist is only interested in providing an accurate account of a traveling accident. There is nothing to tell you that the figure on the ground is St. Paul who, as Saul, was once feared as a persecutor of Christians. And yet, there is something unreal and mysterious about this scene. A powerful light illuminates the figures and makes them stand out boldly against the dark background. This could hardly be described as a natural light. More like a spotlight, it originates outside the picture, making it something of a mystery. Its purpose goes beyond making it easy for you to see what is going on. Caravaggio uses it to add drama to the scene. He uses light in the same way a technician skillfully snaps on and directs a spotlight on a darkened stage. The brilliant flash of light reveals St. Paul at the exact moment that he hears God's voice. This voice cuts through the darkness like the light. It demands to know, "Saul, why do you persecute me?"

Criticism

What is happening here? Describe the actions and expressions of the two men. Is there any sign that this is a religious painting? Describe the light in the picture—is it natural, artificial, or mysterious? Where does it come from? What mood or feeling is created by the use of this light? Describe the background. How does the treatment of the background contribute to this picture's effectiveness? Point to areas where gradations of value are found. What effect does this gradation have upon the shapes in the painting? How did you judge this painting?

Figure 14.6   Caravaggio. *The Conversion of St. Paul.* c. 1601. Santa Maria del Popolo, Rome [Photo Alinari]

Controversial Portrayal of Religious Subjects

Caravaggio's desire to use ordinary people in his portrayal of religious subjects met with mixed reactions. Some of his paintings were refused by the Church officials who had commissioned them. They disliked the fact that Christ and the Saints were shown in untraditional ways.★ Often the figures looked like peasants and common beggars. The people of Caravaggio's time were used to seeing religious figures pictured as majestic and supernatural beings. Since he refused to do this, they turned to lesser artists whose works were more in keeping with their tastes.

A Reckless Life

Caravaggio's reckless life was as shocking to the public as many of his pictures. During the last decade of his life, he was in constant trouble with the law because of his brawls, sword fights, and violent temper. Finally he was forced to flee Rome after killing a rival during a quarrel over a point in tennis. Through all this, he continued to paint, and, surprisingly, the pictures from this period are among the most gentle he ever created. Caravaggio died of malaria in 1610 when he was just thirty-seven years old. But his dynamic style of art helped to change the course of European painting during the seventeenth century. Spreading north into Flanders and Holland, it provided inspiration for Rubens, Rembrandt, and a host of other artists.

Artemisia Gentileschi

Among Caravaggio's many Italian followers were Orazio Gentileschi and his daughter Artemisia. Artemisia was an artist of such skill that her fame, in time, surpassed that of her father. Her skill was such that she became the first woman in the history of Western art to have a significant impact upon the art of her time. During her career, she went to Florence, Venice, Naples, and Rome. The paintings she did on these travels helped spread Caravaggio's style throughout Italy. Her debt to him can be seen in her works. A good example is *Judith and Maidservant with the Head of Holofernes* (Figure 14.7), painted when she was at the peak of her career.

The biblical story of Judith is one of great heroism. She used her charms to capture the fancy of Holofernes, the enemy of the Jewish people and general of King Nebuchadnezzar. Waiting in his tent until Holofernes was asleep, Judith struck suddenly, cutting off his head. Artemisia captures the tense scene just after this

act. Judith stands with the knife still in her hand as her servant places the severed head in a sack. A mysterious noise has just interrupted them. Judith raises a hand in warning and both wait quietly, hardly daring to breathe, staring intently into the darkness. The dark, cramped quarters of the tent are an effective backdrop for the two figures illuminated by the light from a single candle. Judith's raised hand partially blocks the light from this candle and casts a dark shadow on her face. Her brightly lit profile is thus accented, and this adds force to her anxious expression. Has she been discovered? Are soldiers even now gathering outside the tent to block her escape? Or was the noise nothing more than the wind tugging at the flaps of the tent? Artemisia's lifelike treatment of the subject matter, her use of light and dark contrasts for dramatic effect, and her skill as a forceful storyteller are all evidenced in this painting.

History

Why is this artist so important in the history of art? Which artist greatly influenced her painting style? In what way is that influence evident in this picture?

Figure 14.7 Artemisia Gentileschi [Italian, 1593-c.1651]. *Judith and Maidservant with the Head of Holofernes.* **c. 1625. Oil on canvas, 1.84 x 1.42 m [72½ x 55¾"]. Courtesy of The Detroit Institute of Arts, Detroit, Michigan. Gift of Mr. Leslie H. Green. 52.253**

★ Enrichment   In one of these paintings, Caravaggio showed St. Matthew with his legs crossed and the dirty sole of his bare foot turned outward toward the viewer.

In what way does this painting remind you of works by the following artists: Jan van Eyck, Michelangelo, Titian, and Caravaggio? Make a list of the most obvious Baroque features found in this work.

Figure 14.8 Peter Paul Rubens. *The Elevation of the Cross.* 1610. Approx. 4.62 x 3.4 m [15′ 2″ x 11′ 2″]. Antwerp Cathedral, Antwerp, Belgium

Once, in a letter, Artemisia declared that she had the spirit of Caesar. Only a woman of extraordinary self-confidence would have dared to write such words at that time in history. But it was no idle boast. Artemisia's paintings are proof that her confidence in her abilities was well deserved.

Peter Paul Rubens

Of all the European artists of the seventeenth century, Peter Paul Rubens most completely captured the exciting spirit and rich effects of the Baroque style. While still a young man, he spent eight years in Italy. There he came to know Italian sixteenth-century painting and the works of Caravaggio. When he went back to his native Antwerp, he set up his own studio. This studio soon became the busiest in Europe. Assisted by many helpers, he turned out portraits, religious pictures, and scenes from myths.

The Elevation of the Cross

Rubens liked powerful and exciting subjects, and this is evident in his painting of *The Elevation of the Cross* (Figure 14.8). This was the first major altarpiece he finished after his return to Flanders from Italy and shows how much he learned from the Italians. He was inspired by the rich color of Titian and the dramatic composition of Tintoretto. Both are evident in this work. In addition, he created powerful, twisting figures which were inspired by Michelangelo's Sistine Ceiling. And from Caravaggio he learned to use light to illuminate the most important parts of his work. However, Rubens did not ignore his Flemish roots. He shows a concern for realistic detail, which had been a feature of Flemish painting since van Eyck. This concern for detail is noted in the carefully painted leaves of the tree, the armor of the soldier, and the marvelous dog in the lower left corner of the picture. He blends these realistic details with a swirling mixture of colors and shapes to produce a picture of great dramatic force.

Rubens carefully arranged his figures to form a solid pyramid of twisting, straining bodies. However, this is no stable, balanced pyramid. It tips dangerously to the left, and the powerful figures seem to push, pull, and strain in an effort to restore balance. Like many other Baroque artists, Rubens makes use of a strong diagonal axis line in this picture. It follows the vertical section of the Cross through the center of the pyramid. Notice how it runs from the lower right foreground to the upper left background. In this way the axis line not only organizes the direction of movement in the painting, but also adds to the feeling of space. It serves to draw your eye deep into the work. The figures arranged on either side of this axis line form the unbalanced pyramid which sweeps across the canvas like an overflowing stream at springtime.

The action in this painting is so intense that it embraces the viewer—you are made to feel as though you are part of it. This attempt to draw the viewer into the work is a trademark of the Baroque style. You will see it demonstrated over and over again in architecture and sculptures as well as in painting.

Perhaps more than any other artist, Rubens was able to give his pictures a feeling of energy and life. He did this by avoiding stiff, geometric forms: you will rarely find straight contour lines or right angles in a painting by Rubens. Instead, he used curving lines which join with one another to create a feeling of movement. Then he softened the contours or edges of his forms and placed them against a swirling background of color. The effect is one of violent and continuous motion.

A comparison of Rubens' *Elevation of the Cross* with Raphael's *Alba Madonna* (Figure 11.21, page 204) should aid your understanding of both the Baroque and Renaissance styles. This comparison brings out the restraint and dignity of the *Alba Madonna* in contrast to the action and drama of *The Elevation of the Cross.* Rubens replaces the calm, peaceful balance of the Renaissance with motion, power, and tension. Raphael, with much care, plans the placement of his figures to gain balance and stability. Rubens, on the other hand, uses a lively diagonal composition to tempt the viewer into the scene. Then he blurs contours, makes colors more intense, and spotlights powerful figures. This all adds to the excitement. Raphael's work invites you to leisurely view and think about its subject. Rubens' work gives you no time for this. It immediately reaches out and pulls you into the work where you become emotionally involved. You *look* at the Raphael and *experience* the Rubens.

Daily Routine

Rubens gained fame during his lifetime not only because of his painting. He was also a diplomat and a man of learning who was very active in the intellectual, political, and spiritual life of his country. His energy and accomplishments were truly amazing. In an account of his daily routine, a contemporary wrote that Rubens rose every morning at 4:00 A.M. and began his day by going to church. Following this, he retired to his studio to paint. A paid reader read to him from the classics while he worked. Rubens chose to eat sparingly during the day because he did not want to become uncomfortable while at work. At 5:00 in the afternoon, he would set aside his palette and brushes and call for his horse in order to take a relaxing ride in the country. When he returned home, he usually found several friends waiting for him, and they would enjoy dinner together. However, Rubens never engaged in any excesses in food, drink, or entertainment. His greatest joys were to mount a good horse, read an interesting book, or busy himself with a collection of precious stones.

His Use of Assistants

In order to meet all the demands for his art and because he could not give all his time to painting, Rubens had to rely on many assistants. This was especially true when he worked on the large pictures he preferred to paint. Most artists would have avoided the nearly impossible assignments he accepted routinely. One of these assignments was to paint twenty-one huge paintings showing events from the life of the French queen, Marie de Médicis. Some of these pictures were as large as 3.6 x 6.1 m [12 x 20 feet], and yet Rubens managed to complete the task in four years. While assistants worked with him on this project, Rubens painted some of these pictures by himself and applied the finishing touches to all of them. In a letter he once wrote to a representative of the king of England, Rubens said of himself: "My talent is such that no undertaking, no matter how large or complex, has taxed my courage." From most artists, this would be dismissed as vain and boastful. From Rubens, it was a simple statement of fact.

Criticism

Do the lions look authentic? Are they about to attack the man? Where is this event taking place? Point to the light source. How is the figure of the man made to stand out? What is he doing? What clues tell you that he was not the first to be placed in this situation? Do you think this man will suffer the same fate as his predecessors? Who is he hoping will save him?

Figure 14.9   Peter Paul Rubens. *Daniel in the Lions' Den.* **c. 1615. Oil on canvas, 2.24 x 3.3 m [7′ 4¼″ x 10′ 10⅛″]. The National Gallery of Art, Washington, D.C. Ailsa Mellon Bruce Fund, 1965**

Figure 14.10   Peter Paul Rubens. *Lion.* **c. 1614. Black and yellow chalks heightened with white, 25.4 x 28.2 cm [10 x 11 ⅛″]. The National Gallery of Art, Washington, D.C. Ailsa Mellon Bruce Fund**

Daniel in the Lions' Den

A painting that Rubens did without the aid of assistants illustrates the Bible story of *Daniel in the Lions' Den* (Figure 14.9).★ The prophet, illuminated by the light coming in from a hole overhead, stands out against the dark interior of the lions' den. He raises his head and clenches his hands in an emotional prayer. God's answer is indicated by the behavior of the lions—they pay no attention at all to Daniel. His faith in God has saved him. As in all of Rubens' works, there is a great deal of emotion here, but not at the expense of realism. The lions are accurately painted and arranged at different angles in natural poses. Rubens painted them after making a number of drawings of lions at a nearby zoo (Figure 14.10).

★ **Enrichment** Interestingly, this picture once hung for years in the boardroom of an English business house. Everyone assumed it was nothing more than a copy of a work by the great artist. Only after the painting was sold did the new owner discover that it was a lost original.

Dutch Art Takes a New Direction

In 1648, a treaty with Spain (known as the Peace of Westphalia) divided the Low Countries into two parts.★ Flanders in the South remained Catholic and a territory of Spain. But Holland in the North, which was largely Protestant, finally gained its independence from Spain. In Holland, the Baroque style had little impact. Although some features appear in Dutch art, the Baroque was limited mainly to Catholic countries, where it was the style of the Counter-Reformation.

Dutch Protestants did not want religious sculptures or paintings in their churches, and this presented a problem for artists. If you think back over the kind of art that had been produced in western Europe before this time, the problem becomes obvious. Religious subjects had been one of the principal concerns of artists since early Christian times. Now there was no market for such paintings. What then was left for the Dutch artist to paint? Trade and colonization had brought wealth to the country, and so people could certainly afford art. But if religious art no longer interested patrons, what did? The search for an answer eventually leads to an examination of the Dutch people themselves.

Typical Dutch citizens enjoyed their comfortable homes and profitable businesses. In art, they favored works which reminded them of these as well as their loyal, hardworking wives; polite, obedient children; and good-natured friends. They wanted to surround themselves with paintings of the things they loved most. Realizing this, artists began to paint people and places, city squares and streets, the countryside and the sea. Many of these works were scenes from daily life, or "genre" paintings. The market for portraiture, landscape, still life, and genre paintings grew to such an extent that artists began to specialize. For instance, some painted only pictures of the sea, while others did views of the city or interior scenes of carefree groups in taverns and inns.

Frans Hals

One artist, Frans Hals, preferred to paint portraits of people: laughing soldiers, brawling fish vendors, and happy merrymakers. He used quick, dashing brushstrokes to give his works a fresh, just-finished look. His portraits are so successful in capturing a fleeting expression that they look like candid photographs. In one of Hals' portraits (Figure 14.11), an officer looks as if he has just turned to glance over at the painter. Perhaps he has been posing for some time and is tired. Abandoning pretense for a moment, he is shown behaving in a completely natural way. Placing one hand impatiently on his hip and flashing a sly grin, he appears to be saying, "Really, Mr. Hals, aren't you finished yet?"

While Hals' portraits may look as though they were done in a matter of minutes, they actually took a great deal of time. His genius lies in the illusion that he creates. You are led to believe that Hals, in an instant, has caught a characteristic expression of the subject and recorded it in paint.

For many years, Frans Hals was among the busiest and most prosperous portrait painters in Holland. But as he grew older the public turned to other, more fashionable painters. His carefree life, huge family, and constant lawsuits for past debts finally drove him to accept a meager assistance from the pauper's fund in Haarlem where he lived. The last payment from this fund, in 1666, was "four florins to the gravedigger to open a tomb in the Groote Kerk for a Meester Frans Hals."

Rembrandt van Rijn

No discussion of Dutch seventeenth-century art could be complete without mention of Rembrandt van Rijn, often referred to as the greatest Dutch painter of his era. His works alone make Dutch painting outstanding in the history of Western art.

★ **Enrichment** Today, the Low Countries, located north of France, is a region made up of Belgium and Holland. The term *Low Countries* comes from the word "Netherlands," another name for Holland. "Netherlands" means "lowlands," an appropriate label since much of that country is below sea level.

Frans Hals specialized in painting which of the following: landscapes, religious pictures, portraits, battle scenes, still lifes? Was it unusual for artists at this time and in this country to specialize in certain subjects for their paintings? List the things in this painting that make it seem so lifelike. What does this painting have in common with a photograph?

Figure 14.11   Frans Hals. *Portrait of an Officer.* **c. 1640. Oil on canvas, 86 x 69 cm [33¾ x 27"]. The National Gallery of Art, Washington, D.C. Andrew W. Mellon Collection, 1937**

Light is an important element in this picture. Why is it so important? Does this light come from the right or the left? Point to the main characters in this crowded scene. What are they doing? Describe the actions of the other figures. If sound could be added to this picture, what would you hear? Is this a successful work? Would it be as effective if you could see every detail clearly?

Figure 14.12 Rembrandt van Rijn. *The Company of Captain Frans Banning Cocq* (*The Night Watch*). 1642. Oil on canvas, 3.7 x 4.4 m [12′ 2″ x 14′ 7″]. Rijksmuseum, Amsterdam

The Night Watch

Like other artists of his time, Rembrandt painted portraits, everyday events, historical subjects, and landscapes. But, unlike most, he refused to specialize and was skilled enough to succeed in all. If he specialized at all, it was in the study of light, shadow, and atmosphere. The results of this study can be observed in one of Rembrandt's best-known paintings, *The Night Watch* (originally titled *The Company of Captain Frans Banning Cocq*) (Figure 14.12).* Light can be seen throughout this picture, although it is brightest at the center. There an officer in charge gives instructions to his aide. The shadow of the officer's hand falls across the aide's uniform, telling you that the light comes from the left. The light falls unevenly on the other features in the picture. Several, including a young woman and a drummer, are brightly illuminated, while others are barely

★ **Enrichment** When this painting was cleaned in 1946-47, it was discovered that the work was not a night scene at all, but a morning scene. It shows a militia company preparing to welcome the queen of France, who was making a visit to the Netherlands.

visible in the shadows. Rembrandt's skill in handling light for dramatic effect, so obvious in this painting, was one of his most remarkable accomplishments.

Before leaving this painting, use your imagination to add movement and sound. When you do, you will find that you become a spectator at a grand pictorial symphony. Light flashes across the stage, a banner is unfurled, a musket is loaded, lances clatter, and boots thud softly on hard pavement. At the same time, a dog barks at a drummer and instructions are heard over the murmur of a dozen conversations. Rather than paint a picture showing continuous movement, Rembrandt has frozen time, allowing you to study different actions and details. The visual symphony before you is not as loud and emotional as that of a Rubens. This melody is quieter and more soothing. *The Night Watch* holds your attention with highlights and challenges your imagination with hints of half-hidden forms.

The Mill

Few artists have been as successful as Rembrandt in arousing the viewer's curiosity and rewarding it with a warm and comfortable feeling. Nowhere is this more evident than in his painting of *The Mill* (Figure 3.9, page 48). This is his largest and probably most famous landscape. *The Mill* is an example of the highly personal work that Rembrandt did after the death of his wife, Saskia, in 1642. Deeply saddened, the artist took long walks in the country. The peace and quiet he found in

nature may have helped him overcome his grief. He shares this peace and quiet with you through his painting of the mill.

An Artist in His Studio

Early in his career, Rembrandt painted a small picture of an artist in his studio, (Figure 14.13). It may be a self-portrait—after all, he painted over ninety in his lifetime—or it could be a picture of one of his first students. In either case, it seems to be more than a faithful record of a young painter before his easel. Could it be that Rembrandt uses this painting to tell the viewer something about his ideas on art? In the picture, the artist is not actually working on his painting, nor is the painting visible to you. Instead, he stands some distance away and seems to be studying it. This could be Rembrandt's way of saying that art is a deliberate, thoughtful process requiring much more than skill with a brush. Rembrandt once advised visitors to his studio to stand back from his pictures because the smell of the fresh paint might offend them. Was he hoping that if they stood back they might share the same thoughts that passed through his mind as he studied his paintings? And if so, how remarkably similar this is to the ideas expressed by Leonardo da Vinci almost 150 years earlier when he said that men of genius sometimes produce the most when they do not seem to be working at all.

Criticism

Describe the room illustrated in this picture. Does it seem comfortable? Why are there no chairs? Is the figure here young or old, active or still? What is he staring at? Describe the texture of the wall, the artist's clothing. Point to the most obvious contrasts of value. What dominates in this picture—the artist or the easel with the painting? What idea or message do you receive from this work?

Figure 14.13 Rembrandt van Rijn [Dutch 1609-1669]. *An Artist in His Studio.* **1628. Oil on panel, 25 x 31.5 cm [10 x 12½"]. Courtesy of the Museum of Fine Arts, Boston. The Zoe Oliver Sherman Collection, 38.1838. Given in memory of Lillie Poor Oliver**

Jan Steen

During the same period in which Hals and Rembrandt were working, a group of artists doing only genre paintings supplied the Dutch with pictures for their fashionable homes. These artists are now called the "Little Dutch Masters." However, this label should not in any way suggest that these artists were lacking in skill or sensitivity. Indeed, one of the greatest painters of this period, Jan Vermeer, is often associated with this group of artists. But before discussing Vermeer, some time should be spent examining a painting by one of these Little Dutch Masters, an artist by the name of Jan Steen. It will be time that is well rewarded.

Steen's painting of *The Eve of St. Nicholas* (Figure 14.14) demonstrates again how a painting can be used to tell a story. Here the story is not religious or historical. It is a simple story involving common people and familiar events. When you inventory the literal qualities in this picture, the story becomes clear. It is the Christmas season, and St. Nicholas has just visited the children in this Dutch family. At the right, a young man holding a baby points up to something outside the picture. The child beside him looks upward, his mouth open in wonder. You can almost hear the man saying, "Look, out the window! Isn't that St. Nicholas?"

However, this is not a joyous occasion for everyone in Steen's picture. The boy at the far left has just discovered that his shoe is not filled with gifts at all.★ Instead of candy or fruit, his shoe contains a switch. This can only mean that he did not behave himself during the year and now must suffer the consequences. A child in the center of the picture smiles at you and points to the shoe's disappointing contents. This child makes you feel like a welcomed guest, enjoying the holiday along with this family.

★ **Enrichment** In Holland, holiday gifts were placed in shoes rather than in stockings.

Criticism

How many people are there in this picture? Are they rich or poor? What is each one doing? Point to all the diagonal lines you can find on the right side of this picture. Where do these lines lead? Find the one figure that looks directly at you. Where is this figure pointing? Why is the boy at the left crying? What clues reveal that this is a family gathering to celebrate some holiday? What American holiday is similar to the one being celebrated here? What do you think the man at the right is pointing to?

Figure 14.14   Jan Steen. *The Eve of St. Nicholas.* **c. 1660-65. Approx. 81.9 x 70.5 cm [32¼ x 27¾"]. Rijksmuseum, Amsterdam**

Compare the two rooms shown in this painting. In which room are you, the viewer? Describe the dress, expressions, and actions of the two women. Which is the servant and which is the mistress of the house? How can you tell? Describe their behavior toward one another. Does this behavior have anything to do with the letter held by the seated woman? There is a clue in this picture to suggest that this letter came from far away. Can you find it? Who do you think could have sent the letter?

Figure 14.15 Jan Vermeer. *The Letter*. 1666. Approx. 43.8 x 38.7 cm [17¼ x 15¼"]. Rijksmuseum, Amsterdam

Because he was such an excellent storyteller, you could easily overlook the care that Steen took in organizing this painting. He used diagonal lines to lead you into and around his picture. The long cake at the lower left guides you into the work where the diagonal lines of the table, chair, and canopy direct your attention to the crying boy at the left. Jan Steen not only recognized a good story—he knew how to tell it.

Jan Vermeer

With Jan Vermeer, Dutch genre painting reached its peak. Unfortunately even though he is regarded today as one of the greatest artists of all time, little is known about him. For over two hundred years, Vermeer was all but forgotten, until his genius was recognized during the second half of the nineteenth century. It is known that he lived and died in Delft and that he was the father of eleven children. He most probably had difficulty providing food and shelter for all those children because he was such a slow worker. Less than forty pictures are known to have been painted by Vermeer.★ Of these forty, most illustrate events taking place in the

same room. Because so many of his paintings show inside scenes, Vermeer is often thought of as a painter of interiors. Even though there are people in his paintings, they seem to be less important than the organization of the composition and the effect of light on colors and textures.

The Letter (Figure 14.15) demonstrates Vermeer's mastery as an artist. He has taken an ordinary event and transformed it into a timeless masterpiece of perfect poise and serenity. Everything seems frozen for just a

★ Enrichment Vermeer painted few pictures and fewer still survive, so when his painting of *The Letter* was cut out of its frame and stolen in 1971, the art world was in shock. Eventually the painting was found in a small apartment above a restaurant where the thief worked as a waiter. The painting was rolled up and hidden under the bed. The thief's knife had cut several centimeters [an inch or so] of canvas from around the edge of the picture, and areas of paint had flaked away. It was restored, but, sadly, it would never be the same.

moment as if cast under some magic spell. You are soon made to feel as if you are actually in the painting, standing in a darkened room which looks very much like a closet. A curtain has been pulled aside and a door opened, allowing you to peer into another room where a cool, silvery light filters in from the left. The black and white floor tiles lead your eye into this room where you see two women. The dress of the standing woman suggests that she is a servant. A basket of laundry rests on the floor beside her. She has just handed a letter to the seated woman. This second woman is richly dressed and, until this moment, has been amusing herself by playing the lute. The facial expression and exchange of glances tell you that this is no ordinary letter. The young woman holds the letter carefully and avoids looking at it. Instead, she glances shyly up to the face of the servant girl. No words are uttered, and none are needed. A reassuring smile from the servant girl is enough to tell the young woman that it is indeed a very special letter—no doubt from a very special young man.

On the wall behind the two women are two pictures; both serve a purpose. The landscape in the upper picture curves to repeat the diagonal sweep of the curtain above the door. In this way, it connects the foreground and the background. The second picture is a marine painting showing ships at sea. Perhaps Vermeer is using this picture to tell you that the letter is from someone at sea or someone who has been transported afar by sea. This is quite possible. Dutch artists were fond of painting pictures of people reading letters, and a remarkable number of those paintings include pictures of ships.

The two figures in Vermeer's paintings seem to be surrounded by light and air. This contributes to a feeling of space which is increased by placing the viewer in the darkened closet. Moreover, the doorway of this closet acts as a frame for the scene in the next room. Thus, the foreground is an introduction to the story unfolding deeper in the work.

Vermeer died in 1675 at the age of forty-three. He left behind no romantic legends, no hint of mysterious intrigues, no stories of brawling or tragic love affairs. He left behind much more, a precious few paintings which rank among the greatest works of art ever produced.

Judith Leyster

You may think it unusual, but turning the pages of history ahead to the year 1893 helps to introduce another noteworthy Dutch painter. In that year, officials at the Louvre in Paris decided to clean a painting in the museum collection long thought to have been painted by Frans Hals. Imagine their shock when they discovered that the name on the painting was not that of Hals at all. Adding to their amazement was the fact that the signature was that of a woman—Judith Leyster.

Who was this artist whose work looked so much like that of the great and famous Frans Hals? Surprisingly, it was found that there was little written information available on Judith Leyster. At first, some historians considered her little more than an imitator of Hals. But in the years since, it has been determined that Leyster was a great deal more than that. She is now recognized as a unique and talented artist whose work had its own impact on Dutch art of the seventeenth century.

Judith Leyster was born in 1609 to a brewer in Haarlem. By the time she was seventeen years old, she was already gaining a reputation as a painter of considerable promise. She stood alone in her choice of subject matter of different types. Women artists at the time were expected to paint delicate still lifes. Leyster also painted still lifes, but chose in addition to do genre subjects and portraits. A serious student of art, Leyster studied the works of others and skillfully applied what she learned to her own painting. From artists who had visited Italy she learned about Caravaggio's dramatic use of light and dark. This sparked her own interest in the effects of light on her subjects under varying conditions. It was an interest which remained with her for years to come.

Leyster also learned from the pictures painted by her fellow Dutch artists. She was not only familiar with Hals' work but was a friend of his as well. Records show that she attended the baptism of one of his many children. However, their friendship was strained several years later when Hals coaxed one of Leyster's students to leave her studio and study with him. She brought a lawsuit against him and won, and Hals was required to pay her the money she would have received from the student.

Leyster and Hals had their differences, but this did not interfere with Leyster's appreciation of Hals' technique. She, in fact, imitated it in several instances. It is clear that she saw much to be learned from Hals' remarkable brushwork. However, the influence of Hals on Leyster's style was not far-reaching. The majority of her works give less an impression of the fleeting moment and more the feeling that care and time have been taken to achieve an overall elegant effect. While the subjects in Leyster's portraits often smile and gesture toward the viewer as they do in Hals' pictures, they do so more quietly and with greater dignity. Nowhere is this more evident than in a self-portrait she did at about the time she was involved in her lawsuit with Hals (Figure 14.16). Here you are made to feel as if you have been looking over her shoulder as she worked on a painting of a laughing fiddler. She has just turned to see how you like it. The smile on her attractive face is friendly, and she seems to be completely at ease. Her manner convinces you at once that you are in the company of a good friend. It was just this kind of psychological interaction between subject and viewer that Leyster sought in her paintings of people. And in this self-portrait, she succeeded in achieving it.

Not long after this painting was completed, Leyster married a fellow artist named Meinse Molenaer. Unfortunately, she painted less and less after her marriage. Although she may have worked with her husband on his paintings, it is probable that their three children kept her too busy to return to her easel. Judith Leyster, the artist who shocked the art world with a painting mistaken for a Frans Hals, died in 1660 when she was only fifty years old.

Religious Subjects Continue in Spanish Art

Dutch artists at this time, then, were busy painting portraits, landscapes, and genre subjects. At the same time, however, Spanish artists continued to paint saints, Crucifixions, and martyrdoms. Religious subjects always interested Spanish artists more than other subjects. This had certainly been true in the sixteenth century. At that time, El Greco's art led the mind of the viewer to a mysterious, spiritual world. The seventeenth century was to see a slight change, however. Artists at this time often used the same religious subjects as El Greco, but their works brought the viewer back to earth. Their paintings had a more realistic look. One of the first to show greater realism in his works was Jusepe de Ribera.

History

In what ways is this painting similar to portraits done by Frans Hals? How is it different? What connection did Leyster have with Hals? Does the woman in this picture seem startled, annoyed, or relaxed? Would you describe her as warm and friendly, or cold and aloof? Identify things in the picture to support your decision.

Figure 14.16   Judith Leyster. *Self-Portrait.* c. 1635. Oil on canvas, 72.3 x 65.3 cm [29⅜ x 25⅝"]. The National Gallery of Art, Washington, D.C. Gift of Mr. and Mrs. Robert Woods Bliss, 1949

Which had the greatest influence on Ribera's work: (a) El Greco's mysterious, deeply spiritual pictures, (b) Rubens' complicated paintings filled with active figures, (c) Caravaggio's dramatic lighting and realism, or (d) van Eyck's symbolism and precise detail?

Figure 14.17   Jusepe de Ribera. *The Blind Old Beggar.* **c. 1638. Oil on canvas, 1.24 x 1.02 m [49 x 40¹⁄₁₆″]. Allen Memorial Art Museum, Oberlin College, Oberlin, Ohio. R.T. Miller, Jr. Fund, 55.9**

Jusepe de Ribera

Ribera was born near Valencia, Spain, but moved to Italy while he was still a young man. Because of his short stature, he came to be known to the Italians as "Lo Spagnoletto" or "The Little Spaniard." He lived and studied art in Rome for several years and then moved to Naples, where he remained for the rest of his life. Caravaggio had died only a few years before Ribera arrived in Rome, and the latter's paintings show that he was strongly influenced by that Italian Baroque artist.

The Blind Old Beggar

In his painting of *The Blind Old Beggar* (Figure 14.17), Ribera used Caravaggio's dramatic lighting and realism to paint an old man and a young boy standing together in the shadows. Their faces stand out clearly against a dark background. A light originating outside the painting illuminates these faces and allows you to see every detail. The wrinkles, creases, and rough beard of the old man's face contrast with the smooth freshness of the boy's. The old man's unseeing eyes are tightly closed, but the lively eyes of the boy stare openly at you.

Who are these people that Ribera introduces to you? Some have suggested that they are the main characters from an autobiography published about eighty years before Ribera painted this picture. This book describes the life of a penniless wanderer named Lazarillo de Tormes, or "Little Lazarus of Tormes." It starts with an account of how Lazarillo's mother, unable to feed her many children, gave him to a blind man to act as his guide. In return for his help, Lazarillo was to be cared for by the old man. Forced by a brutal world to depend on each other for survival, they went through many adventures together. But the relationship between the crafty, often cruel old man and the innocent boy was unhappy from the beginning. Gradually the boy became just as shrewd and hardened as his master. Nothing could shock, or surprise, or frighten Lazarillo, and the same can be said for the boy who stares boldly at you from the shadows of Ribera's painting.

A Simple, Calm Style

Baroque painters like Rubens liked to paint large complicated pictures with masses of active people. Ribera's paintings, however, were much simpler. He preferred to paint a single tree rather than a forest, one or two figures instead of a crowd. He also avoided excitement and action in favor of calmness in most of his works. While Rubens' pictures were like a rousing symphony played by a grand orchestra, Ribera's were more like a sonata softly played by a small string quartet.

Works Popular in His Native Spain

Although he chose to live in Italy, Ribera's fame was not limited to that country. He was well known in his native Spain as well and was even visited by the court painter to the Spanish king who came to Italy to purchase works for the royal collection. This court painter's name was Diego Rodríguez Velázquez, destined to be honored as the greatest of Spanish Baroque artists.

Diego Velázquez

Velázquez was born in Seville to a noble family. This presented some problems for him since it was considered improper at that time for a nobleman to earn his living as a common artist. He could follow a career as a painter only if he found a position at the royal court. With this in mind, the young artist went to Madrid with a letter of introduction to one of the king's attendants.

Criticism

The two men in the center are the main characters in this scene—what has been done to make them stand out? What are they doing? What is the one at the left offering the other? How do these figures act toward one another? The soldiers at the right hold their lances erect; how does this differ from the behavior of the soldiers at the left? Does this offer a clue as to which army is the victor and which is the defeated? Does this picture emphasize the horror and brutality of war, or its glory and gallantry?

Figure 14.18   Diego Velázquez. *Surrender of Breda.* 1634-35. Oil on canvas, approx. 3.07 x 3.65 m [10′1″ x 12′]. The Prado, Madrid. Courtesy of Scala/Art Resource, New York, NY

His talent was soon recognized, and he was asked to paint a portrait of the king, Philip IV. When it was finished, Philip was so pleased that he said no one but Velázquez would ever again paint his picture. He was a man of his word. In all, Velázquez painted Philip thirty-four times. No artist ever painted a king so often.

Surrender of Breda

When he was thirty-five years old, Velázquez completed his largest painting. This work celebrated the Spanish victory over the Dutch city of Breda nine years earlier (Figure 14.18). The picture shows the moment when the commander of the Spanish army receives the key to

History

Two figures, one at each side of the picture, stare out at the viewer. They position the viewer directly in front of the two main characters in this scene.

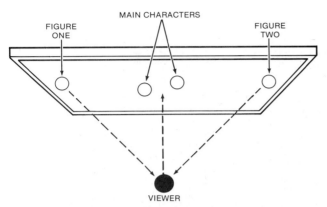

Figure 14.19   Diagram of the viewer's position before Surrender of Breda by Velázquez

the conquered city. Clearly, the two commanders are the main characters in this scene. However, the two figures at either side of the picture are also important. It is they who direct your attention to these main characters. Both side figures stare directly at you. Their gaze, coming from different places in the picture, pinpoints your position in front of the painting (Figure 14.19). From this position, you can observe the meeting of the two rival commanders. So you will know exactly what is happening, the key to the city being passed from one commander to the other is silhouetted against a light background. At the right, the position of a horse helps to lead your eye deeper into the painting where you see the lances and the flag of the Spanish army. The soldiers of this army proudly hold their lances erect. After all, they are the victors. How different are their actions when compared to the careless manner in which the defeated Dutch soldiers at the left hold their lances! Repeating the diagonal movement of the Spanish flag is the smoke rising from the captured city in the background. In this way, Velázquez unites the triumphant army with the city they conquered.

The Maids of Honor

Later in his career, Velázquez painted one of his best-known works, *Las Meninas* (or *The Maids of Honor*) (Figure 14.20). In it he placed the young daughter of the king surrounded by ladies-in-waiting, attendants, and a dog. The artist also shows himself standing at his easel. Further back in the picture, reflected in a mirror, are the faces of the king and queen Velázquez's use of a mirror in this way may remind you of Jan van Eyck's picture of Giovanni Arnolfini and his bride (Figure 12.1, page 211). It is quite possible that Velázquez was influenced by van Eyck's painting since it was a part of the Spanish royal collection at that time.

But what is happening here? Has the princess just entered the room where the artist is painting a portrait of the king and queen? Perhaps the girl at her right is trying to persuade the princess to go with her to another room so that the painter can go on with his work. On the other hand, the artist may be trying to paint the princess while the king and queen watch. But the princess, tired of posing, turns her back to him. Generations of curious viewers have tried to discover what is happening in this picture. But is it really so important? If one sees the painting as nothing more than a picture of everyday life at the palace, it is still interesting. The scene is peaceful, quiet, and natural. There are no surprises or sudden movements. Even the playful boy at the right seems gentle and unhurried as he arouses a sleeping dog with his foot. The dog, only half-awake, seems unconcerned. As soon as he is left alone, he will go back to sleep.

One of the most striking things about Velázquez's painting is the way he creates the illusion of space. You can see the scene stretched out before you as well as a continuation of it behind you reflected in the mirror. But Velázquez goes even further by suggesting the world beyond the room, which he allows you to glimpse through an open door. Light from a window illuminates the foreground, while the background is veiled in soft shadows. You not only see space here—you can almost feel it. If you could enter that room, you would first pass through the bright, warm sunlight in the foreground and, with each step, move deeper and deeper into the shadowy coolness of the interior. If you wished, you could then walk through the open door, up the steps, and out of the room. On the stairs you would have to squeeze by a man who seems to be adjusting a curtain. Perhaps, as you pass, he will tell you that he is trying to give the artist more light by which to paint.

Criticism

How many people are in this picture? Is the open door at the back of the room the only place where light enters? If not, from which direction does additional light come? How is the illusion of space created in this painting? How is space beyond the room suggested? Do you think this is an important event, or just a common occurrence for these people? What do you find most appealing about this picture?

Figure 14.20   Diego Velázquez. *Las Meninas* (*The Maids of Honor*). 1656. Oil on canvas, 3.18 x 1.08 m [10′ 5″ x 9′]. The Prado, Madrid. [All rights reserved]

Compare the clothing worn by the two men in the center. What does this tell you about them? Describe their actions toward one another. Would you say that your eye is drawn *into* this picture, or does it sweep *across* it? What do you think is happening here? Do you think that this story will have a happy ending?

Figure 14.21 Bartolomé Esteban Murillo. *The Return of the Prodigal Son.* **Between 1670 and 1674. Oil on canvas, 2.36 x 2.61 m [7′ 9″ x 8′ 6″]. The National Gallery of Art, Washington, D.C. Gift of the Avalon Foundation, 1948**

Bartolomé Esteban Murillo

While Velázquez was working at the royal court in Madrid, another artist named Bartolomé Esteban Murillo was building a reputation for himself in Seville. Like Velázquez, Murillo was born in Seville, but not to a noble family. Orphaned at ten, he was raised by an uncle. Murillo showed an early interest in art by drawing in his schoolbooks and on walls. His uncle realized that Murillo had talent and placed the boy with a local artist where he could study art. Later, Murillo was forced to earn a living by painting and selling pictures in the marketplace. At first, people stopped to look at his work out of curiosity and were surprised to find that they liked what they saw. They bought his works, and Murillo's reputation began to grow, until he was recognized as the leading artist in the city.

The Prodigal Son

Many of Murillo's paintings were done for monasteries and convents. One of these tells the familiar tale of *The Prodigal Son* (Figure 14.21). All of the characters and objects described in the Bible story are included. You see the father welcoming his wayward son; the calf to be prepared for the celebration feast; and servants bringing a ring, shoes, and new garments. Notice the contrast between excited and calm feelings in the picture. On the one hand, you see a little dog barking excitedly and servants conversing in an earnest manner. On the other hand, you see that the tone of the reunion between father and son is tender and quiet. Murillo avoided sharp lines and color contrasts in order to keep his composition simple and harmonious. In this way, the viewer would not be distracted from observing the joy associated with the son's return.

Church Division Has Lasting Effect on Art

It seems fitting for a discussion of the seventeenth century to close with a painting of *The Prodigal Son.* This subject accurately reflects the Catholic Church's attitude during this period of the Counter-Reformation. Like the forgiving father, it welcomed back those who had followed Martin Luther and other Protestant Reformers. Many did return, but many others did not. The religious map of Europe was now complete, and it has stayed about the same ever since.★ For artists, this meant that they could no longer seek out or depend upon a universal Church for commissions. At the same time, they experienced a new freedom. Rather than producing works solely for the Church, they were able to paint, carve, and build for a variety of patrons. Their freedom also extended to subject matter, for most of these patrons did not ask for religious works. In fact, most of them taxed the artists' ingenuity with demands for art that was not inspired by religion.

★ Enrichment The Catholic countries were located in the southern portion of western Europe and included Portugal, Spain, France, Flanders, Italy, Austria, and parts of Germany. The Protestant countries occupied the northern section of western Europe and included Holland, England, and the remaining parts of Germany.

Studio Experiences

Lesson One: Drawing a Shape Moving in Space

In your reading you discovered that Baroque forms and figures do more than occupy space —they seem to move about freely in that space. Notice how the illusion of movement in space is captured in Bernini's *The Ecstasy of St. Theresa* (Figure 14.4) and Rubens' *The Elevation of the Cross* (Figure 14.8). Try to create that same sensation of movement in space during this drawing activity. First, draw a simple geometric shape at the top left corner of a sheet of paper. Then draw the same shape at the lower right corner of the paper. Now, imagine that the shape you have drawn is made of rubber. Your picture shows the first and last positions of that rubber shape after it has been dropped and bounced on the floor. Reproduce the shape as it twists, turns, and bounces through space from its starting position to its resting place. You will, of course, have to draw the shape over and over again and overlap these drawings to suggest a *continuous movement through space*. At least one bounce should be indicated.

Lesson Two: Ink Drawings Emphasizing Value Contrasts for Dramatic Effect

Baroque artists are recognized for the way they make use of contrasts of light and dark values for dramatic emphasis (see Figures 14.6, 14.7, 14.12, 14.17, and 14.20). Ask a friend or fellow student to act as a model and position him or her in an action pose (throwing, chopping, pushing, etc.). Complete several quick preliminary sketches in which you try to capture the action or gesture of the model. (You can use pencil, charcoal, crayon, or chalk for these preliminary sketches.) Then darken the room and direct a spotlight on the model. With India ink and brush, paint the *shadowed areas* observed on the model. Do several of these ink drawings, concentrating on bold contrasts of light and dark values and simplified shapes. Finished drawings should reveal a concern for dramatic impact rather than accuracy in representing the physical form.

Chapter 15

In Search of Pleasure: Rococo Art

Courtly Beginnings

On a pleasant evening in 1661, the young king of France, Louis XIV, attended a celebration in his honor at a great château owned by his minister of finance. The king viewed the fine home of his minister and grew jealous and suspicious. He decided, correctly, that the minister must be stealing from him in order to live in such luxury. Angered, he sent his minister to prison for life. Then he hired the minister's architects, artists, decorators, and gardeners to work for him on the greatest building project of the age.

At Versailles, a short distance from Paris, the king's father had built a hunting lodge, and this became the site for the largest, most elegant palace in the world (Figure 15.1). It was to be the king's home as well as the capital of France. The royal family moved into it in 1682, but the palace continued to undergo changes.

Louis and his followers were always making improvements and adding new decorations. Walls were torn down and new ones built; windows, balconies, and staircases were added; and paintings and sculptures purchased.

Within the palace, Louis was treated as if he were a god. He chose the sun as his emblem and was known as the "Sun King." Fences, balconies, and even the roof of the palace were gilded to reflect the golden rays of the sun. In this luxurious setting, court life was a continuous pageant with the king always in the spotlight. To make sure that there was an audience for this display of power and wealth, people were free to enter and wander about the palace as long as they were properly dressed. There they could stare at the artworks, the tapestries, the mirrors. They could even watch the king and queen eat their spectacular meals. Every action of the king was made into a royal ceremony with strict rules. Thus, only high-ranking noblemen were allowed to dry the king after his bath or hand him his shirt during the dressing ceremony.

Versailles was considered to be an example of the Baroque style in France. However, in this elegant, aristocratic setting were also the seeds of a new style which was to see fruition at the beginning of the eighteenth century. This new style had its origins in the luxurious court of Louis XIV, but more truly reflected the character of the court of Louis XV, great grandson of the Sun King. The style was marked by a free, graceful movement, a playful use of line, and bright colors. Sometimes referred to as "Late Baroque," it differed enough from the Baroque that it deserved its own label. It received one when artists at the beginning of the next century irreverently called it "Rococo."★

★ **Enrichment** "Rococo" comes from the French *rocaille*, meaning "pebble" or "rockwork" of the kind used to decorate artificial grottoes. The reason for the selection of this word to describe the ornamental, decorative art style of the eighteenth century is unknown. However, it is certain that when the word was first used towards the end of the century, it was meant to indicate disrespect for this style of art.

Rococo art placed emphasis on the carefree life of the aristocracy rather than on grand heroes or pious martyrs. Love and romance were thought to be more fitting subjects for art than history and religion. At a time when poets were creating flowery phrases of love, painters were using delicate, pastel colors to express the same sentiment. Both showed a zest for describing a light-hearted world filled with people looking for pleasure and happiness.

New Directions in French Painting

In painting, the dramatic action of the seventeenth century gave way to this new carefree Rococo style. The constant movement of the Baroque lost its force in Rococo art, which favored greater control and elegance. Paintings made greater use of rich colors and curved, graceful patterns. This made them look more light-hearted and decorative. When seen in the palaces and châteaux for which they were intended, these paintings added a final touch of gaiety and elegance.

Figure 15.1   Louis Le Vau and Jules Hardouin-Mansart. Garden façade of the Palace at Versailles, France. 1669-85

Describe the dress and manners of these people. Do you think they are poor, middle-class, or wealthy? Can you find many dark, heavy outlines, or do the colors and shapes seem to blend together? Does this look like a real or an imaginary setting? If you had to use a single word to describe the mood of this picture, what would it be?

Figure 15.2 Antoine Watteau. *Embarkation for Cythera*. 1717-19. Approx. 1.3 x 1.9 m [4′ 3″ x 6′ 4½″]. The Louvre, Paris

Antoine Watteau

The greatest of the Rococo painters was a Frenchman named Antoine Watteau. Watteau began his career as an interior decorator and rose to become the court painter to King Louis XV. Although he painted religious works and portraits, Watteau is best known for pictures of characters or scenes from the theater as well as paintings showing the French aristocracy at play.

In *Embarkation for Cythera* (Figure 15.2), he combines both these themes in a work that demonstrates the elegance of the Rococo style. The subject of this painting comes from a play and shows a happy group of young aristocrats about to set sail from Cythera, the legendary island of romance. The soft, dreamlike atmosphere, luxurious costumes, dainty figures, and silvery colors give the picture its unique feeling, or mood. Nothing is still, but nothing seems strained either. The figures move with graceful ease. Arranged like a garland, they curl over a small hill and down into a valley bordering the sea. A similar garland made of cupids playfully twists around the mast of the ship. In many ways, Watteau's figures look like fashion dolls—although the fashion may look odd to you. No doubt, you would look twice if you saw men wearing high-heeled shoes and carrying walking sticks today, but in the eighteenth century that was considered to be the height of fashion.★

★ **Enrichment** Women's fashions were also unusual, especially if judged by today's standards. Hairdos grew taller and taller until they made a woman's face appear to be located in the middle of her person. At the same time, the heels of their shoes were raised to amazing heights. All this made it necessary, at times, for architects to raise or widen doors in order to allow the fashion-conscious ladies to pass through.

Embarkation for Cythera appears to be a happy scene, but it is tempered by a touch of sadness. One figure in particular seems to sum up this feeling. It is the woman in the center who casts one final backward glance as she reluctantly prepares to join her companions in boarding the boat. Along with her friends, she has spent a carefree day on the island paying homage to Venus, the goddess of Love (whose flower-covered statue is seen at the far right of the picture). But the day is now coming to a close. It is time to leave this world of make-believe and return to reality. The woman lingers for just a moment, but her companion reminds her to hurry —the dream is ending.

Many of Watteau's works hint at the fleeting nature of happiness. Perhaps the sadness in his pictures reflects the sadness in his own life. Watteau was always in poor health, and four years after this painting was completed, he died. He was only thirty-seven years old.

Jean-Honoré Fragonard

Ignoring the growing signs of unrest that led to the French Revolution, the upper class continued to devote their lives to pleasure. They liked to frolick in park-like gardens, gaze dreamily through telescopes, pamper their pets, play on elegant swings, or engage in idle gossip. All of these trivial pastimes are found in a painting by Jean-Honoré Fragonard (Figure 15.3).

Fragonard, like Watteau, was a court painter. Until the revolution, he was also one of the most popular artists in France. He painted pictures about love and romance using glowing, pastel colors applied in a sure, brisk manner. But these pictures also reveal that Fragonard was a master designer as well. In *The Swing* he used axis lines and contour lines to tie the parts of his composition together. The arrangement of the figures, the ropes of the swing, the water from the lion fountains, even the position of the telescope form a series of parallel diagonal lines in the lower part of the picture.

Criticism

Identify the different activities found in this painting. What sort of people would have the opportunity to spend their days in this way? Note the rounded contours of the clouds—can you find the same rounded contours repeated elsewhere in this picture? Why do you think this was done? Which term seems most appropriate to describe the colors here—bold, clashing, dull, or dainty?

Figure 15.3 Jean-Honoré Fragonard. *The Swing.* Probably c. 1765. Oil on canvas, approx. 2.2 x 1.8 m [85 x 73"]. The National Gallery of Art, Washington, D.C. Samuel H. Kress Collection, 1961

He tied the sky and the landscape together with repeated, rounded contours; the clouds at the right repeat the curved contours of the trees at the left.

The French Revolution brought a swift end to Fragonard's popularity. Near the end of his life he stopped painting entirely. At the time of his death (he died of a stroke while eating ice cream), he was all but forgotten. Today his works are reminders of a bygone era and an outdated way of life. But to the sensitive viewer they still whisper softly of pleasant outings in the park, idle talk, and romance.

Jean-Baptiste Siméon Chardin

Not all artists in eighteenth-century France accepted the elegant court style of Watteau and Fragonard. Jean-Baptiste Siméon Chardin disliked the delicately painted subjects of the court artists. He preferred subjects that were more in keeping with those painted by the Little Dutch Masters. His works showed peasants and the middle-class going about their simple daily chores. He chose to show this rather than aristocrats engaged in frivolous pastimes.*

Chardin saw in the arrangement of simple objects the symbols of the common man. He painted still lifes (Figure 15.4) of humble, everyday items. Earthenware containers, copper kettles, vegetables, and meat were his subjects. Chardin took delight in showing slight changes of color, light, and texture. The way he painted these objects made them seem important and worthy of close examination.

★ **Enrichment** Chardin's career as a painter began in an unusual way. Asked by a surgeon to paint a sign for his shop, Chardin decided not to paint the customary symbols for the profession—a shaving dish and a surgical knife. Instead, he painted a scene showing a wounded dualist being cared for by a surgeon on his doorstep. As soon as it was hung, the sign began to attract great crowds of people who marveled at the skill of the young artist.

History

How did Chardin's work differ from the works of court artists like Watteau and Fragonard? Of which earlier artists are you reminded when looking at Chardin's paintings? What was his purpose in painting these unimportant, common objects?

Figure 15.4 Jean-Baptiste Siméon Chardin. *Still Life with Rib of Beef.* **1739. Oil on canvas, 40.6 x 33.2 cm [16 x 13¹⁄₁₆"]. Allen Memorial Art Museum, Oberlin College, Oberlin, Ohio. R. T. Miller, Jr. Fund, 45.32**

Criticism

Is this woman engaged in an important task? Do you think she enjoys what she is doing? How can you tell? How do the dark and light values help to emphasize the main parts of this painting? Point to places where there is a contrast of value; a gradation of value.

Figure 15.5   Jean-Baptiste Siméon Chardin. *The Attentive Nurse.* **Probably c. 1738. Oil on canvas, 46.2 x 37 cm [18½ x 14½"]. The National Gallery of Art, Washington, D.C. Samuel H. Kress Collection, 1952**

Toward the middle of his career, Chardin began to paint simple genre scenes. One such scene is *The Attentive Nurse* (Figure 15.5). There is a gentle, homespun quality in this work that is unforced and natural. His brush illuminates beauty hidden in the commonplace. Chardin shows you a quiet, orderly, and wholesome way of life. You are welcomed into a comfortable household where a hardworking nurse is carefully preparing a meal. Light filters in softly to touch the figure and the table in the foreground. The rest of the room is partly hidden in the shadows. The light reveals the rich textures and creates the changes of value on cloth, bread, and kitchen utensils. The colors are silvery browns and warm golds, which add to the calmness, the poetry of this common domestic scene.

In his old age, Chardin gave up oil painting in favor of pastels because of his failing eyesight.[*] The best of these pastels were self-portraits and portraits of his wife. Weakened by illness, he died in 1779.

★ **Enrichment** Other reasons have been suggested for Chardin's decision to work in pastels. Some historians have indicated that he used pastels because they allowed him to work more quickly than did oil paints. And, because pastels require less time and effort for preparation, Chardin may have found them more relaxing to work with.

Does this figure seem tense or relaxed? Point to the warm and cool colors used in this painting. Are the warm colors used in the foreground or in the background? Where are the cool colors used? When judging this picture, to which aesthetic qualities—literal, visual, or expressive—did you refer most often?

Figure 15.6 Sir Joshua Reynolds. *Lady Betty Hamilton.* **1758. Oil on canvas, 1.17 x 0.84 m [46 x 33″]. The National Gallery of Art, Washington, D.C. Widener Collection, 1942**

The Movement in England

Up until this time, England could boast of only a few outstanding painters and sculptors. No doubt, the Protestant Reformation was partly to blame for this. Reformers were against religious images, and this had a crushing effect on art. However, with the return of the fun-loving Stuarts to the English throne and the growth of a wealthy aristocracy, the visual arts gained in importance. Portrait painting in particular grew in popularity. But, instead of making use of English artists, the wealthy invited foreign portrait painters such as Hans Holbein to England. This practice continued until around the middle of the eighteenth century. By then the talents of native English painters were finally being appreciated.

Sir Joshua Reynolds

Sir Joshua Reynolds was one of a number of English artists who painted the fashionable portraits that the English nobility desired. Highly respected as an artist and a scholar, he was also a kindly man who was genuinely fond of children. No doubt this enabled him to capture on canvas their sensitive and fleeting expressions. This helped make him one of the most popular artists of his time. His appealing portrait of the five-year-old daughter of the Duke of Hamilton (Figure 15.6) shows that he could make his young subjects seem completely natural and at ease.

Thomas Gainsborough

Reynolds' great rival was Thomas Gainsborough, who began his career by painting landscapes. Ultimately he became the favorite portrait painter of English high society. Gainsborough was admired for his delicate brushwork and rich, glistening pastel colors. His works showed the shining silks and buckles, fragile lace, and starched ruffles of fashionable clothing.

A professional rivalry with Reynolds resulted in one of Gainsborough's best-known paintings, *Blue Boy* (Figure 15.7). In a lecture to the Royal Academy of Art, Reynolds had stated that blue, a cool color, should always be used in the background. He said it should never be used in the main part of a portrait.★ When Gainsborough heard this, he accepted it as a challenge and began planning a blue portrait. According to one account, he had a blue satin costume prepared and then set about finding someone to model it for the painting. The "someone" turned out to be a delivery boy whom Gainsborough met in his own kitchen. He quickly arranged to have the surprised youth pose for him and completed the painting. The finished portrait showed a princely-looking boy dressed in a shimmering blue satin suit standing in front of a warm brown background. The work was an immediate success in the eyes of most viewers—although Reynolds never publicly admitted that Gainsborough had proved him wrong.

This story does not end here, however. Later, when Gainsborough was dying, Reynolds paid him a visit. What they said to one another is unknown. But we do know that when Gainsborough died, Reynolds, with tears in his eyes, delivered another lecture to the Royal Academy, this time praising the rival who had challenged him.

★ **Enrichment**   Notice that Reynolds' portrait of Lady Hamilton shows the child dressed in a warm red dress before a blue background. Sir Joshua practiced what he preached.

History

How does the use of warm and cool colors here differ from the use of warm and cool colors in Reynolds' picture of Lady Betty Hamilton? Reynolds and Gainsborough were alike in that both became famous for which of the following: (a) genre scenes of middle-class subjects, (b) portraits of English aristocracy, or (c) deeply religious subjects inspired by the Bible?

Figure 15.7   Thomas Gainsborough. *Blue Boy*. 1770. The Huntington Library, San Marino, California

From your reading, can you identify the main characters in this drama? What clues can you find to suggest that the marriage being planned will not be a happy one?

Figure 15.8 William Hogarth. *Scene I* from *Marriage à la Mode, The Marriage Contract.* **1744. Oil on canvas. Reproduced by courtesy of the Trustees of the National Gallery, London**

William Hogarth

Other artists in England at this time refused to cater to the tastes of the aristocracy in the manner of Reynolds and Gainsborough. William Hogarth was one of these. Hogarth began his career as a commercial artist in London, a city that he must have enjoyed. In all his sixty-seven years, he left it only twice. He was more interested in painting the common people he found on London streets and in taverns than in painting portraits for wealthy patrons. Nothing gave him more pleasure than exposing the immoral conditions and foolish customs of his time. He used his art to tell a story, scene by scene, picture by picture, with great wit and attention to detail. His pictures were a stage filled with colorful performers from every level of society: lords, ladies, lawyers, merchants, beggars, thieves, and lunatics.

In a series of six paintings entitled *Marriage à la Mode,* Hogarth criticized the practice of arranged marriages. In the first of this series, *The Marriage Contract* (Figure 15.8), he introduces the main characters in his story. At the right, a nobleman with gout points proudly to the family tree to prove that his son is a worthy groom.★ He is speaking to a wealthy merchant seated across from him who is eager to have his daughter marry into a noble family. The merchant peers through his thick

---

★ **Enrichment** Gout is a disease causing swelling and severe pain, especially in the big toe. It was believed to be caused by a rich life-style and so was regarded as an ailment affecting only the very wealthy.

spectacles studying the marriage agreement as if it were nothing more than a business contract. Meanwhile, the future bride and groom, their backs to each other, seem uninvolved and uninterested. A lawyer flirts with the young woman, while her bored fiancé prepares to take a pinch of snuff.

The other five pictures in this series show the progress of the marriage from this unfortunate start. It moves from boredom to unfaithfulness to death. Each scene is painted with the same brilliant, biting satire. The paintings demonstrate Hogarth's uncanny ability to remember and use what he saw in the world around him. The gestures and expressions that he uses were learned during long observations of the way real people behave in different situations. Interestingly, Hogarth was too impatient to carry a notebook or a sketchpad, although he sometimes used his thumbnail as a tiny surface on which to sketch. In Hogarth's case, nothing else was necessary.

Hogarth was a small man, slightly over 152 cm [5 feet] tall, although this did not prevent him from being stylish. As soon as he could afford one, he bought a sword and wore it at all times. He was proud and cocky and never hesitated to voice his opinion on any subject. But the quality of his art and his great wit won him the admiration of many intellectuals and the affection of the English public.

While it took English painters a long time to gain acceptance in their native country, this was not the case with architects. In fact, many of the most impressive buildings in London are due to the efforts of a single English architect: Sir Christopher Wren.

Sir Christopher Wren

At 1:00 A.M. on September 2, 1666, a fire broke out in a baker's shop in Pudding Lane in the sprawling city of London. The blaze spread quickly from building to building and raged for four days. Before it could be brought under control, it had destroyed eighty-nine churches, the city gates, a large number of public buildings, and some fourteen thousand houses. For years after this fire, Sir Christopher Wren was responsible for designing churches and other buildings to replace those that had been destroyed. St. Paul's Cathedral and fifty-one parish churches were built according to his designs. As if this were not enough, he also played an active role in supervising the construction of each. He routinely walked from one building site to the next jotting down notes as he went along. Because Wren assumed the entire responsibility for each construction, he felt free to make changes. And make changes he did: workers would rarely know what to expect from one day to the next. Each day he would present them with

rough plans which were often sketched on the spot. If he did not like the results, even if they were done according to his plans, he would order the work torn down and rebuilt according to a new design.

It was not easy to design churches to fit comfortably within specified areas. Many of these areas were small and awkward. Yet Wren was able to design churches which were ideally suited for their settings. Often, he used a tall, slender steeple to crown these churches. Soaring proudly above surrounding buildings which threatened to hide the church, this steeple became an inspiration for later architects in England and America.

The best known of Wren's work is St. Paul's Cathedral (Figure 15.9). Before the fire, he had been hired to restore the old cathedral which had been built late in the eleventh century. The fire, however, destroyed the building, and Wren was asked to design a new cathedral instead. Like most of his other buildings, St. Paul's was constantly changed as it was being built.

History

Find the tympanum and the dome of this cathedral. How has the architect directed your eye to these two important features? How do the columns here differ from those you have seen in earlier buildings? In what ways is this building similar to Borromini's San Carlo alle Quattro Fontane? In what ways is it different?

Figure 15.9 Sir Christopher Wren. St. Paul's Cathedral, London. 1675-1710

The façade of St. Paul's is marked by a pattern of light and dark values. This pattern is created by the use of deep porches at two levels. Each porch is supported by huge columns arranged in pairs. The top porch is narrower than the one below and draws your eye upward to the tympanum and the great dome above. Two towers flank the façade and frame the dome.

You may feel that St. Paul's reminds you of Borromini's San Carlo alle Quattro Fontane (Figure 14.2, page 245), which was constructed over forty years earlier. Of course, Wren's building is much larger and does not have concave and convex surfaces. But, like Borromini's church, it does make use of light and dark value contrasts. On San Carlo these contrasts create a feeling of movement, while on St. Paul's they suggest stability and strength.

The London skyline is Wren's legacy—and his monument. The Latin inscription on his tomb calls attention to this skyline with a simple but appropriate statement that reads: "If ye seek my monument, look around." Only when you do can you fully appreciate this great architect's remarkable imagination, skill, and energy.

Spanish Rococo Art: Francisco Goya

This discussion of eighteenth-century art ends in Spain with the work of Francisco Goya, an artist who eventually rejected the past and looked to the future. Goya's early works were in the Rococo style imported from France.

The Marquesa de Pontejos

His fashionable portrait of *The Marquesa de Pontejos* (Figure 15.10), shows a doll-like figure standing stiffly in a park bathed in a soft Rococo light. The woman's stylish gown has been painted to reveal every fold, ribbon, and flower. The silver-grays and pinks are similar to the colors used by Watteau and Fragonard. A straw hat and an elegant hairdo circle a face that reveals little emotion. The Marquesa neither smiles nor frowns. In fact, it is difficult to say if she is happy or sad. Was she afraid that a smile would create lines that might mar her smooth complexion? Her pose is as stiff and unnatural as the expression on her face and suggests that she was trying very hard to look dignified and important.

Criticism

List the colors found in this painting. Is there a great deal of contrast in hues? Would you say this figure's pose is casual and natural, or stiff and unnatural? What has been done to attract your eye to this woman's face? Describe the expression on this face—is it sad, happy, angry, or expressionless?

Figure 15.10   Francisco Goya. *The Marquesa de Pontejos*. Possibly 1786. Oil on canvas, 2.11 x 1.26 m [83 x 49¾"]. The National Gallery of Art, Washington, D.C. Andrew W. Mellon Collection, 1937

Criticism

What is about to happen here? Describe the actions of each figure at the left. Describe the actions of the group of figures at the right. Where have repeated shapes and axis lines been used to create a sense of movement? What is the direction of that movement? Which is the most important figure in this composition? How has that figure been made to stand out? What feeling or emotions do you receive from this picture?

Figure 15.11 Francisco Goya. *The Third of May, 1808.* 1814. Oil on canvas, approx. 2.64 x 3.43 m [8′ 8″ x 11′ 3″]. The Prado, Madrid

The Third of May, 1808

Goya was satisfied to be a fashionable society painter until he was forty-five years old. But then, after seeing the brutality and the suffering caused by war, his art changed and he became Goya the Rebel. He was in Madrid when the French invaded Spain. One of his most memorable paintings commemorates an uprising of the people of Madrid after the French had occupied the city (Figure 15.11). On May 2, 1808, people had gathered in anger before the royal palace. They had heard that the children of the king were to be taken to France. A fight broke out and Spanish civilians and French soldiers were killed. That night and the next morning, French troops executed the Spanish patriots they had taken prisoner. It was a tragic scene that Goya may have witnessed personally from his balcony.

Goya's view of this grim event shows the patriots, including a clergyman, lined up and about to be shot. The morning sky is almost black, and a lantern placed on the ground lights the scene. In the glare of this lantern, you see the wild gestures of the helpless victims, in contrast to the cool efficiency of the French troops.

The soldiers lean forward pointing their rifles like lances, their faces hidden from view. But their faces are unimportant here. They are like robots—cold, unfeeling, unthinking. The wedge of light from the lantern reveals the different reactions of the men facing death. The central target is a figure in white with his arms raised. His pose suggests an earlier sacrifice—Christ on the Cross. To his right, a monk seeks refuge in prayer. The three others exhibit less courage. One stares blindly at the rifle barrels. Another holds his ears so he will not hear the crack of the rifles. The third buries his face in his hands.

Goya's painting does not echo the traditional view of war. Unlike his countryman Velázquez (Figure 14.18, page 263), he placed no importance on chivalry and honor or bravery and glory. To him, war meant only death and destruction, and he used his art to pass his feelings on to others.

On what is this figure sitting? What does this tell you about his size? Point to places where there are contrasts in value; gradations in value. Do you find anything frightening about this figure? Whom or what do you think he represents? Where did Goya turn for inspiration?

Figure 15.12   Francisco Goya. *The Giant* **(etching). c. 1820. The Metropolitan Museum of Art, New York. Harris Brisbane Dick Fund, 1935, 35.42**

The Giant

As he grew older, Goya became even more bitter and disillusioned. Increasingly he turned away from the subject matter found in the real world because it could not be used to communicate his thoughts and feelings. Instead, he began to rely on his dreams and visions for subject matter. The drawings, paintings, and etchings that he produced were unlike anything that had been created before. For the first time, an artist reached deep into his own mind for inspiration. By doing this, Goya made it difficult for others to understand exactly what he was trying to say. But he also challenged them to use their imaginations to arrive at their own interpretations of his work.

One of Goya's most unforgettable prints shows a giant sitting on the edge of the world (Figure 15.12). A small landscape in the foreground is dwarfed by the towering presence of this giant. Who is he and what is he looking up at? Could this be Goya's vision of war—a giant who could, with one swipe of his mighty hand, cause widespread destruction and suffering? He glances up as if something has just disturbed him. Perhaps he is being summoned into action at this very moment. If so, what does this hold in store for the unsuspecting world resting peacefully in the moonlight?

Breaking the Bounds of Tradition

The eighteenth century began with artists creating works which stressed the lighthearted and fanciful. Artists like Watteau and Fragonard painted the beauty, wealth, and gaiety of court life. But a more middle-class view of life was provided by the works of Chardin and Hogarth. Goya's works ranged from the courtly Rococo style to the more realistic and finally to the realm of his imagination. By using his own visions and dreams as the inspiration for his art, Goya opened the door for others to follow. From this point on, artists no longer felt bound by tradition. Like Goya, they could rely on their own personal visions to move in any direction they wished. For this reason, Goya is regarded as the bridge between the art of the past and the art of the present.

Studio Experiences

Lesson One: Still-Life Drawing in Pastels

Compare and contrast paintings in the Rococo style by Watteau (Figure 15.2) and Fragonard (Figure 15.3) with works by Chardin (Figures 15.4 and 15.5). Then, focusing on Chardin's paintings, observe the subtle changes of color, value, and texture. Set up a still life consisting of several familiar objects. Then make a simple viewfinder by cutting a piece of cardboard into two "L" shapes. Join the two "L" shapes together to frame different views of the still life. In this way you can frame small or large portions of the still life. Select a neutral-tone drawing paper (or construction paper) and use white chalk to draw the most pleasing view framed in your viewfinder. Study the still-life objects thoroughly and try to reproduce them as accurately as possible. Then use pastels to add color to your drawing. When using pastels keep the following suggestions in mind:

• First apply "base colors" that closely match the colors of the still-life objects.

• Blend in lighter values to suggest highlights.

• Add details and blend in the darkest values.

• Observe how gradations of light and dark values can be used to suggest the roundness of certain shapes.

Make certain to reproduce as accurately as possible the varied textured surfaces noted in your still-life objects.

Safety Note

Inhaling chalk dust may be harmful to your health, particularly if you are asthmatic or have breathing difficulties. If your physician cautions against using art materials that may cause dust *bring this to the attention of your instructor immediately*. A substitute material can easily be found. In this lesson, for example, watercolor or tempera paints could be substituted for pastels.

Lesson Two: Expressing an Emotion or Mood in an Ink Drawing

Study the actions, expressions, and gestures of the figures in Goya's painting of an actual event entitled *The Third of May, 1808* (Figure 15.11). Select a newspaper or magazine article dealing with an unusual or exciting contemporary event. Complete several pencil sketches in which you illustrate the event described in the article. Be sure to emphasize the expressive qualities in these sketches—you should be trying to communicate feelings or moods rather than provide an objective illustration. Transfer your best sketch to white drawing paper and go over the pencil lines with India ink (using pen, brush, or both). Ink washes of varied values should then be used to tint different areas or shapes. Include contrasts of value to emphasize the most important parts of the picture. Before doing this, you may want to refer back to Goya's painting to see how he did this.

Chapter 16

Era of Change: New Styles in Nineteenth-Century Art

Artists you will meet in this chapter

Jacques Louis David (*zjahk* loo-*ee* dah-*veed*), 1748-1825. His painting of an assassinated political figure was intended to stir the viewer's emotions.

Marie Louise Elisabeth Vigée-Lebrun (*mah*-ree *lu*-eez aye-*lee*-zah-bet vee-*zhaye* luh-*brun*), 1755-1842. Her friendship with the ill-fated Queen of France helped assure her reputation.

Jean-Auguste-Dominique Ingres (*zjahn* oh-*gust* doh-min-*eek ahn*-gr), 1780-1867. After an eighteen-year absence from his native France, he wondered how his newest painting would be received when he returned. If it was a failure, he vowed to leave Paris at once.

Théodore Géricault (*tay*-oh-door jay-ree-*coe*), 1791-1824. His painting of the *Raft of the Medusa* signaled the birth of a new art style.

Eugène Delacroix (oo-*zhen* del-lah-*kwah*), 1798-1863. His love of exotic settings, dramatic action, and bold colors is evident in his paintings.

John Constable (*jahn kahn*-stuh-buhl), 1776-1837. His landscapes captured the look and feel of a scene as it appeared at a particular moment in time.

Joseph M. W. Turner (*joh*-sef *ter*-ner), 1775-1851. Light and atmosphere became the most important ingredients in his paintings.

Gustave Courbet (*guss*-tav koor-*bay*), 1819-77. His painting of a funeral established him as the leader of a new style and made him famous at the age of thirty.

Edouard Manet (aye-doh-*are* ma-nay), 1832-83. He was more interested in technique than in subject matter.

Rosa Bonheur (*roe*-zah bahn-*err*), 1822-99. Her paintings of animals made her one of the most popular painters in Europe.

Claude Monet (*kload* muh-*nay*), 1840-1926. He spent a lifetime trying to capture in paint the effects of sunlight on subject matter.

Pierre Auguste Renoir (pee-*err* oh-*gust* ren-*wahr*), 1841-1919. He continued to paint his happy pictures even in his old age when, crippled by rheumatism, brushes had to be tied to his wrists.

Suzuki Harunobu (soo-*zoo*-key hor-oo-*noh*-boo), 1718-70. His works and those produced by other Japanese printmakers inspired French painters in the nineteenth century.

Edgar Degas (ed-*gahr* dug-*ah*), 1834-1917. The ballet studio and the race track provided him with his favorite subject matter.

Mary Cassatt (*mair*-ee cah-*sat*), 1845-1926. Degas challenged her to paint a picture of real merit—and was so impressed with the result that he bought it!

Berthe Morisot (*bairt* moh-ree-*zoh*), 1841-95. Fellow artists considered her work equal to theirs, but critics failed to take her seriously—until after her death.

Auguste Rodin (oh-*gust* roh-*dan*), 1840-1917. Light and shadows on the bumpy surfaces of his sculptures give them life and vitality.

Looking to the Past

The growth of academies, or art schools, in France and England during the seventeenth and eighteenth centuries changed the way artists were taught. No longer were they apprenticed to established masters to learn their craft. Instead, art was taught in the same way as other school subjects. The academies urged their students to study the famous works of the past as the best way of developing their own skills.

The emphasis on the greatness of the past was not limited to the academies. The people who bought paintings also showed a preference for artworks produced by the great masters. Thus, when a wealthy French merchant decided to buy a painting for his new country home, he preferred a work by one of the old masters rather than one done by a living artist. Of course, this presented a problem for contemporary artists seeking buyers for their works. In an effort to correct this problem, the academies in Paris and London began to hold yearly exhibitions of art created by their members. These exhibitions were called *Salons.* They became important social events and aroused great interest and even controversy. Reputations were made and destroyed during these annual events. For this reason, artists worked long and hard on the works they submitted. However, the artists who won honors at these exhibitions were not always the most gifted. Those who best reflected the tastes of the academies were acclaimed while others were ignored or ridiculed.

Neoclassicism

In France, the Academy endorsed a new style of art based on the art of Greece and Rome. This style had been born late in the eighteenth century. When Pompeii and Herculaneum were found in the 1730s and 1740s, the world became interested in the Classical.★ This interest was true of artists as well. They studied and copied the Classical sculptures. Their aim was to learn to draw and, in time, equal what legendary ancient artists had done. These French artists rejected the earlier Baroque and Rococo styles. Instead, they used Classical forms to express their ideas on courage, sacrifice, and love of country. Their new art style was known as Neoclassicism. One of the first artists to work in this style was the painter Jacques Louis David.

★ **Enrichment** A revival of interest in Classical art forms was also due to the work of Johann Winckelmann, who explored Pompeii and Herculaneum and wrote the first modern history of art. In his writing, Winckelmann praised Classical art as the most perfect ever produced. His opinion strongly influenced contemporary artists and intellectuals.

What do you see in this work? Would you describe it as complex and exciting, or simple and calm? Point to an area of smooth texture. Now find an area with a contrasting rough texture. Are the colors mainly warm or cool? What effect is created by the use of these colors? What has happened to this man? What does the knife on the floor suggest? Does this picture look lifelike? If so, how has this been achieved? What idea or mood does it communicate to you?

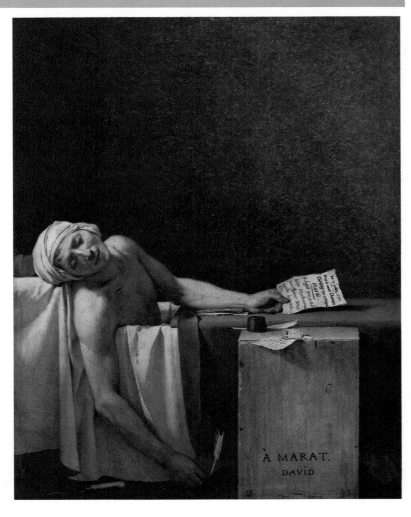

Figure 16.1   Jacques Louis David. *The Death of Marat.* 1793. Oil on canvas, approx. 1.6 x 1.24 m [5′ 3″ x 4′ 1″]. Musées Royaux des Beaux-Arts de Belgique, Brussels

Jacques Louis David

David's involvement in politics,★ his love of ancient art, and his skill as a painter are all noted in his picture of *The Death of Marat* (Figure 16.1).

★ Enrichment In addition to being an artist, David played an important role in the French Revolution, the most violent period in French history. Known as the official painter of the Revolution, he became the artistic dictator of France. David felt that the spirit of freedom that swept across the country could best be illustrated in artworks inspired by Greek and Roman models.

The Death of Marat

David admired the noble simplicity and calm beauty of Greek art and tried to achieve the same qualities in this tribute to Jean Paul Marat, one of the major figures of the French Revolution. Marat suffered from a skin ailment which required him to spend time each day in a medicinal bath. Not a man to waste time, he placed a board across the tub and covered it with a cloth to serve as a desk.★ On the day of Marat's assassination, a young

---

★ Enrichment David had a fresh image to draw upon when he painted this picture because he had seen Marat in his bath the day before his death.

woman was allowed into the room with a petition. While Marat was reading it, she stabbed him. David shows Marat still holding his pen in one hand and the petition in the other.

This painting often produces an emotional shock in the viewer seeing it for the first time. You see the dead figure of the political leader slumped over the side of his bathtub. The murder weapon still lies on the floor where it was dropped by the assassin. The clear, cool lighting illuminates a room that is almost bare. A simple wooden box and a plain green cloth are placed before a rough, greenish-brown wall. The textured wall contrasts with the smooth skin of the dead politician. Marat, wearing a white turban, leans back against a white cloth which lines the tub. His color is cool except for the red around the small wound. As you can see, warm colors have been used sparingly in this painting.

David's study of Greek and Roman sculptures taught him how to paint a figure so that it looks realistic and noble. He learned how to avoid details that could interfere with a simple, direct statement. Like the *Dying Gaul* (Figure 6.17, page 102), David's picture was meant to stir your emotions. He wants you to become involved in the drama, to share the pain and anger he felt at the "martyrdom" of Marat.

But David's work gives you only one side of the story. It fails to tell you that Marat's fanatical support of violence and terror during the Revolution led to his own violent end. You may have seen a picture or photo in a magazine which tried to influence your opinion about something. This was called "propaganda." David's painting is a fine work of art, but it is also a form of propaganda because he was trying to influence public opinion about Marat.

Napoleon in His Study

Later under Napoleon, David became the court painter. The emperor and the artist were well suited to each other because Napoleon recognized the value of propaganda and David had already proved that he knew how to produce it. In a portrait of Napoleon (Figure 16.2), David presents the emperor standing by a desk covered with important papers of state. The clock tells you that it is after 4:00 and the candle, that it is nighttime rather than afternoon. The message here is clear. While his subjects sleep peacefully, the emperor toils far into the night for their well-being.

Criticism

Describe everything you see in this room. What time of day is it? How do you know it is nighttime rather than daytime? What makes this man look important? Using the clues presented, what do you think he has been doing? Has he been doing this for some time, or has he just begun? How can you tell? Can you find the man's initial in the picture? What sort of personality do you associate with this man—weak and unsure of himself, determined and self-confident, or nervous and confused?

Figure 16.2   Jacques Louis David. *Napoleon in His Study.* 1812. Oil on canvas, 2.04 x 1.25 m [80¼ x 49¼"]. The National Gallery of Art, Washington, D.C. Samuel H. Kress Collection, 1961

Marie Louise Elisabeth Vigée-Lebrun

David chose to stay in France and take an active part in the Revolution. However, another artist, Marie Louise Elisabeth Vigée-Lebrun, left France and did not come back until peace was restored. Vigée-Lebrun is one of history's most celebrated women artists. Her life story would, in fact, have made a fine film. Before she was twenty, she had studied in a convent and had received private art lessons. She had also painted portraits of important members of the French aristocracy. By the age of twenty-five, she was employed by Queen Marie-Antoinette. Vigée-Lebrun's wit, beauty, and talent made her a favorite of the queen, whose portrait she painted some twenty times.

On the night the king and queen were arrested, Vigée-Lebrun escaped from Paris.* While the Revolution interrupted her career in France, it did not keep her from working. She was able to continue painting with equal success in other capitals of Europe. Everywhere she was warmly received and flooded with requests. Many of the leading social figures asked that she do their portrait. By the age of thirty-five, Vigée-Lebrun estimated that she had earned over a million francs from her painting. This was a huge sum for any artist. Unfortunately, she needed every bit of it to pay her husband's debts. Jean Baptiste Lebrun liked nothing better than to visit houses of chance, and he usually emerged a loser.

Vigée-Lebrun's portraits frequently were extremely flattering to the sitter (Figure 3.11, page 52). Especially in her self-portraits, Vigée-Lebrun tended to be quite generous. To all of her sitters, the artist gave large, expressive eyes, and played down realistic—and unique —details of the face.

Madame de la Châtre

Madame de la Châtre was just twenty-seven years old when she had her portrait painted by Vigée-Lebrun (Figure 16.3). As in most of her portraits, the artist selected a pose that was simple and direct. Madame de la Châtre glances up from an open book and turns slightly to face in your direction. However, she takes little notice of you. Instead, there is a faraway look in her eyes, and it seems as though her thoughts still linger on the words she has been reading. Notice how the artist has made use of repeating contour lines to achieve harmony in this picture. The sweeping contour of the woman's hat is repeated by the curve of the sofa back, and the angle of the forearm is duplicated by the edge of the pillow. The diagonal of the upper arm is found again in the deep crease of the skirt. The color scheme is subdued by the extensive use of gray for the background and of white for the dress. Needed contrast is provided by the green velvet sofa, the blue-gray sash and hat ribbon, and the gold trim on the pillow.

Vigée-Lebrun preferred simplicity in her portraits, and this is evident in her treatment of costumes. Her memoirs reveal that she often wore white muslin dresses with little decoration other than a sash or a scarf. In addition, she tried to convince many of her sitters, presumably including Madame de la Châtre, to adopt this classic style for their portraits.

A Fitting Memorial

Vigée-Lebrun outlived her husband and children by twenty-two years. She was cared for during those last years by two nieces. When she died, her will specified that a relief sculpture of a palette and brush be carved on her gravestone. It is certainly a fitting reminder of a painter who left behind over eight hundred paintings.

Jean-Auguste-Dominique Ingres

By the start of the nineteenth century, the art of Europe was influenced by France and France, by the Academy. The Academy itself was influenced by Neoclassic artists who followed David. The Neoclassic style was carried to its highest point by Jean-Auguste-Dominique Ingres. He was the best known of David's students. In 1801, Ingres won the coveted *Prix de Rome* (Rome Prize). It was a prize given by the Academy and allowed him to study in Rome for three years.* However, once he

---

★ Enrichment King Louis XVI was executed on January 21, 1793, and Queen Marie-Antoinette, on October 16 of the same year. They joined over twenty thousand victims of the guillotine during the French Revolution.

★ Enrichment During this time, the winner had to produce one work of art every year to send back to Paris where it was exhibited. This award was highly valued because it usually meant that fame and fortune would follow. The importance placed on the *Prix de Rome* is shown by the fact that David attempted suicide after several failures to win this prize.

History

How did the France of Vigée-Lebrun's time differ from the France of Watteau's time? How did Vigée-Lebrun's actions concerning the revolution in France differ from those of David? Who was Vigée-Lebrun's most famous patron? What happened to that patron?

Figure 16.3 Marie Louise Elisabeth Vigée-Lebrun. *Madame de la Châtre.* **1789. Oil on canvas, 1.14 x 0.88 m [45 x 34½″]. The Metropolitan Museum of Art, New York. Gift of Jessie Woolworth Donahue, 1954**

arrived in Italy, he stayed for eighteen years. When he finally returned to Paris, the Neoclassic movement was without a leader. David was by then an old man living out his final years in Brussels. Ingres brought with him a large religious painting he had been commissioned to paint for a cathedral in southern France.★ He was not sure how this work would be received since the Academy had criticized many of his earlier works. He need not have worried; the painting, which borrowed heavily from Raphael's pictures of the Madonna and Child, was a great success. In fact, it was so successful that it made Ingres the leader of the Neoclassic movement in France.

★ **Enrichment** The title of this work was *The Oath of Louis XIII.*

Criticism

Judging by her manner, dress, and surroundings, what sort of woman is this? Describe the contour lines of the shoulder, arms, and face. Do you think this woman is preparing to (a) go to work, (b) go to the theater, (c) make dinner, or (d) play with her children? Would you describe her expression as excited, angry, happy, or serious?

Figure 16.4   Jean-Auguste-Dominique Ingres. *Madame Moitessier.* 1851. Oil on canvas, approx. 1.47 x 1 m [57¾ x 39½"]. The National Gallery of Art, Washington, D.C. Samuel H. Kress Collection, 1946

Madame Moitessier

Ingres preferred to paint large historical paintings and said that he disliked painting portraits. But today his portraits are ranked among his most impressive works. He took years to complete a portrait of *Madame Moitessier* (Figure 16.4) and probably grumbled the entire time about having to do it.★

★ **Enrichment** Ingres actually completed two versions of this portrait.

Madame Moitessier looks as though she is about to leave for an evening at the opera. In her left hand, she holds a small fan with which to cool herself if the theater becomes too warm. She stands before a dark violet wallpaper. The dress she is wearing is elegant and black. The light source is behind the viewer to eliminate the shadows on the figure. Thus, Ingres could show more clearly the smooth, graceful contour line of the shoulders, arms, and face. This free-flowing line is repeated in the pearl necklace, which directs your attention upward to the head. The dark hair is parted in the middle and frames a face which is attractive but serious.

Ingres took delight in painting smooth contours. This is certainly evident in his portrait of Madame Moitessier. He believed that line was the most important element in painting and that color was secondary. In fact, he placed so little importance on color that he once said that an artist could learn all there is to know about it in an afternoon.

Romanticism

Even though the Neoclassic style of David and Ingres became the official style of the Academy, it did not go unchallenged. Not all artists shared these painters' enthusiasm for Classical art, noble subject matter, and free-flowing lines. In 1819, a young French artist named Théodore Géricault exhibited a painting called the *Raft of the Medusa* (Figure 16.5). It signaled the birth of a new art style in France known as *Romanticism.* This new style emphasized emotions which were painted in a dramatic manner.★

Théodore Géricault

Théodore Géricault was an artist with great natural ability. Many have wondered what heights he might have reached if he had lived a longer life. Unfortunately, he died at the age of thirty-three as a result of a fall from a horse.★★

★ **Enrichment** Romanticism was widely evidenced throughout the Western world in literature, music, and philosophy as well as the visual arts. Generally speaking, it flourished around the first half of the nineteenth century.

★ **Enrichment** A horse lover, Géricault had at one time
★ thought about becoming a jockey.

In what ways does this painting remind you of works created by Michelangelo and Rubens? In what ways does it differ from works created by Neoclassic artists? How have opposing diagonal axis lines been used to organize and balance this composition?

Figure 16.5   Théodore Géricault. *Raft of the Medusa.* 1818-19. Oil on canvas, approx. 4.9 x 7 m [16 x 23']. The Louvre, Paris. [Cliché des Musées Nationaux, Paris]

Raft of the Medusa

Géricault's *Raft of the Medusa* shows a contemporary event as it actually happened rather than something from the Classical past. In July of 1816, the French ship Medusa was wrecked in a storm off the west coast of Africa. When it was certain that the ship was sinking, 149 passengers and crew members were placed on a large raft made from parts of the ship. The raft was then towed by officers aboard a lifeboat. Later, it was claimed that the officers, concerned with their own survival, cut the raft adrift. By the time they were rescued, only 15 men on the raft remained alive.

As you study Géricault's picture, you may be reminded of the diagonal compositions of Rubens. Or perhaps you will think of the sculpturesque painted figures of Michelangelo. Géricault arranged his figures in a design based on two opposing diagonals. The major diagonal runs from lower left to upper right. It carries you into the work and leads you over a series of twisting figures. These figures express a range of emotions from complete despair to hope. A second diagonal begins with the corpse at the lower right. It moves upward to the mast of the crude raft at the upper left. This serves to balance the composition. The diagonal design, twisting figures, strong emotion, and dramatic use of light are important elements. They marked Géricault's break with the Neoclassic style, which stressed calmness and balance.

Criticism

Describe the way the artist has organized this composition. Are the edges blurred or distinct? What seems to dominate here—color or line? Are the colors and shapes varied or harmonious? Which of the following adjectives would you use when interpreting this work: rigid, calm, ordinary, swirling, exciting, dramatic? Which aesthetic qualities would you use when judging this work?

Figure 16.6   Eugène Delacroix. *The Lion Hunt*. 1861. Oil on canvas, 76.2 x 97.8 cm [30 x 38½"]. Collection of The Art Institute of Chicago. Potter Palmer Collection, 22.404

This work was displayed in the Academy show of 1819. Its title was *Shipwreck*. All knew the subject though, and the work drew much attention. The final version may lack some of the excitement of Géricault's early sketches, but it still ranks among the most powerful paintings ever done. It also had a strong influence on another young French artist. That artist was Eugène Delacroix.

Eugène Delacroix

When Géricault suddenly died, his position of leadership in the Romantic movement fell to Delacroix. Glowing colors and swirling action are marks of Delacroix's style. But Ingres and his followers disliked such work. They found it violent, crude, and unfinished. This resulted in a long rivalry between Delacroix and Ingres. The former spoke for Romanticism, while the latter was the champion of the Neoclassical cause. These two artists disliked each other's art, and they disliked each other as well. Delacroix once described Ingres' art as "the complete expression of an incomplete intelligence."

The Lion Hunt

Delacroix's love of dramatic action and exotic settings is evident in his painting of *The Lion Hunt* (Figure 16.6). He took a six-month trip through Morocco, Tangiers, and Algiers in 1832, and the trip fired his enthusiasm for the Near East. The sketches he did during that trip gave him the inspiration and subject matter for paintings done long after his return to France. *The Lion Hunt* was among these.

The theme of *The Lion Hunt* is action. The excited movement of hunters, horses, and lions is arranged in a circular pattern placed within an oval of light. The violent action is made more convincing by the use of blurred edges, rapidly applied brushstrokes, and spots of bold color. Again, there are reminders of Rubens; you find them in the swirling action, the dramatic use of color, and the bold contrasts of light and dark. The scene looks as though it has been caught up in a tornado. Everything has been swept up into the swirling spiral, making colors and forms blur as they whirl around and around.

His Belief in Color

Color was the most important element in painting for Delacroix. "A painting," he said, "should be a feast for the eye." Unlike Ingres, he did not begin his paintings with lines. When painting a figure, for example, he did not draw the outline first and then fill it in with color. Instead, he ignored the use of an outline and began painting at the center of the figure. He then worked outward to the edges to complete the figure.

Delacroix learned a great deal from studying the work of the English landscape painter John Constable, who used patches of color placed side by side instead of blending them smoothly together.★ But when Delacroix did this, he was criticized for the rough finish of his works.

At first, the honors and awards in the battle between Neoclassicism and Romanticism went to Ingres. Six times in a row the French Academy refused to admit Delacroix as a member. When he was finally admitted, it was too late to mean very much to him. Romanticism had been generally accepted by then, and other, younger artists were already beginning to paint pictures in a new style known as "Realism." However, before looking at the work of the Realists in France, the paintings of two extraordinary English artists should be examined.

English Landscape Painting

By 1800, qualities which were to characterize English painting throughout the nineteenth century could be found in the works of John Constable and Joseph M. W. Turner. Both artists were mainly landscape painters. However, they went in different directions in the way they painted their landscapes.

John Constable

John Constable formed his own personal way of looking at things among the trees and meadows of the English countryside. His approach to painting was like that of the seventeenth-century Dutch masters. Like them, he wanted to paint the sky, meadows, hills, and streams as the eye actually sees them. He delighted in trying to capture the light and warmth of sunlight, the coolness of shadows, and the motion of clouds and rain. He painted wide-open landscapes with great detail, recreating the exact look and feel of the scene.

During long walks through the fields, Constable would carry a small pocket sketchbook. The pages of this sketchbook measured little more than 76 x 102 mm (millimeters) [3 x 4 inches]. On these tiny pages he drew views of the landscape from different angles. He was especially interested in the way changes in sunlight altered the look of things. Later, when working on his large paintings, he referred over and over again to these small sketches.

★ **Enrichment** According to a popular story, Delacroix repainted completely the background of one of his early works after seeing one of Constable's landscapes at a Parisian art dealer's gallery. He did this in the four days before the opening of the Salon in which his picture was to be exhibited.

The Haywain

Constable's *Haywain* (Figure 16.7), with its sparkling color and dewy freshness, is a scene of quiet charm. It shows a hay wagon slowly crossing a shallow stream near a cottage. Behind the cottage are full, rich trees that cast shadows which are cool and inviting. Clouds overhead appear to be moving swiftly across the sky. A stream of sunlight breaks through to light up a lush, grassy meadow. It is not too difficult to imagine the sounds of the flowing stream, the creak of the wagon, and the rustle of leaves as a soft breeze stirs the trees.

Wivenhoe Park, Essex

Wivenhoe Park, Essex (Figure 16.8) offers Constable's view of an estate belonging to a friend of the artist's father. The landowner, a retired army general, commissioned the painting and asked that certain things be included in it. In fact, when Constable finished the picture, the general objected because he thought the artist had not shown enough of the estate. Constable then had to sew pieces of canvas to both sides of his painting to widen the scene. He added interest by including a pony cart, swans, cattle, and birds. The

Criticism

List the things you see in this painting. What makes this picture look so real? Is the overall feeling of texture rough or smooth? What kinds of shapes are used for the clouds? Are there similar shapes found elsewhere in the picture?

What *sounds* are suggested by this picture? What mood does it communicate to you? Do you consider this a successful work? Why or why not?

Figure 16.7   John Constable. *The Haywain*. 1821. Oil on canvas, 1.28 x 1.69 cm [4' 3" x 5' 6½"]. Reproduced by courtesy of the National Gallery, London

painting conveys the look and feel of the scene as Constable saw it. He caught the light airiness of the atmosphere and the sweeping movement of the clouds. The sparkle of light across the dark green leaves of the trees and the lighter green of the rolling hills are shown. In addition, the artist captured the stately look of the red brick house. The entire scene has a feeling of the momentary—as though you have been given a quick glimpse of nature as it exists at a particular moment in time.

Joseph M. W. Turner

Joseph M. W. Turner began his career as a watercolor painter and later turned his attention to painting landscapes in oils. A talented artist, he first exhibited in the Royal Academy when he was only sixteen years old. As his career progressed, he became less and less interested

in showing nature in realistic detail. Instead, he turned his attention to the effects that light and atmosphere have upon subject matter. In time, light and atmosphere became the most important part of his works (see Figure 2.23, page 35). They added a kind of magic to his pictures, even pictures of the most ordinary scenes. When painting a landscape with a castle, for example, Turner would not make the castle the center of interest as you might expect. Instead, he would paint a glowing atmosphere as a way of arousing your curiosity and luring you closer for a longer look. And what would you find? The blurred forms and intense colors would be changed by way of your imagination. In the indistinct forms you would see a blazing sunset, violet mountains, and the silhouette of a Medieval castle. No wonder that Constable, when talking about Turner's pictures, said, "Turner has golden visions, glorious and beautiful. . . . One could live and die with such pictures."

History

Constable was interested in showing how sunlight affected the subject matter in his pictures. In this respect, he was a great influence on a style of art developed by Claude Monet, Pierre Auguste Renoir, and others. What was that art style called?

Figure 16.8   John Constable. *Wivenhoe Park, Essex.* 1816. Oil on canvas, approx. 0.56 x 1.01 m [22⅛ x 39⅞"]. The National Gallery of Art, Washington, D.C. Widener Collection, 1942

How does this picture differ from traditional pictures of ships at sea? What is the most important thing in this picture—the steamship or the storm? Turner's mature works reveal his interest in which of the following: (a) precise detail, (b) genre scenes, (c) light and atmosphere, (d) symbolism?

Figure 16.9   Joseph M. W. Turner. *Snow Storm: Steam-Boat off a Harbor's Mouth.* **1842. Oil on canvas, 0.91 x 1.22 m [36 x 48″]. The Tate Gallery, London**

Snow Storm: Steam-Boat off a Harbor's Mouth

Turner's painting entitled *Snow Storm: Steam-Boat off a Harbor's Mouth* (Figure 16.9) is his view of nature at its most violent. He captures this violence with a bold use of sweeping light and color rather than detail. However, when this painting was exhibited at the Royal Academy in London, critics were shocked and angered. They were used to traditional pictures of ships at sea and failed to find any value in this painting of blurred and violent impressions. Why, it was impossible to find the ship in the picture, they claimed. It was all but lost in the swirling action of light and color.

What the critics failed to understand was that Turner was painting things that have no shape or form—things like speed, wind, and atmosphere. To learn how to do this, he boarded a small steamship during a snowstorm and, as the storm grew, asked crew members to tie him to the mast. For four hours he remained bound to the mast, at times certain that he would not survive. But he was determined to witness the full fury of the storm and then paint it exactly as he saw it. His picture shows the steamship in the middle of the swirling composition, but it is almost lost in the mist, smoke, and windblown snow. The ship is not the most important thing in the work. Of most importance is the violent mood of the storm raging about the ship. The powerful but majestic violence of nature is painted without the distraction of unnecessary details.

Space and Light

Turner's later paintings of space and light became even more abstract. They were so formless that he had to attach rings to the frames so galleries would know which way to hang them.

An insight into this artist's views about his work is provided by a conversation between Turner and a gentleman viewing one of his landscapes. After studying the painting a few minutes, the gentleman turned to the artist and complained that he had never seen skies as Turner painted them. The artist only nodded and replied, "Possibly—but don't you wish you could?"

Turner died on December 19, 1851, a death listed simply as "natural decay." His last words were, "The sun is God."

Realism

Meanwhile, in France, many young artists were looking for subject matter that did not glorify the past or present romantic views of current events. They rejected both Neoclassicism and Romanticism. Gustave Courbet was in the forefront of this group of artists. He and his followers became known as *Realists.*

History

In what ways does this scene differ from El Greco's *Burial of Count Orgaz* (Figure 13.8)? Do the people in this picture seem deeply saddened by the loss of a friend and relative? Why did the critics find fault with this painting? What

argument did Courbet use to defend his picture? What was the name given to the art style developed by Courbet and his associates?

Figure 16.10 Gustave Courbet. *Burial at Ornans.* 1849. Approx. 3 x 6.7 m [10 x 22′]. The Louvre, Paris. [Cliché des Musées Nationaux, Paris]

Gustave Courbet

To understand the Realist movement you must look at conditions in France at that time in history, roughly one hundred years ago. More and more factories were using new machines to increase production. This drew great numbers of people from rural areas to the cities. Artisans who took pride in their hand-made products were replaced by factory workers who mass-produced the same products more cheaply and in greater quantities. These factory workers were usually unskilled and poorly paid. They lived in crowded conditions in drab, unhealthy slums. In a short time, this "industrial revolution" pushed aside old beliefs, habits, and institutions.

These changes had an effect on artists who were sensitive to what was going on around them. They realized that Classical models and Romantic subject matter were out of place in their world. A peasant, they felt, was as good a subject for their brush as a Greek goddess, and the life of a factory worker offered as much inspiration as a lion hunt in some far-off land. But

they also knew that they could not paint the world around them by using old techniques. They would have to invent new ones. So they discarded the formulas of Neoclassicism and the theatrical drama of Romanticism to paint familiar scenes and trivial events *as they really looked.*

Burial at Ornans

In *Burial at Ornans* (Figure 16.10), Courbet painted the funeral of his grandfather. It is a common scene, certainly not what you would call an important event. Unlike El Greco's *Burial of Count Orgaz* (Figure 13.8, page 231), you will find no saints assisting at this burial. Nor will you see an angel bearing the soul of the departed upward to be welcomed by Christ and a host of heavenly inhabitants. Courbet shows nothing more than a large group of almost-full-sized figures standing beside an open grave in front of a somber landscape. There is no mystery or miracle here to marvel over; the painting communicates little in the way of grief or piety.

Indeed, not one person looks at the cross or at the grave. So why are they there? The people attending this funeral do so out of a sense of duty. The priest routinely reads the service. After all, he has done this many times before, and there is nothing about this funeral to set it apart from all the rest. The kneeling gravedigger looks bored and impatient to get on with his work. The women at the right go through the motions of mourning, but they are not very convincing.

Courbet's friends had posed for the painting, and, in most cases, they could be identified. He used them because they were important to him and were a part of his life. But when he exhibited his painting in Paris, he was criticized for this. His work was considered insulting because he had dared to use plain, ordinary people painted on a scale which was by tradition reserved for important people or great events.

Courbet felt that an artist should draw upon his or her own experiences and paint only what could be seen and understood.★ He *did* experience this funeral, and he painted it just as he saw it. It is an actual scene painted honestly. The work shows real people behaving the way real people behave.

Edouard Manet

Among the artists who took part in the Realist movement was Edouard Manet. He exhibited with Courbet and was often attacked by critics for the same reasons. However, unlike Courbet, he was more concerned with *how* to paint than with *what* to paint.

Gare Saint-Lazare

In *Gare Saint-Lazare* (Figure 16.11), he uses his technical knowledge and skill to paint a simple, everyday scene. A woman is sitting with a sleeping puppy nestled in her lap. She has just looked up from a book she has been reading. You are made to feel as though you have come upon her by chance and she looks up to see who it is.

You exchange casual glances, and, at the same time, your eye takes in the black fence of a railway station. A little girl stands with her back to you, peering through this fence at the steam and smoke left by a passing locomotive. The girl's left arm unites her with the figure of the woman while also breaking up the strong vertical pattern of the fence. At the same time, the curving shapes of the figures contrast with the repeated verticals of the railings. In this way, Manet adds variety and interest to his composition.

Manet did not pose the figures in his pictures. He painted them as he found them—and as he saw them. Details were avoided because he wanted his picture to show what the eye could take in with a quick glance. His concern with technique is seen in the way he placed his colors on the canvas. In some places, the paint is stroked on carefully. In others, it is dabbed on or pulled across the canvas. The result is a richly textured surface that adds even more to the variety and interest of the picture.

Rosa Bonheur

An artist who effectively combined the flair of Romanticism with the accuracy of Realism was Rosa Bonheur. Few artists were as successful or as admired in their lifetime as this remarkable woman.

Rosa Bonheur received her first painting lessons from her father, who was a painter and art teacher. When her mother died, the young Rosa was forced to leave school and help her father raise her two brothers and a sister. This did not prevent her from continuing to paint, however. The family had moved to Paris when she was seven years old, and Bonheur often copied the works of the masters found in the many galleries there. But she soon showed a preference for sketching live animals rather than copying paintings. During her teens and early twenties, she journeyed regularly to country fields and to the stockyards outside Paris to draw the animals. Bonheur also found subjects for her works at cattle markets and fairs where horses were being sold. To facilitate her work, she substituted comfortable men's clothing for the restrictive women's clothing of the day. (However, this was done only after permission had been obtained from the authorities.) Men's clothing was much more suitable for walking and sketching among the animals, and it helped her avoid the jeers of the workers and spectators.

When she was just nineteen, two of Bonheur's paintings were chosen for exhibition at the Salon. Four years later, she was given a medal. This was the first of many honors and awards she earned during her long career. Eventually, she was made an officer of the Legion of Honor, the first woman to be so recognized.

★ **Enrichment** Courbet once said that it was impossible for him to paint an angel because he had never seen one.

Criticism

In what ways does this look like a simple, everyday scene? At what is the little girl looking? What does the woman hold in her hands? Describe the lines in this picture. How have these lines been used to tie the composition togeth-er? Is this composition asymmetrically or symmetrically balanced? To what aesthetic qualities would you refer when judging this picture? Having applied those qualities, do you judge it to be successful or unsuccessful?

Figure 16.11   Edouard Manet. *Gare Saint-Lazare.* **1873. Oil on canvas, 0.93 x 1.14 m [36¾ x 45⅛"]. The National Gallery of Art, Washington, D.C. Gift of Horace Havemeyer in memory of his mother, Louisine W. Havemeyer, 1956**

The Horse Fair

Bonheur's accurate anatomical studies of animals enabled her to successfully undertake such large, sweeping works as *The Horse Fair* (Figure 16.12). In it, she combines her knowledge and admiration of horses with an understanding of the emotion and vigor found in paintings by Géricault and Delacroix. She shows horses being led by their handlers around the exhibition area of a fair. The scene is crackling with tension and excitement. High-strung horses rear up suddenly and wildly flail the air with their hooves. Others trot and prance about, barely held in check by grooms who ride them or guide them on foot. The imaginative viewer will have no difficulty adding the sounds of pounding hooves and the sharp commands of the handlers. The result is a thrilling blend of movement, drama, and reality that echoes the accomplishments of both the Romantic and Realist artists.

There is little about Rosa Bonheur's paintings that you could call delicate or timid. Her animals are painted boldly with a heavy, rich application of paint. She possessed the skill and the confidence to paint pictures of great size. *The Horse Fair*, for example, is over 4.8 m [16 feet] wide. In another work entitled *Horses Thrashing Corn*, she painted ten life-size horses. At the time, it was the largest animal picture ever done.

A Lasting Popularity

Rosa Bonheur chose a life without marriage, and a life-work which set her apart from others. By any measure, she was an unusual woman. She was talented, kindly, uninhibited, and sure of herself. Her animal paintings made her one of the most popular painters in Europe. It is a mark of her talent that her popularity has not lessened over the years.

Impressionism

The generation of artists that followed Courbet and were associated with Manet carried even further the quest for realism. They took their easels, paints, and brushes outdoors to paint rather than work from sketches in their studios. These artists contributed to a new style of painting which stressed the effects of sunlight on subject matter. They tried to reproduce this effect by using quick, short brushstrokes. This approach resulted in paintings made up entirely of small dabs, or

History

This artist is primarily known for her paintings of which of the following: (a) landscapes, (b) genre scenes, (c) portraits, (d) animals? In what ways does this painting remind you of the works of Géricault and Delacroix? How is it similar to Realist paintings by Courbet and Manet?

Figure 16.12   Rosa Bonheur. *The Horse Fair.* **1853-55. Oil on canvas, 2.4 x 5 m [8′¼″ x 16′ 7″]. The Metropolitan Museum of Art, New York. Gift of Cornelius Vanderbilt, 1887**

Why did Monet frequently paint the same subject over and over again? What technique did he use to apply his paint to the canvas? Can you find any clear, precise lines in this picture? Name the hues found in the work. What did Monet try to show in his pictures? How did the critics react to his work? What effect did this have on the artist?

Figure 16.13 Claude Monet. *Rouen Cathedral, West Façade.* 1894. Oil on canvas, 1 x 0.66 m [39½ x 26″]. The National Gallery of Art, Washington, D.C. Chester Dale Collection, 1962

spots, of color. When viewed from a distance, these dabs of color were blended together in the eye of the viewer to create the desired effect. Because these artists were concerned with momentary effect, they avoided posed or staged compositions. Instead, they preferred an informal, casual arrangement in their paintings. In many ways, their pictures have the same natural look as quickly snapped photographs. This "snap-shot" approach to composition added a lively, more realistic appearance to their paintings.

Claude Monet

In 1874, a group of artists using this new style of painting held an exhibition of their work in Paris. One of these artists was Claude Monet, who exhibited a picture entitled *Impression: Sunrise.* It was this painting that gave the new movement a name: *Impressionism.* Outraged critics took the word "Impression" from Monet's title and used it as a label when referring, unkindly, to all the works in this exhibition.

Monet's painting of the west façade of Rouen Cathedral (Figure 16.13) shows the famous building bathed in bright, shimmering sunlight. It is one of twenty-six paintings of this same church produced by this artist. Why twenty-six paintings of the same object? When you find the answer to this question, you will have a better understanding of what the Impressionists tried to accomplish with their paintings.

Criticism

What is the subject matter in this painting? Describe the outlines around the shapes—are they firm or blurred? What effect does this create? Point to areas where the most intense colors are used. Does the surface of this picture look smooth or rough? Do you think it would be accurate to call this a "super-realistic work?" Why or why not?

Figure 16.14   Claude Monet [French, 1840-1926]. *Haystack at Sunset near Giverny.* **1891. Oil on canvas, approx. 74.9 x 94 cm [29½ x 37"]. Courtesy of the Museum of Fine Arts, Boston. The Juliana Cheny Edwards Collection, 25.112. Bequest of Robert J. Edwards in memory of his mother.**

Haystack at Sunset Near Giverny

It may seem odd, but a good place to begin a search for an answer is a farm near Paris on a sunny afternoon in 1891. There, in a field of haystacks, a middle-aged man in a wide-brimmed hat stands before an easel. On the easel is a half-finished painting of a haystack (Figure 16.14). The man takes his brush and continues to work on the picture by adding dashes and dots of brightly colored paint. His eyes dart quickly from the haystack in the field to the canvas and back again. Suddenly the sunlight changes, and the artist glances upward to see that a cloud has passed in front of the sun. He notices the way the sunlight filters through the clouds and the effect this has on the haystack he is painting. Removing the unfinished painting, he places it carefully on the ground and picks up a new canvas from a stack beside him. He sets this new canvas on the easel and smiles. "Of course," he says softly to himself, "when the sunlight changes, the colors change." The artist is Claude Monet.

Several times during the day, Monet changes his canvas, until by sunset he has started more than a dozen paintings of the same haystacks. Each of these captures a different moment of light.

For months, Monet worked in the field painting the same haystacks. Often he worked on several pictures at once, rushing from one to another as the light changed. He painted the haystacks at all hours of the day, always trying to record in paint the exact colors he saw reflected from them. Sometimes the sun was so brilliant that the outlines of the haystacks became blurred and seemed to vibrate. Monet tried to capture this effect in his pictures, painting exactly what his eye saw rather than what he knew to be there.

However, when Monet exhibited his haystack paintings later in Paris, most critics responded in anger. It was not so much the bright colors or the common subject matter that they objected to; it was the way the paintings were done. They looked crude and hastily completed, as if they were no more than sketches which had to be developed further to be considered finished works. The critics thought it was an insult to put a frame around a quick oil sketch and then call it art. But after all, they said, it was what could be expected from an artist like Monet who had a reputation for being stubborn and defiant.

The Poplar Trees

But Monet refused to be discouraged. Instead, he began work on another series of paintings showing a row of poplar trees along a river. This time he was not only interested in painting the colors reflected from the subject, but how these colors looked in the rippling water of the stream as well. He anchored a small boat in the river and painted this new "slice of life" in every kind of light. The area he wanted to show in his pictures was not large, but he wanted to show all of it. He tried to show it as if it had been experienced all at once in a single glance at a particular moment in time.

Later, when they were shown in Paris, Monet's poplar trees were more warmly received than his haystacks had been. Monet, however, was not impressed. "What do the critics know?" he asked.

Rouen Cathedral

That winter, exhausted, Monet visited his brother who lived in the cathedral city of Rouen. Late one afternoon he stopped to make a purchase in a little upstairs shop. Through a window, he spied the towers and the doorway of the great church looming in the twilight. He sent home for his canvases and soon set up his easel in the window of the little shop. Day after day during three winters, Monet painted the doorways and towers of the cathedral. At the end of the second winter, he wrote, "What I have undertaken is very difficult. I have not the strength to pick up my canvases. The more I continue, the more I fail."

One of Monet's paintings of Rouen Cathedral (Figure 16.13, page 299) uses complementary colors—blues and oranges. These colors were applied in separate brushstrokes, which look like an uneven mixture of colored dabs and dashes when seen up close. But viewed from a distance they blend together. As a result, what the viewer sees is not solid form, but a rich visual impression.

When the critics saw Monet's pictures of Rouen Cathedral, they marveled at last. But the highest tribute to Monet's genius may have come from another great artist, Paul Cézanne, who said, "Monet is only an eye, but what an eye!"

The credit line for this work is found on page 310.

Figure 16.15

Figure 16.16

The credit line for this work is found on page 310.

The credit line for this work is found on page 310.

Figure 16.17

Try to answer the question in the text concerning Figures 16.15, 16.16, and 16.17 before reading the credits.

Main Features of the Style

Now that you have learned something about Impressionism, do you think you could pick out the Impressionist painting among several works of art representing different styles (Figures 16.15, 16.16, and 16.17)? Try it; you will find that it is not difficult if you keep in mind some of the main features of Impressionism. Perhaps the most obvious one is the use of dabs and dashes of bright colors that seem to blend together as you look at them. But there are other features as well, and some of these are listed here:

• Blues and violets are used in place of grays, browns, and blacks, even in the shadows.

• Smooth, slick surfaces are replaced by rich, textured surfaces made up of short brushstrokes.

• Because they are composed of strokes and patches of color, solid forms lose some of their solidity.

• Hard, precise outlines are replaced by blurred edges.

• Often there is *no* emphasis or center of interest to which your eye is guided by perspective lines.

• Details are missing because the artist includes only those things that can be taken in with a single glance. This gives the picture a casual, almost accidental look.

• The subject matter used comes from the contemporary world, which may seem unimportant when compared to the grand subjects painted by earlier artists.

Why were the Japanese able to mass-produce art prints like this? How did western European artists become aware of them? In what ways were these prints an influence of French Impressionist painters? How is the handling of space in this Oriental print different from the traditional Western method of showing space on a flat surface?

Figure 16.18 Suzuki Harunobu. *Drying Clothes.* **1767-68. Color woodcut. Philadelphia Museum of Art. The S. S. White Collection**

304

Pierre Auguste Renoir

Have you decided which is the Impressionist painting? You would be correct if you selected Figure 16.16. It is a landscape by Pierre Auguste Renoir, whom you may remember from the discussion in Chapter 3 (pages 42-46). Like many Impressionist paintings, the work is quite small, only 29 x 45 cm (centimeters) [11.5 x 17.75 inches]. Why so small? Because the Impressionists painted outdoors and the canvases on which they painted had to be easy to carry.

Renoir's paintings are happy paintings. He delighted in showing the happiest side of nature. You will never find anything evil or ugly in his pictures. He even avoided painting night or winter scenes and could not understand how Monet and the other Impressionists could. "For me," he declared, "a picture must be an amiable thing, joyous and pretty—yes, pretty! There are enough troublesome things in life without inventing others."

Renoir loved to paint and did so up to the day he died. Even though he was crippled by rheumatism during his final years, he continued to paint by having his brush tied to his wrist. Shortly before his death, he was honored in an unusual way—he was invited to visit the great Louvre Museum in Paris as its only guest. Seated in a wheelchair, he was pushed from one gallery to the next. What pride he must have felt when he viewed his own works exhibited alongside the great artists of the past.

Major Influences

Monet, Renoir, and the other Impressionists sought inspiration everywhere. Certainly, one source of inspiration was the Japanese print.

A century before, the Japanese had perfected an inexpensive way of printing pictures in several colors. In fact, it was such an inexpensive process that it became possible to produce huge quantities of prints which could be sold at modest costs to large numbers of people. These prints were made by using several wood blocks. Each block was covered with a different-colored ink, applied to one piece of paper. The prints produced in this way were usually landscapes or genre scenes (Figure 16.18). They were done with an elegant pattern of lines and delicate, flat colors. No attempt was made to create an illusion of depth by using perspective or shading. Further, Japanese printmakers revealed new and unusual ways of looking at and representing the world. For one thing, they did not hesitate to show only part of a figure. Sometimes a curtain or even the edge of the print was used to "cut off" a figure so that all parts of it could not be seen. This was something that European artists had never done.

The Japanese did not place much value on these inexpensive, mass-produced prints. As a result, when trade was begun with Europe in the nineteenth century, they were often used as packing material, just as old newspapers are today. In time, the Impressionists discovered the prints. Then, awed by their beauty, they began to collect them. Before long, some of the features found in the Japanese prints began to appear in their paintings.

In addition to Japanese prints, the Impressionists were influenced by the new art of photography. The camera opened their eyes to the possibilities of candid, or unposed, views of people. They were startled and then excited by the way snapshots showed familiar subjects from new and unusual points of view.

Describe the two figures and their setting. How does the artist guide your eye from the objects on the nearest table to the figures? Did you notice that something is missing in this work? What is it and why has it been eliminated? What are the two figures doing? Do you think they enjoy a close relationship? What is the mood of the woman? Why is she in this mood? What are your feelings toward this woman?

Why did Degas prefer ballerinas and horses as subjects for his paintings and sculptures? What explanation can you give for the lack of detail on this sculpture?

Figure 16.20 Edgar Degas. *Galloping Horse.* 1865-81. Bronze, 31.1 cm [12¼″] high. The St. Louis Art Museum

Figure 16.19 Edgar Degas. *The Glass of Absinthe.* 1876. Oil on canvas, approx. 92 x 68 cm [36 x 27″]. The Louvre, Paris [Cliché des Musées Nationaux, Paris]

Edgar Degas

Another artist who found inspiration in these new discoveries was Edgar Degas. His pictures reveal that he learned a great deal from studying Japanese prints and photographs. Cut-off figures, unusual points of view, and candid poses can be found in many of his paintings. Some of these features are evident in his painting entitled *The Glass of Absinthe* (Figure 16.19).

The Glass of Absinthe

Beginning with the slightly out-of-focus items on the nearest table, you are led indirectly to the two figures at the upper right. A folded newspaper acts as a bridge enabling you to cross from one table to the next and from there across to the woman and man. Degas wanted nothing to interfere with this journey into and across his painting. He decided not to paint legs on the

tables because they might lead your eye away from the route he wanted you to travel. His carefully planned tour is well rewarded. At journey's end you meet a woman you will not soon forget. Lonely, sad, lost in her own thoughts, she is seated next to a man who casually smokes his pipe and looks at something outside the picture. The woman is empty of feeling and past caring, drained like the empty bottle on the table beside her. Looking at her you know she leads a dull, dreary life and that the man with her is incapable of feeling any genuine sympathy or affection for her.

Although he was in sympathy with many of their objectives, Degas did not consider himself to be an Impressionist. He always painted in his studio using sketches made from life. *The Glass of Absinthe* may well have originated as a sketch made while Degas was seated in a Paris café. Perhaps those out-of-focus items on the nearest table are some of his drawing instruments. They may have been intentionally painted out of focus because Degas wanted nothing to delay your journey into his painting. Carefully painted, detailed objects at the "starting point" of that journey might have caused such a delay.

His Interest in Drawing

Degas' great interest in drawing also set him apart from the other Impressionists. This interest may have come from his admiration for Ingres. Degas' drawings, and the paintings that he developed from those drawings, show that he was concerned with the line, form, and movement of the human body. This explains why so many of his pictures show scenes from the ballet. They offered him the chance to capture the split-second movement of a dancing ballerina. Along with scenes of

Would you describe this girl as pretty? Do you think she is wealthy? Why do you think this? With you finger, trace along the contour and axis lines of this figure—where do these lines lead? Has the artist made effective use of the elements of art in this picture? Explain. What do you think the artist wanted to say with this work? Do you consider it a successful painting?

Figure 16.21 Mary Cassatt. *Girl Arranging Her Hair.* 1886. Oil on canvas, 75 x 62.3 cm [29½ x 24½"]. The National Gallery of Art, Washington, D.C. Chester Dale Collection, 1962

the racetrack, these views of ballerinas became his favorite subject.

Sculpture

An interest in the figure carried over into Degas' work in sculpture. He may have turned to sculpture because his eyesight was beginning to fail and he was trying to make up for this by drawing upon his sense of touch. The subjects for his sculptures were the same ones he used for his paintings—ballerinas and horses (Figure 16.20). And, because he wanted to capture the illusion of swift movement, he avoided the use of details. After all, he reasoned, it is impossible to observe all the details of a horse as it dashes by.

Mary Cassatt

Degas played an important role in the development of one of America's finest painters, Mary Cassatt. The daughter of a wealthy Pittsburgh banker, Cassatt spent several years in Paris as a child. During the Civil War, she studied art in Philadelphia even though her father disapproved. He said he would almost rather see her dead than become an artist. But Cassatt was also

strong-willed, and, at the age of twenty-three, she returned to Paris to continue her studies. She soon found that as a woman she had to work twice as hard to gain recognition in the competitive nineteenth-century Paris art world.

One day, a work by Degas in a shop window caught her eye. It was Cassatt's introduction to Impressionism, and it had an immediate and lasting effect on her. "I used to go and flatten my nose against the window," she said later. "It changed my life."

Cassatt's admiration for Degas' work was not one-sided. Her own paintings soon attracted his attention, and they became good friends. Degas introduced her to the Impressionists, and they liked her paintings so much that she was invited to show her work at their exhibitions.

Girl Arranging Her Hair

Cassatt painted *Girl Arranging Her Hair* (Figure 16.21) in answer to a challenge made by Degas. He may have been expressing his doubts that a woman could ever become a serious artist. Or perhaps he wanted to spur his friend into putting forth her best effort. In any event, Degas urged Cassatt to produce a painting of real merit—if she could. She responded by painting a subject Degas had used often in his own work. Her finished painting demonstrated that she was a first-class painter, and Degas was so impressed that he bought it. "Now here is someone who sees as I do," he exclaimed.

Like many of Degas' subjects, the girl in Cassatt's picture is not pretty. She was a young Irish kitchen maid with big teeth. Cassatt dressed her in a baggy nightgown and had her pose in an awkward position in front of a cheap washstand. Concentrating on the design of her picture, Cassatt tried to make certain that the viewer's eye would be attracted to the model's face. How did she do this? You can answer this question for yourself by examining the contour and axis lines in the work. With your finger, trace the contour lines along the model's back upward and around her right shoulder. Do the same thing with the axis line formed by the right arm and the top of the nightgown. Finally, run your finger upward along the front of the nightgown. All these lines lead to the girl's face. And, the more you look at this face, the more interesting and appealing it becomes —just as Cassatt knew it would. She proves that any subject, even one that is not very attractive, can be made to look beautiful by a skilled artist.

A Changing Role

When Cassatt reached her mid-sixties, she began to go blind—just as Degas did. This made it impossible to continue her painting. As a result, she turned her attention to a new task. Acting as an adviser for her wealthy American friends, she persuaded them to buy artworks by old and new masters—especially the Impressionists. When she died at the age of eighty-two, Mary Cassatt had succeeded in enriching the world with her art, and she had enriched America with some of the world's great masterpieces.

Berthe Morisot

Mary Cassatt was not the only woman artist included in the Impressionist group. Berthe Morisot had a long and important career and took part in all the Impressionist exhibitions but one. That one she missed only because she was awaiting the birth of a child.

Morisot's entire life was entwined with art. A great-granddaughter of Jean-Honoré Fragonard, she was born into a family with a rich artistic tradition. From the time she was a child, she was certain that she would become a painter. At fifteen, following the advice of her teacher, she began to study painting by copying pictures in the Louvre. At that time, it was common practice to learn from the masters of the past by copying their works. In the Louvre, Morisot often saw Edouard Manet. They met and became good friends. Several years later, she married Manet's brother Eugène.

Throughout her lifetime, Morisot was uncertain about her talent. She always valued the opinions and suggestions about her work from those she respected, especially Manet. When she was twenty-nine years old, she finished a portrait of her mother and sister and asked Manet to give his opinion of it. He was pleased with it, but suggested a few changes. Carried away with his critique, he suddenly picked up a brush and spent several hours retouching parts of the portrait. While he was still working, a carriage arrived to take the picture to the Salon where it was to be considered for the annual exhibition. Of course, Morisot was furious with Manet because he had worked on her painting. But there was nothing else to do but send the picture as it was. Her anger did not last long though, because the painting was much acclaimed by the judges.

The Sisters

Like Manet, Morisot concentrated on portraits and interior scenes. However, she added a fresh, delicate vision that was entirely her own. In *The Sisters* (Figure 16.22) two young women dressed in identical ruffled gowns sit quietly on a sofa. They are almost exactly alike in appearance and manner. They are attractive and properly reserved. Neither would be so bold as to stare directly at you. Instead, they shyly lower their gaze and hold their pose patiently. It is unlikely that they had to do so for very long. Morisot usually posed her models for short periods of time and then painted them largely from memory. In that way she was able to capture the more natural but fleeting expressions of her sitters. She avoided the stiff, artificial expressions displayed when poses were held over long periods.

Did you attach any importance to the two fans in this picture? They are not only decorative, but also act as a way of bridging the space between the sisters. The framed fan over the sofa and another held casually by the girl at the right form a semicircle. It acts as a bridge linking the two figures seated at either end of the sofa.

Criticism

How are the two figures in the picture similar? Would you describe their pose as relaxed and natural, or stiff and artificial? Explain how the two fans serve to unite the figures. Do these women appear to be loud and bold, or quiet and shy? On what do you base your opinion?

Figure 16.22   Berthe Morisot. *The Sisters.* 1869. Oil on canvas, 52.1 x 81.3 cm [20½ x 32″]. The National Gallery of Art, Washington, D.C. Gift of Mrs. Charles S. Carstairs, 1952

Overlooked in Her Lifetime

As with so many fine women artists throughout history, Morisot's achievements as a painter were largely overlooked in her day. Critics during her lifetime ignored her or refused to regard her as a serious, talented artist. Often this was just because she was a woman. Her fellow Impressionists, however, considered her work equal to theirs. It was not until after her death at age fifty-four that Morisot's work finally received the widespread acclaim it deserved.

Auguste Rodin

One man dominated the world of sculpture at the end of the nineteenth century and beginning of the twentieth. He was the Frenchman Auguste Rodin. Like the Impressionists, he was able to capture in his work the most fleeting moments of life. His technique in sculpture was similar to that of the Impressionists in painting. As he modeled in wax or clay he added pieces bit by bit to construct his forms, just as the painters added dots and dashes of paint to create their pictures.

Criticism

Does the surface of this sculpture appear to be even or bumpy? In what ways is this work similar to an Impressionist painting? What is the man doing? What feeling or mood is communicated to you by this work?

Figure 16.23 Auguste Rodin. *The Prodigal Son.* 1889. Bronze, black patina; 1.38 m [54¼″] high. Allen Memorial Art Museum, Oberlin College, Oberlin, Ohio. R. T. Miller, Jr. Fund, 55.32

The Prodigal Son

The uneven surfaces of Impressionist paintings are also found on Rodin's sculptures, such as *The Prodigal Son* (Figure 16.23). The way light and shadow play over the uneven surface of this figure gives it life and vitality. Rodin was more than just an Impressionist sculptor, however. The prodigal son with head and arms reaching upward is a powerful image. His wealth and self-esteem gone, at the edge of despair, he pleads for forgiveness. Rodin said he wanted to express joy and sorrow and pain as he saw them. His vision of pain and desperation is so effective here that, like the father to whom the son pleads, you are moved to show mercy.

Review

Rodin ends this discussion of the Impressionists, and with them this chapter draws to a close. Before moving on to Chapter 17, you might pause a moment and briefly review the artists covered so far in the nineteenth century. An outline of the artists and movements (Figure 16.24) may help you with this review.

Figure 16.24

NINETEENTH-CENTURY ART STYLES AND ARTISTS (David to Rodin)

Movement or Style	Representative Artists
NEOCLASSICISM This was the official style of the French Academy throughout the century, but particularly during the first half. This style made use of ancient Greek and Roman sculptures as models. It stressed the importance of balanced compositions, flowing contour lines, figures modeled in light and dark, subdued colors, and noble gestures and expressions.	Jacques Louis David Marie Louise Elizabeth Vigée-Lebrun J.-A.-D. Ingres
ROMANTICISM This style developed and flourished during the first half of the century. It favored the use of rich, dramatic color and a sense of movement rather than balance. Paintings done in this style did not begin with contour lines, but with patterns of color which were used to create shapes and figures.	Théodore Gericault Eugène Delacroix
REALISM This style favored contemporary subject matter, which was ignored by both the Neoclassic and Romantic artists. Realists wanted to create images that were as close to reality as possible. (Rosa Bonheur is included here even though her works, combining Romanticism and Realism, could be considered as unique and individual.)	Gustave Courbet Edouard Manet Rosa Bonheur
IMPRESSIONISM Impressionists studied nature and tried to capture the effect of sunlight on subject matter. They used short brushstrokes to reproduce the flickering quality of sunlight. Their pictures show that they were less interested in the solid look of forms. They concentrated instead on the changing effects of light and atmosphere. In his sculptures, Rodin tried to capture the fleeting moment, as did the Impressionists. He used small pieces of clay or wax to form his works. This technique was like that of the Impressionists, who used small dabs of paint to create their pictures. The uneven surface of his works also looks like the rough-textured surfaces of their paintings.	Claude Monet Pierre Auguste Renoir Edgar Degas Mary Cassatt Berthe Morisot Auguste Rodin
Note: **ENGLISH LANDSCAPE PAINTING** English landscape painting contained elements of several styles, including Romanticism, Realism, and Impressionism. Constable's paintings (especially his sketches painted outdoors) are close to the Impressionist style. However, he remained mostly interested in showing the world as he saw it. Like the Impressionists, Turner was fascinated by the effects of light and atmosphere. However, he showed less concern for authentic appearances than did they. Instead, he used light and color to suggest moods in a more Romantic manner.	John Constable Joseph M. W. Turner

Studio Experiences

Lesson One: Watercolor Still Life in the Style of Delacroix

Compare Delacroix's painting of *The Lion Hunt* (Figure 16.6) with Ingres' portrait of *Madame Moitessier* (Figure 16.4). Which of these artists emphasized color in his painting? Which emphasized line? Set up a still life consisting of five or more objects. Working with watercolor, paint this still life starting with the objects that are closest to you. However, *do not* paint the contours of these objects and then fill them in with color. Instead, begin painting in the center of each object and work outward to the edges. Complete the entire still life by painting in this manner. When the watercolor is dry, add contour lines with pen and India ink. These contour lines should define as accurately as possible the shape of each object in your still life. Do not be concerned if some of your colors extend beyond the contour lines or fail to reach them. This is a characteristic of a painterly style in which precise contours are less important than the application of color. Examine your finished composition. In what way is it similar to Delacroix's painting style? How is it similar to Ingres' painting style?

Lesson Two: Landscape Painting in the Style of Impressionism

Examine the paintings by Monet and Renoir (Figures 16.13, 16.14, and 3.3, page 42) and review the main characteristics of their Impressionistic style. Obtain a large photo poster of a landscape, measuring about 46 x 30 cm [18 x 12 inches]. (These posters can be purchased in most department stores.) Fix a piece of 23 x 30.5-cm [9 x 12-inch] white paper to your poster with sections of rolled masking tape. You may attach this paper wherever you wish. With tempera, paint in the concealed section of your poster on the white paper. However, try to do this as an Impressionist might. This means including characteristics found in paintings done by Monet, Renoir, and the other Impressionists. Special attention should be paid to the following:

- Use a variety of colors, applied as small dabs and dashes of paint placed closely together.
- Place hues so that from a distance they will seem to blend together to suggest other hues.
- Contrast the smooth, slick surface of the poster with a painted surface which is rich in actual texture.

Chapter 17

A Time for Rebels: Art of the Later Nineteenth Century

Artists you will meet in this chapter

Paul Cézanne (*pawl* say-*zahn*), 1839-1906. What drove this stubborn artist to spend his days painting pictures that no one bought?

Vincent van Gogh (*vin*-sent van *goe*), 1853-90. He painted landscapes flooded with color in which trees and flowers spiraled upward as if they were about to tear themselves from the earth.

Paul Gauguin (*pawl* go-*gan*), 1848-1903. Many people could not understand how this successful businessman could give up everything for art.

Winslow Homer, 1836-1910. He is considered to be one of the most skillful and forceful painters of the sea.

Thomas Eakins (*tahm*-us *ay*-kins), 1844-1916. Many failed to appreciate his highly realistic style—especially when he used it to paint pictures of surgeons performing operations!

Albert Pinkham Ryder, 1847-1917. He lived the life of a hermit, leaving his apartment at night to roam the barren streets of New York alone.

Henry Tanner, 1859-1937. In France, he received the recognition that was denied to him in his native United States.

Europe in the Late Nineteenth Century

During the last two decades of the nineteenth century, some artists who had been connected with Impressionism began to find fault with it. They felt that it sacrificed too much by trying to capture the momentary effects of sunlight on forms and colors. These artists wanted to continue painting the contemporary world, but hoped to overcome some problems with the Impressionist style.

Post-Impressionism

The most important of these artists were Paul Cézanne, Vincent van Gogh, and Paul Gauguin. They belong to a group of artists who are now called *Post-Impressionists.* Each of these artists wanted to discover what was wrong or missing in Impressionism. Their search for an answer led them in different directions and had an important effect on the course of art history.

Paul Cézanne

Early in his career, Paul Cézanne was associated with the Impressionists and even took part in their first exhibition in 1874. But he never lost his strong affection for the art of the old masters. His studies of the great artists in the Louvre led him to believe that Impressionist paintings lacked form, solidity, and structure. He spent the rest of his life trying to restore those qualities to his paintings, although he did not turn his back entirely on Impressionism. Indeed, he wanted to make Impressionism "something solid like the art of museums."

History

Cézanne's use of color planes placed next to each other at different angles is similar to the placement of the bricks in this curved wall.

Figure 17.1   Curved brick wall

Cézanne's effort to change this began with experiments with still-life painting followed by pictures with figures and landscapes. Often he painted the same object over and over again until he was completely satisfied.★ If a picture did not please him, he would throw it out the window, or leave it in the field where it had been painted, or give it to his son to cut up for a jigsaw puzzle. In time, his patience paid off; he arrived at a technique in which he applied his colors in small, flat patches. These patches of color were placed side by side so that each one represented a separate plane. When he painted a round object such as an apple, these planes were joined together to follow the curved form of the object. Each of these planes had a slightly different color as well because Cézanne knew that colors change as they come forward or go back in space. And so he used cool colors that seemed to go back in space and warm colors that seemed to advance in space to make his painted objects look more three-dimensional.

It might be easier for you to understand Cézanne's technique if you imagine that someone gave you a pile of bricks and asked you to build a high, curved wall. You would have to arrange each brick so that it turned slightly in order to make the wall round (Figure 17.1). Now, try to imagine painting that same wall by using patches or planes of color to make it look round. Each plane of color would be placed next to another at a slightly different angle just as the bricks had been placed next to each other. To show that the planes were coming forward or going back into space, you would have to change the color of each plane slightly. With this technique, Cézanne was able to create the solid-looking forms that he felt were missing in Impressionist pictures.

The style that Cézanne worked so hard to perfect was not realistic. He was not concerned with reproducing exactly the shapes, colors, lines, and textures found in nature. It is true that nature was his starting point, but he did not feel bound to it. He felt free to discard anything that he thought was unnecessary. Further, he carefully placed the objects in his works rather than paint them as he found them. Thus, Cézanne reversed a trend in art that had its origin with the great Italian artist Giotto. Giotto had abandoned the flat, decorative style of Medieval art and turned to nature as his teacher and his model. And for six hundred years, artists followed his example and did the same, trying to reproduce nature as faithfully as possible in their pictures.

★ **Enrichment** One amusing story should serve to demonstrate Cézanne's great patience and determination. When painting a portrait of Ambroise Vollard, an art dealer, Cézanne required his subject to pose on 115 different occasions. When the portrait was finally completed, Cézanne said that he was satisfied—with the way he had painted the front of Vollard's shirt!

Criticism

What do you see in this picture? Can you find some things that do not look accurate? Find as many straight lines as you can—then find lines that curve and contrast with these straight lines. Which hue dominates? Point out shapes that are painted with a color that is a complement to this dominant hue. Do the shapes look solid and heavy, or thin and fragile? When judging this work, would you refer most often to the literal qualities or the formal qualities?

Figure 17.2   Paul Cézanne. *Still Life with Peppermint Bottle.* **c. 1894. Oil on canvas, 65.9 x 82.1 cm [26 x 32⅜"]. The National Gallery of Art, Washington, D.C. Chester Dale Collection, 1962**

Cézanne developed this painting technique with still-life pictures. You can learn more about it by studying one of those paintings (Figure 17.2). Earlier artists like Chardin (Figure 15.4, page 272) painted still lifes because this type of subject matter allowed them to choose objects for their unique shapes, colors, lines, and textures. But Cézanne was interested in still-life objects because they did not move and he could study them closely. In portrait painting the subject often moved. Still-life painting, on the other hand, gave him the chance to study and paint objects over long periods of time. Sometimes he even used artificial fruit and flowers because they would not spoil or wilt over the long hours in which he studied and painted them.

Up close, everything in Cézanne's still life seems flat because your eye is too near to see the relationships between the colored planes. But, when viewed from a distance, these relationships become clear and the forms take on a solid, three-dimensional appearance.

Notice how every object in Cézanne's still life has been carefully positioned. There are no "happy accidents" here. Like a master builder, he has placed objects so they balance and complement each other. All the pieces in his picture fit neatly together to form a unified design. The dark vertical and horizontal bands on the wall not only hold the picture together, but also direct your eye to the most important objects. To balance the strong horizontal lines at the right, Cézanne has strengthened the contour of the white napkin at the left by placing a shadow behind it. Because the firm line on the wall to the right of the glass jug might compete with the jug, he blends it out. Then he adds a dark blue line to strengthen the right side of the jug. To add interest and variety, Cézanne contrasts the straight lines with the curved lines of the drapery, fruit, and bottles.

The blue-green hue used throughout this painting helps to pull the parts together into an organized whole. Also, Cézanne showed a preference for blue tones whenever he wanted to show depth. Observe how the fruit placed throughout the middle of the still life seem to float forward toward you and away from the blue-green cloth and wall. This illusion is due to the warm reds and yellows used to paint this fruit. These hues are complements to the cool blue-green. When placed before a blue-green background, they appear to come forward.

Cézanne's still life does not look very realistic—the drapery fails to fall naturally over the edge of the table, and the opening at the top of the jug is too large. But he was willing to sacrifice realism in order to achieve another goal. He wanted the apples to look solid and heavy, and the napkin and tablecloth to appear as massive and monumental as mountains.

History

What did Cézanne try to show in paintings like this that he felt was missing in Impressionist works? Did the public or the critics of his time appreciate Cézanne's paintings? How is this artist regarded today?

Figure 17.3 Paul Cézanne. *Pines and Rocks (Fontainebleu?)*. 1896-99. Oil on canvas, 81.3 x 65.4 cm [32 x 25¾"]. Collection, The Museum of Modern Art, New York. Lillie P. Bliss Collection

History

Cézanne, like Claude Monet, often painted the same subject over and over again. Were the objectives of these two artists the same? How did they differ? Can you recall some of the subjects that Monet painted several times? Select two adjectives from the following list to describe this painting: monumental, transparent, two-dimensional, solid, flimsy, formless.

Figure 17.4   Paul Cézanne. *Mont Sainte-Victoire as Seen from Bibemus Quarry.* c. 1898-1900. Oil on canvas, 64.8 x 81.3 cm [25½ x 32″]. The Baltimore Museum of Art. The Cone Collection, formed by Dr. Claribel Cone and Miss Etta Cone of Baltimore, Maryland

This same solid, massive quality is found in Cézanne's landscapes. Notice how the rock in the foreground of his *Pines and Rocks* (Figure 17.3) looks heavy and solid. Small brushstrokes have been used to suggest the form of this rock, giving it the weight and volume of a mountain. The foliage of the trees is painted as a heavy mass of greens and blue-greens. Like everything else in the work, the foliage is created with cubes of color. The work has the appearance of a three-dimensional mosaic. Some cubes seem to tilt away from you, while others turn in a variety of other directions. They lead your eye in, out, and around the solid forms that make up the picture. In some places outlines are firm and strong, and in others they fade out, allowing forms to blend together to unify the composition.

Cézanne did his best to ignore the critics who scorned or laughed at his work. Even the people in the little town where he lived thought that he was strange. They wondered about a man who spent his days alone painting in the fields, creating works that no one bought. What sort of an artist would stand for long periods of time staring at a little mountain? And then, when he finally put his brush to canvas, he would make no more than a single stroke before returning to his study. Cézanne painted more than sixty versions of the little mountain known as Sainte-Victoire (Figure 17.4 and Figure 1.2, page 12). In each, he used cubes of color to build a solid form that is both monumental and durable.

One day while he was painting in the fields, it began to rain. But Cézanne refused to stop working and seek shelter. Finally, he collapsed. He was picked up by a man in a passing laundry cart and taken home. A few days later he died of pneumonia.

Describe the people in this picture. Is this home warm and comfortable? What are these people doing? Do you think this family is well-to-do, or poverty-stricken? Give your interpretation of this painting; be sure to mention why you think the people do not seem to be enjoying themselves.

Figure 17.5   Vincent van Gogh. *The Potato Eaters.* 1885. National Museum Vincent van Gogh, Amsterdam

Vincent van Gogh

There are few people today who are not familiar with the tragic story of Vincent van Gogh. It has been told and retold in scores of books and motion pictures. And this is unfortunate because the story of this unhappy artist's life has probably lured attention away from his art.

As a young man, van Gogh worked as a lay missionary in a poor Belgian mining village. But he was a failure at this vocation. More and more he withdrew into himself and turned to his art. He loved art; wherever he went he visited museums and would draw and paint at every opportunity. His early pictures were painted in browns and other drab colors and showed peasants going about their daily routines. One of these early paintings was *The Potato Eaters* (Figure 17.5).★ In this picture, a peasant family has gathered around a table to eat their humble meal of potatoes. In most families, this would be a happy time, a time to share experiences and talk over the events of the day. But there is no happy chatter here. This day is no different than any other day. It has meant the same back-breaking work in the dark mines for the men and the usual dull routine in and around the drab cottage for the women. The interior of the cottage is dark and cool. Steam rises from the potatoes and from the tea, and everyone wears heavy clothing. There is little color; the walls, clothing, and even the faces of the people have an earthen hue. It looks as if the entire scene is taking place underground. Look at the faces a moment; what do they remind you of? Surprisingly, they look like the potatoes that grow in the ground and provide this poor family with its only nourishment.

★ Enrichment Van Gogh's first large paintings were three versions of *The Potato Eaters,* which were painted in dismal browns and dark, earthy greens.

Large flat areas of bright color and a strange perspective are noted in this painting of Van Gogh's narrow room.

What two influences contributed to the development of this artist's painting style?

Figure 17.6   Vincent van Gogh. *The Bedroom at Arles.* 1888-89, Oil on canvas, 73.7 x 91.4 cm [29 x 36″]. Collection of The Art Institute of Chicago

You have seen paintings before that draw you into them and make you feel like a participant in the event. Jan Steen's *Eve of St. Nicholas* (Figure 14.14, page 258) is an excellent example of such a painting. But in *The Potato Eaters* van Gogh prevents you from joining the family around the dinner table. His figures form a tight circle and one, the young girl, even turns her back to you. Why do you think the artist has done this? Possibly he is trying to tell you that you can never join this family circle without first experiencing the poverty and the hardship they have experienced. You are allowed to be no more than a silent witness to their actions. You can never share their hopelessness without being hopeless yourself.

In 1886, van Gogh moved to Paris to be with his brother Theo, an art dealer.⁎ Recognizing his brother's abilities as an artist, Theo gave van Gogh an allowance so that he could continue painting. While he was in Paris, van Gogh came under the influence of Impressionism. As a result, his colors became brighter and his brushstrokes more spirited. At about this same time, he saw his first Japanese woodcut prints. These also had an effect on his painting style. He began to use large flat areas of color and tilt his subject matter to present a strange new kind of perspective (Figure 17.6).

★ Enrichment Van Gogh's nearly one thousand letters to his faithful brother Theo are among the most moving documents of modern art.

Describe the texture of this painting. Is this an example of actual texture, or simulated texture? Do you think this picture represents what the artist *saw,* or what he *felt*? Explain your answer. Which of the following terms would you use when interpreting this work: calm, peaceful, dull, exciting, forceful? What does this picture tell you about nature?

Figure 17.7   Vincent van Gogh. *Starry Night.* 1889. Oil on canvas, 73.7 x 92.1 cm [29 x 36¼″]. Collection, The Museum of Modern Art, New York. Acquired through the Lillie P. Bliss Bequest

In 1888, when he was thirty-five years old, van Gogh traveled to the city of Arles in the south of France. He hoped to find there the brilliant colors he saw in Japanese prints. But, because it did not suit his restless and excitable personality, he began to turn away from Impressionism to develop his own painting style. This style was marked by a use of bright colors, twisting lines, bold brushstrokes, and a thick application of paint. The bright sunshine of southern France offered him a landscape of vivid colors. He began to paint fields bathed in sunlight, and trees and flowers that twisted and turned as if they were alive. In his eagerness to capture these colors and forms in his pictures, he would squeeze yellows, reds, and blues from the paint tubes directly onto his canvas. Then he used his brush and even his fingers to spread the paint with swirling, curving strokes.

During this period, the last two years of his life, van Gogh painted his best works—portraits, landscapes, interiors, and night scenes. In one of his night scenes, *Starry Night* (Figure 17.7), you can see how quick slashes of paint were used to create the dark cypress trees that twist upward like the flame from a candle. Overhead the sky is alive with bursting stars that seem to be hurtled about by violent gusts of wind sweeping across the sky. Short, choppy brushstrokes are combined with sweeping, swirling strokes, which gives a rich texture to the painting's surface. Unlike Cézanne, van Gogh did not try to think his way through the painting process. He painted what he *felt,* not what he thought. And here he felt the violent energy and creative force of nature. In order to capture that energy and force he had to develop a painting style that was energetic and forceful.

Van Gogh was an unstable personality who suffered from epileptic seizures during the last two years of his life. Informed that there was no cure for his ailment, he grew more and more depressed. He lived in fear that his seizures would become more frequent and more severe. And, if this were not enough, he worried about the burden he placed upon his brother Theo who had been providing him with money for years. Theo had married and had a son, and van Gogh felt that he was a greater burden to his brother then ever. Finally, on a July evening in 1890, in a wheat field where he had been painting, van Gogh shot himself. The wound was not immediately fatal, however, and he was able to return to his room where Theo rushed to his side. He died two days later. Like Raphael and Watteau before him, van Gogh died at the age of thirty-seven.

As for Theo, the faithful brother, he was so heartbroken that he died six months later. He is buried in Auvers, beside the artist brother he unselfishly encouraged, supported, and loved.

Vincent van Gogh received only one favorable review and sold only one painting during his lifetime. But his art served as an inspiration for many artists who followed. And today the works of this lonely, troubled man are among the most popular and most acclaimed in the history of painting.

Paul Gauguin

Like Cézanne and van Gogh, Paul Gauguin passed through an Impressionistic period before moving in another direction. He was a successful broker who began painting as a hobby. Under the influence of some of the Impressionists, he exhibited with them in the early and mid-1880s. Then, at the age of thirty-five, he left his well-paying job and turned to painting as a career. This was not a popular decision for Gaugin's wife and family. They could not understand how a successful businessman could give up everything for art. To make matters worse, his paintings did not sell, and he and his family were reduced to poverty. Still, Gauguin never lost heart. He felt that he was destined to be a great artist.

Throughout his career, Gaugin moved from one location to another in search of an earthly paradise with exotic settings that he could paint. His quest took him from Paris to Brittany to Provence to the South Seas.★ In Tahiti, he painted a strange picture entitled *Spirit of the Dead Watching* (Figure 17.8). In a letter to his wife, Gauguin tried to describe and explain this work. First, he painted a young girl lying on a bed. She has been frightened by the spirit of a dead woman appearing behind her. Gauguin explained that this girl was a Maori and that these people had a great fear of ghosts and spirits. He made the ghost in the painting look like a little woman because the girl believed that ghosts looked like the people they were in life.

★ **Enrichment** In the South Seas, Gauguin lived with the natives and shared their way of life.

Criticism

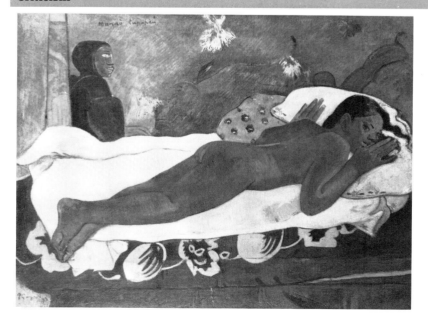

Describe the things you see in this painting. Do you see any three-dimensional forms? Is the girl on the bed relaxed; is she sleeping? Do you think she looks frightened? If so, why is she frightened? Who is the little woman? Do you think the girl knows the woman is there? Why doesn't the girl turn around and face her?

Figure 17.8 Paul Gauguin. *Spirit of the Dead Watching.* **1892. Oil on burlap mounted on canvas, approx. 72.4 x 92.7 cm [28½ x 36⅜"]. Albright-Knox Art Gallery, Buffalo, New York. A. Conger Goodyear Collection, 1965**

Criticism

What do you see in this picture? Can you find some shapes that look flat and others that look round? What has been done to create the illusion of depth? Identify the most intense color. Are there many straight lines in this work?

Describe the contour lines. Would you judge this work mainly in terms of its literal, formal, or expressive qualities? Do you think it is successful?

Fatata te Miti

Figure 17.9   Paul Gauguin. *Fatata te Miti (By the Sea).* 1892. Oil on canvas, 67.9 x 91.5 cm [26¾ x 36"]. The National Gallery of Art, Washington, D.C. Chester Dale Collection, 1962

Gauguin was more interested in creating a decorative pattern than a picture that looked real. Flat areas of bright colors are combined with forms that look round and solid. Notice how the shapes which surround the girl are arranged in a relatively flat pattern, while the body of the girl looks three-dimensional. Gauguin felt that the artist should be free to use light and shadow when he wanted, but should never feel bound to do so.

Gauguin's pictures started with the exotic subject matter he searched for in his travels. But as he painted,

he allowed his imagination to take over. "I shut my eyes in order to see," he said. What he saw were crimson rocks, gold trees, and violet hills. He used color in new and exciting ways to make his pictures more decorative. "How does that tree look to you?" he asked. "Green? All right, then use green, the greenest on your palette. And that shadow—a little blue? Don't be afraid. Paint it as blue as you can."

Gauguin's novel ideas about color are demonstrated in another picture he did in Tahiti entitled *Fatata te Miti*

(Figure 17.9). This means "By the Sea" in the Maori language which Gauguin learned. Beyond a huge twisted tree root, two native girls wade out into the blue-green sea for a swim. In the distance, a fisherman with spear in hand stalks his quarry. Flat areas of bright colors, especially in the foreground, give the picture the look of a Medieval stained-glass window. Except for the figures, the forms are flattened into planes of color which overlap to lead you into the work. Gauguin is not really interested in creating the illusion of real space here. He is more concerned with combining flat, colorful shapes and curving contour lines to produce a decorative pattern.

Although he returned to Paris for a short time, Gauguin's last years were spent in the Pacific Islands. Unfortunately, he had little money, was in poor health, and was always arguing with local officials. In 1903, he was sentenced to three months in prison for an insulting letter sent to a government official. Before he could serve his sentence, he died, alone and helpless in his hut.

Gauguin always believed he would be a great artist, and he was right. His contribution to the history of art is unquestioned. He succeeded in freeing artists from the idea of copying nature. After Gauguin, artists no longer hesitated in using a bright red color to paint a tree which was only touched with red, or an intense blue to paint a shadow with a bluish cast. Later artists felt free to change the curve of a branch or a shoulder to the point of exaggeration. They felt at liberty to paint any way they wished.

The Influence of Cézanne, van Gogh, and Gauguin

Cézanne, van Gogh, and Gauguin saw the world in different ways and developed their own methods to show others what they saw. Cézanne sought weight and solidity in his carefully composed still lifes, landscapes, and portraits. He used planes of warm and cool colors that advance and recede to model his forms, creating a solid, enduring world with his brush. Van Gogh used vibrating colors, distortion, and vigorous brushstrokes to show a world throbbing with movement and energy. And Gauguin took the shapes, colors, and lines he found in nature and changed them into flat, simplified shapes, broad areas of bright colors, and graceful lines. Then he arranged these elements to make a decorative pattern on his canvas. Each of these artists experienced loneliness, frustration, even ridicule. But their work had a tremendous influence on the artists of the twentieth century. Cézanne inspired Cubism. Van Gogh influenced the Fauves and the Expressionists. And Gauguin showed the way to different groups of primitive artists and, closer to the present day, American Abstract Expressionists.

America in the Late Nineteenth Century

The United States came of age in the nineteenth century and began to be aware of itself as a nation. It was a time of great change and growth. There was growth westward, growth in trade and industry, growth in population, and growth in wealth. Although the Civil War stopped the rate of progress for a time, it continued with a new vigor after Appomattox. American scientists, inventors, and businessmen provided new products to make life easier for people. These were products such as the typewriter, sewing machine, and electric lamp. Meanwhile, immigrants from all over Europe brought their knowledge and skills to the new world. Great fortunes were made. Wealthy industrialists and businessmen like Carnegie, Rockefeller, and Morgan funneled some of their riches into schools, colleges, and museums. Interest in education grew due to the efforts of Horace Mann, Henry Barnard, Emma Willard, and others. The first state university was founded in 1855 in Michigan, and others quickly followed. By 1900, the United States had become a world leader.

Changes in American Art

Change and growth were also noted in American art. Works were produced by self-taught artists traveling from village to village. Other works were created by more sophisticated artists who journeyed to the art centers of Europe to study. Some chose to remain there, where they became part of European art movements. Others returned to the United States to develop art styles that were American in subject matter and technique. One of these artists was Winslow Homer.

★ Enrichment You will recall that Mary Cassatt was one of those who chose to remain in Europe, where she became an important member of the Impressionists.

323

Winslow Homer

Homer was born in 1836 in Boston, Massachusetts. When he was six, his family moved to Cambridge, and it was there, growing up with his two brothers in the country, that Homer learned to love the outdoors. This was a love of a lifetime that he expressed through his paintings.

Homer's interest in art began while he was quite young. He was about ten years old when his talent for drawing became obvious to those around him. His mother was an amateur painter, and she as well as other members of his family approved of the boy's enthusiasm for art. When he was nineteen, Homer was accepted as an apprentice at a large printing firm in Boston even though he had little formal training. However, he soon tired of designing covers for song sheets and prints for framing and decided to become a magazine illustrator.

For seventeen years, Homer earned his living as an illustrator, chiefly for *Harper's Weekly* in New York. During the Civil War, *Harper's* sent him to the front lines where he drew and painted scenes of army life. His first public recognition came in 1866 for a painting entitled *Prisoners at the Front.*

After the war, Homer decided to strike out on his own as a painter. He traveled a great deal, drawing and painting the things he saw. The income from the sale of his works financed two trips to Europe. In between these trips, he painted the American scene: pictures of schoolrooms, croquet games, and husking bees, pictures which were popular with everyone but the critics. They felt his works were too sketchy and looked unfinished.

From 1883 until his death, Homer lived in Prout's Neck, Maine, where the ocean crashing against majestic

Criticism

How has this scene been made to look lifelike? What is the man in the boat doing? Where is he going? What do you see on the horizon? Describe the action of the sea—is it calm or rough? Do you think the fisherman is in danger? If so, what do you think he will do next? Is this a good work of art? Why or why not?

Figure 17.10   Winslow Homer [American, 1836-1910]. *The Fog Warning.* **1885. Oil on canvas, 76.2 x 121.7 cm [30 x 48″]. Courtesy of the Museum of Fine Arts, Boston. Otis Norcross Fund, 94.72**

Criticism

Describe the actions of the two ducks. Can you find any evidence of a human figure in this picture? Why does one duck seem to be falling? From what point of view are you witnessing this scene? Explain how the background is organized; be sure to discuss how lines, shapes, and values are used. What do you think are the most successful features of this work?

Figure 17.11   Winslow Homer. *Right and Left.*   1909. Oil on canvas, approx. 71.8 x 122.9 cm [28¼ x 48⅜"]. The National Gallery of Art, Washington, D.C. Gift of the Avalon Foundation, 1951

cliffs inspired many of his great seascapes. His paintings followed hours in which he studied the ocean in all its moods, as well as the sun and clouds, rain and fog. Long regarded as one of the most skillful and powerful painters of the sea, Homer is seen at his best in works like *The Fog Warning* (Figure 17.10).

In this painting, a lone fisherman in oilskins rests the oars of his small dory and takes advantage of his position on the crest of a wave to get his bearings. He turns his head in the direction of a schooner on the horizon, although his eyes are locked on the fog bank beyond. Apparently the fisherman is returning to the schooner after a successful day of fishing for there are two or three large fish amid the items in the dory. The sea is very rough. Whitecaps are clearly visible, and the bow of the light dory is lifted high in the air, while the stern settles deep into a trough of waves. Overhead the sky is still clear, but touched with the fading colors of late afternoon and marred by the fog bank lying low on the horizon. All the signs evident in the sea and the sky point to an approaching storm.

Different values separate the sea, sky, and fog. The horizontal contour lines of the oars, boat seats, horizon, and fog bank contrast with the diagonal axis lines of the dory and portions of the windblown fog. But notice in particular how effectively Homer directs your attention to the right side of the picture. A diagonal line representing the crest of the wave on which the dory rests leads your eye in this direction. Furthermore, the curving axis line of the fish in the dory guides you to the same destination. There you discover the schooner and the advancing fog bank. Why was he so interested in making certain that you did not overlook these two items? Because they make it clear that this is not just a

pleasant, very realistic picture of a man in a fishing boat. The concerned gaze of the fisherman, the choppy sea, and the fog bank suggest a great deal more. Homer has caught the exact moment that the fisherman recognizes the danger he is in. He stops rowing for just a few seconds. Even the dory seems frozen at the top of a wave as he calculates whether or not he will be able to reach the schooner before it is hidden by the windswept fog. For a moment, he cannot catch his breath. His pulse quickens. You know that in the next instant he will begin rowing as he has never rowed before in a desperate race to beat the fog to the schooner. His survival depends on whether or not he can win that race. If he loses, he will be lost, alone, and at the mercy of the storm.

Homer's unique imagination and organizational skills are further shown in a painting finished a year before his death, *Right and Left* (Figure 17.11). The horizontal and diagonal lines of the waves and clouds provide a backdrop for two ducks. One is plunging into the sea, while the other rises upward and is about to fly out of the picture. You may be so engrossed with the startling realism of the ducks that it comes as a surprise when you realize that you are looking directly at a hunter who has just shot the duck at the right. Homer has placed you at the same height as the ducks where you can look down at the stormy sea and the hunter.

Not long after painting *Right and Left*, Homer completed a picture entitled *Driftwood*. It shows a small, solitary human figure observing the sea in a storm. It was Homer's final tribute and farewell to the sea he loved. When it was finished, he set aside his easel and his brushes, never to paint again. A short time later, after a full and active life, Winslow Homer died.

History

Eakins and Homer were considered to be among America's first (a) Impressionists? (b) Realists? (c) Romanticists? Homer painted scenes of nature; what subject matter did Eakins prefer for his pictures? Which artists greatly influenced Eakins? Why did many Americans object to his portraits? What did he do to make his figures look so authentic?

Figure 17.12   Thomas Eakins. *The Gross Clinic.* 1875. Oil on canvas, 2.44 x 1.98 [96 x 78″]. The Jefferson Medical College of Thomas Jefferson University, Philadelphia

Thomas Eakins

Winslow Homer and Thomas Eakins are considered to be among the first *Realists* in American painting. Both were firmly rooted to their time and place and drew upon this for their work. The subjects they chose differed, however. Homer, as you know, chose to portray the drama of nature, especially the sea. Eakins, by contrast, was mainly interested in painting the people and scenes of his own Philadelphia setting.

Early in his career, Eakins studied in the Paris studios of a Neoclassic artist and was certainly influenced by the realism of Courbet.★ But his most important teachers were the seventeenth-century masters Velázquez, Hals, and the painter he called "the big artist," Rembrandt. From Rembrandt, Eakins learned to use light and dark values to make his figures look solid, round, and lifelike.

When he returned to the United States, Eakins found that Americans did not like his highly realistic style. They preferred sentimental scenes and romantic views of the American landscape. Many felt his portraits were too honest. Eakins painted only what he saw. He would not flatter his subjects. Even though it reduced his popular appeal, Eakins never varied his realistic style during a career that spanned forty years.

One of Eakins' best works and one of the great paintings of the era was *The Gross Clinic* (Figure 17.12). The famous surgeon Dr. Gross has paused for a moment during an operation to explain a certain procedure. Eakins draws attention to the head of the doctor by placing it at the tip of a pyramid formed by the foreground figures. Behind, in the darkness of the medical arena, the doctor's students watch and listen attentively.

The artist's attention to detail and his portrayal of figures in space give the painting its startling realism. For some viewers, it was too real.★ They objected to the blood on the scalpel and hand of the surgeon. But it would have been impossible for Eakins not to show everything he saw exactly as he saw it. You may wonder why the doctors and attendants around the patient are shown in street clothes. This was the custom before science discovered that a sterile environment was needed to protect the patient from infection. You may be relieved to learn that the cringing figure at the left is not a doctor but a relative of the patient. The law at that time required that a relative be present during surgery.

Throughout his life, Eakins was fascinated by the study of the human body. He was an enthusiastic student of the anatomy by dissection and required his students to dissect corpses to learn how to make their figures look more authentic. His knowledge of the human body was vast. In fact, he once gave a paper on this topic to a scientific group. It was this knowledge that enabled Eakins to paint figures that look as if every bone and muscle has been taken into account.

★ **Enrichment**   The artist with whom Eakins studied was Jean Léon Gérôme.

★ **Enrichment**   The painting was rejected by the committee selecting artworks for Philadelphia's Centennial Exhibition in 1876. Eakins had to be content with having it shown among the medical exhibits of the Centennial.

Albert Pinkham Ryder

Eakins and Homer painted realistic scenes from everyday American life. The works of Albert Pinkham Ryder, on the other hand, were inspired by the Bible, Chaucer, Shakespeare, and nineteenth-century Romantic writers. Ryder went to Europe several times. However, he had little interest in the works of other artists. He lived as a hermit apart from the rest of the world and looked within himself for inspiration.

Ryder was born in New Bedford, Massachusetts, when it was still a thriving fishing port. When he was a young man, his family moved to New York City, where an older brother helped pay his expenses to art school. At first Ryder lived in Greenwich Village, but later moved to a humble rooming house on the city's West Side. There he slept beneath piles of old overcoats on a floor littered with stacks of yellowing newspapers, empty cans, and other trash. Troubled with poor eyesight, he remained indoors during the day and roamed the streets of the city alone at night. Passersby must have

---

★ Enrichment At least one of his paintings was taken from the opera. He was greatly inspired by Wagner, and after hearing *Siegfried* he went home and started work on his *Siegfried and the Rhine Maidens*. He worked on this painting for forty-eight hours without sleep or food.

---

wondered about the big bearded man dressed in tattered clothing, especially when they observed him staring for long periods of time at the moon. Perhaps, during those walks alone down dark city streets, ideas were formed which Ryder eventually expressed in his paintings.

In *Jonah* (Figure 17.13), Ryder shows the Old Testament figure flailing about helplessly in a sea made turbulent by a raging storm. Jonah has been tossed from the frail boat by a crew who are filled with fright and who hold him responsible for their misfortune. The whale, in whose stomach Jonah was to spend three days, is fast approaching at the right. It is almost lost in the violent action of the water. Ryder's version of the whale may look strange to you. He had never seen the real thing, so he had to rely on his imagination when painting it. At the top of the picture, barely visible in a golden glow, God, Master of the Universe, looks on.

Color and texture were as important to Ryder as the objects or events he painted. His small pictures were built up carefully over months and even years until the forms were nearly three-dimensional. At one time

---

★ Enrichment Ryder found it difficult to think of a work as finished. Often he took back paintings he had sold and redid them completely.

Criticism

Find the following principal characters in this drama: (a) a man in the sea, (b) a whale, (c) a boat manned by a frightened crew, (d) God. Which elements of art dominate in this picture? What is your interpretation of this scene? Is this a good work of art? What aesthetic qualities would you use to defend your decision?

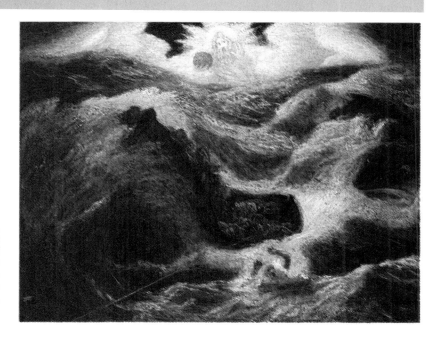

Figure 17.13 Albert Pinkham Ryder. *Jonah.* **c. 1885. Oil on canvas, approx. 69.2 x 87.6 cm [27¼ x 34⅜″]. National Museum of American Art (formerly National Collection of Fine Arts), Smithsonian Institution, Washington, D.C. Gift of John Gellatly, 1929.6.98**

Where did Ryder often turn to find ideas for his paintings? In what ways does this picture seem more like a scene from a dream than from real life? If sound could be added to this picture, do you think it would be loud and stirring, or soft and mysterious? What sounds would you hear?

Figure 17.14   Albert Pinkham Ryder. *Flying Dutchman.* **c. 1887. Oil on canvas, 36.1 x 43.8 cm [14¼ x 17¼"]. National Museum of American Art (formerly National Collection of Fine Arts), Smithsonian Institution, Washington, D.C. Gift of John Gellatly, 1929.6.95**

these simple, massive forms had the rich color of precious stones. But now the colors have faded because his paints were of poor quality or were applied improperly. However, there is more to Ryder's pictures than texture, form, and color. If you have seen the fury of a storm at sea or been in a boat during such a storm, you will be aroused by his pictures. Even if you have never seen or experienced the sea in this way, Ryder's paintings act as a springboard for your imagination (Figure 17.14). This would please Ryder, who withdrew from the world around him and relied upon his own imagination.[★] In this way, he discovered a dreamworld where dark boats sail soundlessly on moonlit seas, mysterious forests are bathed in an unearthly light, and death rides a pale horse around a deserted racetrack.

The Contributions of Afro-American Artists

Afro-American artists have contributed a great deal to the growth of art in the United States. In colonial times, many artists were black. They gained much success traveling from one town to the next and practicing their craft. One such artist, Joshua Johnston of Baltimore, was in demand among wealthy Maryland families who sought him out to paint their portraits. However, after his death, others were often given credit for pictures that were actually painted by Johnston. Such mistakes are now being corrected, and Johnston's place in history is being confirmed.

Two years after the Civil War, a black artist was angered by an article in a New York newspaper. The artist was Edward Bannister from Providence, Rhode Island. The writer claimed that blacks were especially talented in several arts, but not in painting or sculpture. Bannister later shattered that claim by becoming the first American black painter to win an award at a national exhibition. His landscape *Under the Oaks* received first prize at the Philadelphia Centennial Exhibition.[★] It is of interest to note that when the judges learned that he was black, they considered withdrawing the award. But the other artists in the show insisted that Bannister receive the award he had won.

★ **Enrichment** Living a completely solitary life after 1900, Ryder spent his last years reworking old paintings and never undertaking any new works.

★ **Enrichment** Unfortunately, this painting by Bannister has been lost.

Criticism

What do their surroundings tell you about the kind of life these people lead? Why do you think music might be very important to them? How would you answer someone who claimed that this picture was too sentimental?

Figure 17.15   Henry Tanner. *The Banjo Lesson.* 1893. The Hampton Institute's Archival and Museum Collection, Hampton Institute, Hampton, Virginia

Henry Tanner

The most famous Afro-American artist of the late nineteenth and early twentieth centuries was Henry Tanner. Tanner was born and raised in Philadelphia. His father was a Methodist minister, who later became a bishop. Tanner's interest in art began by chance when he was just twelve. One day he and his father were on an outing in a city park when they happened to see a landscape painter at work. The boy was fascinated, and this fascination grew with the years. Finally, against his father's wishes, he enrolled at the Pennsylvania Academy of the Fine Arts. There he studied with Thomas Eakins. They became friends, and Eakins influenced Tanner to turn from landscapes to genre scenes. Eakins also convinced his student to stay in the United States rather than go to Europe. Eakins saw little need to go abroad when there was so much of interest to paint in the U.S. Tanner took his advice and went south to North Carolina and Georgia when he had finished his studies at the Academy.

Tanner's painting of *The Banjo Lesson* (Figure 17.15) grew out of his experience among the blacks of western North Carolina. Here, under the watchful eye of an old man, a boy strums a tune on a worn banjo. Man and boy are lost in concentration, forgetting for a precious few moments their humble surroundings. This music lesson represents more than just a pleasant way to pass the time for them. For the old man, music is his legacy to the boy, one of the few things of value he has to pass on to him. For the boy, music may be his only hope for pleasure in a world that will surely be difficult and unexciting. Tanner tells this story simply and without sentimentality. And, because he does, it is not likely to be forgotten.

In time, Tanner decided to ignore Eakin's advice to remain in the United States. He was not enjoying financial success—a one-man show in Cincinnati failed to sell a single work. Furthermore, his strong religious upbringing made him eager to paint biblical subjects. It was time for a new start. So following the route of many leading artists of his day, Tanner journeyed to Paris, arriving there when he was thirty-two years old. Five years later his painting of *Daniel in the Lion's Den* was hanging in a place of honor in the Paris Salon. The next year, another religious painting was awarded a medal and purchased by the French government. The recognition Tanner failed to receive in his homeland was finally his.

Review

As a review of later nineteenth-century artists, examine the list of statements provided in Figure 17.16. Then try to identify the artist referred to in each statement. To check your answers, turn to page 436.

Figure 17.16

NINETEENTH-CENTURY ARTISTS
(Cézanne to Tanner)

Post-Impressionists

1. His early paintings were done in browns and other drab colors, but the Impressionists introduced him to brighter colors and a more lively brushstroke.

2. He wanted to make Impressionism solid, like the art of the old masters found in museums.

3. Instead of realistic pictures, he preferred to paint decorative patterns made from flat, colorful shapes and curving contour lines.

4. Ignoring a centuries-long tradition, he chose not to paint objects as he found them. Instead, in his quest for form and structure, he carefully arranged and even changed the appearance of the objects in his pictures.

5. His pictures started with the exotic subject matter that he found on his travels, but, as he painted, he allowed his imagination to take over.

6. He moved away from Impressionism to develop his own painting style because Impressionism did not suit his restless and excitable personality.

7. His works have the look of three-dimensional mosaics because they were composed of small flat planes of color.

8. He left a well-paying job as a broker to become a painter; even when his paintings were not well received, he was confident that he was destined to be a great artist.

9. His mature style made use of bright colors, twisting lines, bold brushstrokes, and a heavy application of paint.

American Artists

1. Uninterested in the work of other artists, he drew his inspiration from the Bible, Shakespeare, Chaucer, and Romantic writers.

2. A student of Thomas Eakins, he went to Paris to achieve financial success and critical acclaim.

3. His paintings of the American scene were popular with everyone but the critics, who said they looked unfinished and sketchy.

4. He is one of the most celebrated Afro-American artists of the late nineteenth and early twentieth centuries.

5. He was fascinated by the study of the human body and felt this study was necessary to make his figures look more lifelike.

6. He is recognized as one of the most skillful and powerful painters of the sea.

7. Concerned with texture, he would apply layers of paint to his small canvases until the forms were almost three-dimensional.

8. Regarded as one of the first American Realists, he painted the people and scenes of his native Philadelphia.

Studio Experiences

Lesson One: Designing a Painting Based on van Gogh's *The Potato Eaters*

Study van Gogh's painting of *The Potato Eaters* and respond to the following questions dealing with the aesthetic qualities in this work:

Literal Qualities

1. How many people are in this picture?
2. What are these people doing?
3. What kind of clothing are the people wearing?
4. From what you can see, how would you describe this home?
5. How would you describe the economic condition of this family?

Visual Qualities

6. Which color or colors dominate in this picture?
7. Are the values used in this picture light or dark?
8. What textures can you identify in this picture?
9. How would you describe the quality of the line used?
10. What has been done to direct the viewer's eyes to the main parts of the painting?

Expressive Qualities

11. Do you think this home is warm and cozy, or cold and uncomfortable?
12. What word best describes the expressions on the faces of these people?
13. How do you think these people feel at this moment?
14. What might cause them to feel this way?
15. What feelings or moods does this work evoke in you?

Design and paint a picture which incorporates at least five of your answers to the questions above.

Lesson Two: Tempera Batik in the Style of Gauguin

Gauguin's decorative painting style featured (1) flat, overlapping shapes, (2) intense colors, and (3) curving contour lines. His subject matter often consisted of scenes observed in a remote South Sea paradise. His unique painting style and exotic subject matter are evident in his painting entitled *Fatata te Miti* (Figure 17.9). Create a tempera batik in which you use shape, color, and line as Gauguin did in this painting. (The batik method of dyeing cloth involves the use of removable wax to repel the dye on parts of the design where dye is not desired. Your picture, though involving different materials, will have a batik-like appearance.) For subject matter, illustrate a scene from contemporary society—but imagine that those who see your work are completely unfamiliar with life in contemporary society. Your work will be viewed by natives of a remote South Sea paradise. The batik process you are to use involves the following steps:

- After completing several sketches of the subject matter, reproduce the best of these on a sheet of light-colored construction paper. Make certain that the shapes used are flat and overlap each other to suggest a shallow space. Fill the paper completely.
- Trace over the main lines in your picture with white chalk. Emphasize the curved contour lines as you do this. You may elect to use a variety of thick and thin chalk lines.
- Paint your picture with a heavy application of tempera paint. Use bright, intense hues. The chalk lines are to remain exposed, so *do not paint over them.*
- When your picture is dry, cover it with a coating of India ink.
- When the ink is completely dry, place the picture on a flat surface (such as a food tray) and hold it under a light stream of water at the sink. Gently rub the surface to remove the ink and create a batik-like appearance.

Chapter 18

A New Vision: Art of the Early Twentieth Century

Henri Matisse (ahn-*ree* mah-*teess*), 1869-1954. He wanted his paintings to bring happiness and pleasure to others.

Georges Rouault (*zjorzj* roo-*oh*), 1871-1958. His early training as a stained-glass maker greatly influenced the paintings he did later.

Ernst Ludwig Kirchner (*airnst lood*-vig *keerk*-ner), 1880-1938. He was a member of a group of German artists who wanted their works to communicate deep, emotional feelings.

Käthe Kollwitz (*kay*-teh *kahl*-wits), 1867-1945. Her art was a protest against the tragedy and suffering brought about by war and poverty.

Edvard Munch (*ed*-vard *moonk*), 1863-1944. The fear, suffering, and death of loved ones he experienced in his own life provided him with the subject matter for his haunting paintings.

Vasily Kandinsky (vass-*see*-lee can-*din*-skee), 1866-1944. One of his watercolor paintings altered the course of art history.

Pablo Picasso (*pah*-blow pee-*cahs*-oh), 1881-1973. No artist achieved as much fame during his own lifetime —or produced such varied and powerful artworks.

Georges Braque (*zjorzj brahk*), 1882-1963. He used heavy layers of paint and attached fragments of paper, cloth, and other materials to his canvases to make them more "touchable."

Aristide Maillol (ah-riss-*teed* mah-*yahl*), 1861-1944. He discovered his true vocation as a sculptor after an eye disease made it impossible to continue his career as a weaver of tapestries.

Diego Rivera (dee-*ay*-goh ree-*vay*-rah), 1886-1957. He created the first modern mural painting in Mexico.

José Clemente Orozco (ho-*say* cleh-*men*-tay oh-*ross*-coh), 1883-1949. He used art to express his anger for all kinds of tyranny.

David Alfaro Siqueiros (*day*-vid al-*far*-oh see-*kayr*-ohss), 1898-1974. Just as involved in political activities as in art, he was imprisoned and driven into exile several times for his political beliefs.

John Sloan, 1871-1951. He was a member of a group of artists who were laughingly referred to as "The Ashcan School."

George Bellows, 1882-1925. He had been an outstanding athlete himself so it is not surprising that some of his best known paintings showed athletes in action.

Alexandre Gustave Eiffel (al-ex-*an*-der *gus*-tahf *eye*-fel), 1832-1923. His "temporary" monument for the Paris Industrial Exposition still stands—and is one of the best-known landmarks in Europe!

Antonio Gaudi (ahn-*toe*-nee-oh *gow*-dee), 1852-1926. His architecture has no links with the past—it is the product of a fertile imagination.

Julia Morgan, 1872-1957. Her reputation as an architect was built upon a strict concern for detail and an appreciation for high-quality work.

Louis Sullivan, 1856-1924. The simplicity and logic of his buildings inspired many architects who followed.

European Art

The turn of the century saw the end of the Academy's influence and the beginning of a new series of art movements in Europe. The first of these movements came to public attention in 1905. It was then that a group of younger French painters under the leadership of Henri Matisse exhibited their works in Paris. Their paintings were so simple in design, so brightly colored, and so loose in brushwork that an enraged critic called the artists *Fauves,* or "Wild Beasts."

The Fauves

The Fauves carried on the ideas of Vincent van Gogh and Paul Gauguin. They took the colors, movement, and concern for design stressed by those earlier artists and built an art style that was unrealistic, free, and wild. Their works looked hectic when compared to those of van Gogh and Gauguin because they tried to extend and intensify the ideas first expressed by those Post-Impressionists. They were more daring than van Gogh in their use of color, and bolder than Gauguin in their use of broad, flat shapes and lively line patterns.

Henri Matisse

Henri Matisse, the leader of the Fauves, was the son of a middle-class couple from northern France. When he was a twenty-year-old law student, he suffered an appendicitis attack. His mother, who was interested in art, gave him some paints to help him pass the time while recovering, and he began his first painting. Later Matisse said, "I felt transported into a paradise in which I felt gloriously free." Eventually Matisse convinced his father to allow him to study art rather than law. He spent a brief period as a student of an academic painter, but found this experience almost as frustrating as studying law.★ Then he studied with another artist, who was not as rigid and strict.★★ In this class, Matisse was encouraged to exercise greater freedom in his use of color. It was while he was in this class that Matisse met Georges Rouault and some of the other artists who became associated with Matisse in the Fauve movement.

★ Enrichment The painter with whom he studied was Adolphe Bouguereau.

★★ Enrichment This artist was Gustave Moreau.

What is the subject of this picture? Can you find any corners or shadows? Are there areas where gradation of color is used? Point to shapes that look three-dimensional. Now find some that are two-dimensional. Find some shapes that are painted with the complement of red. Find examples of the different types of lines used—straight, curved, light, dark, heavy, and thin. Does this picture present a realistic view of a room? What aesthetic qualities would you use when judging this picture?

Figure 18.1   Henri Matisse. *The Red Studio.* 1911. Oil on canvas, approx. 1.8 x 2.7 m [5′ 11¼″ x 7′ 2¼″]. Collection of the Museum of Modern Art, New York. Mrs. Simon Guggenheim Fund

By 1905, Matisse had developed a style that made use of broad areas of color that were not meant to look like the shape or colors found in nature. This style is shown in his painting entitled *The Red Studio* (Figure 18.1). Many artists including Velázquez (Figure 14.20, page 265) and Rembrandt (Figure 14.13, page 257) used their studios as subjects for their paintings. Unlike them, Matisse did not include himself in his picture. He does show a number of his paintings, however, which hang from or lean against the walls in a haphazard way. He welcomes you into his studio by using linear perspective. A table at the left and a chair at the right direct you into the room and invite you to look around. Of course,

Matisse's studio could hardly have looked like this. The room has been flattened out into a solid red rectangle. The walls do not have corners; round objects look flat; and there are no shadows. Red is found everywhere—it covers the walls, floor, and furnishings. It is a strong, pure red that is in no way descriptive.

Matisse was mainly interested in organizing the visual qualities in this picture rather than providing you with a lifelike view of his studio. He used the studio as a starting point. It suggested the colors, shapes, lines, and textures that he could use in new and exciting ways to create a colorful decorative pattern. The objects in his work seem to be suspended by the intense red hue. This allows you to glance casually about the room where surprising contrasts of greens, pinks, blacks, and whites serve to attract and hold your interest. Unnecessary details are stripped away. The result is a balanced design in which tables, dresser, and chairs exist as colors, lines, and shapes. With paintings like this, Matisse was able to realize his goal of "an art of purity and serenity without depressing subject matter."

Today it is difficult to understand why Matisse's paintings were so shocking to people when they were first exhibited. Perhaps critics were upset by the simplicity of his pictures. But Matisse used simplicity because he wanted a more direct form of personal expression. In a way, he is like a writer who chooses to use a few sentences and simple, easy-to-understand words to make his or her message as precise and direct as possible.

During the last years of his life, Matisse devoted most of his efforts to making paper cutouts. These were shapes which he cut from papers that he had painted earlier. Sometimes he cut these shapes at random, sometimes with a certain idea in mind. After cutting out the shapes, he would spend days and even weeks arranging and rearranging them until he was satisfied with the results. *La Negresse* (Figure 18.2) was a cutout inspired by an American entertainer, Josephine Baker, who was very popular in Paris during the 1920s. Large, bright flowers and contrasting black birds surround the figure. The same shapes used to suggest the wings of the birds are used for the arms and legs of the entertainer. She moves as if she is dancing, and her large, fluttering hands add a lightness and grace to her movement.

Matisse had no complicated theories to explain his paintings or cutouts. He relied on his own instincts when composing his works. And what purpose were they intended to serve? Throughout his career, Matisse claimed that they had only one purpose: to give pleasure. He felt that paintings should have a calming influence on the mind. "Art," he once said, "is something like a good armchair which provides relaxation from physical fatigue."

History

What technique and materials were used to create this work? How has the figure been made to stand out from the other shapes? What does the figure appear to be doing? Does this figure seem to be light and active, or clumsy and slow? What did Matisse hope to achieve with pictures like this—to give pleasure, or to tell a story?

Figure 18.2   Henri Matisse. *La Negresse.* 1952. Approx. 4.5 x 6.2 m [14′ 10¾″ x 20′ 5½″]. The National Gallery of Art, Washington, D.C. Ailsa Mellon Bruce Fund, 1973

Georges Rouault

This point of view was not shared by George Rouault, another artist associated with the Fauves. Instead of trying to show happiness and pleasure in his art, Rouault chose to illustrate the more sorrowful side of life.

Matisse thought that art could solve problems—he would prop his colorful pictures around the beds of sick friends to cheer them up and speed their recovery. But Rouault used his art in a different way—to point out the problems he saw in the world. His works were bold visual sermons condemning the world's injustices and suffering.

When he was a boy, Rouault was apprenticed to a stained-glass maker. Later he used heavy, dark lines to surround areas of thick, glowing colors, creating paintings that looked like Medieval church windows. In this manner he painted clowns, landscapes, and biblical figures. He claimed that he did not belong to the age in which he lived. "My life," he said, "is back in the age of the cathedrals."

Rouault's heavy lines do more than make his painting of *The Old King* (Figure 18.3) look like stained glass. They also tie his picture together while stressing the sorrowful expression of the figure. Rouault may have been trying to arouse your curiosity with this picture.

Criticism

What makes this painting look like a stained-glass window? Are all the shapes in this painting outlined? What colors are the outlines? Are all the lines the same thickness? Do all the lines connect with each other? Why does this also occur in stained glass? Is this man a merchant, a king, or a soldier? How can you tell? Describe the expression on his face. How does this picture make you feel? Is this a successful work? Why or why not?

Figure 18.3 Georges Rouault. *The Old King.* **1916-36. Oil on canvas, approx. 76.8 x 54 cm [30¼ x 21¼″]. Museum of Art, Carnegie Institute, Pittsburg. Museum Purchase: Patrons Art Fund, 1940**

Who is this king and why is he so sad? Certainly this is no proud, joyful ruler. Is Rouault trying to tell you that even a king, with all his power and wealth, cannot find comfort in a world of suffering? Or is he suggesting that no king is powerful enough to offer his subjects the happiness needed to guarantee his own happiness?

Rouault hated to part with his pictures because he was never completely satisfied with them. He always felt that with a little more time he could make them much more effective. Sometimes he kept them for as long as twenty-five years, during which he would endlessly study and change them, hoping to achieve perfection. One night, late in his life, he arose suddenly from his bed and padded into his studio in bare feet. Picking up one of his pictures, he tossed it into the fireplace and then, relieved, returned to bed. Like Cézanne before him, Rouault did not hesitate to destroy a painting if it failed to please him. It did not bother him in the least that the picture he casually threw away could have been sold for thousands of dollars.

German Expressionism

Rouault and Matisse felt that art is a form of personal expression. It was a way for them to present their own thoughts and feelings about the world. In Germany, this view was eagerly accepted by several groups of artists who came to be known as *Expressionists*. These artists were interested in representing deep emotional feelings with their work.

Ernst Ludwig Kirchner

Street, Berlin (Figure 18.4) is a painting by Ernst Ludwig Kirchner, who used clashing angular shapes to express one of his favorite themes—the tension and artificial elegance of the city. The people here are jammed together on a street, part of a never-ending parade. They look strangely alike, as if cut from the same piece of cardboard with the slashing strokes of a razor-sharp knife. They are uninterested and uninteresting people who appear to be concerned only with themselves and going their own way. Or are they? Look at the faces; they are more like masks. Behind those masks are their *real* faces, but these are hidden because they might betray the people's true feelings. This picture was painted in Berlin just before the outbreak of World War I. It may be the artist's attempt to suggest the tension lurking just beneath the phony elegance of the German capital on the brink of war.

Kirchner was a troubled artist; a persistent nervous condition kept him out of the war and sent him to Switzerland seeking relief. But even there, trouble followed him. In 1938, his works were condemned by Hitler. Kirchner, ill and upset about the conditions in Germany, was unable to face up to this insult and took his own life.

Describe the people in this painting. What makes them look so much alike? How do they act toward one another? Are the shapes mainly circular, angular, or both? What do you find most interesting in this work—the literal qualities or the expressive qualities? Is it an effective work of art?

Figure 18.4   Ernst Ludwig Kirchner. *Street, Berlin.* **1913. Oil on canvas, approx. 120.6 x 90.8 cm [47½ x 35⅞"]. Collection of the Museum of Modern Art, New York. Purchase**

Criticism

What principles of art have been used to make the line more interesting in this work? Describe the expression on the woman's face. Why is she holding the child so tightly? Whom do you think the third figure represents? How do you think this drama will end?

Figure 18.5   Käthe Kollwitz. *Death and the Mother.* 1934. Lithograph. Private Collection

Käthe Kollwitz

Käthe Kollwitz was another of Germany's great Expressionists. She used her art to protest against the tragic plight of the poor before and after W.W. I. Hoping to reach the greatest number of viewers, she chose to express her ideas with etchings, woodcuts, and lithographs. Her lithograph *Death and the Mother* (Figure 18.5) is an example of this work. It shows the terrifying struggle of a mother trying to protect her child from the skeleton-like figure of Death. The desperate fear of the mother is seen in her wide-open eyes and the powerful arms and hands which grip and protect the helpless child. But it is a struggle the mother cannot win. In the end, her child, like so many children of the poor, will be snatched from her.

Kollwitz and many of the other German Expressionists were greatly influenced by Vincent van Gogh, the Fauves, and a Norwegian painter named Edvard Munch.

The Influence of Edvard Munch

Munch's childhood was marked by tragedy. His mother died when he was five and one of his sisters, when he was fourteen. His father was a doctor in a poor district, and Munch's own health was never strong. The fear, suffering, and death of loved ones that he experienced in his own life became the subject matter for his art.

How much his own suffering contributed to his work can be seen in a picture entitled *The Sick Child* (Figure 18.6). It was a subject he returned to several times in paintings and prints and was no doubt inspired by the death of his older sister. In it Munch captures the pale complexion, colorless lips, and hopeless stare of a child weakened and finally conquered by illness. Beyond caring, she looks past her grieving mother out of the picture to a certain, tragic future.

Pictures like this shocked viewers when the paintings were first seen. Munch's figures seemed crude and grotesque when compared to the colorful and light-hearted visions of the Impressionists who were enjoying great popularity at the time. But Munch's works were in keeping with the period in which he lived. It was a period when writers and artists were turning their attention inward. Like Munch, they were interested in exploring feelings and emotions rather than describing outward appearances.

Have you ever heard someone say that they were so upset that they could not see clearly? Munch tried to show the world as seen through the eyes of such a person. Before, artists showed people in anguish as they appeared to a rational, objective viewer. But with Munch and the other Expressionists this changed. They showed the world as viewed through the eyes of people in anguish. Seen that way, the colors and shapes of familiar objects change. Trees, hills, houses, and people are pulled out of shape and take on new, unexpected colors.

The painting style based on this view of the world is illustrated in Munch's painting of *The Scream* (Figure 18.7). In it you can see that he used curved shapes and colors that are expressive rather than realistic. Everything is distorted to make you feel a certain way and thus share with the artist a particular emotion. How does this picture make you feel? Happy? Of course not. Sad? Possibly, but this does not seem strong enough.

Afraid? Yes, that is more like it; the subject of this picture is fear. Although it is impossible to determine why, there is no mistaking the fact that the person in this painting is terrified. The body bends and twists as a scream builds and erupts from deep within. It is a scream so piercing that the figure clasps its hands tightly over its ears. The entire scene vibrates with the intensity of this scream—it echoes across the landscape like ripples across still water.

History

How did this artist's own life influence his art? Which artists were influenced by Munch's works? How did the public react to his paintings and prints? In what ways did his works reflect the concerns of other artists and writers working at this time?

Figure 18.6   Edvard Munch. *The Sick Child.* **1896. The Tate Gallery, London**

Criticism

How many figures can you find in this work? What is the nearest figure doing? Describe the background. Would you say that the shapes and colors here are natural and familiar, or new and surprising? What emotion do you associate with the nearest figure—joy, anger, or fear? List the things in the picture that will support your decision.

Figure 18.7   Edvard Munch. *The Scream.* **1893. Casein on paper, approx. 91 x 73.5 cm [36 x 29″]. Nasjonalgalleriet, Oslo, Norway**

In what way did works like this change the course of art history? What are works without recognizable subject matter called? If this artist was not interested in subject matter, what was he interested in? Which aesthetic qualities would you use when judging and supporting your judgment of this painting?

Figure 18.8   Vasily Kandinsky. *Improvisation 28* (Second Version). 1912. Oil on canvas, 1.11 x 1.62 m [3′ 7⅞″ x 5′ 3⅞″]. Collection, The Solomon R. Guggenheim Museum, New York

Nonobjective Art: Vasily Kandinsky

About two years after Munch did his haunting picture of *The Scream,* a twenty-nine-year old Russian lawyer strolled into an exhibit of French Impressionist paintings in Moscow. His name was Vasily Kandinsky. He was overwhelmed by the paintings, mainly one by Claude Monet. After several hours, he left the exhibit with reluctance. But in the weeks and months that followed, his thoughts kept returning to the works he had seen. Finally, he left his legal career and went to Munich, Germany, to study painting. In 1900, five years after his visit to the Impressionist exhibit, he received his diploma from the Royal Academy in Munich.

For several years, Kandinsky changed from one style to another. He tried Impressionism, Post-Impressionism, Fauvism, and Expressionism. His work did not seem greatly original, though. Then, around 1909, he turned away from these outside influences and listened to his own instincts. A year later he finished a watercolor painting that changed the course of art history. It was brightly colored and may have been based on some earlier landscape studies. But most importantly, no subject matter could be seen in the work. With this painting, Kandinsky's place in history as a founder of *nonobjective* art was assured.★

★ **Enrichment** Nonobjective art is a style which employs color, line, texture, and unrecognizable shapes and forms. These works contain no apparent reference to reality. Kandinsky is generally regarded as *the* founder of the movement, although this is by no means certain.

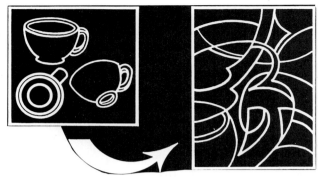

Figure 18.9 A student's drawings of a coffee cup in the style of Cubism

After that start, Kandinsky went on to do paintings that lacked subject matter, even as a starting point (Figure 18.8). His main goal was to convey moods and feelings. This could be done, he felt, by arranging the art elements in certain ways. The colors, values, lines, shapes, and textures he used were selected and carefully placed on the canvas for a certain effect. He felt that art elements, like musical sounds, could be arranged to convey emotions and feelings. In fact, Kandinsky believed that a painting should be the "exact duplicate of some inner emotion." He did not believe that art should be an illustration of objects as they appear in nature. Thus, Kandinsky was able to free painters completely from relying on nature as they had in the past.

Cubism

Earlier you learned that German Expressionism, with its concern for expressing moods and feelings, can be traced back to the works of van Gogh and Gauguin. Another twentieth-century art movement, *Cubism*, can be linked in much the same way to the work of Paul Cézanne in the nineteenth century. Cubist artists like Pablo Picasso and Georges Braque started with Cézanne's idea that all shapes in nature are based on the sphere, the cone, and the cylinder. They carried this idea further by trying to paint three-dimensional objects as if they were seen from many different angles at the same time. Cubism, then, was a style of painting in which artists tried to show all sides of three-dimensional objects on a flat canvas.

Perhaps the Cubist approach to painting can be illustrated with the simple sketches provided here (Figure 18.9). In the first sketch, an ordinary coffee cup has been drawn from several different points of view. After these first sketches have been done, the artist studies them to find the parts of the cup that are most interesting and most characteristic of coffee cups. These parts are then arranged in a composition. Thus, parts from the top, sides, and bottom of the cup are blended together to complete the picture. Of course, this illustration is very simple, but it may help you understand the process a Cubist artist used when painting a picture like *Glass of Absinthe* (Figure 18.10).

History

Did Cubist artists like Picasso want to (a) show inner feelings and emotions in their paintings instead of outward appearances, (b) paint three-dimensional objects as if seen from many different points of view at the same time, or (c) create designs that were flat, brightly colored, free, and exciting?

Figure 18.10 Pablo Picasso. *Glass of Absinthe.* 1911. Oil on canvas, approx. 38.7 x 46.4 cm [15⅛ x 18¼"]. Allen Memorial Art Museum, Oberlin College, Oberlin, Ohio. Mrs. F. F. Prentiss Fund, 47.36

Do not be surprised if you fail to recognize any of the objects in this Cubist painting. Recognition is eliminated by the breaking up of shapes and the reassembling of these shapes in the composition. This produces a complex arrangement of new shapes that is often very confusing to the viewer. You can never be sure when one shape is ahead of another because part of it seems to be in front and part behind. This confusion is heightened by the use of lines that end suddenly when you expect them to continue, or continue when you expect them to end. Colors associated with the objects are not used. Instead, the artist chose grays, browns, and other drab colors, which painters before this time had avoided.

Cubists were also interested in making the surfaces of their paintings richer and more exciting by adding a variety of actual textures. Around 1911, Picasso, Braque, and others began to add materials such as newspaper clippings, pieces of wallpaper, and labels to the picture surface. This technique, known as *collage*, further blurred the recognizable connection between the painting and any represented object. The materials arranged in shapes on the surface of the painting seemed to take on a reality of their own.

Now that you know what a Cubist work looks like and how it was done, you might be wondering why artists painted this way. Cubism was an *intellectual* approach to art rather than a descriptive or emotional one. Cubist artists thought their way through their paintings trying to show not what they saw or felt, but what they knew was there. Picasso may have summed up the intent of Cubism best when he said, "We have kept our eyes open to our surroundings, but also our brains." It was the product of their brains, not their eyes or hearts, that they wanted to share with viewers.

Criticism

Make a list of everything you recognize in this painting. Describe the shapes used. Find the large triangular shape used to tie all the elements in the picture together. In what ways does this work bring to mind the appearance of newspaper print and photographs? What message do you receive from this painting?

Figure 18.11   Pablo Picasso. *Guernica*. 1937. Oil on canvas, approx. 3.5 x 7.8 m [11′ 6″ x 25′ 8″]. The Prado, Madrid

Pablo Picasso

Pablo Picasso led a long and productive life. As an artist, he passed through many different stages. For some time, he worked in the Cubist style, then returned to paintings of the human figure. It was at this time that he began to use a greater range of colors. Then, in 1937, he painted his famous anti-war picture, *Guernica* (Figure 18.11).

Guernica was a large mural (3.5 × 7.8 m [11.5 × 25.7 feet]). It was made for the Pavilion of the Spanish Republic at the Paris International Exposition. The work was inspired by the bombing of the ancient Spanish city of Guernica by German planes during the Spanish Civil War. Guernica was not an important military target. Its destruction apparently served no other purpose than to test the effectiveness of large-scale bombing. As a result of the "tests," the city and most of its inhabitants were destroyed.

The large triangle in the center of Picasso's painting may remind you of the way earlier artists organized their work. It was a technique used in the Renaissance by artists like Botticelli and Raphael. Here it effectively links a series of tragic images. At the far right, a woman crashes through the floor of a burning building. In front of her, another woman dashes forward blindly in panic. A horse with a spear in its back screams in terror. A severed head with staring eyes rests on an outstretched arm, its hand reaching for nothing. Another hand tightly clutches a broken sword. A woman holds a dead child and raises her head skyward to scream out her horror at the planes overhead.

In this work, Picasso combines Expressionism and Cubism. Like the Expressionists, he exaggerates and distorts forms. At the same time, he overlaps flat shapes in an abstract design as did the Cubists. Picasso uses bold blacks, whites, and grays instead of color to give the impression of newsprint or newspaper photographs. Adding to the look of newsprint is the stippled effect on the horse. But the painting's powerful images convey the full impact of the event far more effectively than could the words in a newspaper account or even photographs.[*] The artist makes no effort to show the event itself. Instead, he combines a number of vivid images to form a forceful and moving statement about the horror, the agony, and the waste of modern warfare.

Just who was this artist who was not only the most famous artist of his time, but may be the most famous artist of all time? People who have never heard of Giotto, or Rubens, or Matisse know of Picasso. They may not understand or like his work, but they know that he was a major figure in the modern art movement. Pablo Picasso was born in Malaga, Spain, in 1881. As a boy, he never stopped drawing. In fact, his mother claimed that he could draw before he could talk. And when he did talk, she went on to say, his first word was "piz," baby talk for *lapiz*, or *pencil*. Wherever he went, the young Picasso took his pad and pencil: even to the bullfights he attended with his father. There, while others roared and jumped about, he would draw. He enjoyed betting his friends that he could draw anything —in one continuous line. And he always won.

One day his father, a painter and teacher, arrived home to find that his young son had finished a portrait. After comparing it with his own work, he gave all his art materials to Pablo and vowed never to paint again. His son, he said later, had surpassed him and he could work no longer.

Later Picasso's father took a position with the Barcelona School of Fine Arts. Pablo wished to enroll in the school but was required to take the entrance exam. This exam was so difficult that it often took a month to complete. But Picasso took it in one day and was admitted to advanced classes the next.

★ **Enrichment** A *London Times* correspondent wrote: "Reflections of the flames could be seen in the smoke above the mountains from ten miles away. Throughout the night houses were falling until the streets became long heaps of red impenetrable debris."

Criticism

Describe this man and his actions. What hue dominates here? How does this hue add to the emotional effect of the picture? Would another hue have been just as effective? How does this picture make you feel?

Figure 18.12 Pablo Picasso. *The Blind Man's Meal.* 1903. Oil on canvas, 95.25 x 94.62 cm [37½ x 37¼"]. The Metropolitan Museum of Art, New York. Gift of Mr. and Mrs. Ira Haupt, 1950

When he was nineteen, Picasso went to Paris, the art capital of the world. There he fell under the spell of the great museum collections and exhibitions of contemporary art. Two years later, he started a series of paintings which were marked by a deep blue background color. The paintings done during this "Blue Period" focused on scenes of loneliness, poverty, or suffering. A painting from this period (Figure 18.12) shows a blind man searching with sensitive fingers for the items that make up his meager meal.

In a "Pink Period" that followed, Picasso's mood softened, and he began to paint pictures of acrobats and circus performers with warm, rose-colored hues. The works from both these periods were greatly admired, but Picasso was too restless to continue for long working in the same style. It was at this point that he and Braque began the experiments that led to Cubism.

Picasso lived a long and full life; he was ninety-one years old when he died in 1973. Although he said he had no fear of death, he admitted that he was afraid that he might suffer from an illness that would keep him

from working. He need not have worried. On the night before he died, he worked until 3:00 A.M. as was his custom. The next morning he awoke at 11:30 but could not get out of bed. Ten minutes later he was dead of a heart attack. He left behind a tremendous number of paintings, prints, and sculptures—and a profound influence on twentieth-century art.

Georges Braque

Unlike Picasso, Georges Braque did not go through a series of style changes during his career. He always maintained that a painting is a flat surface and should remain a flat surface. He remained involved throughout his life with ways to make that surface more interesting with the use of colors, lines, shapes, and textures.

From 1907 to 1914, Braque and Picasso worked closely together to develop Cubism. But when World War I broke out, Braque went into the army and, in 1915, was seriously wounded. In 1917, following long months in recovery, he returned to his painting. His work from that point shows a growing respect for subject matter, more playful curves, and brighter colors. Always interested in texture, he applied his paint in layers to build a rich, heavy surface. In this way, he said, his pictures were more "touchable." He painted still lifes (Figure 18.13) but instead of using fruits and flowers, concentrated on more permanent man-made objects, such as tables, bottles, mandolins, books, and pipes. These were objects people used when they were relaxing and enjoying pleasant thoughts. These quiet, elegant still lifes did exactly what Braque intended them to do—they put viewers in a gentle, comfortable mood.

Criticism

Can you identify any of the objects in this still life? Make a list of the different lines used. Is texture an important element here? Point to areas with different textures. Where are the darkest values found? Do you think the artist was interested in showing three-dimensional forms, or was he more concerned with creating an interesting two-dimensional design?

Figure 18.13 Georges Braque. *Blue Guitar.* 1943. Oil on canvas, 72.4 x 53.3 cm [28⅜ x 21″]. Allen Memorial Art Museum, Oberlin College, Oberlin, Ohio. R. T. Miller, Jr. Fund, 48.297

Criticism

Would you describe this figure as slim and graceful, or solid and sturdy? Does she seem nervous and tense, or quiet and restful? How many triangular shapes can you find in this work? What purpose do these triangular shapes serve? What mood or feeling do you receive from this sculpture?

Figure 18.14 Aristide Maillol. *The Mediterranean.* 1902-05. Bronze, 104.14 cm [41″] high, at base 114.3 x 75.6 cm [45 x 29 ¾″]. Collection of the Museum of Modern Art, New York. Gift of Stephen C. Clark

Balance and Simplicity: Aristide Maillol

The same kind of gentle, comfortable feeling is experienced when you stand before the sculptures of Aristide Maillol. Unlike Rodin, Maillol was not interested in dramatic gestures and expressions, or with a sculptured surface made up of bumps and hollows. Nor did he seek to shock or surprise the viewer. He admired the balance, simplicity, and peacefulness of ancient Greek sculptures and tried to capture these same qualities in his own work.

Maillol began his career as a painter, but, since he did not enjoy great success in that medium, he later turned to tapestry making. In his workshop, he designed the tapestries and dyed the materials himself. Then, when he was forty years old, an eye ailment prevented him from weaving. Although he must have been discouraged, he refused to abandon his career in art. Instead, he became a sculptor. To his amazement, he discovered that sculpture was his true medium. Almost immediately he mastered a style that he used for the rest of his life.

Maillol had been a sculptor for only a few months when he created a seated woman entitled *The Mediterranean* (Figure 18.14). This work contained all of the main features of his style. A sturdy woman is posed in a quiet, restful position without a hint of movement. There is no sign of nervousness or tension or any sign that she is even aware of what might be going on around her.

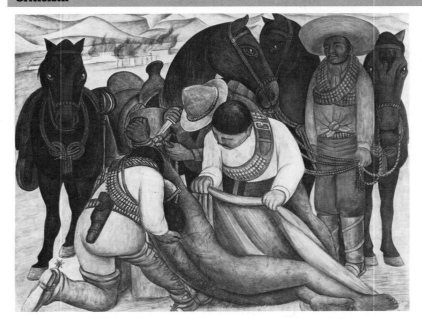

Do you think the soldiers shown here are responsible for the man's death? How did he die? Can you find clues to indicate that the man's death has been avenged?

Figure 18.15 Diego Rivera. *Liberation of the Peon*. 1931. Fresco of plaster, approx. 1.9 x 2.4 m [74 x 95″]. Philadelphia Museum of Art. Given by Mr. and Mrs. Herbert Cameron Morris

From the side, the figure forms a large triangular shape, which gives it a balanced, stable look. Smaller triangles are created by the raised leg and the arm supporting the head. The repetition of these triangular shapes is important here because it helps to unify the work in the same way that a certain color used over and over again can unify a painting. There is nothing about this woman to suggest that she is a specific individual. Maillol was not attempting a portrait. He was using the woman's figure to represent a particular mood or feeling. In this case, that mood was thoughtful, gentle, and calm.

Mexican Art

The early twentieth century in Mexico was marked by much unrest. It was a time when the poor, landless peons tried to make a better life for themselves. They increased their efforts to be free of corrupt landlords who treated them no better than feudal serfs. In 1911 this struggle reached a bloody climax with the fall of the dictator, Porfirio Diaz, and the start of the Mexican Revolution. The revolt ended in 1921.

The Muralists
The years following the conflict saw the emergence and rise of Mexican mural painting. A group of Mexican muralists became known world-wide. As their subject matter, they chose the political and social problems of the Mexican people and adorned both the inside and outside walls of buildings with their murals. Buildings in the United States as well benefited from their art.

Can you think of other times when art was done on building walls? You may recall the mosaics in Byzantine churches, like Italy's San Vitale. These mosaics were meant to show the Christian message (Figure 8.12, page 134, and Figure 8.13, page 135). Later Giotto, Masaccio, and others used a fresco technique to illustrate stories from the Bible on the interior walls of Italian churches (Figure 10.20, page 177, and Figure 11.1, page 182). Several Mexican artists revived that ancient practice, but they did so to tell different kinds of stories. They told of revolutions, native traditions, festivals, and legends. Painting their pictures on the walls of public buildings allowed these artists to take their work directly to the people. They did not want their paintings placed in museums, galleries, or private homes where only a few people would see and respond to them. Instead, their works were intended to be public property and not the private property of the wealthy and powerful.

Diego Rivera
One of the first and most famous of these Mexican mural painters was Diego Rivera. It was he who created the first modern mural painting in Mexico. As a young man, Rivera studied the art of the great Italian fresco artists. This study helped him to achieve his own artistic goal—to record in art the gallant struggle of the Mexican peasant.

In the *Liberation of the Peon* (Figure 18.15), Rivera draws equally upon his skills as a painter and as a master storyteller to create one of his finest works. It shows a group of somber revolutionary soldiers cutting the

How many different colors can you identify in this work? Point to places where there are contrasts of line. Do the shapes have sharp or blurred edges? Are the shapes simple or complex? Would you describe these shapes as small and delicate, or large and heavy? Where has repetition of line and shape been used? Explain how movement and rhythm have been achieved in this painting. What is the mood of these people?

Figure 18.16 José Clemente Orozco. *Zapatistas*. 1931. Oil on canvas, approx. 1.1 x 1.4 m [45 x 55″]. Collection of the Museum of Modern Art, New York. Given anonymously

ropes which bind a dead peon. A blanket is held ready to cover the peon's naked, whip-scarred body. In the distance, a hacienda burns. This tells you that the landowner responsible for the peon's death has already been punished by the soldiers. Now, silently and sorrowfully, they do what they can for their dead comrade. Rivera's story is not difficult to read or to understand —the peon has been "liberated" from a life of oppression and suffering. Like scores of other poor peasants, his liberation has come in the form of death.

Can you point to any similarities between Rivera's painting and Giotto's *Lamentation* (Figure 10.20, page 177)? Like Giotto's figures, Rivera's have bulk and weight and seem to move in space. They also act out their story with easily understood gestures and expressions. Both works succeed in stirring in the viewer a feeling of helplessness, sorrow, and anger.

José Clemente Orozco

Another of the Mexican muralists, José Clemente Orozco, developed a style of painting that earned him the title of the Mexican Goya. It is a style stripped of everything but emotion. Orozco used it to paint pictures that expressed his anger for all forms of tyranny. Even in pictures that at first seem calm and quiet there is an undeniable undercurrent of power and fury. *Zapatistas* (Figure 18.16) is such a painting. In it the followers of the revolutionary leader Emiliano Zapata are shown going to war. The determined plodding of the grim peons and the rhythm created by their forward-pressing bodies gives the impression of a steady, marching movement across the work. The repeating hats, swords, and serapes reinforce this vigorous movement. The use of movement and rhythm in this painting is both powerful and frightening. Orozco's peons are joined together by a common cause. They are determined to overcome their wealthy and powerful oppressors. United, they are a tremendous force. Like an avalanche that builds in strength as it rumbles down a mountain, more and more people will swell their ranks. Nothing will stop them until they have crushed the enemy, restored justice, and gained freedom.

David Alfaro Siqueiros

Orozco painted his first mural in 1922. It was for the National Preparatory School of Mexico City. Working next to him was another, younger painter, who was also doing his first mural. That painter's name was David Alfaro Siqueiros. He, along with Rivera and Orozco, was to be known as a founder of Mexican mural painting.

Siqueiros was just as involved in politics as he was in art. Several times he was put in prison or exiled for his political beliefs. *Echo of a Scream* (Figure 18.17) is a nightmarish protest against war. It was done in the year that Picasso finished his masterpiece on the same theme —*Guernica*. If you compare these two works, you will see how two artists expressed the anti-war theme in completely different ways. In his painting, Picasso used overlapping flat shapes, a variety of contrasting light

History

Compare this picture with Picasso's *Guernica* (Figure 18.11). In what ways are these two paintings alike? How are they different? Which one do you prefer? Why?

Figure 18.17 David Alfaro Siqueiros. *Echo of a Scream.* **1937. Duco on wood, 124.5 x 91.4 cm [49 x 36″]. Collection of the Museum of Modern Art, New York. Gift of Edward M. M. Warburg**

and dark values, and an abstract design. Siqueiros, on the other hand, used gradations of value to model three-dimensional forms that look as if they are flowing forward and backward in space. This three-dimensional quality makes his work more vivid, like a horrible dream brought into sharp focus. Siqueiros also centers his attention on one of the most innocent and helpless victims of a war—a baby. The infant is shown sitting amid the rubble of a shattered city. But what purpose is served by the addition of a second, larger head? It may be a symbol for all children killed, crippled, orphaned, or made homeless by war. Its magnified scream of terror pierces an unnatural stillness, but this scream is destined to fade without having reached a single ear. The child alone survives but, fragile and alone, it cannot survive much longer.

The Impact of These Artists

Clearly the art of Rivera, Orozco, and Siqueiros reveals a strong preoccupation with suffering and war. The reason for this is obvious. These artists, with their strong social and political views, were products of their time. Much of their art was concerned with telling the story of the peons' bitter struggle to overthrow the corrupt landowners who had used and abused them for generations. They told this story in bold murals that brought about a revolution in painting. The changes in painting were just as intense as the political upheaval that altered the course of events in their country.

At various times, all three of these Mexican artists visited and painted murals in the United States. There they had a great impact on many young artists. Some of these American artists even went on to show the same concern for social and political problems in their own works. And, in the late forties and fifties, the idea of huge wall paintings was so appealing to a number of artists that they abandoned their easels and small canvases to paint on a monumental scale. Many of their works were so large in fact that they came to resemble walls. One of the most notable of these American artists was Jackson Pollock, whom you will meet later.

American Art

The start of the twentieth century was a time of Henry Ford, George Bernard Shaw, J. P. Morgan, Harry Houdini, the Wright Brothers, and Teddy Roosevelt. The United States was a growing industrial nation. It was a land of assembly lines, locomotives, airships, steam shovels, telephones, and buildings that rose ten or more stories high. Large city sidewalks overflowed with shoppers. The elevated train rumbled past the windows of

What was the name given to the group of artists with whom Sloan was associated? Why was this name given to these artists? What past experiences did these artists have in common? How did their paintings differ from those created by more academic artists? Describe the way in which Sloan guides the viewer's eye through this picture.

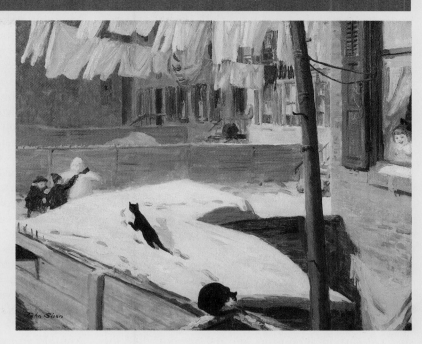

Figure 18.18 John Sloan. *Backyards, Greenwich Village.* **1914. Oil on canvas, approx. 66 x 76.2 cm [26 x 32"]. Collection of the Whitney Museum of American Art, New York**

shabby tenement buildings. As it passed, windows, furniture, and occupants shook. Laundry hung limply from fire escapes. In the coal fields of Pennsylvania, miners lived in small company houses and bought their food and clothes at company stores. After digging 2.7 t [3 tons] of coal a day, they were paid $1.60. In the South, workers stripped tobacco leaves for $.06 an hour.

American art at the start of the twentieth century was conservative. Though artists like Homer, Eakins, and Ryder were still working, art as a whole did not show much progress or excitement. Many American artists still felt that they must study in Europe. However, once there, they met with stale academic approaches. They learned to accept traditional painting techniques and subject matter. As a result, they failed to look for new approaches and images.

The Ashcan School

This conservative trend was challenged early in the century by a group of young realistic painters. These artists rebelled against the idealism of the academic approach. Instead they chose to paint the life around them. Most of these painters had been newspaper artists, and that work had opened their eyes to the contemporary world. In a way, they had much in common with the Dutch artists of the seventeenth century. The Americans had the same feeling for the sprawling, bustling city of the twentieth century as the Dutch had had for the countryside. For subject matter, the Americans turned to the city's nightlife, cafés, streets, alleys, and theatres. Their goal was to record all of the city's color, excitement, and glamor. However, when this group held its first show in New York in 1908, they were laughingly called the "Ashcan School." The name came from the subjects they chose, the most ordinary features of the contemporary scene.

John Sloan: Backyards, Greenwich Village

An example of the kind of painting produced by members of this group is John Sloan's *Backyards, Greenwich Village* (Figure 18.18). If you examine this picture carefully, you will be impressed with Sloan's skill as he guides you from one important item to the next.

As your eye sweeps over this picture, it eventually comes to rest on the cat at the bottom center. This cat sits contentedly on the fence facing you. From there, your gaze moves to the second cat gingerly picking its way through the snow toward the two children who are putting the finishing touches on their snowman. One child uses a small shovel to pat the snowman into shape.

The diagonal formed by his arm and the shovel directs your attention to the fence at the right. This fence leads you across the painting to the face of a smiling girl peering out of a tenement-building window. This child is placed at the very edge of the picture, and it would have been easy for you to miss her if Sloan had not carefully organized his picture to lead you to this spot. Then, to prevent your eye from roaming off the right side of the picture, he used the lines of the window, shutter, and bricks to take you further back into the work. Here you discover more buildings, fences, and clothes hanging out to dry on lines strung high overhead.

You may have expected to feel some sadness when looking at Sloan's picture. After all, it is a painting of a working-class residential area in a large city. The dingy tenement buildings are crowded tightly together, giving the children little space in which to play. But the picture is not sad at all. It does not dwell on the unhappy aspects of tenement living. Instead it is a happy scene painted with sensitivity and affection. It illustrates the gift that children everywhere seem to have—the gift to find joy and pleasure in almost any kind of situation. It is the memory of that joy and pleasure that you will carry away with you from Sloan's painting.

George Bellows: A Similar Style

George Bellows, while not a member of the Ashcan School, created paintings that were similar in many ways to those of Sloan and his companions. Realizing that anything could be used as subject matter for art, Bellows concentrated on the subject he loved most—sports. An outstanding athlete throughout his school years in Ohio, he may have been the only artist who ever had a choice between being an artist or a major-league baseball player. His background in sports led to a desire to capture in his pictures the strength and movement of athletes in action.

Bellows left Ohio while he was still a young man and spent the rest of his short life in New York. He had a studio across the street from an athletic club where he could see the boxing matches he loved to paint. Applying his paint to the canvas with slashing brushstrokes, he was able to reproduce the violent action of the ring in works like *Stag at Sharkey's* (Figure 18.19). The action of the two fighters charging into one another at the center of the ring is viewed from a ringside seat. There you share the wild excitement of the fight crowd as they cheer the favorite and boo his opponent. Illuminated by the lights overhead and silhouetted against the dark background, the two boxers abandon all caution to flail away at each other. Both are willing to accept brutal punishment rather than give ground. Bellows captures this powerful determination and swift action with strong diagonal lines and blurred contours.

There is no telling how Bellows may have developed as an artist had he lived a long life. Ignoring stomach pains that would have sent most men scurrying for a doctor, he died of a ruptured appendix when he was just forty-three years of age.

Criticism

What has been done to make the two boxers stand out in this painting? Why are there so few details? How do the blurred contours add to the feeling of violent action? What kinds of lines are used? In what way do these lines contrast with one another? Do you think this picture is more successful in capturing the appearance or the excitement of a prizefight?

Figure 18.19 George Bellows. *Stag at Sharkey's.* **1909. Oil on canvas, approx. 92.1 x 122.6 cm [36¼ x 48¼"]. The Cleveland Museum of Art. Hinman B. Hurlbut Collection**

The Armory Show of 1913

The Ashcan School played a major role in American art from about 1908 until the opening of the famous Armory Show in 1913.★ This exhibit was organized by a group of artists who knew of the exciting new art being done in Europe. They wanted to introduce the American public to the works of such artists as Cézanne, van Gogh, Gauguin, Matisse, Munch, and Picasso. In the show were some thirteen hundred works by three hundred artists. Most were Americans, but about one hundred were Europeans. It was their work that caused the greatest controversy. Well over a quarter of a million people saw the exhibition.★ For most, it was their first contact with modern European and American art, and

★ **Enrichment** The show was so named because it was held in the Sixty-ninth Regiment Armory in New York City.

★ **Enrichment** After it closed in New York, a smaller version of the show traveled to Chicago and then to Boston.

Figure 18.20

EARLY TWENTIETH-CENTURY ART STYLES AND ARTISTS

Movement or Style	Representative Artists
EUROPE	
FAUVISM The Fauves took the colors, movement, and concern for design stressed by van Gogh and Gauguin to build a style that was unrealistic, free, and wild. Their pictures made use of recognizable subject matter, but were done as a flat pattern made with a patchwork of brilliant color.	Henri Matisse Georges Rouault
EXPRESSIONISM This was a style that grew out of the work of van Gogh and flourished among German artists of the World War I period. Expressionists were interested in representing deep emotional feelings in their work rather than painting outward appearances. They used expressive color, distortion, and exaggeration to express highly personal feelings of fear, anxiety, anger, and love.	Earnst Kirchner Käthe Kollwitz Edvard Munch
NONOBJECTIVE ART Works done in this style did not make use of recognizable subject matter. Colors, lines, shapes, and textures were selected and placed on the canvas to achieve an effective design or to communicate emotions or feelings.	Vasily Kandinsky
CUBISM This style is built on Cézanne's ideas about the use of cubes of color to show form and volume. Cubist artists tried to present objects as though viewed from several angles at the same time. This often resulted in a complex arrangement of geometric shapes. It was an intellectual approach to painting rather than a descriptive or emotional approach. Artists wanted to show what they knew to be there rather than paint what they saw or felt.	Pablo Picasso Georges Braque
MEXICO	
MURAL PAINTING Mexican muralists chose to illustrate the political and social problems of their people in large murals which adorned the walls of public buildings. There everyone could see and respond to their efforts to illustrate the struggle of a people determined to fight for justice and freedom. These powerful and easy-to-understand visual statements were intended to stir the emotions and enlist the sympathy of all who viewed them.	Diego Rivera José Clemente Orozco David Alfaro Siqueiros
AMERICA	
ASHCAN This style was a revolt against conservatism and the academic approach. It was a style in which artists tried to capture the look and flavor of the contemporary world. For subject matter, they turned to the color and excitement of the twentieth-century city—its cafés, streets, alleys, and theaters.	John Sloan (George Bellows is often associated with this style.)

they did not know what to make of it. Unlike the French public who had seen modern art evolve slowly, step by step, the American public were caught by surprise. Americans were unprepared for the strange-looking pictures they found in the exhibition. Some tried to understand the new works; others tried to explain them; while most either laughed or was enraged. The room where the Cubist paintings were hung was called the "Chamber of Horrors." Furthermore, it was said of Matisse, "It is a long step from Ingres to Matisse, but it is only a short one from Matisse to anger."

The Armory Show has been called an ending and a beginning. It marked the end of one era and the start of another. Both younger and more mature American artists saw the new styles of the Fauves, Expressionists, and Cubists. As a result, many Americans turned away from traditional academic art to carry on their own daring experiments. Thus, the Armory Show set the stage for the development of modern art in America. In the years that followed, New York replaced Paris as the art capital of the world.

Review

Before going on to the work of architects in Europe and America, take some time for review of this chapter. Briefly look at the outline in Figure 18.20, (page 351), which shows the art styles and artists of the early twentieth century. You will see that a large role was played by the Post-Impressionists, whose ideas and techniques had a great effect on many of the artists who followed.

European and American Architecture

During the nineteenth century, architects were content to use ideas from the past. This practice became widespread, and buildings in Europe and America showed a variety of styles. Among them were Greek, Roman, Romanesque, Gothic, and Renaissance. But some architects in the late nineteenth and early twentieth centuries saw the exciting potentials for use of the new industrial methods and materials. It was they who broke the ground for others who followed in the years to come.

The Beginnings of Change: Alexandre Gustave Eiffel

Late in the nineteenth century, a French builder and engineer named Alexandre Gustave Eiffel saw the value of iron and steel, which he used to build bridges and industrial plants. However, he is best known for the 300-m [984-foot] tower which he built for the Paris Industrial Exposition of 1889 (Figure 18.21).

The Eiffel Tower is a spire boldly made of exposed ironwork. To build it, Eiffel used open beams made of small angle irons and flat irons. The entire structure was prefabricated. It was riveted together without accident by only 150 men in just seventeen months. This was an amazing feat at that time. It was made even more amazing by Eiffel's confident claim that his tower was strong enough to stand forever. At first it appeared unlikely that it would stand until the end of the Exposition because it produced such howls of protest from artists, architects, and leading citizens. They felt that it was a disgrace to their beautiful city and should be removed. But it was not taken down, and within two decades it became one of the most popular landmarks in Europe. Although it had been planned as a temporary monument for the Exposition, it still stands—and Eiffel's boast that it could stand forever no longer seems quite so absurd.

Eiffel's tower was one of a series of engineering feats that demonstrated how new materials and construction techniques could be used in major building projects. The use of cast iron and steel made it possible to erect buildings more quickly and more economically. It also seemed to offer added protection against fire. However, a series of serious fires in the United States near the end of the century showed that this was not the case. This led to the practice of adding an outer shell of masonry to iron and steel buildings, making them both strong and fire-resistant.

What was Eiffel's background? How did this background prepare him to design this famous tower? What new materials and techniques were used? How did artists, architects, and others react to the tower? What have other builders learned from this structure?

Figure 18.21   Alexandre Gustave Eiffel. Eiffel Tower. Paris. 1887-89

New Inspirations: Antonio Gaudi

The work of the Spanish architect Antonio Gaudi reflects his belief that an entirely new kind of architecture was possible. Gaudi turned away from current practices. He was inspired instead by nature and his own vivid imagination. Gaudi felt that if one listened very closely to nature, its secrets could be learned. He believed these secrets could be used by the sensitive artist in architectural designs. Thus, the roof of a building could resemble a mountain with its ridges and slopes. Ceilings could look like the wind- and water-worn walls of caves, and columns could suggest the stout, sturdy legs of elephants.

In 1900, a rich textile manufacturer named Güell asked Gaudi to design a city which would show the latter's ideas on town planning. It was to be a garden city of sixty dwellings. The proposed site was a hill which overlooked the sprawling city of Barcelona, Spain. Sadly, Gaudi's busy schedule kept him from completing the project. Building was limited to the main entrance with two gatehouses, fountains, play area, gardens, roads, and footpaths. Later, the 15.3-ha [38-acre] site was given to the city to be used as a public park.

Where did Gaudi receive ideas for his work? Can you find any straight lines in Gaudi's creations? What was the original purpose of this park? Was it ever finished? What makes Gaudi's work so unique?

Figure 18.22   Antonio Gaudi. Gatehouse, Güell Park. Barcelona, Spain. c. 1900-1906

Figure 18.23   Antonio Gaudi. Staircase and fountains, Güell Park

Figure 18.24   Antonio Gaudi. Children's game terrace, Güell Park

What feature of this house did critics attack? Describe the working relationship between architect and patron during the construction of the house. Why are this architect's many accomplishments not better known?

Figure 18.25 Julia Morgan. San Simeon. Between San Francisco and Los Angeles, California. Begun 1919

If you were to visit Güell Park today, you would pass through the main gate with its two fairy-tale gatehouses on either side (Figure 18.22). Your eye would be dazzled by the pieces of brightly colored ceramic tiles on the walls and roofs. However, this is nothing to what you would see inside. There you would find yourself in an enchanted garden with a double staircase curling around bubbling fountains (Figure 18.23). A huge, colorful dragon would great you as you climbed the stairs. At the top, you would find a great Doric colonnade supporting a children's game terrace (Figure 18.24). A snake-like bench covered by mosaics made from pieces of glazed pottery completely surrounds this terrace. It is an enchanted world that Gaudi created here, a world with no direct link with the past, a world that owes its existence to a truly unique imagination.

As he grew older, Gaudi showed little interest in anything except his art. On June 7, 1926, while crossing a busy street, he was hit by a streetcar. He was so poorly dressed that people thought he was a street beggar. Taxi drivers refused to drive him to the hospital, and so

several passersby finally carried him to a local clinic. Later, he was moved to the hospital and placed in a charity ward. Several hours passed before friends found the famous architect in a pauper's bed. Gaudi never regained consciousness and, three days later, he died.

Drawing on the Past: Julia Morgan

In the United States a widespread fondness for the art styles of the past continued from the late nineteenth into the early twentieth centuries. Many architects planned structures with the public's fondness for the past in mind. Both architects and patrons considered certain styles to be right for certain types of buildings. For instance, Gothic was thought right for churches, Roman for banks, and Classical for museums and libraries. Byzantine was used for synagogues. Tudor was the style in which houses were built. Eighteenth-century French was the style for mansions. A fine example of this eclectic, or "borrowed," style is the estate designed for William Randolph Hearst by Julia Morgan. It is located at San Simeon, California (Figure 18.25).

History

Was Sullivan greatly influenced by the architecture of the past, or was he concerned with discovering new approaches? What material was used for the frame of this building?

What was used to cover this frame? What provides the support for the building—the walls or the frame?

Figure 18.26 Louis Sullivan. Wainwright Building. St. Louis, Missouri. 1890–91

Morgan was the first woman to graduate as an architect from the famous Ecole des Beaux Arts in Paris. She ranks as one of America's top architects. Between 1902 and 1952 Morgan designed well over seven hundred structures. Yet, she is barely known today. She chose not to publicize her work, but preferred instead to have it speak for her. For this reason, Morgan would not have her name placed at construction sites. She did not attend professional meetings and turned down interviews. And when she retired in 1952, she destroyed her records.

In 1919, this shy, retiring woman was already successful. In that year she was chosen to plan the estate of the flamboyant journalist and congressman, William Randolph Hearst. Its location at San Simeon was some two hundred miles south of San Francisco.★ The main structure on this huge estate is the house of one hundred rooms, which was started three years later. The critics had a name for its free use of many styles. They called it the "Spanish, Moorish, Romanesque, Gothic, Renaissance, Hang-the-Expense" style of architecture. It is easy to see why. The façade includes two towers which rise 41.8 m [137 feet] high. They are replicas of a tower found on a sixteenth-century Moorish Cathedral in Ronda, Spain. Each tower is topped by a prominent weather vane. These vanes were brought from Venice and date from the seventeenth century.

★ **Enrichment** San Simeon is now a California state monument visited by nearly a million tourists each year. This makes it the state's most popular historic monument.

The two towers are joined by a teakwood gable roof which came from a Peruvian palace. The main doors were taken from a Spanish convent of the sixteenth century. They are flanked by Spanish Gothic relief sculptures.

Morgan was known for doing her best to satisfy the needs and desires of her clients. This is certainly evident at San Simeon. Surely though, her patience must have been put to test in the face of Hearst's tendency to change his mind and redo things. For example, Hearst approved Morgan's plans for the towers, but once they were up they did not please him. At great expense, he had them torn down and replaced by the more decorative versions that now stand. When he wanted to move a large French Renaissance fireplace in one of the guest houses, it was moved. Later, when he decided that he liked it better in its original position, it was moved back again. Both times it was necessary to remove the wall and ceiling around it. In a like manner, the Roman-style swimming pool was built and destroyed twice before it satisfied him.

Julia Morgan died in 1957, six years after Hearst. Over the years she had built a reputation as an architect with a strict concern for detail and a stubborn appreciation for high-quality work. Her many projects, especially the grand design for San Simeon, speak eloquently for this frail, quiet woman who refused to speak up for herself.

A New Style: Louis Sullivan

America's pioneering architect of the late nineteenth and early twentieth centuries was Louis Sullivan. Other architects at this time were inspired by the past. Unlike them, Sullivan was busy exploring new approaches. Early in the 1890s, he designed the Wainwright Building in St. Louis (Figure 18.26). It is a structure that owes little, if anything, to earlier styles. For its basic support, Sullivan used a large frame, or cage, made of steel beams. This frame was then covered with vertical strips of brick. Windows and decorative panels filled in the spaces between. The cage-like frame can be plainly seen from the outside of the structure. It is evident that this steel frame and not the walls supports the building.

History

What are the main features of structures like this which were built according to the International Style of architecture? Why was this label used to describe these buildings?

Figure 18.27   Skidmore, Owings, and Merrill. Lever House. New York. 1952

The simplicity and logic of buildings like Sullivan's were not lost to architects who followed. During the twentieth century, buildings made with steel frames covered with glass and concrete were built everywhere, resulting in an *International Style of architecture*. The Lever House in New York City (Figure 18.27) is an excellent example of this style.

Studio Experiences

Lesson One: Drawing in the Cubist Style

Cubist artists tried to paint three-dimensional objects as if seen from many different angles at the same time. Often, as in Picasso's *Glass of Absinthe* (Figure 18.10), their works became so abstract during these attempts that it is difficult to identify the objects portrayed. Prepare to do your own Cubist drawing by selecting a single familiar object as your subject matter. (You might use a coffee cup, a tennis shoe, or a musical instrument.) Complete a series of *precise and detailed* line drawings of the object viewed from a number of different angles. Then study these drawings and identify the sections on each which are most interesting or which include the most characteristic features of the object. Outline these sections on each drawing with a heavy line. On a large (30.5 x 46-cm [12 x 18-inch]) sheet of white paper, combine all the sections outlined on your earlier drawings. Sections should overlap and, to assure harmony, some sections may be repeated. When finished, you will have a complex, abstract composition composed of a variety of lines and shapes. In all likelihood, you will be unable to identify the object in your work.

Lesson Two: Painting in the Cubist Style

Often Cubist artists selected neutral browns and grays when painting their compositions (Figures 18.10 and 18.11). Paint the Cubist drawings completed in the previous lesson with a variety of light and dark values. These values should be obtained by mixing white and black tempera paint. Use a mini-mum of five different values throughout the composition to assure variety and visual interest. Value contrasts may be used in areas of your composition where emphasis is desired. Gradation in value could be included to suggest three-dimensional forms.

Lesson Three: Expressive Paper-Cylinder Faces

Observe how the works of several artists associated with the Expressionists portray people with different moods or emotions (Figures 18.3, 18.4, and 18.6). During this studio experience, you will construct a three-dimensional face of a particular character expressing an emotion of some kind. To begin, make a list of occupations ranging from the legitimate and serious to the whimsical and humorous. Your list might begin with "doctor" and "professor" and end with "pirate" and "Pharaoh." When your list is complete (it should be lengthy), compile three other lists under the labels "adjectives," "verbs," and "adverbs." Identify the character and the emotion you intend to portray by making a single selection from each of your four lists. For instance, you may arrive at "furious pirate shouting loudly," or "sleeping knight snoring violently." Select a sheet of 30.5 x 46-cm [12 x 18-inch] colored construction paper, roll it into a cylinder, and staple it in place. Use scrap pieces of construction paper, yarn, cloth, cotton balls, and other items to transform the paper cylinder into the character you have identified. Be sure to use a variety of actual and simulated textures on your paper construction.

Chapter 19

NEW DIRECTIONS: ART TO THE PRESENT

Artists you will meet in this chapter

Joan Miró (*zjoh*-ahn mee-*roh*), 1893-1983. He painted a fascinating world of dreams and the subconscious.

Salvador Dali (*sahl*-vah-door *dah*-lee), born in 1904. Many of his images are so bizarre that some people have labeled them the products of a madman.

Paul Klee (*pawl clay*), 1879-1940. He wanted his works to be as simple and innocent as those done by children and primitive artists.

Kay Sage, 1898-1963. In *No Passing*, she created a work that communicates an unsettling sense of isolation and loneliness.

Grant Wood, 1892-1942. You have probably seen his painting entitled *American Gothic* many times—and may be surprised to discover how much you can still learn from it.

Edward Hopper, 1882-1967. He tried to capture the emptiness and loneliness that characterize life in the big city.

George Grosz (*jorj growss*), 1893-1959. He portrayed the absurd, evil face of war in his drawings and paintings.

Jack Levine, born 1915. A sharp wit took some of the sting out of his paintings of anger and protest.

Stuart Davis, 1894-1964. Trying to become an abstract painter, he nailed an electric fan, a pair of rubber gloves, and an egg beater to a table and painted nothing else for an entire year.

Georgia O'Keeffe, 1887-1986. She was most comfortable painting the things of nature.

Alice Neel, 1900-1984. She collected and preserved people's faces on canvas.

Jacob Lawrence, born 1917. The brightly colored shapes in his painting of *Tombstones* mask an undercurrent of despair.

Horace Pippin, 1888-1946. His first artworks were designs burned into wood with a hot poker.

Willem de Kooning (*vill*-em duh *koe*-ning), born 1904. He claimed that he always started out to paint attractive young women—but they turned out to be something quite different.

Jackson Pollock (*jack*-sun *pah*-lock), 1912-56. He felt more a part of the painting when he placed a huge canvas on the floor and walked onto and around it while working.

Helen Frankenthaler, (*hell*-en frank-en *tahl*-er), born 1928. Applying swirls and drips of thinned paint to the canvas enables her to create graceful, intensely colored shapes.

Henry Moore, 1898-1986. He combined rounded abstract forms with holes and openings to suggest unique human images.

Barbara Hepworth, 1903-75. She applied what she learned as a student of nature to her work as a sculptor.

Jacques Lipchitz (*zjahk lip*-sheets), 1891-1973. Weary of solving sculptural problems, he turned to creating sculptures that were exciting and emotional.

David Smith, 1906-65. Early experience as a riveter and welder on an automobile assembly line helped him when he turned his attention to sculpture.

Alexander Calder, 1898-1976. He designed hanging sculptures that were set in motion by air currents.

Louise Nevelson, born 1900. Discarded wood scraps from a remodeling project were the inspiration for a unique sculptural style.

Isamu Noguchi (is-*sah*-moo noh-*goo*-chee), born 1904. Will his version of Humpty Dumpty match your mental picture of the well-known fairy-tale character?

Allan Houser, born 1914. An extremely successful sculptor today, this American Indian artist once considered a career as a housepainter!

Le Corbusier (luh core-*boo*-see-*aye*), 1887-1965. His design for a French chapel included walls that bend and curve like gigantic slabs of soft clay.

Frank Lloyd Wright, 1867-1959. His unusual design for a New York museum broke with tradition—and sparked controversy!

I.M. Pei (I.M. *pay*), born 1917. An awkwardly shaped building site represented a challenge for him when he planned an addition for the National Gallery of Art.

Claes Oldenburg (*klahss old*-en-berg), born 1929. His works may cause you to take a closer look at things you take for granted.

Bridget Riley, born 1931. The surfaces of her paintings seem to heave in and out.

Yaacov Gipstein, called **Agam** (*ya*-kov *gip*-styne, a-*gahm*), born 1928. He incorporates several designs in a single work of art.

Barnett Newman, 1905-70. His sculpture entitled *Broken Obelisk* turns viewers' thoughts from the outside world to the world within.

Ronald Bladen, born 1918. His gigantic abstract sculptures reach out boldly to claim space and become an active part of the environment.

Kenneth Noland, born 1917. He is one of a group of artists known as Hard-edge painters.

Frank Stella, born 1936. He often painted designs that complemented the unusual shapes of his canvases.

Josef Albers, 1888-1976. He influenced artists working in several different styles.

Alfred Leslie, born 1927. He painted monumental genre paintings—with a twentieth-century flavor.

Andrew Wyeth (*an* droo *wye* uth), born 1917. One of the most famous of today's painters, he continues in the tradition of his father, a well-known book and magazine illustrator.

Lawren Stewart Harris, 1885-1970. He created lively paintings of the Canadian wilderness that were inspired by the work of the Fauves.

Alexander Young Jackson, 1882-1974. His work is noted for its intense color, curvilinear shapes, and energetic brushwork.

Emily Carr, 1871-1945. Experiencing difficult times as an artist, she had to support herself by making and selling carpets and pottery before achieving success.

Art in the Past Few Decades

During the past few decades, artists in Europe and America continued to show much interest in new materials and techniques. Painters seemed more anxious than ever before to work with visual and expressive qualities. Their works showed fewer literal qualities and were more abstract and nonobjective. Sculptors used traditional and modern materials in new ways. Through new kinds of processes they found unique ways to combine forms. Like painters, sculptors no longer were just concerned with subject matter and realism. Their works also became more and more abstract and nonobjective. The focus of their work was now on formal elements and principles. Architects working with iron, steel, reinforced concrete, and glass were also discovering new techniques. This allowed them to change rapidly the look of homes, office buildings, museums, churches, and factories.

Painting in Europe: Dada, Surrealism, and Fantasy

The years following World War I in Europe were marked by revolution and inflation, anxiety and unrest.

To many it was apparent that the "war to end all wars" was not going to bring about a prolonged period of peace and prosperity. It was a time of disillusionment, and this was apparent in much of the art that was produced.

One group of artists expressed their disillusionment in an art movement known as *Dada*. The movement is said to have received its name when one of its members stuck a pin into the word "dada" on a page of a dictionary opened at random. The word, which sounded like baby talk, made no sense at all. However, since the members of the movement believed that European culture had lost all meaning and purpose, this word seemed appropriate.

Dada artists like Marcel Duchamp exhibited the most ordinary and absurd objects as works of art. These included an electric iron with tacks glued to it and a fur-covered cup, saucer, and spoon. But perhaps no work sums up the Dada point of view as well as Duchamp's photograph of the *Mona Lisa*—with a carefully drawn mustache. With works like this, the Dada artists sought to ridicule the art of the past.

The Dada movement ended in 1922. However, it set the stage for later artists who were attracted to the idea of creating art that was whimsical, humorous, and fantastic.

This was among the first works to be called Surrealist. What were the Surrealists interested in showing in their paintings? How were their works similar to the works of Bosch and Goya? How were they different? Which of the following words would you include in your description of this painting—playful, frightening, pious, fantastic, dreamlike, logical?

Figure 19.1   Joan Miró. *Carnival of Harlequin.* 1924-25. Oil on canvas, approx. 66 x 92.7 cm [26 x 36⅝"]. Albright-Knox Art Gallery, Buffalo, New York. Room of Contemporary Art Fund, 1940

Joan Miró

He was a forgetful, modest little man who looked as if he should be working in a bank rather than in a painting studio. He lived on the island of Majorca off the eastern coast of Spain and painted in a room so small that he had difficulty moving around in it. Because he never lost his childhood curiosity, his house was filled with toys which he collected and studied with enthusiasm and amusement. Especially fond of jack-in-the-boxes, he owned hundreds. He was a friend of Picasso, who bought one of his early paintings. But when the two artists visited each other, they usually hurried off to a movie together rather than discuss art. Both enjoyed seeing a good film, and seeing it together made it even more enjoyable. Ernest Hemingway purchased one of this artist's first important pictures and then offered to

teach him to box. Early in this man's career, he experienced so much frustration trying to express himself through his art that he would strike his head against a wall in despair. When he was a student in his native Spain, a teacher made him draw objects by feeling them and thinking about them rather than by looking at the objects. Nothing could have been better for him; he was always more fascinated by the world within than by the world around him. In all his years as an artist, he never tried to be popular or to gain public favor. His name was Joan Miró.

In 1925, Miró startled the Paris art world with a painting called *Carnival of Harlequin* (Figure 19.1). It was among the first paintings to be called "Surrealist." This work served notice that the shy little Spanish artist was a major figure in twentieth-century art.

The *Surrealists* were a group of artists who rejected control, composition, and logic. They preferred instead to paint the world of dreams and the subconscious. The world of dreams had been explored before by Bosch, Goya, and others. However, in even the most fantastic of their works, the subjects could be recognized. This is not true of Miró's paintings. His pictures take you into a misty world of dreams and half-forgotten memories. There time is meaningless, space is ignored, and imaginary creatures frolic. Nothing makes sense in this fairy-tale world. A ladder reaches into the sky as an escape route from the real world, cats dressed as harlequins unravel a ball of yarn, and an assortment of large and small creatures float about without effort. It is a fantasy ballet in which familiar figures and objects have been transformed by Miró into new, extraordinary shapes.

Miró saw many hardships, and these led to the visions which inspired paintings like *Carnival of Harlequin.* When he arrived in Paris in 1919, he forced himself to live on one meal a week, chewing gum to deaden his appetite and eating dried figs for energy. Then, when he began painting, forms came to him as if seen in a vision. Sometimes an accidental brushmark suggested the beginnings of a picture. But this period of unconscious experiment would only last for so long. He would then work on each detail. The result of this effort was a carefully controlled design.

After seeing *Carnival of Harlequin,* a writer said that Miró's pictures were for children. The statement was meant to belittle Miró's paintings, but it contains a certain amount of truth. Miró's playful paintings, you see, appeal to the child in everyone.

Salvador Dali

Miró's countryman Salvador Dali joined the Surrealist movement late and used his skills as a master showman to become its most famous member. In *The Persistence of Memory* (Figure 19.2), he created an eerie world in which death and decay are symbolized by a dead tree and a strange sea monster decomposing on the deserted beach. Ants swarm over a watch in an unsuccessful attempt to eat it. The meaning of this unusual picture seems clear: in time, everything will die and decay except time itself. Time alone is indestructible. The limp watches indicate that someone has the power to twist time as he or she sees fit. That person is the artist who painted them this way. Thus, Dali tells you that the artist alone, through his or her works, is able to conquer time and achieve immortality.

The meanings in Dali's other works are not always as clear. In some, the symbolism is lost to everyone but the artist. Further, his images are frequently so bizarre and grotesque that some people have called them the products of a madman. Dali, enjoying the controversy caused by his works and his unusual behavior, has responded by saying, "The difference between a madman and myself is that I am not mad."

Criticism

Describe what you see in this painting. Point to areas where there are gradation and contrast in value. Describe the shapes used. In what ways do these shapes differ from each other? What could the objects in this work symbolize—life and energy, or death and decay? List the things in the work that support your choice. To which aesthetic qualities would you refer when making a judgment about this painting?

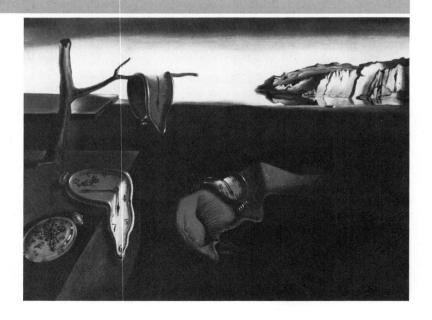

Figure 19.2 Salvador Dali. *The Persistence of Memory.* **1931. Oil on canvas, approx. 24 x 33 cm [9½ x 13″]. Collection of the Museum of Modern Art, New York. Given anonymously**

Paul Klee

Although the Swiss painter Paul Klee was never a Surrealist, fantasy was an important part of his painting. On scraps of burlap, paper, glass, and linen, he produced pictures based on his own imagination and wit. Often he worked on several paintings at the same time, sitting before his easels for hours, puffing on his pipe. He was fascinated by a world which he said was filled with wonders and spent hours studying shells, coral, butterfly wings, stained glass, and mosaics. His reactions to the world resulted in pictures that can free you from accustomed ways of looking at things or cause you to smile with delight and amusement.

One such picture is the *Twittering Machine* (Figure 19.3). Here Klee shows a machine which, when cranked, does nothing but imitate the sound of twittering birds. The picture, which shows bird-like figures as machine parts, asks you to look at machines in a different way. You are asked to see them not as useful objects which help with such tasks as washing clothes, telling time, or stamping out parts for more machines, but as devices which do nothing but make sounds. Klee singled out the stubborn squeak which he believed to be a feature of nearly every modern machine and made that the *only* feature of his machine. In so doing, he made a comment on the quality of modern mechanization in general.

A further comment can perhaps be seen in the bird-like apparatus which produces the twittering sound. You may be thinking that this little machine is surely ridiculous. After all, real birds can certainly do a better job, and there is no need to turn a crank to hear them. What does this aspect of the painting say about machines? Perhaps Klee is trying to tell you that in the mad rush to mechanization, people have forgotten that there are things in nature that machines cannot reproduce or replace. He may be telling the viewer that it is important not to get carried away with the use of mechanical devices.

Also important is the feeling you have when looking at this work. Perhaps you will smile at the child-like interpretation of the subject. Are not children, in their simple, happy innocence, more likely to be fascinated by the squeak of a machine than by its function?

Criticism

What art element dominates in this work? What do you think is pictured here? What is it supposed to do? Is it practical? Why or why not? How do you react to this picture—are you amused, tense, depressed? Is it a successful work?

Figure 19.3   Paul Klee. *Twittering Machine.* 1922. Watercolor, pen, and ink, 41.3 x 30.5 cm [16¼ x 12″]. Collection of the Museum of Modern Art, New York. Purchase

Would you describe this painting as complex and sophisticated, or simple and innocent? After whom did Klee pattern his art? Why? Did he have a clear idea in mind when he started working on a painting? What procedure did he follow when painting a picture like this?

Figure 19.4   Paul Klee. *Fish Magic.* 1925. Oil on canvas mounted on board, approx. 77.5 x 97.8 cm [30⅜ x 38½″]. Philadelphia Museum of Art. The Louise and Walter Arensberg Collection

In 1902, while in Italy, Klee visited the Aquarium in Naples. For hours he stood with his nose almost pressed against the glass watching the fish in the huge tanks dart, turn, and glide gracefully by. He was bewitched by the colorful fish, the flora which swayed gently in the current, and the bubbles that drifted lazily upward. Later, Klee recalled that marvelous dreamworld he saw in the Aquarium. Inspired, he took his brush and slowly began to make lines and shapes on a canvas. He had no definite idea in mind, but, as he worked, forms slowly began to take shape. These forms suggested real or imaginary fish and plants and even human beings. He followed these hints when they seemed "right" and painted them out when they did not seem to fit the mood of the moment. With these "found" images as a guide, he thought his way along until his picture was finished.★ He painted many pictures this way, each showing a marvelous dreamworld suggested by the things he had seen in the Aquarium. One of those pictures was named *Fish Magic* (Figure 19.4).

You may think that Klee's pictures look childish or primitive; few would disagree with you, including the artist. Klee hoped to regain the unspoiled imagination of the child. He wanted his works to be simple and innocent, and so he patterned his art on the drawings of children and primitive artists. It enabled him to record his impressions of the world in an uncomplicated style that made use of delicate lines and soft colors.

Klee created almost nine thousand paintings and drawings. Some were beautiful; others, weird; and still others, especially those done near the end of his life, frightening. In 1933, after years spent painting, teaching, and writing in Germany, he returned to his native Switzerland where he died seven years later. On his tombstone is an inscription which is a testament to his immortal imagination: "I cannot be understood in purely earthly terms. For I can live as happily with the dead as with the unborn."

Painting in America: A Mixture of Styles

American art from the time of the Armory Show until the start of World War II owed much to the modern art movements that sprang up in Europe at the start of the century. Some artists were influenced by the bright, decorative style of the Fauves, or explored their own personal approaches to Cubism. Others took the path of the Expressionists or the Surrealists.

★ **Enrichment** Found images, in this case, are images that are not preplanned. Instead, they are discovered in the maze of colors, lines, and shapes created randomly without plan or purpose.

Surrealism: Kay Sage

Kay Sage, for example, shared an interest in Surrealism with her husband, the French-born painter Yves Tanguy. In *No Passing* (Figure 19.5) she shows you a fantastic world of beautifully built but meaningless structures. Complex and illogical, these architectural forms are repeated over and over again until they disappear into infinity. To experience the full impact of this mysterious painting, place yourself in the picture. Almost immediately you sense the loneliness, the nightmare quality of the work. You seem to be standing on some strange, deserted planet. Nothing moves; no sounds are heard. You look up to see huge forms towering over you. They look like the painted scenery left over from a stage play produced in the distant past by a race of giants. Their colors are dull and earthy as if time had dimmed their brilliance. You may ask, Who built them and why have they been abandoned? How have they managed to stay upright? They look so insecure that you are certain that if you brush up against one you would start a chain reaction that would eventually topple them all. Like a giant game of dominoes, they would continue to fall as far as the eye could see. And somehow you know that the sound of their falling would continue to reach your ears long after you had lost sight of them on the horizon. And, more disturbingly, you are convinced that yours would be the only ears to hear them.

Criticism

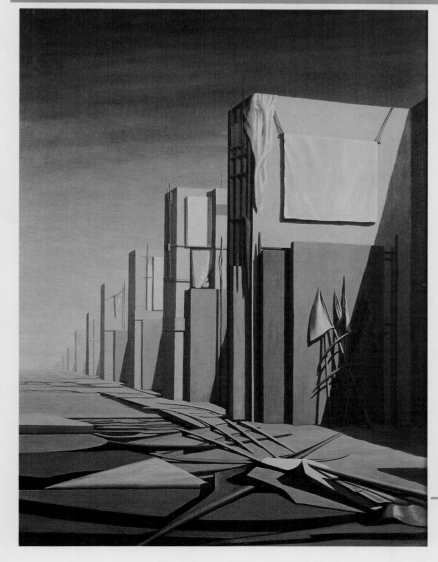

Is there any recognizable subject matter in this picture? Describe the colors, lines, and shapes used. In what ways have the principles of harmony, variety, and gradation been employed? Has the artist succeeded in creating the illusion of deep space? If so, how has this been done? Imagine yourself standing inside this painting—what are your feelings?

Figure 19.5 Kay Sage. *No Passing*. 1954. Oil on canvas, 130.2 x 96.5 cm [51¼ x 38″]. Collection of the Whitney Museum of American Art, New York

With what group of artists was Wood associated? Why were these artists given this name? What other artists were members of this group? These artists were interested in which of the following: (a) using symbols to express their ideas, (b) painting subjects in a clear manner so that everyone could understand them, or (c) creating interesting designs from the colors, values, shapes, lines, textures, and spaces suggested by nature?

Figure 19.6   Grant Wood. *American Gothic.* 1930. Oil on beaver board, approx. 76.2 x 63.5 cm [29⅞ x 24⅞"]. Courtesy of The Art Institute of Chicago. Friends of American Art Collection, 30.934

How has Sage created this vision that disturbs and attracts you at the same time? It is composed of repeated angular forms placed in what appears to be a limitless space. A strange light from an unknown source illuminates these forms. Each form is painted in a slightly lighter value and on a slightly smaller scale until they fade away into a gray mist. The brushwork is almost invisible and the image difficult to describe exactly. But there is no denying the impression that no matter how far you walk into this picture you will always face that row of absurd forms stretching to the horizon and beyond.

Regionalism and the American Scene

Unlike Sage, other American artists chose not to follow the art movements of Europe because they felt those doctrines were too complicated. They wanted to paint the American scene in a clear, simple way so that it could be understood and enjoyed by all. These artists were called "Regionalists" because of the subjects they chose. They painted the scenes and events that were typical of their sections of America. Thomas Hart Benton painted his native Missouri; John Steuart Curry, Kansas; and Grant Wood, Iowa. During the 1930s, *Regionalism* was a popular art style in the United States.

Grant Wood

Like the other Regionalists Benton and Curry, Grant Wood studied in Europe. In Paris, he was exposed to the modern art styles. But the art he saw on a trip to Munich, Germany, in 1928 impressed him more deeply. The fifteenth- and sixteenth-century Flemish and German paintings he saw there were to affect much of his later work. When Wood returned to his native Iowa, he painted rural scenes using a style of realism modeled after that of the Flemish and German works. His well-known painting *American Gothic* (Figure 19.6) captures some of the simple faith and determination of the European Gothic period.

Because it is such a familiar picture, you may think that there is little still to be learned from it. But when you go beyond description to conduct a thorough analysis, you will be impressed by the way the artist has organized this painting. A curved contour line is repeated over and over again throughout the work as a way of adding harmony. You can find these contour lines for yourself, beginning with the curve representing the top of the woman's apron. Trace this line with your finger, and then see how many similar curves you can find in the rest of the picture. As you do this, you might notice that the pattern of the pitchfork is repeated in the seam of the man's overalls. And, did you see how the heads of the figures are linked by the horizontal lines of the porch roof and the diagonals forming the peak of the house?

As you interpret Wood's painting, consider the following questions:

- What kind of people are these?
- What mood or expression do you "read" on their faces?
- What is their attitude toward you, the observer?
- Why are the curtains and shades in the house pulled shut?
- How is the closed house like the people in this picture?

Answering questions like these may lead to some interesting discoveries and add new meaning to a familiar work of art.

You may have decided that these are midwestern farming people accustomed to working hard for everything they have and proud of their accomplishments. You have just walked up to them, and the man has placed his pitchfork out in front of him. He stares directly at you in a determined manner. Meanwhile, the woman seems willing to go along with any decision the man might make in this matter. The position of the pitchfork and the expressions on the faces could hardly be taken as a sign of welcome. These people seem reluctant to extend a welcome until they get to know you better. The inside of their house is closed to your gaze, just as their feelings are closed to you. They will remain closed until these people are certain that you cherish the same wholesome values that they do. Only then will they set the pitchfork aside, break out in smiles, extend a welcoming hand, and invite you into their home and into their lives.

Edward Hopper

Edward Hopper was not a Regionalist in the true sense of the word, although he did paint the American scene in a realistic manner. As a student of Robert Henri, Hopper had early ties with the Ashcan School.* But unlike the Ashcan artists who used the city as a setting for their pictures, Hopper concentrated on the look and feel of the city itself. Ignoring the glitter and excitement of the city life, he set out to capture the emptiness and loneliness that were also a part of the urban scene. Many of his pictures did not include people—they were not needed. He was able to communicate a feeling of loneliness, isolation, and monotony with pictures of deserted streets and vacant buildings. When he did show people, they were often seen through the windows of all-night diners, huge empty houses, and drab apartments. At other times, they were glimpsed as if seen from a fast-moving car. His pictures recreate the mystery and the loneliness which, for many people, are as much a part of a great city as its wide boulevards, towering skyscrapers, and endless traffic.

★ **Enrichment** Robert Henri was a well-known artist and teacher who argued against the conservatism of academic art. Eventually he started his own school where many famous artists studied.

Criticism

Describe the setting in which these people find themselves. Would you describe the colors and shapes used here as simple and uncomplicated, or intricate and complicated? What kinds of lines are used—straight, curved, horizontal, vertical, diagonal? How has value contrast been used to emphasize the figures? How do the figures relate to one another? What mood or feeling does this painting suggest?

Figure 19.7   Edward Hopper. *Nighthawks*. 1942. Oil on canvas, 76.2 x 152.4 cm [2′ 6″ x 5′]. Courtesy of The Art Institute of Chicago. Friends of American Art Collection, 42.51

Typical of Hopper's paintings of loneliness and isolation is *Nighthawks* (Figure 19.7). An all-night diner with its cool, white light stands like an oasis in a dark, empty city. Within the diner's blank walls, four people converge and briefly come into contact with each other. Their meeting will be short and uneventful. They are separate travelers drawn to the artificial glare of the diner like moths to a flame. The men do not even bother to remove their hats. The counterman routinely performs his duties, while the woman stares blankly at something in her hand. In a few minutes, the people at the counter will rise, leave the diner, and resume their aimless wandering over barren streets. Strangers when they entered the diner, they will continue to be strangers when they return to the darkness outside.

Hopper's design for *Nighthawks* is masterful. The organization of horizontals, verticals, and diagonals; the sharp contrasts of light and dark values; and the simplicity of the color scheme all contribute to the mood of the picture. It is a mood Hopper captured in many of his paintings. In one, he showed an isolated lighthouse, but offered no hint of the ocean, its only reason for existence. In another, he presented a bored attendant at a gas station waiting for a car that might never come. With pictures like these, Hopper was able to recreate the same feeling you have when you find yourself all alone in strange surroundings with nothing to do.

An Art of Protest

By the end of the 1930s, Regionalism was declining in popularity and importance. A concern for international events caused artists to look beyond their local regions for subject matter. For one thing, the Great Depression of the 1930s made them aware of the economic ills of society. Then came World War II. The suffering and destruction of that conflict had an enormous impact on artists. No longer content to paint outward appearances, many chose to express their feelings about the tragedy and pain brought about by these events. Artists felt that art should be used to criticize and protest the injustice and suffering in the world. One of these artists was George Grosz.

George Grosz

George Grosz had been a painter of social themes and was a well-known cartoonist in Germany in the years following World War I. In 1932, he arrived in America as a refugee from the political tension in his own country and took a position as a professor of art in New York City. He remained in New York until 1959 when, shortly before his death, he returned to Germany.

World War II was the inspiration for Grosz's powerful watercolor, *Waving the Flag* (Figure 19.8). It is a nightmare vision of a skeleton-like figure stubbornly carrying on the fight amid the rubble of a bombed-out world. The figure stands with legs braced, hands tightly gripping a tattered flag. Almost stripped of his clothing, his hair smoldering, he refuses to surrender. His wide eyes glare defiantly, and his mouth is set in grim determination. But what is there left to fight for? Everything worth defending or conquering has been destroyed; the man himself is little more than a corpse. The markings on his flag are long gone, so it is impossible to say for which cause he fights. Still, he mindlessly continues to fight on, a haunting symbol for the insanity that causes and prolongs the horrors of war.

Criticism

Describe the condition, the expression, and the pose of this figure. What is the condition of the world around him? What is he holding in his hands? With your finger, trace along the dominant line in this picture. What other lines can you find? How has the figure been made to stand out from the background? Do you think this picture is a tribute to man's bravery, or does it condemn war and those who willingly participate in it? How would you defend your answer? What aesthetic qualities would you use when making a judgment about this work? Do you think that it is successful?

Figure 19.8 George Grosz. *Waving the Flag.* 1947-48. Watercolor, 63.5 x 45.7 cm [25 x 18″]. Collection of the Whitney Museum of American Art, New York

What international events in the 1930s and 1940s resulted in the decline of Regionalism? What impact did these international events have upon the artists of that time?

The works of Jack Levine and George Grosz differed even though they often used the same themes in their works. In what ways did the works differ?

Figure 19.9 Jack Levine. *Welcome Home.* **1946. Oil on canvas, 101.5 x 152.3 cm [39¹⁵⁄₁₆ x 59¹⁵⁄₁₆″]. The Brooklyn Museum. John B. Woodward Memorial Fund, 46.124**

Jack Levine

Jack Levine's visual statements about the war were more satirical and less frightening than those of Grosz. His pictures of anger and protest were tempered by a sharp wit. The scornful but humorous *Welcome Home* (Figure 19.9) was inspired by his own wartime experience as an army private. Levine presents a grand banquet staged to welcome home an important army officer at the end of the war. The officer is seen at a table, napkin tucked

firmly beneath his chin. He is busy salting a stalk of celery. His companions at the table are a woman who tries without success to look elegant and glamorous and an elderly gentleman who self-consciously sips his coffee. These three figures are arranged along a diagonal axis reinforced by the strong diagonal contour of the table. Levine wants to make sure your attention will keep returning to these three main characters. He uses the figure of the waiter to help achieve this purpose.

This waiter goes about pouring champagne with a flourish, bending his body in such a way that it keeps your attention from straying off the picture. It lures your eye upward along the bottle to the arm, on to the head, and finally around to the wreath in the background. This wreath, bearing flowers, that spell out "welcome," leads back to the three main characters.

Who are these people that Levine is so anxious for you to meet? Since he is placed in the center and the "welcome" on the wreath leads directly to him, it is safe to assume that the gentleman in uniform is the guest of honor. Several rows of campaign ribbons and two stars decorate his uniform. But why is he so glum? He fails to show any sign of happiness or relief even though the war is over and he has returned in triumph. Is it possible that he is upset that the war is over? This may be so. After all, in peacetime he will not command the respect and admiration of his compatriots; he will be regarded as just another soldier. Wartime certainly presented no real danger for him—one glance is enough to tell you that he is not a battle-hardened combat soldier. More than likely, he spent the war in safety well behind the lines. While younger men fought the battles, he reaped the glory.

But what about the officer's companions? They look equally forlorn. If the woman is the general's wife, she may be thinking how the end of the war is going to affect her social life. As the wife of a general during wartime, she enjoyed a lofty position in society. However, when things return to normal she will be no better than any other officer's wife. The other gentleman is too old to have served in the military. In addition to looking unhappy, he seems uncomfortable in such distinguished company. As he raises his cup, he holds his napkin daintily and extends the finger of his hand in what he thinks is the socially correct manner. It is still a novel experience for him to mix in high society. Recently acquired wealth may have allowed him to climb the social ladder quickly. He enjoys his new status but knows that it will soon come to an end. His wealth could have come from business dealings resulting from the war. Perhaps he is a manufacturer of war materials who realized huge profits while the conflict continued. But now that the war is over, his profits will dwindle and his position in society will plunge.

All these people profited in one way or another from the war. Levine places you at a raised position so that you can look down upon them as they gorge themselves at a banquet bought by the lives of thousands of soldiers. They cannot conceal their unhappiness that the war has come to an end; nor can you deny the feeling of contempt generated by Levine's scathing portrait of them.

Some Other Directions for Art

Levine was always concerned with people and their problems and tragedies. Throughout his career he remained convinced that art should make use of subject matter. Other artists, however, did not share this same commitment to subject matter. Included among these was Stuart Davis.

Stuart Davis

Although Stuart Davis' early works were influenced by the Ashcan School, the Armory Show introduced him to new models.★ Almost at once, he set out to find a new visual language with which to express himself. At first, he did colorful landscapes that looked like the work of the Fauves. Then in 1927 he nailed an electric fan, a pair of rubber gloves, and an egg beater to a table and for an entire year painted nothing else. It was a turning point for the young artist because it drew him away from a reliance on subject matter and opened his eyes to the possibilities of abstraction.

★ **Enrichment** The son of the art director of a Philadelphia newspaper, Davis knew several of the Ashcan artists who were employed there and admired their work.

Davis' best works reveal his affection for the modern office buildings, gas stations, neon signs, and traffic that are such important features of urban America. He tried to capture on canvas the sights, sounds, and movements of his time and place. Sometimes, as in his *Swing Landscape* (Figure 19.10), he used bits and pieces of recognizable objects in his works. At other times, he used only the colors, shapes, and textures suggested by the world around him. He took the blaring colors, twisting lines, crisp edges, and angular shapes to project his personal image of America. Often, he added letters and words that seem to flash like neon across his pictures. He painted the American scene as he saw it, felt it, and heard it.

Davis was certain that pictures could communicate the same exciting rhythms as the music played by jazz musicians in downtown night spots. He created a visual rhythm by using contrasts—contrasts of color, value, shape, line, and texture. Flaming oranges vibrate against brilliant blues; blaring reds dance before subdued greens. Colors rush forward or push backward, while light values clash with neighboring dark values.

Shapes of every kind point up, down, and sideways as planes tilt in all directions. There is no place for your eye to rest because no matter where you look there is movement. It is this movement that gives Davis' work its excitement and energy. Your eye, drawn by this excitement and energy, darts from one color to another, one shape to another. Like your foot which insists on tapping to the rhythm of a jazz band, your eye keeps moving across, up, down, and into the picture, keeping time to the rhythm of Davis' "visual jazz."

Georgia O'Keeffe

Stuart Davis drew his inspiration from urban America, but Georgia O'Keeffe was more at ease when she based her art on the things of nature. O'Keeffe studied art in Chicago, New York, and Virginia before taking a position as a high school art teacher in Amarillo, Texas. She was immediately fascinated by the beauty of the dry, open western landscape. While in Texas, she began to paint watercolors based upon her response to the flat, stark landscape where, she said, one could see the weather coming for a week.

Criticism

Make a list of the objects you recognize in this picture. Describe the objects you cannot recognize in terms of their colors, shapes, lines, and textures. Point to areas where there are contrasts between these elements. In what directions do the different lines point? Does this work exhibit a great deal of movement and excitement, or does it seem calm and still? What has been done to make some shapes seem closer than others? In what way is this painting like the musical rhythms played by a jazz band?

Figure 19.10   Stuart Davis. *Swing Landscape.* **1938. Oil on canvas, approx. 2.2 x 4.4 m [7′ 2¾″ x 14′ 5⅛″]. Indiana University Art Museum, Bloomington**

Describe the colors and shapes used in this painting. Point to places where contrast and gradation of value are found. Are the shapes and lines in sharp focus, or are they fuzzy?

Why do you think an artist would want to paint such a close-up view of a flower?

Figure 19.11   Georgia O'Keeffe. *The White Calico Flower.* 1931. Oil on canvas, 76.2 x 91.4 cm [30 x 36″]. Collection of the Whitney Museum of American Art, New York

Without her knowledge, a friend took a group of O'Keeffe's paintings to the gallery of Alfred Stieglitz in New York. Stieglitz was a talented and well-known photographer. He admired the works of Cézanne, Matisse, Picasso, and Rodin and encouraged the new American abstract painters by showing their works in his gallery. Stieglitz was impressed with O'Keeffe's paintings at once, exhibited them, and became her most enthusiastic supporter. Their friendship grew and eventually they were married.

During her long career, O'Keeffe painted pictures of flowers, the angular shapes of New York skyscrapers, and the clean white bones, desert shadows, and mountains of her beloved Southwest. In the 1920s, she began to feel that the world was moving too fast. No one seemed to have the time or inclination to stop and think. She decided to slow things down a bit by painting something that people were too busy to notice, some-

thing that they took too much for granted. She decided to paint a flower. But because a flower is so small, so easy to overlook, she determined to paint it in such a way that it could not be ignored. The result was a startling close-up view, painted in sharp focus. The results were so pleasing that she painted others. In each, the flower is simplified and enlarged to fill the entire canvas. When you study one of these paintings (Figure 19.11), you will find nothing to interfere with your vision of graceful curved surfaces and flowing contours. The beauty of each petal is seen many times over in the greater beauty of the complete flower. In a painting of a single flower, O'Keeffe records with great sensitivity and affection the splendor, wonder, and mystery that nature offers to all. She reminds you that this can be enjoyed at any time. All you have to do is take a moment to bend down and look.

Alice Neel

Alice Neel found the inspiration for her art in people's faces. Her portraits are not realistic, but somehow they still manage to look alive. Nor are they portraits of famous or wealthy clients. They are teachers (Figure 19.12), businesspeople, salespersons, artists, authors, and children. Neel collected people and preserved them on canvas. And, like an avid collector always looking for new specimens, she found them everywhere. She often stopped strangers on the street and asked them to pose and painted portraits of salespersons who came to her door. Her portraits are all unique—some smile, others frown, still others seem as though they are about to speak. Some of her portraits are done with great care

History

What subject matter did this artist prefer to paint? Where did she find this subject matter? Why did she often paint the same subject several times?

Figure 19.12 Alice Neel. *Portrait of Ellen Johnson.* 1976. Oil on canvas, 111.8 x 81.3 cm [44 x 38″]. Allen Memorial Art Museum, Oberlin College, Oberlin, Ohio. R. T. Miller, Jr. Fund and gift of the artist in honor of Ellen Johnson on the occasion of her retirement, 77.39

and precision. Others appear to be casually painted, reflecting perhaps the casual look and attitude of the sitters.

Frequently, Neel painted the same person several times. However, because they *were* painted at different times, each portrait looks different. People are, after all, complex and always changing. Their appearances change to reflect their moods and feelings. And moods and feelings can change at any moment. Take a few minutes to study Neel's portrait of Ellen Johnson. How would you describe the expression on this face? What mood do you think this person is in? Notice that Neel has managed to create the impression that her sitter's mood is a fleeting thing. It might change at any momentand with it her expression and her appearance. Studying Neel's portraits will cause you to look more closely at the faces of people you come into contact, with, people you meet in school, at parties, in the street. Like Neel's portraits, you will find all those faces unique and memorable.

Afro-American Art

Some of the best known Afro-American artists of recent times emerged during the 1930s and 1940s. Among these were Jacob Lawrence and Horace Pippin.

Jacob Lawrence

Jacob Lawrence came out of the same tradition of social protest that produced Grosz and Levine. He and Levine had something else in common—both had their start in art in a New York settlement house. The flat, brightly colored shapes that marked his mature style can be traced back to the work with poster paints and cut paper Lawrence did as a boy. In *Tombstones* (Figure 19.13), he simplified these flat colorful shapes to tell a story of hopelessness. Notice how the postures and gestures of the figures in this painting provide clues to their despair. None of these people seem inclined to go anywhere or do anything. They even ignore the crying infant in the baby carriage who has dropped her doll. The cries of the child fail to disturb or irritate because these people are accustomed to hearing children cry. At first, it seems as if the people in this picture are just waiting. But what are they waiting for? Perhaps they are just "putting in their time" as best they can, routinely going through the motions of a drab, meaningless existence. In the basement apartment of the building in which they live is a tombstone dealer. Every day they pass the tombstones on display or peer down on them from their apartment windows. This sight is a constant reminder that the only change in their dreary lives will come when their own names are carved on one of those tombstones.

How would you describe the lines in this picture? Does the artist stress the three-dimensional quality of his shapes? What is the mood of these people? Do any of them appear to be in a hurry to go somewhere? Do they communicate with one another? To what aesthetic qualities would you refer when judging this work? What is your judgment?

Compare this painting with Rembrandt's *An Artist in His Studio* (Figure 14.13, page 257). What makes these paintings of the same subject so different? What hardships did this artist have to overcome to become a painter? What subjects did he prefer to paint? What is the most impressive thing about this self-portrait? Explain your answer.

Figure 19.13 Jacob Lawrence. *Tombstones.* 1942. Gouache, 73 x 52 cm [28¾ x 20½"]. Collection of the Whitney Museum of American Art, New York

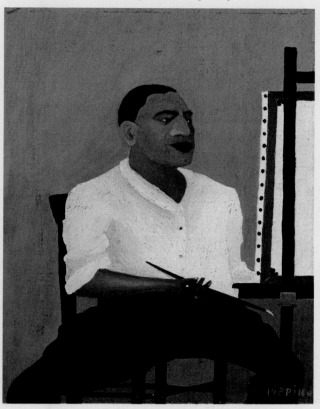

Figure 19.14 Horace Pippin. *Self Portrait.* 1941. Oil on canvas mounted on cardboard, 35.6 x 27.9 cm [14 x 11"]. Albright-Knox Art Gallery, Buffalo, New York. Room of Contemporary Art Fund, 1942

Horace Pippin

Horace Pippin was a self-taught artist who did not begin painting seriously until he was forty-two years old. As an infantryman during the final year of World War I, he was badly wounded and lost the use of his right arm. When the war ended, he married and settled in his hometown of West Chester, Pennsylvania. However, this did not mark the beginning of a "life lived happily ever after." To earn a meager living, Pippin's wife took in laundry and he delivered it.

In the mid-1920s, Pippin began to produce his first pictures. However, these were not paintings but designs burned into wood with a hot poker. He did not complete his first oil painting until 1930—after having spent three years working on it. Because he could not move his right arm, he had to guide it as best he could with his left hand.

From that first painting, Pippin went on to paint the ideas and events that had meaning and importance to him. These included family reunions, biblical stories, scenes observed in the Pennsylvania countryside, and events in the life of John Brown.* His *Self Portrait* (Figure 19.14) shows the artist seated before an easel supporting a canvas. His crippled right arm holds a long paint brush. He is gazing thoughtfully at the picture he

---

★ **Enrichment** John Brown, obsessed with the idea of abolishing slavery by force, was convicted of treason for having seized the U.S. government arsenal at Harper's Ferry, Virginia. Hanged on December 2, 1859, he was regarded as a martyr by Northern sympathizers. Pippin's grandmother, a freed slave, witnessed Brown's hanging. No doubt her account of that event made a deep impression on him.

Can you identify the subject in this painting? Are the shapes here mostly angular or mostly rounded? Point to areas of contrasting warm and cool colors. Does it seem as if the paint has been applied in a careful, precise way, or with swift, sweeping strokes? In your opinion, is this subject made to look ugly and grotesque? Or does it take on a unique look because the painting shows a familiar subject in a completely different way? What do you feel is the main concern here—is it outward appearances, or has the exterior been stripped away to allow the viewer to see within the subject?

Figure 19.15   Willem de Kooning. *Woman VI.* 1953. Oil on canvas, 1.74 x 1.49 m [68½ x 58½"]. Museum of Art, Carnegie Institute, Pittsburg. Gift of G. David Thompson, 1955

has been working on, but it is turned so that you are unable to see it. Perhaps Pippin did this so that you would focus your attention on his portrait rather than on the picture he is painting. It seems that he will return to work at any moment—he has only to decide what he will do next. This painting represents a clear and simple statement, stripped of any details that might lead to clutter or confusion. The easel, figure, and chair are made of contrasting blacks and whites with little gradation in value. A solid blue background is like a final period at the end of this straightforward statement. It seems to tell you that nothing else follows because nothing else matters. There is no hidden message here, no symbolism, no surprises. Everything worth seeing has already been included in the picture for you to see.

Abstract Expressionism

After World War II, a new art movement that came to be known as *Abstract Expressionism* sprang up and took hold in America. Probably no other movement ever gained such instant recognition or caused so much confusion and anger. The roots of this new movement can be traced back to the works of Kandinsky, Picasso, and especially the Surrealists. Abstract Expressionists rejected the idea of realistic subject matter. They did not try to create the illusion of space filled with figures and buildings and landscapes. They thought of the picture surface as if it were a flat wall and emphasized the physical action it took to paint it. Instead of carefully planned brushstrokes, artists dribbled, spilled, spattered, and slashed paints onto their pictures. As they applied colors in this way, they looked for and emphasized areas of interest as they began to emerge. These areas of interest added structure to their work. Several artists were identified with the development of this new style. Included among these artists were Willem de Kooning, Jackson Pollock, and Helen Frankenthaler.

Willem de Kooning

Willem de Kooning was born in Holland but moved to the United States in 1926. Among his most powerful and shocking paintings are those showing the female figure, which he began to paint in the late 1940s. Of course, many artists had painted women before, and some, including Raphael, Botticelli, Titian, and Rubens, were famous for their pictures of female subjects. So what was so unusual about de Kooning's pictures? Even a quick glance at one of his women (Figure 19.15) should provide an answer to that question. It was not his choice of women as subject matter but his way of showing them that aroused so much controversy. People said that his women were grotesque, insulting, and ugly. De Kooning claimed that he always started out to paint attractive young women, but the image changed as he worked. Partly humorous, his paintings poke fun at the typical wholesome, pretty all-American-girl image. But on a more serious level, they reveal de Kooning's feeling that a woman is a great deal more than just a pretty face and an attractive figure. She is revealed as a complex human being with unique interests, skills, and responsibilities. Her emotions range from hate to pity, anger to love, and sorrow to joy. De Kooning knew that it would be impossible to show all this by painting a traditional picture of a woman limited to outward appearances. As he painted, de Kooning stripped away the "façade" to show the person *within*.

De Kooning's new vision of women grew out of the creative act of painting. Using sweeping, violent strokes, he applied an assortment of rich colors to his canvas. Giving full reign to impulse and accident, he worked until the image slowly came into focus. But he never allowed the images to come completely into focus; a great deal is left to your imagination. For example, how many women do you see in this picture? One? Two? More than two? Do you see anything else? Why is the figure painted in warm hues, while the background is cool? As you answer questions like these, you become aware of just how complicated de Kooning's picture really is. You might even say that it is as complicated as the subject he tried to paint in such a new and novel manner.

Jackson Pollock

De Kooning's style was unique, yet his method of painting was more traditional than that of Jackson Pollock. De Kooning worked from a position in front of his paintings with brush in hand. Pollock, by contrast, placed his huge canvases on the floor while he worked. He walked onto and around them, using brushes, sticks, and knives to drip and spatter his paints on the canvas. In this way, he could work from any direction he wished. This technique enabled him to get as involved as possible with the creative act.

Pollock abandoned the idea that the artist should know beforehand how the painting will look when it is finished. He began each new work by randomly dripping paint over the entire canvas. After this, he went through a "get-acquainted period," during which he studied what he had done by accident. Then he added to some areas and changed others. He would often destroy entire sections in order to repaint them and bring them into harmony with the rest of the work. Any number of solutions were possible—Pollock recognized that it was up to him, as the artist, to choose the best one to express his feelings.

The purpose of Pollock's art was to *express* his feelings and not just to illustrate them. Other artists chose to picture feelings by painting figures crying, laughing, suffering, or rejoicing. Pollock's pictures were created while he was experiencing those feelings, and they influenced his choice of colors and how he applied them.

Looking at a small reproduction of a painting by Pollock may not stir much interest and excitement in you. One of the things a reproduction fails to do is show the large scale of his works. Pollock's power and vitality could not be contained in a picture measured in centimeters or inches. His *Lavender Mist* (Figure 19.16) measures about 2 x 3 m [7 x 10 feet]. It is intended to pull you in, to wash over you, to surround you. Such a large scale enables you to feel that you are a part of the painting, as Pollock felt when he created it. It is like a sea of color, bottomless and constantly moving. Once you fall under its spell, you will forget that there are no images here. They are not necessary; the painting *is* the image.

Helen Frankenthaler

Helen Frankenthaler developed her own unique painting technique as an extension of Pollock's method of applying swirls and drips of paint onto a canvas spread out upon the floor. She has moved away from a heavy application of paint, however, to use paint thinned with turpentine. This thinned paint is then poured onto an unprimed, or uncoated, canvas so that it will sink into the canvas and stain it. The paints, poured onto a flat canvas in this manner, produce flowing, graceful, free-form shapes of intense color. These shapes, some with soft edges, others with hard edges, overlap, contrast, or blend with other shapes. Frankenthaler's concern centers upon the way these shapes work in relation to each other. She avoids preplanning, preferring to allow the painting to "grow" in a spontaneous way as she moves about and applies paint to the huge canvas stapled to the floor. She pours paint from cans and pushes and spreads it across the canvas. She uses her shoulders and upper body in this action rather than just her hand and wrist. Often she spreads the paint with a sponge rather than with a brush.

By concentrating on shapes and colors, Frankenthaler permits a fantasy to take shape on the canvas. And, when she finally recognizes it, she gives it a name. In *Interior Landscape* (Figure 19.17), a flame-like shape emerges in the center of the painting. Like two smaller ones below, it twists and leaps in all directions threatening to burst from the canvas. It is held in check by the dark blue square in the center and the unyielding yellow and slate gray frame surrounding it. Like all of Frankenthaler's works, this painting is nonobjective. Its meaning is for you to discover for yourself. But, whether you are successful or not, your search will be rewarded by a journey through an exciting arrangement of colors and shapes.

History

What was Pollock's painting technique? How did it differ from the technique used by previous artists? Why did he use this technique? How did his approach to feelings and emotions differ from that of other artists? Why did he create paintings on such a grand scale?

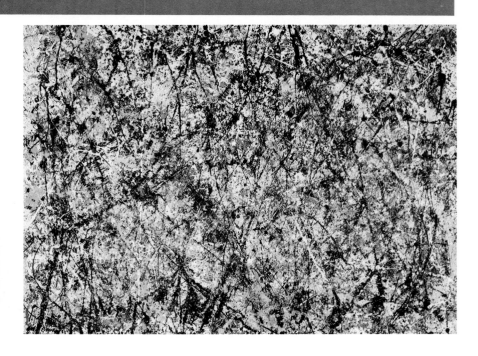

Figure 19.16   Jackson Pollock. *Number 1, 1950 (Lavender Mist).* 1950. Oil, enamel, and aluminum on canvas, approx. 2.2 x 3 m [7′ 3″ x 9′ 10″]. The National Gallery of Art, Washington, D.C. Ailsa Mellon Bruce Fund, 1976

Criticism

Do you think this artist was interested in subject matter? If not, what was she interested in? Do the paints here seem thick and opaque, or thin and transparent? Point to shapes with soft edges; hard edges. Do you feel a sense of energy here? If so, point to the areas of energy and to the shapes that seem to hold that energy in check.

Figure 19.17   Helen Frankenthaler. *Interior Landscape.* 1964. Acrylic on canvas, 2.66 x 2.35 m [8′ 8⅞″ x 7′ 8⅝″]. San Francisco Museum of Modern Art. Gift of the Women's Board, 68.52

Sculpture in Europe and America

The twentieth-century search for new forms was not limited to painters. Many sculptors in Europe and America were engaged in the same quest. Sculptors also felt that they had to break away from their dependence on subject matter to invent new forms. In addition to this, they thought that it was necessary to learn as much as possible about their materials in order to make the best use of them. The material, they argued, could guide the sensitive sculptor in the search for new forms. The work of the English sculptor Henry Moore could certainly be used as evidence in support of their argument.

Henry Moore

Henry Moore sought to create sculptures that would be completely unique and original—images in stone, wood, and bronze that had never been seen before. Because he had no desire to make copies of things, he avoided the use of a model and kept an open mind each time he started a new work. If he chose to do a sculpture in stone, he first studied the block carefully from every angle, hoping that it would suggest something to him. Then, prompted by something he saw or felt, he would take his hammer and chisel and begin to cut into the stone. At first, he worked slowly and cautiously, carving forms from the hard rock. Sometimes the combination of these forms suggested a human figure—the head, torso, arms, and legs. When this happened, he would work more rapidly, although he was always careful not to carve away too much of the stone. He wanted to bring out the figure, but did not want to sacrifice the simplicity and the solidity of the stone.

In what ways does this form resemble a human figure? In what ways does it not resemble a human figure? Are the forms found here straight and rigid, or round and flowing? Is there a straight contour line visible on this sculpture? Describe the texture. Do you think you could learn more about this work by studying it from a fixed position, or by walking around it? What aesthetic qualities would you use when making a judgment about this sculpture?

Figure 19.18 Henry Moore [English, 1898-1986]. *Reclining Figure.* **1939. Elmwood, 94 cm × 2 m × 76.2 cm [37″ × 6′ 7″ × 30″]. Courtesy of The Detroit Institute of the Arts. Gift of the Dexter M. Ferry, Jr. Trustee Corporation, 65.108**

His search for new and unusual forms led Moore to cut holes or openings into his sculptures. This was something that had never been dared before. In his *Reclining Figure* (Figure 19.18), rounded abstract forms and openings combine to suggest a human image that has been eroded and worn smooth by the forces of nature. The work is Moore's tribute to nature. Nature provided him with the raw material from which the sculpture was made and showed him how to transform that material into a work of art. Wind and water were his teachers, instructing him through their example how to form, smooth, and polish the wood to create a unique work of art.

Barbara Hepworth

Barbara Hepworth was also a student of nature and applied what she learned to her work in sculpture. As a girl she often painted the funnel-like caves cut into the cliffs along the Yorkshire coast of England. Having had the same teacher—nature—it is not surprising that many of her works have much in common with Moore's. Beginning in the 1930s, they followed a similar path, opening up their sculptural forms by piercing them with holes and hollowing them out. A bronze figure she completed in 1959 (Figure 19.19) illustrates how Hepworth used holes as a focus in her sculptures. Even though this work is very abstract, it succeeds in capturing a definite movement. A dancer is suggested, but the dance is slow and smooth rather than swift and jerky. With arms stretched upward, it bends gracefully to one side, its head suggested by one of two holes piercing the form.

Hepworth shared with Moore an affection for and knowledge of natural materials. Their search for new sculptural forms led them to a study of these materials. Meanwhile, other sculptors were looking in different directions.

What does this work have in common with Henry Moore's *Reclining Figure* (Figure 19.18)? How does it differ? Which "teacher" did this artist share with Moore?

Figure 19.19 Barbara Hepworth. *Figure (Archaean).* **1959. Bronze, 2.3 m [7′7″] high. Wichita Sate University Endowment Association Art Collection, Edwin A. Ulrich Museum of Art, Wichita, Kansas**

Henry Moore's search for new forms led him to a study of various materials to use for his sculpture. Where did Lipchitz turn for his ideas? What style of painting influenced Lipchitz when he created works like this? What was his main concern here—feeling and expression, or space and form?

Figure 19.20 Jacques Lipchitz. *Sailor with Guitar.* 1914. Bronze, 78.7 cm [31″] high, 21.6 cm [8½″] wide, and 3.8 cm [1 ½″] at base. Philadelphia Museum of Art. Given by Mrs. Morris Wenger in memory of her husband

Jacques Lipchitz

Some, including Jacques Lipchitz, were influenced by the new movements in painting. Lipchitz arrived in Paris from his native Lithuania in 1909. Soon after, he was attracted to the ideas of Cubism. His *Sailor with Guitar* (Figure 19.20) was done in the Cubist style. It is a three-dimensional form with the same kinds of geometric shapes found in paintings by Picasso and Braque.

What figures and objects are found here? Can you determine what is happening? Describe the forms used in this sculpture. How is movement achieved? Does the texture seem rough or smooth? Is value an important element here? What does it contribute to the overall effect of this work? What mood or feeling do you receive from this work?

Figure 19.21 Jacques Lipchitz. *Sacrifice II.* 1948-52. Bronze, 125 x 83.8 x 55.9 cm [49¼ x 33 x 22″]. Collection of the Whitney Museum of American Art, New York

Flat surfaces of different shapes were placed at various angles to one another. The result suggested a jaunty sailor strumming his guitar.

Later, Lipchitz's sculptures became more emotional. He was affected by such events as the Great Depression and World War II, and this showed in his work. Like the Expressionist painters, Lipchitz was no longer satisfied to work on solving design problems of form and space. He felt that art had to say something, that it had to be more exciting and emotional. However, while most of his subjects can be recognized, it is not always possible to agree on the meaning of his works. *Sacrifice II* (Figure 19.21) might refer to an ancient religious ritual.

Can you find anything in this work that makes it look like a landscape? Which element, form or line, is more important here? Describe the various lines used. Describe the shapes. Is this a two-dimensional or a three-dimensional work? Since this work is not realistic and does not express a mood or feeling, what qualities would you consider when judging it?

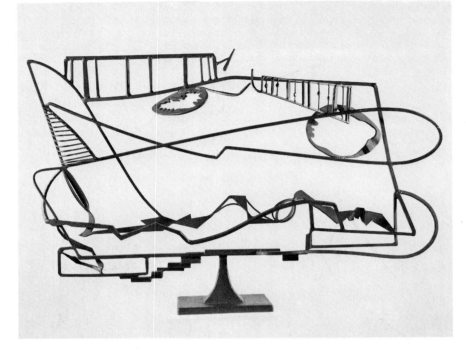

Figure 19.22 David Smith. *Hudson River Landscape.* 1951. Steel, 1.26 x 1.9 x 0.42 m [4′ 1½″ x 6′ 3″ x 1′ 4¾″]. Collection of the Whitney Museum of American Art, New York

On the other hand, it could have something to do with the sacrifices which are caused by war and famine in today's world. In any case, there is no denying the violence here. The figures twist and turn, and the bird issues a piercing cry as the knife strikes its breast.

David Smith

While Lipchitz looked to Cubism and Expressionism for inspiration, another sculptor, David Smith, was attracted to abstract and nonobjective art. Smith was born in 1906 in Decatur, Indiana. He knew from the time he was nineteen that he wanted to be an artist, but it looked like an impossible goal. At that time, art was something often made from expensive materials using techniques that took years to learn.★ Still, Smith decided to try. After studying at Ohio University, he took a temporary job in 1924 working in an automobile factory as a riveter and spot welder. He never dreamed that the skills he developed on the assembly line would help him later as an artist. Two years later, Smith went to New York where he worked as a painter while supporting himself as a taxi driver, seaman, carpenter, and salesman. In

★ Enrichment For example, marble carving and bronze casting, the oldest and most revered methods of creating sculpture, made use of costly materials and tools. In order to use these materials and tools successfully, artists-in-training spent several years enrolled in courses of study offered by colleges, universities, and special art schools.

1930, he met Stuart Davis, who directed him toward abstract art. Not long after that, Smith saw some examples of welded-metal sculptures by Picasso and was so impressed that he decided to turn his attention entirely to sculpture. He realized that the art of sculpture was entering a new era and that he was uniquely qualified to play a leading role.

Before this time, sculpture had been an art of volume and mass, but Smith invented a technique that resulted in a new form. He began to "draw in space" using rods, tubes, and sheet metal which he cut, bent, and welded together. What Stuart Davis was doing in paint, Smith felt he could do in steel. Best of all, he could create this new kind of sculpture by using the skills he had learned earlier as a welder on the automobile assembly line. In the fall of 1933, he bought a welding outfit and eagerly went to work in the back room of his apartment. However, after several fires, he wisely decided to move to an industrial workshop.

While on a train between Albany and Poughkeepsie, New York, Smith completed a number of sketches of the landscape. Later he combined his visual impressions of that landscape with his feelings about it to create a drawing in space which he called *Hudson River Landscape* (Figure 19.22). He used metal rods which were heated, curved, and welded into place. In this way he formed a design composed of curved and straight lines organized along a two-dimensional plane. The work only slightly resembles a landscape. You might think that some parts of it look like hills and other parts like clouds. However, there is a great deal more in the work that will not fit

How did works like this differ from earlier sculptures? What name was given to this type of sculpture? Were all of Calder's works based on natural objects? In what ways do his works resemble the paintings of Joan Miró and Paul Klee? Why is it unnecessary to walk around this work to see all of it?

Figure 19.23 Alexander Calder. *Pomegranate*. 1949. Painted sheet aluminum, steel rods, and wire, 1.8 x 1.7 m [72 x 68″]. Collection of the Whitney Museum of American Art, New York

your ideas of a landscape. But this does not make the work any less successful. It no longer owes anything to the landscape that inspired it. The sculpture exists on its own, the product of Smith's fertile imagination and skill.

A surprising feature of Smith's sculpture is its flatness. You can view it from a single position as you would a painting or a relief sculpture. Since the back is similar to the front, there is no need to walk around the sculpture to see it all.

Alexander Calder

In one respect, many of the works created by Alexander Calder are related to David Smith's sculpture. Although Calder's works are certainly not flat, you do not have to walk around them to see them completely. As with Smith's sculpture, they can be viewed from a single vantage point. Calder's sculptures move, and this allows you to stand still and see all their parts as they change position.

Mobile is a term invented by Calder to describe these sculptures that move. Hanging from a single point, they were made with rods, wires, and delicately balanced shapes made of sheet metal. Air currents set the mobiles in motion, treating the viewer to constantly changing patterns of colors and shapes. Unlike traditional sculpture, the appeal of these works is almost entirely visual. They are most effective when the wire arms and attached shapes begin to quiver, swing, and rotate in space.

Many of Calder's mobiles are based on natural forms —animals, birds, fish, or plants—and the motions were carefully planned to imitate the movement of his subjects. An excellent example is *Pomegranate* (Figure 19.23), where shapes representing the leaves and fruit of the plant turn and bob as if stirred by a gentle breeze. Calder's later works show that he became more interested in shapes and movements that had little to do with natural objects. His concern came to be centered on the

383

How was this work put together? What was used to make it? What has the artist done to unify this composition? Had artworks like this ever been done before?

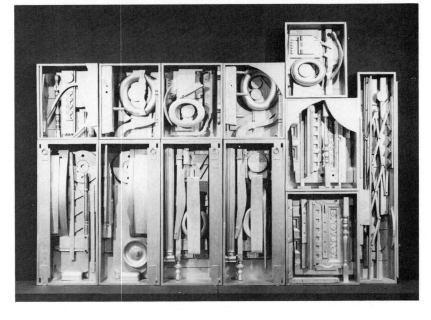

Figure 19.24   Louise Nevelson. *Royal Tide II.* **1961-63. Painted wood, 2.4 x 3.2 x 0.2 m [7′ 10½″ x 10′ 6½″ x 8″]. Collection of the Whitney Museum of American Art, New York. Gift of the artist**

Figure 19.25   Façade, Santa Maria, Sangüesa, Spain. Twelfth to thirteenth centuries

changing relationships of nonobjective shapes. But all of his works reveal his wit and imagination. It is as if he had discovered a way to add life to the fantasy world painted by Joan Miró and Paul Klee.

Louise Nevelson

An interesting contrast to the works of Smith and Calder is offered by the sculptures of Louise Nevelson. Hers is a sculptural style of assemblage, a kind of three-dimensional collage. The massive wooden "walls" of black, white, and gold that she began to construct in

the 1950s firmly established her international reputation.

Louise Nevelson was an excellent athlete in her youth. She was the center and captain of the girl's basketball team in elementary and high school in Rockland, Maine. While she was still in school, a teacher praised her artwork, and that helped her decide to become an artist. Early in her career, she was primarily a painter. However, she did produce some sculptures in bronze, terra-cotta, marble, and wood. Some carpenter's scraps from a remodeling project and the chance find of a discarded wooden box proved to be the inspiration for a series of nonobjective sculptures that soon filled several rooms.

In *Royal Tide II* (Figure 19.24), you can see how she carefully assembled found objects and wood scraps in boxes. These were then stacked together to make a large composition. The result was a rich variety of contrasting angles and curves. These were then unified visually by spray painting the whole structure with one color. What you see is a blend of the familiar and the unfamiliar. Many parts can be recognized easily as odd pieces taken from furniture. Others appear to be scraps from old Victorian houses. However, their original functions have now been ignored. What they are or, more accurately, what they were is no longer important. It is the ingenuity with which they have been precisely fitted together to form a new and novel sculptural form that is important. In some ways they may remind you of Medieval sculptures. The latter were also designed to fit neatly within their assigned niches (Figure 19.25). Unlike the Medieval works, Nevelson's forms are nonobjective. Even so, her works capture some of the same quiet dignity of those earlier religious sculptures.

Isamu Noguchi

Isamu Noguchi's path to international acclaim has been a long one. It has stretched from the United States, where he was born in 1904, to Japan, where he lived until he was fourteen, and back to the United States. At one time he was apprenticed to a cabinetmaker and at another time to a sculptor who told him he would never be an artist.* Discouraged, Noguchi entered Columbia University in New York City to study medicine. However, thoughts of a medical career were permanently discarded when he left school to return to sculpture.

Over the years, Noguchi has shown himself to be a versatile artist. He is a student of both modern and ancient styles of art, both Eastern and Western, and this has been reflected in his work. Noguchi is well-known as a designer of gardens and furniture as well as sculpture. His skill as a carver and his love for smoothly polished stone surfaces are seen in works like *Humpty Dumpty* (Figure 19.26). Each section of this whimsical, abstract figure was carefully modeled from slate and then assembled like a construction. A basic curvilinear shape is repeated throughout the work. Smaller versions of this shape penetrate a larger version at unexpected

---

★ **Enrichment** The sculptor was Gutzon Borglum, who gained fame as the artist who carved Mount Rushmore.

How have value contrasts been achieved in this sculpture? What kinds of shapes have been used in this work? Is repetition important here? Where has it been used? How does repetition contribute to the harmony found in this work? What does this work look like to you? What clues suggested such an idea? Is this, in your opinion, a successful work?

Figure 19.26   Isamu Noguchi. *Humpty Dumpty*. 1946. Ribbon slate, 149.2 x 52.7 x 45.7 cm [4′ 10¾″ x 1′ 8¾″ x 1′ 6″]. Collection of the Whitney Museum of American Art, New York

angles. At the same time, an array of value contrasts breaks up what would otherwise be the solid gray color of the slate. What does all this suggest to you? The title, which refers to a character from a familiar nursery rhyme, may provide an important clue. Perhaps what you see is the result of a not-so-successful effort to "put Humpty Dumpty back together again," treated in a witty, highly imaginative manner.

Allan Houser

Many contemporary sculptors choose to work with abstract or nonobjective forms. Some, on the other hand, prefer more realism. One of these is Allan Houser.

Allan Houser's father was the grandson of the Apache chief Mangus Colorado and a relative of Geronimo. The oldest child in a family of two girls and three boys, he had to leave high school in order to help his father on their Oklahoma farm. However, Houser managed to find time to continue with his favorite pastime—art.

In 1948, having found only slight success with his paintings, Houser was thinking of becoming a housepainter. Fortunately, one of his designs was chosen for a war memorial statue at the Haskell Institute in Lawrence, Kansas.★ Since then he has had little time to think about any other career but sculpture.

Watching for Dancing Partners (Figure 19.27) is a Pink Tennessee marble carving of two Indian women standing side by side at a dance. Their smooth, polished faces contrast with the strands of long hair which encircle them. Over their shoulders they wear heavily textured shawls with fringes. These shawls add further textural contrast to the faces and long, smooth skirts. The textural similarities of the two women tie them together as effectively as do their positions next to each other. A carving like this is meant to be explored slowly with the eyes in order to appreciate the rich surface effects. And, as your eyes move over it, they will linger no doubt on the faces. There you will detect an air of watchfulness and anticipation. The two women do not communicate with one another. They are too busy watching the swirling actions of the dancers sweeping by in front of them. Each eagerly awaits the moment when some young man will approach and ask her to dance.

Architecture in Europe and America

As the twentieth century wore on, the International Style in architecture was seen less and less. This decline was due to uninspired and endless repeating of the style in Europe and America. Gradually, architects began to search for new forms and new approaches.

★ **Enrichment** Houser's finished sculpture entitled *Comrade in Mourning* is of a Plains Indian. It stands 2.4 m [8 feet] tall and is carved from a 3.6-t [4-ton] block of white Carrara marble.

Describe these figures in as much detail as possible. Do they seem to be talking to one another? From their facial features and clothing, what do you know about these people? Is texture an important art element here? How has it been used? Describe the mood of these figures. Is this a successful work of art? Why or why not?

Figure 19.27 Allan Houser. *Watching for Dancing Partners.* 1979. Museum of the Southwest, Midland, Texas

Le Corbusier

One of the most exciting of the new forms was a building in southeastern France (Figure 19.28). This was the Chapel of Notre Dame du Haut, built in the early 1950s by a Swiss-born architect called Le Corbusier. (His real name was Charles-Edouard Jeanneret.) The boxlike forms of the old style are absent here. Instead one finds massive walls that bend and curve like slabs of soft clay and a rounded, billowing roof. The windows look as if they have been cut through the thick walls with great difficulty. It is a sculptured building which combines features found in the abstract figures of Henry Moore and the curving architectural forms of

Antonio Gaudi. At the same time, it suggests the same strength and solidity as a Medieval fortress. Doors are difficult to locate and, when found, lead to an interior illuminated by a mysterious light. A spotlight effect is created by light passing through small stained-glass windows placed almost randomly in the walls (Figure 19.29). This pattern of colored light on the walls provides all the decoration needed on the inside of this unusual church. Part sculpture, part architecture, it is completely unique. It is unlike any church ever built before.

Criticism

How does sunlight enter this building? Are all the windows the same size and shape? Are they placed in the walls according to a particular pattern? What effect is created by the light striking the walls? Do you think this interior is appropriate for a place of worship? Why or why not?

Figure 19.29   Le Corbusier. Notre Dame du Haut. Interior

History

How does this building differ from those built according to the International Style? In what ways does this structure resemble a sculpture? What qualities do you associate with this building—delicacy and charm, or solidity and strength?

Figure 19.28   Le Corbusier. Notre Dame du Haut. Ronchamp, France. 1950-55

Criticism

Do the axis lines here define a horizontal or a vertical emphasis? How do value contrasts contribute to this same emphasis? Point to areas of smooth and rough textures. What has been done to make this house blend with its surroundings? Would you like to live in a house like this? Why or why not?

Figure 19.30   Frank Lloyd Wright. Kaufmann House (Falling Water). Bear Run, Pennsylvania. 1936-39

Frank Lloyd Wright

The American Frank Lloyd Wright was destined to become an architect. Before he was born, his mother hung pictures of the great cathedrals in her room to inspire the unborn child. Years later, Wright withdrew from the University of Wisconsin where he had been studying engineering to join the architectural firm of Louis Sullivan in Chicago. He left the firm to strike out on his own five years later, but never forgot his debt to the head of that firm. Wright called Sullivan his "well-beloved master."

Wright designed over six hundred buildings during his long career. Among them were private homes (Figure 2.12, page 25), apartment buildings, office buildings, factories, churches, and hotels. The Imperial Hotel he built in Tokyo met a special test. It stood through the great earthquake of 1923. That triumph helped to make his reputation as one of the greatest architects of the century.

In the mid-1930s, Wright was asked by a gentleman named Kaufmann to design a house in Bear Run, Pennsylvania. There was a small waterfall on the property that the client loved, and he requested that Wright build his house near it. Wright did more than that; he built the house *over* it, making the stream and waterfall part of the design. In this way, the house, known as Falling Water (Figure 19.30), blends easily with the environment. Two concrete porches extend out over the rock ledges on which the house is built. The porches are parallel to the ledges and, like them, are rectangular in shape. Balancing these porches are the vertical forms of the fireplace and chimney. Variety in texture and value is achieved through the use of smooth, light-colored concrete for the porches, which contrasts with the rough, dark stone used in the vertical forms. Because this stone is from the site, it has the same texture and color of the ledges on which the house is built. This helps to link the house with its surroundings. Falling Water clearly illustrates Wright's ideas. He believed that a house should grow out of the needs and desires of its owners and from the unique character of the setting.

Wright's most controversial building is the Guggenheim Museum in New York City, a gallery for modern art (Figure 19.31). Critics said that the building was Wright's revenge on a city that he hated. They believed he was reacting to unpleasant experiences with officials on earlier projects. Some even claimed that the museum was built from plans for a parking garage. When you look at the building, it is not too difficult to see how such a charge could have been made. Wright wanted to create a museum in which a single continuous ramp spiraled upward (Figure 19.32). This would enable people to move up and down while viewing artworks displayed along the walls. Wright did not care for the maze-like collections of rooms found in traditional museums. His plan was a departure from the usual series of connecting squares. He designed a single, round, windowless room almost 30.5 m [100 feet] in diameter. Around this room he placed a continuous ramp, which was about 5 m [17 feet] wide at the bottom and about 10.5 m [almost 35 feet] wide at the top. The ramp curled upward covering a distance of 0.4 km [.25 mile]. Visitors could either walk up the slight grade or take an elevator to the top and stroll down to the ground level. In either case, the gently curving ramp allowed visitors to walk leisurely past the artworks which hung on the walls.

The controversy surrounding Wright's unusual design for the Guggenheim Museum began before it was finished and has continued up to the present. There are those who have enthusiastically labeled it the most beautiful building in the world. There are also those who think it looks like a giant corkscrew or a cupcake. Had he lived, Wright would have paid little attention to the praise or the disapproval heaped upon his creation. He would have been too deeply involved with new projects. Unfortunately, he died six months before his unusual museum opened its doors to the public.

History

How does this museum differ from more traditional museums? What would you list as its most unusual feature? Did everyone appreciate Wright's design for this museum? What did the critics have to say about it? People have used a variety of descriptions when discussing this building—how would you describe it? Do you think the design is successful? Why or why not?

Figure 19.31   Frank Lloyd Wright. Solomon R. Guggenheim Museum. Exterior. New York. 1943-59

Figure 19.32   Frank Lloyd Wright. Solomon R. Guggenheim Museum. Interior

What problem did this architect face when designing this museum? How did he solve this problem? From the exterior, how is this building like a sculpture? What do you feel are the most appealing features of this building? In what ways is it similar to and different from Frank Lloyd Wright's plan for the Solomon R. Guggenheim Museum (Figures 19.31 and 19.32)?

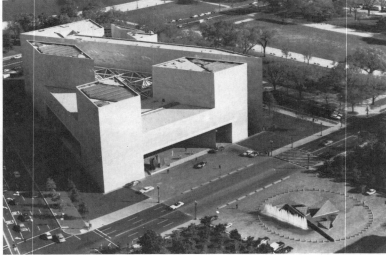

Figure 19.33   I. M. Pei. East Building, National Gallery of Art. Exterior. Washington, D.C. 1968

Figure 19.34   I. M. Pei. East Building. National Gallery of Art. Interior

I. M. Pei

Wright avoided the tradition of square-roomed galleries by using one long circular ramp. I. M. Pei's problem in designing the addition to the National Gallery of Art in Washington, D.C., was of a different kind. The site was shaped like a trapezoid, formed by the meeting of two streets. To make the best use of this site, Pei used two triangular-shaped buildings. The larger was an isosceles triangle, and the smaller, a right triangle (Figure 19.33). These two triangular-shaped structures are linked by a great indoor courtyard. A vast skylight high above the courtyard allows natural light to filter down on trees, sculptures, and visitors. In the upper reaches of this courtyard a huge red, black, and blue Calder mobile floats majestically. Stairways, escalators, and bridges lead from the courtyard to research faciiities and numerous galleries of various sizes and shapes (Figure 19.34). Some of these galleries are small and intimate, while others are spacious enough to accommodate the largest artworks. Visitors moving through these galleries are never allowed to feel as though they are trapped in a maze of rooms and corridors. At no time are they more than a few steps away from views to the outdoors or to the great interior courtyard.

Pei's design is no less impressive from the outside. A stroll around the building is similar to walking around a huge sculpture. Shapes, forms, angles, and surfaces seem to change, and a new view is presented with each step. The result is satisfying and appropriate. After all, what could be more fitting than a work of art to house the artworks of a nation?

Art Today—A Never-ending Quest for New Visual Experiences

In recent years each new generation of artists has included some who were unwilling to continue in the direction laid out by their predecessors. Abstract Expressionist artists were not immune to such challenges. Since 1960, their ideas have been challenged by a series of new art movements worldwide. The loose painting technique and the emphasis placed on personal expression, as seen in the work of de Kooning, Pollock, and other Abstract Expressionists, were replaced by new styles. These new art movements were Pop Art, Op Art, Minimal Art, Hard-edge Painting, and Photo-Realism.

Pop Art

Pop Art emerged in the 1950s in England.★ There a group of young artists broke new ground with their collages made of pictures clipped from popular magazines. Collages, of course, were not new. Cubist, Dada, and other artists had used this technique earlier, but for different reasons. British Pop artists combined pictures of familiar household objects, such as television sets, vacuum cleaners, and canned hams, to state their message. They suggested that people were letting the mass media shape their lives. A typical collage showed a couple in their living room surrounded by many of the trappings of the "good life" as advertised by the media. These artists wanted people to see how meaningless their own lives were becoming, and to change.

Pop art made its way to the United States during the 1960s. Images of popular culture such as billboards, comic strips, magazine ads, and supermarket products appeared throughout Pop works. American Pop artists examined the contemporary scene and reported what they found without satire or criticism. However, they did present their images of Coke bottles, Campbell's soup cans, Brillo boxes, and hamburgers in new ways. Often they showed them in surprising combinations or greatly enlarged their size. In this way they hoped to shake viewers out of accustomed ways of looking at the most trivial trappings of modern life.

Claes Oldenburg

Claes Oldenburg's *Giant Three-Way Plug* (Figure 19.35) shows how artists enlarged the scale of an object in order to call attention to it. You could say that Pop artists like Oldenburg treated ordinary objects found in the manufactured environment in much the same way that Georgia O'Keeffe treated objects found in nature.

★ Enrichment The name "Pop" was given to this movement because its artists used popular objects as subject matter in their works.

In what way is this sculpture a reminder of Georgia O'Keeffe's paintings of flowers (Figure 19.11, page 373)? Why were artists like Oldenburg called "Pop" artists? What were Pop artists trying to accomplish with their works?

Figure 19.35 Claes Oldenburg. *Giant Three-Way Plug.* 1970. Cor-Ten steel and bronze, approx. 1.55 x 1.98 x 3.06 m [5'⅞" x 6' 6" x 10'⅝"]. Allen Memorial Art Museum, Oberlin College, Oberlin, Ohio. Fund for Contemporary Art, 70.38

What kind of effects did Op artists seek to achieve with their works? Was this artist successful in creating these

effects? How did he accomplish this? In what ways is this work different from more traditional paintings?

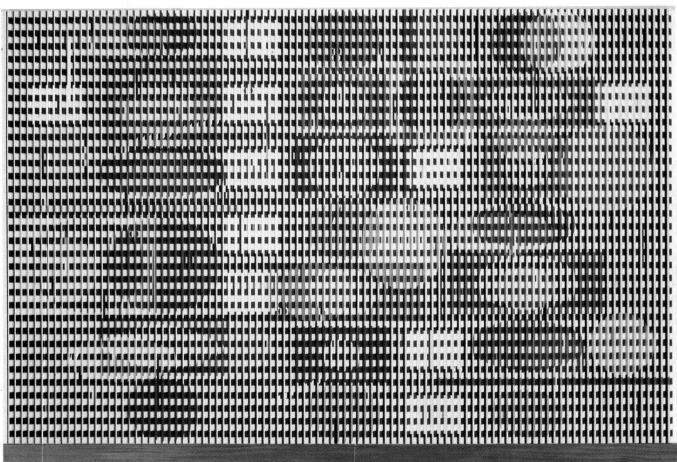

Figure 19.36   Agam (Yaacov Gipstein). *Double Metamorphosis, II.* **1964. Oil on corrugated aluminum, in eleven parts, 2.69 x 4.02 m [8′ 10″ x 13′ 2¼″]. Collection of the Museum of Modern Art, New York. Gift of Mr. and Mrs. George M. Jaffin**

Both enlarged their subjects to increase the impact on viewers. O'Keeffe did this to call attention to the beauty in nature, which is too often taken for granted (Figure 19.11, page 373). Oldenburg wanted viewers to stop and think about the products of the industrial and commercial culture in which they lived. He felt that people had come to rely too readily on these products and hoped to make viewers more conscious of that fact.

In a further effort to call attention to common objects, Oldenburg often changed the material from which they are made. One material he used was brightly colored and stuffed canvas. Out of this he made soft hamburgers, bags of French fries, and even typewriters.★ This

forced viewers to see the mass-produced, antiseptically sealed, chemically preserved products in a new light. It caused them to view these products of their hard-sell culture through more sensitive eyes.

Op Art

Op Art was a nonobjective art movement that developed in the United States after 1960. However, similar movements were evident at about the same time in

---

★ **Enrichment** This was a technique that came to be known as "soft sculpture."

several European countries including Germany and Italy. Op artists sought to create an impression of movement on the picture surface by means of optical illusion. In traditional paintings, the aim was to draw the viewer into the work. In contrast, Op pictures seem to vibrate and reach out to the spectator. Victor Vasarely is generally regarded as the founding father of this movement. He used dazzling colors and precise geometric shapes to create surfaces which appear to move. They seem to project forward in some places and recede backward in others.

Vasarely's Followers: Bridget Riley and Agam

Bridget Riley (Figure 2.4, page 19) used gradual changes of color and waving lines to add movement to her paintings. The effect is a surface that seems to swell out in one place and fade back in another. Israeli-born artist Yaacov Gipstein, known as Agam, was able to create multiple images within a work. This effect was created with rows of thin, fixed strips which project from the surface of his painting in vertical rows (Figure 19.36). He painted the sides of the strips differently from their tops and from the spaces in between. In this way the artist succeeded in combining several designs in a single work. The one you see depends on your position when viewing the work. And, when you change your position, the design will change.

Minimal Art

Minimal artists exercised the greatest restraint and understatement to create works of art that were spare, austere, and betrayed no sign of the artist's involvement. They felt that by doing this they could give their works the same impersonal, anonymous look that would result if the pictures were produced by some kind of machine. This art movement stressed the idea of reducing a work of art to the minimum number of colors, values, shapes, lines, and textures.

Ad Reinhart

Ad Reinhart went further than other artists to reduce the colors, values, shapes, lines, and textures in his paintings. Beginning in the early 1950s, he painted pictures which seemed at first to consist of an even application of black paint. Only after intense study would viewers notice the subtle lines, shapes, or value changes in these works.

Barnett Newman

The Minimalist's point of view can be noted in the sculptures of Barnett Newman. His *Broken Obelisk* is an example (Figure 19.37). It consists of a four-sided pyramid whose tip supports that of an obelisk that

appears to have been broken off at the top.★ The two tips have exactly the same angle (53 degrees) found in ancient Egyptian pyramids. The juncture of the tips forms a perfect "X." You may be wondering what meaning the artist had in mind when he created this work. Perhaps it means whatever you or anyone else viewing it wants it to mean. Or, perhaps it is not

---

★ **Enrichment** An obelisk is a four-sided shaft that tapers gradually from bottom to top. It is topped by a pryamid form. Because of their Egyptian origin, obelisks are sometimes called "Cleopatra's Needles."

Criticism

Describe the forms used in this sculpture. How many forms are there? To what point on this work is your eye drawn? Why do you suppose the top of this sculpture was made to look broken off? What is unusual about the way the forms are joined together? Does this create a feeling of tension? Do you think that was deliberate?

Figure 19.37 Barnett Newman. *Broken Obelisk*. 1968. Rothko Park, Houston, Texas

intended to *mean* anything and acts only as an instrument to stimulate your thoughts and ideas. The sculpture succeeds in drawing your eye to the point where two age-old forms—pyramid and obelisk—daringly meet. At that point, both forms seem to disintegrate, to disappear, leaving you adrift with your own thoughts. Concentrating on that point, you will find your thoughts drifting inward to a meditative state. Thus the work acts as a vehicle by which you enter into a deeply personal experience in which your thoughts are redirected from the world around you to the world within you.

Ronald Bladen

Though often referred to as a Minimalist, Ronald Bladen prefers to be thought of as a geometric abstractionist. His huge sculptural forms are inspired by architecture and industry. They reveal a concern for precise form and finish. Their smooth, even surfaces offer no hint of the artist's hand as they curve, bend, twist, and dramatically reach out into space. Works like *Sonar Tide* (Figure 19.38) are certainly impressive because of their gigantic scale. But sensitive viewers soon recognize the drama and the excitement they can arouse as well. Such a response sometimes comes as a surprise with a structure that is so simple. Bladen's forms are carefully stripped of all excess baggage. *Sonar Tide* is a carefully calculated arrangement of contrasting straight and curved planes and forms which project into space to become an active part of the environment. The work does more than just occupy a great deal of space. It boldly curves and stretches out to claim that space with authority. And, as it does so, it effectively links the architectural forms which surround it.

Sonar Tide was designed to fit within an area of 13.9 m² [150 square feet] in the Civic Center of downtown Peoria, Illinois. It has taken its place with the surrounding buildings to become a familiar object to the hundreds of people who pass it each day. One gently curving section of the form seems to bow with dignity and grace toward the theater. At the other end the form sweeps upward, directing the eye to the City Hall. The sculpture is huge—7.9 m [26 feet] high and over 15.5 m [51 feet] long—but its size in no way detracts from its grace. And, the longer you look at it, the more impressed you become by the space *around* the form. Repeating the angles and curves of the sculpture itself, these negative spaces contribute to a feeling of excitement mixed with satisfaction. Such a feeling is essential if the work is to become, in Bladen's words, "a part of people's lives."

Hard-edge Painters

Hard-edge painters placed importance on the crisp, precise edges of the shapes in their paintings. Often the shape of the canvas helped these artists decide how to organize their compositions. Typical of Hard-edge painters are Kenneth Noland (Figure 19.39), Ellsworth Kelly, and Frank Stella. Their works contain smooth surfaces, hard edges, pure colors, and simple geometric shapes, and were done with great precision.

Frank Stella

Taking the new style a step further, Frank Stella used different canvas shapes for his works (Figure 19.40). Many of his paintings were not rectangular. Working on

---

Criticism

Describe the forms that make up this huge structure. Would you refer to these forms as simple or complex? Point to as many contrasting planes and forms as you can. What can you say about the spaces around the forms, spaces that are often referred to as the negative spaces? Does this work seem rigid and dignified, or active and exciting? List the reasons to support your decision.

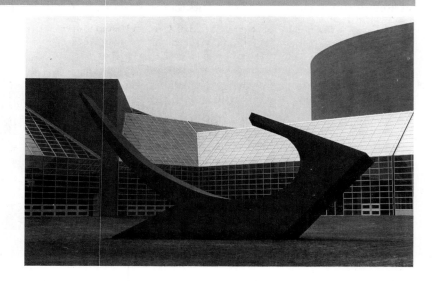

Figure 19.38   Ronald Bladen. *Sonar Tide.* **1982. Civic Center, Peoria, Illinois**

History

What name was given to artists who painted pictures like this? Do you think this name describes clearly their style of painting? Why has it been said that artists like Kenneth Noland were indebted to Josef Albers? How is this painting similar to paintings done by Albers (see Figure 2.18)? How is it different?

Figure 19.39 Kenneth Noland. *Across.* 1964. Acrylic resin on canvas, 2.46 x 3.2 m [8′1″ x 10′6″]. Private Collection, courtesy of the André Emmerich Gallery, New York

Criticism

Identify the colors, lines, and shapes in this work. Are the shapes here simple or complex? Is there any suggestion of space? If so, how is this achieved? How have repetition and contrast been used to unify this painting? What is unusual about the overall shape of this painting?

Figure 19.40 Frank Stella. *Agbatana III.* 1968. Fluorescent acrylic on canvas, 3.05 x 4.57 m [10 x 15′]. Allen Memorial Art Museum, Oberlin College, Oberlin, Ohio. Ruth C. Roush Fund for Contemporary Art and National Foundation for the Arts and Humanities Grant, 68.37

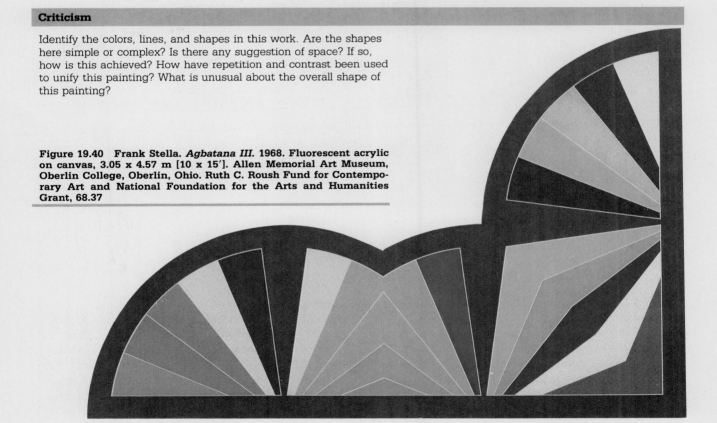

Why do you think this style of art became so popular in the 1970s? Is this a completely new style of painting, or is it a restatement of some earlier style? Explain your answer.

Figure 19.41 Alfred Leslie. *7 A.M. News.* **1976-78. Oil on canvas, 2.13 x 1.52 m [7 x 5']. Allan Frumkin Gallery, New York**

a huge scale, Stella painted designs that would complement the unique shapes of his canvases. He used a wide range of intense colors to create a vivid visual movement. Thin white lines, actually the unpainted white of the canvas, help define shapes and set off the colors. These white lines, along with large repeated protractor-like shapes, act as unifying elements. They hold the brightly colored work together in a unified whole.

A Debt to Josef Albers

Hard-edge painters as well as Minimalists and Op artists all owed a great deal to an artist named Josef Albers. A respected artist and teacher in his native Germany, Albers came to the United States in 1933. From 1949 until the end of his life, he worked on a single series of paintings called *Homage to the Square* (Figure 2.18, page 30). They were all concerned with color and color relationships. All of these paintings had nearly the same dimensions and content. They were composed of symmetrically arranged square shapes of different sizes and colors. By varying the types of colors that he placed next to each other, Albers could create various optical effects. Thus, when you examine one of his paintings at length, you will find that some of the colored squares seem to expand and contract, while others appear to advance or retreat.

Photo-Realism

One of the leading art styles of the 1970s was Photo-Realism. Its instant success may have been due to the exaggerated homage it paid to the literal qualities. It was these qualities that abstract and nonobjective artists had objected to earlier.

Alfred Leslie

Photo-Realists like Alfred Leslie turned away from abstract art and looked to the past for models. One of Leslie's models was Caravaggio. He used that artist's technique to paint huge genre works with a modern flavor. In the *7 A.M. News* (Figure 19.41), Leslie shows a woman alone reading a newspaper. On a table next to her, a television set flickers. The woman's face is illuminated by the harsh, artificial light of the television. In this can be seen a reminder of the divine light found in Carvaggio's painting of *The Conversion of St. Paul* (Figure 14.6, page 249). News comes to this woman from television and the newspaper. The message in *The Conversion of St. Paul* came via a voice from heaven. However, the woman looks as if she senses something is missing in the message she is getting from the mass media. What she sees and reads may leave her feeling empty and alone. (Notice that there are no words on the newspaper.) The message she receives may reflect only the mundane realities of the electronic age in which she lives. As a result, this woman may be trying to re-establish a more meaningful communication with a divine source.

Andrew Wyeth

Although he is not regarded as a Photo-Realist, Andrew Wyeth is noted for paintings in which careful attention is directed to the literal qualities. It would be a mistake, however, to think of his works as merely "photographic." They are much more than this. In his paintings, Wyeth tries to go beyond showing what people or places look like. Instead, he tries to capture their essence.

Criticism

List everything you see in this painting. Would you describe this painting as lifelike? What is the boy doing? What seems to dominate in this picture, the boy or the hill? Describe the colors used. Do these colors suggest warmth or coldness? What mood or feeling do you associate with this picture? How does it make *you* feel? Is this a successful painting? What reasons can you give to support your judgment?

Figure 19.42   Andrew Wyeth. *Winter, 1946.* **1946. Tempera on board, approx. 80 × 122 cm [31 × 48″]. North Carolina Museum of Art, Raleigh, NC.**

Like his father, the well-known illustrator N.C. Wyeth, he feels that an artist can paint well only those things that the artist knows thoroughly. To acquire this knowledge the artist must live with a subject, study it, and become a part of it.

Andrew Wyeth was born in Chadds Ford, Pennsylvania, a small country town in which he still lives. Since he was not a healthy child, he had to stay home for long periods of time and had few friends his own age. His father became his closest friend and constant companion. Before Andrew was sixteen, he began studying art with his father, and from that point on they drew and painted together every day.

In 1945, Andrew Wyeth's father was killed in an automobile-train accident. Perhaps Andrew's grief was increased by the realization that he had never painted a picture of his father. No doubt he thought of his father constantly in the months following his death, particularly when hiking across the Pennsylvania countryside they once roamed together. His paintings of that countryside seem to reflect his grief and loss. Typical of those works is his *Winter, 1946* (Figure 19.42), painted a year after his father's death. In this painting a solitary boy runs down a hill. This particular hill appears in many of his best-known works. The place where his father died is on the other side of this hill, in the direction from which the boy in the painting is running.

Painting in Canada: A Passion for Nature

Modern Canadian art, which barely existed before the twentieth century, can trace its origins to 1920 and a small group of landscape painters working in Toronto. These painters eventually came to be known as the *Group of Seven.*

The Group of Seven

The paintings of this group did much to direct public attention away from a cautious acceptance of European styles by exposing viewers to a unique Canadian art style.

Although the first Group of Seven exhibition was held in 1920, several of the artists involved had been working together for a number of years. They often went on group sketching trips, which sometimes took them to isolated parts of Canada. There they experi-

enced the beauty of their native country. This inspired them to create art that expressed their increased national pride. It was this national pride, so obvious in their work, that won for them the admiration and respect of the public.

As founder and perhaps the best-known member of the group, Lawren Stewart Harris created energetic, Fauve-like interpretations of the Canadian wilderness. Another important group member, Alexander Young Jackson, matched Harris' use of intense color, curvilinear shapes, and spirited brushwork. In 1933 the group decided to change its name to the *Canadian Group of Painters.* After that, members began to drift in various directions to pursue individual interests. Lawren Harris, for example, began creating abstract geometric paintings.

Emily Carr

The work of Harris, Jackson, and other members of the Group of Seven played an important role in the career of Emily Carr, who was to become Canada's best-known early modern artist.

Carr first studied in San Francisco before traveling abroad to perfect her painting skills in London and Paris. Periodically she returned to Canada to teach art and to paint along the coast of British Columbia. Her first exhibition was held following her return to Victoria in 1911. However, her work failed to generate widespread interest or brisk sales. She experienced difficult times and had to support herself by making and selling carpets and pottery with Indian designs. Her lack of success even caused her to seriously consider abandoning her career in art.

But then, in 1927, Carr saw the work of the Group of Seven. This experience rekindled her desire to paint and helped focus her attention even more on the forests of British Columbia as her subject matter.

Carr saw the works of Matisse and the other Fauves while she was in Paris in 1910 and 1911. Like the painters in the Group of Seven, she was greatly impressed by the expressive qualities of those works and adapted these qualities to her own painting style. But in works like *Forest, B.C.* (Figure 19.43) one senses something more. The trees in this forest join together to create a place of great spirituality. Like stout pillars in a Medieval church, they define and protect a quiet sanctuary awaiting anyone in need of security and consolation. Painted with spiraling forms and intense colors, the work presents a personal and powerful vision of nature.

The paintings created by Emily Carr heralded a period of artistic activity that continues to grow in diversity and quality. And today her paintings rank among the most admired in Canadian art.

Criticism

What is the subject of this painting? Is this subject treated in a realistic manner? Describe the lines and shapes used. How are variety and harmony realized? Is this, in your opinion, a successful work of art? What aesthetic qualities would you refer to if asked to defend your decision?

Figure 19.43 Emily Carr. *Forest, British Columbia.* c. 1931–32. Oil on canvas, 129.8 × 86.5 cm [51 3/16 × 34 1/16"]. Collection of Vancouver Art Gallery, Vancouver, Canada. Photo by Robert Keziere.

Studio Experiences

Lesson One: Drawing Expressive Portraits

From your reading you learned that many contemporary artists no longer feel obliged to paint the outside appearances of their subjects. Willem de Kooning's *Woman VI* (Figure 19.15) reveals the person within and bares that person's feelings and emotions. Decide upon an inner feeling or emotion that you would like to use as the subject for a continuous line drawing. You might decide upon "happy," or "sad," or "angry," or "lonely." Have a friend act as a model and assume a facial expression that reflects the inner feeling you have decided upon. On a 30.5 x 46-cm [12 x 18-inch] sheet of white paper, draw your friend's face from the front (full face) in *one continuous line*. Be sure to fill most of your paper with this drawing. Do not aim for accuracy here. Instead, turn to distortion and exaggeration to emphasize the inner feeling you are trying to portray.

Lesson Two: Coloring Expressive Portraits with Oil Pastels

Contemporary artists often use color in expressive ways. They use it to accent or heighten the moods or emotions they wish to communicate through their artworks. In the same manner, using oil pastels, color the expressive portraits completed in the previous lesson. Select hues that you associate with the inner feelings portrayed in your drawing. Press down firmly on the oil pastels to produce rich, vibrant colors. Faces and backgrounds should be colored in this way.

Lesson Three: An Abstract Wire Construction

Henry Moore's *Reclining Figure* (Figure 19.18) shows a concern for volume and mass. David Smith's *Hudson River Landscape* (Figure 19.22) is composed of curved and straight lines organized along a two-dimensional plane. Smith's work represents an abstraction of a landscape. Your task during this studio experience is to design in wire your own abstract landscape. First, complete several small sketches of landscapes. Choose the one that most appeals to you and reproduce it on a larger scale. Eliminate all but the most essential curved and straight lines in this landscape. Next, cut a 91-cm [36-inch] length of 14- or 16-gauge steel wire and fasten one end to a wood base. Carefully bend this wire to replicate your abstract landscape drawing. Your sculpture should reveal a variety of straight and curved lines organized along a two-dimensional plane. Use only the single length of wire and do not solder, tie, or glue the joints to gain support strength. Support should come from the material itself and the forms into which it is bent. The completed freestanding form must reveal an obvious horizontal or vertical emphasis.

Chapter 20

Centuries of Tradition in the East: The Art of China and Japan

Artists you will meet in this chapter:

Lei (lah *ee*), twenty-second century B.C. The sister of an early emperor, she is said to be the first Chinese painter.

Ku K'ai-chih (*koo kih* chuh), born c. 345. One of the early Chinese painters, he was known for his painting, wit, and foolishness.

Han Kan (*hahn kahn*), eighth century. A thorough knowledge of his subject matter was put to good use in a painting of the emperor's favorite horse.

Wu Tao-tze (woo *tow* tzeh), born c. 700. One of his wall paintings was as famous in China as Michelangelo's Sistine Ceiling was in Europe.

Kuo Hsi (*koo* oo *see*), born 1100. His paintings were intended to make viewers feel as if they were in the places pictured.

Ch'ien Hsüan (chee *en* syoo en), c. 1235–1301. His paintings are marked by a carefully studied understatement.

Chao-Meng-fu (*chow* meeng *foo*), 1254–1322. His paintings are marked by a carefully studied understatement.

Sōami Kangaku Shinso (*so* ah mee—*kahng* ah koo *sheen* soh), died 1525. His painted screen of a peaceful landscape was welcomed during a period of turmoil and fear.

Hishikawa Moronobu (hee *shee* kah wah moh *roh* noh boo), 1618–1694. He is credited with producing the first Japanese woodblock prints.

Torii Kiyonobu I (to ree *ee* key *yoh* noh boo), 1752–1815. An actor's son, he often used actors as subjects for his popular prints.

Katsushika Hokusai (kaht soo *shee* kah hoh *koo* sah ee), 1760–1849. He claimed that he was born at age fifty, when he felt he was finally prepared as an artist.

Ichiyū-sai—Ando—Hiroshige (ee chee *ee* sah ee—*ahn* do—hee *roh* shee geh), 1797–1858. His works reveal a sensitive concern for the weather and changing seasons.

Soga Shohaku (*sho* gah sho *hah* koo), 1730–1783. His paintings of two Zen monks suggest that they may not be as foolish as they seem.

The Beginnings of Chinese Civilization

Chinese civilization, which began some two thousand years before the birth of Christ, can lay claim to being the oldest continuous culture in the world. As this civilization grew, its people gained skill and knowledge in many different fields. We are indebted to them for such accomplishments as inventing the compass, paper, printing with carved wood blocks, and porcelain.

Skill in bronze casting was developed at an early date in Chinese history. Bronze vessels found in ancient graves reveal that Chinese artisans were exercising this skill by the first dynasty. This dynasty was known as the *Shang* and was founded in 1766 B.C. Many of the early bronze vessels show extraordinary technical mastery and hint at centuries of development (Figure 20.1). The surfaces of these vessels were covered with decorations that often included dragons, birds, and masks done in bold relief.

The art of painting is mentioned in Chinese literature several centuries before the birth of Christ. Painting has continued to be a valued art form ever since. According to tradition, the first Chinese painter was a woman named Lei. She was the sister of the Emperor Shun (2255 to 2205 B.C.), who numbered among his accomplishments an improved calendar and a standardized system of weights and measures. No doubt he was also fondly remembered by generations of Chinese school children for having reduced the size of the whip used to encourage pupils to attend to their studies.

History

Do you think this bronze vessel shows great technical skill? Why is it safe to assume that centuries of development were required before vessels of this quality could be produced? Describe the decorations noted on the surface of this work. Is this type of decoration crude or sophisticated?

Figure 20.1   Vessel: Li-Ting. Chinese, Shang dynasty. Bronze, 19.1 x 14.6 cm [7½ x 5¾"]. The Metropolitan Museum of Art, New York. Gift of Mrs. John Marriott, Mrs. John Barry Ryna, Gilbert Kahn, and Roger Wolfe Kahn, 1949

Unfortunately, no paintings have survived from these early periods of Chinese history. But written reports tell us that paintings of great skill and beauty were created and were appreciated.

The Chow Dynasty, which followed the Shang Dynasty in 1030 B.C., apparently produced few artistic changes. This dynasty eventually disintegrated into warring states and continued to be fragmented until the powerful Han Dynasty was founded in 206 B.C.

The Arrival of Buddhism during the Han Dynasty

It was near the end of the Han Dynasty that Buddhism, which originated in India, came to China.* This religion had a great impact on the way artists approached their work. It also helped raise artists to a position of respect and admiration in Chinese society. The Chinese people were the first to consider the painting of pictures as an important and honorable task and placed the artist on the same level as poets, who were very highly regarded.

Buddhism offered comfort to the weary and hope for an eternity of peace in the next world. It recognized the existence of people who had attained a state of enlightenment and who had either postponed death or made the decision to return to the world for the purpose of bringing comfort and offering guidance to the living.

★ **Enrichment** More than five hundred years before Christ was born, a prince named Siddhartha Gotama gained fame in India because of his holiness and love for all creatures. He came to be called *the Buddha,* which means "the Enlightened One." Buddha did not claim to be of divine origin, nor did he claim to receive inspiration from gods. He meditated but did not pray to a Higher Being. After his death in 483 B.C., temples were built in his honor and his beliefs spread throughout Asia. Fundamental to those beliefs is the return of the soul or spirit in other forms of life. Evildoers return as animals or unfortunate humans. The good return in progressively higher and more fortunate conditions of life until they are worthy of *Nirvana.* This is a blissful state in which one is free of all desires. Once this final state is attained, the person is never born again.

Such a person was known as a *Bodhisattva* (boh-dee-*saht*-vah) or "Buddha-to-be." Figure 20.2 shows a type of Bodhisattva, a gilt bronze statue called a *Maitreya*, the "Buddha of the Future." It is also one of the largest of its kind to survive to the present day. With a serene smile he extends his open hands in a sign of welcome and a promise of peace that must have been reassuring and calming to those who saw him.

Unlike ancient Greek sculptors who recognized the beauty of the human body and tried to capture that beauty in their sculptures, Chinese sculptors did not regard the body as a thing of beauty. This, combined with the fact that they did not regard sculpture as one of the important arts, caused them to limit their sculpture production to religious portraits like the Bodhisattva in Figure 20.2.

The Importance of Meditation

Buddhism, like other Eastern religions, places great emphasis on meditation. It is important to be aware of this emphasis because it had great impact on Chinese art.

During meditation a person focuses his or her thoughts on a single object or idea. In this way the inherent beauty or meaning of that object or idea can be completely experienced. Thus, it is not unusual for Buddhist monks to remain motionless in meditation for hours, or even entire days. They may contemplate a leaf sagging from the weight of raindrops, or the possible meanings of a single word. Influenced by these monks, Chinese artists found that long periods of time spent in meditation enabled them to recognize the beauty of a leaf, a tree, a rock, or a mountain. They were then better prepared to capture that beauty in their painting.

Ku K'ai-chih

The names of individual artists from the Han period are known because written reports about them and their works have survived. Unfortunately, their paintings did not. * The only artist of the period whose name is linked

★ Enrichment Few Oriental paintings existed for a significant period of time due to the fragile nature of the material on which they were painted. The paintings of the Far East were never done on canvas. Occasionally they were wall frescoes, and in more recent periods they were painted on paper. But for the most part, they were painted on silk, which is not a durable material.

Criticism

Describe the garment this figure is wearing. Does this appear to be a realistic portrait? What kinds of lines are used? How do these lines help unify the sculpture? Does this figure appear to be friendly or unfriendly? What aesthetic qualities are most valuable to you when making and defending a judgment about this sculpture?

Figure 20.2 Standing Buddha (front view). Chinese, Wei dynasty. Fifth century. Gilt bronze sculpture, 1.4 m [4'7"] high. The Metropolitan Museum of Art, New York. Kennedy Fund

to any surviving pictures is Ku K'ai-chih, who was born in the middle of the fourth century.

Apparently Ku K'ai-chih was a man of great talent with a unique personality. Not surprisingly, many legends grew up around him. One of the most popular of these concerns his romance with a young girl who lived in the house next to his. Finally summoning the courage, he proposed to her and was crushed when she refused his offer of marriage. Returning to his house, he painted a picture of her on a wall and stuck a thorn into her heart. Soon the girl mysteriously became ill. When all efforts to cure her failed, her family began preparing for her death. Ku K'ai-chih took this opportunity to renew his proposal of marriage, and this time the girl accepted. Elated, he removed the thorn and the girl was immediately restored to health.

When discussing Ku K'ai-chih, contemporary writers have not limited their discussions to his painting skills or the many legends about him. They also mention his unusual speech and behavior, claiming that he was outstanding in three fields: painting, wit, and foolishness.

Increased Concern for Landscape Painting

For over a thousand years, beginning with the Han Dynasty in 206 B.C., the human figure dominated in Chinese painting, just as it did in the West. But by the ninth century, Chinese artists were beginning to exhibit a greater appreciation for nature. By the eleventh century this trend was complete. While Western artists continued to focus their attention on people, artists in China preferred to concentrate on nature.

The landscape was the primary interest and the major accomplishment of Chinese painting. Artists, like poets, sought out places in which they could meditate and be inspired to create. They valued every opportunity to do this, taking long, leisurely walks across the countryside.

When an artist named Tsung Ping found himself to be too old for such activity, he must have been heartbroken. In a short essay, however, he explained how he was able to overcome this loss. He re-experienced his earlier travels by painting the landscapes that lived in his memories on the walls of his room. Looking at those paintings, he wrote, aroused the same feelings he had experienced when viewing the real scenes.

To gain the knowledge and skills needed to continue in the tradition of painting landscapes, Chinese artists spent years copying the paintings of earlier artists. It was common to base a painting on the work of an earlier artist, but the painter was also expected to add some personal touches as well.

Scroll Painting

In addition to a few murals on the walls of burial chambers, the earliest Chinese paintings that have survived to the present are of two kinds: hanging scrolls and horizontal or handscrolls.

Scrolls were designed to be rolled and carefully stored away. When their owners were in the mood for quiet reflection, the scrolls were taken from the shelf just as we might take down a book to read. Unrolling the scrolls section by section, the viewer gazed on no more than two feet or so at a time. In this way it was possible to journey slowly from scene to scene through the entire painting.

The End of the Han Dynasty

The Han Dynasty produced a culture that rivaled that of the Roman Empire, which was flourishing at this same time in history. The Han Dynasty extended over a four hundred year period, the second longest in Chinese history.

Due to a series of weak emperors, the Han empire ended. It was followed by a period, beginning at the close of the third century A.D., in which China was divided into a number of smaller states. None of these states became strong enough to conquer the others in order to restore a unified empire. After a period of chaos, a new dynasty, the T'ang Dynasty, assumed control in 618 and held control for nearly three hundred years.

The Powerful T'ang Dynasty

During the T'ang Dynasty the people enjoyed prosperity, military campaigns extended the boundaries of the empire, foreign trade increased, and Buddhism grew in strength. It was a period in which China reached the peak of its power and influence.

Sculpture during the T'ang Dynasty

Most of the sculptures produced during the T'ang period were religious. Believers in Buddhism, looking forward to a peaceful life in the next world, commissioned thousands of sculptures of Buddha. Tomb sculptures, chiefly in clay, were also created to honor the dead. Many of these tomb sculptures were of animals. An excellent example is the gilt and polychrome horse illustrated in Figure 20.3.

History

Many clay sculptures like this were found in ancient Chinese tombs. Why do *you* think they were placed there? Do you think this is a successful work of art? Explain your answer.

Figure 20.3   Standing Horse. Chinese, T'ang dynasty. 618-907. Pottery tomb figure, 71 x 84 cm [28 x 33"]. The Metropolitan Museum of Art, New York. Rogers Fund

A T'ang Handscroll

Apparently horses were highly prized by the Chinese. The emperor Ming Huang was said to own over forty thousand. The handscroll in Figure 20.4 shows one of his favorite horses rearing against the tether that binds it to a post.

One of the chief measures of excellence in Chinese painting throughout its long history is the quality of the brushline, which is certainly evident in Figure 20.4. A delicate use of line is combined with subtle value graduations to give a realistic appearance to the animal. The work demonstrates convincingly that the artist, Han Kan, knew his subject well and could apply this knowledge effectively to his art.

The many inscriptions and seals placed on Han Kan's painting indicate that others appreciated his knowledge and skill. They were placed there by collectors who wished to express their approval of the work. These inscriptions and seals, which are found on many Chinese paintings, have become a part of the work and add their own ornamentation and meaning.

Wu Tao-tze

Perhaps the greatest painter of the T'ang period was Wu Tao-tze. He is said to have created three hundred beautiful fresco paintings on the walls of Buddhist temples throughout China. One of these included over one hundred figures and became as famous in China as Michelangelo's Sistine Ceiling or Leonardo's *Last Supper* in Europe. This famous painting by Wu Tao-tze, like all his other works, has not survived. The loss is an important one if we attach any significance to the legends told about this artist's abilities.

Criticism

Does this horse look pampered or abused? What clues did you refer to when answering the previous question? Would you describe the lines used here as delicate or bold? Explain. How has gradation been used in this work? Why does this animal look agitated? Does this work make good use of the literal qualities? Does it make good use of the visual qualities? Does it make good use of the expressive qualities?

Figure 20.4   Han Kan. *Night-Shining White.* Chinese. Between 742-756. Ink on paper, 34 x 30.8 cm [13⅜ x 12⅛"]. The Metropolitan Museum of Art, New York. The Dillon Fund.

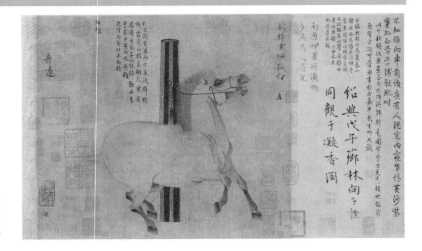

According to one of these legends, Wu Tao-tze was sent by his emperor to draw the scenery along a certain river. When he returned, however, he did not have a single drawing to show the emperor. Asked to explain himself, the artist claimed that he had the scene stored in his head and in his heart. Then, isolating himself in a room in the palace, he drew a hundred miles of landscape.

None of the legends about this remarkable artist are as fascinating as the one concerning his death. When he felt he had lived long enough, he painted a grand landscape. Then, having put his affairs in order, the artist stepped into the mouth of a cave pictured in the painting. He was never seen again.

A Period of Stability and Great Art

Following the collapse of the T'ang Dynasty in 906, China experienced a period of confusion. Finally, reunification was realized in 960 under the Sung Dynasty. The rule of this dynasty proved to be a period of great stability that produced a series of artists who created works of art that were admired for centuries.

The Production of Porcelain

During the Sung period, the production of porcelain ware perfected earlier was carried to new heights. Porcelain is made from a fine white clay known as *kaolin*. This clay is relatively rare and can be found in only a few locations in China. After a vessel is made from this clay, it is coated with a glass-like glaze containing feldspar. Then it is fired in a kiln to a high temperature. The result is a vessel with a hard, white, translucent surface of great beauty.

An excellent example of Sung porcelain ware is illustrated in Figure 20.5. Bowls like this were the first of the classic pieces that were widely imitated but seldom equaled by later artists. The bowl's delicate shape and beautiful translucent surface is enhanced with a subtle pattern of leaves. Because some of these vessels were fired upside down, the rims were left unglazed so they would not fuse to the kiln shelf on which they were placed. These rims were often covered with a metal rim in the manner you see in Figure 20.5.

Sculpture during the Sung Dynasty

Sung sculpture remained strongly tied to Buddhism although the figures that were created were more

History

What material was used to make this bowl? Which of the following terms seems more appropriate when describing this bowl: shiny or dull? crude or delicate? rough or smooth? Do you think handling this bowl would be a pleasant experience? Explain your answer.

Figure 20.5   Bowl. Chinese, Sung dynasty. 960-1230. Hard porcelaneous ware, 11.4 x 24.8 cm [4½ x 9¾"]. The Metropolitan Museum of Art, New York. Gift of Mrs. Samuel T. Peters

informal and natural than those created earlier. A painted and glazed ceramic sculpture of a follower of Buddha (Figure 20.6) is an example of this more relaxed and natural figure style. Here the seated figure is seen casually adjusting his robe. Something has momentarily captured his attention, and he turns his head to investigate.

Landscape Painting during the Sung Dynasty

The Sung Dynasty was noted for its great landscape artists. Painters like Kuo Hsi claimed that the value of landscape painting lay in its capacity to make viewers feel as if they were really in the place pictured. In a handscroll entitled *Clearing Autumn Skies Over Mountains and Valleys* (Figure 20.7), the artist invites you to join the scholars who travel beneath the trees of an enchanted mountain landscape. Such an invitation is difficult to ignore, and so . . .

Imagine that you are seated comfortably with this handscroll in your hands. What will you experience as you slowly unroll it? If you allowed yourself to meditate on each scene as it appeared, you could expect to be carried off on a magical journey alongside gently flowing streams, past quaint cottages and magnificent temples. Perhaps you would choose to pause briefly to spend time with some fishermen before striding through a bamboo grove and into an area of towering pine trees. Another scholar is encountered trudging homeward, and you greet each other with mutual respect. Continuing on, you enter a clearing at the foot of tall mountains, the tips of which peek through a fine mist. The mountains are breathtaking even though dimmed by haze and great distance. Across the clearing, a rustic wine shop offers a perfect place to rest, to experience, to think. Your pace quickens even though you are weary from your long journey . . .

Unlike Western paintings, Chinese art makes use of different vanishing points. Thus, as you unroll a handscroll, you may find that the perspective shifts. This makes you feel as though you are looking at the scene from different vantage points. The result is a strong sensation that you are indeed traveling through the work—journeying *over* worn paths, *under* stately trees, *in front of* distant mountains, and *across* quaint bridges placed there for your convenience by the thoughtful artist. Every opportunity is provided for you to stop to examine a flower heavy with dew or a butterfly perched on a blossom, or to listen to the breeze as it whistles softly through a stand of bamboo. There is nothing to distract you from your quiet contemplation. Even shadows are eliminated from the picture because they might interfere with your efforts to experience and enjoy the painting.

Criticism

Would you describe the pose of this figure as formal or informal? What does the figure seem to be doing? Does he seem to be pleasant, cheerful, or serious? If you encountered this work on a museum visit, would you stop to study it closely? Why or why not?

Figure 20.6   Figure of a Lohan. Chinese, Sung dynasty. Eleventh to twelfth centuries. Pottery. The Metropolitan Museum of Art, New York. Fletcher Fund

History

What is a handscroll? How would you view a handscroll? Why are handscrolls intended to be examined slowly, quietly, and in private? What kinds of subjects were typically painted on these handscrolls? Why was it considered necessary for Chinese artists to spend years copying the paintings of earlier artists?

Figure 20.7   Attributed to Kuo Hsi. *Clearing Autumn Skies Over Mountains and Valleys.* Chinese. Date unknown. Section of a handscroll, ink and light colors on silk, 26 cm [10¼"] high. Freer Gallery of Art, Smithsonian Institution, Washington, DC.

The End of the Sung Dynasty

In 1224 Genghis Khan and his powerful Mongol army swept into northwest China, bringing the Sung Dynasty to an end. Following a period of strife, the Mongols, under Kublai Khan, a grandson of Genghis Khan, took control of the country and established the Yüan Dynasty.

Ch'ien Hsüan

The career of the painter Ch'ien Hsüan covers the period from the fall of the Sung and the establishment of the Yüan Dynasty. Like many other Chinese artists, he chose to retire rather than to serve the new leaders of his country.★ Living in seclusion, he turned to the past for inspiration and continued to paint. His handscroll of a scholar watching geese on a lake (Figure 20.8) repeats a familiar Chinese theme—the quiet contemplation of nature.

★ **Enrichment** The reign of Kublai Khan and his successors was marked by a respect for and support of the established culture in China. These foreign rulers were more eager to make the Chinese culture part of their own culture than to impose their own Mongol culture on the Chinese.

Chao-Meng-fu

The contemplation of nature is also the theme of a painting by Chao-Meng-fu, a pupil of Ch'ien Hsüan's (Figure 20.9). This artist was greatly admired even though he chose to cooperate with the Mongol ruler Kublai Khan. His picture of pine trees, rocks, and distant mountains was done only after the artist had meditated upon the subject at great length. Because he had to be properly prepared to produce on paper the mental images that resulted from such meditation, he practiced his skills at representing trees, rocks, mountains, and clouds in a precise style for years before actually painting the picture. He did this in the traditional way—by carefully studying the paintings of earlier masters rather than by studying nature. Only when his skills were perfected did he attempt to create a painting based on his own response to the natural world.

To fully understand and appreciate a painting like this scroll, you must learn to see more than is there —you must also learn to look for what is *not* in the picture. Observe the carefully studied understatement in this work. Most of the painting is simply left blank. The landscape has been reduced to its barest essentials. Concentrating on each brushstroke, the artist applied the ink to paper with confident strokes. There was no

---

Criticism

Describe the literal qualities in this work. Identify the most important elements of art used. How are the principles of art used to organize these elements? What would be the most appropriate title for this work: "A Great Event in History," "Quiet Contemplation of Nature," "The Turning Point in a Fascinating Story," or "A Portrait of an Important Person"? What appears to be more important in this work—the figures or the setting? Why is it sometimes difficult for Western viewers to appreciate Eastern paintings like this one?

Figure 20.8 Ch'ien Hsüan. *Wang Hsi-chih Watching Geese.* Chinese, late southern Sung to early Yüan dynasty. Handscroll, ink, color, and gold on paper, 23.2 x 92.7 cm [9⅛ x 36½"]. The Metropolitan Museum of Art, New York. Gift of the Dillon Fund, 1973

room for error, no opportunity to erase a misplaced mark. And yet the artist had to work quickly to capture the mental impressions he received when meditating about the scene. Years of practice enabled him to work swiftly and flawlessly.* Further, he knew exactly when it was time to stop and set his brush aside. He painted no more than was absolutely necessary to portray the subject and convey the mood.

It is important to remember that works like this were not done to tell a dramatic story, teach a profound lesson, or decorate a wall of a house. They were intended to inspire the same deep thoughts in the viewer that passed through the mind of the artist while the work was created. A work like this would only be unrolled and savored when the viewer was in the proper state of mind and was certain not to be disturbed.

★ **Enrichment** The art of calligraphy, or fine handwriting, was practiced for years by students before they became painters. This study was regarded as essential because painting depended upon the distinctive quality of each and every brushstroke.

The Art of the Ming Dynasty

The Ming Dynasty, which followed the collapse of the Yüan Dynasty in 1368, signified the end of foreign rule and the beginning of another Chinese dynasty. Thus, it was a time in which artists sought to restore the glories of the past. In painting, nature scenes of great beauty were done on silk and paper. Mainly these were done in a manner that continued the traditions of the past.

A range of different styles and techniques are noted in the ceramics produced during the Ming Dynasty. The use of a stunning cobalt blue glaze at this time is regarded as one of the major accomplishments in the development of Chinese porcelain. An early example of a covered vase (Figure 20.10) is admired for the intricate design that complements its elegant form.

Tribes from Manchuria conquered China in 1644. This brought the Ming Dynasty to an end and ushered in the Ch'ing Dynasty, which continued until 1912. Like other conquerors before them, Manchu rulers were determined to make the Chinese culture part of their own. However, despite the work done by several well-known and talented artists and the encouragement of Manchu emperors, Chinese painting experienced a decline during this period.

History

Why is it important for the viewer to learn what *not* to look for in a painting like this? How does the treatment of space in this work differ from the treatment of space in Western paintings?

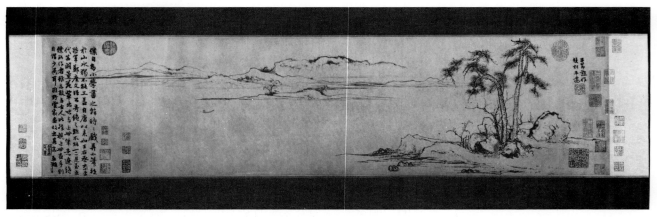

Figure 20.9   Chao-Meng-fu. *Twin Pines Against a Flat Vista.* **Chinese, Yüan dynasty. Early fourteenth century. Handscroll, ink on paper, 26.67 x 106.68 cm [10½ x 42″]. The Metropolitan Museum of Art, New York. Gift of the Dillon Fund, 1973 (1973.120.5)**

History

Why were foreign conquerors determined to preserve and adopt Chinese culture? What important innovation is evident on this vase? What adjectives would you use when describing the decoration and the form of this vase?

Figure 20.10   Vase with cover. Chinese, late Yüan to early Ming dynasties. Third quarter of fourteenth century. Porcelain, painted in underglaze blue, 44.5 cm [17.5″] high. The Metropolitan Museum of Art, New York. Rogers Fund, 1926

Porcelain production fared somewhat better than painting. During this last great age of Chinese porcelain, large quantities of fine works were produced. Unfortunately, rebellion and subsequent warfare in the middle of the nineteenth century resulted in the destruction or closing of most kilns and the flight of craftspeople into a disordered world.

The Early Development of Japanese Art

The first traces of Japanese art date to about 5000 B.C. and a culture known as *Jomon.* The earliest artworks consist mainly of simple, undecorated vessels, figures, and animals made of red clay (Figure 20.11). Curiously, many clay pieces in the form of figures and animals have been discovered in the areas surrounding burial mounds. This has caused some experts to suggest that they were placed there to ward off evil spirits and protect the dead.

Until the end of the ninth century, the art of Japan was largely modeled on that of China and other Oriental cultures. After that time, however, foreign influences became less pronounced and Japanese artists began to develop their own styles. In the centuries that followed, various subjects grew in favor, faded, and were replaced by new ones. At certain times, scenes of life at court, witty caricatures, and portraits were popular. Other favorite subjects included battle scenes, genre scenes, and landscapes.

Our examination of the development of Japanese art begins in 552 A.D., when the ruler of a kingdom in Korea sent a gilt bronze figure of the Buddha to the Emperor of Japan. Along with the sculpture came Buddhist writings and missionaries. This is how Buddhism was introduced to Japan.

At first, there was resistance to the new religion, particularly by those who chose to remain faithful to Shinto,★ the indigenous religion of Japan. But eventually Buddhism became firmly established throughout the country and came to affect every aspect of Japanese culture.

★ **Enrichment** Shinto, or *Way of the Gods,* originated in early Japan. It is a religion based on ancestor worship and a love of nature, family, and, above all, the ruling family, the members of which were regarded as direct descendants of the gods.

Criticism

Would you describe this horse as realistic? Do you think the surface of this sculpture would feel rough or smooth to the touch? Discuss the principles of art used in this work. Does this work communicate any feeling or emotions? If not, does this lessen its appeal? What do *you* find most interesting about this work?

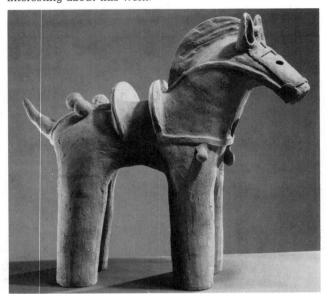

Figure 20.11   Haniwa Horse. Japanese. Third to sixth centuries. Terra cotta, 59.7 x 66 cm [23½ x 26"]. The Cleveland Museum of Art. The Norweb Collection

Temple Construction

In the year 594, the Empress Suiko ordered that Buddhist temples be built throughout her realm. Prince Shotoku was charged with the responsibility of seeing that this edict was carried out. He brought from Korea architects, wood carvers, bronze workers, clay modelers, weavers, and other skilled artisans to build and decorate the temples that soon filled the countryside.

In many respects these temples were similar to those in China. They were, however, more richly decorated and more delicately assembled. Because the Japanese islands were formed from volcanic rock, there was little hard stone suitable for building these temples. Consequently, these and other structures were made of wood.

Japanese builders raised the art of constructing wooden buildings to a sophisticated art form. Their temples and palaces were built on a stone base with wooden posts and rafters that were carefully fitted together in beautifully crafted joints. These buildings had to be especially well designed and constructed to survive the frequent earthquakes and violent storms that plagued the island nation.

The Temple at Horyuji

Among the greatest architectural achievements in Japan was the temple complex at Horyuji (sometimes written as *Horyu-ji*),* built near Nara about the year 616. The temple was built on a square plan surrounded by a double wall. Inside were two pagodas** containing sacred relics, the main hall containing a sculpture of the Buddha, a lecture hall, a library, and a bell tower. It is something of a miracle that one of these ancient wooden structures, a pagoda, has survived countless earthquakes and outlasted thousands of stone edifices. It still stands today as the oldest wooden structure in the world (Figure 20.12). However, its fame does not rest on age alone. Few structures in history have surpassed its simple majesty.

The Temple and Treasures at Todaiji

Perhaps as beautiful, and only slightly younger, is the temple of Todaiji (Todai-ji) in Nara, which was erected by the Emperor Shomu in 752 (Figure 20.13). Four years after the temple was completed the emperor died. Not long after his death, his widow, the Empress Komoyo, presented the treasures of his court to the Great Buddha enshrined at Todaiji. Other gifts were later added to these treasures and were housed and protected in the temple. As a result, no less than ten thousand works of eighth century Japanese art were preserved.

★ **Enrichment** This temple complex was built during a period of Japanese history known as the *Asuka Period,* which spanned the years from 538 to 645. It is customary to name the various periods in Japanese history according to the name of the capital city. The capital at this time was Asuka.

★★ **Enrichment** A pagoda is a tower in which each story is marked by a gently flaring roof.

History

What makes this particular structure so important in art history? Point to the features on this building that are found on all pagodas. What kind of temple complex included this pagoda: Christian, Moslem, or Buddhist? How was this religion introduced to Japan? From were did it come?

Figure 20.12 Pagoda from the temple complex at Horyuji, near Nara, Japan. c. 616

Criticism

What impression is created as you look at the three views of this temple? Describe this structure by referring to the lines used. Does it look pleasant and inviting, or ominous and forbidding? What, in your opinion, makes this a successful work of art?

Figure 20.13 Temple at Todaiji, Nara, Japan. 752

Among the artworks preserved at Todaiji is a painting on silk regarded as one of the temple's greatest treasures (Figure 20.14). It portrays the Buddha, surrounded by Bodhisattvas, preaching in the mountains. Although retouched in the twelfth century, this painting still testifies to the high quality of eighth-century Buddhist painting.

The Japanese took pleasure and pride in building huge sculptures. Examples are plentiful, but certainly one of the most impressive is the Great Buddha at Todaiji. In the year 747, when an epidemic of smallpox broke out in Japan, the emperor ordered this gigantic bronze Buddha to be created to pacify the gods. The sculptor used 437 tons of bronze, 228 pounds of gold, 165 pounds of mercury, seven tons of wax, and several tons of charcoal. Two years and seven attempts were required to successfully complete the casting. The head was cast in a single mold, but the body was formed of several metal plates that were soldered together and then coated with gold. Over 16.2 m [53 feet] high, the figure presents with remarkable simplicity the Buddha as a powerful but gentle teacher and savior.

Criticism

Identify the most important figure in this composition. What has been done to emphasize this figure? (When answering, be sure to mention such elements of art as color, intensity, and shape, in addition to the principles of variety and proportion.) What kind of person do you think this figure represents: an important king, a powerful military leader, or a great religious teacher?

Figure 20.14 *Hokke Mandara Representing the Shaka Trinity Surrounded by Devas, Bodhisattvas and Monks in a Landscape.* **Chinese. Late eighth to early ninth centuries. Silk panel, 107.4 x 144.3 cm [42.3 x 56.8"]. The Museum of Fine Arts, Boston. Bigelow Collection**

A Japanese Painting Style

In 784, Heian (the modern city of Kyoto) was made the capital of Japan. The name Heian has since been used to identify a period regarded as a golden age for Japanese art. During the four hundred years of this period, numerous new temples and monasteries were founded. Also during this period, members of the royal court and the heads of great families commissioned painters to create works of art.

Contacts with China continued until 898 when ties were broken as a consequence of internal strife in Japan. Unable to any longer draw inspiration from China, Japanese artists developed their own unique style of painting, which was known as *Yamato-e,* or "painting in the Japanese manner." Artists using this style created decorative wall paintings showing travelers on the road, nobles admiring cherry blossoms or hunting, and peasants working in the fields. These spirited scenes of everyday life included clear references to particular seasons of the year. Unfortunately, only a handful of works dating to this period have survived.

The Kamakura Period

A series of civil wars prompted by corrupt provincial governments brought an end to the Heian period in 1185. Clan leaders waged war with one another until one leader, Minamoto Yoritomo, was able to establish a military government at Kamakura. As in previous periods, the name of the capital city proved to be a convenient label for the period. A succession of military rulers assumed control over various parts of the country for the next 148 years. These rulers recognized the emperor as little more than a powerless figurehead.

The Great Buddha at Kamakura

The tradition of creating colossal sculptures continued during this period with such works as the Great Buddha at Kamakura, which was cast in bronze in 1252 (Figure 20.15). Today it sits outdoors on a rise surrounded by a pleasant grove of trees. This seems to be an especially appropriate setting for the gigantic Buddha seated in quiet contemplation.

History

What material was used to make this sculpture? Is there a reason why it is located outdoors rather than within a temple? Compare and contrast this sculpture of Buddha with the one done earlier at Todaiji. Which seems more aloof? Which seems more friendly?

Figure 20.15   The Great Buddha at Kamakura. c. 1252

At one time the figure was housed in a temple, but in 1495 a great tidal wave destroyed the temple and the nearby city. When the waters subsided, the huge bronze Buddha was found calmly surveying the widespread destruction surrounding him.

The Burning of the Sanjō Palace

Painting is the most interesting visual art form from the Kamakura period due to the advances made in the Yamato-e style. These advances reflected the artistic tastes of the new military leaders, who preferred paintings that stressed realism and action. Nowhere is this realism and action more apparent than in a handscroll, *The Burning of the Sanjō Palace* (Figure 20.16).

This scroll illustrates with shocking realism a revolt that took place on the night of December 9, 1159. On that tragic night the Sanjō palace was attacked and the emperor taken prisoner. Unrolling the scroll from right to left, the viewer is immediately swept up in the frantic scene. Noblemen and their servants are seen arriving at the palace after hearing of the attack. They are too late. The palace, already ablaze, is surrounded by warriors, some of whom are forcing the emperor into a cart to carry him away. Within the palace itself the horrors of war are presented in graphic and frightening detail: palace guards are beheaded, loyal attendants are hunted down and killed, and ladies-in-waiting are trampled beneath the hoofs of horses.

As the scroll is unrolled further, the viewer is led at a less hectic pace through swarms of soldiers, horses, and carts. Finally, at the very end of the scroll—nearly 7 m [23 feet] long—a warrior astride a rearing horse is seen following a single archer (Figure 20.17). The lone figure of the archer brings the powerful narrative to a quiet end, like the final period at the end of a story. However, the manner in which this story is told is not likely to be quickly forgotten.

The Rise of Zen Buddhism

During the Kamakura period new Buddhist sects were formed. One of these, the Zen sect, was introduced from China. As you will discover, this sect was to have an impact on later Japanese art.

The Fall of the Kamakura Rulers

The power of the Kamakura military rulers ended in 1333. To their great shame this loss of power did not occur on the field of battle. Like their predecessors, they too became corrupted by power. This corruption is evident in the actions of Takatoki, the last in the line of the military rulers. He developed such a passionate fondness for dogs that he neglected the affairs of state. He eagerly accepted dogs as tax payments, and in time he collected from four to five thousand dogs, which he kept in kennels decorated with gold and silver. He fed the dogs fish and fowl and ordered that they be carried

---

Criticism

Describe what you see in this painting. What seems to be happening here? What emotions does the painting evoke in *you*? Is this a successful work of art? What aesthetic qualities would you identify to support your judgment?

Figure 20.16   *The Burning of the Sanjō Palace*. Japanese, Kamakura Period. Second half of thirteenth century. Portion of handscroll: ink and colors on paper, 16.3″ x 12′ [41.3 cm x 7 m]. The Museum of Fine Arts, Boston. Fenollosa Collection

Compare this scene with the scene from the same hand-scroll illustrated in Figure 20.16. Why does the handscroll format seem especially suitable for telling a story of this kind? What emotions are communicated by this final scene in the long narrative? Describe your overall impressions of the two scenes from this handscroll.

Figure 20.17 *The Burning of the Sanjō Palace.* Another portion of the handscroll.

about in covered litters by his servants. The emperor, who was powerless at the time, saw in this unusual behavior a sign of weakness and an opportunity to regain control, and following a series of defeats, the emperor was ultimately able to claim victory. As for Takatoki, he fled to a temple and together with 870 of his generals and servants committed suicide.

Unfortunately political unrest did not end with Takatoki's death. Civil war again broke out and continued until 1573. Somehow the arts managed to flourish during this period of almost continuous unrest and conflict.

The growing appeal of Zen Buddhism resulted in the popularity of art forms associated with that religion. Zen's appeal may have been due to the fact that it offered people an escape from the chaos that marked daily life. A desire to escape reality may have motivated artists as well. For example, when a painter named Sōami took up ink and paper to create a design for a screen, he chose as his subject a quiet and peaceful landscape rather than an event marked by conflict and horror (Figure 20.18). His finished paintings were mounted on two screens illustrating the four seasons. Reading from right to left in the same manner as a

What was Japan like during the period in which this work was completed? Why were works like this popular during this period? How does this painting make you feel?

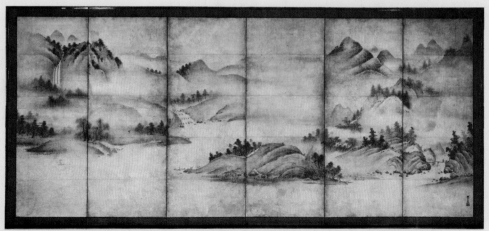

Figure 20.18 Sōami Kangaku Shinso. *Landscape of Four Seasons.* **Japanese. Early sixteenth century. Ink on paper, 1.76 x 3.71 m [5′8″ x 12′2″]. The Metropolitan Museum of Art, New York. Gift of John D. Rockefeller, Jr.**

handscroll, the paintings were intended to gently draw viewers into an imaginary world of beauty and peace in which they could forget the real world of unrest and fear.

This same quest for beauty and peace was undertaken by architects. The result can be seen in carefully proportioned pavilions set in the midst of splendid gardens. One such structure, the Golden Pavilion at Kyoto, was erected in 1397.

A period known as the *Momoyama* marked a time in which a succession of three dictators, or *shoguns*, finally restored unity and brought peace to the troubled land. During this era, huge palaces were built (Figure 20.19). These palaces served two purposes—they were both protective fortresses and symbols of power. Inside these structures sliding doors and large screens were decorated with gold leaf and painted with a range of different subjects.

A Rich Era of Art

In 1615, Iyeyasu Tokugawa overwhelmed the forces of rival military leaders in a battle that left forty thousand dead. Victory enabled him to build a new capital at Edo (Tokyo) and establish the Edo rule, which continued until 1867. This period represents one of the longest periods of peace and one of the richest eras for art in all history.

Peace brought about a prosperous middle class even as the once powerful warrior class declined in importance and number. This new middle class demanded artworks that showed the life of the people rendered in new techniques. Demands such as these led to the development of the Ukiyo-e style, which means *Pictures of the Passing World.*

Woodblock Printing
Since painting produced only one picture at a time, artists searched for other ways to satisfy the increased

History

Discuss the differences between this castle and more familiar European castles such as those illustrated in Chapter 9, Figures 9.8 and 9.9. What two purposes were served by these Japanese castles?

Figure 20.19   Hikone Castle on southeast shore of Lake Biwa, Japan. 1603-23

demand for art. A solution was found in the woodblock printing process that had been introduced from China in the eighth century. This process involved transferring and cutting pictures into wood blocks, inking the surface of these blocks, and printing. Using this technique an artist could produce as many inexpensive prints as needed.

Originally prints were made with black ink on white paper. If color was desired, it was necessary to add it by hand. But in the eighteenth century a process for producing multicolored prints was developed. This process required the talents of a painter, a wood carver, and a printer. The artist first prepared a design in ink, adding color notations to guide the printer. The lines of the design were then transferred to a wood block, and a specialist in wood cutting carved away the wood between the lines. A separate block was prepared for each color. Finally, the printer inked each block and pressed each one against the paper, being careful to align the blocks exactly. Since hundreds of copies could be made from one set of blocks, the prints produced were relatively inexpensive.

Hishikawa Moronobu

Around the middle of the seventeenth century, a designer of dress patterns named Hishikawa Moronobu produced the first woodblock prints. At first these were used as illustrations for books, but later they were sold separately. Moronobu's work was appealing due to the artist's charming style. With clear and precise lines he was able to record the grace of a female figure. At the same time he skillfully organized the interplay of black lines against white paper to achieve a striking effect.

Torii Kiyonobu I

Moronobu paved the way for other artists who soon began producing individual prints with a similar style and technique. Included among these artists is Torii Kiyonobu I, an actor's son who often selected as his subjects actors from the Kabuki theater.★ His picture of a woman dancer (Figure 20.20) uses a characteristic bold line that flows across the paper to create a complex yet graceful rhythm.

★ **Enrichment** The Kabuki theater provided a popular form of drama. It was developed as a more easily understood, enjoyable form of entertainment than the highly stylized plays favored by the nobility.

Criticism

Describe this work in terms of its literal qualities and the elements of art used. Which of the elements—value, line, or texture—seems to be especially important in this work? Explain how variety and harmony are achieved. What does the figure seem to be doing? Does the figure look realistic? If not, is this reason enough to dismiss this as a poor work of art? What aesthetic qualities could you turn to when supporting a positive judgment about this work?

Figure 20.20 Attributed to Torii Kiyonobu I. A Woman Dancer, or possibly Tsugawa Handayu as a dancer holding a fan and a wand and wearing a large hat. Japanese. c. 1708. Woodblock print, 55.2 x 29.2 cm [21¾ x 11½"]. The Metropolitan Museum of Art, New York. Harris Brisbane Dick Fund and Rogers Fund, 1949

Suzuki Harunobu

The first multicolored prints were probably done by Suzuki Harunobu. Examining his prints (see page 304) reveals that he endowed his female figures with an almost supernatural grace. They appear to have weightless bodies with slender waists and tiny hands and feet. Rarely do their faces betray any signs of emotion or stress.

Harunobu, along with Katsushika Hokusai and Ichiyū-sai Hiroshige, produced many of the works that were to inspire the French Impressionists in the nineteenth century.

Katsushika Hokusai

Hokusai was fond of saying that he "was born at the age of fifty." By this he meant that long years of preparation were required before he was able to produce works of merit.

From about 1825 to 1831 Hokusai published his brilliant Mount Fuji series of prints. In spite of its title, "Thirty-six Views of Mount Fuji," there are actually forty-six scenes included in the series. In this group of prints he adopted a low angle of vision to increase the dramatic impact. One of these prints, *The Great Wave off Kanagawa* (Figure 20.21), shows Mount Fuji in the distance, beyond a huge wave that threatens to destroy the fishing boats that are almost lost in the violently churning sea.

Hokusai was a humble man destined to be ranked among the great artists of history. As death approached, he could only claim that "if the gods had given me only ten more years I could have become a truly great painter."

Ichiyū-sai Hiroshige

Although he greatly admired Hokusai and was greatly influenced by him, the younger Hiroshige did not adopt his predecessor's spirited style. Instead, he used delicate lines and a harmonious color scheme to give nature a more subdued atmosphere. He often unified a scene by giving it an overall darkness of tone that captures the sadness of a rainy scene (Figure 20.22). Much of the beauty of his work comes from his sensitive response to variations in the weather and changing seasons.

Criticism

Identify everything in this work. Discuss the way line variety adds to the visual interest of this composition. Discuss the different ways value is used. In what way does the addition of the fishing boats enhance this picture?

What is the only thing in the picture that does *not* seem to be in motion? Could you justify a positive judgment of this work in terms of its expressive qualities? Explain.

Figure 20.21   Katsushika Hokusai. *The Great Wave off Kanagawa.* Japanese. c. 1823-29. Woodblock print. The Museum of Fine Arts, Boston. Spaulding Collection

What technique was used to produce artworks like this? Where did this technique originate? When was it introduced to Japan? Briefly describe the steps involved in this technique. Why did Japanese artists adopt this technique of producing art?

Figure 20.22   Ichiyū-sai Hiroshige. *Evening Rain on the Karasaki Pine,* from the series Eight Views of Omi Province. Japanese. Nineteeth century. Woodblock print, 26 x 38.1 cm [10¼ x 15"]. The Metropolitan Museum of Art, New York. Bequest of Mrs. H. O. Havemeyer, 1929. The H. O. Havemeyer Collection

Soga Shohaku and Zen Buddhism

You read earlier that during the Kamakura period new Buddhist sects originated and grew in popularity. Indeed, the Japanese could select from many variations of Buddhism, including Zen. Those who chose Zen were largely interested in finding self-realization and bliss through quiet meditation. Some of the most interesting Japanese works of art were created by artists who were members of this sect.

In the eighteenth century, one of these artists, Soga Shohaku, completed two hanging scrolls showing a pair of Zen monks. The monks, Kanzan (Figure 20.23) and Jittoku (Figure 20.24), lived in a private world of their own, complete with an imaginary language. A first glance at their pictures might convince you that they are little more than two absurd clowns. Certainly they are not to be taken seriously.

But look more closely. Each succeeds in communicating a thoughtful message, something for viewers to meditate about, perhaps. Kanzan smiles foolishly and holds out a scroll on which one might be expected to read ideas of great significance. But the scroll is blank. Kanzan may be trying to point out the lack of meaning behind many statements that might at first seem thoughtful and profound. Meanwhile, Jittoku seems to be busily sweeping something away with an oversized broom. Perhaps he is tidying up after a long philosophical discourse. The floor is littered with useless and discarded ideas, and he has taken it upon himself to dispose of them.

Each of these ink drawings is rendered with a minimum number of brushstrokes. No more is provided here than is needed. But it is enough to tell the viewer that these two monks may not be as foolish as they look.

History

What was your first impression of these two prints? If you did not know what these two Zen monks were doing, would you have taken the time to study them closely?

What does this tell you about the value of historical inquiry?

Figure 20.23 Soga Shokaku. *Kanzan.* **Japanese. 1730-83. Hanging scroll, sumi ink on paper, painting: 124.7 × 54.4 cm [49⅛ x 21⅜"]. Dallas Museum of Art. Gift of Mr. and Mrs. Lawrence S. Pollock**

Figure 20.24 Soga Shokaku. *Jittoku.* **Japanese. 1730-38. Hanging scroll, sumi ink on paper, painting: 124.7 x 54.4 cm [49⅛ x 21⅜"]. Dallas Museum of Art. Gift of Mr. and Mrs. Lawrence S. Pollock**

Studio Experiences

Lesson One: Negative Shape Painting of a Branch

Chinese artists including Kuo Hsi and Ch'ien Hsüan were noted for the long periods of time that they devoted to studying the objects that they had chosen to use as the subjects for their art. Perhaps the same kind of careful study will add to the quality of your own studio efforts.

Select a large, leafless branch and study it closely. Note how it twists, bends, and divides into smaller branches. Examine the irregularities along its contours. Now draw the branch to show all the features you have observed. This is to be an outline drawing that goes off the paper at the top, bottom, and sides, creating a variety of negative shapes. When you are finished with the drawing, select two complementary colors, such as red and green, and paint the negative shapes. Do not paint the positive shape, the branch itself.

Begin painting by applying one of the colors (red, perhaps) to one of the negative shapes. Then paint the shape next to it with the color you have created by adding a small amount of the complementary color (green) to the first color. Increase the amounts of the complementary color as you paint the remainder of the shapes in your composition. The final shape should be painted with the complement (green). In this way you will create a type of intensity scale using the negative shapes in your design to show the gradual change from one color to its complement. When you are finished painting, use a black marker to emphasize the outline of the branch with a variety of thick and thin lines.

Lesson Two: Detailed Figure Drawings Derived from Preliminary Meditation

Oriental artists placed great emphasis on meditation, which might be helpful to your own studio efforts. Meditating on a subject before you attempt to draw or paint it can be an effective way of identifying the subjects' most interesting features and details.

Assume that you are asked to write a story. The main character in this story is a fascinating individual—and a product of your own fertile imagination. Take the time needed to form a detailed mental image of that character. (He or she could be a combination of several interesting people you know.) Next, write a paragraph that provides a *detailed* description of the character. Finally, draw this character as a full figure seen from the front. Fill the paper assigned for this activity, and make certain to include all the details included in your mental picture and your descriptive paragraph. When you are finished, place your drawing on display along with those produced by other members of the art class. Take turns reading the descriptive paragraphs while the class tries to identify the drawings made from each.

Chapter 21

Out of the Shadows: The Art of Other Non-Western Cultures

Although the focus of this book is on the art of Western countries, you should understand that the production of exceptional artworks is not limited to these countries. By no means does the West have sole rights to creativity or artistic skill.

You have already discovered that artists in China and Japan made important contributions. In this chapter you will discover that equally important contributions were made by tribal artists in Africa, by Moorish artists, and by artists in the Americas before the arrival of Columbus. Often the artworks from these cultures differ in intent and appearance from those produced in the West. But this in no way diminishes their appeal or their significance.

The Art of Tribal Africa

Little was known of the lands and the peoples south of the Sahara Desert until the close of the fifteenth century. At that time Portuguese explorers and traders arrived in Africa and established friendly relations with the Africans, which lasted until the middle of the seventeenth century. But, for most Europeans, there was little reason to believe that the "uncivilized" peoples who populated the region were capable of producing anything of artistic merit.

These Europeans would have been shocked to learn that long before their arrival in Africa, Black Africa had its own highly developed culture with many sophisticated art styles. The religious court of Ife, which was located in what is now southern Nigeria, flourished one thousand years ago. At that time, Europe was still feeling its way cautiously through the Middle Ages. Other highly advanced African empires and city-states

A typical village in central Africa today.

predate even Ife. The earliest was the ancient kingdom of Cush, which conquered Egypt around 700 B.C.

The Benin Empire, also located in what is now southern Nigeria, is another example of highly developed African culture and art. The Benin Empire reached the peak of its power in the sixteenth century. The art of Ife and Benin shows that Africans could achieve artistic levels of quality equal to those of Egypt, Greece, and Renaissance Italy.

Bronze Casting

The Ife and Benin artists achieved their successes in bronze, a material which had limited use in the West. For centuries in the West, bronze had been reserved for the most important works by European masters. Imagine, then, the excitement created in 1897 when a huge shipment of African bronze castings arrived in England.

History

In what century did the Benin Empire reach its peak? What was happening in Europe at this same time? Why was it so unusual for Benin artists to use bronze for their art? Did they become skilled in the use of this medium? What do you find most interesting about this particular work? Do you think it is a successful work of art?

Figure 21.1   Bronze Plaque. Benin culture. Southern Nigeria. The University Museum, University of Pennsylvania, Philadelphia

These castings were brought back to England by the leaders of a British expedition that had captured Benin City earlier that same year. Scholars and artists alike were amazed to discover that technically the Benin bronzes were the equal of the best European work.

The most ambitious of the Benin bronzes are the high-relief sculptures that once covered the walls and pillars of the royal palace from top to bottom. One of these (Figure 21.1) contains the figure of the king, or Oba,* flanked by two chiefs bearing shields. Four smaller attendants are located in the vertical spaces between these major figures. One of the two figures at the top holds bells, while another blows a horn, signaling the arrival of the powerful Oba. At the bottom, one of the remaining small figures carries a ceremonial sword, and the other carries a fan. The Oba wears a tooled-leather loincloth and an eight-ringed coral necklace as well as a coral net helmet. He holds a sword in his right hand and a spear in his left. The Oba's central position, size, weapons, and dress indicate clearly that he is the most important figure in this group. It appears as if he has just arrived and is about to preside over an important ceremonial event.

Without question, the Benin artist who made this bronze relief was in complete command of bronze-casting techniques. Notice how the arms and weapons are thrust forward in space, completely free of the background. This not only adds to the three-dimensional appearance of the figures, but creates an interesting pattern of light and dark values as well. A variety of contrasting textures and a symmetrically balanced design tie all parts of this complex work together in a unified whole.

Wood Carvings

Only a small portion of Africa's contribution to world art has been in the form of bronze casting. The powerfully expressive wooden sculptures and highly stylized masks of tribal art are much more common. These have also greatly influenced Western artist since the late nineteenth century. Picasso, Matisse, and many other European artists incorporated features of African art in their own work. In this way, African art has had an impact on the course of modern art in the West.

★ **Enrichment** As an indication of the Oba's great power, one eighteenth-century visitor to Benin City wrote that the king could raise an army of 100,000 warriors in twenty-four hours.

Oddly enough, African tribal art owes much of its zest to a wood-eating white ant and a damp environment. Both contributed to the rapid destruction of wood carvings. This meant that each new generation of artists had to make new carvings to replace those that had been damaged. Not satisfied with merely copying earlier models, these artists improved upon them. Thus, they continuously revitalized images and forms that were used in traditional tribal rituals.★

★ **Enrichment** Much of what we refer to as African tribal art found in museums today may date from only the nineteenth and twentieth centuries.

Criticism

What material was used to make this mask? Point out the different facial features. Explain how exaggeration has been used in this carving. Do you think this exaggeration contributes to the effectiveness of this work? What feeling or mood is aroused when looking at it?

Figure 21.2 Nimba Headdress. Baga culture. Guinea. Nineteenth to twentieth centuries. Wood, approx. 123 x 41 x 71 cm [48½ x 16 x 28″]. Dallas Museum of Art. The Gustave and Franyo Schindler Collection of African Sculpture. Gift of the McDermott Foundation in honor of Eugene McDermott

There are two main classifications of African wood carving: masks and figures. These carvings varied in style from tribe to tribe, and there were a great many tribes.

Masks

African masks were made to be seen in motion at important tribal ceremonies. A wooden headdress, or *nimba* mask, of the Baga tribe (Figure 21.2) is part of a complete costume worn by a dancer in a farming ceremony. This headdress was made to rest on the wearer's shoulders. Strips of palm fiber were used to conceal the rest of the body. With the mask in place, the dancer stood over 2.4 m [8 feet] tall. He must have been an awesome sight tossing, swaying, and jerking to and fro with the motions of the dance. Witnesses at ceremonies in which this mask was used have claimed that it has a strange, hypnotic effect.

Although they were sometimes used in playful dances, ritual masks were intended to aid efforts to communicate with a world of spirits. They were also thought to have supernatural powers. When Africans donned such masks, they ceased being themselves. Instead, they became the god or the force they sought to contact. For this reason, these masks are regarded by many Africans as very powerful and are to be treated with great respect.

In addition to the shoulder mask represented by the nimba carving, two other types of masks were produced: the face mask and the head mask.

As you might guess, the face mask is designed to be worn over the face. Among the most appealing of all African face masks are the Songe dance masks (Figure 21.3) from the Central Congo (now named Zaire). Observe how the facial features are all indicated in simplified forms, which reflect the overall simplicity of the entire mask. A rich pattern of closely spaced lines accents the geometric planes that divide the face. These lines, which are actually carved into the wood with a sharp instrument, create a textured surface that contrasts and emphasizes the smooth surfaces of the eyes, nose, and mouth. Form, line, texture, and value are combined in this mask to create a unified design that is subtle and dramatic at the same time. A costume made of long strips of raffia★ was attached to the holes at the bottom of the mask. This costume draped over and

---

★ **Enrichment** Raffia is a fiber made from the leaves of an African palm tree. It is used to make mats, baskets, and other products in addition to masks.

Discuss the manner in which the elements of line, texture, shape, and form are used in this mask. Discuss the ways in which the principles of balance, emphasis, harmony, and variety are used. Do you think these elements and principles have been used effectively in achieving an overall sense of unity? Explain your answer.

What three types of masks were produced by African artists? What type is represented by this mask? For what purpose were masks like this used?

Figure 21.3   Songe Face Mask. Zaire, Africa. Nineteenth to twentieth centuries. Wood and paint sculpture, 44.5 cm [17.5″] high. The Metropolitan Museum of Art, New York. The Michael C. Rockefeller Memorial Collection of Primitive Art. Bequest of Nelson A. Rockefeller

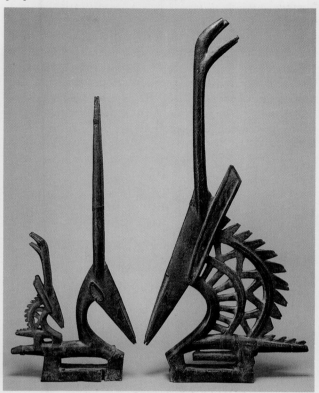

Figure 21.4   Two Antelope Headpieces. Bamana tribe. Mali, Africa. Nineteenth to twentieth centuries. Wood, metal bands, left: 71.2 x 30.9 x 5.4 cm [28 x 12⅛ x 2⅛″]; right: 90.7 x 40 x 8.5 cm [35¾ x 15¾ x 8.5″]. The Metropolitan Museum of Art, New York. The Michael C. Rockefeller Memorial Collection. Gift of Nelson A. Rockefeller, 1964

effectively covered the body of the wearer. Masks like this were originally designed to be worn at the funeral of a chief.

Among the best-known head masks are those carved in the form of antelopes by the Bamana (or Bambara) people of the Sudan. These spectacular wooden carvings are attached to woven caps and worn on top of the head. They are used during dances at the sowing and harvest seasons to pacify evil spirits and insure a bountiful crop. The dances always included both male and female antelope carvings (Figure 21.4). The male is identified by its beautiful stylized mane, while the female carries a baby on her back.

The designs of the headdresses in Figure 21.4 are especially striking. They manage to suggest the grace of the antelopes even though they are highly abstract. The two-dimensional shapes of the wood slabs from which they were carved are clearly evidenced. Note the elegantly curved necks that contrast with the vertical lines of the horns and zigzag pattern of the openings. This adds variety to the overall designs. The repeated use of positive and negative triangular shapes lends the necessary harmony to the pieces.

Various forms of the antelope headdress are found in the villages of the northwest region of Africa known as the Sudan. The admirable aesthetic qualities noted in Figure 21.4 are by no means unique. For this reason, these headpieces are considered to be among the very finest examples of African wood carving.

425

Figures

The carved wood sculptures of West Africa and the Congo take many different forms, although they are all based on the human figure. These wood carvings can be classified into several different types. Included among these are the ancestral figure and the funerary (having to do with burials) figure. Both types exhibit certain characteristics that can be seen in all the figures, no matter where they were produced. These characteristics are:

- little concern for the natural proportions of the figures,
  - a frontal pose,
  - enlarged heads,* and
  - a lack of movement.

Most African figures were carved for two reasons: respect for the deceased and fear of angry spirits. Many Africans believed that at death the soul was separated from the body, and that the soul might even remain in the village to influence the present.** They believed that since these spirits were still present, they were not really dead. They also thought that the spirits might not be pleased with their fate and might even seek revenge against those still living. Therefore, people thought it was wise to please these spirits and make their existence as comfortable as possible. Ancestral figures (Figure 21.5) were created as pleasant resting places for spirits. These sculptures were not created to *symbolize* a spirit; they were created to *contain* the spirit.

It was not necessary for these ancestral figures to be realistic portraits of the deceased. A spirit would immediately recognize his or her figure and inhabit it. The spirit would remain there until it decided to leave or was called to the hereafter. Since the spirit dwelled in the figure, members of the family were accustomed to talking to it as if it were alive. In this way, the carved figure served as an effective link between the past and the present, between the dead and the living.

Another type of African carving is the funerary figure that was produced to protect the dead. Among the best-known funerary figures are the wood and metal sculptures created by the Bakota of central Africa (Figure 21.6). These abstract figures have large oval heads and bodies reduced to open diamond shapes. They are made of wood and partially covered with thin sheets and strips of copper and brass. These serve to emphasize portions of the face, neck, and body. The use of copper and brass indicates the importance attached to these figures since metal is scarce in this part of Africa.

History

Why were carved figures produced in Africa? How did figures such as these act as links between the living and the dead? Would you describe the proportions used in this figure as natural? Does the figure appear to be in motion? Is this figure symmetrically balanced or asymmetrically balanced?

Figure 21.5 Master of Ogol. Standing Female Figure. Dogon culture. Mali, Africa. Late nineteenth century. Wood, patination, metal, beads, approx. 58 x 11 cm [23 x 4½"]. Dallas Museum of Art. The Gustave and Franyo Schindler Collection of African Sculpture. Gift of the McDermott Foundation in honor of Eugene McDermott

★ **Enrichment** Heads may have been enlarged because the people believed that the heads were the storage places for knowledge.

★ **Enrichment** You may have noticed the similarity
★ here with the ancient Egyptian's belief in Ka.

Criticism

Describe this figure. Point to areas of rough and smooth texture. What is the term used to describe the type of texture used here? Do you think the elements and principles of art have been used effectively in this work? Identify several design relationships to support your answer. What do you find more impressive about this work—its visual qualities or its expressive qualities? Explain.

Figure 21.6 Reliquary Figure. Kota tribe. Gabon, Africa. Nineteenth to twentieth centuries. Wood, brass, ivory eyes, 42.2 x 16.5 x 7.4 cm [16⅝ x 6½ x 2⅞"]. The Metropolitan Museum of Art, New York. The Michael C. Rockefeller Memorial Collection. Bequest of Nelson A. Rockefeller.

Note in Figure 21.6 that the head is flanked by large triangular shapes. No one knows for sure what these shapes represent. Some experts have suggested that they are intended to represent hair. Others think they were originally meant to be wings. If they were indeed meant to be wings, the first figures of this kind may have been gods of the dead rather than mere guardians of the dead.

Bakota figures with convex faces represent males, while those with concave faces indicate females. The head is joined to what appears to be a neck, and this is attached to legs with flexed knees.★ It is symmetrically balanced in terms of surface decoration and overall form.

The purpose of these unusual, abstract figures is not entirely certain. It is known, however, that the figures were placed in or on top of baskets containing the skulls of ancestors. This fact suggests that the purpose of the figures was to protect the dead.

The Art of Islamic Spain

Mohammed was born in Mecca in 1570 and was raised by an uncle after the death of his parents. Eventually he became a lowly camel driver and learned the habits and languages of the wandering Arabs with whom he came in contact. His fortunes improved following his marriage to a wealthy widow, and he became a successful merchant. But he was unable to ignore or forget the ignorance and superstitions of the Arabs who worshiped many different idols.

Following years of meditation, Mohammed felt he had a divine call as the last of the prophets and a teacher for his race. At first he taught in secret, converting his wife, cousin, and adopted son to his religious beliefs. Around 613, when he began to teach openly, he was opposed by those who wished to preserve established tribal and religious customs. He persisted, however, and today more than four hundred million followers, called Moslems, honor him as a prophet and founder of the Islamic religion.

★ **Enrichment** Some scholars have suggested that these limbs are arms rather than legs. When placed on a funeral basket, these arms appear to embrace the basket in a protective way.

Mohammed claimed that he received messages from God, which were delivered to him by the angel Gabriel. As he made these messages known, his followers wrote them down. They were eventually assembled into the Koran, the holy scripture of Islam.

Mohammed taught that any Moslem dying in battle for the faith was assured immediate entrance into Paradise. No promise could have been more welcomed by his Arab followers, who were magnificent warriors. At Mohammed's death in 632, all Arabia was united under Islam, and an inspired and impatient army was poised to carry out the Prophet's dream of spreading the faith to the entire world. By 710 all of North Africa had been subdued, and shortly thereafter a Moslem army crossed the Strait of Gibraltar into Spain.

The army advanced swiftly through Spain, encountering little resistance on the part of the disorganized Visigoths who inhabited the peninsula. The Moslems advanced into France where an army under the command of Charles Martel, the grandfather of Charlemagne, finally stopped them at Poitiers in 732. Unable to advance farther, the invaders consolidated their control of Spain. The Moslems, known as Moors in Spain, remained on the peninsula for almost eight hundred years.

Criticism

How would you describe this building? What are some of its most interesting features? After examining it from the outside, how do you think it might look on the inside? What purposes could such a building serve? If you came upon this building unexpectedly, would you be tempted to enter? Why or why not?

Figure 21.7 The Mosque at Cordoba, Spain. Exterior. Thirteenth century

Cordoba

At the height of Moorish power in Spain, Cordoba was one of Islam's most impressive capitals. In the ninth and tenth centuries it was reported to have over 800,000 inhabitants; 300 mosques, or houses of worship; and 600 inns. People came from all over Europe for enlightenment and knowledge. And there they gained the continent's first knowledge of algebra, paper, and glass. At a time when the rest of Europe was groping through the Medieval period, Cordoba was a splendid center of learning* and art. All that survives today, however, are the remnants of a fortress—and the great mosque known as the Mezquita.

The first view of the Mezquita is not a memorable one. Its ancient brown walls marked by unused arched entries offer little hint of the pleasures that await inside (Figure 21.7). Perhaps one of its more surprising features is the lack of a facade.

Passing through an arch, the visitor enters a courtyard known as the Patio of the Orange Trees. Originally there were no walls separating this courtyard and the interior of the mosque. The courtyard and the mosque were linked by the lines of orange trees outside and the rows of columns inside. Today, however, a wall separates them and the trees grow at random.

The Moors worshiped five times a day in the mosque. Preparing for worship involved ceremonial bathing. The fountains placed in the Patio of the Orange Trees were used for this bathing.

Stepping into the dark mosque from the bright Spanish sunshine is a shock to your vision. Once your eyes adjust to the dim light, you find yourself standing in an enchanting world, surrounded by a forest of polished marble columns that extend back into the darkness (Figure 21.8). Each pair of columns supports horseshoe-shaped arches decorated with yellow and red bands. These columns also support stone piers that carry a second tier of arches three feet above the first.

As you walk down one of the endless rows of columns, you cannot help but be impressed by the size of the mosque. The direction of the aisles guides you to the side of the building facing Mecca. This was the direction Moslems faced when praying. Eventually you notice a change in the arches above. They are now more

---

★ Enrichment By the tenth century the city is said to have had a library housing 400,000 manuscripts.

History

Identify the capitals of these columns. Are they Doric, Ionic, or Corinthian? When and where did columns of this type originate? How does the interior of this mosque differ from the interiors of Christian churches you have studied? Describe the manner in which the Moors worshiped in mosques like this.

History

How do these arches differ from the arches shown in Figure 21.8? Why are they different? What name is used to identify the most important part of a mosque?

Figure 21.9   The Mosque at Cordoba, Spain. Interior

Figure 21.8   The Mosque at Cordoba, Spain. Interior

Criticism

You are writing a letter to a friend after having visited this mosque. How would you describe what you saw so that your friend could form a mental picture of it? Would you recommend that your friend visit this mosque if the opportunity presented itself? How would you prepare him or her for such a visit?

ornate, and their colors have changed to a creamy white and dark brown (Figure 21.9). You are nearing the most important part of the mosque, the *mihrab* (Figure 21.10).

The mihrab is a niche in the wall large enough to accommodate a standing figure. It is richly decorated with a delicate stucco relief,★ incorporating passages from the Koran.

★ **Enrichment** This is a method of decoration in which patterns are impressed into wet plaster. Its popularity during Moorish times was due to the fact that it was inexpensive, efficient, and visually appealing.

Figure 21.10   The Mosque at Cordoba, Spain. Interior

Mohammed disapproved of painted or sculptured images or symbols. As a consequence, the interiors of Islamic mosques are unlike the interiors of Christian churches. Christian artists created religious images as a way of encouraging prayer and meditation. Islamic artists, on the other hand, were forbidden to create religious images because it was thought that they would be distracting to prayer and meditation. Instead, they created plaster relief decorations that featured excerpts from the Koran. Their skill in doing this is evident in the rich and varied visual effects concentrated around the mihrab.

The mihrab, a feature found in all later mosques, is something of a mystery. Its origins and purpose are still being debated by scholars. Some think it may symbolize the place where Mohammed stood when teaching in his house. Others challenge this theory because early Islamic art avoids all use of symbols.

Whatever the mihrab's origins and purpose, the viewer does not forget its beauty. It is difficult to take your eyes from it. But eventually your eyes drift up-ward. There, in the dome that covers the area in front of the mihrab, you see how Moorish artists applied their decorative skills to perfection (Figure 21.11).

Granada

The Christian effort to drive the Moors from Spain required over seven hundred years. This effort began in 722 with the resistance of a Visigoth prince named Pelayo in the mountains near Covadonga. It was more than five hundred years after this resistance began that Cordoba was taken by Christian forces. With the fall of Cordoba, Granada, to the southwest, came into prominence.

Granada, which resisted capture by the Christians until 1492, was the last great Moorish city in Spain. In the fourteenth century, while Gothic art spread throughout France and Giotto's paintings heralded a new style of realistic art in Italy, the pinnacle of an artistic period that had been flourishing for five hundred years was reached in Granada.

History

What single adjective best summarizes your reactions to this dome? Where in the mosque is this dome found? Movies and novels have often depicted the Moors as bar-baric and crude. Do you feel that this dome looks like the product of a barbaric and crude people?

Figure 21.11   Dome before the Mirhab. Mosque at Cordoba, Spain

Cordoba and Granada are both known for their impressive examples of Islamic architecture. However, Granada's remarkable Moorish fortress-palace, the Alhambra,* is more than a match for Cordoba's great mosque, the Mezquita.

The Alhambra is protected by an outer wall that can be entered at several well-fortified gates. The massive

---

★ **Enrichment** The Alhambra received its name from the Arabic word *al-hambra,* meaning ''the red.'' This refers to the reddish color of the brickwork of the outer walls.

Justice Gate is the most impressive of these (Figure 21.12). This gate received its name from the tribunals that met there to try petty thieves. On the keystone of the outer horseshoe arch is carved a great open hand; and, on the keystone of the smaller arch within, a key is carved. While it is likely that these carvings represent Moorish law and faith, legend offers another, more colorful explanation. According to an ancient Moorish story, the hand and the key are magical signs on which the fate of the Alhambra depended. The Moorish king who built the palace was a great magician who placed the entire structure under a magic spell. This spell protected the Alhambra over the centuries during

History

What was the Alhambra? Where was it built? How did this gate receive its name? Do you think an enemy would have difficulty gaining entry through this gate?

Figure 21.12 Justice Gate, The Alhambra, Granada, Spain. Fourteenth century

which earthquakes and storms destroyed all other Moorish buildings. The spell would last until the hand on the outer arch reached down and grasped the key. Then the entire structure would crumble and the treasures hidden within by the Moors would be revealed.

Although the Alhambra and its surrounding gardens are enchanting, the Court of the Lions at the heart of the Alhambra is certain to take your breath away (Figure 21.13). It was built in the fourteenth century by Mohammed V around a massive, low-lying fountain, which gave the court its name. A delicate arcade supported by 124 marble columns is a reminder of the cloisters found in Medieval monasteries. This resem-

blance may not be accidental. It is known that Mohammed V was on friendly terms with a Christian king, Peter the Cruel.* Perhaps through this relationship Mohammed V learned about cloisters and decided to use a similar design for this court.

★ Enrichment Peter the Cruel was well named. He was later responsible for the assassination of his friend's son and successor, Mohammed VI.

Criticism

Describe in detail what you see here and how you react to it. Which of the following words seems more appropriate when applied to this court: massive or delicate? light or heavy? cheerful or somber? refined or crude?

Figure 21.13   Court of the Lions, The Alhambra, Granada, Spain

The fountain in the center of the court, with its crudely carved marble lions, seems out of place in this enchanting setting (Figure 21.14). The fountain has twelve sides with a poem carved in Arabic around the rim. A translation is certain to bring a smile. The poem describes how fierce the little lions would be if they were not behaving themselves out of respect for the king.

State apartments surround the Court of the Lions, and nearly every apartment has a legend associated with it. In one of these rooms, for example, a Moorish king is said to have carried out a family massacre. Believing that the family members planned to betray him, he had them assassinated following a grand banquet.

The columns and walls of the arcade and apartments around the Court of the Lions are filled with delicate stucco decorations. These consist of a variety of designs, including bands of inscriptions from the Koran (Figure 21.15). Impressive today, they must have been especially beautiful in the fourteenth century. At that time they were brilliantly colored and gilded.

Moorish kings did not build for the future—they built for the present. Beneath the rich decorations of the Alhambra are assorted bricks and stones. As each new ruler ascended to the throne, he would tear down the structures of his predecessor to make room for his own new palace. These palaces were, however, all similar in that they grouped rooms around a central patio or court.

Criticism

Do the animals carved for this fountain look like lions? What kind of animal do they more closely resemble? If you were limited to discussing just two elements of art noted in this work, which two would you choose? Which princi- ples of art are used to organize these two elements? Do these animals look fierce and dangerous? What feelings do they arouse in you when you look at them? Do you feel that this is a good work of art?

Figure 21.14   Lion Fountain, Court of the Lions, The Alhambra, Granada, Spain

Part II   Seeing to Learn

Part II   Seeing to Learn

Part II   Seeing to Learn

Why were stucco decorations like these popular in Moorish Spain? What famous religious document provided the passages used in these decorations? What do you know about the origins of that religious document? Were Islamic build-ers concerned with erecting long-lasting structures? What feature was common to all Moorish palaces? What may have served as a model for this feature?

Figure 21.15   Detail of Stucco Decorations, Court of the Lions, The Alhambra, Granada, Spain

The End of Moorish Rule in Spain

Although they gradually lost parts of their kingdom to the advancing Christian armies, the Moors managed to maintain a presence in Spain until 1492.* Following a period of intrigue, the Moorish king Boabdil surrendered Granada and the Alhambra to the Christian monarchs, Ferdinand and Isabella. As he left the city with his mother, Boabdil paused on a hillside for a final look at the Alhambra. Noticing that he was crying, his iron-willed mother scolded him saying, "You weep like a woman for what you could not hold as a man." The spot is still known as "The Moor's Sigh."

★ Enrichment   Of course everyone knows that this was the year Christopher Columbus embarked on his voyage of discovery. But did you know that his request to Queen Isabella for financial aid was made while Isabella and King Ferdinand were staying at the Alhambra?

After 781 years Moorish rule in Spain was ended. What happened to the Moors? The American author Washington Irving offers one answer to that question: "Ask the shores of Barbary and its desert places. The exiled remnants of their once powerful empire disappeared among the barbarians of Africa and ceased to be a nation. They have not even left a distinct name behind them, though for nearly eight centuries they were a distinct people."

434

Pre-Columbian Art

The term *pre-Columbian* is used when referring to the various cultures and civilizations found throughout North and South America before the arrival of Christopher Columbus in 1492.

North-American Indian Art

The first settlers in North America probably came by way of the Bering Strait from Asia between twenty thousand and forty thousand years ago. In time, these people spread out to cover all parts of North and South America. Some were hunters, while others grew crops as a way to survive. But all of them created art of some kind.

Frequently, art was created to serve the religious needs of the people. This was the case with the Eskimo mask of the Bear Spirit (Figure 21.16) carved in the Yukon River area of Alaska. The Eskimo shaman, or medicine man, wore such a mask during ceremonial dances. While dancing, he would go into a trance and act as a messenger between the world of the living and the world of the spirits.

Of course, not all Indian masks were of animals. Further south, on the coast of what is now British Columbia, an unknown Eskimo carver created a mask just 25.4 cm [10 inches] high of a frightening woman (Figure 21.17). This mask with its sunken cheeks, small eyes, and large down-turned mouth represented to its creator the spirit of a crazed woman who lived in the woods and ate children. Perhaps you are reminded of the familiar children's tale of Hansel and Gretel. It would seem that the Eskimos also had tales of this kind. Perhaps they were told to their children to keep them from wandering too deeply into the woods and possible danger.

In the southwestern parts of the United States, Pueblo and Apache Indians also created masks. However, their masks were not carved. They were made from various colorful materials. These masks were used during religious ceremonies that included singing, dancing, offerings, and magic rituals.

History

For what purpose were masks like this produced? In what ways are masks like this similar to those carved by African tribal artists?

Figure 21.16   Mask: Bear Spirit. Eskimo. Norton Sound, Yukon River area, Alaska. Late nineteenth century. Wood, paint, fiber, cord, feathers, approx. 72 x 82 cm [28½ x 32″]. Dallas Museum of Art. Gift of Mrs. Robert R. Penn

Criticism

Describe the features of this mask. Can you identify this as the face of a male or female figure? Do you think it is a realistically rendered face? What adjective—friendly, frightening, wise, or happy—best describes this mask's appearance? Identify the features of the mask that you referred to when answering this question.

Figure 21.17   Mask of Tsonoqua, a Mythical Spirit. Kwakiutl culture. Northwest coast of British Columbia, Canada. Approx. 25.4 cm [10″] high. The Denver Art Museum.

Art in Mexico and Central America

The first great civilization in Mexico was the Olmec, which dates to about 1200 B.C. These people lived in the great coastal plain of the Gulf of Mexico. They settled mainly in the areas which are now Veracruz and Tabasco. The Olmecs are thought by many to have made the first Mexican sculptures. They left the earliest remains of carved altars, pillars, sarcophagi, and statues in Mexico. But their most surprising works were great carved heads. These sculptures measured 2.4 m [8 feet] high and weighed up to 36 t [40 tons]. Some of the same features found on those heads can be seen in a realistic jadeite mask that may have once graced the tomb of a ruler (Figure 21.18). The huge heads and this striking mask contain the same mouth that droops at the corners. The face on this mask is certainly not warm or welcoming. Eyes peer out at you from beneath heavy eyelids, and the open mouth suggests a snarl rather

Criticism

Does this face appear to be calm, welcoming, or angry? How does it make you feel? What aesthetic qualities seem most appropriate when making and defending a judgment about this mask? Do you think that knowing when, where, why, and by whom this work was created would affect your response to it? What does your answer to this question tell you about the value of art history?

Figure 21.18   Mask. Olmec culture. Veracruz, Mexico. 800-400 B.C. Jadeite, approx. 18 x 16.5 cm [7⅛ x 6⁹⁄₁₆″]. Dallas Museum of Art. Purchased with a gift from Mr. and Mrs. Eugene McDermott and the McDermott Foundation and Mr. and Mrs. Algur H. Meadows and the Meadows Foundation, Incorporated

than speech. The mask seems to be waiting for you to make the first move, a move you may be reluctant to make. This is not the face of someone who would take kindly to an insult, no matter how unintentional it might be.

When Cortez* waded ashore at Veracruz in 1519, a people called the Aztecs had nearly succeeded in conquering Mexico from the Atlantic to the Pacific as far south as Guatemala. By 1521 the Aztec conquest was

★ **Enrichment** Hernando Cortez was the Spanish conqueror of Mexico.

complete. It was an effort that took less than two hundred years (1324-1521). The Aztecs were a warlike people driven to continuous combat by their religious beliefs. They believed that human sacrifices were necessary to keep the universe running smoothly. Against a backdrop of brilliantly painted architecture and sculpture, these human sacrifices were made to insure that the gods remained in good spirits. And to remain in good spirits the gods demanded human hearts.

Art was closely linked to these rituals. Statues to the gods were carved and placed in temples located at the top of stepped pyramids. There were even statues of priests dressed in the skins of flayed victims who had been sacrificed to the gods (Figure 21.19). Realism is carried to the extreme in this case. The artist has even shown the slash in the skin where the victim's heart was removed.

The most elegant and appealing of the pre-Columbian cultures was the Mayan. The Maya controlled vast lands that included what are now Yucatán, Guatemala, and Honduras. They never advanced technically beyond the Stone Age, but still made much progress in several fields. They became great builders and devised an elaborate system of mathematics as well as the most precise calendar in history.

Mayan artists made rich reliefs for their buildings, altars, and monuments. The first of these carvings were simple and realistic, but later they became more elaborate and complex. Figures were carved with so many ornaments that it is often difficult to separate them from backgrounds filled with symbols and inscriptions referring to various important events.

History

What do you know about the Aztec people who created figures like this? Why were sculptures like this produced? What is the figure wearing? What do you think he might have once carried in his hand? Identify the features of this figure that give it a realistic appearance. Do you think works like this are useful in helping us understand the Aztecs? Explain.

Figure 21.19   Xipe Impersonator. Aztec culture. Mexico. A.D. **1400-1521. Volcanic stone, shell, 69.8 x 27.9 cm [27½ x 11″]. Dallas Museum of Art. Purchased with a gift from the Mr. and Mrs. Eugene McDermott Foundation and the Mr. and Mrs. Algur H. Meadows Foundation, Incorporated**

What were some of the accomplishments of the Mayan people? How is this carving typical of those produced by Mayan artists? What was originally done to separate this intricately carved figure from its elaborate background?

Figure 21.20   Female Dignitary Holding Scepter. Mayan culture. Mexico. A.D. **675-750. Limestone, plaster, traces of paint, approx. 2.2 m [7′2¾″] high, 76.8 cm [2′6¼″] wide, and 12 cm [4¾″] deep. Dallas Museum of Art. Foundation for the Arts Collection. Gift of Mr. and Mrs. James H. Clark**

One of these reliefs (Figure 21.20) shows a royal priestess dressed in a rich costume and wearing an elaborate plumed headdress. She is shown with her face in profile, although her shoulders are turned to present a front view. Observe how the forehead slants back, the large nose dominates, the mouth is open, and the chin recedes. All these are features found in most Mayan heads.

Mayan architecture and sculpture were painted, and in this case traces of pigment still cling to the limestone surface. The carved surfaces were painted in contrasting colors, and this may have helped separate the figure from the background. Usually, red was used for the skin areas, blue and green for ornaments, green for feathers, and blue for garments.

Conclusion

It is not easy to end this story of art—indeed, it is impossible. The story can have no ending. Art has its roots somewhere at the dawn of civilization before recorded history. Throughout the ages, it has continued uninterrupted up to the present day. Every nation has had its art in one form or another. It has survived wars, famines, and periods of prosperity. Art has flourished whether it was admired, ignored, ridiculed, or condemned. Even now, this very minute, there are artists all over the world continuing to dream, to experiment, and to create. Eventually their efforts will add to the precious tapestry of art history. It is a tapestry which may have been started centuries ago when someone picked up a piece of soft stone and, with a few awkward strokes, discovered that it was possible to create an image on the rough wall of a cave. . . .

Studio Experiences

Lesson One: Painting to Distinguish between Positive and Negative Shapes in a Complex Composition

Examine the Mayan relief sculpture, *Female Dignitary Holding Scepter* (Figure 21.20). Notice how this composition consists of so many complex shapes and lines that it is difficult to separate the figure from the background. Apparently Mayan artists used contrasting colors of paint to distinguish the figure from the background.

Set up a still life and carefully draw it with pencil. Then use a ruler to straighten and extend all the lines in your drawing. Extend these lines to break up the positive (still-life objects) and negative (background) shapes. This will create a complex composition. Paint the composition by selecting and applying colors that will emphasize the positive shapes and separate them from the background shapes.

Lesson Two: Expressive Clay Masks

In this chapter you learned that many African tribal masks exhibit exaggerated features and expressions. Examples of masks from the Baga (Figure 21.2) and Songe (Figure 21.3) cultures represent this type. In all likelihood this exaggeration was done to increase the dramatic impact of these masks.

Design a full-size face mask of your own on newsprint. Make certain to exaggerate the facial features and the expression. Lay your finished mask design on a slab of moist clay. You can produce this slab of clay by placing a ball of clay between two wooden 1.3 cm [½ inch] slats and rolling it flat with a rolling pin. Trace over the mask design with a pencil leaving an indentation in the clay. Cut around the mask, saving the excess clay to model such details as eyebrows, hair, lips, and cheeks. (Remember that all these features are to be exaggerated for dramatic effect.)

When you have finished with your mask, roll a stack of newspapers into a cylinder and tape it securely. Gently place your mask on this cylinder so that it will have a slightly curved surface. You may want to add holes at the outer edges of your mask from which to hang raffia or other decorative materials. Holes will also be needed later if you decide to hang your mask. Allow your mask to dry *slowly*. This is important. If the mask dries too quickly there is a good chance that it will crack. After the mask has dried thoroughly and has been fired, you may want to glaze it or add a patina. Refer to Lessons 10.3 and 13.2 for suggestions on creating a patina.

Criticism and History Experiences

Chapter 2

How well can you use the visual vocabulary of elements and principles? To test your skill, select a familiar object and try to describe it to a friend in terms of its elements and principles alone. Then have your friend do the same and you try to identify the object that he or she has selected. As you and your friend get better at this, select more and more difficult items to describe. To add to the challenge, set a time limit in which you must describe the object well enough for your friend to identify it.

Another approach to improving your understanding of the visual vocabulary is to play a variation of the familiar game Twenty Questions. This time three or four of your friends can take part. Taking turns, have them ask questions about the object you have in your possession but hidden from their view. Each of their questions must deal with an element, a principle, or a combination of element and principle. They may ask no more than twenty questions in their effort to identify the object. If they are unable to do so, they lose. If one of them does guess correctly, it is that person's turn to select the item for the next round of questioning.

Chapter 3

(a) Plan a trip to a museum with some of your friends. Perhaps your entire class could go on such a trip. But, to make it more interesting, have each member of the group visit the museum beforehand and write a critical description of a work of art found there. The name of the artist and the title of the work should be omitted from the description. Before entering the museum with your friends, exchange these written descriptions and read them carefully. As you proceed through the museum, each member of the group should be searching for the artwork referred to in the description they received.

(b) Assume that you are a well-known art historian and that you have been asked to conduct research on an art object in your community. Any art object can be used for this purpose provided it is an original work of art and not a reproduction. You are not limited to the art found in museums or galleries, although you may want to look into those sources first. However, an original art object could be that grand church that has always fascinated you, or that elegant old house you pass every day, or that unusual statue in the park, or that painting in the courthouse that no one seems to pay attention to any-more. Gather as much information as you can about the art object, the artist who created it, and the times during which it was done. When you are finished, you should feel as though you are an expert on that work of art.

Of course, when you have completed your research you will want to share what you have discovered with others. The members of your class would make an excellent audience. Make certain though that your presentation is interesting as well as informative. You may want to show slides or pass around photographs, drawings, or diagrams of the art object. Perhaps you could include taped interviews with people who had some association with the object—perhaps even an interview with the artist or someone who knew the artist. Your instructor may feel that a class visit to the art object to see it in person is called for.

Another way of sharing the information you have gathered is to write an article for the school newspaper —or even the community newspaper. You may be surprised to discover how much interest your article may generate if you have done your job as an art historian well.

Chapter 4

As a noted art critic you disagree with another scholar who insists that prehistoric cave paintings are simple and childlike. A friendly debate is scheduled and you must now prepare for it. List all the arguments you will use to demonstrate that prehistoric cave paintings (like the one illustrated here) were expressive and skillfully done.

Figure Standing bison (cave painting), Altamira. c. 15,000-10,000 B.C. Near Santillana, Spain

Chapter 5

In the darkened corner of a small antique shop you come across a small relief carving that looks very much like the panel pictured here. Curious, you ask the owner of the shop to tell you what he knows about it. However, the owner can provide no information at all about the panel. It had been in the shop when he purchased it many years before. Several lengthy searches had failed to turn up any information about the panel.

Based upon what you have learned from your reading, what could you tell the shop owner about this relief? Write out the comments you might make. You may surprise yourself with the amount of (critical and historical) information about the mysterious panel you can supply the shop owner.

It would be interesting to compare your written comments with those prepared by one or more of your friends. For example, were many of the same qualities and facts mentioned? What was mentioned most often? Did anyone make an observation that no one else had made?

To find out more about the mystery panel, turn to page 436.

Allen Memorial Art Museum, Oberlin College, Oberlin, Ohio. R. T. Miller, Jr. Fund, 43.302

Chapter 6

Greek artists learned a great deal from Egyptian artists, although there are many differences between the art-works they created. See if you can tell which statements in the chart refer to Egyptian artists and which to Greek artists.

Painting

They preferred to use flat, bright colors.

They showed the same concern for realism in their paintings as they did in their sculptures.

They followed a strict set of rules when painting the human figure.

The most important figures in their paintings were made to look larger than the other figures.

Sculpture

They used flowing, graceful lines to create elegant figures that seemed to move in space.

Many of their sculptures kept the solid, block-like form of the stones from which they were carved.

Their sculptured figures, like their painted figures, rarely showed any signs of emotion or feeling.

Eventually, their sculptures in bronze and marble became more dramatic and even violent.

Architecture

They had such an affection for color that they painted their buildings as well as their sculptures.

Their concern for life after death influenced their architecture just as it did their painting and sculpture.

They thought of their temples as dwelling places for their gods.

Because their religious ceremonies took place in front of their temples rather than inside, they made the outside of these buildings as attractive as possible.

Their tomb design evolved gradually over the centuries.

The basic design of their temples did not change over the centuries.

Their tombs were fortresses designed to house and protect the body of their dead king whom they believed to be a god.

Chapter 7

Ask several of your friends or the members of your class to identify on separate sheets of paper the most impressive building in the community. When they are finished, have them pass their papers to you so you can list the buildings on the board. Was one building mentioned more frequently than any others? Why did those mentioning it think that it was so impressive? Keep a written account of the answers to these questions and any others that might arise during this discussion.

Each person now selects one of the buildings mentioned, visits it, and completes a written study of it using the four art-criticism operations (Figure 3.17, page 56). If several students select the same building, they may elect to make this a group activity. Later, when the criticism operations have been completed, have the groups and individuals present their findings. Slides, photos, and drawings of the buildings would be very helpful here.

Finally, ask everyone to list on separate sheets of paper the building they *now* regard as the most impressive. Does a list of these buildings differ from the original list? If some people now selected different buildings, what changed their minds? Was there an agreement on any single building, or was the group still divided?

Chapter 8

You learned in this chapter that Early-Christian artists used symbols as a kind of code. Their paintings of animals, birds, and plants had special meanings for them, although these meanings were lost to the Romans who were unfamiliar with Christian religious beliefs.

Of course, symbols—visual signs that represent something else—remain popular today. If asked, for example, to name a symbol for the United States, you would probably respond quickly by describing the well-known elderly gentleman in a red, white, and blue outfit known as Uncle Sam.

Given a limited amount of time, say five to ten minutes, prepare a list of as many familiar symbols as you can. You may find it interesting to compare your list with those compiled by several of your friends. No doubt many of the same symbols would be found on several lists, but some unique ones may also be discovered.

With a pencil, quickly sketch a symbol for any one of the following ideas:

World Peace

Justice for All

Freedom of the Press

Freedom of Religion

Equal Opportunity under the Law

Perhaps several friends or other members of the class could do the same thing using the same list of ideas. However, make certain that everyone keeps secret the ideas he or she is attempting to symbolize. Then, when finished, each person can show his or her symbol to the others—who try to match the symbol to the correct idea.

Chapter 9

You may wish to play this game with some of your friends or with the members of your class. First, have everyone take a few minutes to reexamine the painting of *Christ in Majesty* from San Clemente (Figure 9.25, page 158). As they do, ask them to think of a single word which best describes their feelings when looking at this painting. Then take a large sheet of paper and pass it around so that each person can write the word he or she decided upon. Have the first person write his or her word at the top of this paper and fold it over before passing it on to the next person who does the same thing. In this way, no one can see what the others have written. When everyone is finished, open the paper to reveal all the words written on it. If this is done in class, write the words on the board so that everyone can see them. How often did several people use the same word to describe their reactions to this painting? Which was the word used most frequently? Which was the next most popular word? Ask the people using those words to explain why they used them. Were some words only mentioned once? What were those words and why were they used?

When you have finished, you may wish to play this same game with some other works discussed in this chapter. Some suggested works are provided below:

St. Matthew from the *Gospel Book of Archbishop Ebbo of Reims* (Figure 9.6, page 144).

Adam and Eve Reproached by the Lord after the Fall (Figure 9.7, page 145).

Annunciation from a Swabian Gospel Manuscript (Figure 9.24, page 157).

Chapter 10

Prepare a walking tour through a building in your community that you feel is worthy of closer examination. You might wish to tour a new building, or an older one that has been in place for so long that most people now take it for granted. It is a good idea to prepare a list of questions before beginning this tour. This could be done alone or with the help of other members of your class. The questions you prepare and try to answer during your tour might include some of the following:

- Is the façade of the building welcoming, or does it seem forbidding?
- What effect does light have on the outside of this building?
- How is the outside of the building decorated?
- From the outside, does it appear that the interior will be spacious or cramped; light or dark; ornate or plain?
- Does the outside of the building prepare you for what you find inside, or are you surprised by the contrast?
- Is the space inside the building easy or difficult to define? Is it cluttered or open?
- Is the emphasis inside on breadth, depth, or height?
- Is there some dominant focus of attention and, if so, what is it?

- Does one art element seem to dominate in the building—is it color, value, line, texture, shape, form, space?
- What effect, if any, does light have on the interior of this building?
- Do you sense a feeling of movement in the way the forms have been used? If so, what is the direction of that movement?
- What was your first impression of this building?
- What is your lasting impression of this building?

When you have completed your tour, share what you have learned with your class.

Chapter 11

In this chapter you were introduced to several important sculptors of the Renaissance period. Of course, these were not the only notable sculptors working in Italy at that time. The names of six others are Jacopo della Quercia, Nanni di Banco, Andrea del Verrocchio, Luca della Robbia, Antonio Pollaiuolo, and Desiderio da Settignano.

Select one of the artists named above and then refer to the art-history books in your school or community library to learn more about him and his art. Choose a sculpture by that artist that you find most interesting and do a written study of it, using the four art-criticism operations (Figure 3.17, page 56). Make certain that you select a sculpture that is clearly illustrated in one or more

of the art-history books you are using. When you are finished, you may want to present what you have learned about this sculpture to the members of your class. If you do, it would be helpful if you brought to class a large illustration or a slide of the sculpture and referred to it as you discussed the sculpture's aesthetic qualities.

Save some time at the end of your presentation for questions. If there are questions indicating that the class wants to know more about the sculptor, someone—perhaps you—may volunteer to do a written study of this artist and his works, using the four art-history operations (Figure 3.7, page 46). A report to the class could be scheduled for delivery at a later date.

Chapter 12

In this chapter you studied three fifteenth-century northern artists—Jan van Eyck, Rogier van der Weyden, and Hugo van der Goes. Choose one of these three artists and then visit your school or community library to learn even more about him from the art-history books found there. Of course, you will come across several paintings by that artist that you have never seen before. Select one of these unfamiliar works and do a written study of it using the four art-criticism operations (Figure 3.17, page 56). When you have done this, ask your instructor if you can present what you have learned about the

work in class. Make sure you bring to class an illustration or a slide of the work you are discussing, *but do not reveal the name of the artist.* At the end of your presentation, ask if anyone can determine which of the three artists studied in this chapter painted the picture. You may find that there are differences of opinion on the identity of the artist. Once the discussion is over, it will be up to you to provide the name of the artist and any new information about him that you learned as a result of your library study.

Chapter 13

(a) The paintings created in Venice during the late fifteenth and early sixteenth centuries differed in many ways from the paintings produced in Florence and Rome at about the same time. These differences become apparent when you compare the works of two well-known Venetian artists, Giorgione and Titian, with the works of such Florentine and Roman artists as Piero della Francesca, Sandro Botticelli, Leonardo da Vinci, Michelangelo, and Raphael (see Chapter 11).

As a self-test, examine the list of statements below and decide which describe works by Venetian artists and which describe works by Florentine and Roman artists.

(b) Some artists choose to show every detail of the subjects they paint. Others choose not to include every detail, preferring instead to have viewers use their imaginations to fill in the parts that are missing or hidden from view in some way. Look closely at the paintings illustrated in Chapters 12 and 13. Can you identify at least two works in which the artist went to great lengths to include each and every detail? Can you find two works in which the artist did not include all the details and even hid some of the important parts of the painting from view? Of these four works, which one is most appealing to you? Is it appealing because it is very detailed, or because the lack of detail forced you to use your own imagination to "fill in" what was missing or hidden?

They were interested in drawing and less interested in color.

They discarded the old, established rules of composition and used color and light to unify their paintings.

They tended to use less intense, grayer tones of color.

They were concerned with the relationship and balance of lines in their compositions.

They employed a full range of bright colors in their paintings.

They introduced themes without either religious or Classical traditions and which had no other purpose than to provide visual pleasure.

They sought complete harmony in their paintings by means of perfect design and balanced arrangements.

They were more concerned with the use of light and dark to suggest three-dimensional, solid bodies and objects existing in real space.

Their preference for color, light, and texture can be traced to centuries of close contact with the East.

They used the ancient Classical momuments of Greece and Rome as the inspiration for their artworks.

Chapter 14

Included on the following page is an illustration of a painting done by an artist discussed in Chapter 14. Match this mystery painting to each of the paintings studied in this chapter and try to identify the artist who painted it. Then, on a sheet of paper, list the reasons for your choice.

When you are finished, you may wish to share your list of reasons with the members of your class. Perhaps they were asked by the instructor to do the same thing. If so, did everyone identify the same artist as the creator of the mystery painting? You may find that there are some differences of opinion about the identity of this artist and this could lead to a lively discussion.

Would you like to know who painted the mystery picture? The following clues, taken from Chapter 14, will help you make a positive identification:

- This artist's paintings demonstrate how pictures can be used to tell stories.
- Often, these stories were not religious or historical, but were simple tales involving common people and familiar events.

- This artist owned an inn and often painted the people who came there to joke, sing, and enjoy themselves.

To find out who painted the mystery picture, turn to page 436.

Allen Memorial Art Museum, Oberlin College, Oberlin, Ohio. R. T. Miller, Mrs. F. F. Prentiss, Charles F. Olney Funds, 57.14

Chapter 15

Compare Goya's painting of *The Third of May, 1808* (Figure 15.11, page 279) with Velázquez's *Surrender of Breda* (Figure 14.18, page 263). Clearly, both these paintings deal with war, but the attitudes of the two artists toward this subject are quite different. Prepare a short report in which you discuss how their attitudes toward war differed. Be sure to base your arguments on the information found in each of their paintings. End your report by stating which of these two artworks made the deepest impression on you—and explain why.

Chapter 16

(a) Do a written study using the four art-history operations (Figure 3.7, page 46) on Courbet's *Burial at Ornans* (Figure 16.10, page 295) and El Greco's *Burial of Count Orgaz* (Figure 13.8, page 231).

From what you have learned of these two artists during this assignment, explain why they interpreted the same subject in such different ways.

(b) The illustrations you find in books and short stories are often very helpful in presenting a vivid image of important characters, settings, and events. At other times these illustrations provide in visual form the ideas and emotions that the author is trying to communicate to readers. Examine thoroughly Figures 16.15, page 302, and 16.17, page 303, and select one of these as the illustration for a short story you will write. Make certain that your story takes into account everything you find in the illustration, including characters, setting, events, ideas, and emotions.

Once your story is written, have some of your friends read it, or read it out loud to the members of your class. When this has been done, ask them to answer the following questions:

• Did the story make effective use of the images provided by the illustration?

• Were there important things in the illustration that were overlooked in the story?

• Did the story reflect the same moods or feelings found in the picture?

• What was the most important thing they learned from the story? Could they have learned the same thing from the picture alone?

• What was their opinion of the picture before they read or heard the story?

• Did their opinion of the picture change as a result of the story?

• How might their stories differ from the one you wrote?

(c) As a celebrated critic, you are angered after reading the following paragraph in a letter published in a New York newspaper:

> . . . and perhaps the biggest joke in the entire Metropolitan Museum collection is Rosa Bonheur's *Horse Fair*. This is clearly a bad work of art and its lack of quality is magnified because the painting is so big. It is time that real appreciators of art mount a movement to have this picture removed from the museum and hidden somewhere out of sight!

What is there about this paragraph that angers you so much? Write your own letter in support of *The Horse Fair*, but make certain that you do not make the same mistakes found in the letter above. Use the four art-criticism operations (Figure 3.17, page 56) to help you prepare such a letter.

Chapter 17

Prepare a number of small cards and, on each, write the name of one of the theories of art discussed in Chapter 3. Place these cards in a box and pass it around a group of friends or members of your class so that each person can select one. Everyone should then reexamine the paintings and sculptures illustrated in Chapter 17 and select one that possesses the aesthetic qualities stressed by the theory written on his or her card. In a short presentation, each student should do the following:

• Identify the theory of art he or she received.

• Describe the aesthetic qualities favored by that theory.

• Single out the work of art he or she feels possesses those aesthetic qualities.

• Point out the aesthetic qualities in the work of art.

Some interesting questions may arise from this activity that you may wish to discuss. For example, how many times was the same work selected and discussed in terms of one particular theory? How many times was the same work selected and discussed in terms of different theories? Does this mean that someone made a mistake? If not, how can this be explained? Was one work mentioned more than any other illustrated in this chapter? If so, what was there about this work that caused so many to select it?

Chapter 18

In this chapter you learned that Henri Matisse was regarded as the leader of a group of artists who were known as the Fauves. You also learned that Georges Rouault was associated with this group. But who were the other Fauves and how did their paintings compare with those of Matisse and Rouault?

To find out, consult the art-history books in your school or community library. There you will discover a great deal about the other Fauve artists and see examples of their paintings. After you have examined those paintings, select one that is especially appealing to you and do a written study of it using the four art-criticism operations (Figure 3.17, page 56). Once you have done that, you may find that your curiosity is aroused and you will want to find out more about the artist who painted it. To help accomplish this, do another written study, this time using the four art-history operations (Figure 3.7, page 46).

Ask your instructor for an opportunity to share your findings with the other members of your class. When you do this, be sure to bring in an illustration of the Fauvist painting you selected for study so they can see it.

Chapter 19

Select the work of art illustrated in Chapter 19 that you liked the *least*. Do a written study of this work, using the four art-criticism operations (Figure 3.17, page 56) as you have in previous chapters. However, in this case, you must arrive at a *positive judgment*.

Chapter 20

(a) In the eighteenth century, a Chinese emperor invited two European artists to paint decorations for several of his palaces. Unfortunately, this particular meeting of East and West was not destined to end happily. Even though the European artists were recognized as highly skilled painters in their native countries, their work was rejected by the emperor. Discuss with other members of your class why you think this might have happened.

(b) For a moment, place yourself in the role of the Chinese emperor. You are accustomed to seeing paintings like the ones illustrated in Figures 20.7 and 20.9. What would your reactions be to European paintings like those illustrated in Figures 11.14 and 11.21? Discuss with other members of the class your answer to this and the following questions:

• Would you be pleased with the way the human figures dominate in both these paintings?

• Would you be impressed with the way the artists used aerial and linear perspective to create the illusion of deep space in their pictures?

• How would you react to the presence of shadows and other details that add to the realistic appearance of these works?

• Would you marvel at the way both these paintings imitate reality?

• Would you enjoy the rich, textured surface of the oil paint applied to the canvas?

In recent times, artists from the West have learned a great deal from their study of Oriental art. The same can be said for Oriental artists, who have come to regard with less suspicion many of the innovations made by Western artists. This exchange can be beneficial, but it is not without some drawbacks. It is hoped that the unique qualities that distinguish each will not be forgotten and lost as a consequence. What are *your* thoughts on this matter?

Chapter 21

While browsing in a shop that specializes in exotic imports you notice an unusual mask (such as the mask in Figure 21.4) and spend several minutes examining it. The owner of the shop, noticing your interest, tells you that the mask is African, but that he has no other information about it. He is willing, however, to sell it for a modest amount to make room for some new items that have just arrived. The amount quoted is well within your means and would be a bargain for an authentic African mask. Should you buy it? Take a position pro or con and prepare an argument to defend this position. In this argument be sure to say:

• Whether or not you think the mask is authentic.

• What clues you relied on when making that decision.

• If you think the mask is a successful work of art.

• What aesthetic qualities you relied on when making that decision.

Appendix: Art-Related Careers

There are many reasons why people choose to study art. Some find it enlightening and exciting to learn more about the artists and artworks they encounter in books, galleries, and museums. Others, eager to develop their own skills as artists, recognize that past and present masters can be among their most valuable teachers. Still others, hoping to learn more about past civilizations, regard works of art as windows to those past civilizations. They realized that information about any previous civilization would be meager indeed if it were not for that civilization's art.

No matter what the reason, if you enjoy studying or creating art you may want to consider the many career opportunities in the art field. Every year challenging and rewarding positions are available in the visual arts. Schools, museums, galleries, small businesses, and large corporations look for creative and knowledgeable persons for visual arts jobs. An awareness of some of these opportunities may help you as you begin thinking about your own career plans. It may also prompt you to respond to the experiences you undergo in your art class with even greater interest and enthusiasm. For this reason, a brief discussion of just a few career opportunities involving the visual arts is presented here. For more detailed information concerning careers in art, consult your art teacher, guidance counselor, and librarian. You may be surprised to find that art and art-related career opportunities are so plentiful and so varied.

Advertising Art

The advertising industry is concerned with selling products and services to people. The history of advertising can be traced far back into history to a time when people with goods and services to sell or messages to deliver realized that they would be more successful if they could communicate to as many people as possible. It is not altogether surprising then that on a papyrus found among the ancient ruins of Egypt there is an advertisement offering a reward for runaway slaves. In Pompeii, there were political ads that advised readers to vote for certain candidates for public office and not to vote for others. And, in the Middle Ages, the town crier often mixed his news announcements with "commercials" for various local business establishments.

Today, when a manufacturing company develops a new product, it faces the same task of trying to tell as many people as possible about it. The advantages of the new product are presented to potential buyers through a variety of media including television, radio, newspapers, magazines, and billboards. Imaginative, creative people are needed to produce the visual materials and write the messages delivered by these media.

For example, suppose that the Acme Company has created a revolutionary new product known as the Gadget. The success of the company and everyone associated with it may depend upon how well the Gadget is received in the marketplace. Thus, an advertising firm is contracted to coordinate a campaign aimed at introducing the Gadget to the buying public.

The art director of the advertising firm works with a team of experts who gather information about the potential market and the consumer. After closely studying this information, a selling strategy is agreed upon and formally presented to Acme Company executives. If they approve it, specialists within the advertising agency would be asked to prepare newspaper and magazine advertisements, while others would be assigned to plan radio and television commercials. People with art skills, working closely with copywriters, would design the illustrations and photographs to be used in newspaper and magazine ads. An important part of their assignment would be to select and arrange the proper kind of type for those ads.

In the case of the Gadget, the artist and copywriter would probably discuss several different ways to showcase their product in ads. Some of these different ways might include the following:

• Showing the Gadget in such a way that its streamlined design would make it an attractive addition to any home.

• Showing the Gadget being used by someone who is obviously enjoying its efficiency and ease of operation.

• Showing a smiling man taking a nap because he finished an unpleasant household chore so quickly and effortlessly with the aid of the Gadget.

• Showing the Gadget in elegant surroundings to suggest that it is used in the most fashionable households.

• Showing the Gadget rolling off the production line at a modern factory, making it obvious that only the best workers, materials, and machines were used in its manufacture.

• Showing the Gadget in the hands of a well-known movie star or sports figure who urges readers to be the first in their neighborhood to own one.

It might help you gain a better understanding of the planning that goes into a magazine ad if you select an ad from a magazine and study it closely. You may be surprised to discover how the artist and copywriter who produced it succeeded in arousing your interest and directing your eye to the most important objects and copy. To do this, they had to have an understanding of the visual vocabulary—the elements and principles of art (which you learned about in Chapter 2 and applied to your encounters with art throughout this book).

Television commercials require a host of people to create costumes, sets, and props. Even more people serve as filmmakers, interior designers, fashion designers, makup specialists, and fine artists. All these people working together are needed to produce a video message which, if successful, will arouse viewer curiosity and eventually have them eager to purchase the Gadget.

If an advertising campaign is effective, a product such as the Gadget could become a familiar item in thousands of households. As a result, the Acme Company and its employees would prosper. Further, the people associated with the advertising firm would be rewarded with new contracts from other companies hoping to have their products sold as effectively as the Gadget. As for consumers, they might well wonder how they ever managed to get along without the Gadget.

Graphic Design

The next time you watch television, pay attention to the symbols used by the networks to identify themselves. The people who design such symbols, or logos, are known as graphic designers. Just think of the many different symbols that you have come to associate with various corporations and manufacturers—the CBS "eye," the Izod alligator, the golden arches of McDonald's. And, how many times have you purchased a pair of jeans because of the special symbol sewn onto a back pocket? Of course, graphic designers do more than create symbols for companies. Who do you think designed the colorful box that contains the indispensable Gadget?

Graphic designers are also employed as magazine and book designers. Before a new magazine or book is published, an artist is often selected to design the layout. The designer of a magazine can make it look sophisticated, glamorous, humorous, folksy, homey, or inform-

ative to appeal to a particular type of reader. You can see how effectively they do this by comparing two different kinds of magazines, perhaps a newsmagazine like Time or Newsweek with a fashion magazine like Glamour. These magazines differ in more than just the kind of articles and advertisements they contain. The newsmagazine is designed to look as though it will convey timely and important information to readers in a fast, efficient manner. The fashion magazine typically has a more elegant, unhurried look about it. It may contain longer, in-depth articles and large, colorful photographs that explain and illustrate how readers can make themselves look and feel more attractive and appealing.

Book designers are employed by publishing houses or independent agencies to plan the layouts for the books that are produced. They must carefully consider and integrate the ideas and requirements presented by representatives of the publishing house and the author. Then they may select the style of type, create line drawings and color illustrations, and secure photographs for the book. Further, they may decide how these items are to be arranged on each page. Included among the decisions they might make are how much white space to use, where color could be most effective, and what colors to choose to dramatically or subtly attract the reader's attention. Frequently, the designer submits a design for the cover and dust jacket of a book as well.

How important are book designers? They are very important. Their contribution to the success of a book is evident when you consider that an effective design will invite people to pick up a book, flip through the pages, and begin reading. An unsuccessful design, on the other hand, may cause potential readers to push the book aside after flipping through pages that lack visual appeal.

Fashion Design

Fashion designers learn to use fabrics of different colors, textures, and weights to create garments that people wear for different occasions. A designer creating a design for a winter jacket, for example, must make certain that the jacket is warm, comfortable, and attractive. This means selecting the most suitable fabric and fashioning a garment that meets these specifications. If one of these specifications is ignored, the jacket may be rejected by buyers. After all, no one wants a winter jacket that may look stunning, but fails to protect the wearer from the cold. Every garment that the fashion designer creates has different specifications. These must be taken into account if the garments are to be favorably received by buyers.

Interior Design

Interior designers direct their talents to making our living, working, and playing areas more attractive and useful. They plan and supervise the design and arrangement of building interiors and furnishings. When planning the interior space for a home, they take into account the desires and needs of each family member as they go about selecting furniture, fabrics, floor coverings, lighting fixtures, and accessories. Interior designers also consider the various activities associated with each room in the house when designing attractive and functional areas for eating, sleeping, working, and playing and estimate what the work and furnishings will cost for each. In order to help their clients visualize their plans, interior designers work on floor plans and elevations and prepare sketches or perspective drawings. After the client approves the plans and the costs, the designer may make arrangements for purchasing the furnishings and supervises the work of painters, carpet layers, cabinet makers, and other craftspersons.

No one would deny that people are happier and work more efficiently in surroundings that are pleasant and comfortable. For this reason, interior designers are being called upon in greater numbers than ever before to plan the work spaces for entire office buildings, hospitals, libraries, stores, and even factories. Generally, their plans include the complete layout of the rooms within the space allowed by the exterior walls and the framework. Sometimes they are called in by clients who want them to redesign and furnish the interiors of older buildings. Business people realize that when their employees are comfortable and content their efficiency increases. This in turn leads to lower production costs, which means that the items or services provided by the business will be more competitive. No wonder then that the drab, disagreeable interiors that characterized many of the work spaces of the past are being replaced today with colorful, pleasant places in which to work.

Industrial Design

What do toys, tools, furniture, home appliances, light fixtures, and automobiles have in common? All those items and just about anything else with which you come into contact every day of your life have been carefully designed to function easily and look appealing. Specialists whose job it is to create those designs are known as industrial designers. These specialists are called upon by manufacturers to work on things as simple as a tamper-proof cap for an aspirin bottle, or as complex as an information-processing system.

The Gadget, for example, owes its modern, streamlined appearance to the efforts of industrial designers who worked closely with the engineers who developed it. Those designers were not satisfied that the Gadget was easy to use and did the job that it was supposed to do. They wanted it to have an eye-catching appearance as well.

The public has wide choices of styles in products such as radios, television sets, and furniture. For this reason, a primary objective of industrial designers is to design products that will compete favorably with similar goods on the market. Only a few months after the Gadget reached the store shelves, other manufacturers were coming out with their versions of the handy appliance. The industrial designers at the Acme Company had to be ready to meet this challenge. They made certain that new models of the Gadget looked more attractive, were easier to use, could make use of a host of accessories, and were less expensive than the competition.

To be successful, industrial designers must know about various production processes as well as the characteristics of the different materials used in those processes. Moreover, they must understand completely the function of each product with which they are working. The most successful products are those in which design and function complement each other. After all, who would want to buy a Gadget that looked fantastic but was so delicate that it required constant maintenance and expensive repairs? Of course, the same question could be asked of a Gadget that was a marvel of efficiency but looked so clumsy and unattractive that it had to be hidden away when not in use.

Art Education

Many people with an interest in art and a desire to work with children and young people decide to become art teachers. These people realize that there can be as much creativity and excitement involved in planning and presenting stimulating art lessons as there is in designing and executing a painting or a sculpture.

A teaching career in art requires a college education which combines a broad background in art materials and techniques with instruction pertaining to child development, learning theory, teaching techniques, and curriculum planning. Effective art teachers are prepared to provide their students with a wide variety of art experiences. Consequently, they offer students opportunities to create their own art forms and to respond to the art forms created by others. An art teacher's responsibilities are not limited to helping talented students develop their artistic skills. They also include preparing as many students as possible to be intelligent consumers of art. In order to do all of this, art teachers design their programs to include educational experiences in studio, history, and criticism.

Today art teachers can be found working in a variety of settings. While it is true that most teachers continue to be employed in elementary and secondary schools, others work in museums, hospitals, retirement centers, nursery schools, and day-care centers. Those interested in teaching at the college or university levels continue their formal educations by working for graduate degrees in art studio, history, or education. Some obtain graduate degrees in such related areas as museum science and arts administration.

Museum Science

The basic and traditional tasks of a museum are to acquire, conserve, display, and study art. By doing these things, the museum, like the university and the library, performs the valuable service of passing on to each new generation the rich cultural heritage of the past. Here curators with advanced degrees in art history and museum science are responsible for securing and exhibiting artworks for the general public and scholars to view, enjoy, and study. Drawing upon their knowledge of human attention, perception, and learning, curators seek to impart specific knowledge as well as teach general ideas. To do this, carefully selected objects are labeled and exhibited in such a way that they teach and inform viewers. Thus, each visitor undergoes an educational experience while walking through the halls of a museum.

However, museum curators are also scholars. As such they carry on research into their own specialized areas of interest. Eventually they report their findings in books, lectures, and papers prepared for publication in scholarly journals. You met two such scholars, Helen and Robert, in Chapter 3. Helen, you will recall, was a historian and Robert a critic.

Of course, modern museums must not limit themselves to the needs of scholars alone. They must also devote themselves to the spread of knowledge to an ever-increasing and interested general public. For this reason, major museums in the United States have set up education departments. Educators within these depart-

ments teach volunteer guides, known as docents, to take groups of adults and children through the museum's exhibitions. These educators are also responsible for preparing various publications, providing lectures, producing radio and television programs, and planning special educational displays and exhibitions. Frequently, too, they are in charge of after-school or Saturday art programs for people of different ages and levels of ability. However, the art programs offered in museums are designed to supplement rather than duplicate the art programs provided in the schools.

Arts Administration

People who choose to become arts administrators assume administrative responsibilities in public and private museums, libraries, theaters, concert halls, and art centers. These administrators oversee the daily operations of their institutions, and this involves them in a variety of important tasks. They are in charge of securing operational funds, preparing budgets, organizing volunteers, arranging publicity, and working closely with various groups to make the institution a vital and active part of community life.

Art Therapy

Art therapy is a profession which combines interests in the visual arts with psychiatry. A career in art therapy is especially rewarding for people with the personality and patience needed to work with the emotionally disturbed. The therapist uses art as a means of opening the lines of communication with patients. This is done by encouraging patients to discuss freely the meaning or meanings of the images that they create with various art media. Thus art can serve as a way for patients to express their pent-up feelings and emotions. Moreover, patients who project these repressed emotions into images are often able to interpret the meanings of these images for themselves, thereby aiding the efforts of the therapist.

Some art therapists work as members of therapeutic teams in psychiatric wards of large hospitals, in clinics, in community health centers, and in prisons. Others are employed at institutions and special schools for students who are emotionally disturbed or have learning disabilities. Therapists also work with individuals who are blind, deaf, or are in some other way physically handicapped.

Corporate Art Advising

A few years ago only a handful of major corporations in the United States sought advice from critics and museum personnel when purchasing works of art. At that time art was acquired mainly for decorative purposes. Pictures and sculptures were used to add interest to executive offices and reception rooms. Recently, however, a growing number of corporations have exhibited a desire to develop their art collections. With this increased activity in corporate collecting, a new profession was born—the corporate art adviser.

The duties of corporate advisers include purchasing artworks, developing a unified collection, and advising the corporation on laws and taxation as they apply to art. They also speak to various groups about the collection and organize traveling exhibitions. Consultants are either full-time employees of corporations or work as free-lance advisers for several companies at the same time.

This list of art-related careers is by no means complete. Furthermore, it is unlikely that any such list could remain complete for very long. Even now new demands prompted by new technology offer unique career opportunities for people with interests and talent in art. Many of these careers were unheard of just a few years ago. One need look no further than the rapid development and widespread use of computers to see an example of this. In the next few years, more and more artist-technicians will be needed to create increasingly sophisticated graphics and animations with computers for a wide range of uses. Their unique creations will go beyond the wildest dreams of even the most imaginative of yesterday's artists.

Glossary

Abstract art Artworks which stress the importance of the elements and principles of design rather than subject matter. Abstract artists select and then exaggerate or simplify the forms suggested by the world around them. The paintings of Picasso (Figure 18.10) and Braque (Figure 18.13) as well as the sculptures of Moore (Figure 19.18), Hepworth (Figure 19.19), and Lipchitz (Figure 19.20) are examples of abstract art.

Abstract Expressionism A twentieth-century painting style in which artists applied paint freely to their huge canvases in an effort to show feelings and emotions. It is characterized by a strong dependence on accident and chance, and there is no effort to represent subject matter. Some artists who painted in this style were de Kooning (Figure 19.15), Pollock (Figure 19.16), and Frankenthaler (Figure 19.17).

Academic A term used to describe works of art that were done according to established, traditional ways and so were not original.

Acropolis This is the Greek word meaning "high city." Ancient Greek builders chose to erect their towns around fortified hills upon which their main temples were placed. The most famous acropolis is in Athens (Figure 6.4). It was here that the Parthenon was built.

Aerial perspective Aerial, or atmospheric, perspective is a method of showing the effect of distance on a flat surface. It is achieved by using bluer, lighter, and duller hues for distant objects in a picture. The change in hue suggests the effects of light, air, and distance. One of the first artists to use this technique was Masaccio (Figure 11.3).

Aesthetic qualities Cues within a work of art, such as literal, visual, and expressive qualities, which are studied during the art-criticism process. See also "Literal qualities," "Visual qualities," and "Expressive qualities."

Aisle A long, narrow space on either side of the nave of a church, usually between a row of columns and the outer wall. It is often referred to as a "side aisle."

Altamira A cave in northern Spain where a large number of prehistoric paintings of animals were discovered (Figures 4.1, 4.4, and 4.5).

Ambulatory A semi-circular aisle curving around the apse of a church behind the main altar. Developed during the Romanesque period, it made it easier for large religious processions to move about inside the church. The addition of the ambulatory led to the construction of radiating chapels, each with its small altar for worship (Chapter 9).

Analogous colors Colors that are next to each other on the color wheel (Figure 2.3) and are closely related, such as blue, blue-green, and green.

Apse The semicircular area at the end of the church opposite the main entry. It was here that the altar was placed (Figure 9.15).

Aqueduct A channel built to carry water to towns and cities. In some places these channels were supported by a series of arches. The Romans built many aqueducts, including those found in Spain at Tarragona (Figure 7.6) and Segovia (Figure 7.7).

Archaic This name is given to the early stage in the development of an art style. It is at this stage that the characteristics of the fully developed style are found, although in simpler forms. The term is often used to describe the art of ancient Greek artists whose early sculptures (Figures 6.9 and 6.10) were a step in the direction of more natural figures.

Armory Show This was the first large exhibition of modern art in America. It was held in the 69th Regiment Armory building in New York City in 1913. Although the show was soundly criticized by the public and the press, it had a great impact on American artists who were influenced by the works of modern European artists (Chapter 18).

Ashcan School A group of early twentieth-century American artists who painted pictures of city life. Critics who did not appreciate their choice of subject matter—alleys, tenements, and slum dwellers—called this group The Ashcan School, a label that is now better known than the group's original name, "The Eight." Sloan (Figure 18.18) is one of the best known artists in this group.

Asymmetrical balance A way of organizing the parts of a design so that one side differs from the other without destroying the overall harmony. Also known as "informal" balance, it can be observed in Diebenkorn's painting entitled *Woman by a Large Window* (Figure 2.19). Asymmetrical and symmetrical are the two kinds of balance, which is a principle of art.

Axis line An imaginary line which indicates movement and the direction of movement. It can be observed in Lawrence's painting entitled *War Series: Another Patrol* (Figure 2.9).

Balance A principle of art, it refers to the way the art elements are arranged to create a feeling of stability in a work. Balance can be symmetrical, or formal (Figure 2.18), or it can be asymmetrical, or informal (Figure 2.19).

Baptistry A building used for baptism in the Christian church. A famous example is the baptistry of the cathedral in Florence, Italy.

Baroque The art style of the Counter-Reformation in the seventeenth century. Although some features appear in Dutch art, the Baroque style was limited mainly to Catholic countries. It is a style in which painters, sculptors, and architects sought movement, contrast, and variety in their works. The dramatic flair in painting and sculpture can be seen in the works of Rubens (Figure 14.8) and Bernini (Figure 14.4). In architecture, Borromini used curved surfaces to create a pattern of light and dark as well as a sense of movement on his church facades (Figure 14.2).

Barrel vault A half-round stone ceiling made by placing a series of arches from front to back. Also known as a *tunnel* vault, it was developed by the Romans and adopted later by Romanesque church builders (Figure 9.15).

Basilica A type of public building erected in ancient Rome. Basilicas had a rectangular plan with two or four rows of columns placed along the longer axis to support the roof. This plan was later adopted by Early Christian church builders (Figure 8.4).

Batik A method of dyeing cloth which involves the use of removable wax to repel the dye on parts of the design where dye is not desired.

Benin A people and former kingdom of western Africa. Benin artists of the sixteenth and seventeenth centuries realized a high level of quality in their bronze castings (Postscript Figure 1).

Book of Hours A book for private devotions containing prayers for different hours of the day. Often these books were richly illustrated. One of the most famous was produced by the Limbourg brothers for the Duke of Berry (Figure 10.17).

Brayer A roller used to ink a surface by hand.

Buddhism A religious belief based on the teachings of Gautama Buddha, who held that suffering is a part of life but that mental and moral self-purification can bring about a state of illumination, carrying the believer beyond suffering and material existence.

Buttress A support or brace which counteracts the outward thrust of an arch or vault. A flying buttress is an arch which reaches over a side aisle to support the heavy stone roof of a cathedral (Figure 10.4).

Byzantine art The art of the Eastern Roman Empire. Byzantine paintings and mosaics are characterized by a rich use of color and figures which seem flat and stiff. Intended as religious lessons, they were presented clearly and simply in order to be easily learned (Figures 8.12 and 8.13). Byzantine architects favored the central plan covered by a huge dome. An example is Hagia Sophia in Constantinople (Figures 8.6 through 8.9).

Campanile A bell tower near, or attached to, a church (Figure 8.3).

Capital The top element of a pillar or column. There are three basic types of capitals which originated with the ancient Greeks: Doric, Ionic, and Corinthian (Figure 6.5).

Catacombs Underground tunnels in which the Early Christians in Rome and other communities buried their dead (Figure 8.1). Some catacombs also contained chapels and meeting rooms. The painted decorations found in the catacombs are the earliest known forms of Christian art (Figure 8.2).

Cathedral The principal church of a diocese, which contains the *cathedra,* or "bishop's chair." An excellent example is the Cathedral of Chartres in France (Figure 10.7).

Ceramics The art of pottery making. Objects are made of

clay and fired at high temperatures in a kiln or oven to make them stronger.

Chapel An area or compartment in a church containing an altar dedicated to a particular saint.

Classical This term has come to have several meanings. Originally it was used when referring to the art of ancient Greece produced during the fifth and fourth centuries B.C. Later it included all works of art created from 600 B.C. until the fall of Rome. Still later it was used to describe any art form thought to be inspired or influenced by ancient Greek or Roman examples. Today, *Classical* is used to describe perfection of form, with an emphasis on harmony and unity and restraint of emotion. Usually, it is applied to works that are representational but idealistic.

Clerestory This term describes a wall of a building which is raised above an adjoining roof. Thus the walls of a nave in a Christian church are higher than the roof over the side aisles. The clerestory contains windows for light and ventilation. Because of the heavy walls, the clerestory windows of a Romanesque church were small and admitted little light. Development of the pointed arch, piers, and flying buttresses in the Gothic cathedral made possible the enlargement of this window area.

Cloister A covered walkway around an open court or garden. It was a common feature of Medieval monasteries such as San Juan de la Peña in northern Spain (Figure 9.4).

Collage A picture or design created with such elements as paper, photographs, cloth, string, etc. Introduced by the Cubist artists, it was widely used by artists who followed and is a familiar technique in contemporary art (Figure 2.13).

Colonnade A line of columns supporting lintels or arches. Colonnades have been used along streets, courtyards, and around temples such as the Parthenon (Figure 6.1).

Color An element of art with three properties: (1) hue, the color name, e.g., red, yellow, blue, etc.; (2) intensity, the purity and strength of a color, e.g., bright red or dull red; and (3) value, the lightness or darkness of a color (Chapter 2).

Column An upright post used to bear weight. Columns usually consist of a base at the bottom, a shaft, and a capital (Figure 6.5). A half-column is attached to a wall and does not bear weight. Half-columns were used for decorative purposes on the Temple of Fortuna Virilis in Rome (Figure 7.1).

Complementary colors Colors that are directly opposite each other on the color wheel, such as red and green, blue and orange, and violet and yellow. When complements are mixed together in the right proportions, they form a neutral gray (Figure 2.3).

Complexity Closely related to variety, a principle of art, this term refers to a way of combining art elements in involved ways, to create intricate and complicated relationships. A picture composed of many shapes of different colors, sizes, and textures would be called complex (Figure 2.22). See also "Variety."

Composition The organization of the elements of art in a work, usually according to the principles of art.

Content The subject matter in a work of art.

Contour drawing A drawing in which contour lines alone are used to represent subject matter.

Contour line A line or lines that surround and define the edges of an object or figures. Dark, heavy contour lines can be found in Toulouse-Lautrec's painting entitled *A Corner of the Moulin de la Galette* (Figure 2.7).

Contrapposto A way of sculpting a human figure in a natural pose with the weight of one leg, the shoulder, and hips counterbalancing each other. It was a technique developed late in the Greek period. An excellent example is the *Doryphoros* (or *Spear Bearer*) by Polyclitus (Figure 6.16).

Contrast Closely related to emphasis, a principle of art, this term refers to a way of combining art elements to stress the differences between those elements. Thus, a painting might have bright colors which contrast with dull colors, or angular shapes which contrast with rounded shapes. Used in this way, contrast can emphasize and direct attention to points of interest (Figure 2.20). See also "Emphasis."

Cool colors Colors often associated with water, sky, spring, and foliage and suggest coolness. These are the colors which contain blue and green and appear on one side of the color wheel opposite the warm colors (Figure 2.3).

Cross-hatching Shading created by crossed parallel lines.

Cubism A twentieth-century art movement developed by Picasso and Braque in which the subject matter is broken up, analyzed, and reassembled in an abstract form. Picasso's *Glass of Absinthe* is an example of this style of art (Figure 18.10).

Dada An early twentieth-century art movement which ridiculed contemporary culture and traditional art forms. It was born as a consequence of the collapse of social and moral values which developed during World War I. Many artists associated with this movement later went on to become Surrealist artists.

Design The organization, plan, or composition of a work of art. An effective design is one in which the elements and principles have been combined to achieve an overall sense of unity (Chapter 2). Since the nineteenth century, this term has also been applied to the production of attractive and well crafted utilitarian objects.

Diagonal Having a slanted direction. A clear example of a bold diagonal line is the flag pole in George Grosz's painting entitled, *Waving the Flag* (Figure 19.8).

Distort To deform or stretch an object or figure out of its normal shape to exaggerate its proportions. El Greco's elongated figures (Figure 13.7) are examples of moderate distortion. More extreme examples of distortion are found in Picasso's painting entitled *Guernica* (Figure 18.11).

Dome A hemispherical vault or ceiling over a circular opening. It rises above the central part of a building. Sometimes it is elevated further by being placed on a circular drum. Examples of domes are found on the Pantheon (Figure 7.13), Hagia Sophia (Figure 8.6), and the Cathedral of Florence (Figure 11.12).

Drum The cylindrical wall supporting a dome. The drum used by Brunelleschi on the Cathedral of Florence (Figure 11.12) served to raise the dome to a more lofty position above the building.

Elements The basic components used by the artist when producing works of art. The elements consist of color, value, line, shape, form, texture, and space.

Elongate Stretching an object or figure lengthwise, thus altering its proportions and making it look taller and more slender. For example, the figures of the Madonna and Christ Child in Parmigianino's *Madonna with the Long Neck* (Figure 13.4) have been elongated.

Emotionalism A theory of art which places emphasis on the expressive qualities. According to this theory, the most important thing about a work of art is the vivid communication of moods, feelings, and ideas.

Emphasis A principle of art, it refers to a way of combining elements to stress the differences between those elements and to create one or more centers of interest in a work. Often, contrasting elements are used to direct and focus attention on the most important parts of a composition. See also "Contrast."

Engobe A kind of slip often used when pottery is to be glazed. See also "Slip."

Engraving A method of cutting or incising a design into a material, usually metal, with a sharp tool. A print can be made by inking such an engraved surface. An example is *Knight, Death, and the Devil* by Dürer (Figure 13.10).

Epistle A message or letter; in the New Testament, any of the letters written by an Apostle.

Etruscans Before the days of Rome's greatness, Italy was the home of a people of advanced civilization known as the Etruscans. These people rose to prosperity and power, then disappeared, leaving behind many unanswered questions conerning their origin and their culture. Because little Etruscan literature remains and the language of inscriptions on their monuments has been only partially deciphered, scholars have gained most of their knowledge of the Etruscans from studying the remains of their buildings, monuments, and tombs.

Evangelists The four writers of the Gospels in the New Testament: Matthew, Mark, Luke, and John. Frequently, they are represented in works of art by their symbols: an angel, a lion, an ox, and an eagle (Figure 10.12).

Expressionism A twentieth-century art movement in which artists tried to communicate their strong emotional feelings through artworks. Kollwitz's *Death and the Mother* (Figure 18.5) is an example of a painting done in this style.

Expressive qualities The feelings, moods, and ideas communicated to the viewer through a work of art. This aesthetic quality is favored by emotionalism.

Façade The front of a building (Figures 10.7, 14.1, 14.2). The façade accents the entrance of a building and usually prepares the visitor for the architectural style found inside.

Fauvism An early twentieth-century style of painting in France. The name Fauves, or "Wild Beasts," was given to artists adhering to this style because it was felt that they used brilliant colors in a violent, uncontrolled way. The leader of the Fauves was Henri Matisse (Figure 18.1).

Fettling knife A special knife for working with clay.

Firing A process of applying heat in the making of pottery, done in an oven-like enclosure called a "kiln."

Flying buttress See "Buttress."

Foreground The area of a picture, usually at the bottom, that appears to be closest to the viewer.

Foreshortening A way of drawing or painting an object or person so that it seems to go back into space. Uccello used foreshortening when painting the figures, horses, and broken spears in his *Battle of San Romano* (Figure 11.8).

Form An element of art that is three-dimensional (height, width, *and* depth) and encloses volume. Cubes, spheres, pyramids, and cylinders are examples of various forms.

Forum A central gathering place for the citizens of a city. It was a typical feature of ancient Roman cities.

Formalism A theory of art which places emphasis on the visual qualities. According to this theory, the most important thing about a work of art is the effective organization of the elements of art through the use of the principles.

Fresco A method of painting in which pigments are applied to a thin layer of wet plaster so that they will be absorbed and the painting becomes part of the wall. Giotto's painting of the *Lamentation* (Figure 10.20) was done in this manner.

Frieze A decorative horizontal band usually placed along the upper end of a wall. Parts of a processional frieze that once decorated the outside wall of the Parthenon are in museums in London (Figure 6.13), Paris (Figure 6.14), and Athens.

Function Refers to the intended use or purpose of an object. The term is usually applied to manufactured products, particularly crafts. It is also used when discussing designs for architecture.

Gargoyle A rainspout carved or formed to resemble a grotesque monster. It is a common feature of Gothic cathedrals (Figure 10.15).

Genre The representation of subjects and scenes from everyday life. Genre painting achieved its greatest popularity in seventeenth-century Holland with the works of Steen (Figure 14.14) and Vermeer (Figure 14.15).

Geometric Refers to mechanical, man-made shapes such as squares, rectangles, circles, spirals, and bands. Also, refers to a period in ancient history when decorative patterns made from these shapes were used on pottery. For example, the earliest Greek vases were decorated with bands of simple geometric patterns covering most of the vessel (Figure 6.20).

Glaze A term used in ceramics to describe a thin coating of minerals which produces a glass-like coloring on earthenware. The glaze is fixed by baking the earthenware in a kiln or oven. This makes the surface smooth, shiny, and waterproof.

Gospel The story of Christ's life and His teachings as found in the first four books of the New Testament written by the evangelists Matthew, Mark, Luke, and John.

Gothic The name given to the style of architecture, painting, and sculpture which flourished in western Europe, mainly France and England, between the twelfth and sixteenth centuries. The cathedral is the most impressive example of the Gothic style (Figure 10.7).

Gradation A principle of art, it refers to a way of combining art elements by using a series of gradual changes in those elements. Unlike contrast which stresses sudden changes in elements, gradation refers to a step-by-step change. A gradual change from dark to light values or from large to small shapes would be called gradation (Figure 19.5).

Groin vault A vault formed when two barrel vaults meet at right angles. Groin vaults were used by Roman builders in the construction of the central hall of the Baths of Caracalla (Figure 7.9).

Grout A mortar used for filling cracks and crevices.

Hagia Sophia A church in Istanbul (formerly Constantinople) considered to be the masterpiece of Byzantine architecture. It was commissioned by the Emperor Justinian and built in A.D. 532-537. Hagia Sophia (meaning "Holy Wisdom") is crowned by a dome which is 56.08 m [184 feet] high (Figures 8.6 through 8.9).

Hard-edge Refers to a twentieth century movement in painting in which the edges of shapes are crisp and precise rather than blurred (Figures 19.39 and 19.40).

Harmony A principle of art, it refers to a way of combining elements to accent their similarities and bind the picture parts into a whole. It is often achieved through the use of repetition and simplicity. See also "Repetition" and "Simplicity."

Hellenistic A period of Mediterranean culture influenced by the Greek world following the conquests of Alexander the Great. The expression of inner emotions was more important than beauty to the artists of this period. Many of the features of the Hellenistic Style can be found in the sculpture of the *Dying Gaul* (Figure 6.17).

Hieroglyphics The characters and picture-writing used by the ancient Egyptians.

Highlight The area on any surface which reflects the most light.

Hue See "Color."

Illuminations A term applied to manuscript paintings, particularly those done during the Medieval period. An example of such an illumination is the *Annunciation* from a Swabian Gospel Manuscript of the twelfth century (Figure 9.24).

Illuminated manuscript A manuscript, popular during the Medieval period, in which the pages are decorated with silver, gold, and rich colors. Often these manuscripts contain small pictures known as illuminations or miniatures.

Imitationalism A theory of art which places emphasis on the literal qualities. According to this theory, the most important thing about a work of art is the realistic representation of subject matter. A work is considered successful if it looks like and reminds the viewer of what is seen in the real world.

Impressionism A style of painting that started in France during the 1860s. Impressionist artists tried to paint candid glimpses of their subjects and emphasized the momentary effects of sunlight. The leaders of this movement included Monet (Figure 16.14) and Renoir (Figure 3.3)

Intensity See "Color."

Intermediate (or tertiary) colors Colors produced by mixing unequal amounts of two primary colors. For example, adding more red to the combination of red and yellow will produce the intermediate color of red-orange. Intermediate colors are located between the primary and secondary colors on a color diagram (Figure 2.3).

Keystone The central and highest stone in an arch. It cannot fall out of place because it is wedge-shaped, with the widest part of the wedge at the top. It is the last stone to be set in place during the construction of an arch. By pressing equally on either side, it holds the arch together (Figure 7.4).

Kiln An oven in which earthenware objects are fired or baked. Kilns may be electric, gas, or wood-fired.

Kouros A Greek statue of a male youth who may have been a god or an athlete (Figure 6.9).

Kore A Greek statue of a clothed maiden (Figure 6.10).

Landscape A painting, photograph, or other work of art which shows natural scenery such as mountains, valleys, trees, rivers, and lakes. Constable's painting of *Wivenhoe Park, Essex* (Figure 16.8) is an example of a landscape painting.

Line An element of art which refers to the continuous mark made on some surface by a moving point. It may be two-dimensional (pencil on paper), three-dimensional (wire), or implied (the edge of a shape or form). Often, it is an outline, contour, or silhouette.

Linear A painting technique in which importance is placed on contours or outlines. Toulouse-Lautrec's picture entitled *A Corner of the Moulin de la Galette* (Figure 2.7) is an example of a painting done in this manner.

Linear perspective A system of drawing or painting in which the artist attempts to create the illusion of depth on a flat surface. The lines of buildings and other objects in a picture are slanted inward making them appear to extend back into space. If lengthened, these lines will meet at a point along an imaginary horizontal line representing the eye level. The point at which the lines meet is called a "vanishing point" (Figure 11.2).

Lintel A horizontal beam spanning an opening between two walls or posts (Figure 5.4).

Literal qualities The realistic presentation of subject matter in a work of art. This aesthetic quality is favored by imitationalism.

Lithography A method of printing from a prepared flat stone or metal plate invented in the late eighteenth century. A drawing is made on the stone or plate with a greasy crayon and then washed with water. When ink is applied, it sticks to the greasy drawing but runs off the wet surface, allowing a print to be made of the drawing. (For color lithography, separate drawings are made for each color). *Death and the Mother* (Figure 18.5) by Kollwitz is an example of a work done in this way.

Mannerism A European art style that developed between 1520 and 1600. It was a style that rejected the calm balance of the High Renaissance in favor of emotion and distortion. Works of art done in this style reflected the tension that marked Europe at this time in history. *The Madonna with the Long Neck* (Figure 13.4) by Parmigianino is an example of a painting done in this style.

Mass Refers to the outside size and bulk of a form such as a building or a sculpture. Also, the celebration of the Eucharist in a Christian Church.

Mastaba A low, rectangular Egyptian tomb made of mud brick with sloping sides and a flat top. It covered a burial chamber.

Medium The material used by the artist to produce a work of art. It may also refer to the liquid with which powdered pigments are mixed to make paint.

Minimal art A twentieth-century style of painting and sculpture that stressed the idea of reducing a work of art to the minimum number of colors, values, shapes, lines, and textures. An example of this style is Newman's *Broken Obelisk* (Figure 19.37).

Mobile A construction made of shapes that are balanced and arranged on wire arms and suspended from the ceiling so as to move freely in the air currents. Alexander Calder, a twentieth-century American artist, originated this art form (Figure 19.23).

Modeling (or modelling) A sculpture technique in which a three-dimensional form is shaped in a soft material such as clay. The term also refers to the effect of light on a three-dimensional form. The three-dimensional quality of such a form is emphasized by means of light and shadow. Reproducing the effect of light and shadow in a drawing of such a form makes it seem more realistic. For example, Masaccio modeled the figures in his painting of *The Holy Trinity* (Figure 11.1) to make them appear solid and round.

Modeling tools Tools for working with, or modeling, clay.

Molding A decorative strip that adds variety and interest to a surface by creating areas of light and shadow. Brunelleschi used dark moldings along with pilasters and columns to divide and organize the flat, white walls inside the Pazzi Chapel (Figure 11.13).

Monastery The dwelling place of persons under religious vows (Figure 9.3).

Monasticism Refers to a way of life in which individuals voluntarily joined together in isolated communities called monasteries, where they spent their days in prayer, manual labor, and self-denial.

Monochromatic Consisting of only a single color or hue.

Mosaic A work of art made of small cubes of colored marble or glass set in cement. It was a technique used by the Romans to decorate the floors of their villas (Figure 7.20) and later adopted by Byzantine artists to tell the Christian story on the walls of their churches. The mosaics in the church of San Vitale at Ravenna (Figures 8.12 and 8.13) are among the best known examples of this technique.

Movement A principle of art, it is a way of combining elements to produce the look of action or to cause the viewer's eye to sweep over the work in a certain manner (Figure 2.24).

Mural A large design or picture, generally created on the wall of a public building.

Nave The major, central part of a church where the congregation gathers. It leads from the main entrance to the altar and is usually flanked by side aisles (Figure 8.4).

Neoclassicism A nineteenth-century French art style that originated as a reaction to the Baroque. It sought to revive the ideals of ancient Greek and Roman art. Neoclassic artists used classical forms to express their ideas about courage, sacrifice, and love of country. One of the first artists to work in this style was Jacques Louis David (Figure 16.1).

Nonobjective art   Artworks that have no recognizable subject matter such as houses, trees, or people. Also known as non-representational art. Pollock's painting entitled *Lavender Mist* (Figure 19.16) is an example of nonobjective art.

Obelisk   A tall, four-sided shaft of stone, usually tapering, that rises to a pyramidal point (Figure 19.37).

Oil paint   Slow drying paint made when pigments are mixed with an oil base. The oil dries with a hard film, and the brilliance of the colors is protected. Oil paints are usually opaque and traditionally used on canvas.

Op art   A twentieth-century art style in which artists sought to create an impression of movement on the picture surface by means of optical illusion (Figure 2.4).

Painterly   A painting technique in which forms are created with patches of color rather than with hard, precise edges. Monet's painting of a *Haystack at Sunset near Giverny* (Figure 16.14) is an example of a work done in this manner.

Pastel   Pigments mixed with gum and pressed into a stick form for use as crayons. Works of art done with such pigments are referred to as pastels.

Perspective   A method for representing three-dimensional objects on a two-dimensional surface. See also "Aerial perspective" and "Linear perspective."

Pier   A massive vertical pillar that is used to support an arch, vault, or other kind of roof (Figure 10.3).

Pietà   A sculpture or painting of the Virgin Mary holding the body of the dead Christ on her lap. The term comes from the Italian word for "pity." Perhaps the best known of all pietàs is the sculpture completed by Michelangelo which is now in St. Peter's, Rome (Figure 11.18).

Pilaster   A flat, rectangular column attached to a wall. It may be decorative or used to buttress the wall.

Pop art   An art style that had its origins in England in the 1950s and made its way to the United States during the 1960s. Pop artists focused attention upon familiar images of the popular culture such as billboards, comic strips, magazine ads, and supermarket products (Figure 19.35).

Post and lintel   The simplest and oldest way of constructing an opening. Two vertical posts were used to support a horizontal beam, or lintel, creating a covered space (Figure 5.4).

Portal   A door or gate, usually of importance or large in size. In most Gothic cathedrals there were three portals in the main façade (Figure 10.7).

Portrait   The image of a person's face. It can be made of any sculptural material or any two-dimensional medium. Holbein's painting of *George Gisze* is an example of portraiture (Figure 13.14).

Post-Impressionism   A French art movement that immediately followed Impressionism. The artists involved showed a greater concern for structure and form than did the Impressionist artists (Figure 17.2).

Primary colors   The basic colors of red, yellow, and blue from which it is possible to mix all the other colors of the spectrum (Figure 2.3).

Principles of art   Refers to the different ways that the elements of art may be used in a work of art. Artists "design" their works by controlling and ordering the elements of art. To do this, they use such principles as balance, emphasis, harmony, variety, gradation, movement, rhythm, and proportion (Figure 2.26).

Proportion   A principle of art, it refers to the relationship of elements to the whole and to each other. Often proportion is allied with another principle of art, emphasis. For example, if there is a greater proportion of intense hues than dull hues in a work, emphasis is suggested. Proportion may also refer to size relationships. For example, if one figure is made to look larger compared to other figures in a composition, it is said to be out of proportion and is given greater importance. See also "Distort" and "Elongate."

Realism   A mid-nineteenth-century style of art in which artists discarded the formulas of Neoclassicism and the theatrical drama of Romanticism to paint familiar scenes and events as they actually looked. Courbet's *Burial at Ornans* (Figure 16.10) is an example of a painting done in this style.

Reformation   A religious revolution in western Europe that took place during the sixteenth century. It began as a reform movement within the Roman Catholic Church but evolved into the doctrines of Protestantism.

Regionalism   A style of art that was popular in the United

States during the 1930s. The artists who worked in this style wanted to paint the American scene in a clear, simple way that could be understood and enjoyed by everyone. Wood's painting entitled *American Gothic* (Figure 19.6) is a work executed in this style.

Relief A type of sculpture in which forms project from a background. In high relief, the forms stand far out from the background. In low relief (also known as "bas-relief"), they are shallow. An example of relief carving is found on the north portal of San Miguel in Estella, Spain (Figure 9.20).

Renaissance A revival or rebirth of cultural awareness and learning that took place during the fourteenth and fifteenth centuries, particularly in Italy. It reached its peak in the visual arts with the works of Leonardo (Figure 11.16), Michelangelo (Figure 11.20), and Raphael (Figure 11.21).

Repetition Closely related to harmony, a principle of art, this term refers to a way of combining art elements so that the same elements are used over and over again. Thus, a certain color or shape might be used several times in the same picture (Figure 2.21). Repetition also can contribute to movement and rhythm in a work of art. See also "Harmony," "Movement," and "Rhythm."

Rhythm A principle of art, it refers to a way of combining art elements to produce the look and feel of movement, especially with a visual tempo or beat. It is often achieved through the careful placement of repeated elements which

invites the viewer's eye to jump rapidly or glide smoothly from one to the next (Figure 2.24).

Rococo An eighteenth-century art style which placed emphasis on portraying the carefree life of the aristrocracy rather than on grand heroes or pious martyrs. Love and romance were considered to be better subjects for art than historical or religious subjects. The style was characterized by a free, graceful movement; a playful use of line; and delicate colors. Watteau is often referred to as the greatest of the Rococo painters, and his picture of the *Embarkation for Cythera* (Figure 15.2) demonstrates the elegance of this style.

Romanticism A style of art that flourished in the early nineteenth century. It emphasized the emotions painted in a bold, dramatic manner. Romantic artists rejected the established art of the times to paint pictures filled with dramatic action or showed exotic settings (Figure 16.6).

Rose window Large circular windows of stained glass found in Gothic cathedrals. A fine example is observed on the façade of the Cathedral of Burgos in Spain (Figure 10.2).

Sarcophagus A coffin, usually of stone, although sometimes made of wood, metal, or clay. In ancient times they were often decorated with carvings of the deceased or with some religious or mythological subject. Some of the earliest Christian art is found in sarcophagi, where scenes from the Old and New Testament were carved.

Sculpture A three-dimensional work of art. Such a work may

be carved, modeled, constructed, or cast. Michelangelo's sculpture of *Moses* (Figure 11.20) is a life-size carving in marble, while Nevelson's *Royal Tide II* (Figure 19.24) is a painted construction made of wood.

Secondary colors The colors obtained by mixing equal amounts of two primary colors. The secondary colors are orange, green, and violet (Figure 2.3).

Sgraffito A method of decorating a surface, as of a clay pot, by scratching into the top layer to expose a different color underneath. Comes from the Italian word meaning "to scratch."

Shape An element of art, it is an enclosed space defined and determined by other art elements such as line, color, value, and texture. In painting and drawing, shapes may take on the appearance of solid three-dimensional objects even though they are limited to two dimensions—length and width. This two-dimensional character of shape distinguishes it from form, which has depth as well as length and width.

Side aisle See "Aisle."

Simplicity Closely related to harmony, a principle of art, this term refers to the practice of using a limited number of similar elements to secure a more uniform appearance (Figure 19.39). See also "Harmony."

Sketch A quick drawing that captures the appearance or action of a place or situation. Sketches are often done in preparation for larger, more detailed works of art. Rubens' *Lion* (Figure 14.10) was done in preparation for his painting of *Daniel in the Lions' Den* (Figure 14.9).

Slip A mixture of clay and water used in the making of pottery to cement together parts that have been formed separately.

Space An element of art that refers to the distance or area between, around, above, below, or within things. It can be described as either three-dimensional (Figure 2.16) or two-dimensional (Figure 2.10).

Stained glass The art of cutting colored glass into different shapes and joining them together with lead strips to create a pictorial window design. It was a popular art form during the Medieval period. In Gothic cathedrals such as Chartres in France and León in Spain (Figure 10.5), large areas were devoted to stained glass.

Still life A painting of inanimate objects. Chardin, for example, painted many pictures of everyday items, including kettles, vegetables, and earthenware containers, in which he showed slight changes in color, light, and texture (Figure 15.4).

Style An artist's characteristic manner of expression. Also, works of art by different artists may have certain features in common. Such works are said to have a group style. Some examples of group styles are Impressionism, Expressionism, and Surrealism.

Stylobate The platform or foundation for a row of columns. On the Parthenon (Figure 6.1), the top step of the three-step platform is known as the stylobate.

Subject That which is represented in a work of art. For example, a hay wagon crossing a shallow stream near a quaint cottage is the subject in Constable's painting entitled *The Haywain* (Figure 16.7).

Surrealism A twentieth-century art style in which dreams, fantasy, and the subconscious served as the inspiration for artists. Often, the images found in Surrealist works are confusing and even startling. Surrealist works can be representational, as in the works of Dali (Figure 19.2), or more abstract, as in the works of Miró (Figure 19.1), who was one of the first Surrealists.

Symbol A form, image, or subject representing a meaning other than the one with which it is usually associated. Van Eyck included several symbols in his painting of *Giovanni Arnolfini and His Bride* (Figure 12.1).

Symmetrical balance A way of organizing the parts of a design so that one side duplicates, or mirrors, the other. Also known as "formal balance," it can be observed in Albers' painting entitled *Homage to the Square: "Ascending"* (Figure 2.18). Symmetrical and asymmetrical are the two kinds of balance, which is a principle of art.

Tactile Of or relating to the sense of touch.

Tapestry A textile wall hanging that is woven, painted, or embroidered with decorative designs or colorful scenes.

Technique Any method of working with art materials to create an art object.

Tempera paint A painting method which was popular before the invention of oil painting. In tempera paint, the pigments or colors are mixed with an emulsion of egg yolk rather than oil.

Template A pattern used as a guide in making a form.

Tertiary colors See "Intermediate colors."

Tesserae Small pieces of glazed clay used in mosaics.

Texture An element of art which refers to the surface quality or "feel" of an object, its smoothness, roughness, softness. Textures may be actual or simulated. Actual textures can be felt with the fingers (Figure 2.13), while simulated textures are suggested by the way the artist has painted certain areas of a picture (Figure 2.14).

Thrust The outward force produced by the weight of an arch or vault. It is counterbalanced by buttressing.

Transept An aisle between the apse and nave. It cuts across the nave and side aisles to form a cross-shaped floor plan (Figure 9.16).

Tympanum The half-round panel that fills the space between the lintel and the arch over a Romanesque or Gothic doorway. It is a perfect place for relief carvings. An example is provided above the west portal of Leyre Monastery (Figure 9.17).

Unity The quality of wholeness or oneness that is achieved through the effective use of the elements and principles of art. Often it is realized through a deliberate or intuitive balancing of harmony and variety. However, this balance does not have to be of equal proportions—harmony might outweigh variety, or variety might outweigh harmony. Harmony aids efforts to blend picture parts together to form a whole. Variety adds visual interest to this unified whole.

Variety A principle of art that refers to a way of combining art elements in involved ways to achieve intricate and complex relationships. Variety is often obtained through the use of diversity and change by artists who wish to increase the visual interest of their work. A painting which makes use of many different hues, values, lines, textures, and shapes would reflect the artist's desire for variety (Figure 2.22). See also "Complexity."

Vault An arched roof or covering made of brick, stone, or concrete. A barrel vault is made up of a continuous row of arches joined to one another. A groin vault consists of two barrel vaults intersecting each other at right angles. A dome is a hemispherical vault.

Value An element of art that describes the lightness or darkness of a color (Figure 2.3). See "Color."

Often, value is found to be an important element in works of art even though color is absent. This is true with drawings, woodcuts, lithographs, and photographs. It is also true with most sculpture and architecture. Sudden or gradual changes in value can add greatly to the visual impact of these art forms. Changes in value can also be used to help the artist express an idea (Figure 2.5).

Vase A usually round vessel which is deeper than it is wide. It can be decorative, functional, or both.

Vessel A hollow container, such as a cup, bowl, or vase, for holding something. See also "Vase."

Visual qualities The careful organization of the elements and principles of design in a work of art. This aesthetic quality is favored by formalism.

Volume Refers to the space within a form. Thus, in architecture, volume refers to the space within a building.

Warm colors Colors often associated with fire and sun and suggest warmth. These are colors which contain red and yellow and appear on one side of the color wheel opposite the cool colors (Figure 2.3).

Watercolor Any paint that uses water as a medium. Paintings done with this medium are known as watercolors. Grosz painted his powerful picture entitled *Waving the Flag* (Figure 19.8) in watercolor.

Woodcut A print made by cutting a design in a block of wood. The ink is transferred from the raised surfaces to the paper (Figure 16.18).

Zen A Chinese and Japanese school of Buddhism that claims that enlightenment can be attained through meditation, self-contemplation, and intuition rather than through the scriptures. (Postscript Figures 10 and 11).

Metric Terms Used in This Book		
Metric Unit		**Approx. U.S. Equivalent**
mm (millimeter)	=	0.04 inch
cm (centimeter)	=	39.37 inches
m (meter)	=	0.39 inch
km (kilometer)	=	0.62 mile
m^2 (square meter)	=	10.76 square feet
ha (hectare)	=	2.47 acres
t (metric ton)	=	1.1 tons
L (liter)	=	1.057 quarts (liquid)

Books for Further Reading

Chapter 2: Learning a Visual Vocabulary

Bevlin, Marjorie Elliott. *Design through Discovery:* Brief Edition. Holt, Rinehart & Winston, New York. 1980

Cheatham, Frank, and Cheatham, Jane Hart. *Design Concepts and Application.* University Park Press, Baltimore, Md. 1983

Gatto, Joseph A.; Porter, Albert W.; and Selleck, Jack. *Exploring Visual Design.* Davis Publications, Worcester, Mass. 1978

Laver, David A. *Design Basics.* 2nd ed. Holt, Rinehart & Winston, New York. 1979

Malcolm, Dorothea C. *Design: Elements and Principles.* Davis Publications, Worcester, Mass. 1972

Chapter 3: Seeing, Knowing, Understanding, and Judging

ART HISTORY

Brommer, Gerald F. *Discovering Art History.* Davis Publications, Worcester, Mass. 1981

Cleaver, Dale G. *Art: An Introduction.* 3rd ed. Harcourt Brace Jovanovich, New York. 1977

Davis, Beverly Jeanne. *Chant of the Centuries: A History of the Humanities—The Visual Arts and Their Parallels in Music and Literature.* W. S. Benson & Co., Austin, Texas. 1969

Elsen, Albert E. *Purposes of Art.* 4th ed. Holt, Rinehart & Winston, New York. 1981

Feldman, Edmund B. *The Artist.* Prentice-Hall, Englewood Cliffs, N.J. 1982

Gombrich, Ernst H. *The Story of Art.* 13th ed. Prentice-Hall, Englewood Cliffs, N.J. 1983

Great Ages of Man. 16 vols. Time-Life Books, Alexandria, Va. 1970

Great Museums of the World. 16 vols. Newsweek Book Division, New York. 1968

Harris, Ann Sutherland, and Nochlin, Linda. *Women Artists: 1550-1950.* Alfred A. Knopf, New York. 1976

Janson, H. W., and Janson, Dora Jane. *The Story of Painting from Cave Painting to Modern Times.* Harry N. Abrams, New York. 1962

Monro, Eleanor. *The Encyclopedia of Art.* Golden Press, New York. 1961

Norwich, John Julius, ed. *Great Architecture of the World.* Random House and American Heritage Publishing Co., New York. 1975

Phaidon Encyclopedia of Art and Artists. E. P. Dutton, New York. 1978

Splendors of the Past: Lost Cities of the Ancient World. National Geographic Society, Washington, D.C. 1981

Time-Life Library of Art. 6th ed., 28 vols. Time-Life Books, Alexandria, Va. 1981

Wasserman, Burton. *Exploring the Visual Arts.* Davis Publications, Worcester, Mass. 1976

AESTHETICS AND ART CRITICISM

Feldman, Edmund Burk. *Varieties of Visual Experience.* 2nd ed. Prentice-Hall, Englewood Cliffs, N.J. 1981

Pepper, Stephen C. *Principles of Art Appreciation.* Reprint of 1949 ed. Greenwood Press, Westport, Conn.

Read, Herbert. *The Meaning of Art.* Reprint of 1931 ed. Arden Press, Denver, Colo. 1977

Stolnitz, Jerome. *Aesthetics and Philosophy of Art Criticism: A Critical Introduction.* Houghton Mifflin Co., Boston. 1960

Taylor, Joshua. *Learning to Look: A Handbook for the Visual Arts.* 2nd ed. The Univ. of Chicago Press, Chicago, Ill. 1981

Weitz, Morris. *Problems in Aesthetics: An Introductory Book of Readings.* 2nd ed. Macmillan Publishing Co., New York, 1970

Chapter 4: The Magic Picture: Prehistoric Art in Western Europe

Graziosi, Paolo. *Paleolithic Art.* McGraw-Hill Book Co., New York. 1960

Lerio-Gourhan, André. *Treasures of Prehistoric Art.* Harry N. Abrams, New York. 1967

Chapter 5: Art for Eternity: The Art of Ancient Egypt

Hoving, Thomas. *Tutankhamun: The Untold Story.* Simon & Schuster, New York. 1978

Jordan, Paul. *Egypt, the Black Land.* Phaidon, Oxford, England. 1976

Macaulay, David. *Pyramid.* Houghton Mifflin Co., Boston. 1975

Steward, Desmond. *The Pyramids and the Sphinx.* Wonders of Man Series. Newsweek Book Division, New York. 1971

Woldering, Irmgard. *Gods, Men, and Pharoahs: The Glory of Egyptian Art.* Harry N. Abrams, New York. 1967

Chapter 6: The Age of Beauty: Greek Art

Boardman, John. *Greek Art.* World of Art Series. Oxford University Press, New York. 1973

Boardman, John; Dörig, José; Fuchs, Werner; and Hirmer, Max. *Greek Art and Architecture.* Harry N. Abrams, New York. 1967

Bruno, Vincent J., ed. *The Parthenon.* W. W. Norton and Company, Inc., New York. 1974

Lullies, Reinhard, and Hirmer, Max. *Greek Sculpture.* Harry N. Abrams, New York. 1960

Richter, Gisela M. A. *The Sculpture and Sculptors of the Greeks.* 4th ed., rev. Yale Univ. Press, New Haven, Conn. 1970

Robertson, Martin. *Greek Painting.* Rizzoli International Publications, New York. 1979

Chapter 7: Age of the Conquerors: Roman Art

Brown, Frank E. *Roman Architecture.* Great Ages of World Architecture Series. George Braziller, New York. 1961

Kähler, Heinz. *The Art of Rome and Her Empire.* Art of the World Series. Crown Publishers, New York. 1963

Quennell, Peter. *The Colosseum.* Wonders of Man Series. Newsweek Book Division, New York. 1972

Ward-Perkins, J. B. *Roman Imperial Architecture.* Pelican History of Art Series. Penguin Books, New York. 1981

Chapter 8: In Quest of Salvation: Early Christian and Byzantine Art

Grabar, André. *Byzantine Painting.* Rizzoli International Publications, New York. 1979

Swift, Emerson. *Hagia Sophia.* Columbia Univ. Press, New York. 1940

Volbach, W. F., and Hirmer, Max. *Early Christian Art.* Tr. by Christopher Ligota. Harry N. Abrams, New York. 1962

Chapter 9: The Age of Faith: Early Medieval and Romanesque Art

Beckwith, John. *Early Medieval Art.* World of Art Series. Oxford Univ. Press, New York. 1964

Grabar, André. *Romanesque Painting.* Tr. by Stuart Gilbert. Great Centuries of Painting Series. Skira, Geneva, Switzerland. 1958

Grabar, André, and Nordenfalk, Carl. *Early Medieval Painting from the Fourth to the Eleventh Century.* Tr. by Stuart Gilbert. Great Centuries of Painting series. Skira, Geneva, Switzerland. 1957

Timmers, J. J. M. *A Handbook of Romanesque Art.* Harper & Row, Publishers, New York. 1976

Chapter 10: The Age of Faith Continued: Gothic Art

Dupont, Jacques, and Gnudi, Cesare. *Gothic Painting.* Tr. by Stuart Gilbert. Great Centuries of Painting Series. Skira, Geneva, Switzerland. 1954

Frankl, Paul. *Gothic Architecture.* Tr. by Dieter Pevsner. Pelican History of Art Series. Penguin Books, Baltimore, Md. 1962

Fremantle, Anne. *Age of Faith.* Great Ages of Man Series. Time-Life Books, Alexandria, Va. 1965.

Macaulay, David. *Cathedral: The Story of Its Construction.* Houghton Mifflin Co., Boston. 1973

Chapter 11: A Time of Titans: Renaissance Art in Italy

Fanning, Ralph, and Myron, Robert. *Italian Renaissance.* Pitman Publishing Co., New York. 1965

Hartt, Frederick. *History of Italian Renaissance Art: Painting, Sculpture, Architecture.* 2nd ed. Harry N. Abrams, New York. 1980

Pope-Hennessy, John. *Italian Renaissance Sculpture.* Phaidon, New York. 1971

Chapter 12: With Sight and Feeling: Fifteenth-Century Art in the North

Benesch, Otto. *The Art of the Renaissance in Northern Europe.* Rev. ed. Phaidon, London. 1965

Blunt, Anthony. *Art and Architecture in France: 1500-1700*. Pelican History of Art Series. Penguin Books, Baltimore, Md. 1977

Friedlander, Max J. *From Van Eyck to Bruegel: Early Netherlandish Painting*. Rev. ed. Phaidon, London. 1981

Chapter 13: Crisis and Transition: The Art of the Sixteenth Century

Friedlaender, Walter. *Mannerism and Anti-Mannerism in Italian Painting*. Shocken Books, New York. 1965

Russell, Francis, *World of Dürer, 1471-1528*. Library of Art Series. Time-Life Books, Alexandria, Va. 1967

Wolf, Robert Erich, and Millen, Ronald. *Renaissance and Mannerist Art*. Harry N. Abrams, New York. 1968

Chapter 14: A World of Light and Shadow: Baroque Art

Kitson, Michael. *The Age of Baroque*. McGraw-Hill Book Co., New York. 1968

Nash, J. M. *The Age of Rembrandt and Vermeer: Dutch Painting in the Seventeenth Century*. Phaidon, Oxford, England. 1979

Portoghesi, Paolo. *The Rome of Borromini*. George Braziller, New York. 1968

White, Christopher. *Rubens and His World*. Viking Press, New York. 1964

Wittkower, Rudolf. *Art and Architecture in Italy: 1600-1750*. 3rd ed. Pelican History of Art Series. Penguin Books, Baltimore, Md. 1973

Chapter 15: In Search of Pleasure: Rococo Art

Fosca, Francois [Georges de Traz]. *The Eighteenth Century: Watteau to Tiepolo*. Tr. by Stuart Gilbert. Great Centuries of Painting Series. Skira, Geneva, Switzerland. 1952

Kalnein, Wend Graff, and Levey, Michael. *Art and Architecture of the Eighteenth Century in France*. Pelican History of Art Series. Viking Press, New York. 1973

Schneider, Pierre. *World of Watteau*. Library of Art Series. Time-Life Books, Alexandria, Va. 1967

Pignatti, Terisio. *The Age of Rococo*. Tr. by Lorna Andrade. The Hamlyn Publishing Group, Middlesex, England. 1969

Chapter 16: Era of Change: New Styles in Nineteenth-Century Art

De Francia, Peter. *Impressionism*. Methuen, London, England. 1957

Friedlaender, Walter. *David to Delacroix*. Harvard Univ. Press, Cambridge, Mass. 1952

Gaunt, William. *Impressionism: A Visual History*. Praeger Publishers, New York. 1970

Hitchcock, Henry-Russell. *Architecture: Nineteenth and Twentieth Centuries*. Pelican History of Art Series. Penguin Books, Baltimore, Md. 1977

Pool, Phoebe. *Impressionism*. World of Art Series. Oxford Univ. Press, New York. 1967

Chapter 17: A Time for Rebels: Art of the Later Nineteenth Century

Rewald, John. *Post-Impressionism: From Van Gogh to Gauguin*. Rev. 3rd ed. Museum of Modern Art, New York. 1979

Sloane, Joseph C. *French Painting between the Past and the Present: Artists, Critics, and Traditions from 1848 to 1870*. Princeton Univ. Press, Princeton, N.J. 1973

Wallace, Robert. *World of Van Gogh, 1853-1890*. Library of Art Series. Time-Life Books, Alexandria, Va. 1969

Chapter 18: A New Vision: Art of the Early Twentieth Century

Brown, Milton W. *The Story of the Armory Show*. The Joseph H. Hirshhorn Foundation, New York. 1963

Brown, Milton W. *American Painting from the Armory Show to the Depression*. Princeton Univ. Press, Princeton, N.J. 1970

Crespelle, Jean Paul. *The Fauves*. The Graphic Society, New York. 1962

Goodrich, Lloyd, and Baur, John I. H. *American Art of Our Century*. Praeger Publishers, New York. 1961

Hamilton, George H. *Painting and Sculpture in Europe, 1880-1940*. Pelican History of Art Series. Rev. ed. Penguin Books, Baltimore, Md. 1978

Prown, Jules D. *American Paintings: Vol. I, from the Colonial Period to the Armory Show*. Rizzoli International Publications, New York. 1980

Rose, Barbara. *American Art since 1900*. Rev. ed. Praeger Publishers, New York. 1975

Seltz, Peter. *German Expressionist Painting*. Univ. of California Press, Berkeley and Los Angeles. 1957

Chapter 19: New Directions: Art to the Present

Canaday, John. *Mainstreams of Modern Art.* 2nd ed. Holt, Rinehart & Winston, New York. 1981

Dover, Cedric. *American Negro Art.* Graphic Society, Greenwich, New York. 1969

Johnson, Carlotte Buel. *Contemporary Art.* Davis Publications, Worcester, Mass. 1973

Lippard, Lucy R. *Pop Art.* Oxford Univ. Press, New York. 1966

Read, Herbert. *A Concise History of Modern Painting.* World of Art Series. Oxford Univ. Press, New York. 1974

Read, Herbert. *A Concise History of Modern Sculpture.* World of Art Series. Oxford Univ. Press, New York. 1964

Rose, Barbara. *American Painting: Vol. II, The Twentieth Century.* Rizzoli International Publications, New York. 1980

Rubin, William S. *Dada and Surrealist Art.* Harry N. Abrams, New York. 1969

Scully, Vincent. *Modern Architecture: The Architecture of Democracy.* George Braziller, New York. 1961

Chapter 20: Centuries of Tradition in the East: The Art of China and Japan

Baker, J.S. *Japanese Art.* Thames & Hudson, London, England. 1984

Cahill, James. *Chinese Painting.* Rizzoli International Publications, New York. 1985

Cahill, James. *Chinese Painting, 11th-14th Centuries.* Crown Publishers, New York. 1960

ANSWERS TO STATEMENTS ON PAGE 330:

Post-Impressionists	American Artists
1. van Gogh	1. Ryder
2. Cézanne	2. Tanner
3. Gauguin	3. Homer
4. Cézanne	4. Tanner
5. Gauguin	5. Eakins
6. van Gogh	6. Homer
7. Cézanne	7. Ryder
8. Gauguin	8. Eakins
9. van Gogh	

Lee, Sherman E. *Chinese Landscape Painting.* The Cleveland Museum of Art, Cleveland, Ohio. 1954

Lee, Sherman E. *A History of Far Eastern Art.* Harry N. Abrams, New York. 1982

Munsterberg, Hugo. *Art of the Far East.* Harry N. Abrams, New York. 1968

Rawson, J. *Ancient China: Art and Archaeology.* Harper & Row, Publishers, New York. 1980

Terukazu, Akiyama. *Japanese Painting.* Rizzoli International Publications, New York. 1977

Waley, Arthur. *An Introduction to the Study of Chinese Painting.* Charles Scribner's Sons, New York. 1923

Wichmann, Siegfried. *Japonisme: The Japanese Influence on Western Art in the 19th and 20th Centuries.* Harmony Books, New York. 1981

Chapter 21: Out of the Shadows: The Art of Other Non-Western Cultures

Antequera, Marino. *The Alhambra and the Generalife.* Editorial "Padre Suarez," S.L., Granada, Spain. 1965

Attenborough, David. *The Tribal Eye.* W.W. Norton and Company, Inc., New York. 1979

Christensen, Erwin O. *Primitive Art.* Thomas Y. Crowell Co., New York. 1955

Emmerich, André. *Art before Columbus.* Simon & Schuster, New York. 1983

Hamlyn, Paul. *Benin Art.* Batchworth Press, London, England. 1960

Highwater, Jamake. *Arts of the Indian Americas: North, Central and South: Leaves from the Sacred Tree.* Harper & Row, Publishers, New York. 1983

Inverarity, R.B. *Art of the Northwest Coast Indians.* 2nd ed. Univ. of California Press, Berkeley. 1967

Irving, Washington. *Tales of the Alhambra.* Grefol, S.A., Nostoles (Madrid), Spain. 1976

Leonard, Jonathan Norton. *Ancient America.* Great Ages of Man Series. Time-Life Books, Alexandria, Va. 1967

Leuzinger, Elsy. *Africa: The Art of the Negro Peoples.* McGraw-Hill Book Co., New York. 1960

Whiteford, Andrew. *North American Indian Arts.* Golden Press, New York. 1970

Willet, Frank. *African Art.* World of Art Series. Thames & Hudson, London, England. 1985

Willett, Frank. *African Art, An Introduction.* Praeger Publishers, New York. 1971

Page 441: (Mystery relief panel) *Relief from a Mastaba* (Tomb of Ny-ankh-Nesut). Egyptian, Sakkara, first half of VI Dynasty. c. 2300 B.C. Painted limestone, approx. 38 x 123 cm [15 x 48½"]

Page 446: (Mystery painting) Jan Steen. *A Merry Company.* c. 1667-69. Oil on panel (oak), approx. 44.5 x 36.8 cm [17⅝ x 14⅝"]

Chronology of Selected Periods, Styles, and Artists

Prehistory

30,000 B.C.
15,000 B.C. Cave paintings at Lascaux and Altamira
10,000 B.C.

Ancient Egypt

5000 B.C. Prehistoric hunters and their families settle in Nile River Valley

2686 B.C. Old Kingdom: Architecture (Mastabas, Step Pyramids, Pyramids); Sculpture (Sphinx, Portrait of Khafre); Relief Sculpture and Painting (Portrait of Hesire)

2160 B.C. Old Kingdom ends

2050 B.C. Middle Kingdom: Sculpture (Portrait)

1800 B.C. Middle Kingdom ends

1570 B.C. New Kingdom: Architecture (Temple of Karnak); Sculpture (Portrait of Ikhnaton, Portrait of Nefertiti); Relief Sculpture and Painting (Tomb of Nakht paintings)

Ancient Greece

1100 B.C. Dorian invasion of Greece, followed by growth of small city-states

900 B.C. Geometric Period: Vase Decoration (Geometric Jug, Vase from Dipylon Cemetery)

700 B.C. Archaic Period: Vase Decoration (Exekias' *Ajax and Achilles Playing Draughts*); Sculpture (*Kouros*, *Hera of Samos*)

480 B.C. Classical Period: Architecture (Parthenon, Shrine to Athena Nike, The Erechtheum, Monument to Lysicrates); Sculpture (Myron's *Discobolus*, Phydias' Parthenon Sculptures, Polyclitus' *Doryphorus*)

338 B.C. Philip of Macedonia conquers Greece

323 B.C. Hellenistic Period (Greek culture spreads after conquests of Alexander the Great): Sculpture (*Dying Gaul, Nike of Samothrace, Seated Boxer*)

146 B.C. Greece conquered by Romans

Ancient Rome

509 B.C. Romans drive the Etruscans from their city and establish a republic: Architecture—Temples (Temple of Fortuna Virilis, Sanctuary of Fortuna Primigenia, Pantheon); Public Buildings and Monuments (Baths of Caracala; Colosseum; Amphitheater at Tarragona, Spain; Basilica of Constantine; Arch of Constantine; Arch of Bara, Tarragona, Spain)/Sculpture (Portrait of a Roman)/Mural Painting (Architectural View, Pompeii; *Maiden Gathering Flowers*, Pompeii)

A.D. 330 Constantine moves his capital from Rome to Constantinople

A.D. 476 Roman Empire in the West comes to an end

Early Christian and Byzantine Periods

A.D. 313 Early Christian Period begins when Constantine legalizes Christianity: Painting (Catacomb of Sts. Pietro and Marcellino)

A.D. 330 Byzantine period begins with dedication of Constantinople: Architecture and Mosaics (Hagia Sophia, San Vitale)

A.D. 476 Roman Empire in the West comes to an end, but Christian art continues to grow throughout western Europe.

Early Medieval Period

A.D. 476 Fall of the Roman Empire in the West marks start of Early Medieval Period: Architecture Churches built like Roman basilicas; growth (of monasteries like San Juan de la Peña); Illuminated Manuscripts (*St. Matthew* from the *Gospel Book of Archbishop of Reims*); Sculpture (*Adam and Eve Reproached by the Lord, St. Michael's, Hildesheim, Germany*)

About 1050

469

Romanesque Period

1050 Churches with similar features built throughout western Europe. This new artistic style comes to be known as Romanesque: Architecture (Castles at Peñafiel and near León, Spain; City Walls, Avilá, Spain; San Sernin, Toulouse, France; Cathedral of St. James, Santiago de Compostela, Spain); Relief Sculpture (Leyre Monastery, Spain; Santa Maria, Sangüesa, Spain; *Three Marys at the Tomb*, San Miguel, Estella, Spain); Capital Carving (Santes Creus Monastery, Spain); Miniature Painting in Religious Manuscripts (*Annunciation* from a Swabian Gospel); Church Wall Painting (*Christ in Majesty, San Clemente, Tahull, Spain*)

1150 Romanesque style gives way to Gothic style

Gothic Period

1150 Church construction moves away from Romanesque heaviness and solidity to structures which are light and graceful: Architecture (Cathedrals of Tarragona, Burgos, Chartres, and León); Stained Glass (Cathedral of León); Sculpture (Cathedrals of Chartres and Tarragona; *Golden Virgin*, Cathedral of Amiens; Gargoyles, Monastery of Santes Creus); Relief Sculpture (Sarmental Portal, Cathedral of Burgos; *Death of the Virgin*, Cathedral of Pamplona); Manuscript Illumination ("Christ Child in the Temple," *Queen Mary's Psalter*; Limbourg Brothers' *Book of Hours*); Painting (Duccio, Giotto)

1500 Gothic style gives way to new Renaissance style in western Europe

Sixteenth Century

1500 **Venice, Italy:** Painting (Giorgione, Titian)

Italy: Painting—Mannerism (Parmigianno, Tintoretto)

Spain: Painting—Mannerism (El Greco)

Northern Europe: Painting (Grünewald, Dürer also prints, Bosch, Bruegel, Holbein)

Baroque Period

1600 **Italy:** Architecture (Borromini); Sculpture (Bernini); Painting (Caravaggio, Artemisia Gentileschi)

Flanders: Painting (Rubens)

Holland: Painting (Hals, Rembrandt, Steen, Vermeer, Leyster)

Spain: Painting (Ribera, Velázquez, Murillo)

1453 Ottoman Turks capture Constantinople, bringing to a close the Byzantine Period

Renaissance in Italy

1400 Italian artists study Classical sculpture and nature to make their own works look more lifelike: Painting (Masaccio, Fra Angelico, Uccello, Piero della Francesca, Botticelli, Leonardo, Michelangelo, Raphael, Sofonisba Anguissola); Sculpture (Ghiberti, Donatello, Michelangelo); Architecture (Brunelleschi)

1520 Death of Raphael signals an end to the Renaissance and the rise of Mannerism

Renaissance in the North

Northern artists uninterested in Classical art. They focus attention on precise detail and symbolism in their work: Painting (Jan van Eyck, Rogier van der Weyden, Hugo van der Goes)

Rococo Period

1700   **France:** Architecture (Palace of Versailles);
Painting (Watteau, Fragonard, Chardin)

England: Painting (Reynolds, Gainsborough,
Hogarth); Architecture (Wren)

Spain: Painting (Goya)

Early and Mid-Nineteenth Century

1800   **France:** Painting—Neoclassicism (David,
Vigée-Lebrun, Ingres); Romanticism (Géricault,
Delacroix); Realism (Courbet, Manet, Bonheur);
Impressionism (Monet, Renoir, Degas, Cassatt,
Morisot)/Sculpture (Rodin)

England: Painting (Constable, Turner)

Late Nineteenth Century

About   **France:** Painting (Cézanne, Gauguin)
1880
  Holland: Painting (van Gogh)

United States: Painting Homer, Eakins, Ryder,
Bannister, Tanner)

Early Twentieth Century

About   **France:** Painting—Fauvism (Matisse, Rouault);
1900   Nonobjective Art (Kandinsky [born in Russia]);
Cubism (Picasso, Braque)/Sculpture (Maillol)/
Architecture (Eiffel)

Germany: Painting—Expressionism (Kirchner,
Kollwitz)

Norway: Painting (Munch [influenced the
Expressionists])

Spain: Architecture (Gaudi)

Mexico: Mural Painting (Rivera, Orozco,
Siqueiros)

United States: Painting (Sloan [Ashcan
School], Bellows); Architecture (Morgan,
Sullivan)

Mid-Twentieth Century

About   **France:** Painting—Dada (Duchamp);
1920   Architecture—(Le Corbusier [born in Switzer-
land])

Spain: Painting—Surrealism (Miró, Dali)

Switzerland: Painting—Fantasy (Klee [often
referred to as a German artist])

About   **England:** Sculpture—Abstract (Moore,
1980   Hepworth)

United States: Painting—Surrealism (Sage);
Regionalism and the American Scene (Benton,
Curry, Wood, Hopper); Social Protest (Grosz,
Levine); Other Directions (Davis, O'Keeffe,
Neel, Lawrence, Pippin); Abstract Expression-
ism (de Kooning, Pollock, Frankenthaler)/
Sculpture (Lipchitz [born in Lithuania], Smith,
Calder, Nevelson, Noguchi, Houser/Architecture
(Wright, Pei)

American Art Today

About   **United States:** Painting—Pop Art (Oldenburg);
1960   Op Art (Vasarely, Agam, Albers [influenced Op,
Minimal, and Hard-edge artists]); Minimal Art
(Reinhart, Newman, Bladen); Hard-edge Painters (Noland, Kelly, Stella); Photo-Realism (Leslie)

Present

471

Index

A

Abstract art, 28
Abstract Expressionism, 376–378
Acropolis, 91, *Figure 6.4*
Across (Noland), *Figure 19.39*
Activities, 440–448
Adam and Eve Reproached by the Lord after the Fall, 145, *Figure 9.7*
Adoration of the Lamb (van Eyck), 212–213, *Figure 12.2*
Adoration of the Magi, The (Botticelli), 24, 195, *Figures 2.10, 11.14*
Adoration of the Shepherds, The (Giorgione), 29, *Figure 2.17*
Adoration of the Shepherds, The (van der Goes), 217–218, *Figures 12.6, 12.7*
Advertising, careers in, 449–450
Advice to a Young Artist (Daumier), Frontispiece
Aerial perspective, 184
African art, 422–427
Afro-American artists, 328–329, 374–376
Agam, 360, 393; *Double Metamorphosis, II,* 393, *Figure 19.36*
Agbatana III (Stella), 394–396, *Figures 1.1, 19.40*
Ajax and Achilles Playing Draughts, Vase with (Exekias), 106, *Figure 6.22*
Akhenaton. *See* Ikhnaton
Alaric, 123
Alba Madonna, The (Raphael), 204–205, 252, *Figure 11.21*
Albers, Josef, 360, 396–397; *Homage to the Square: ''Ascending,''* 31, 396–397, *Figure 2.18*
Alexander the Great, 74, 101
Altamira, cave paintings of, 64–70, *Figures 4.1, 4.4, 4.5*
Altarpiece, 174
Ambulatory, 150
Amenhotep, 74
American art, 323–329, 348–352
American Gothic (Wood), 367, *Figure 19.6*
Amiens, Cathedral of, 166, 170, *Figure 10.14*
Amon-Re, Temple of, 76–78, *Figure 5.4*
Amphitheater at Tarragona, *Figure 7.5*
Analogous colors, 18
Anatomical Studies (Leonardo), 196, *Figure 11.15*
Ancestral figures, African, 426, *Figure 21.5*
Angelico, Fra, 181, 185–186; *The Annunciation,* 185–186, *Figure 11.4*
Anguissola, Sofonisba, 181, 206–207; *Double Portrait of a Boy and a Girl of the Attavanti Family,* 207, *Figure 11.23*

Annunciation (manuscript illumination), 156, *Figure 9.24*
Antonello de Messina, 221
Apse, 119
Aqueducts, 113, *Figures 7.4, 7.6, 7.7*
Arabs Skirmishing in the Mountains (Delacroix), *Figure 16.17*
Archaic period of Greek art, 94, 104
Arches, pointed, 161–162, round, 110–112, *Figures 7.3, 7.4;* triumphal, 120
Architecture, Baroque, 244–245; Byzantine, 131; Early Medieval, 140–143; Egyptian, 75–78; English, 277–278; Gothic, 161–167, 174; Greek, 89–94; Renaissance, 192–193; Roman, 108–120; Romanesque, 146–152; twentieth-century, 352–357, 386–391
Architrave, 89
Arch of Bara, 120, *Figure 7.18*
Arch of Constantine, 120, *Figure 7.17*
Armory Show, 351–352
Art, elements of, 11, 15–30; principles of, 15, 30–38
Art criticism, 11, 48–61
Art education, careers in, 451–452
Art history, 12, 41–47, 60–61
Artist and His Mother, The (Gorky), 46–47, *Figure 3.8*
Artist in His Studio, An (Rembrandt), 257, *Figure 14.13*
Arts administration, careers in, 452
Art therapy, careers in, 452
Ashcan School, 349–352
Atmospheric perspective, 184
Attentive Nurse, The (Chardin), 273, *Figure 15.5*
Augustus, Roman Emperor, 114
Axis, 23
Aztec art, 436–437

B

Backyards, Greenwich Village (Sloan), 349–350, *Figure 18.18*
Balance, 30–31
Banjo Lesson, The (Tanner), 329, *Figure 17.15*
Bannister, Edward, 328; *Under the Oaks,* 328
Baptism of Christ (Piero), 190–191, *Figure 11.9*
Baroque art, 243–267
Barrel vault, 115, *Figure 7.3*
Basilicas, 118–119, 127–129, *Figures 7.15, 7.16*
Bas-relief, 155
Baths, Roman, 114–115, *Figures 7.8, 7.9*

Battle of San Romano, The (Uccello), 189, *Figure 11.8*
Beauvais, Cathedral of, 166
Bedroom at Arles, The (van Gogh), 319, *Figure 17.6*
Bellows, George, 332, 350; *Stag at Sharkey's,* 350, *Figure 18.19*
Benedict, St., 140–141
Benin, bronze casting from, 423, *Figure 21.1*
Benton, Thomas Hart, 366
Bernini, Gianlorenzo, 243, 247–248; *David,* 248, *Figure 14.5; The Ecstasy of St. Theresa,* 247–248, *Figure 14.4*
Berry, Duke of, 173
Between Two Appearances (Krasner), 25, *Figure 2.13*
Bison from Altamira, 64–66, *Figure 4.1*
Bladen, Ronald, 360, 394; *Sonar Tide,* 394, *Figure 19.38*
Blind Man's Meal, The (Picasso), 344, *Figure 18.12*
Blind Old Beggar, The (Ribera), 262, *Figure 14.17*
Blue Boy (Gainsborough), 275, *Figure 15.7*
Blue Guitar (Braque), 345, *Figure 18.13*
Bonheur, Rosa, 282, 296, 298; *The Horse Fair,* 298, *Figure 16.12*
Borglum, Gutzon, 385
Borromini, Francesco, 243, 245; San Carlo alle Quattro Fontane, 245, *Figure 14.2*
Bosch, Hieronymus, 220, 236–237; *Death and the Miser,* 237, *Figure 13.11*
Botticelli, Sandro, 181, 194–195, 201; *The Adoration of the Magi,* 24, 195, *Figures 2.10, 11.14*
Bouguereau, Adolphe, 333
Braque, Georges, 332, 344–345; *Blue Guitar,* 345, *Figure 18.13*
Broken Obelisk (Newman), 393–394, *Figure 19.37*
Bruegel, Pieter, 220, 237–238, *The Parable of the Blind,* 237–238, *Figure 13.12*
Brunelleschi, Filippo, 181, 183, 187, 192–193; Cathedral of Florence, 192–193, *Figure 11.12;* Pazzi Chapel, 193, *Figure 11.13; The Sacrifice of Isaac,* 186–187, *Figure 11.6*
Burgos, Cathedral of, 168, *Figures 10.2, 10.3, 10.4, 10.9, 10.12*
Burial at Ornans (Courbet), 295–296, *Figure 16.10*
Burial of Count Orgaz, The (El Greco), 231–232, *Figure 13.8*
Buttresses, flying, 161–162
By the Sea (Gauguin). *See Fatata te Miti*

Byzantine art, 125–136

C

Calder, Alexander, 359, 383–385; *Pomegranate*, 383, *Figure 19.23*

Calling of the Apostles Peter and Andrew, The (Duccio), 175, *Figure 10.19*

Campanile, 128

Capitals, Greek, 89, 92; Romanesque, 156

Caracalla, Baths of, 115, *Figures 7.8, 7.9*

Caravaggio, Michelangelo da, 243, 248–250; *The Conversion of St. Paul*, 249, *Figure 14.6*

Careers, 449–453

Carnival of Harlequin (Miró), 361–362, *Figure 19.1*

Carolingian Dynasty, 138

Carthage, 108

Cassatt, Mary, 282, 307–308; *Girl Arranging Her Hair*, 307–308, *Figure 16.21*

Castelfranco, Giorgione da. *See* Giorgione da Castelfranco

Castles, 146–147. *Figures 9.8, 9.9*

Catacombs, 125–127, *Figures 8.1, 8.2*

Cave painting, 64–70

Cézanne, Paul, 313–317, 323; *Mont Sainte-Victoire as Seen from Bibemus Quarry*, 317, *Figures 1.5, 17.4*; *Pines and Rocks*, 317, *Figure 17.3*; *Still Life with Peppermint Bottle*, 315–316, *Figure 17.2*

Chao-Meng-fu, 400, 407–408, *Twin Pines against a Flat Vista*, 408, *Figure 20.9*

Chardin, Jean-Baptiste Siméon, 268, 272–273; *The Attentive Nurse*, 273, *Figure 15.5*; *Still Life with Rib of Beef*, 272, *Figure 15.4*

Charlemagne, 138–139

Chartres, Cathedral of, 165, *Figures 10.7, 10.10*

Charts, Art-Criticism Operations, 56; Art-Criticism Operations and Aesthetic Qualities, 57; Art-History Operations, 46; Art Theories and Aesthetic Qualities, 53; Chronology of Selected Periods, Styles, and Artists, 469–471, Comparison of van Eyck and Masaccio, 213; Design, 37, 50; Early Twentieth-Century Art Styles and Artists, 352; Nineteenth-Century Artists (Cézanne to Turner), 330; Nineteenth-Century Art Styles and Artists (David to Rodin), 311; Sequence of Art-History and Art-Criticism Operations, 60

Cheops. *See* Khufu

Chephren. *See* Khafre

Chinese art, 400–409

Chinese Restaurant (Weber), 34, *Figure 2.22*

Christ Child in the Temple (manuscript illumination), 171, *Figure 10.16*

Christ in Majesty, 158, *Figure 9.25*

Churches, Early Christian, 140; Romanesque, 148–152, *Figure 9.16*

Cicero, 117

Cimabue, 176

Classical period of Greek art, 94, 96, 104

Clerestory, 140

Cloister, 143

Cloud, The (De Creeft), 26, 28, *Figure 2.16*

Cluny Abbey, 150

Collage, 25, 342

Color, 16–20

Colosseum, 115–117, *Figures 7.10, 7.11, 7.12*

Company of Captain Frans Banning Cocq, The (Rembrandt). See *Night Watch, The*

Complementary colors, 18

Concert, The (Giorgione), 222–223, *Figure 13.3*

Constable, John, 282, 291–293; *The Haywain*, 292, *Figure 16.7*; *A View of Salisbury Cathedral*, 58–59, *Figure 3.19*; *Wivenhoe Park, Essex*, 292–293, *Figure 16.8*

Constantine I, Roman Emperor, 123, 125

Constantinople, 123, 131

Contour line, 21

Conversion of St. Paul, The (Caravaggio), 249, *Figure 14.6*

Cool colors, 18

Corbusier, Le. *See* Le Corbusier

Corinthian order, 94, *Figure 6.5*

Corner of the Moulin de la Galette, A (Toulouse-Lautrec), 21, *Figure 2.7*

Cornice, 89

Corporate art advising, careers in, 453

Courbet, Gustave, 282, 294–296; *Burial at Ornans*, 295–296, *Figure 16.10*

Creation of Adam, The (Michelangelo), 201, *Figure 11.19*

Crucifixion, The (stained glass), *Figure 10.6*

Cubism, 341–345

Curry, John Steuart, 366

Curved lines, 22

Cyrano (Kaz), 20, 22, *Figure 2.5*

D

Dada, 360

Dali, Salvador, 359, 362; *The Persistence of Memory*, 362, *Figure 19.2*

Daniel in the Lions' Den (Rubens), 253, *Figure 14.9*

Daniel in the Lion's Den (Tanner), 329

Dating, radiocarbon, 66

Daumier, Honoré, *Advice to a Young Artist*, Frontispiece

David (Bernini), 248, *Figure 14.5*

David, Jacques Louis, 282, 284–285; *The Death of Marat*, 284–285, *Figure 16.1*; *Death of Socrates*, *Figure 16.15*; *Napoleon in His Study*, 285, *Figure 16.2*

Da Vinci, Leonardo. *See* Leonardo da Vinci

Davis, Stuart, 359, 371–372, 382; *Owh! in San Paõ*, 40, *Figure 3.2*; *Swing Landscape*, 372, *Figure 19.10*

Death and the Miser (Bosch), 237, *Figure 13.11*

Death and the Mother (Kollwitz), 338, *Figure 18.5*

Death of Marat, The (David), 284–285, *Figure 16.1*

Death of Socrates (David), *Figure 16.15*

Death of the Virgin, 169, *Figure 10.13*

De Creeft, José, *The Cloud*, 26, 28, *Figure 2.16*

Degas, Edgar, 282, 306–307; *Galloping Horse*, 307, *Figure 16.20*; *The Glass of Absinthe*, 306, *Figure 16.19*

De Kooning, Willem, 359, 377; *Woman VI*, 377, *Figure 19.15*

Delacroix, Eugène, 282, 290–291; *Arabs Skirmishing in the Mountains*, *Figure 16.17*; *The Lion Hunt*, 291, *Figure 16.6*

Descent from the Cross (Rogier van der Weyden), 214–215, *Figure 12.4*

Design, elements of. *See* Elements of art

Design, principles of. *See* Principles of art

Design, unified, 30

Design chart, 37–38, 50–51

Design relationships, 37–38

Diagonal lines, 22

Diamond Painting in Red, Yellow, Blue (Mondrian), 54, *Figure 3.15*

Diebenkorn, Richard, *Woman by a Large Window*, 31, *Figure 2.19*

Discobolus (Myron), 96–97, 104, *Figure 6.11*

Doge Andrea Gritti (Titian), 224–225, *Figure 13.3*

Donatello, 181, 191–192; *St. George*, 191–192, *Figure 11.11*; *St. Mark*, *Figure 11.10*

Doric order, 92, *Figure 6.5*

Doryphorus (Polyclitus), 100, 104, *Figure 6.16*

Double Metamorphosis, II (Agam), 393, *Figure 19.36*

Double Portrait of a Boy and a Girl of the Attavanti Family (Anguissola), 207, *Figure 11.23*

Driftwood (Homer), 325

Drying Clothes (Harunobu), *Figure 16.18*

Duccio di Buonnisegna, 160, 174–176; *Maestà Altarpiece*, 174–175, *Figure 10.19*

Duchamp, Marcel, 360

Dürer, Albrecht, 220, 233, 235–236; *Knight, Death, and the Devil*, 235–236, *Figure 13.10*

Dutch art, 254–261

Dying Gaul, 102, *Figure 6.17*

E

Eakins, Thomas, 313, 326; *The Gross Clinic*, 326, *Figure 17.12*

Early Christian art, 125–136

East Building, National Gallery of Art (Pei), 390–391, *Figures 19.33, 19.34*

Echo of a Scream (Siqueiros), 348, *Figure 18.7*

Ecstasy of St. Theresa, The (Bernini), 247–248, *Figure 14.4*

Edward VI as a Child (Holbein), 239, *Figure 13.13*

Egypt, history of, 73–74

Egyptian art, 72–86

Eiffel, Alexandre Gustave, 332, 352; Eiffel Tower, 352, *Figure 18.21*

Elements of art, 11, 15–30, 49

Elevation of the Cross, The (Rubens), 251–252, *Figure 14.8*

El Greco, 220, 229–233; *The Burial of Count Orgaz*, 231–232, *Figure 13.8*; *The Martyrdon of St. Maurice and the Theban Legion*, 230, *Figure 13.7*

Embarkation for Cythera (Watteau), 270–271, *Figure 15.2*

Emotionalism, 52–55

Emphasis, 30, 32

Entablature, 89

Entice 2 (Riley), 19, *Figure 2.4*

Entombment, The (Titian), 223–224, *Figure 13.2*

Entrance of St. Ignatius into Paradise, The (Pozzo), 247, *Figure 14.3*

Erechtheum, 92–93, *Figure 6.7*

Eskimo masks, 435–436, *Figures 21.16, 21.17*

Etruscans, 108

Eve of St. Nicholas, The (Steen), 258–259, *Figure 14.14*

Exekias, 87; *Vase with Ajax and Achilles Playing Draughts*, 106, *Figure 6.22*

Expressionism, 337–339

Eyck, Jan van. *See* Van Eyck

F

Falling Water (Wright). *See* Kaufmann House

Fashion design, careers in, 450–451

Fatata te Miti (Gauguin), 322–323, *Figure 17.9*

Fauvism, 333–337

Female Dignitary Holding Scepter, 438, *Figure 21.20*

Feudalism, 139, 146

Figure (Archaean) (Hepworth), 380, *Figure 19.19*

Fish Magic (Klee), 364, *Figure 19.4*

Flemish art, 210–218

Florence, Cathedral of, 192–193, *Figure 11.12*

Flying buttresses, 161–162

Flying Dutchman, The (Ryder), *Figure 17.14*

Fog Warning, The (Homer), 325, *Figure 17.10*

Form, 27–28

Formalism, 52–55

Forum, 117

Fragonard, Jean-Honoré, 268, 271–272; *The Swing*, 271–272, *Figure 15.3*

Franco-Saxon Gospels, *Figure 9.5*

Frankenthaler, Helen, 359, 378; *Interior Landscape*, 378, *Figure 19.17*

Fresco, 176

Frieze, 89

G

Gainsborough, Thomas, 268, 275; *Blue Boy*, 275, *Figure 15.7*

Galloping Horse (Degas), 307, *Figure 16.20*

Gare Saint-Lazare (Manet), 296, *Figure 16.11*

Gargoyle, 170, *Figure 10.15*

Gaudi, Antonio, 332, 353–355; *Güell Park*, 353–355, *Figures 18.22, 18.23, 18.24*

Gauguin, Paul, 313, 321–323; *Fatata te Miti*, 322–323, *Figure 17.9*; *Spirit of the Dead Watching*, 321–322, *Figure 17.8*

Gentileschi, Artemisia, 243, 250–251; *Judith and Maidservant with the Head of Holofernes*, 250, *Figure 14.7*

Gentileschi, Orazio, 250

Geometric period, 105

George Gisze (Holbein), 241, *Figure 13.14*

Géricault, Théodore, 282, 288–290; *The Raft of Medusa*, 288–290, *Figure 16.5*

Gesù, Il. *See* Il Gesù

Ghiberti, Lorenzo, 181, 186–188, 192; ''The Gates of Paradise,'' 188, *Figure 11.7*; *The Sacrifice of Isaac*, 186–187, *Figure 11.5*

Giant, The (Goya), 280, *Figure 15.12*

Giant Three-Way Plug (Oldenburg), 391–392, *Figure 19.35*

Ginevra de' Benci (Leonardo), 199, *Figure 11.17*

Giorgione da Castelfranco, 220–223; *The Adoration of the Shepherds*, 29, *Figure 2.17*; *The Concert*, 222–223, *Figure 13.1*

Giotto di Bondone, 160, 176–178; *Lamentation*, 177–178, *Figure 10.20*

Giovanni Arnolfini and His Bride (van Eyck), 210–211, *Figure 12.1*

Gipstein, Yaacov. *See* Agam

Girl Arranging Her Hair (Cassatt), 307–308, *Figure 16.21*

Girl with a Watering Can, A (Renoir), 42–46, *Figure 3.3*

Glarner, Fritz, *Relational Painting*, 33, *Figure 2.21*

Glass of Absinthe (Picasso), 341–342, *Figure 18.10*

Glass of Absinthe, The (Degas), 306, *Figure 16.19*

Glossary, 454–464

Goes, Hugo van der. *See* Hugo van der Goes

Golden Virgin, 170, Figure 10.14

Gorky, Arshile, 46–47; *The Artist and His Mother*, 46–47, *Figure 3.8*

Gospel Book of Archibishop Ebbo of Reims, 144–145, *Figure 9.6*

Gothic art, 160–180, 209

Goya, Francisco, 268, 278–280; *The Giant*, 280, *Figure 15.12*; *The Marquesa de Pontejos*, 278, *Figure 15.10*; *The Third of May, 1808*, 279, *Figure 15.11*

Gradation, 30, 35

Graphic design, careers in, 450

Greece, history of, 87–89, 101, 106

Greek art, 87–107

Groin vault, 115, *Figure 7.3*

Gross Clinic, the (Eakins), 326, *Figure 17.12*

Grosz, George, 359, 369; *Waving the Flag*, 369, *Figure 19.8*

Grünewald, Matthias, 220, 233–235; *The Small Crucifixion*, 55, 234–235, *Figures 3.16, 13.9*

Güell Park (Gaudi), 353–355, *Figures 18.22, 18.23, 18.24*

Guernica (Picasso), 343, 348, *Figure 18.11*

Guggenheim Museum (Wright), 388–389, *Figures 19.31, 19.32*

Guglielmi, Louis, *Terror in Brooklyn*, *Figure 3.13*

Gutenberg, 182

H

Hagia Sophia, 131–132, *Figures 8.6, 8.7, 8.8, 8.9, 8.10*

Hals, Frans, 243, 254; *Portrait of an Officer*, 254, *Figure 14.11*

Hard-edge painters, 394–396

Harmony, 30, 33–35

Hartley, Marsden, *Painting Number 5*, 32, *Figure 2.20*

Harunobu, Suzuki, 282; *Drying Clothes*, *Figure 16.18*

Haystack at Sunset near Giverny (Monet), 301, *Figure 16.14*

Haywain, The (Constable), 292, *Figure 16.7*

Head of the Procession (Phidias), 99, *Figure 6.14*

Hellenistic period, 74, 101, 104

Henri, Robert, 367

Hepworth, Barbara, 359, 380; *Figure (Archaean)*, 380, *Figure 19.19*

Hera of Samos, 96, *Figure 6.10*

Hobbema, Meindert, *A Pond in the Forest*, 40, *Figure 3.1*

Hogarth, William, 268, 276–277; *The Marriage Contract*, 276–277, *Figure 15.8*

Holbein, Hans, 220, 233, 238–241; *Edward VI as a Child*, 239, *Figure 13.13*; *George Gisze*, 241, *Figure 13.14*

Holy Trinity, The (Masaccio), 182–183, *Figure 11.1*

Homage to the Square: ''Ascending'' (Albers), 31, 396–397, *Figure 2.18*

Homer, Winslow, 313, 324–325; *Driftwood*, 325; *The Fog Warning*, 325, *Figure*

17.10; *Prisoners at the Front*, 324; *Right and Left*, 325, *Figure 17.11*

Hopper, Edward, 359, 367–368; *Nighthawks*, 368, *Figure 19.7*

Horizontal lines, 22

Horse Fair, The (Bonheur), 298, *Figure 16.12*

Horsemen (Phidias), 99, *Figure 6.13*

Houser, Allan, 360, 386; *Watching for Dancing Partners*, 386, *Figure 19.27*

Hudson River Landscape (Smith), 382–383, *Figure 19.22*

Hue, 17

Hugo van der Goes, 216–218; *The Adoration of the Shepherds*, 217–218, *Figures 12.6, 12.7*

Humpty Dumpty (Noguchi), 385, *Figure 19.26*

Hyksos, 74, 80

I

Ikhnaton, 74; portraits of, 81–82, *Figure 5.8*

Il Gesù, 244, *Figure 14.1*

Illuminated manuscripts. *See* Manuscript illumination

Imitationalism, 52–55

Impressionism, 44–46, 298–310

Impression: Sunrise (Monet), 299

Improvisation 28 (Kandinsky), 341, *Figure 18.8*

Industrial design, careers in, 451

Ingres, Jean-Auguste-Dominique, 282, 286–288; *Madame Moitessier*, 288, *Figure 16.4*

Intensity, of color, 17

Interior design, careers in, 451

Interior Landscape (Frankenthaler), 378, *Figure 19.17*

Interior of the Pantheon (Panini), *Figure 7.14*

Intermediate colors, 18

International Style (architecture), 357

International Style (manuscript illumination), 173, 209

Ionic order, 92, *Figure 6.5*

J

Japanese art, 305, 409–420

Jeanneret, Charles-Edouard. *See* Le Corbusier

Jittoku (Shohaku), 419–420, *Figure 20.24*

Johnston, Joshua, 328

Jonah (Ryder), 327–328, *Figure 17.13*

Julius, Pope, 201, 205

Justinian, Emperor, 131–135

Justinian and Attendants, 134–135, *Figure 8.12*

K

Kandinsky, Vasily, 332, 340–341; *Improvisation 28*, 341, *Figure 18.8*

Kanzan (Shohaku), 419–420, *Figure 20.23*

Karnak, 76–78

Kaufmann House (Wright), 388, *Figure 19.30*

Kaz, Nathaniel, *Cyrano*, 20, 22, *Figure 2.5*

Kelly, Ellsworth, 394

Keystone, 111, *Figure 7.3*

Khafre, portrait of, 78–79, *Figure 5.5*; sphinx of, 80, *Figures 5.1, 5.6*

Khufu, pyramid of, 75, *Figure 5.2*

Kirchner, Ernst Ludwig, 332, 337; *Street, Berlin*, 337, *Figure 18.4*

Klee, Paul, 359, 363–364; *Fish Magic*, 364, *Figure 19.4*; *Twittering Machine*, 363, *Figure 19.3*

Knight, Death, and the Devil (Dürer), 235–236, *Figure 13.10*

Kollwitz, Käthe, 332, 338; *Death and the Mother*, 338, *Figure 18.5*

Kouros, 94–95, 104, *Figure 6.9*

Krasner, Lee, 25; *Between Two Appearances*, 25, *Figure 2.13*

Kroll, Leon, *Still Life with Lemon Tree*, *Figure 2.15*

L

Lady Betty Hamilton (Reynolds), 274, *Figure 15.6*

Lamentation (Giotto), 177–178, *Figure 10.20*

Landscape at Cagnes (Renoir), 305, *Figure 16.16*

Lascaux, cave paintings of, 66–69, *Figure 4.2*

Las Meninas (Velázquez). *See Meninas, Las*

Last Judgment, The (Michelangelo), 202

Last Supper, The (Leonardo), 197–198, *Figure 11.16*

Lavender Mist (Pollock), 378, *Figure 19.16*

Lawrence, Jacob, 359, 374; *Tombstones* 374, *Figure 19.13*; *War Series: Another Patrol*, 23, *Figure 2.9*

Le Corbusier, 360, 386–387; *Notre Dame du Haut*, 386–387, *Figures 19.28, 19.29*

León, Cathedral of, 162, *Figure 10.5*

Leonardo da Vinci, 181, 196–199, 233; *Anatomical Studies*, 196, *Figure 11.15*; *Ginevra de'Benci*, 199, *Figure 11.17*; *The Last Supper*, 197–198, *Figure 11.16*; *Mona Lisa*, 199

Leslie, Alfred, 360, 397; *7 A.M. News*, 397, *Figure 19.41*

Letter, The (Vermeer), 259–260, *Figure 14.15*

Lever House, 357, *Figure 18.27*

Levine, Jack, 359, 370–371; *Welcome Home*, 370–371, *Figure 19.9*

Leyre Monastery, *Figure 9.17*

Leyster, Judith, 243, 260–261; *Self-Portrait*, 260–261, *Figure 14.16*

Liberation of the Peon (Rivera), 346–347, *Figure 18.15*

Limbourg Brothers, *Les Tres Riches Heures du Duc de Berry*, 173, *Figure 10.17*

Line, 20–24

Linear art, 21–22

Linear perspective, 183

Lintels, 77, 89

Lion (Rubens), 252, *Figure 14.10*

Lion Hunt, The (Delacroix), 291, *Figure 16.6*

Lipchitz, Jacques, 359, 381–382; *Sacrifice II*, 381–382, *Figure 19.21*; *Sailor with Guitar*, 381, *Figure 19.20*

Lippi, Fra Filippo, *Madonna and Child*, *Figure 3.5*

Lochner, Stephen, *The Virgin of the Rose-Bower*, *Figure 3.6*

Louis XIV, 268–269

Lysicrates, Monument to, 94, *Figure 6.8*

M

Madame de la Châtre (Vigée-Lebrun), 286, *Figure 16.3*

Madame Moitessier (Ingres), 288, *Figure 16.4*

Madonna and Child (Lippi), *Figure 3.5*

Madonna with the Long Neck, The (Parmigianino), 226–227, *Figure 13.4*

Maestà Altarpiece (Duccio), 174–175, *Figure 10.19*

Maiden Gathering Flowers, 122, *Figure 7.22*

Maids of Honor, The (Velázquez). *See Meninas, Las*

Maillol, Aristide, 332, 345–346; *The Mediterranean*, 345–346, *Figure 18.14*

Manet, Edouard, 282, 296; *Gare Saint-Lazare*, 296, *Figure 16.11*

Mannerism, 225–233

Manuscript illumination, 143–145, 156–167, 171–173

Marquesa de Pontejos, The (Goya), 278, *Figure 15.10*

Marriage Contract, The (Hogarth), 276–277, *Figure 15.8*

Martyrdom of St. Maurice and the Theban Legion, The (El Greco), 230, *Figure 13.7*

Masaccio, 181–185; *The Holy Trinity*, 182–183, *Figure 11.1*; *The Tribute Money*, 184–185, *Figure 11.3*

Masks, African, 424–425, *Figures 21.2, 21.3, 21.4*, Eskimo, 435–436, *Figures 21.16, 21.17*; Olmec, 435–436, *Figure 21.18*; Pueblo and Apache, 435

Mass, 27

Mastaba, 76

Matisse, Henri, 332–335; *La Negresse*, 335, *Figure 18.2*; *The Red Studio*, 334–335, *Figure 18.1*; *Young Girl Seated*, *Figure 3.12*

Mayan art, 437–438

Mazzola, Francesco. *See* Parmigianino

Medieval art, Early, 137–146

Menes, 74

Meninas, Las (Velázquez), 264, *Figure 14.20*

Metric terms, 464

Mexican art, 346–348

Michelangelo Buonarroti, 181, 200–203; *The Last Judgment*, 202; *Moses*, 202, *Figure 11.20*; *Pietà*, 200, *Figure 11.18*; Sistine Chapel, 201–202, *Figure 11.19*

Mill, The (Rembrandt), 257, *Figure 3.9*

Minimal Art, 393–394

Miró, Joan, 359, 361–362; *Carnival of Harlequin*, 361–362, *Figure 19.1*

Mona Lisa (Leonardo), 199

Monasteries, 140–143

Mondrian, Piet, *Diamond Painting in Red, Yellow, Blue*, 54, *Figure 3.15*

Monet, Claude, 21, 282, 299–301; *Haystack at Sunset near Giverny*, 301, *Figure 16.14*; *Impression: Sunrise*, 299; *Rouen Cathedral, West Façade*, 299, 301, *Figure 16.13*

Mont Sainte-Victoire as Seen from Bibemus Quarry (Cézanne), 317. *Figures 1.5, 17.4*

Monument to Lysicrates, 94, *Figure 6.8*

Moore, Henry, 359, 379–380; *Reclining Figure*, 380, *Figure 19.18*; *Reclining Figure (Hand)*, 22, *Figure 2.8*

Moreau, Gustave, 333

Morgan, Julia, 332, 355–357; San Simeon, 355–357, *Figure 18.25*

Morisot, Berthe, 282, 308–309; *The Sisters*, 308, *Figure 16.22*

Mortlake Terrace (Turner), 35, *Figure 2.23*

Mosaics, Byzantine, 132–135; Early Christian, 128

Movement, 30, 35–36

Munch, Edvard, 332, 338–339; *The Scream*, 339, *Figure 18.7*; *The Sick Child*, 338, *Figure 18.6*

Muralists, Mexican, 346–348

Murillo, Bartolomé Esteban, 243, 266; *The Return of the Prodigal Son*, 266, *Figure 14.21*

Museum science, careers in, 452

Myron, 87; *Discobolus*, 96–97, *Figure 6.11*

N

Nakht, wall paintings from tomb of, 84–85, *Figures 5.11, 5.12*

Napoleon in His Study (David), 285, *Figure 16.2*

Nash, John, The Royal Pavilion, *Figure 3.20*

Nave, 119

Neel, Alice, 359, 374; *Portrait of Ellen Johnson*, 374, *Figure 19.12*

Nefertiti, Queen, 82

Negresse, La (Matisse), 335, *Figure 18.2*

Neoclassicism, 283–288

Nevelson, Louise, 359, 384–385; *Royal Tide II*, 385, *Figure 19.24*

Newman, Barnett, 360, 393–394; *Broken Obelisk*, 393–394, *Figure 19.37*

Nighthawks (Hopper), 368, *Figure 19.7*

Night Watch, The (Rembrandt), 256–257, *Figure 14.12*

Nike Fastening Her Sandal, 100, *Figure 6.15*

Nike of Samothrace, 102–103, *Figure 6.18*

Nimba Headdress, 424, *Figure 21.2*

Noguchi, Isamu, 359, 385; *Humpty Dumpty*, 385, *Figure 19.26*

Noland, Kenneth, 394; *Across*, *Figure 19.39*

Nonobjective art, 340–341

No Passing (Sage), 365–366, *Figure 19.5*

Notre Dame, Cathedral of (Paris), 166

Notre Dame du Haut (Le Corbusier), 386–387, *Figures 19.28, 19.29*

O

Obelisks, 78

Ogol, Master of, *Standing Female Figure*, 426, *Figure 21.5*

Oil paints, 210

O'Keeffe, Georgia, 359, 372–373, 391–392; *The White Calico Flower*, 373, *Figure 19.11*

Oldenburg, Claes, 360, 391–392; *Giant Three-Way Plug*, 391–392, *Figure 19.35*

Old King, The (Rouault), 336–337, *Figure 18.3*

Olmec art, 436

Op Art, 392–393

Orders of Decorative Style, 92–94, *Figure 6.5*

Orozco, José Clemente, 332, 347; *Zapatistas*, 347, *Figure 18.16*

Owh! in San Paõ (Davis), 40, *Figure 3.2*

P

Painterly art, 21–22

Painting, Abstract Expressionist, 376–378; American, 323–329, 348–352, 366–378; Baroque, 248–266; cave, 64–70; Chinese, 401–408; Dada, 360; Dutch, 254–261; Early Christian, 143–145; Egyptian, 82–85; English, 274–278, 291–294; Expressionist, 337–339; Fauvist, 333–337; Flemish, 210–218, 236–238; French, 269–273, 294–309; German, 233–236, 238–241; Greek, 104–106; Impressionist, 42–46, 298–310; Italian, 182–187, 189–191, 194–207, 220–228, 246–251; Japanese, 412–416, 419–420, Mannerist, 225–233; Mexican muralist, 346–348; Neoclassical, 283–288; nonobjective, 340–341; Post-Impressionist, 313–323; Realistic, 294–298, 324–326; Regionalism, 366–367; Renaissance, 182–187, 189–191, 194–207; Rococo, 269–280; Roman, 120–123; Romanesque, 156–158; Romantic, 288–291; sixteenth century, 220–241; Spanish, 229–232, 261–266, 278–280; Surrealist, 361–362, 365–366; twentieth century, 332–352, 359–378, 391–397

Painting Number 5 (Hartley), 32, *Figure 2.20*

Pamplona, Cathedral of, 156, 169, *Figures 9.23, 10.13*

Panini, Giovanni Paolo, *Interior of the Pantheon*, *Figure 7.14*

Pantheon, 118, *Figures 7.13, 7.14*

Parable of the Blind (Bruegel), 237–238, *Figure 13.12*

Parmigianino, 220, 225–227; *The Madonna with the Long Neck*, 226–227, *Figure 13.4*

Parrhasius, 105

Parthenon, 89–91, *Figures 6.1, 6.3*

Pattern, 105, 107, 245, 305, 323, 333, 334, 367

Pazzi Chapel, 193, *Figure 11.13*

Pediment, 89

Pei, I. M., 360, 390–391; East Building, National Gallery of Art, 390–391, *Figures 19.33, 19.34*

Pericles, 88–89

Persistence of Memory, The (Dali), 362, *Figure 19.2*

Perspective, aerial, 184; linear, 183

Perugino, 201

Peterdi, Gabor, *Tidal*, 36, *Figure 2.24*

Phidias, 87, 91; frieze on Parthenon, 97–99, *Figures 6.13, 6.14*; statue of Athena, 97, *Figure 6.12*

Philip II of Macedonia, 101

Photography, 299, 305

Picasso, Pablo, 332, 341–344; *The Blind Man's Meal*, 344, *Figure 18.12*; *Glass of Absinthe*, 341–342, *Figure 18.10*; *Guernica*, 343, 348, *Figure 18.11*

Piero della Francesca, 181, 190–191; *Baptism of Christ*, 190–191, *Figure 11.9*

Pietà (Michelangelo), 200, *Figure 11.18*

Pilasters, 120

Pilgrimage churches, 148–149

Pines and Rocks (Cézanne), 317, *Figure 17.3*

Pippin, Horace, 359, 375–376; *Self Portrait*, 375–376, *Figure 19.14*

Pisano, Andrea, 186

Pliny the Elder, 104–105

Poblet, Monastery of, *Figure 10.18*

Pollock, Jackson, 359, 377–378; *Lavender Mist*, 378, *Figure 19.16*

Polyclitus, 87; *Doryphorus (Spear Bearer)*, 100, 104, *Figure 6.16*

Pomegranate (Calder), 383, *Figure 19.23*

Pond in the Forest, A (Hobbema), 40, *Figure 3.1*

Pop Art, 391–392

Portinari Altarpiece (van der Goes), 217–218, *Figures 12.6, 12.7*

Portrait of a Lady (Rogier van der Weyden), 215–216, *Figure 12.5*

Portrait of an Officer (Hals), 254, *Figure 14.11*

Portrait of a Roman, 121, *Figure 7.19*

Portrait of Ellen Johnson (Neel), 374, *Figure 19.12*

Portrait of Hesire, 82–83, *Figure 5.10*

Post-and-lintel construction, 77, 111
Post-Impressionism, 313–323
Potato Eaters, The (van Gogh), 318–319, *Figure 17.5*
Pozzo, Fra Andrea, 243, 247, *The Entrance of St. Ignatius into Paradise*, 247, *Figure 14.3*
Pre-Columbian art, 435–438
Prehistoric art, 64–71
Presentation of the Virgin (Tintoretto), 288, *Figure 13.5*
Primary colors, 18
Principles of art, 15, 30–38, 51
Prints, Japanese, 305; Chinese, 416–418
Prisoners at the Front (Homer), 324
Prodigal Son, The (Rodin), 310, *Figure 16.23*
Proportion, 30, 36–37
Pyramids, 72–73, 75–77

Q

Queen Mary's Psalter, 171, *Figure 10.16*
Queen Nefertiti, 82, *Figure 5.9*

R

Radiocarbon dating, 66
Raft of the Medusa (Géricault), 288–290, *Figure 16.5*
Raking cornice, 89
Raphael Sanzio, 181, 203–206; *The Alba Madonna*, 204–205, 252, *Figure 11.21*
Realism, 294–298, 324–326
Reclining Figure (Moore), 380, *Figure 19.18*
Reclining Figure (Hand) (Moore), 22, *Figure 2.8*
Red Studio, The (Matisse), 334–335, *Figure 18.1*
Regionalism, 366–367
Reims, Cathedral of, 165, *Figure 10.8*
Reinhart, Ad, 393
Relational Painting (Glarner), 33, *Figure 2.21*
Relief, 74, 155
Religion, Christian, 126–127; Egyptian, 76, 78, 83
Rembrandt van Rijn, 243, 254, 256–257; *An Artist in His Studio*, 257, *Figure 14.13*; *The Mill*, 49–51, 257, *Figure 3.9*; *The Night Watch*, 256–257, *Figure 14.12*
Renaissance art, Italian, 181–208
Renoir, Pierre Auguste, 42–46, 282, 305; *A Girl with a Watering Can*, 42–46, *Figure 3.3*; *Landscape at Cagnes*, 305, *Figure 16.16*
Return of the Prodigal Son, The (Murillo), 266, *Figure 14.21*
Reynolds, Sir Joshua, 268, 274; *Lady Betty Hamilton*, 274, *Figure 15.6*
Rhythm, 30, 35–36
Ribera, Jusepe de, 243, 262; *The Blind Old Beggar*, 262, *Figure 14.17*
Right and Left (Homer), 325, *Figure 17.11*

Riley, Bridget, 19, 360, 393; *Entice 2*, 19, *Figure 2.4*
Rivera, Diego, 332, 346–347; *Liberation of the Peon*, 346–347, *Figure 18.15*
Robie House (Wright), 24, *Figure 2.12*
Rococo art, 268–281
Rodin, Auguste, 282, 309–310; *The Prodigal Son*, 310, *Figure 16.23*
Rogier van der Weyden, 209, 213–216; *Descent from the Cross*, 214–215, *Figure 12.4*; *Portrait of a Lady*, 215–216, *Figure 12.5*
Roman art, 108–124
Romanesque art, 146–158
Romanticism, 288–291
Rome, history of, 108, 123, 130
Rouault, Georges, 43, 332–333, 336–337; *The Old King*, 336–337, *Figure 18.3*; *Three Clowns*, 43, *Figure 3.4*
Rouen Cathedral, West Façade (Monet), 299, 301, *Figure 16.13*
Royal Pavilion (Nash), *Figure 3.20*
Royal Tide II (Nevelson), 385, *Figure 19.24*
Rubens, Peter Paul, 243, 251–253; *Daniel in the Lions' Den*, 253, *Figure 14.9*; *The Elevation of the Cross*, 251–252, *Figure 14.8*; *Lion*, 252, *Figure 14.10*
Ryder, Albert Pinkham, 313, 327–328; *The Flying Dutchman*, *Figure 17.14*; *Jonah*, 327–328, *Figure 17.13*

S

Sacrifice of Isaac, The (Brunelleschi), 186–187, *Figure 11.6*
Sacrifice of Isaac, The (Ghiberti), 186–187, *Figure 11.5*
Sacrifice II (Lipchitz), 381–382, *Figure 19.21*
Safety Note, 62, 71, 107, 136, 159, 180, 242, 281
Sage, Kay, 359, 365–366; *No Passing*, 365–366, *Figure 19.5*
Sailor with Guitar (Lipchitz), 381, *Figure 19.20*
St. George (Donatello), 191–192, *Figure 11.11*
St. John (manuscript illumination), *Figure 9.5*
St. Mark (Donatello), *Figure 11.10*
St. Matthew (manuscript illumination), 144–145, *Figure 9.6*
St. Michael's Cathedral of Hildesheim, 145, *Figure 9.7*
St. Paul's Cathedral, 277–278, *Figure 15.9*
Salon, 283
San Carlo alle Quattro Fontane (Borromini), 245, *Figure 14.2*
San Clemente, Church of, 158, *Figure 9.25*
San Juan de la Peña, Monastery of, 141–143, *Figures 9.3, 9.4*
San Miguel, Church of, (Estella), 36–37, 154, *Figures 2.25, 9.20*

San Sernin, Church of, 151–152, *Figures 9.14, 9.15, 9.17*
San Simeon (Morgan), 355–357, *Figure 18.25*
Santa Maria, Church of, (Sangüesa), 153–154, *Figures 9.11, 9.18, 9.19, 19.25*
Sant' Apollinare in Classe, *Figures 8.3, 8.4, 8.5*
Santes Creus Monastery, *Figure 9.21*
Santiago de Compostela, Cathedral of, 149, *Figure 9.12*
San Vitale, 133–135, *Figures 8.11, 8.12, 8.13*
Sarcophagus, 76
Sautuola, Marcelino de, 69–70
Scale, intensity, 17; value, 17
Scream, The (Munch), 339, *Figure 18.7*
Scriptoria, 143
Sculpture, African, 422–427; Baroque, 246–248; Egyptian, 78–83; Gothic, 167–170; Greek, 94–104; Impressionist, 307, 309–310; Italian, 186–188, 191–192, 246–248; pre-Columbian, 435–438; Renaissance, 186–188, 191–192; Roman, 120–121; Romanesque, 152–156; twentieth-century, 345–346, 379–386, 391–397
Seated Boxer, 103–104, *Figure 6.19*
Secondary colors, 18
Self-Portrait (Leyster), 260–261, *Figure 14.16*
Self Portrait (Pippin), 375–376, *Figure 19.14*
Serf, 139
Sesostris III, Fragment of a Head of King, 80, *Figure 5.7*
7 A.M. News (Leslie), 397, *Figure 19.41*
Sgraffito, 107
Shape, 27
Shohaku, Soga, 400, 419–420; *Jittoku*, 420, *Figure 20.24*; *Kanzan*, 420, *Figure 20.23*
Sick Child, The (Munch), 338, *Figure 18.6*
Signorelli, 201
Siqueiros, David Alfaro, 332, 348; *Echo of a Scream*, 348, *Figure 18.7*
Sisters, The (Morisot), 308, *Figure 16.22*
Sistine Chapel, 201–202, *Figure 11.19*
Sloan, John, 332, 349–350; *Backyards, Greenwich Village*, 349–350, *Figure 18.18*
Small Crucifixion, The (Grünewald), 234–235, *Figures 3.16, 13.9*
Smith, David, 359, 382–383; *Hudson River Landscape*, 382–383, *Figure 19.22*
Snow Storm: Steam-Boat off a Harbour's Mouth (Turner), 294, *Figure 16.9*
Soft sculpture, 392
Solomon R. Guggenheim Museum (Wright), 388–389, *Figures 19.31, 19.32*
Sonar Tide (Bladen), 394, *Figure 19.38*
Space, 28–29
Spear Bearer (Polyclitus), 100, 104, *Figure 6.16*
Sphinx, Great, 80, *Figures 5.1, 5.6*

Spirit of the Dead Watching (Gauguin), 321–322, *Figure 17.8*

Stag at Sharkey's (Bellows), 350, *Figure 18.19*

Stained-glass windows, 162–165, *Figures 10.5, 10.6, 10.7*

Starry Night (van Gogh), 320–321, *Figure 17.7*

Steen, Jan, 243, 258–259; *The Eve of St. Nicholas*, 258–259, *Figure 14.14*

Stella, Frank, 360, 394–396; *Agbatana III*, 394–396, *Figures 1.1, 19.40*

Step Pyramid of King Zoser, *Figure 5.3*

Stieglitz, Alfred, 373

Still Life with Lemon Tree (Kroll), *Figure 2.15*

Still Life with Peppermint Bottle (Cézanne), 315–316, *Figure 17.2*

Still Life with Rib of Beef (Chardin), 272, *Figure 15.4*

Street, Berlin (Kirchner), 337, *Figure 18.4*

Stylobate, 89

Suitor's Visit, The (Ter Borch), 26, *Figure 2.14*

Sullivan, Louis, 332, 357; Wainwright Building, 357, *Figure 18.26*

Surrealism, 361–362, 365–366

Surrender of Breda (Velázquez), 263–264, *Figure 14.18*

Swing, The (Fragonard), 271–272, *Figure 15.3*

Swing Landscape (Davis), 372, *Figure 19.10*

Symbols, Christian, 126–127

T

Tanguy, Yves, 365

Tanner, Henry, 313, 329; *The Banjo Lesson*, 329, *Figure 17.15; Daniel in the Lion's Den*, 329

Tapestries, 146

Tarragona, Cathedral of, 156, *Figures 9.22, 10.1, 10.11*

Tempera, 210

Temple of Athena Nike, 92, *Figure 6.6*

Temple of Fortuna Primigenia, 109–111, *Figure 7.2*

Temple of Fortuna Virilis, 109, *Figure 7.1*

Temples, Egyptian, 76–78; Greek, 89, *Figure 6.2;* Roman, 109–110

Ter Borch, Gerard, *The Suitor's Visit*, 26, *Figure 2.14*

Terror in Brooklyn (Guglielmi), *Figure 3.13*

Tertiary colors, 18

Tesserae, 136

Texture, 24–27

Theodora and Attendants, 134–135, *Figure 8.13*

Theotocopoulos, Domenico. *See* El Greco

Third of May, 1808, The (Goya), 279, *Figure 15.11.*

Three Clowns (Rouault), 43, *Figure 3.4*

Three Marys at the Tomb, The, 37–38, 154–155, *Figures 2.25, 9.20*

Thutmose III, 74

Tidal (Peterdi), 36, *Figure 2.24*

Tintoretto, 220, 227–228; *Presentation of the Virgin*, 228, *Figure 13.5*

Titian, 220, 223–225; *Doge Andrea Gritti*, 224–225, *Figure 13.3; The Entombment*, 223–224, *Figure 13.2*

Toledo, Cathedral of, 24, *Figure 2.11*

Tombstones (Lawrence), 374, *Figure 19.13*

Toulouse-Lautrec, Henri de, 21; *A Corner of the Moulin de la Galette*, 21, *Figure 2.7*

Transept, 140

Trapezoid, 205

Très Riches Heures du Duc de Berry, Les (Limbourg Brothers), 173, *Figure 10.17*

Tribute Money, The (Masaccio), 184–185, *Figure 11.3*

Triumphal arch, 120, *Figure 7.17*

Turner, Joseph M. W., 282, 293–294; *Mortlake Terrace*, 35, *Figure 2.23; Snow Storm: Steam-Boat off a Harbour's Mouth*, 294, *Figure 16.9*

Twin Pines against a Flat Vista (Chao-Meng-fu), 408, *Figure 20.9*

Twittering Machine (Klee), 363, *Figure 19.3*

Tympanum, 152–153

U

Uccello, Paolo, 181, 189; *The Battle of San Romano*, 189, *Figure 11.8*

Under the Oaks (Bannister), 328

Unity, 15, 37

V

Value, of color, 17; apart from color, 20

Van Eyck, Jan, 209–213; *Adoration of the Lamb*, 212–213, *Figure 12.2; Giovanni Arnolfini and His Bride*, 210–211, *Figure 12.1*

Van Gogh, Vincent, 313, 318–321, 323; *The Bedroom at Arles*, 319, *Figure 17.6; The Potato Eaters*, 318–319, *Figure 17.5; Starry Night*, 320–321, *Figure 17.7*

Vanishing point, 183

Variety, 30, 34–35

Vasarely, Victor, 393

Vasari, Giorgio, 186

Vases, Greek, 105–106

Vaults, 110, 115, *Figure 7.3*

Velázquez, Diego, 243, 262–265; *Las Meninas*, 264, *Figure 14.20; Surrender of Breda*, 263–264, *Figure 14.18*

Venetian art, 221–225, 227–228

Vermeer, Jan, 243, 259–260; *The Letter*, 259–260, *Figure 14.15*

Versailles, 268–269, *Figure 15.1*

Vertical lines, 22

View of Salisbury Cathedral, A (Constable), 58–59, *Figure 3.19*

Vigée-Lebrun, Marie Louise Elisabeth, 282, 286; *Madame de la Châtre*, 286, *Figure 16.3; The Marquise de Peze and the Marquise de Rouget with Her Two Children*, *Figure 3.11*

Virgin and Child with the Emperors Justinian and Constantine, 132, *Figure 8.10*

Virgin of the Rose-Bower, The (Lochner), *Figure 3.6*

Volume, 27–28

W

Wainwright Building (Sullivan), 357, *Figure 18.26*

Walls, town, 148

Warm colors, 18

War Series: Another Patrol (Lawrence), 23, *Figure 2.9*

Watching for Dancing Partners (Houser), 386, *Figure 19.27*

Watteau, Antoine, 268, 270–271; *Embarkation for Cythera*, 270–271, *Figure 15.2*

Waving the Flag (Grosz), 369, *Figure 19.8*

Weber, Max, *Chinese Restaurant*, 34, *Figure 2.22*

Welcome Home (Levine), 370, *Figure 19.9*

Weyden, Rogier van der. *See* Rogier van der Weyden

White Calico Flower, The (O'Keeffe), 373, *Figure 19.11*

Winckelmann, John, 283

Wivenhoe Park, Essex (Constable), 292–293, *Figure 16.8*

Woman by a Large Window (Diebenkorn), 31, *Figure 2.19*

Woman VI (de Kooning), 377, *Figure 19.15*

Wood, Grant, 359, 366–367; *American Gothic*, 367, *Figure 19.6*

Wood carvings, African, 423–427

Wren, Sir Christopher, 268, 277–278; St. Paul's Cathedral, 277–278, *Figure 15.9*

Wright, Frank Lloyd, 360, 388–389; Kaufmann House (Falling Water), 388, *Figure 18.30*; Robie House, 24, *Figure 2.12*; Solomon R. Guggenheim Museum, 388–389, *Figures 19.31, 19.32*

X

Xipe Impersonator, 437, *Figure 21.19*

Y

Young Girl Seated (Matisse), *Figure 3.12*

Z

Zapatistas (Orozco), 347, *Figure 18.16*

Zeuxis, 105

List of Studio Experiences Included in the Text

Ceramics Experiences

Lesson 6-2 (Functional Coil Vases), 107
Lesson 6-3 (Clay Slab Pitcher with Sgraffito Design), 107
Lesson 8-1 (Making Ceramic Tesserae), 136

Craft Experiences

Lesson 3-3 (A Nonobjective Composition with an Emphasis on Expressive Qualities), 62
Lesson 8-2 (Using Ceramic Tesserae to Make Mosaic Wall Plaques), 136
Lesson 17-2 (Tempera Batik in the Style of Gauguin), 331

Design Experiences

Lesson 9-1 (Crayon Etching in the Style of Romanesque Manuscript Illustrations), 159
Lesson 12-2 (Designing a Visual Symbol), 219
Lesson 13-1 (Bizarre Creatures from Expanded Paper Shapes), 242

Drawing Experiences

Lesson 5-2 (Designing a Sarcophagus Cover in the Egyptian Style), 86
Lesson 6-1 (Drawings of Buildings with Greek Features), 107
Lesson 7-1 (Drawing Exterior Views of Buildings —As They Are), 124
Lesson 7-2 (Drawing Exterior Views of Buidings —As They Could Be), 124
Lesson 10-2 (Drawing Personal Tympana), 179
Lesson 12-1 (Expanding Detail Drawing), 219
Lesson 14-1 (Drawing a Shape Moving in Space), 267
Lesson 14-2 (Ink Drawings Emphasizing Value Contrasts for Dramatic Effect), 267
Lesson 15-1 (Still-Life Drawing in Pastels), 281
Lesson 15-2 (Expressing an Emotion or Mood in an Ink Drawing), 281
Lesson 18-1 (Drawing in the Cubist Style), 358
Lesson 19-1 (Drawing Expressive Portraits), 398
Lesson 19-2 (Coloring Expressive Portraits with Oil Pastels), 398
Lesson 20-2 (Detailed Figure Drawings Derived from Preliminary Meditation), 421

Painting Experiences

Lesson 3-1 (A Still Life with an Emphasis on Literal Qualities), 62
Lesson 3-2 (A Still Life with an Emphasis on Visual Qualities), 62
Lesson 4-1 (Creating the Appearance of Three Dimensions), 71
Lesson 5-1 (Painting with Flat Shapes and Monochromatic Color), 86
Lesson 5-3 (Painting a Sarcophagus Cover in the Egyptian Style), 86
Lesson 11-1 (Painting a Landscape with Gradations of Value to Emphasize Space), 208
Lesson 11-2 (Painting a Landscape with Gradations of Intensity to Emphasize Space), 208
Lesson 16-1 (Watercolor Still Life in the Style of Delacroix), 312
Lesson 16-2 (Landscape Painting in the Style of Impressionism), 312
Lesson 17-1 (Designing a Painting Based on van Gogh's *The Potato Eaters*), 331
Lesson 18-2 (Painting in the Cubist Style), 358
Lesson 20-1 (Negative Shape Painting of a Branch), 421
Lesson 21-1 (Painting to Distinguish Between Positive and Negative Shapes in a Complex Composition), 439

Printmaking Experiences

Lesson 9-2 (Woodblock Prints of Fantastic Creatures), 159
Lesson 10-1 (String Print of a Gothic Cathedral), 179

Sculpture Experiences

Lesson 4-2 (Modeling a Three-Dimensional Animal in Clay), 71
Lesson 10-3 (Carving Personal Tympanum Reliefs in Clay), 180
Lesson 13-2 (Modeling Expressive Figures in Clay), 242
Lesson 18-3 (Expressive Paper-Cylinder Faces), 358
Lesson 19-3 (An Abstract Wire Construction), 398
Lesson 21-2 (Expressive Clay Masks), 439

Picture Credits

The author and publisher are grateful to the museums, galleries, libraries, and private collectors who furnished photographs and granted permission to reproduce artworks from their collections in this book. Owners and custodians of the works are listed in the captions accompanying each work. In addition, the following sources of photographs are gratefully acknowledged:

Dr. Pauline Ahmad: Fig. 3.20; Photo copyright Allen Memorial Art Museum, Oberlin College, Oberlin, Ohio: Figs. 2.15, 2.19, 3.1, 3.4, 3.12, 16.16, 16.23, 18.10, 18.13, 19.12, 19.35, 19.40, photos for Experiences on pages 441 and 446; Jorg P. Anders, Berlin: Fig. 13.14; Photo Wayne Andrews: Fig. 18.27; © James Austin F.I.I.P.: Fig. 10.14; The Museum of Fine Arts, Boston: Figs. 20.14, 20.16, 20.17, 20.21; Copyright, The British Library, London: Fig. 10.16; Photograph courtesy of the Trustees of the British Museum, London: Fig. 6.13; Copyright, The British Tourist Authority, London and New York: Fig. 15.9; Museu d'Art de Catalunya, Barcelona, Spain: Fig. 9.25; Courtesy of the Art Institute of Chicago: Figs. 16.6, 17.6, 19.6, 19.7; The Cleveland Museum of Art: Fig. 20.11; Color Slide Enterprises, Oxford, Ohio: Figs. 6.19, 11.11, 11.18; Dallas Museum of Art: Figs. 20.23, 20.24; © Denver Art Museum: Fig. 21.17; Copyright © 1983 Founders Society, Detroit Institute of Arts: Fig. 19.18; The Photograph Collection, Dumbarton Oaks, Center for Byzantine Studies, Washington, D.C.: Figs. 8.9, 8.10; eeva-inkori: Fig. 2.13; Egyptian Museum: Fig. 5.10; Stanley L. Franzos, Pittsburgh: Fig. 18.3; Freer Gallery of Art, Smithsonian Institution, Washington, D.C.: Fig. 20.7; Dr. Michael Gilliatt: Fig. 5.3; Photographie Giraudon: Fig. 10.17; The Gramstorff Collection, Photographic Archives, National Gallery of Art, Washington, D.C.: Fig. 6.8; Carmelo Guadagno: Fig. 18.8; Italian Government Travel Office, New York: Figs. 7.13, 8.4; Italian State Tourist Office—ENIT, Chicago: Figs. 7.8, 8.3, 8.12, 8.13; Sidney Janis Gallery, New York: Fig. 2.4; Photo © Beth Linn, 1983: Fig. 19.38; Dr. Jessie Lovano-Kerr: Figs. 7.10, 7.12, 10.10; David Manso: Figs. 13.7, 18.3; Bildarchiv Foto Marburg: Figs. 5.5, 5.8, 5.9, 6.11, 6.17, 9.1, 9.7, 9.14 (both photos), 9.15, 9.24, 11.1, 11.5, 11.6, 11.20, 14.2, 14.4, 14.5; Robert E. Mates: Figs. 19.31, 19.32; Photograph Services, The Metropolitan Museum of Art, New York: Figs. 1.2, 5.7, 6.9, 6.21, 7.21, 15.12, 16.3, 16.12, 16.15, 18.12, 20.1, 20.2, 20.3, 20.4, 20.5, 20.6, 20.7, 20.8, 20.9, 20.10, 20.18, 20.20, 20.22, 21.3, 21.4, 21.6; The Museum of Modern Art, New York: Figs. 17.3, 17.7, 18.1, 18.14, 18.16, 19.36; Photo Superintendence to the Artistic and Historic Property—Naples: Fig. 13.12; Photos courtesy of the Navarra Museum, Pamplona, Spain: Fig. 9.23; © Copyrighted by the University Museum, U. of Pennsylvania: Fig. 21.1; Dr. Denny Pett: Figs. 6.1, 6.7 (bottom); Photographed by the Philadelphia Museum of Art: Figs. 16.18, 18.15, 19.4, 19.20; Dr. Marvin Platten: Figs. 20.12, 20.13, 20.15, 20.19; Pont. Comm. di Archaeologia Sacra, Rome—Benedettine di Priscilla, Rome: Fig. 8.2; Dr. Nancy Reed: Figs. 5.4 (left), 7.11, 7.17; The St. Louis Art Museum: Fig. 16.20; Dept. of Parks & Recreation, San Simeon, California: Fig. 18.25; Photo copyright, Steven Sloman: Fig. 19.39; © SPADEM, Paris/ VAGA, New York, 1983: Fig. 18.11; Spanish National Tourist Office, New York: Fig. 9.10; Bill J. Strehorn: Figs. 21.2, 21.5, 21.16, 21.19, 21.20; Photograph by Ken Strothman and Harvey Osterhoudt: Figs. 6.20, 19.10; Copyright, The Tate Gallery, London: Figs. 16.9, 18.6; Photo courtesy, Division of Architecture, Texas Tech University, Lubbock, Texas: Figs. 5.4 (right), 6.12, 8.1, 11.12, 19.30; Dr. Nancy Reed: Fig. 8.6; University Prints: Fig. 7.9; Vancouver Art Gallery: Fig. 19.43; Photo Vatican Museums, Italy: Fig. 6.22; Lorin D. Whittaker: Figs. 5.1, 5.2, 5.6; Women's Architectural League, St. Louis Chapter, A.I.A.: Fig. 18.26 (both photos); Dr. Terry Zeller: Figs. 6.4, 6.6, 6.7 (top)